# COMPREHENSIVE HEALTH CARE FOR EVERYONE

*A Guide for
Body, Mind, and Spirit*

# COMPREHENSIVE HEALTH CARE FOR EVERYONE

## A Guide for Body, Mind, and Spirit

THOMAS M. COLLINS, D.C.

Blue Dolphin Publishing
1995

Published by Blue Dolphin Publishing, Inc.
P.O. Box 1920, Nevada City, CA 95959

Orders: 1-800-643-0765

ISBN: 0-931892-97-X


Library of Congress Cataloging-in-Publication Data

Collins, Thomas M., 1952–
    Comprehensive health care for everyone: a guide for body, mind, and
  spirit / Thomas M. Collins
        p.      cm.
    Includes bibliographical references and index.
    ISBN 0-931892-97-X
    1. Medicine, Popular.   2. Self-care, Health.   3. Holistic medicine.   I. Title.
  RC81.C7133   1995
  362.1—dc20                                                    95-18693
                                                                    CIP

ACKNOWLEDGMENTS: There are innumerable people who have contributed to this
book. Special thanks go to Jeannene Chase Langford for graphic design above and
beyond the call of duty, Cathy Luchetti and Steve Koke for superb editing, Robert
Rand, Deeanna Cariola, and Sara O'Hara for research, Michael Brackney for his
careful indexing, and Steve Wall for his invaluable advice concerning biofeedback
and health integration.

DISCLAIMER: Everyone benefits when more information is disseminated on effective
health enhancement programs. This book was written as an inspirational health
education resource for the average person, as well as health care providers, and
recognizes that people are generally in need of more instruction from knowledgeable professionals on assisted health care. Also, it is hoped that such a book will
bring together health practitioners from different disciplines to consult with clients
so their multifaceted health concerns can be more wisely addressed.

    This book should not, however, take the place of a physician in the role of
diagnosing, prescribing, or treating illness in a patient. The author and publisher
are not medically or legally responsible for any adverse effects or consequences
resulting from the ideas, procedures, and suggestions contained in this book, and
encourage each person to seek a physician who will work closely with them
regarding their health concerns. This book is published, in part, to help *reduce*
people's health risks.

Printed in the United States of America by
Blue Dolphin Press, Inc., Grass Valley, California

10   9   8   7   6   5   4   3   2   1

# CONTENTS

# ILLUSTRATIONS

# TABLES

# PREFACE

"**Health Care Crisis!**" read the headlines everyday across the land. Yes, there are many things wrong with health care today, but there are also many exciting and promising developments. To remedy the former and encourage the latter, proper perspective is of the utmost importance. Many exposés have been produced detailing the countless failings of institutions that affect our health. Not all have been fair. There are innumerable documents proposing solutions to these problems, but they too span a broad range of qualities: absurd, questionable, untested, biased, outdated, possible, probable, obvious, ingenious, superbly viable.

A new perspective is needed. It requires a reevaluation of past errors in the light of a comprehensive synthesis of what really does work—an ongoing process. As new information is gained, reassessment must continue. This book hopes to accommodate that living process of change while still providing concrete, sound advice for the everyday world.

This book comments not only on how to work within the health care delivery system, but also on how to build greater health in spite of the faults of that system. It also points out ways to change the inequities of the institutional systems that determine the quality of our health.

We will first frame universally accepted concepts of "holistic health" around new paradigms in order to build a springboard for future investigations. We will present some of the most effective,

as well as least effective, avenues toward health and provide tools to discover the right path of action at any particular time. This will include:

- self-care
- professional function assessment and instruction leading to more effective self-care
- professional intervention with healing modalities outside the realm of self-care.

This book is not meant to be a compendium of all possible healing practices, regardless of whether they are valid. Other such works exist. Other volumes show a wide variety of health services and wellness practices but are often not very helpful in guiding the reader in beneficial directions. In many instances the resources for effective follow-up activities are not presented either. This book will provide a systematic inquiry into systems that are known today to be of high value or to have great promise.

Providing resources for further investigation, and in particular, periodicals and organizations which continually update valuable information, is an important aspect of this book. Obviously, *all* valuable resources will not be identified within these pages. We have tried to choose the most important works and organizations that would fit into the mosaic of comprehensive care. Some excellent examples will have inadvertently been omitted. The reader has our apologies for any lack of thoroughness. The size and complexity of the health care field lends itself to these occasional oversights. Some resources which are excellent in themselves may have been omitted because others that were similar were chosen. If all the resources which provide some good information were included, the lists would be overwhelming. Other omissions may be deemed by some readers as inexcusable. If so, this criticism will be duly noted and considered. In order to make the most efficient use of the resource sections in the book, some useful limits were established. Well-known works in the field, and obvious classics, were omitted, not because of any lack of respect for their value, but because it seems more relevant to cite the less well known but equally valuable resources.

Resources for professional health care workers are also included so that the average reader can present that information to health professionals for their consideration in delivering better care. Many knowledgeable readers might also want to refer to these more technical references for their own edification.

In many resource sections, there are particularly important entries highlighted with a ★ to denote that they are one of the Best Resources on that subject.

*Many past wrongs can never be righted*
*But many future wrongs can still be prevented.*
**Ashleigh Brilliant**

# INTRODUCTION

*Health is the proper relationship between the microcosm, which is man,*
*and the macrocosm, which is the Universe.*
*Disease is a disruption of this relationship.*

**Yeshe Donden,**
**the Dalai Lama's personal physician**

The Ultimate Journey is the lifelong Path of Wholeness. We have the sense that we once knew what it felt like to be Whole. We are just trying to find our way back. Use this book as a map to help you along the Way. It will show you the landscape of our present day lack of wholeness—physically, psychologically, economically, educationally, socially, ecologically, spiritually. We use the word "health" to describe wholeness and the integration of these aspects of our being, but it is very important to realize that the root meaning of the word *health* comes from the ancient references to "whole" and "holy."

## THE CAUSES OF ILL HEALTH

Reasons for our lack of wholeness or poor health are elucidated early in the book. One primary reason for our poor health is that the lay public and members of the health care industry live their lives and perform their jobs as if they believed that health was merely the absence of symptoms. This misconception creates a cascade of other tragic notions.

With health being the elimination of uncomfortable symptoms, what should be comprehensive "health care" systems are transformed into fragmented "disease care" systems. Modern medicine continues to perpetuate the belief that symptoms are best categorized into specific, discrete conditions or diseases that have one cause and one cure. Because the most powerful and predominant disease care system, medicine and surgery, has as its primary tools "drugs and knives," it has deemed that the best way to deal with these uncomfortable symptoms, conditions, and diseases is to use medicines and surgery. These cures are usually regarded as relatively unrelated to psychodynamics, environment, human relationships, or spirit. Only token credence, money, time, research, and energy are given to prevention, improving function, health promotion, or a transformation of being.

These misconceptions and misdirections are deeply ingrained by an economic and cultural steamroller consisting of doctors, nurses, therapists, hospital administrators, researchers, public relations specialists, insurance executives and claims agents, pharmaceutical manufacturers, advertisers, regulators, lawyers, and surgical instrument manufacturers. Besides those directly involved in the "health care" industry, there is also the tremendous influence of special interests pushing for "economic progress" despite its terribly damaging effects on many other aspects of health, such as consumer safety or environmental protection.

It is no wonder then that the overwhelming majority of citizens ends up deeply programmed to fall into the vicious cycle of:

- Believing that they don't have to do much, if anything, to maintain their health. In fact, too many believe they can blatantly abuse their health.

- Then, they can just wait until symptoms get so bad they can't stand it. At which time the almighty doctor can fix them with a pill, potion, lotion, or extraction of an organ.

It is only after many years of this routine working, usually with progressively deteriorating results, that some individuals start to question those beliefs. What alternatives are then available?

## ATTEMPTS AT HOLISTIC HEALTH CARE

There are a number of health care systems, both ancient and modern, that claim to be "holistic" or imply it. They are known by different names: Ayurvedic, American Holistic Medicine, Traditional Chinese Medicine, Complementary Medicine, Macrobiotic, Third Line Medicine, Patanjali Yoga, Psychoneuroimmunology, Mind-Body Medicine, and Era III Medicine, to name a few. Hippocrates, the Father of Medicine, spoke of health as the harmony of body and mind. He also discussed the importance of harmony between man and the natural world. Even certain segments of Naturopathy, Chiropractic, Osteopathy, and Homeopathy claim the label of holism.

The grand vision of each of these systems certainly leans more towards a unified concept of health and being than does modern medicine. But in practice they fall far short of their theoretical best intentions. There are a number of reasons for this.

The older systems have for the most part failed to integrate modern advances into their practices. Traditional Chinese Medicine might be improved by incorporating modern electronic instrumentation in acupuncture, as well as advances in exercise prescription in the Tai Chi Chuan exercise regimen. Ayurvedic medicine could utilize more elaborate and descriptive methods of psychophysical testing and classification. Macrobiotics could benefit from complementing its Oriental perspective on healthy diet with modern biochemical, nutritional, and toxicological analysis.

These older systems also tend to be more simplistic than reality dictates. This is in part due to the level of knowledge about human physiology and the laws of the natural world that prevailed at the time these systems were developed. Hippocrates, for instance, theorized that health depended on a balance of "humours"—phlegm from the brain, blood produced in the heart, yellow bile from the liver, and black bile coming from the spleen. Quite a bit off base! Oversimplification also comes from a hesitancy to recognize progress.

As for some of the more modern approaches, one pervasive problem is that each system has a predominant therapeutic focus that overlooks a truly balanced, unified view of the client's health. This despite eloquent pronouncements about balance and a holistic perspective from the advocates of these systems. Too often this is just lip service.

Individual exceptions aside, when you go to a chiropractor, the major focus of care is going to center around spinal manipulation. Homeopaths, no matter how much affinity they feel for some of the original holistic philosophies, spend ninety percent of their time figuring out and prescribing homeopathic "remedies." Naturopaths, depending on the particular orientation of the practitioner, will focus on one or two favorite therapeutic modalities. Medical doctors or osteopaths practicing "preventive" or "holistic" care have their own unique, but limited, "little bag of tricks." The contents vary every few months depending on what new seminar the doctor recently attended, or what new products are being hawked by their local detail men. Those "holistic" practitioners that have a psychological bent often focus too exclusively on the psychosomatic axis of care and ignore other important elements.

This limited mode of health care, working under the umbrella of holism, occurs so often for several reasons. *One,* it is difficult, if not impossible, to acquire the knowledge and skill to personally deliver all therapeutic modalities. Many health care workers were practicing, and became accomplished in, a particular specialty prior to coming into the fold of "holistic health care." They were thus trained in a particular method of practice, and then they tried to fit those modalities of care into a new, expanded philosophy of practice. *Two,* it is also difficult to assemble and coordinate a "team of specialists approach." No matter how good it might sound in theory, centers attempting this most often end up just "ping-ponging" patients from one therapist to another so that each can try his or her specialty on the "problem." *Three,* no real, systematic, team approach exists that effectively evaluates priorities of health enhancement strategies for each aspect of one's being. Nor do any health centers use a well defined protocol for integrating all of these factors.

*A team effort is a lot of people doing what I say.*
                                                              **Michael Winner**

Another major problem preventing these types of established "holistic" attempts from actualizing the full promise of comprehensive health care is that they are trying to survive economically in an atmosphere totally hostile to their philosophical tenets. Medical boards revoke licenses of doctors using some "alternative" methods. The legal system imposes potential economic and professional ruin in the form of malpractice lawsuits for those not willing to strictly abide by the "community standards of care," no matter how archaic they might be. Pharmaceutical advertisers relentlessly condition the masses to think that health can be bought in a pill, potion, or lotion.

## A NEW MODEL OF HOLISTIC HEALTH

The model of health that is proposed here is based on several major foundations. *One,* health = wholeness = physical, psychological, economic, intellectual, social, ecological, and spiritual well-being. Each person has a unique pattern in which these and other elements of wholeness are integrated. The more factors that can be accurately assessed and enhanced, the more one can determine the level of wholeness one will obtain. This is why multi-disciplinary cooperation is encouraged

for regaining health in the most effective way. *Two,* all energy and matter in the Universe are intimately interrelated. All life has an inborn drive towards this wholeness and unity. *Three,* illness and symptoms should not be seen as just uncomfortable experiences to be rid of. It is far more useful to view them as signals of *meaning* and encouragement to go into deeper, more comprehensive transformations in all aspects of being. It is more valuable to look at health on a spectrum of varying levels of functioning rather than depend on the old model in which "you are either symptomatic *or* you are healthy." Holistic health is not some ideal state to be acquired, but rather a process of engaging Life in the best way we can. It is a Path of Unity. *Four,* health is more dependent on what people do for themselves and with others than it is on professional intervention. This demands that individuals know their rights and responsibilities regarding health. It also speaks of the importance of right relationship with our fellow beings.

These are not revolutionary ideas. They are well accepted concepts. But people are not living these principles. Health care practitioners are not delivering services that reflect these principles. Paying lip service, yes, but not much more.

Part of this model of health can be illustrated by a "Spectrum of Holistic Functioning." (See next page.)

The diagram attempts to show that a useful philosophy of health is one that identifies varying degrees of functioning rather than simply sick (symptomatic) or well (no symptoms).

Other "spectrum analyses" are used to evaluate other aspects of our health. A prime characteristic of such diagrams is that they identify a range of functioning from very poor to optimal. Symptoms are just one small part of any of these broad spans of human functioning. Physical symptoms, which our medically oriented "disease care system" focuses on with so much tunnel vision, are most often just late warning signs showing that aspects of one's wholeness (psychodynamics, relationship, environment, education, economics, spirituality) are not integrated or working well. By moderating the focus on physical symptoms and expanding our vision of life and wholeness, better models for health care can be designed.

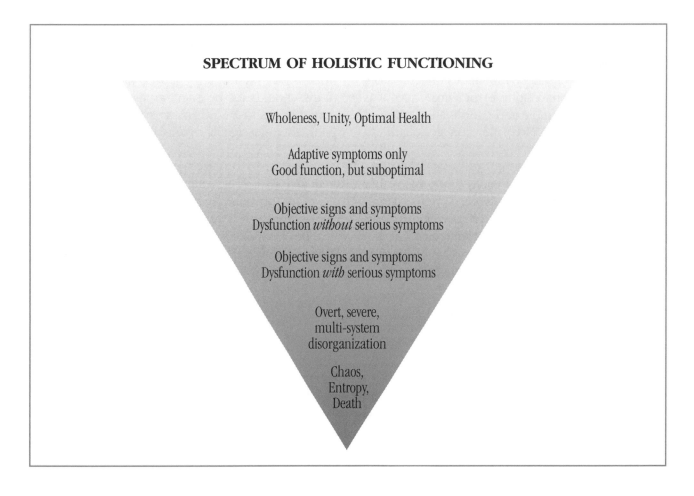

The models of health care proposed here are not the *only* good ones that exist. They are not exact duplicates of reality. They do not imply that they are the *sole* cure of disease. They are not the *best* models. Better maps of paths to wholeness will continually be found as long as we keep our eyes and minds open. The models proposed here *are* good springboards to newer, better paths. The models proposed in this book are designed to address paths of care that are:

- determined, initiated, and performed by oneself, or
- undertaken by oneself after assessment and/ or instruction from a more knowledgeable person, or
- performed by others expert in a particular health care intervention procedure.

This book, used as a map for health, should help a large number of individuals, and thus all life on Earth.

## MAP TO HEALTH

If we use the analogy of "Life as a Journey," we can continue with our "maps for wholeness" metaphor. On any journey it is helpful to have four essentials:

1. to know where you are now
2. to know *how* you got here. (so you don't get lost again)
3. to know where you are going
4. to have a safe, efficient route from here to there.

(Some gurus may argue that it is only necessary to know you are here, now. This will be discussed later.)

The more aspects of health one tests, and the more accurate the tests are, the more precisely we can locate our state of health on the map of wholeness. In many instances simple, self-administered tests are adequate for our needs. At other times limited, inexpensive professional assistance is helpful. Tests such as computerized diet assessments, body flexibility tests, laboratory assays (of blood, urine, hair, and feces), personality inventories, life stress indicators, aerobic conditioning limits, home radon levels, electromagnetic pollution gauges at work, and social typing scales are all examples. If these tests are chosen wisely, rarely is there a need for the elaborate, expensive, sometimes dangerous examinations for which modern medicine is known and feared.

Realizing how you obtained the health, or lack of it, that you have now is also important. It helps to understand onto which difficult, harmful, and dangerous trails you may have walked. Only then can you get off the wrong track and not stumble down that way again. If you realize that those thirty extra, unwanted pounds you are carrying around came from eating the wrong foods, not getting enough of the right kind of exercise, and not adequately nourishing your emotional needs, then proper steps can be taken to change to a healthier diet, maintain a good exercise regimen, and tend to those psychological elements.

After coordinating all the various tests with a scientific eye, it is then wise to take an intuitive, silent look deep within ourselves. This balanced vision into our past and present, and into the interrelatedness of all the parts of our wholeness, will give a more lucid picture of healthy possibilities for the future.

As we see the inadequacy of medicine and surgery in preventing disease, or even in the efficient correction of most of the maladies of man, we realize how grossly inappropriate it is for providing us with health and wholeness. The tables on pages xvi and xvii illustrate what is at the root of the major health problems that plague our society. Again and again we see the importance of multidimensional, natural, self-care measures that are needed to prevent and correct most of the ill health and premature death we experience.

The "Circle of Health" chart might better illustrate what contributes to true health. (See page xviii.)

It must be remembered that for each individual the contribution from each aspect of health (how large each wedge of the circle is) will be different. And it will be different for each individual at different times in his life. Overall, from a statistical perspective, the ratio between what we can do for our own health and what the direct intervention of therapists can do for us is approximately 90% to 10%. So for most individuals the vast bulk of our potential to improve our health comes from things we do for ourselves and things we do for ourselves with just a bit of assistance in assessment or instruction.

Only a small percentage of possible health improvements will come from direct intervention by physicians. And only a fraction of this needs to fall in the realm of medicine and surgery, even though that portion of our disease care system is where most of our money is spent. It should be noticed that in the section of the pie diagram marked "direct professional intervention," a large segment of this is reserved for less invasive, more natural, and safer types of care other than medicine and surgery. This does not diminish the important contribution of medicine and surgery when it is indeed needed, as in cases of crisis and emergency care. It just means that this type of care cannot solve everyone's health problems, as developed countries seem to think it can.

In later chapters we will present methods of evaluating each aspect of health. Upon using these methods, it will be easier to analyze how each affects our total health. After appraising all the different aspects, a comprehensive picture, one's own "Circle of Health," can be drawn to clearly show where emphasis needs to be placed in giving more effort, time, money, assistance, and intervention in order to promote better health. It is often surprising to find how much energy one has wasted in inappropriate areas with little result. It is also enlightening to find whole new avenues of care not yet fully utilized.

# LEADING CAUSES OF DEATH

| Health Problem | Incidence / Year | Major Originating Factors |
|---|---|---|
| 1. Heart Disease | 769,353 | diet, smoking, lack of exercise, stress, poor health education |
| 2. Cancer | 476,927 | diet, smoking, environmental pollution, poor health education |
| 3. Cerebrovascular Diseases | 149,835 | diet, smoking, stress, lack of exercise, poor health education |
| 4. Accidents | 95,020 | alcohol, education, lack of governmental and business safety protection |
| 5. Pulmonary Diseases | 78,380 | smoking, lack of exercise, nutrition |
| 6. Pneumonia and Influenza | 69,225 | nutrition, poverty, stress, poor health education |
| 7. Diabetes mellitus | 38,532 | nutrition, poverty, stress, poor health education |
| 8. Suicide | 30,796 | psychological stress, poverty, nutrition |
| 9. Liver Disease | 26,201 | alcohol, stress, poverty, nutrition, poor health education |
| 10. Atherosclerosis | 22,474 | nutrition, smoking, lack of exercise, stress, poor health education |
| 11. Kidney Diseases | 22,052 | diet, alcohol, smoking, poverty, poor health education |
| 12. Homicide | 21,103 | poverty, psychological stress, alcohol, drugs, gun availability |
| 13. Septicemia | 19,916 | nutrition, hospitals, poverty, poor health education |
| 14. Perinatal Conditions | 18,222 | poverty, nutrition, poor health education |
| 15. Congenital Anomalies | 12.33 | alcohol, drugs, poverty, poor health education |

## LEADING CAUSES OF DISABILITY, DIS-EASE, AND DYSFUNCTION

| Health Problem | Incidence | Major Contributing Factors |
|---|---|---|
| Back and Neck Pain | 80% of Americans will suffer | lack of balanced exercise, insufficient safety precautions, low usage of manipulative therapy |
| Upper Respiratory Tract Infections | #1 complaint for doctor's visit | poor nutrition, psychological stress, poverty, poor health education |
| Headaches | $25 billion per year in production lost | psychological stress, poor diet, low usage of manipulative therapy |
| Accidental and Over-use Injuries | 17 disabilities every minute | alcohol, drugs, poor fitness, poor sleep, insufficient safety precautions at home and work |
| Sexually Transmitted Disease | 9 million new cases per year | poor health education, insufficient safety precautions |
| Allergies and Asthma Chemical Sensitivity | 80% of population | wrong diet, stress, environmental pollution, dependence on medicine instead of natural therapies |
| Obesity | 10-50% of population | poor diet, lack of exercise, psychological stress, junk food advertising, poor health education |
| Digestive Disorders | widespread | poor diet, psychological stress, dependence on medicine instead of natural therapies |
| Menstrual Disorders | 30% of all women | poor nutrition, psychological stress, lack of exercise, low usage of manipulative therapy |
| Learning Disabilities | 3-15% of the population | poor nutrition, psychological stress, light deficits, inadequate holistic education |
| Sleep Disorders | widespread | caffeine, tobacco, poor diet, insufficient exercise, natural light deficits, unhealthy lifestyle habits |
| Arthritis | 80% of those over 50 | poor diet, lack of exercise, low usage of manipulative therapy, poor health education |
| Physician-caused Disease | 100,000+ deaths per year in U.S. | dependence on medicine instead of natural therapies and self-health responsibilities |
| Psychological Distress | widespread | inadequate nutrition, poverty, poor parenting, insufficient preventive mental health services |

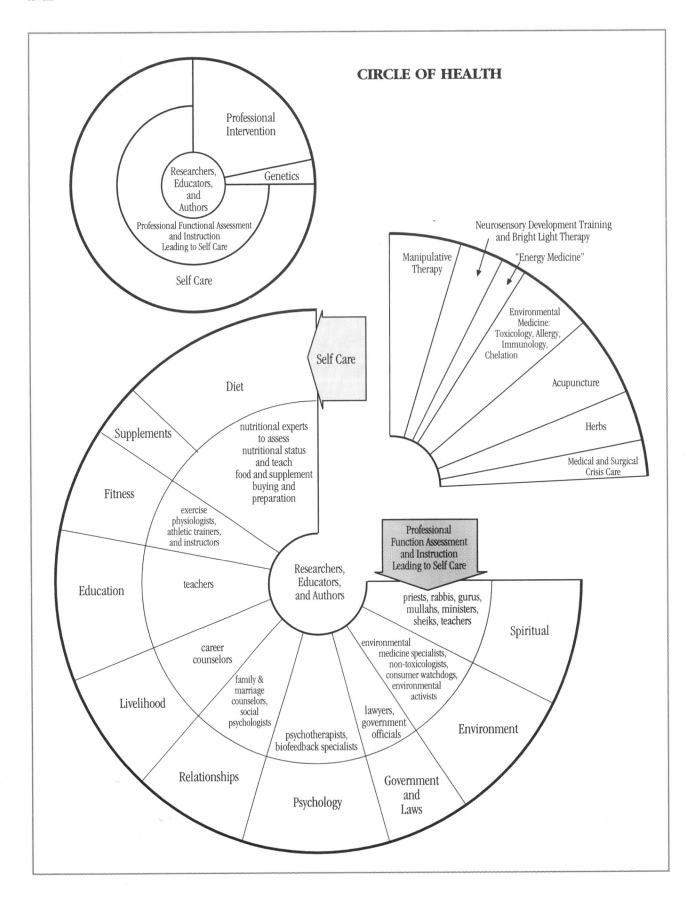

CIRCLE OF HEALTH

# PART ONE

# Health Care

# CHAPTER ONE

# CAUSES OF ILL HEALTH

*Men of superior minds busy themselves first in getting at the root of things,
and when they have succeeded in this, the right course is open to them.*

**Confucius**

The causes of ill health in our society are many. They are not isolated within the bounds of our dysfunctional "health care system." Attitudes, goals, values, conditioning, and behavior which create sub-optimal health are pervasive throughout every aspect of our being. Indicted are:

- the way we relate to our natural environment

- the way we put our religious beliefs into actions

- how our political system works

- how we shape our minds

- how we express our emotional selves

- the way we relate to family, friends and other people

- the impact of the legal system in our lives

- the economic choices that we make

- our failure, at the heart of the problem, to recognize how these varied and interrelated aspects of our being affect our health.

We can start by looking at our entire modern system of health care. It is dysfunctional, in part, because we are trying to apply modern technology to old out-of-date concepts about health. The outmoded philosophy of health we are still operating under, still trying to make the transition from, is one that has been around for thousands of years.

In ancient times knowledge of the human body, its workings, and its interactions with the natural world were very limited. Many misconceptions were prevalent about what caused ill health and what restored health when it was lost. Much of these earlier concepts were based on supposed actions in the spirit realm affecting the material world of humans. When things went wrong with crops, or ill health struck, this could not be understood by the knowledge of the time. So it was logical to assume that invisible "gods" were in control and that they had "reasons."

As knowledge about the world increased, either by trial and error or by the intuition of the more "intelligent" members of the community, important information was accumulated and transmitted from generation to generation.

Soon these wise men were identified as special and unique, seeming to have an exclusive rapport with the powers of the natural world and/or the realm of spirits. They became sorcerers, shamans, wise men, leaders, witch doctors, etc. Their knowledge and position usually brought them power, authority, respect, and wealth. We can assume that some used that power and wealth wisely, and that some did not.

Deep in the jungles of Borneo, thousands of years ago, the village medicine man stood over a feverish child. Long into the dark night he chanted in tongues unfamiliar to his people. His mind "illumined" by the ingestion of hallucinogenic plants, he danced in a frenzy around the stricken child for hours. The blackness of the night shrouded most of the village except for the small, sacred fire used to prepare the healing potion.

What we had eons ago were communities where the vast majority of individuals were ignorant about how the body works, health, or how health relates to the natural world. There were also a few, special individuals on pedestals that had the power to heal, however crudely. The masses, not knowing much about how best to take care of their health, would eventually get sick. They would then turn to the witch doctor or shaman to intervene and fix them. This intervention would usually be between the person and the natural world, as in the use of herbs which the shaman had "mastered," or between the ill person and members of the community as the shaman played social psychologist. Or the medicine man might speak in a strange language with the gods and then intervene between the spirit world and the sick person.

They all stood over the critically ill child, masked in traditional costume for the occasion. There was no frenzied dancing now. It was morning. Bright light shone on the bloody scene. "Cauterize that bleeder. Number 3 cat gut suture. Add 3 cc's of epinephrine to the I.V. Get the methylmethacrylate ready. I need better imaging on the scope. . . ."

Not much has changed. The light may be better. Everyone's level of knowledge has increased, both among the general public and the doctors. But, the great majority of people have not increased their knowledge to the appropriate level, nor have they achieved the level of understanding sufficient to give them more of the health that they desire. There are still many misconceptions about health.

The unknowledgeable masses still relinquish their health care by depending on doctors to fix them when something goes wrong. The "witch doctors" of today are still a select few with special knowledge, power, authority, and wealth, sitting on a pedestal dispensing "disease care" to the commoner. As they did thousands of years ago, some use that knowledge, power, and wealth wisely, others do not. The doctors still intervene between the patient and another world—pharmaceuticals and science—speaking a strange language, Latin and *medicalese*.

This ancient concept of "ignorant" masses being "treated" by a select few has persisted throughout time and is now counterproductive for true holistic health. Comprehensive health cannot be dispensed by that type of disease care system.

When we thought that the spirit realm caused ill health, incantations of a sorcerer entreating the "gods" to intervene was the system we used. When we thought that germs were the sole cause of disease and that modern-made chemicals could kill germs, the system of disease care remained essentially the same.

> *Doctors are men who prescribe medicines*
> *of which they know little,*
> *to cure diseases of which they know less,*
> *in human beings of whom they know nothing.*
>
> **Voltaire**

Even now, when doctors have become so skilled they can cut out diseased organs or surgically repair parts, or even replace them, the masses do little or nothing to enhance their health, wait until they get so sick they can't stand it, then relinquish their responsibility for health care to a doctor who will "fix" them.

> *The great tragedy of science—the slaying of*
> *a beautiful hypothesis by an ugly fact.*
>
> **Thomas Huxley**

Now the scientific literature is alive with a better model of what holistic health is. Most doctors know how much all the aspects of our being are related to health. Many people have at least a hint of what holistic health is, and certainly many more realize at some level that the disease care system that we use is not "right." But what perpetuates our use of a disease care system not designed to build health in an age where multi-faceted health care is desired, needed, and potentially accessible?

> *When the deep meaning of things*
> *is not understood,*
> *the mind's essential peace*
> *is disturbed to no avail.*
>
> **The Third Patriarch of Zen**

We are conditioned and programmed by innumerable forces encouraging us to succumb to old, counterproductive models for living rather than to reach into the totality of existence and choose new, more viable, vibrant pathways to wholeness. These old programs are ingrained in our beliefs, attitudes, goals, and behaviors. They are unrelentingly reinforced countless times every day of every year. They are driven by parental scripts taught in childhood and never changed, added to by peer pressure, etched into our brains by an inadequate educational system, compounded by dogmatic, misinterpreted religious beliefs, imprinted by a multitude of economic forces, ingrained by complex legal mechanisms and propelled by our social and cultural institutions. Looking at examples of these unhealthy programs will tell us much about why we are not healthy and what we have to do to erase these outdated, conditioned patterns.

## MISCONCEPTIONS ABOUT HEALTH CARE

"If it ain't broke don't fix it," says the mechanic. "Sure I'm healthy. I'm not in bed sick, am I?" he adds.

This attitude illustrates some of the root causes of ill health—the misconception that health is merely the absence of symptoms. Many people think that just not feeling bad is equivalent to being healthy. Nothing could be further from the truth. *For forty percent of all people who have heart attacks, the first symptom is death.* No progressively increasing chest pain in days prior. No unusual shortness of breath. Many have normal blood pressure. A frightening percentage recently had a medical exam where no signs of the problem were found. Were their hearts and blood vessels healthy the moment before their cardiac arrest and death? The day before? A week? A month? Obviously not. The course of heart disease is slow, silent, and insidious.

Cancer, too, works silently, often without prelude. For cancers to go from the initial conception of one aberrant cell to a clinically apparent mass requires, on the average, ten years of progressive dysfunction. No matter what the outward appearance, is the body healthy during those ten years? Obviously not.

## SYMPTOMS ARE NOT ACCURATE SIGNALS TO BEGIN CARE

What *are* symptoms? Part of the misconception about health comes from the idea that symptoms are accurate early warning signs that signal when we should start doing something about our health. A more accurate way of looking at symptoms is that they usually arise only after serious tissue damage or dysfunction has occurred, frequently over a long time. Only in the instances of acute injury, where the pain and muscles protect the injured area, do physical symptoms remotely reflect the need to begin doing something differently in attending to one's health. And even then, that does not address the reasons why the injury occurred in the first place. If the injury was due to an automobile accident, was there a lapse in alertness? Was the seat belt worn? If the injury was back pain after the first springtime softball practice of the year, was fitness maintained over the winter? Were sufficient warm-up and cool-down exercises done?

This misconception carries over into other aspects of life, such as our emotions. When do people usually begin working on their psychological health? When they have stuffed their emotions inside them for so many years that they go into a deep depression, or lash out at others, or have the pent-up emotional energy start to erupt in physical symptoms—ulcers, headaches, a "pain in the neck"? There are so many unattended emotional pains inside most people that the world is filled with dysfunctional individuals contributing their own maladaptive behaviors to society. Most of these emotional scars were created in childhood. And we are all much worse for how they have lingered on. You cannot open a newspaper or view television news without another account of a brutal rape, a senseless, bloody assault over some trivial argument, a murder of passion, or a mass killing at the hands of someone who finally "snapped."

Look at financial matters. How many people adequately tend to the minor little signs of financial dysfunction long before those minor problems can grow into major financial symptoms? The millions of bounced checks written every year would give some idea, or the thousands of personal bankruptcies annually. Look at the very low personal savings rate in the U.S. compared to other industrialized countries.

The same holds true with regard to ecological health. We smoke until we are so emphysemic that we lose our ability to breathe before we quit. We consume cheap, pesticide laden food until we have repeated miscarriages or cancer, then suddenly look at that aspect of our health. We devour the land in the name of progress, ignoring the small signs of loss of nature, then desperately rally to save the last remaining few of an endangered species.

## THE QUICK FIX

*There is always an easy solution to every human problem—neat, plausible, and wrong.*

**H. L. Mencken**

Whenever we begin with the idea that health is merely the absence of symptoms, and that the appearance of physical symptoms is the time to begin dealing with the problem, we set the stage for another ill-fated concept to activate itself—the quick fix. This is one of the most tragic and deceptive obstacles to health. In fact, it perpetuates a cycle of progressive health degradation.

"Just give me some pain medication, Doc, so I can get back to work. I don't have time for that job safety class."

"Just patch me up enough so I can play in the game on Sunday. I don't need that rehabilitation stuff."

"Can't you just give me some drugs to lower my blood pressure and cholesterol? I don't want to give up 'good' food."

*One of the first duties of the physician is to educate the masses not to take medicine.*

**Sir William Osler**

The disease care industry, like many other parts of our society, is so short-sighted it accommodates and perpetuates those attitudes and behaviors. The more quick fixes taken today guarantee that there will be more serious problems arising in the future by ignoring dysfunction, health promotion, and self-responsibility. This just means more extensive corrective and emergency services costing much more money than preventive and/or maintenance health care. This short-sightedness comes from focusing too narrowly on quick symptom relief and short term economic profit.

*Drug companies sell approximately $1 billion of aspirin per year.*
*Pharmaceutical companies spend $10 billion every year in advertising trying to perpetuate the behavior of just popping a pill for pain rather than solving the causes for the dysfunction that elicits the pain.*

*In 1990, the pharmaceutical companies spent over $8 billion on research and development of new drugs. During that time they also spent $5 billion in advertising and marketing new drugs.*

So the misconceptions that health is merely the absence of symptoms, and that the appearance of symptoms is the time to begin a "remedy," perpetuate maladaptive attitudes like "the quick fix." These bad attitudes then drive self-destructive behaviors that extend beyond avoiding good preventive care of one's health. It perpetuates downright health abuse.

## THE DISEASE CARE INDUSTRY'S PERPETUATION OF HARMFUL ATTITUDES

*It should be the function of medicine to have people die young as late as possible.*

**Ernst L. Wynder, M.D.**

The disease care industry compounds the problem by encouraging unhealthy attitudes and behaviors in individuals. There is certainly not much effort in discouraging them. The disease care industry adds to the problem by its very structure, power, wealth, and tools of the trade.

## Structural Factors That Perpetuate Problems

In the power hierarchy of the A.M.A., hospitals, insurance company board rooms, research organizations, pharmaceutical company executive suites, and in law firms that do a lot of malpractice and personal injury work, there seems to be a lack of a compassionate and nurturing attitude towards others. Could this power hierarchy be described as economically motivated high-achievers who have a primary focus on acquiring power, recognition, and wealth?

That very power structure has fought very hard for decades, spending millions of dollars to assure a nearly exclusive monopoly on the dispensation of health care. Nearly every step of the way they have fought the very existence of osteopaths, chiropractors, dentists, podiatrists, optometrists, physical therapists, homeopaths, acupuncturists, psychologists, and health food store owners. Only after overwhelming public support and documented research on the efficacy of other modalities of care was "modern medicine" begrudgingly forced to accept these "alternative" health care providers as colleagues.

Part of the result of this effort at monopoly has been a fragmentation of health care. Whenever we conceptually polarize issues—separate us versus them, Marcus Welby, M.D. versus "quacks," rather than seeing the benefits of interdisciplinary cooperation, problems arise. Rather than caring for the whole person with cooperation amongst many health professionals, modern medicine has persisted in looking at only one problem from one perspective.

You have back pain. You go to a general practitioner. He gives you pain medication and muscle relaxants, tells you to rest in bed. He doesn't mention manipulation, acupuncture, nutrition, exercise, prevention, or psychological stress. You go to an orthopedic surgeon. He wants to perform surgery. You go to an acupuncturist. He sticks needles in you. You see an herbalist. He gives you some nasty tasting herbal tea to drink. You go to a pharmacist. He suggests over-the-counter pain medication and anti-inflammatories. You go to a massage therapist. He kneads your

muscles. You go to a physical therapist. He uses some ultrasound and gives you some stabilization exercises to do. You go to a chiropractor. He adjusts your joints. You go to a psychotherapist. He talks to you about your non-assertiveness and "spine-less" behavioral conditioning. You go to your Aunt Mabel, and she covers you with hot mustard plasters. *This is fragmented disease care!* Is one of the above therapists right and the others wrong? Or are they all wrong for looking at themselves, their clients, and health care in a fragmented, narrow-minded way?

*It seems to me that people who admit they're wrong get a lot farther than people who prove they're right.*
**Beryl Pfizer**

## Adversarial Impediments to Health

Money (along with health) is drained from millions, transferred and concentrated into the hands of a few doctors, lawyers, and insurance company executives through the adversarial legal system. This is another cause of ill health. Doctors, lawyers and insurance companies have long used their enormous wealth, and their power over legislators, to manipulate the wheels of justice in such a way as to turn what should be a health care system into an adversarial system of economic aggrandizement.

As another example, look at how the insurance industry has structured itself to the detriment of its policy holders. Claims agents are given promotions, raises, and bonuses dependent upon their ratio of claims made to claims paid. So they have an economic incentive to deny as many claims as they can get away with. Too many will go to great lengths to construct as many obstacles and hassles as possible to deter the policy holder from either filing claims or challenging claim denials. You can almost hear the conversation:

"Mrs. Smith, you didn't read the ultra-fine print in your policy. If you get an extra large magnifying glass you will see where it says you are not covered for 'acts of God.' I interpret your policy like a biblical literalist—everything is an act of God. So unless you are good at squeezing blood out of a rock, you'll find it quite frustrating getting any of your claim paid."

Some insurance companies have made it a policy, often an unwritten policy, to process claims as they are filed but delay payment for as many weeks or months as possible so that the money will be sitting in their investment portfolio earning interest rather than in the pockets of their policy holders who paid their physician's or druggist's bill and are waiting for reimbursement. This, done with millions of policy holders for claims in the hundreds of millions of dollars, transfers vasts amounts of wealth from poor and middle class individuals to rich insurance companies.

Insurance company coverage is nearly always oriented to the quick fix. On the one hand, little is paid for preventive care or health promotion procedures. On the other hand, when expensive tests or prolonged rehabilitation is needed, claims agents balk, delay authorization, request a second opinion from a doctor whom they pay to say that the policy holder doesn't need the procedure, or deny the claim outright. Health Maintenance Organizations (HMO) are sometimes worse, providing a few token preventive procedures but limiting services and available specialists.

Some insurance companies and HMOs will also lure individuals, companies, organizations, and labor unions away from their existing coverage with the appeal of much lower costs of coverage. Falling for this ploy, many discover that although they are paying less initially, they are not being covered for any "pre-existing" condition which their other policy would have covered. Then, whenever their coverage for those conditions is activated six months to a year later, their premiums have also risen to equal or exceed their previous policy.

Another way in which insurers fragment health care services and inhibit a holistic perspective is the adoption of Diagnostic Related Groups (DRG's). Through these narrowly defined clinical entities insurers deem what is appropriate, cost-effective symptom relief and pay physicians accordingly. As we will continually see throughout the rest of the book, humans are complex beings. Trying to simplify lack of wholeness or health by categorizing people into neat, pre-packaged diagnostic codes so that one problem has one best,

cheap cure is scientifically unsound, clinically dangerous, and universally rejected as a practical way to health.

The magnitude of the insurance problem can be seen when comparing U.S. and Canadian health statistics. Billing and administrative costs account for 18% of health care expenditures in the U. S. as opposed to 8% in Canada. U.S. insurance companies spend approximately 27% of health care dollars on administration, whereas provincial spending on administration of Canada's national health insurance system hovers around 2%. And it should be remembered that the Canadian system could be improved upon dramatically.

### "Question Authority" Power and Wealth Inequities Contributing to Poor Health

The AMA and the pharmaceutical industry combine to form one of the most powerful and wealthy legislative lobbies in the world. Their efforts have many times adversely affected health care for millions. They have been responsible for restricting funding of research, making it overwhelmingly oriented to medicinal and high-tech corrections of health problems rather than towards causes and prevention. They have limited funding for alternative health professionals while heavily subsidizing medical education. This powerful special interest group has minimized insurance reimbursements for safe, alternative, viable health care procedures while supporting near carte blanche payment of useless, unnecessary, potentially dangerous, expensive medical care and surgical operations. The AMA has stifled nearly all accountability for incompetence, corrupt ethics, and malpractice by allowing doctors to virtually police themselves.

Medicine's wealth and power has bestowed upon doctors unimaginable influence socially and culturally. Television entertainment programming, news, print media, and movies have, over the decades, seldom put medical care in a poor light, nearly always painting the image that medicine wanted to convey—the caring, brilliant, dedicated physician with impeccable bedside manners, unconcerned about his economic rewards, always there for his patients at any hour of the day to make that lifesaving miracle cure. Only recently, with the boldness of the new investigative journalists and the transition to realism among film and television producers, have drug addiction, incompetence, greed, questionable ethics, and other problems in the medical community been exposed.

### The Tools of the Trade— Part of the Problem

*It is the best Physician that knows the Worthlessness of most Medicines.*

**Ben Franklin**

When the most dominant force in our modern disease care system, medicine, has as its primary tools of trade drugs and knives, do we wonder why the system has problems preventing disease, building, promoting, and maintaining health, or significantly helping people to achieve their fullest potential? Doctors trained in medicine—using drugs, scalpels, magnetic resonance imagers, and working in sterile, regimented, economically-motivated hospitals—will not be conducive to teaching people how to become whole.

Doctors who hide behind the veil of technology and treat a "disease" with chemicals, machines, and sharp, cold steel, cannot address a person's wholeness. Ultimately it also detracts progressively from the doctors' own humanness.

"Here's a prescription for a new medication. If your symptoms aren't better in two weeks, make another appointment and we'll 'try' a different one. If the symptoms get worse or new ones arise, stop taking it and make another appointment immediately," says the intern or general practitioner.

How many times is this experiment in trial and error repeated every day in modern medical offices? Too many. Will this scene, familiar to nearly everyone who has ever visited an M.D., the standard of care, teach anyone how to be more healthy? Not likely.

"I'll take care of those uncomfortable menstrual symptoms for you. We'll schedule you for a hysterectomy next week. Since you already have some children, you don't need and won't miss those organs anyway," said the gynecological surgeon.

*650,000 hysterectomies are performed in the U.S. per year.*
*20,000,000 American women have had their uteruses removed.*
*By various estimates 25-80% are unnecessary.*
*Half of all hysterectomies are followed by complications.*

Does extracting organs make people whole? Doubtful.

"You don't like the way your nose looks? Sure, I can change that to look any way you want. And for $20,000 more I'll raise those cheekbones, plump up those breasts and give that tummy a tuck, too," says the cosmetic surgeon.

Why be concerned about the root psychological, social, and spiritual causes for people not being satisfied with how their bodies look? Because that is what wholeness and health are about, not vanity surgery. (This is in no way an indictment of legitimate plastic surgery that truly performs miracles, restoring function and normalcy to the injured and disfigured.)

*But, 2.3 million American women underwent breast implant surgery every year.*
*Because of leakage, bodily reaction, or a degradation of the silicon, 40% of those women will suffer hardening and pain in their breasts.*

Even the natural process of childbirth has become a high-tech surgical procedure. The United States has the highest rate of Cesarean section surgical births of any country in the world. One quarter of all American children are born by C-section, yet our infant and maternal mortality rates are some of the worst in the industrialized world. Expensive Cesarean surgical deliveries are 3-5 times more likely to be performed in for-profit hospitals than in public hospitals.

*Fifty percent of the yearly 967,000 C-sections in the U.S. are unnecessary.*

Insurance policies often cover services that are unproven, ineffective, dangerous, and obscenely expensive, yet deny payment for services that are effective, safe, and inexpensive.

"No, Mrs. Jones, your 'disease' insurance will not cover nutritional counseling, vitamins, exercise programs, or chelation therapy to *reverse* the atherosclerotic plaquing in your arteries, save you from an early death, and improve your overall functioning. But your policy will pay a surgeon ten times as much to *temporarily* by-pass just the most crucial coronary arteries if you are willing to risk the serious complications and chances of dying from having your chest pried open with bolt cutters and the minimal brain damage that is most likely to occur from being placed on a heart-lung machine," says the claims agent for the Caring Hands Insurance Company . . . if the truth be told.

It would be refreshing to hear truth in advertising.

Instead of this, "Irregular? Take gentle, fast-acting, natural EXPEL, the laxative guaranteed to work before breakfast," we would prefer a more truthful ad: "Stopped up with concrete-like shit, cause you'd rather eat junk food than high fiber natural fruits, vegetables, and whole grains? Why worry about what serious health problems arise and are perpetuated by this lack of responsibility to your diet? Eat whatever you want. EXPEL will ream it out of you with the pop of a pill."

Should we be bombarded relentlessly by drug companies on television and radio, in magazines, scientific journals, billboards, and on store displays by appeals to relieve every conceivable pain with a pill, potion, lotion, or spray? Wouldn't it be money better spent, if the pharmaceutical industry were really concerned with people's welfare, to educate people about how to take care of their health so they wouldn't need to mask their malfunctions with pain erasures? Anthropologists and medical historians of the future will comment on this era of prolific utilization of pain medication and say, "Barbaric! Stupid! Our civilization knew better and still persisted in ignoring prevention and correction of the physiological, psychological, and social causes of the symptoms."

They will tell the story of the M.D. who was driving back to his mansion from the party given by the pharmaceutical company for physicians who prescribed a certain quota of a new pain killer. Midway home, one of the red "idiot" lights saying "HOT" lit up on the dash of his luxury car. The brightness annoyed his vision, so the skilled and intelligent doctor pulled to the side of the road, reached under the dash and yanked out wires until the light went off saying, "There, that light won't bother my eyes now."

Fortunately, the other disconnected wires did not prevent him from proceeding.

Unfortunately, just as his engine was about ready to seize up due to lack of water in the radiator, he came to a steep downhill curve and discovered that one of the wires he had pulled was to the power brake mechanism. But the ever efficient ambulance service with highly trained emergency medical technicians were there within minutes to meet the rescue team with their "jaws of life." An attorney was on the scene before they had him whisked from the ambulance to the "Life Flight" helicopter. The doctor's life was saved. The hospital got 3 million dollars more in funding for their Acute Care Unit. The attorney made millions for suing the company that made the "idiot" light bulb *too* bright. And the system continues.

*But there can hardly be a doubt that we are descended from barbarians.*
**Charles Darwin**

## NOT JUST THE DISEASE CARE SYSTEM

We see the same "quick fix" attitudes played out in a multitude of other facets of our lives, not just in our hospitals and doctors' offices. These attitudes exist with regards to nutrition, exercise, personal financial planning, choice of livelihood, ethics in business, corporate responsibility to the community and environment, educational quality, social interaction, political campaigning, legislative action, ecological protection, etc. These further reinforce our quick fix preference over prevention, long term planning, and building wholeness.

We want the rights and privileges of a Great Society but are unwilling to take the responsibility to work hard and contribute to those ends. We want to be healthy but are unwilling to exercise, eat right, and learn about health in a way that will achieve this goal. We not only want a doctor to give us health in a pill or potion, we even want it for free. We want happiness but want others—

spouses, children, friends—to provide it for us. Few of us engage in the difficult psychological and relational "homework," giving, and therapy that would assure it. We all want a clean, safe, beautiful environment but are unwilling to partake in significant lifestyle changes in order to adequately protect our ecology.

We want a well paying job to buy all the imagined benefits that we think "things" will give us but are unwilling to educate ourselves to perform well on the job. We also abrogate our societal responsibility to pursue occupations that do no harm to others and contribute to the overall health of the planet.

We support our government's military spending and exporting of arms, yet cry to our representatives when we spend a miniscule fraction of our military budget on foreign humanitarian aid and U.N. peacekeeping efforts. We all want a government that provides us with the rights, protection, services, and representation of the greatest country in the world, but only half of us vote with any regularity, and far fewer communicate with their elected representatives about important issues. When we do vote, it is for the politician who can get us the most pork barrel benefits while limiting our contribution. We avoid jury duty like the plague. We decry taxes and go to extreme lengths to contribute as little as we can to the common till.

We choose conditioned reactions over unconditioned, properly analyzed responses, ease and comfort over rewarding, fulfilling productivity, instant gratification over long-range planning, destiny and fate over control of our own life, self-centeredness over consideration of others, and fragmentation over unity.

Some would say the root causes of our lack of wholeness and health are more elemental, more spiritual. Maybe we are not practicing that unconditional love which spiritual leaders of all religions advocate. Maybe we just don't give enough or care enough. Maybe we need to be more mindful of our thoughts, words, and actions. Perhaps, if we could just take care of these simple but seemingly difficult foundations of humanness, the rest of the solutions would be easy.

> *Love is the only satisfactory answer to the problem of human existence.*
>
> **Erich Fromm**

The core of the problem, this lack of health, *is* a lack of wholeness, a deficit in our ability to fully understand and embrace our unity. All of what this chapter has shown is that at the root of every causative factor is the disease of separation, the illness of fragmentation. We have become so conditioned to separating our minds from our bodies, our thoughts from our feelings, our creativity from our logic, work from play, nature from civilization. We fragment our earth with boundaries of barbed wire, ideology, language, tradition, belief, weapons, economics, and race. We isolate religion to Sunday morning and wild animals to zoos. We divide our children into grades, male and female, boy toys and girl toys, teams, and levels of achievement. We dissect patients into diagnostic related groupings, financial ability to pay, personality, and body parts. We split up our likes from our dislikes, our friends from our enemies. It is us versus them, plaintiff and defendant, locals and foreigners, blood relatives and non-relations—cities, counties, tribes, provinces, nation states, cultures, alliances—all divided.

We do this comparing and drawing distinctions so much we forget to see our unity. It is not that we have to quit making *necessary* discriminations in daily life. But we have to balance that with a continual awareness of the intricate webs which bind us as One. We must recruit this wisdom of Unity Consciousness to make our comparisons and distinctions useful ones.

It is time to look more closely at this unity.

# CAUSES FOR A DYSFUNCTIONAL HEALTH CARE SYSTEM

These influences ingrain and intensify problems
impeding transformation to a new era of holistic health for everyone.

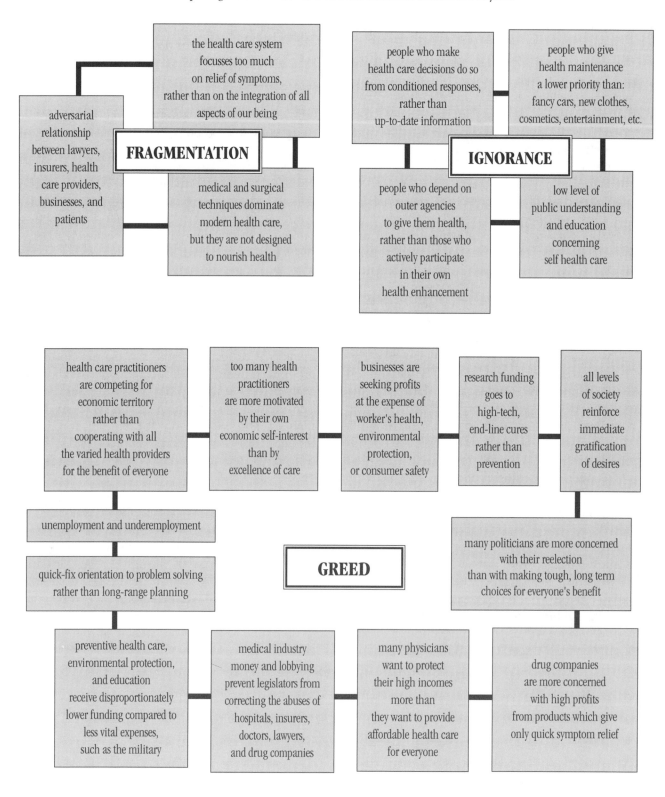

## THE CAUSES OF ILL HEALTH RESOURCES

*I have yet to see any problem, however complicated, which,*
*when you looked at it the right way, did not become still more complicated.*

**Paul Anderson**

★ Denotes Best of the Best Resources

### *Books*

Bogdanich, Walt. *The Great White Lie: How America's Hospitals Betray Our Trust and Endanger Our Lives.* Simon and Schuster, 1991.

Carter, James. *Racketeering in Medicine: The Suppression of Alternatives.* Hampton Roads Publishing, 1992; (800) 766-8009.

Illich, Ivan. *Medical Nemesis: The Exploration of Health.* Pantheon, 1982.

Inlander, Charles B. and Pavalon, Eugene I. *Your Medical Rights: How to Become an Empowered Consumer.* Little, Brown & Company, 1990.

Konner, Melvin. *Medicine at the Crossroads: The Crisis in Health Care.* Pantheon, 1993.

Mendlesohn, Robert S. *Confessions of a Medical Heretic.* Contemporary Books, 1979.

Mendlesohn, Robert S. *Malpractice: How Doctors Manipulate Women.* Contemporary, 1982.

Nelkin, Dorothy & Tancredi, Laurence. *Dangerous Diagnostics.* Basic Books, 1989.

The New Medical Foundation. *Dissent in Medicine: Nine Doctors Speak Out.* Contemporary Books, 1985.

Public Citizen Litigation Group Staff. *Questionable Doctors: Over 7,000 Doctors Disciplined by States or the Federal Government.* Public Citizen, 1991.

Shealy, C. Norman. *Third Party Rape: The Conspiracy to Rob You of Health Care.* Galde Press, Inc., 1993.

Silver, Lynn & Wolfe, Sidney. *Unnecessary Cesarean Sections: How to Cure a National Epidemic.* Public Citizen, 1989.

Smith, Wesley. *The Doctor Book.* Public Citizen, 1994. Available for $10 from The Doctor Book, Public Citizen, P.O. Box 19367, Washington, DC 20036.

Starr, Paul. *The Social Transformation of American Medicine.* Basic, 1984.

West, Stanley. *The Hysterectomy Hoax.* Doubleday, 1994.

★Wolfe, Sidney; Hope, Rose-Ellen; & Public Citizen Health Research Group. *Worst Pills, Best Pills II: The Older Adult's Guide to Avoiding Drug-Induced Death or Illness.* Public Citizen, 1993.

★Wolfe, Sidney & Jones, Rhoda. *Women's Health Alert: What Most Doctors Won't Tell You About.* Addison-Wesley, 1990. From Public Citizen Health Research Group.

Wolinsky, Howard & Brune, Tom. *The Serpent and the Staff: The Unhealthy Politics of the American Medical Association.* Tarcher, 1994.

### *Periodicals*

*Never go to a doctor*
*whose office plants have died.*

**Erma Bombeck**

★*Health Letter,* Public Citizen Health Research Group, 2000 P Street, N.W., Washington, D.C. 20036.

### *Organizations*

*If we do not change our direction,*
*we are likely to end up where we are headed.*

**Chinese proverb**

★People's Medical Society, 462 Walnut Street, Allentown, PA 18102, (215) 770-1670. Their goal is to reform American health care with an emphasis on prevention, exposing incompetence and overcharging, protecting one's freedom to choose alternative health care services, and informing and empowering consumers. They publish a newsletter and offer other publications.

*There are some remedies worse than the disease.*

**Publilius Syrus, 1st century B.C.**

---

## PROFESSIONAL RESOURCES

### *Books*

Monagle, John, et al. *Medical Ethics: Policies, Protocols, Guidelines, and Programs.* Aspen.

Monagle, John and Thomasma, David. *Health Care Ethics.* Aspen, 1994.

### *Organizations*

Physicians Committee for Responsible Medicine, P.O. Box 6322, Washington, DC 20015; (202) 686-2210. They promote nutrition and preventive medicine and question the ethics of animal research.

# CHAPTER TWO

# A NEW MODEL OF HOLISTIC HEALTH

*Love is the pursuit of the whole.*

**Plato**

In this chapter we want to move away from those old concepts about health being just the absence of physical symptoms. We also want to move beyond looking at health as just physical health, even move far past the idea that health is just mind-body health of that entity encapsulated by our skin. We will be expanding our concept of what "self" is, along with expanding our ideas about what health is.

In part, we end up having a narrow-minded concept of what health is because we have a contracted view of who "I" is. When our view of ourselves is a clearly demarcated physical body, then the best view of our health can only be one in which the body parts—organs, arms, legs—are fully functional and well integrated. Even when we view ourselves as a mind-body entity, the result is that we still look at health as only an interplay between the physical, the psychological, and the intellectual parts of our being. There are very good arguments for having a more inclusive identification with different aspects of being.

*All Creatures seek after unity;*
*all multiplicity struggles toward it—*
*the universal aim of all life is always this unity.*

**Johann Tauler**

Proposed here is a model of being with no boundaries—a model of health involving full and integrated functioning of all those infinite aspects of that all-inclusive being. (Refer to the diagram, "Different Orders of 'Self'" on page 15.) We want to investigate comprehensive health transformations, not piecemeal tinkering with symptoms.

To put in a workable form what is relevant to our individual needs on the Path of Wholeness, let us look at eight aspects of ourselves and how each aspect might be made to function more fully, and be integrated more completely, with each of the others.

We have a physical aspect to our being which most people recognize as the atoms, molecules, cells, tissues, organs, and systems of the body encapsulated by our skin. In reality, physicists have scientifically proven that this boundary of skin is only an arbitrary, sometimes useful conceptualization, rather than a discrete entity. We will expand that view later in the chapter on Physical Health. When describing varying degrees of health of the physical body, we look at the range of proper function, coordination, and integration of all these cells, tissues, organs, and systems.

There is a psychological portion of our being. A definition of a healthy psychological self depends on what model of psychology one uses. Freudian psychologists would look for a healthy, strong ego allowing the person to function happily in the world. A strict Buddhist psychologist might classify that as pathologic. We will use transpersonal models of psychological health to illustrate the need to integrate the many elements of various perspectives.

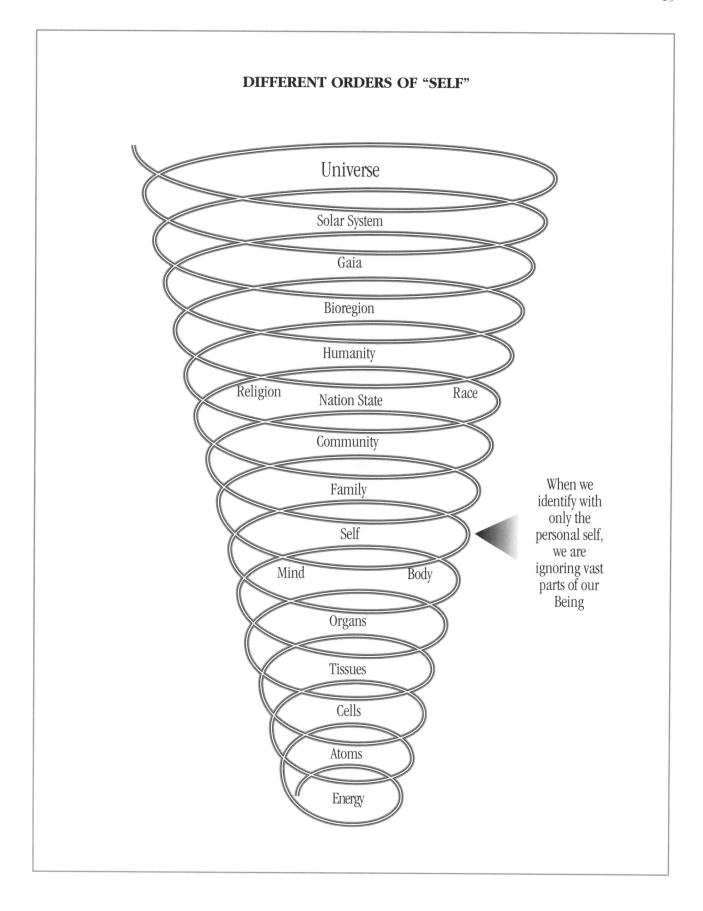

**DIFFERENT ORDERS OF "SELF"**

Universe

Solar System

Gaia

Bioregion

Humanity

Religion    Nation State    Race

Community

Family

Self

Mind    Body

Organs

Tissues

Cells

Atoms

Energy

When we
identify with
only the
personal self,
we are
ignoring vast
parts of our
Being

We have an economic/occupational identification also. There are fluctuating levels of economic status and health. We define ourselves in many cases, and to a large degree, by our occupation. Our livelihood affects other aspects of our health in many ways.

Our educational background and intellectual skills are other factors making up who we are and contributing to holistic functioning. Logic, creativity, intuition, communication skills, reasoning powers, job skills, and educational certification all contribute different qualities to our humanness, helping or hindering our overall health.

Most people do not recognize their political and legal selves. Usually not much thought is given to how these spheres of living affect our day-to-day well-being—at least not until legal turmoil ensues and impacts our emotional stability head on. Politics and government also seem far removed from that which we usually identify as "self." But as will be pointed out in detail, they are not.

It is easier to see how closely each of us is intertwined in being and health to those around us—family, friend, enemy, even our faceless society.

Our progressively increasing environmental awareness makes it easier for us to understand how we interface with the rest of life on the planet and see our health in relation to the sun's energy, the cycle of water and wind, and the flux and movement of the inorganic elements of existence.

Our spiritual lives, too, must be integrated into this total picture of self, wholeness, and health. Some would say that the spiritual component *is* the embrace of that totality. This viable viewpoint will be investigated.

For now, a useful model of these various aspects of self and health and their interrelationships can be illustrated by the following diagram.

As can be seen by the illustration, each aspect is connected with each other. This represents both its effect on the other and the effect of the other on itself. We will consider examples of every interac-

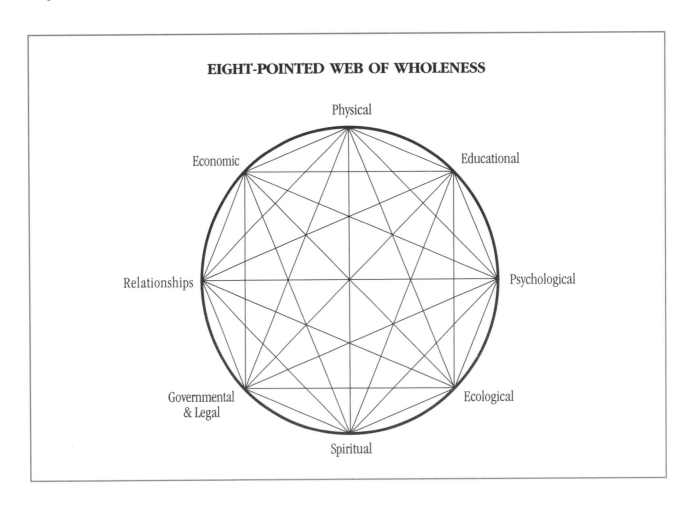

**EIGHT-POINTED WEB OF WHOLENESS**

Physical

Economic

Educational

Relationships

Psychological

Governmental & Legal

Ecological

Spiritual

tion. Some are very straightforward and easily recognized. Other relationships are more difficult to see. Some relationships will have very powerful impacts. Some only minor. The reader can reflect upon his or her own experience of these influences. In subsequent chapters the opportunity for closer self-examination will be presented with these relationships in mind.

It will also be helpful to keep in mind the Spectrum of Holistic Functioning concept and diagram first presented in the Introduction. Understanding health as a broad band of functioning, rather than just an either-healthy-or-ill dichotomy, contributes to a more accurate model of reality which will serve us well in our discussion of each different interrelationship of the aspects of our being.

There is no predefined description of perfect physical health, ideal psychological functioning, optimal ecological balance, the highest intellectual accomplishment, or perfect spiritual enlightenment distinctly separate from sickness, insanity, ecological disaster, stupidity, or moral depravity. Instead, there is a gradual band of different levels of functioning. Everyone has his own unique mental and physical limitations. Those who are physically and/or mentally handicapped (or in preferable terminology, "alternatively-abled") have more prominent limitations. The capacity to overcome "apparent" limitations is greater than most people imagine. Never be surprised by the miraculous ability of humans to overcome ostensible disability. Holistic health is not out of reach for the alternatively-abled. Their challenge may be greater, and many have seen their "physical disabilities" as gifts that have provided enormous opportunity for the growth of other health aspects in ways unimaginable. Everyone can travel the Path of Wholeness—to the best of his abilities. Dynamic growth on the Path of Wholeness has no endpoint.

So too with each relationship between the various aspects of our health. Because of the very complex nature of each interaction, describing the "ideal" relationship is impossible. But it is helpful to define many of the positive influences so that we can encourage their use. We will also delineate the negative influences so that we can diminish their activity.

## THE COMPLEXITY OF THESE INTERCONNECTIONS

*When Health is absent*
*Wisdom cannot reveal itself,*
*Art cannot become manifest,*
*Strength cannot be exerted,*
*Wealth is useless, and Reason is powerless.*
**Herophilus, 300 B.C.**

When we consider our personal health, we must analyze and contemplate all human interactions. Which ones are major forces in our life? Which are real problem areas at this time? Which relationships are my strengths? How do I work on the problem areas at the same time I take advantage of my strengths? What plan for integration can I develop for all these interconnections?

These questions can best be answered after more intimate exploration of each aspect of health in later chapters. But before we break our analysis down into manageable parts, it might prove useful to expand the model of interconnectedness to acquire an even better sense of its complexity and interweaving nature.

To understand in a more detailed, relevant way how these interrelationships combine in everyday life, we can draw a flow chart of just a hypothetical fraction of interconnected influences that can occur in a seemingly simple activity, particularly when multiplied by millions of people. (See pages 18-19.)

We can enlarge our diagram of the interconnected aspects of being to a thirteen-faceted Web of Wholeness (on page 20). Again, each line between each aspect of health is a complex, two-way interrelationship. Every positive quality encourages the development of other positive, unifying attributes. These effects then ramify through the entire system in very complex, and many times unknown, patterns.

Now let us look at this interconnectedness from a different perspective. Take the diagram of the Web of Wholeness as a representation of personal health—a wheel that rolls smoothly and healthfully along the path of life as long as all the spokes in the wheel (the two-way interrelationships between different aspects of being) are strong and fully functional. Slightly weaken just one of the spokes,

# TANGLE OF NEGATIVE INTERCONNECTEDNESS

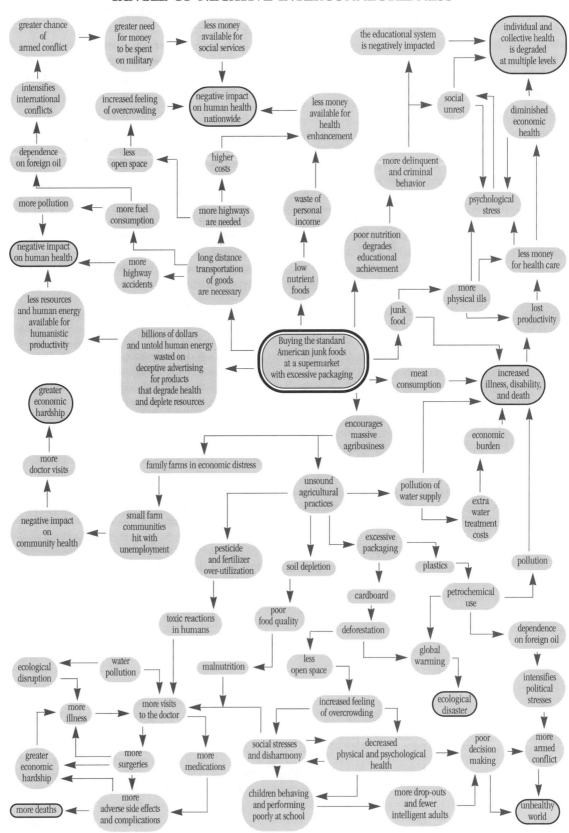

# WEB OF POSITIVE INTERCONNECTEDNESS

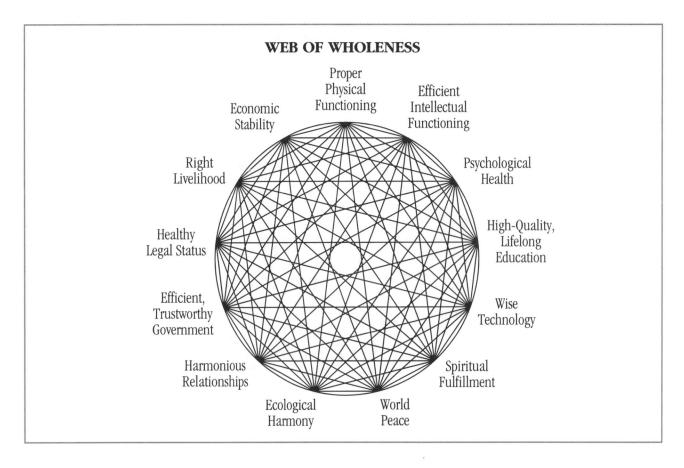

**WEB OF WHOLENESS**

Proper Physical Functioning
Efficient Intellectual Functioning
Economic Stability
Psychological Health
Right Livelihood
High-Quality, Lifelong Education
Healthy Legal Status
Wise Technology
Efficient, Trustworthy Government
Spiritual Fulfillment
Harmonious Relationships
Ecological Harmony
World Peace

one interconnection, and there will be some minute strain throughout the entire system. But very likely it will go unnoticed because of the great complexity, and interconnected support, of all the other spokes.

But severely disrupt one aspect of health plus its multiple interrelationships, and the strain on the system becomes so great that symptoms arise in many different areas. The wheel goes wobbly. Take as an example Jim losing his job. (See page 21.) It totally collapses his economic security. He cannot afford to eat ideally or take his usual vitamin supplement. Unemployment affects his psychological self-worth. This and the reprioritization of his finances puts enormous stress on his relationship with his wife. Her wheel also starts going wobbly. He has to forego his plans to finish his degree, which in turn adversely impacts his future earning potential. Since he isn't paying taxes, the government is poorer, and this ultimately hurts the nation. Even though the effect of just one person unemployed has a negligible impact with regard to macro-economics, the effect is still there

and, when multiplied times millions, does produce noticeable nationwide symptoms.

Notice how the broader, less personal aspects of one's being can do much to support the more personal, fragile elements. Good government, fairly clean environment, available appropriate technology, a peaceful portion of the world to live in, which all noticeably affect Jim, are all major support systems preventing a total collapse of his health.

Jim's wheel of wholeness is not going to roll smoothly along the path of life as long as his unemployment is a factor. Imagine yourself and others you know. What do those wheels of wholeness look like? How well do they roll? Think of the unfortunate souls who suffer severe dysfunction in many aspects of their health. Is it any wonder why so many people have trouble recovering from illness by using medicine and surgery without tending to all the varied aspects of dysfunction in their lives? Do we get a better appreciation for the importance of lifestyle changes that build multiple facets of health in preventive ways? Subsequent

## WEB OF WHOLENESS AFTER JIM LOSES HIS JOB

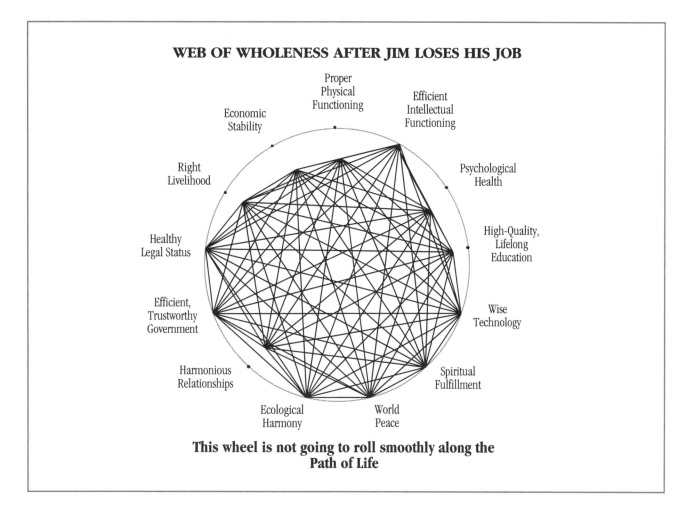

**This wheel is not going to roll smoothly along the Path of Life**

chapters and recommended resources will allow for a greater in-depth investigation of each health aspect, and all the various relationships, so that a more accurate evaluation can be made of each spoke in your wheel. The more carefully each interconnection is analyzed, the easier it will be to choose and prioritize what health enhancement efforts are needed to best heal that Web of Wholeness.

It is evident upon observing the complexity of human activities that mindfulness is very important. Being aware of all the complex influences our actions can have helps us become more responsible to our wholeness, our health. This is particularly so when our individual actions are multiplied by millions, or even billions, of people.

*You never know how something you may think, say or do today will influence the lives of millions tomorrow.*

**B. J. Palmer**

If we were all truly aware of the profound impact that our simple choices, thoughts, and behaviors have on the world, and ourselves for that matter, we would be much more careful and deliberate in our lives. So much of everyone's daily life is run on "automatic." We operate from our unconscious conditioning rather than choosing mindfully, deliberately, after careful analysis of facts and feelings.

Part of the purpose of this book is to open our eyes to the true impact of our actions and give resources for further discovering these effects. By showing readers specific health-enhancing activities, this book hopes to empower readers with wise choices they may not have realized existed before.

*Joy is the feeling that comes from fulfillment of one's potential.*

**William C. Schutz**

# PRIORITIES FOR CARE OF OUR HEALTH

*Eat when you are hungry. Sleep when you are tired.*
*When nature calls, answer. When it's cold, go inside.*
*Don't think of anything else while making love.*

**Irving Oyle**

Establishing effective, logical, conscious priorities for our health, our wholeness, is essential. Establishing these priorities occurs at many different levels in all the varied aspects of health on a continual basis throughout life. Most often we are making these priorities on a daily basis without knowing it. Many of these priorities are chosen by our conditioned behaviors in day-to-day life.

Taking an aspirin when a headache arises, rather than dealing with the issues that create the chronic neck muscle tension that elicits the head pain, is to unconsciously choose a priority of care for one's health—a quick chemical fix instead of counseling for the relationship problem and biofeedback to retrain the muscle tension pattern.

Another example is drinking coffee to wake up in the morning and keep moving and alert throughout the day, rather than working on a multi-tiered effort to improve physiologic function and energy levels by:

- getting more rest and eliminate sleep deprivation
- using light therapy to restore normal biological rhythms
- eating better to sustain energy evenly throughout the day
- aerobic training to improve even further the energy utilization pathways in the body.

*Men have never fully used the powers they*
*possess to advance the good in life,*
*because they have waited upon some power*
*external to themselves and to nature*
*to do the work they are responsible for doing.*

**John Dewey**

What needs to be done instead of this haphazard, health-degrading, unconscious, conditioned, prioritization of health care by default is a deliberate, planned, logical, mindful, daily evaluation of priorities for gaining wellness and wholeness. The different levels of priorities which must be considered include timing—when to implement the following types of care:

- wholeness enhancement endeavors
- prevention of disease or dysfunction approaches
- early detection of dysfunction or disease
- non-invasive, conservative therapies for either acute illness or chronic, degenerative conditions
- aggressive, invasive, medicinal or surgical, corrective treatment protocols
- emergency, crisis care.

This needs to be done for each aspect of health with the Web of Wholeness in mind. Although there is some overlap between the above categories of health care, it is important to be aware of some distinctions in order not to get confused. Wholeness enhancement is designed to build health by integrating all the different aspects of our being, and it should be the primary mode of health care efforts. It should be an integral part of our daily living. It naturally will prevent disease and involve early detection of body-mind-spirit dysfunction. On occasions these endeavors will also include the other elements of interventional care.

We should be wary of modern medicine's view of priorities, particularly in the way that it is practiced. Modern medicine's efforts to present preventive medicine as the new, enlightened, progressive health care approach that will help fill all the needs of Americans might be defined differently by a more objective analysis. If we look at the new, improved, AMA version—"doctor of preventive medicine"—we will find someone who stresses immunization for young and old, which many would classify as an invasive, medicinal approach which injures and kills thousands every year. We will also find a concept of prevention which primarily centers around early detection of things like high blood pressure and high cholesterol, which are then treated with medications. It is a far cry from the health enhancement measures recommended in this book.

## SELF-CARE, ASSISTANCE, OR DIRECT INTERVENTION?

There is also prioritization relative to how much energy, time, and money is allotted for:

- purely self-directed care
- assisted evaluations
- professional instruction of client-centered, therapeutic activities
- direct, professional intervention in therapeutic services the individual is unable to provide for himself or herself.

*The doctor of the future will give no medicine, but interest his patients in the care of the human frame, in diet, and in the cause and prevention of dis-ease.*
**Thomas Edison**

Remembering our "Circle of Health" diagram, we know that only a small proportion of our total health is determined by direct intervention of professionals, and only a fraction of this is contributed by medicine and surgery. But medicine and surgery account for the most expensive component and the one with the greatest likelihood of complications and adverse reactions. One of the important principles that this book hopes to convey is that *everyone should more realistically evaluate where time, money, and energy are exerted to achieve the greatest health for the least cost, and in the safest manner.*

Obviously, it is important not to mistakenly prioritize what is truly a medical/surgical emergency with some inappropriate self-care measure. It can be equally tragic to use a radical, high-risk, surgical procedure for something that can more appropriately be corrected (or even prevented) by less invasive, less expensive means. It is important to mention again the great value in utilizing:

- preventive approaches
- early detection methods
- health promotional techniques.

*Those practices done now* reduce the necessity for more drastic care in the future. This in itself makes prioritizing health care alternatives easier. But we still have to choose how much we are willing to change our lifestyle to encompass greater wholeness. Some people are very attached to their illnesses and fragmentation. We have to choose to redirect money away from unproductive ventures into healthy ones. We have to choose to put effort into breaking bad health habits. How much can we tackle at one time? We have to restructure our time commitments. All of this involves priorities. The more clearly we can delineate our priorities, the easier it will be to shift around our economic, time, and energy resources to most effectively accommodate beneficial transformations.

Knowledge about major health risks and meaningful wellness programs greatly assists good judgment in caring for our health. Statistically, some of the most important factors that contribute to health and longevity are:

- no smoking or breathing secondhand smoke
- minimal and judicious alcohol consumption
- use of proper safety restraints in autos
- diet high in fiber, vegetables, whole grains, vitamins A and C; low in fat and meat
- regular aerobic exercise
- plenty of rest.

Obviously we should adhere to these guidelines which are universally applicable. But we also have to be attentive to our own individual weaknesses and risks. We can't eliminate all risks in our life. We can't partake in every health improvement endeavor. But if we use the guidelines and resources identified in these pages, we will be able to make wiser decisions that are individualized for our own personal, ever-changing circumstances and values.

Most people initiate health care activities only after symptoms arise (usually these arise from neglecting health for a long time prior to the eruption of symptoms). Because of poor health

## HEALTH TESTING CATEGORIES

So how do we evaluate our health? Health testing can be categorized by value based upon:

- importance of the findings
- appropriateness to the situation
- accuracy, sensitivity, and specificity
- depth of information
- availability
- expense
- simplicity and ease of application
- invasiveness
- danger of complications or adverse side effects just from the testing procedure.

Health testing can also be categorized by which aspect of our lives it is testing:

**Physical**

I. Health risk assessments
   A. Smoking
   B. Alcohol consumption
   C. Seat belt use
II. Nutritional status
   A. Intake—computerized diet diaries
      1. vitamins
      2. minerals
      3. fats
         *a.* saturated
         *b.* trans-fatty acids
         *c.* cholesterol
         *d.* polyunsaturated
      4. protein—broken down by amino acids
      5. complex carbohydrates
      6. simple sugars
      7. fiber
   B. Tissue levels—hair, urine, blood
      1. vitamins
      2. minerals
      3. cholesterol
III. Fitness level
   A. Aerobic conditioning
      1. step test
      2. time it takes to run/walk a mile
      3. $VO_2$ max (an indicator of aerobic fitness)

   4. FEV and FEV-1 (respiratory fitness tests)
   B. Strength
      1. how much weight per ten repetitions
      2. computerized strength curves
   C. Flexibility—measured distance one can stretch a joint
   D. Coordination
      1. sport-specific skill tests
      2. neurological tests
IV. Physical examination by a health care professional
   A. Screening procedures
      1. history
      2. observation
      3. inspection
      4. traditional Oriental medicine pulse diagnosis
      5. heart rate, blood pressure, temperature, height/weight ratio
      6. skinfold measurement of body fat
      7. auscultation of heart, lungs, and blood vessels
      8. opthalmoscopic eye exam
      9. otoscopic ear exam
      10. joint range of motion
      11. gait evaluation
      12. neuromuscular reflexes
   B. Biochemical laboratory tests
      1. standard blood or urine chemistry panels
      2. specialized blood, stool, or urine chemistry panels
         *a.* anemia profile
         *b.* calcium metabolism profile
         *c.* diabetes profile
         *d.* hepatitis profile
         *e.* lipid profile
         *f.* liver profile
         *g.* multiple sclerosis profile
         *h.* parathyroid profile
         *i.* rheumatoid profile
         *j.* systemic lupus erythematosus profile
         *k.* thyroid profile

        *l.* plasma or urine organic acids

        *m.* plasma or urine amino acids

        *n.* plasma or urine fatty acid analysis

        *o.* functional liver detoxification capacity

        *p.* digestive evaluation from comprehensive stool analysis

    C. Instrumentation-mediated tests that are more complex and expensive

       1. ECG (heart test)

       2. EMG, sensory evoked potentials (nerve and muscle tests)

       3. diagnostic ultrasound

       4. plethysmography (blood flow studies)

       5. phonocardiogram

       6. x-rays

       7. computerized tomography

       8. magnetic resonance imaging

       9. brain electrical activity mapping

  V. Genetic testing

    A. Errors in metabolism

    B. Predisposition to disease

    C. Disease markers—Huntington's, etc.

## Psychological

  I. Psychometric tests (There are hundreds. Below are some examples.)

    A. Minnesota Multi-Phasic Personality Inventory (MMPI)

    B. Experiential World Inventory (EWI)

    C. Hoffer-Osmond Diagnostic (HOD)

    D. Myers-Briggs

  II. Evaluation by psychological interview

  III. Stress adaptation analysis

    A. Biofeedback

       1. EMG

       2. GSR

    B. Salivary Cortisol

    C. Holmes-Rahe Stress Scale

## Cognitive

  I. Perceptual tests

  II. I.Q.

  III. Reading Level

  IV. Mental status exams

## Relationship

  I. Interpersonal communications effectiveness evaluation

  II. Parent Effectiveness Training skills assessment

## Personal Legal Health

  I. Self-help book checklist

  II. Attorney interview

## Environmental

  I. Potential Exposure

    A. Home and work tests

       1. radon

       2. formaldehyde

       3. pesticide

       4. water

       5. lead

  II. Body Burden

    A. Hair

       1. lead

       2. aluminum

       3. cadmium

    B. Blood levels

       1. lead

       2. toxic levels of medicines

       3. pesticides and chemical contaminants

    C. Urine

       1. mercury

       2. drugs

    D. Tissue biopsy

       1. chemical contaminants

       2. pesticides

  III. Immunological Reactivity

    A. Immediate reactions—RAST IgE

       1. dust

       2. pollen

       3. dander

    B. Delayed reactions—ELISA/ACT™

       1. food

       2. chemicals

       3. microbes

  IV. Challenge with suspected reactants for symptom reproduction

    A. Inhalant

    B. Sublingual

    C. Intradermal

## Spiritual

  I. Interview with respected spiritual teacher, priest, minister, rabbi, rinpoche, etc.

education, most people continue at this point to make improper decisions on how to regain their health. They either choose drug store "quick fixes," folk remedies, "pop" therapies, or direct medical intervention, all of which too many times turn out to be the wrong choices at the wrong time, wasting time, money, and energy.

*Attack problems before they appear.*
*Cultivate peace and order before confusion*
*and conflict arise,*
*A towering tree springs from a tiny sprout.*
*A journey of a thousand leagues*
*begins with the first step.*
**Lao Tzu**

The approach advocated in this book is deliberate prioritization of health enhancement programs before health crises are too severe. Self-care with testing and/or instructional assistance is often the most rewarding way to begin this journey to better health.

Health assessments can be categorized in levels according to their cost to specific findings ratio. Level 1 tests are those which can inexpensively and simply screen large numbers of people to find very prevalent dysfunctions or hidden health problems. More specialized testing in levels 3 and 4 increase with expense and are designed to find very specific and usually more rare clinical diseases or functional faults.

Level 1 "preventive" and "early detection" assessments include:

- pen and paper tests such as psychological evaluations
- simple fitness tests for aerobic capacity, strength, and flexibility
- lifestyle risk or stress questionnaires
- diet diaries for computerized food composition analysis
- urine dip stick tests
- hair analysis
- blood pressure monitoring

- percentage body fat appraisals with skinfold calipers
- at-home testing kits—colon cancer, radon, formaldehyde, lead, electromagnetic radiation.

Examples of Level 2 health evaluations are:

- more complex blood, saliva, stool, and urine laboratory analysis
- physical, neurological, orthopedic type examinations
- EMG's, EEG's, ECG's, and similar technological or biofeedback tests
- complex, expensive fitness tests like Cybex muscle strength curves.
- preconception and prenatal genetic testing.

Level 3 specialized testing encompasses procedures like:

- diagnostic ultrasound
- magnetic resonance imaging
- computerized tomography
- x-rays and mammography.

Level 4 "Very specialized" testing includes more invasive procedures:

- radioactive isotope scanning
- cineradiology
- arthroscopy, laparoscopy, and other procedures using video imaging from surgical introduction of fiberoptics
- exploratory surgery.

By utilizing preventive, early detection, and sometimes Level 2 professional evaluations at health stages short of emergency crisis intervention, we gain several benefits. *First,* we find out more about our health, which empowers us with greater decision-making control over life and health. *Second,* these early stage tests are usually very cost-effective if chosen according to guidelines in this book. Another benefit is that it prevents much wasted effort and wrong courses of action precipitated by uninformed decisions made in error because of lack of data. Preliminary evaluation, even if simple, reduces the chances that excessive procedures will be utilized by direct intervention before other, more conservative, possibly self-care, methods are tried.

Some of the preventive and early detection health assessments are designed to detect beginning stages of body-mind dysfunction such as fitness tests and personality inventories. Some evaluations do not detect dysfunction but rather indicate risk of potential problems such as lifestyle risk assessments. Others are early detection monitors of disease such as monitoring for high blood pressure or heavy metal toxicity shown in the hair. Still others are for evaluation of contamination in one's surroundings before it starts to cause serious body or mind dysfunction.

Once some initial evaluation is done, more appropriate, specific, powerful self-care approaches can then be instituted with greater likelihood of success. This is particularly helpful if there are symptomatic problems that need to be addressed.

## SELF-CARE

*Each patient carries his own doctor inside him.*
*They come to us not knowing that truth.*
*We are at our best when we give the doctor*
*who resides within each patient*
*a chance to go to work.*
**Albert Schweitzer**

Many self-care approaches require little, if any, pretesting. There are many good diets, exercise programs, how-to psychotherapy and relationship books, meditation approaches, and environmental health guidelines that are, to a large degree, applicable for a large number of people. They follow general principles of preventive care. There are tests that help self-care, are readily available without assistance, and are self-scoring. Many individuals are very knowledgeable about health matters and can do a greater degree of self-care without depending on professional assistance. Others are not as knowledgeable. They might be better suited to engage in self-care only after evaluation and instruction by professionals. This is even more true as one's health status diminishes, symptoms arise, and complex issues begin intertwining themselves.

There is an important element to consider with regards to self-care. The inner powers of healing are unimaginable! When patients or clients perceive that the agency of health improvement is primarily oneself, dramatic internal forces can be recruited for self-healing. But when people perceive that the agency responsible for their own health improvement is some outside entity like a doctor, loved one, or even an insurance company, these powerful inner mechanisms for healing are sabotaged.

*You are never given a wish without also being*
*given the power to make it true.*
*You may have to work for it, however.*
**Richard Bach**

## DIRECT INTERVENTION BY HEALTH CARE PROFESSIONALS

*The physician is nature's assistant.*
**Galen**

When one finds the need for professional help of a particular kind, then one should look at

- the type of advanced testing ideal for determining the exact nature of the problem, and then
- the appropriate techniques best suited to restore health.

This is a very critical point in the process of regaining health when it is lost. Just the right amount and type of testing is important for determining proper treatment. If we choose the predominant medical approach and consult a general practitioner, he will have access to a wide range of testing possibilities including the most advanced technologies. But he will usually be inclined to use more testing than necessary in order to protect himself against malpractice and to gain income from the tests and necessary reviews.

*Defensive medicine, the overutilization of diagnostic testing by doctors in order to protect them from malpractice claims, wastes $15 billion of health care consumer money per year in the U. S. This is particularly egregious since 90% of all malpractice claims are filed against 10% of the doctors, the incompetent ones. This is because the medical community does not adequately police its ranks.*

*Clinical medical laboratories that are wholly or partially owned by physicians have 45% more tests run and charge 75% more per test.*

These tests are also oriented to acquiring information which will support medical and surgical options—those options which health care consumers want to use only as a last resort. Many medical doctors are uninformed about natural, noninvasive procedures, and thus they seldom recommend or route clients to these options.

On the other hand, there can be problems if the initial consultation is with health professionals such as massage therapists, health food store personnel, or self-proclaimed nutritionists. The lower end of the health care services spectrum is not knowledgeable enough about a broad spectrum of diagnostic and treatment possibilities to ideally guide the ill towards the best alternatives. Limited attempts at intervention in their own specialty might preclude proper testing that would reveal a better approach.

An ideal approach is initial consultation with a physician who specializes in natural health care procedures detailed in this book and is also qualified and licensed to do more advanced testing if necessary. Then there is a balance. Problems are approached naturally, conservatively, inexpensively. This kind of physician will also have the knowledge and skills to recognize emergency or serious health problems and to either deal with them or refer them directly to advanced testing and/or treatment. Chiropractic physicians, naturopaths, and medical practitioners specializing in holistic, natural methods are good first choices.

Because of their ability to prescribe pharmaceuticals, osteopaths and medical doctors who are holistically oriented can be particularly valuable in the *wise* management of medications. As the seriousness of conditions increases, the need to use medications intelligently along with other, more natural, therapeutics becomes greater. There are a number of conditions which benefit from incorporating pharmaceuticals into the entire scheme of health care. Below are some examples:

- Intravenous Nutrient Therapy
- low dose thyroid hormone for hypothyroidism
- in treating Chronic Fatigue Immune Deficiency Syndrome, drugs often are helpful in eradicating *Candida* and parasitic infections
- low dose hormone replacement therapy
- insulin dependent diabetes
- Sclerotherapy (Prolotherapy) for the strengthening of unstable ligaments.

Chiropractors who follow the professional practice guidelines of the American Chiropractic Association will assure at least some level of dedication to a broad spectrum approach to health care. If medical doctors, chiropractors, or naturopaths are members of the American Holistic Medical Association/Foundation, International Academy of Nutrition and Preventive Medicine, American Association of Orthomolecular Medicine, or the International Society for Orthomolecular Medicine, they have been exposed to many progressive health care approaches and leading-edge practitioners.

Referrals to specialists can be most effective when they come from holistic physicians. Also, they will often know the best specialists to see, who will fit their particular skills into a comprehensive treatment plan. Optometrists, podiatrists, dentists, psychotherapists, surgeons, have invaluable skills and knowledge.

## WHICH ASPECTS OF HEALTH NEED PRIORITY ACTION?

As we prioritize, we must keep in mind the overall goals of total unity and integration of all the various aspects of health. Priorities must be evaluated with reference to energy, time, and money spent on each health aspect (nutrition, fitness, psychological, economic, educational, spiritual, etc.) to gain the best integration of being. It is not sufficient to begin work on one or two health aspects, get a dramatic improvement or resolution of symptoms that is satisfying, and then stop there. Many times we work on a high priority aspect of health and get the impression from the dramatic results that this one avenue is a panacea for all kinds of ills. This is a frequent cause of attributing to particular therapies cures of certain health problems in everyone. It might be more accurate to say that a particular therapy made dramatic, positive changes in one or more conditions because it built on those weak strands in the Web of Wholeness. It was then able to eliminate the obvious problems. But those isolated modalities, techniques, or approaches may not have sufficiently strengthened other strands of the Web that are in great need of repair but have yet to manifest in symptoms.

This brings up the questions: How healthy do I want to be? How committed am I to reaching my greatest potential? Am I willing to tackle problems in difficult areas of my life to insure greater integration and health in the other areas? Too often these questions are blocked by the question: What will the insurance company pay to simply eliminate the symptoms?

One way of putting this system of priority evaluations in perspective is with the flow chart on page 30.

The process of setting priorities is a dynamic one. It will change with time, stresses, the seasons, crises, outside influences, and personal growth. Some people look at all the problems they have and all the options available for health enhancement and are befuddled about where to start or where to turn next. In simple terms, you start from where you are, and you do the best you can. Tackling the most crucial problems that have the greatest impact on the widest array of health aspects is a good start.

Never ignore potentially serious health problems, as did Mary, a sales representative in a high pressure job. She has always had frequent, periodic headaches, but they had been increasing in intensity as her job got more hectic. Mary was never inclined to exercise or watch her diet. She never read much about health issues, being instead highly focused on making money and being "successful." At the first sign of a sniffle or pain, she would immediately turn to drug store remedies for the quick alleviation of symptoms. When this failed it would be off to the doctor for expensive tests and stronger drugs. "My insurance pays for it. Why not use it?"

These actions already determined much of her care through unthinking, automatic responses. Television ads programmed her to pop pills to make everything all right. TV shows told her she could always depend on her M.D. to fix her. When the aspirin, acetaminophen, and ibuprophen were no longer effective, Mary started missing work and losing commissions. This was enough to make her run to her M.D. worrying about a brain tumor.

After giving her a physical examination, her general practitioner was 98% certain that there was nothing more serious than stress and tension, with possible contributions from allergies. But Mary was so concerned about cancer of the brain, after being programmed by TV to think only of the melodramatic, miraculous medical cure, that the doctor ordered an entire battery of blood tests which he was sure would turn out normal—a $1000 Magnetic Resonance Imaging (MRI) series— and referred her to a neurologist, "just to be certain."

What were the physician's priorities? He was part owner of the Radiology Imaging Center where the MRI was done, so he profited from that radiographic study. The more tests he reviewed, and the more blood tests he ran, the more he could charge the insurance company for his time. Because of a past malpractice suit for negligence, the referral to the neurologist was used more to cover his butt in case of another malpractice suit. Since the doctor had no financial stake in referring Mary to a psychologist, biofeedback specialist, nutritionist, exercise physiologist or chiropractor, he did not. That would also require that he inform himself of what his allied health professionals were doing to help people with these problems. Not only would this require time and effort on his part, but he also would have to relinquish his "high on a pedestal, above the rest" image of himself in the world of health professionals.

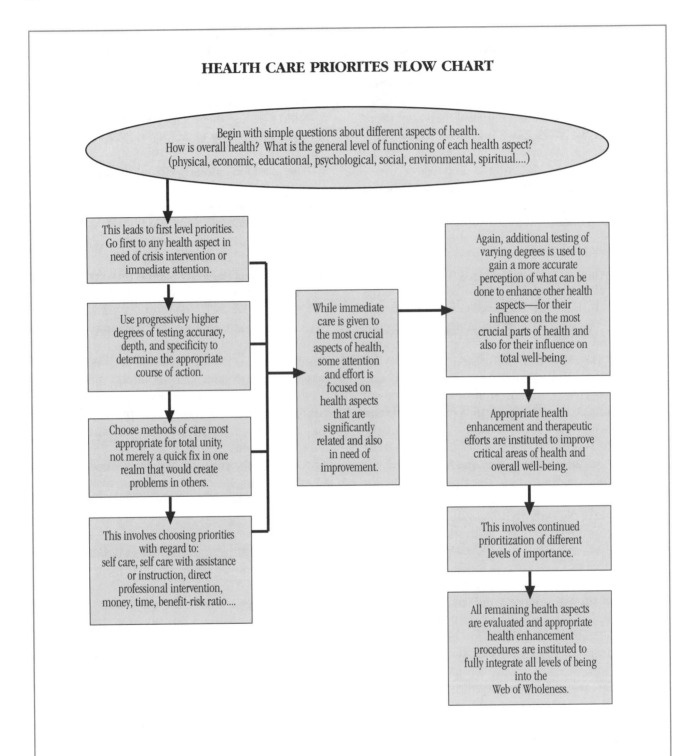

**HEALTH CARE PRIORITES FLOW CHART**

Begin with simple questions about different aspects of health.
How is overall health?  What is the general level of functioning of each health aspect?
(physical, economic, educational, psychological, social, environmental, spiritual....)

This leads to first level priorities.
Go first to any health aspect in
need of crisis intervention or
immediate attention.

Use progressively higher
degrees of testing accuracy,
depth, and specificity to
determine the appropriate
course of action.

Choose methods of care most
appropriate for total unity,
not merely a quick fix in one
realm that would create
problems in others.

This involves choosing priorities
with regard to:
self care, self care with assistance
or instruction, direct
professional intervention,
money, time, benefit-risk ratio....

While immediate
care is given to
the most crucial
aspects of health,
some attention
and effort is
focused on
health aspects
that are
significantly
related and also
in need of
improvement.

Again, additional testing of
varying degrees is used to
gain a more accurate
perception of what can be
done to enhance other health
aspects—for their
influence on the most
crucial parts of health and
also for their influence on
total well-being.

Appropriate health
enhancement and therapeutic
efforts are instituted to improve
critical areas of health and
overall well-being.

This involves continued
prioritization of different
levels of importance.

All remaining health aspects
are evaluated and appropriate
health enhancement
procedures are instituted to
fully integrate all levels of being
into the
Web of Wholeness.

Throughout this entire life-long process, continual efforts are made to incorporate
preventive and early detection measures into the Path of Wholeness.
Continual efforts are also made to integrate, in a balanced fashion, all aspects of Life into this Web of Wholeness.

As is often the case, all the expensive, high-tech tests proved negative, unnecessary, and simply drove the cost of health care up for everybody. The doctor prescribed some stronger pain medication, some muscle relaxants, and some tranquilizers. His parting words to Mary were, "You might want to take it a little easier for a while." The classic understatement.

Mary's headaches decreased slightly for a short while but then returned full force, accompanied with very disturbing digestive complaints which a nursing friend told her were probably due to the medication. At the insistence of a co-worker, Mary set an appointment with a local naturopath who had a good reputation and was well versed in holistic principles of natural health care.

On her first office visit with Dr. Smith, she laid on the naturopath's desk a thick file of all the tests that were done by the other doctors. While the doctor surveyed the files, she questioned Mary for a full forty-five minutes about every aspect of her life: what she ate for breakfast, lunch, dinner, and snacks; what type of activities and exercise she participated in; her social life, sleep patterns, recreation; and all aspects of her work and relationships. Finally Mary thought she was "prying" just a bit too far, not recognizing the importance or relevance of these aspects to her head pain. "What are all these 'personal' questions going to tell you that those complex, scientific tests aren't?"

By now Dr. Smith had a good overview of the situation. Not only from the lack of substantial findings in her previous medical file, but more so in what Mary revealed about all the unhealthy aspects of her life. "Well, I think I've got your problem figured out. And the problem isn't called headaches. Your condition is 'lifestyle dysfunction.' Head pain is just one of the symptoms of that more complex syndrome."

"Well, headaches are what I'm here to have you correct," Mary said, a bit confused, a bit put off.

"Head pain may be the most annoying symptom you have. Focusing on it alone diverts attention from the totality of the problem, as seen by all the unsuccessful high-tech tests done previously. You have admitted many other symptoms which fit into a pattern, as I look at it. You are stressed out at work and often feel tense. That is a symptom and

a sign that your job could be causing the muscles of your face and neck to chronically contract. I noticed this happening as you discussed your job. This muscle tightness is a major cause of the type of head pain you describe. Your fists also clenched. You are exhibiting signs of what is called a 'sympathetic mass action effect,' or 'fight or flight stress response' which can result in all sorts of disorders: heart palpitations, digestive upset, susceptibility to infection, allergies, poor sleep—all of which you said are periodic or on-going problems."

"But I do okay with taking over-the-counter medications for those problems. That's not why I'm here. The headaches are what really bother me. Besides, stress at work comes with the territory. I don't earn all that money with some cushy job. Can't you give me some herbs for the muscle tension just to get rid of the headaches?"

"I do think *we* can resolve your headaches. It won't be simple. And I'll just play one small part. Much will be up to you. The more you help, the faster and more complete the resolution will be. The side effects hopefully will include resolving a lot of your other annoying symptoms. And we can start today if I have a willing partner in this effort."

"Sure, I'm good at working hard. And I'll do just about anything to stop this pounding in my head."

"OK, first thing we will do is move on to some brief examinations to confirm some of my suspicions about where the causes lie. Then we will start by doing some procedures which will help to immediately lessen the pain while some of the other techniques will be directed at the long-standing causes of the symptoms."

The naturopath then performed some examinations not done by the other doctors. She probed deeply into the muscles of the neck and jaw to determine how tight and tender they really were. The pressure caused Mary's headache to intensify in its characteristic way. "A large part of the problem is in the muscles, and we'll address that in several ways. Muscle relaxant medications won't be one of them," said Dr. Smith.

"Those pills didn't seem to help anyway," Mary replied.

The doctor felt the joints of the spine as they moved in different directions, and she noticed restrictions and abnormalities in their motion. "Part of the reason for the continued muscle tightness seems to be some severe joint motion problems which are sending nerve signals to the muscles to stay tight. So here is how we will address this part of the problem, knowing full well that it is only *part* of the problem. To elicit some immediate relief, I'm going to refer you to a massage therapist to relax those muscles."

"I like the sound of that."

"Well I'm sure it will be relaxing overall, but this is going to be some deep massage aimed at correction, and not every minute will be soothing. Then, to make sure that therapy lasts, I'm going to have a good chiropractor manipulate your spine, and joints in your skull, to eliminate the abnormal nerve signals to the muscles which those joint restrictions are sending. I can determine that there are restrictions there, but a chiropractor also skilled in cranial manipulation would be better able to correct those problems. Also, because that muscle tension is being driven by your work pressures, I'd like you to see a biofeedback specialist to help you train your muscles not to respond to stress in such a pathological fashion. In that way we will have some therapists working on you, some teaching you, and then you learning to take control of your life more."

"Well, I'm a take charge kind of person, and although the treatment by the masseuse and chiropractor sound attractive, I will enjoy participating in my own recovery. I've always wondered what it would be like to be hooked up to a machine that could help me control my inner workings," Mary replied, now intrigued by the new ideas.

"I kind of thought you would take to the biofeedback suggestion, but there are other reasons for recommending that approach. The specialist I would like you to see is also a psychotherapist. She uses guided imagery to get at the emotional reasons for relaxing the body. I am very suspicious that you have made some basic lifestyle choices that you may want to reevaluate in order not to have this condition return in some other form."

"What are you suggesting?" asked Mary defensively.

"Look at your life, particularly at how your job and the focus on making money are not only contributing directly to your headaches but are also influencing other aspects of your health. You are only controlling the symptoms with drug store remedies. You eat the same junk food every day. Not only will that cause hypoglycemic headaches, but the hypoglycemia will cause severe drops in energy which you then 'remedy' by drinking caffeine. Well, caffeine causes vascular headaches. So can being allergic to coffee. Even the pesticide residue in the beans can cause headaches and any number of the other symptoms that you are complaining about. You are probably also allergic to some, if not many, of the foods you are eating. So I will recommend some allergy tests to identify those, since the allergy tests that the hospital ran were inaccurate and obsolete.

"The caffeine and the nature of your job hypes you up so much that you feel too tired to exercise. By not getting sufficient exercise, more problems arise. That contributes to your being overweight— probably 25 pounds. As an experiment to illustrate how much energy it takes to lug that 25 extra pounds of useless fat around, carry a back pack to work with three gallons of water jugs in it and see how that makes you feel. Not exercising also disturbs metabolism and biorhythms when added to the caffeine, and stress makes sound, natural sleep difficult. This then forces you to use caffeine in the morning to jump start a poorly functioning machine—your body. Your sleep is probably also disturbed, and your body rhythms are out of sync from all the time spent indoors under artificial light with little exposure to natural sunlight. This will contribute to visual deficits which reinforce your headaches."

"I'm starting to see some of those complex interconnections between my life and health. But I'm not sure if I like what that means. It sounds like you want to change everything about my life," Mary said nervously.

"No, but I am asking you to carefully look at all those elements that impact your health and decide which behaviors are too costly to perpetuate and which new lifestyle patterns, if adopted, will give you worthwhile rewards. It might entail a lot of painful soul searching, difficult decisions, agonizing withdrawal from bad habits, and hard work, but the rewards are always worth it, and you said you are a glutton for hard work. Maybe now you will get paid with something more valuable than money—good health."

"Well, you certainly know how to challenge me. Let's start."

"Next on the agenda we will test your acupuncture meridians to see if there are significant imbalances that can be corrected. This might be a way also to do some treatment today to start easing the pain." Dr. Smith pulled out an electronic acupuncture instrument. Knowing that Mary was still enamored with high-tech medicine, she thought that the patient would respond better to the Western electronic methods of acupuncture than to the traditional pulse diagnosis and needles.

"I'm ready!"

As Dr. Smith began the testing, she continued to inform Mary of the other parts of the comprehensive protocol that would give the most optimal results. "Before you leave the office today, I also want you to fill out a computerized diet evaluation so our software can combine the results of the allergy tests with your apparent deficiencies in diet. That will give us a readout of allowed and disallowed foods as well as sample menus, recipes, and a calculation of what vitamin and mineral supplements might be appropriate." Dr. Smith knew that Mary would respond to dietary change more if a scientific computer told her how bad her diet was, and what corrections to make, rather than just suggesting some healthy cookbooks and giving her some general vitamins.

"It would also be good to start using your company's health club membership. I hear they have an excellent non-impact, singles aerobics class. You could get your exercise and some needed socializing at the same time. Also, many chiropractors in town use their yoga teacher as a trainer for therapeutic stretching, which will go hand-in-hand with the chiropractic work."

"Where will I find the time to do all this therapy?"

"You will be amazed at how much time you will gain from being healthy and energized. Also, you will come to reprioritize your time, leaving out unhealthy activities and making room for healthy ones. Most of the therapies will last only a short time until you have adopted sufficient skills and lifestyle changes to perpetuate the corrections that are made by the various therapists. Then you will be pretty much on your own, only taking advantage of periodic tests to determine progress, work on prevention, or build even greater levels of wholeness."

And that seemed to become an accurate prognosis. The acupuncture started to ease the head pain on that first visit. The next day was her first massage, and although it was painful at times when the masseuse worked deeply on chronically tense muscles, Mary was amazed at how relaxed she felt. She couldn't even remember when she was so at ease, because she had carried that tension for so many years. The massage lessened her headaches even more dramatically. When her spine and cranial joints were adjusted by the chiropractor the following day, she could tell how stiff her joints had become by the relief she felt and the greater range of motion that was restored to her neck. This seemed especially to help the pain behind her eyes. The chiropractor gave her some flexibility exercises to do, first under the direction of a stretching coach at the spa, then, once she knew the regimen well, on her own. She needed only a few more sessions of manipulative therapy to restore good joint function, but she realized how important periodic joint mobility checkups could be for maintaining her newly found sense of well-being. So a checkup was scheduled for every few months.

After just a few electronic acupuncture treatments, her meridians seemed fairly well balanced, and the incidence and severity of her headaches were so diminished that no more acupuncture was needed. The biofeedback really amazed Mary. She couldn't believe how tense her muscles could become just *thinking* about work while hooked up to the biofeedback instrumentation. But she was a good student and quickly learned more relaxed ways of interacting with the world.

More importantly, these sessions inspired Mary to face those parts of her life that she was tense and unhappy with and take action to change them. She realized she was spending a disproportionate amount of time earning money but not enjoying those fruits of her labor. The things that she valued most earlier in life and nearly forgot about, such as friends and creative expression, were not getting any time. So she cut her hours at work (mostly overtime hours anyway) and resumed her once cherished photography with new friends through a community class. This gradually turned into an offer of a full-time position as a magazine photographer with wonderful travel opportunities.

Months after her headaches disappeared and Mary was well on her way to becoming another person, happier and healthier, she made another appointment with the naturopath. Dr. Smith almost didn't recognize her. "I take it from how good you look that you have been doing well? Eating better and exercising too, I'd bet," said Dr. Smith with some amazement. But it was also a confirmation of her earlier intuition that Mary had great potential for pulling off a dramatic change in her health.

"Looking back, I can hardly believe I used to eat such junk and not exercise at all. Now I can't imagine myself not swimming and bicycling and playing tennis and doing my stretches. And it's so fun! But one part of my headaches still remains. I am still sensitive to sunlight, and the squinting still causes problems seeing. I have to wear dark glasses most of the time outdoors. And although my sleep is better, I still have trouble going to sleep, sleeping soundly, and then getting up refreshed. You had mentioned relationships of natural sunlight and biological rhythms as part of my problem, but I was doing so well that I never followed up on that aspect of the therapy because I thought everything was getting better. Now that I'm more involved with the photography, I'm noticing these visual problems more. Even though they are not that bad, I want to make sure I'm doing everything I can to get healthy. I don't want to settle for less than I deserve."

She referred to the option of Neurosensory Development Training, popularly known as "colored light therapy." This is a system that triggers the nervous system to process light more efficiently by flashing different colored lights before the eyes. This had not been offered to her earlier for several reasons. One, the other approaches seemed to address the most important issues that were at the root of the problem. Two, she was doing so well with these procedures that adding this one seemed inappropriate. Three, she was also heavily committed to a number of different activities, and it was important to avoid a therapy overload, particularly with all the other changes that were occurring in her life. It was now a better time to start that type of care, since it would apparently directly affect those remaining symptoms, and she now had the time for it.

And indeed, once Mary began to retrain her nervous system to accept and utilize natural sunlight more efficiently, her visual problems disappeared, and her sleep patterns returned to normal. Not needing sunglasses to be outside greatly increased the quantity of light entering her eyes and neurohormonal pathways, granting better balance in her biological rhythms and more efficient biochemical functions. She felt better, slept more soundly, and had more energy.

Would any of the many health improvements Mary made have occurred if she had continued the standard, orthodox, allopathic, disease care she started with her general practitioner? Probably not. She actually had been getting worse from that care. One reason: the initial diagnosis as a headache had only located a symptom of a much bigger picture. This first flaw sent the medical machinery down an unfulfilling path of misdirected energies.

By the naturopath's correct prioritization of appropriate levels of testing, initial approaches were quickly and inexpensively rewarding. She didn't look for exotic brain tumors when there were no simple indicators pointing in that direction. She tested for the most common causes of these conditions and didn't lose sight of the big picture with its many facets. She chose inexpensive natural therapies with few known side effects to initially address the symptoms of pain, but she also included therapies that got at the deeper roots of the problem. As a good holistic physician, she integrated the professional expertise of colleagues to assist in areas outside her area of specialty with no thought of the economic effects on her own practice. As circumstances improved, the regimen adapted also. Ultimately this naturopath was involved in not just the cure of some headaches but the total transformation of a person's life, touching the psyche, occupation, nutrition, aerobic fitness, flexibility, socialization, and education, at *less* cost than just one of the tests previously done medically.

In addition, there were significant side benefits to the world. Mary now had more energy which could be directed into other avenues. She did more volunteer work for the disadvantaged. She became more ecologically aware with her new knowledge of nutrition, allergy, and toxic substances in the environment. She felt more obligated to act responsibly in a representative democracy by writing legislators, attending hearings, and sharing her experience with others so everyone might know more about holistic health—things she had to learn the hard way.

We can look at another case which will illustrate some other important principles of priorities in health care.

Sally, too, has had increasingly intense headaches. Unlike Mary, Sally guards her health in many ways. She eats a healthy vegetarian fare and exercises regularly. She seldom is sick, so she hardly ever needs to see a doctor and doesn't like to. Sally has had bad experiences with M. D.'s not acknowledging her desire to know about her choices and have control of her treatment. She avoids them as much as possible, so much so that she has tended to favor modes of health care far from the realm of logical, technological medicine. Lately Sally has been involved in channeling, crystal healing, and radionics. This, she thought, along with her regular yoga program and an increase in herbs and vitamin supplements, would surely rid her of the dreadful headaches.

Sally had been programmed to make certain health care choices because of her past experiences, not so much by a critical analysis and prioritization of her needs in a fully integrated program of care. As Sally continued with her self-guided approach, fearing another negative experience with an M. D., she tried this and that esoteric New Age therapy for her ever-increasing headaches. She was sure that they had to do with several of her past lives where she was beheaded as a Sumerian queen and run over by a chariot in a great Roman holy war. But however interesting and cathartic her hypnotic regressions, no help with the headaches occurred, despite the assurances of many New Age therapists.

Finally, she relented to a friend's pressure to see a chiropractor. Since this wasn't a "real doctor" in a

hospital-like setting, it was a bit easier to tolerate. During the initial consultation with the chiropractor, Dr. Jones, she stated her firm reservations about doctors and modern technology. He nodded and recommended taking a history and performing some simple, low-tech, inexpensive, physical, orthopedic, and neurological examinations. This way he could test out the simplest and most likely causes while explaining each test as they went along. He could also rule out some more serious problems with simple tests. If further tests, such as x-rays, would be needed, he would discuss all the reasons and implications first.

The history revealed few clues. Since Sally took good care of herself by eating and exercising well, plus managing stress effectively, there were few clues by which Dr. Jones could suspect some of the more typical causes of headache. She had no allergies, no head or neck trauma, only intense headaches with some visual disturbances that had begun several months ago for no apparent reason. She had made no improvement with self-care approaches.

Early on, the exams eliminated the most likely possibilities one after another. No muscle tension in the neck or jaws. No significant joint restrictions in the spine or cranium. No evidence of infection or allergy. Then, upon performing a simple test by using an opthalmoscope to look at the back wall of the inside of her eyes, the chiropractor discovered evidence of increased pressure from within Sally's skull, as if there might be some space-occupying lesion. A few other simple nerve tests confirmed that something unusual and abnormal was occurring inside the cranial vault.

Dr. Jones said, "With these simple tests I've ruled out almost all of the usual causes, and my findings lead me to suspect some central nervous system abnormalities." He suggested to Sally that she see a neurologist to verify his findings and possibly do further studies, such as an MRI. He knew she would be unhappy with that suggestion, but he made it clear that there was nothing else significant he could find that might have any impact on the problem, and there might be great risk in not following up with further studies. After some emotional discussion, Dr. Jones agreed to first order the MRI and give Sally the results before making an appointment with a neurologist.

He made an appointment the next day with the radiologists to have an MRI identify any soft tissue abnormalities in Sally's brain. The radiologist called Dr. Jones that afternoon, informing him of a definite structural abnormality near the middle of the brain and suggesting a neurosurgeon to consult with. The chiropractor then called the neurosurgeon, explained the findings, and then discussed the situation with Sally. Sally made an immediate appointment.

It so happened that Sally needed neurosurgery for a rare abnormality of the blood vessels in her brain. It was just an unusual weakness, probably since birth, of a crucial artery. Her healthy activities throughout life probably allowed her to survive all those years and were instrumental to her rapid recovery and return to a vibrant lifestyle. But her delay in seeking appropriate testing, while depending on esoteric practices with little or no documented validity or success with these problems, put her life at dire risk. Part of the cause of this was an unresponsive, inhumane, high-tech, medical care system that so disenchanted Sally (and many others) that she rejected out of hand nearly all medical approaches after several bad experiences. She then turned to other inappropriate modalities on the "fringe" side of the health care field, further jeopardizing her health.

Eventually a solution, a graded assessment of priorities, was found. This did not totally invalidate the things she tried to help herself with. It was just the discovery of the most appropriate course of action, once the right amount and type of evaluation was done. Choosing the best health enhancement programs at the right times is best done with careful analysis. Even though many New Age therapies may have health benefits, there is sparse information for rational and cost-effective decisions.

Sally also realized that true caring can go hand in hand with a high-tech approach. The chiropractor was well trained in neurological testing and the appropriate use of methods such as magnetic resonance imaging (MRI). But he added to that careful explanation and consent, and doctor-patient and physician-to-physician consultation. The radiologist who read the films sent Sally flowers in the hospital, even though he spent more time getting to know the inside of her brain than talking directly with her. He realized he was helping another human being and not just reading light and dark images on a film. The neurosurgeon, with his technical skill and his caring manner, also helped renew Sally's confidence in medical science. Advanced technology in the hands of dedicated health care workers can be used judiciously with right timing to benefit self-care efforts. All the doctors involved had reinforced the importance of multi-disciplinary cooperation which helps all future patients.

## LOOKING WITHIN

Now, for our own priorities. First, take a general overview of our individual Web of Wholeness. What aspects of our health put the greatest strain on our total well being? What strands of the Web are most frayed? What area needs most work? Which area am I willing to work on? What strengths will support me?

Looking for answers to these questions can take us to different depths of evaluation as illustrated by the flow chart on page 30. We will start at rather superficial levels of inquiry in order to acquire a general picture of our Web of Wholeness. This will insure that we look to any crisis areas first. We can then inquire more deeply into each health aspect. What can we expect?

- A simple spectrum analysis will be done for most aspects of health.

- Resources will be identified to point individuals toward other, more specific testing when needed.

- Revisions of priorities will be accommodated and encouraged as new knowledge and health are gained.

Initially, it may appear that certain aspects of one's health are the prime problems in one's life and thus need the major portion of attention and care. But deeper investigation often uncovers long overlooked connections and causes that change the picture.

For instance, Albert struggled for years with all kinds of health problems. He went from one therapist to another for different treatments of all his different symptoms with little success. Upon doing the Initial General Spectrum Analysis, he was sure that his major problem area was going to be "physical functioning." The health aspect he thought would be the least problem was his livelihood. He was a highly paid computer operator for a very stable company. He always remarked to his wife that "They pay me more than I'm worth." He even liked the people he worked with. But after doing all the spectrum analyses of each health aspect, he discovered an important fact: his unfulfilled desire was to be a successful science fiction writer, which he did for fun in his limited free time. He also realized that although his job was good to him in significant ways, he really didn't like going to work. His physical symptoms would diminish on weekends and disappear on vacations, which he always took out in the country with his family. Everyone in his family liked the country more than the city where his job was. Suspecting that many of his physical symptoms were related to his submerged dissatisfaction with work and city life, Albert was confronted with the difficult proposition of leaving an unusually well-paid job in order to learn to write for a living.

While reading further about environmental health issues, he realized that there were a number of long-time employees who shared his symptoms. He found that the ventilation ducts that supplied his office were connected to the chemical manufacturing portion of the plant. Further investigation (with resources found in this book) revealed that the chemicals produced were highly toxic. After contacting the Occupational Safety and Health Administration and the Environmental Protection Agency, he concluded that the building was a toxic time bomb. Not only were the odorless chemical fumes from the manufacturing division a problem, but the new paneling and carpet in Albert's office complex was emitting poisonous formaldehyde fumes. Although the company drew up a two-year plan of reconstruction to remedy the situation, Albert and a dozen other employees decided it wasn't worth the wait.

It was a frightening step, but Albert and his family moved to the country. He became so concerned over the environmental health nightmare he had suffered with for so many years that he wrote some magazine articles on the subject. They were so good that he was offered a part-time job with reasonable pay writing for the local newspaper. This supported him and his family sufficiently and gave him enough time to finish his first sci-fi book and get it published with a contract for a sequel. He and his family couldn't be happier. Nearly every one of Albert's symptoms disappeared.

How much of his ill health was due to environmental hazards, and how much was due to other stresses of city life and unfulfilled desires of the heart? Retrospectively, figuring out a percentage of contribution has little meaning. What is more valuable is to investigate carefully and systematically all aspects of one's being for those hidden, or obvious, detriments to wholeness. Then, just as systematically, engage in health enhancement efforts to strengthen all the strands in our Web of Wholeness. Remember that a too superficial evaluation might miss an important element. The more accurate, specific, and deep the testing, the better the map will be to guide us on the Path of Wellness.

Use the following questions and statements to help you calculate the relative health of each aspect of your being. Then mark on the Initial General Spectrum Analysis a 0 to 10 rating for each category.

I experience

- 10: Optimal functioning. The very best imaginable.

- 9: Excellent, but not perfect functioning.

- 8: High levels of good health.

- 7: Acceptable health that doesn't need much attention.

- 6: Minor negative qualities have started to impose on adequate functioning.

- 5: An even mixture of positive and negative qualities.

- 4 to 1: Ever decreasing positive attributes and progressive accumulation of negative characteristics.

- 0: The pits—*major* crisis needing immediate attention.

## Proper Physical Functioning

Do I eat according to the nutritional guidelines on page 63? Or does my diet read like a convenience food store inventory?

Do I participate in enough aerobic exercise to keep my cardiovascular system well conditioned? Or, was the last time I remember my heart rate getting into a training zone when I got overly excited watching the 1981 Bowling Championship on TV?

Do I participate in vigorous stretching exercises at least four times per week sufficient to maintain good flexibility in all my joints? Or, is my stretching limited to that which is required to cut my toenails once a month?

Am I energetic throughout the day? Or do I feel like slush moving downhill?

Do I go to bed at a reasonable hour, sleep soundly, then arise fully refreshed and energized for the day? Or do I often get to bed or finally fall asleep in the wee hours of the morning, only to awake to a semiconscious state sufficient to drag my hulking carcass to the coffee pot in hopes that the brown liquid will transform me into something resembling a humanoid before work?

Do I get out into plenty of sunshine every day? Or do I spend most of the daylight hours under artificial indoor lighting and shade my eyes from the sun when I do go out?

## Economic Stability and Right Livelihood

Do I have enough money for whatever health enhancement programs I feel are necessary? Or do my financial circumstances detract from my health?

Does my livelihood support and enhance all the aspects of my life? Or does my job degrade my physical and psychological health and harm humanity and the environment?

## Intellectual Stimulation and Educational Opportunity

Is my life filled with creative intellectual stimulation? Or do I feel like I'm in a black hole of mental mediocrity?

Are there educational opportunities that are readily available to me? Am I on track for educational advancement to suit my needs and desires?

Is my continuing education relevant to my development as a whole person?

## Psychological Health

Am I happy?

## Interpersonal Relationships

Do I have close, loving, intimate relationships that enhance my life? Do I have a good social support system of friends to interact with in life's daily joys and struggles? Or am I alienated from friends, family, and society?

## Ecological Health

Is my immediate environment clean and supportive of health? Or am I surrounded by smoggy air, polluted water, contaminated food, or a toxic home or workplace? Or do I even know the difference?

I contribute time, money, energy, and awareness to protecting our environment.

Or, I live *my* life as I please without any conscious effort to improve ecological harmony.

## Spiritual Well-Being

I am at peace in my heart with the whole universe.

Now score the Initial General Spectrum Analysis in each category from 0 to 10. Observe strengths. Note weaknesses. Are there serious emergency aspects that need attention? Although this book was meant to be read at first in sequence, the chapters in Part 2 can be read in order of individual priorities. Just remember that the essence of the book lies in integrating all the various aspects of health; it is important to read and consider all subjects.

## INITIAL GENERAL SPECTRUM ANALYSIS

| Aspect of Health | Score |
|---|---|
| Physical | ——— |
| Economic/Occupational | ——— |
| Intellectual/Educational | ——— |
| Psychological | ——— |
| Relationships | ——— |
| Ecology | ——— |
| Spirituality | ——— |

## A RATING OF HEALTH ENHANCEMENT STRATEGIES

There are a mind-boggling number of "therapies" designed to enhance health or to correct a health problem, cure a disease, or eliminate a symptom. This section is meant to assist in the prioritization of these therapies for consideration. First, Table A can be used with every potential approach to health in any life situation to help ask relevant questions on how any particular technique might assist specific problems at hand or overall general health. The questions are divided into three categories corresponding to their most likely degree of importance.

The first category contains those therapies of highest potential value for the greatest number of individuals. Most of our time, money, and effort should be concentrated in this arena of health enhancement.

The second category contains therapies that have the potential to help particular individuals at times, but there is some question about their universal applicability and significance in broad terms. More research needs to be done on therapies in this category to find how to best apply them and who will benefit the most from them. These therapies can be considered after health enhancement strategies from category one have been integrated into a comprehensive holistic health program.

Category three contains the more doubtful approaches that need much more research to verify any validity. Although some may be valuable in particular instances, it is difficult to give recommendations in a book like this when the research substantiating their efficacy is so sparse. This "Consumer Beware" category might be further divided into four subheadings:

- outdated, ineffective, standard medical practices
- snake oil scams
- "good heart, attractive concept, but doubtful benefits"
- investigational, with possible benefits—but more research is needed

Many standard medical practices are virtually worthless. Some of these began as conscientious efforts to improve health. Other medical services are basically rip-offs. These would then fall under the classification of "snake oil."

Some "New Age" techniques could fall under this deceptive category, but most are developed with good intentions following some attractive idea that just doesn't come through with substantial enough benefits to warrant the time, money or effort spent in that direction. Many of the so-called "new age" healing systems have arisen out of progressive-minded efforts to make sense of observed phenomena that traditional health care has not adequately researched or explained. Unique models of unseen energy dynamics are postulated to fill in the gaps between observed phenomena and our understanding. These models will prove useful only if they stand the test of unbiased scientific inquiry. Some will fail. Some show more promise and will prove useful after more scientific evidence accumulates. Still others have certain elements that are beneficial and will be modified to accommodate new knowledge.

In every era there is a band of progressive explorers who push the edges of conventional thinking—fearless innovators who experiment with their intuition. The establishment, safe in their comfortable habits, always brands these mavericks as heretics, crazies, Satan's workers, outcasts. Yes, many of their ideas are crazy. Their theories may not pan out. What seems like fantastic results in the exhilarating aura of a new idea becomes the placebo effect upon closer scrutiny. But some of those ideas, health care techniques, and transformational approaches do prove to be revolutionary. That is the purpose of new age thought and activities. Not to be always right, but not to be afraid of being wrong—taking the risk to probe the inner and outer limits of experience—to push the rest of us out of our unseen shackles.

As it is now, there are so many unproven "New Age" therapies peddled and hawked to unknowing, ill people desperately looking for answers, that the situation may be counterproductive. There is a backlash in the scientific community which frowns on the undocumented, "flaky" claims and hype of approaches on the fringes of present knowledge. But the public is also becoming more skeptical of advertising claims in general, just from the constant false hype assaulting us on a daily basis.

### The believer is happy, the doubter wise.
#### Greek saying

If a fraction of the time, money, and energy that goes into promoting the therapies in this category of "Consumer Beware" were spent on valid, documented, independent research into their efficacy, we would all know much more about how to take better care of our health. Part of the responsibility for performing the necessary research lies with the individuals and organizations profiting from these therapies. Part also belongs to the established clinical and scientific community who have the research experience, facilities, and funding to do relevant research in these promising fields.

Unfortunately, there are often strong walls of bias preventing certain types of research from receiving funding or even being published. Even if a new form of therapy should get funding, research is done, efficacy is proved, and the findings are published, it takes a very long time for validation trials to be performed and published. Longer still is the time it takes to disseminate the results effectively in some usable form to doctors and therapists. There must be a better joining of forces between innovation and scientific validation that can keep unwarranted approaches from assaulting the public while at the same time allowing a more rapid development of new ideas.

Table B contains examples of therapies rated for physical health by the author. Table C contains examples of categorized psychotherapies. Many readers will undoubtedly disagree with this author's classification of certain therapies. My only answer is: provide the research and write your own book. They were arranged this way here because of available research and personal clinical experience.

Also, remember to be wary of false extrapolation and false attribution. False extrapolation is a phenomenon that occurs when an individual, or several, improve under a therapy and an enthusiastic, optimistic conclusion is drawn assuming *everybody* will improve under this procedure. Or, if everybody doesn't benefit, unjustified large numbers of people. Or, when one condition seems to benefit from minute empirical data, other health problems, related or unrelated, are assumed to also benefit without adequate experimental research to prove it.

### Science is the great antidote to the poison of enthusiasm and superstition.
#### Adam Smith

False attribution occurs when a person undergoes a treatment modality and his condition improves because of some other, unrecognized reason. He may then wrongly attribute success to the treatment modality. This mistake often occurs in degrees where the treatment contributed only a small amount of benefit, but the patient and/or the therapist attributed a much greater importance to it.

Remember that one of the major tenets of holistic health care is that one must identify the multiple paths that will lead him or her to continual, total health enhancement at any particular time. Many times when we approach a therapist, his goal, consciously or unconsciously, is to fit you into his repertoire of techniques—whether they are among the most effective approaches or not. So each individual has to be discriminating about what therapies are most appropriate. But health care practitioners, too, have to be broadly educated and use the concepts of multifaceted, inter-disciplinary care presented in this book to help their clients decide on the most beneficial priorities of care.

Also, as we concentrate here primarily on physical and psychological therapies, do not forget the health enhancement requirements in other aspects of life, such as occupational health, economic stability, environmental health, spiritual well-being, relationship harmony. . . .

---

## TABLE A

### *High Priority Health Enhancement Strategies*

- Proven over time
- Have significant impact on many aspects of health
- Have significant impact on one primary aspect of health
- Applicable to large population segments
- Cost/effectiveness ratio good

- Favorable benefit to risk ratio
- Have good preventive and early detection capabilities
- Excellent opportunity for self-directed care
- Well-respected, quality training, certification, or licensing of therapists

### *Second Priority Therapies for Physical Health*

- Empirical data suggests effectiveness, but good scientific research is either equivocal or unavailable
- Applicable to only smaller population segments
- Cost / effectiveness ratio marginal or difficult to calculate

- Benefit/risk ratio difficult to assess due to: significant number, or seriousness, of the side effects or complications; or there are questions regarding the significance of the benefits
- Some opportunity for self-directed care
- Some valid certification of therapists

### *Consumer Beware!*
### *More Research Needed or Snake Oil?*

- Unproven, disproved, and/or very sparse supportive empirical data (often accompanies grand hype, fantastic claims without documentation, testimonials, heavy salesmanship, high emotionality of therapists in presenting claims . . .)
- May be relevant to an isolated, small number of individuals

- Minimal health impact
- Highly questionable cost-effectiveness when compared to therapies in the upper levels of this chart
- Highly questionable benefit to risk ratio
- Few opportunities for self-directed care
- Poor therapist training programs

## TABLE B

### First Priority Strategies for Physical Health

- High complex carbohydrate, low fat, vegetarian diet void of allergenic foods (i.e., McDougall, Anderson, Macrobiotic)
- General nutritional supplementation
- Specific, individualized supplementation program when particular imbalances are present
- Balanced, regular exercise program:
  - a. Aerobic exercise in a low-risk, non-impact form
  - b. Stretching exercise in a systematic, individualized format
  - c. Strength conditioning in a safe, programmed routine sufficient to maintain protection of the body during the demands of daily living
  - d. Tai Chi Chuan
- Spinal, extremity, soft tissue manipulation:
  - a. Chiropractic: Motion Palpation, Diversified, Cox Flexion-Distraction
  - b. Therapeutic Massage
- Awareness Enhancement—Meditation, mindfulness practices, biofeedback
- Stress Management and Stress Reduction Strategies—Biofeedback, lifestyle change, relaxation techniques, voluntary simplicity . . .
- Environmental Medicine (Clinical Ecology—involves the most progressive aspects of Immunology, Toxicology, and Allergy)
- Traditional Oriental Medicine—acupuncture and herbs
- Optimal sleep supporting a harmonized biological rhythm
- Optimal exposure to full spectrum light:
  - a. Plenty of time outdoors in natural sunlight
  - b. Full-spectrum lights indoors
- Accident Prevention: Auto, home, work, and recreational safety

### Second Priority Therapies for Physical Health

- Herbalism (Western formulations used alone)
- Chiropractic techniques—Gonstead, Biophysics
- Neurosensory Development Training with colored lights
- Non-contact Healing techniques: Therapeutic Touch, Prayer . . .
- Modified, Protein-sparing Fasting
- Chelation therapy
- Colonics
- Ayurvedic Medicine
- Homeopathy
- Feldenkrais
- Structural Integration (Rolfing)
- Alexander Technique
- Hellerwork
- Qi Gong
- Properly prescribed medications integrated with a comprehensive health enhancement program
- Necessary surgery expertly performed and integrated with a comprehensive health enhancement program

**TABLE B (Cont.)**

*Consumer Beware!*
*More Research Needed or Snake Oil?*

- A large percentage of hospital food
- 80% of hysterectomies
- 50% of C-sections
- A large percentage of tonsillectomies
- Silicone breast implants
- 90% of ear tubes for chronic otitis media
- Ritalin for hyperactivity
- 40% of heart bypass surgeries
- Iridology
- Subliminal message tapes
- Medical Astrology
- MORA Therapy
- Bio-Electronic Vincent
- Scalar Wave Electroacupuncture
- Electronically assisted Tui-Na
- Bio-Photon Light Therapy
- Biokinesiology with Vegatest
- Flyberg Sound Therapy
- Orthobionomy
- Questionable chiropractic techniques:
  Activator
  Biosacral
  Toftness
  Ayurvedic Kinesiology
  Meric
  Neural Organizational Technique
  Directional, Non-Force Technique
  Spinal Stressology
  Concept Therapy
  BioEnergetic Synchronization Technique
    (BEST)
  Micro-Manipulation
  Vickery Method

- Exclusive upper cervical methods—
  NUCCA, Grostic, Blair, Duff, HIO, Kale,
  Life, Herring, Atlas Orthogonality
- Parfango Therapy—volcanic ash and
  paraffin applied to body
- Crystal Healing
- Infra-Red Crystal Therapy
- Absuchan Ka—"a highly evolved method
  of healing and bodywork taught by Mafu,
  an illumined Lord who is channeled by
  his oracle, Swami Paramanand Saraswati
  which involves massaging the energy
  vortices of the body, stimulating of
  soulular meridian points, and the
  application of crushed crystals,
  poultices, and copper wire"
- Chakra balancing
- Foot reflexology
- Polarity therapy
- Cymatic Therapy (specific sound
  frequencies transmitted through the body)
- Radiance Technique
- Reiki
- OMEGA
- Aural healing
- Gemstone therapy
- SHEN—Physio-emotional Release Therapy
- Angelite

**TABLE C**

### *First Priority Strategies for Psychological Health*

Each psychological health enhancement strategy listed in this section provides enormous opportunity for self-directed psychological growth over a vast array of different individual circumstances. They are most likely to help the greatest number of individuals in the most productive way. This is in part due to the universality and power of the techniques themselves. It should be remembered though that one of the prime determinants of success in psychotherapeutic practice is the relationship between the client and the therapist. So if you are using the services of a therapist, be sure that you have the utmost confidence in that person. It must also be remembered that many psychotherapists practice an eclectic form which incorporates aspects of many techniques to best fit the client and the circumstances. This is a valuable, open-minded approach. Use the resources on page 46 to find organizations that will make referrals to qualified therapists.

Keep in mind the importance of aerobic exercise, meditative techniques, sufficient sleep, and optimal sunlight for their profound effects on psychological health, even though they are not listed as direct psychotherapeutic approaches. They could all be included in first priority approaches.

---

**TABLE C**

### *First Priority Strategies for Psychological Health*

The first four lead the list because of their self-care opportunities and broad scope:

- Psychosynthesis
- Progoff's Journal Work
- Focusing
- Personality assessments like the Myers-Briggs and Palmer's *Enneagram*
- Orthomolecular Psychiatry leads the list too, but is in a bit of a different category since it focuses on altering the biochemical aspects of psychological health through diet, allergy control, elimination of toxic substances from irritating the nervous system and distorting biochemistry, and nutrient supplementation. All other psychotherapies can be enhanced if the nervous system is working efficiently with nutrients, biochemicals, and hormones balanced in optimal quantities.

- Biofeedback also heads the list because of its universal benefit. It too is unique as a non-psychotherapeutic modality *per se*. Learning harmonious, physiological integration through biofeedback training powerfully reinforces psychodynamic harmony.

### *Other First Priority Strategies for Psychological Health*

- Process-Oriented Psychotherapy
- Integrative Body Psychotherapy
- Diamond Heart Approach

- Object Relations Psychotherapy
- Family-Based Psychotherapy

## TABLE C (Cont.)

### *Second Priority Psychotherapies*

Please note that the following therapies are categorized as "second priority" not because of their lack of efficacy. They have been put in this category primarily because they have either a more limited focus on particular types of psychological problems, there is less opportunity for self directed work outside the therapist's office, thus lowering the cost-benefit ratio, or the availability of these services is limited. Finding a high-quality therapist utilizing one of the approaches below, when that therapy is ideally suited to help your particular problem, should prove worthwhile.

The first three therapies need to be separated out from the following ones in the same way that orthomolecular psychiatry and biofeedback were in category one. They do not focus on psychotherapy *per se.* They are oriented to improving brain biochemistry and neurophysiological integration, and via that route they have a dramatic impact on specific psychological problems.

- Acupuncture
- Neurosensory Development Training
- Cranial Electrical Stimulation
- Hypnotherapy—by licensed psychologists or counselors—(Ericksonian and Alchemical are two valid types of therapy)

- Cognitive Therapy
- Transactional Analysis
- Rational-Emotive Therapy
- Bioenergetics
- Guided Imagery
- Voice Dialogue
- Jungian Therapy
- Gestalt Therapy
- Holotropic Breathwork
- Neuro Linguistic Programming
- Reichian and Neo-Reichian Therapy
- Sand Play
- Bonding Therapy
- Art Therapy
- Music Therapy
- CORE—Energetics
- Hakomi
- Dreamwork
- Rebirthing
- Eye Movement Desensitization and Reprocessing (EMDR)
- Light Spectrum Assisted Psychotherapy/ Confluent Somatic Therapy

### *Consumer Beware!*
### *More Research Needed or Snake Oil?*

- A large percentage of psychopharmacology
- Subliminal message tapes
- Firewalking
- Aromatherapy
- Bach flower essences

- Dianetics
- Stance of Light
- HUNA
- SHEN.
- Aura Soma

# HOLISTIC HEALTH RESOURCES

*We ourselves are responsible for our own happiness and misery.*
*We create our own heavens. We create our own hells.*
*We are the architects of our fate.*

**Narada Mahathera**

★ Denotes Best of the Best Resources

## Catalogs, Directories, Encyclopedias, Bibliographies

*Backus, Karen, ed. *Encyclopedia of Medical Organizations and Agencies.* Gale Research, 1989. Gale Research Inc., Book Tower, Detroit, MI 48226; (800) 877-GALE.

*Backus, Karen, ed. *Medical and Health Information Directory.* Gale Research, 1990.

*Directory of National Helplines: A Guide to Toll-Free Public Service Numbers,* The Perian Press, P.O. Box 1808, Ann Arbor, MI 48106; (800) 678-2435 (313) 434-5530. An annual listing of approximately 500 toll-free phone numbers providing assistance and support in many aspects of health—physical, psychological, social, economic, legal, and environmental.

Fink, John. *Third Opinion: An International Directory to Alternative Therapy Centers for the Treatment and Prevention of Cancer.* Avery Publishers, 1988.

*Lesko, Mathew et al. *What to Do When You Can't Afford Health Care.* Information, U.S.A., 1993. Information, U.S.A., P.O. Box E, Kensington, MD 20895.

*Life Sciences Catalog,* CRC Press, 2000 Corporate Blvd., N.W., Boca Raton, FL 33431; (800) 272-7737; Fax (407) 998-9114. Specialized books, periodicals, and computer software related to health.

Lowfat Lifeline, P.O. Box 1889, Port Townsend, WA 98368; (800) 294-9801; (206) 379-9724. Resources for nutritional wellness programs.

★Rheingold, Howard. *The Millennium Whole Earth Catalog.* HarperSanFrancisco, 1994. An essential resource.

★*Self-Care Catalog,* 5850 Shellmound St., Emeryville, CA 94608; (800) 345-3371; Fax (800) 345-4021. Excellent catalog for wide variety of resources for providing oneself better health. Includes books; self testing kits; and useful health devices and aides.

Strasburg, Kate, et al. *The Quest for Wholeness: An Annotated Bibliography in Patient-Centered Medicine.* 1991. Available from Commonweal, P.O. Box 316, Bolinas, CA 94924; (415) 868-0970.

★White, Barbara and Madara, Edward. *The Self-Help Sourcebook: Finding and Forming Mutual Aid Self-Help Groups.* Available from the American Self-Help Clearinghouse. Lists 7500 self-help headquarters throughout the U.S.

*Wasserman, Paul, ed. *Encyclopedia of Health Information Sources.* Gale Research, 1987.

*Wilson, Robert, ed. *Consumer Sourcebook.* Gale Research, 1989. Gale Research Inc., Book Tower, Detroit, Michigan 48226; (800) 877-GALE.

* Note—These are expensive, extensive, often multi-volume compilations, but the best resources for organizations that can assist people in their health objectives. Every library should have them!

Note—The National Health Information Center (NHIC) is a service of the Office of Disease Prevention and Health Promotion of the U.S. Department of Health and Human Services. NHIC, P.O. Box 1133, Washington, DC 20013-1133; (800) 336-4797; In Maryland, (301) 565-4167; Fax (301) 984-4256. In their HEALTHFINDER series are two helpful, free publications, *Toll-Free Numbers for Health Information* and *Federal Health Information Centers and Clearinghouses.*

Note—The Public Information Division, National Institutes of Health, Room 305, Bethesda, MD 20892; (301) 496-4143. They have a free catalog (NIH Publication List) that itemizes the publications which are available from all of the Institutes. While not holistic or progressive *per se,* useful information is available inexpensively in these publications.

## Books

Anderson, Robert. *Wellness Medicine.* Keats, 1987.

★Boston Women's Health Book Collective Staff. *The New Our Bodies, Ourselves.* Touchstone, 1992.

★Murray, Michael and Pizzorno, Joseph. *Encyclopedia of Natural Medicine.* Prima Publishing, 1991. Prima Publishing, P.O. Box 1260MP Rocklin, CA 95677; (916) 624-5718.

Travis, John and Ryan Regina. *Wellness Workbook.* Ten Speed Press, 1986.

Ware, John and Stewart, Anita. *Measuring Functioning and Well-Being.* Duke University Press, 1992.

## *Periodicals*

★ *Alternative & Complementary Therapies,* Mary Ann Liebert, Inc., Publishers, 1651 Third Ave., New York, NY 10128; (800) M LIEBERT; (212) 289-2300; Fax (212) 289-3347.

★ *Natural Health,* P.O. Box 57320, Boulder, CO 80322-7320.

★ *New Age Journal,* P.O. Box 53275, Boulder, CO 80321-3275.

★ *In Context,* P.O. Box 11470, Bainbridge Island, WA 98110.

★ *Utne Reader,* LENS Publishing, 1624 Harmon Place, Suite 330, Minneapolis, MN 55403; (612) 338-5040; for subscriptions—(800) 736-UTNE; (614) 382-3322. Shares with *Whole Earth Review* the top echelon of journals that glean the best from the alternative press.

★ *Whole Earth Review,* P.O. Box 38, Sausalito, CA 94966-9932; (415) 332-1716; (800) 938-6657. One of the most progressive and extensive documenters of new information related to holistic living.

## *Computer Software, Networks, and Databases*

Allied and Alternative Medicine Database—From Medical Information Service. It surveys 350 biomedical journals as well as books and newsletters for varied non-allopathic literature on subjects from Acupuncture to Yoga.

★ *Alternative Medicine Connection Online Service,* P.O. Box 683, Herndon, VA 22070; (703) 471-4734; BBS (703) 471-8465; Fax (703) 471-6170.

Combined Health Information Database—(800) 955-0906, BRS Online.

Ed Del Grosso, 1 Ball Farm Way, Wilmington, DE 19808; (302) 994-3772. He has a listing of 300 health-related computer bulletin boards.

Ferguson, Tom. *Consumer Health Informatics (Proceedings of the First National Conference on Consumer Health Informatics),* Self-care Productions, 1993. Available from Mailcomm Plus, 2729 Exposition Blvd., Austin, TX 78703; (512) 472-1296. Information on how computers can help people care for their own health.

GO GOODHEALTH, P.O. Box 292496, Kettering, OH 45429; (513) 445-6441; CompuServe E-Mail: 76702,562; (Internet: 76702,562@compuserve.com). CompuServe's "Health and Fitness Forum."

Health Periodicals Database—from Information Access Company. Over 180,000 health related articles, summaries, abstracts from technical medical journals and consumer health publications. Updated weekly and going back to 1983.

Health *Response*Ability Systems, P.O. Box 220775, Chantilly, VA 22022-0775; (703) 904-8484; Fax (703) 904-8485; America Online E-Mail: ESillveous or ADouma; (Internet: ESilveous@AOL.COM or ADouma@AOL.COM). They operate the "Better Health and Medical Forum" on America Online. For information or an on-line trial—(800) 827-6364.

*Mindware Catalog,* 1803 Mission St., Suite 414, Santa Cruz, CA 95060; (800) 447-0477. Computer software and CD-ROMs for better care of one's health.

## *Organizations*

***Love cures people—both the ones who give it and the ones who receive it.***
**Karl Menninger**

★ American Self Help Clearinghouse, St. Clares-Riverside Medical Center, Denville, NJ 07834; (201) 625-7101. The place to find self-help groups.

Center for Frontier Sciences, Temple University, Ritter Hall 003-00, Philadelphia, PA 19122; (215) 787-8487. A networking and educational exchange for scientific advances leading towards wholeness.

Global Education Associates, 475 Riverside Drive, Suite 570, New York, NY 10115; (212) 870-3290. Nonprofit research and educational institution that focuses on issues of peace, sane economic development, ecological balance, and human rights.

★ Institute of Noetic Sciences (IONS), P.O. Box 909, Sausalito, CA 94966-0909; (800) 383-1586; (800) 383-1394; (415) 331-5650. A nonprofit, public foundation for broadening knowledge of the nature and potentials of mind and consciousness, and to apply that knowledge to the enhancement of the quality of life on the planet. It gives grants for scientific and scholarly research. Some of this work has been involved in: The Inner Mechanisms of the Healing Response, Exceptional Human Abilities, Emerging Paradigms in Science and Society, and Altruism. It publishes books, a journal, a newsletter, special reports, and sponsors a national public television series *Thinking Allowed.*

★ National Wellness Institute, P.O. Box 827, Stevens Point, WI 54481-0827; (715) 342-2969. One of the best organizations promoting multidimensional well-being through self-care and assisted self-care. Their wide array of educational services is directed at health care professionals and the general public.

National Women's Health Network, 514 10th St. NW, Suite 400, Washington, DC 20004; (202) 628-7814.

RESOURCES

## ★ *Consumer Health Information Libraries and Consumer Health Research Organizations*

AIC Services, P.O. Box 8030, Ann Arbor, MI 48107; (313) 996-5553.

The Center for Medical Consumers, 237 Thompson St., New York, NY 10012; (212) 674-1705.

Consumer Health Information Center, Mission Hospital Regional Medical Center, 27700 Medical Center Rd., Mission Viejo, CA 92691; (714) 582-2919.

Consumer Health Information Research Institute, 3521 Broadway, Kansas City, MO 64111; (816) 753-8850.

Consumer Health Information Service, MacNeal Hospital, 3249 Oak Park Ave., Berwyn, IL 60402; (708) 795-3089.

Family Resource Center, Good Samaritan Medical Center, 1015 NW 22nd Ave., Portland, OR 97201-5198; (503) 229-7348.

First Edition, W.O. Boswell Memorial Hospital, 13101 N. 103rd Ave., Sun City, AZ 85351; (602) 974-7848. Consumer health library.

Gateway Health Library, Gould Medical Group, 500 Coffee Rd., Suite D, Modesto, CA 95335; (800) 52-GOULD.

Health Answers, Bronson Methodist Hospital, 252 E. Lovell, Kalamazoo, MI 49007; (616) 341-6318. Consumer health library.

Health Education Center, Kaiser Permanente Medical Center, 280 W. MacArthur Blvd., Oakland, CA 94611; (510) 596-6150.

Health Information Network, 4527 Montgomery Drive, Suite E, Santa Rosa, CA 95409; (800) 743-6996; in Sonoma County (707) 539-3967; FAX (707) 539-8234. A computer-linked, health research service that will provide information on nearly any health topic.

The Health Library, Stanford University Hospital, 248 Stanford Shopping Center, Palo Alto, CA 94304; (415) 725-8400.

Health Network, Battle Creek Health System, 80 N. 20th St., Battle Creek, MI 49015; (616) 964-5616. Consumer health library.

The Health Resource, 564 Locust St., Conway, AR 72032; (501) 329-5272. A health research service that will provide literature searches and reports on conditions and therapies.

Healthwise, 1602 W. Franklin St., Boise, ID 83702; (208) 345-1161; Fax (208) 345-1897. Health promotion and education materials. They are also developing a computer-based, consumer medical database.

Learning Center, Kaiser Permanente, 13652 Cantara St., Panorama City, CA 91402; (818) 375-3018. Consumer health library.

Los Gatos Medical Resource Facility, 815 Pollard Rd., Los Gatos, CA 95030; (408) 866-4044.

McCauley Health Information Library, Catherine McCauley Health System, P.O. Box 995, Ann Arbor, MI 48106; (313) 572-3121.

Medsearch Unlimited, 4515 Merrie Lane, Bell Aire, TX 77401; (800) 748-6866.

Patient Education Resource Center, Veterans Affairs Medical Center, 4150 Clement St., San Francisco, CA 94121; (415) 221-4810, ext. 3477.

Patient Information on Chronic Illness, 41 Green Valley Court, Kleinburg, Ontario, Canada, L0J1C0. Patient information service including a newsletter, consultations, seminars, and physician referrals.

Patient's Library, James A. Haley VA Medical Center, 13000 Bruce B. Downs Blvd., Tampa, FL 33512; (813) 972-2000, ext. 7531.

Peoples Medical Society, 462 Walnut St., Allentown, PA 18102; (215) 770-1670. Consumer information service on health issues.

Planetree Health Resource Center, California Pacific Medical Center, 2040 Webster Street, San Francisco, CA 94115; (415) 923-3680 and San Jose Medical Center, 98 N. 17th St., San Jose, CA 95112; (408) 977-4549. A nonprofit clearinghouse, search service, public library, bookstore, referral directory, and educational center oriented to informing and empowering the health care consumer.

Sutter Resource Consumer Health Library, 2800 L St., Sacramento, CA 95816-5600; (916) 733-3880.

Valley Care Health Library, Valley Care Medical Center, 5575 W. La Positas Blvd., Suite 120, Pleasanton, CA 94588; (510) 734-3315.

Vintage Health Library, Alta Bates-Herrick Hospital, 2001 Dwight Way, Berkeley, CA 94704; (510) 540-4475. Consumer health library.

Wadley LifeSource, Wadley Regional Medical Center, 57 Central Mall, Texarkana, TX 75501; (214) 793-5433. Consumer health library.

World Research Foundation, 15300 Ventura Blvd, Suite 405, Sherman Oaks, CA 91403; (818) 907-5483. A nonprofit clearinghouse and search service specializing in health care alternatives, also those used in other countries without acceptance in the U.S. Their computer database includes over 5,000 journals published throughout the world. Their in-house library for public use has over 10,000 volumes.

## Interconnectedness Resources

*Wonderful how completely everything in*
*wild nature fits into us,*
*as if truly part and parent of us.*
*The sun shines not on us, but in us.*
*The rivers flow not past, but through us,*
*thrilling, tingling, vibrating every fiber and cell*
*of the substance of our bodies,*
*making them glide and sing.*

**John Muir**

### *Books*

Hamilton, John and Morrison, Nancy. *Entangling Alliances: How the Third World Shapes Our Lives.* 1990. Seven Locks Press, Box 27, Cabin John, MD 20818.

Kellert, Stephen & Wilson, Edward. *The Biophilia Hypothesis.* Island Press, 1993.

Lemkow, Anna. *The Wholeness Principle: Dynamics of Unity Within Science, Religion, and Society.* Quest Books, 1990.

Macy, Joanna. *World as Lover, World as Self.* Parallax Press, 1991.

Russell, P. *Global Brain: Speculations on the Evolutionary Leap to Planetary Consciousness.* Tarcher, 1983.

Sheldrake, Rupert. *The Presence of the Past: Morphic Resonance and the Habits of Nature.* Times Books, 1988.

Sheldrake, Rupert. *The Rebirth of Nature: The Greening of Science and God.* Bantam New Sciences, 1991.

Swimme, Brian and Berry, Thomas. *The Universe Story: A Celebration of the Unfolding of the Cosmos.* Harper San Francisco, 1993.

Talbot, M. *The Holographic Universe.* HarperCollins, 1991.

Wilson, Edward. *The Diversity of Life.* Harvard U. Press, 1992.

### *Videotapes*

★Media Network, 39 W. 14th St., Suite 403, New York NY 10011; (212) 929-2663. A clearinghouse for over 4,000 films on alternative, progressive subjects.

The Video Project, 5332 College Ave., Suite 101, Oakland, CA 94618; (510) 655-9050. A media center that distributes over 250 videos covering a broad range of topics.

See also the video resource section in the chapter on Educational Health.

## PROFESSIONAL HOLISTIC HEALTH RESOURCES

*An apple a day bugs the AMA.*

**Unknown**

### *Books*

Jamison, Jennifer. *Health Promotion for Chiropractic Practice.* Aspen, 1991.

★Pizzorno, Joseph & Murray, Michael. Eds. *A Textbook of Natural Medicine.* Bastyr College Publications, 144 N.E. 54th Street, Seattle, WA 98105; (206) 523-9585. Quarterly updates to this volume are also available.

The following books are available from the National Wellness Institute.

Bellingham, Richard & Cohen, Barry. *The Corporate Wellness Sourcebook.* Human Res. Dev. Pr., 1987.

Kimble, Cathy and Longe, Mary. *Health Promotion for Older Adults.* AHPI, 1989.

O'Donnell, Michael & Harris, Jeffrey, eds. *Health Promotion in the Workplace.* Delmar, 1993.

Queen, Sandy. *Wellness Activities for Youth.* Whole Person, 1992.

Sol, Neil and Wilson, Philip, eds. *Hospital Health Promotion.* Human Kinetics, 1989.

Travis, John. *Wellness for Helping Professionals: Creating Compassionate Cultures.* Wellness Assoc., 1990.

### *Journals*

*Advances: Journal of Mind-Body Health,* The Fetzer Institute, 9292 W. KL Ave., Kalamazoo, MI 49009; (616) 375-2000.

*Alternative Health Practitioner: The Journal of Complementary and Natural Care,* Springer Publishing, 536 Broadway, New York, NY 10012; (212) 983-1983; (212) 431-4370.

*Alternative Medicine Journal*—(617) 899-2702.

*Alternative Therapies in Health and Medicine,* 101 Columbia, Aliso Viejo, CA 92656; (800) 899-1712.

*American Journal of Health Promotion,* P.O. Box 6646, Syracuse, NY 13217-9990. The largest peer-reviewed journal in its field.

*Journal of Alternative and Complementary Medicine,* Mary Ann Liebert, Inc., Publishers, 1651 Third Ave., New York, NY 10128; (800) M LIEBERT; (212) 289-2300; Fax (212) 289-3347.

RESOURCES

*Journal of Naturopathic Medicine,* Journal Management Group, 10 Morgan Ave. Norwalk, CT 06851; (203) 866-7664.

*Journal of Holistic Nursing,* SAGE Publications, Inc., P.O. Box 5084, Newbury Park, CA 91359; (805) 499-0721.

*Health Values: The Journal of Health Behavior, Education & Promotion,* PNG Publications, P.O. Box 4593, Star City, WV 26504-4593; (304) 293-4699.

*Quarterly Review of Natural Medicine,* Natural Product Research Consultants, 600 First Ave., Suite 205, Seattle, WA 98104; (206) 623-2520; Fax (206) 623-6340.

## *Computer Programs*

*Lifestyle Assessment Questionnaire.* Available from the National Wellness Institute.

## *Organizations*

★American Academy of Environmental Medicine, P.O. Box 116106, Denver, CO 80216, (303) 622-9755. Progressive group of physicians practicing "clinical ecology" who would be most likely to use the most updated methods for identifying and treating toxic and allergic reactions to the environment.

American Association of Holistic Nurses, 4101 Lake Boone Trail, Suite 201, Raleigh, NC 27607; (919) 787-5181.

American Association of Naturopathic Physicians, 2366 Eastlake Ave. East, Seattle, WA 98102; (206) 323-7610.

American Chiropractic Association, 1701 Clarendon Blvd., Arlington, VA 22209; (703) 276-8800.

American College for Advancement in Medicine, 23121 Verdugo Dr., Suite 204, Laguna Hills, CA 92653; (714) 583-7666; (800) 532-3688. Educational and research organization for physicians using chelation therapy.

American Holistic Medical Association / Foundation, 4101 Lake Boone Trail, Suite 201, Raleigh, NC 27607; (919) 787-5181.

American Preventive Medical Association, 459 Walker Rd., Great Falls, VA 22066; (703) 759-0662; Fax (703) 759-6711. A multi-disciplinary professional society promoting progressive, effective health care. They operate a patient referral network and book ordering service.

Center for Professional Well-Being, 21 West Colony Place, Suite 150, Durham, NC 27705, (919) 489-9167; Fax (919) 490-5587. Provides support, education, and counseling for health care professionals so they can become more capable of dealing with the stresses of their livelihood. This is also the address for the Society for Professional Well-Being, a membership-based, mutual support forum for professionals to exchange information and ideas on the subject.

★Health Comm, Inc., 5800 Soundview Drive, #E-102, P.O. Box 1729, Gig Harbor, WA 98335; (800) 843-9660. Best place to get an education in clinical nutrition. Dr. Bland's organization offers seminars on different nutritional subjects; periodicals in written and audio format on medical nutrition, preventive medicine, and food science; and books.

Institute for the Transformation of Medicine, 1400 Shattuck Ave., Suite 7-126, Berkeley, CA 94709; (510) 233-5626. Resource center for professionals and the public aimed at transforming health care by emphasizing mind/body/spirit integration with the inclusion of complementary therapies to comprehensive medical practices.

★International Academy of Nutrition and Preventive Medicine, P.O. Box 18433, Asheville, NC 28814, (704) 258-3243.

Office of Alternative Medicine, National Institutes of Health, 6120 Executive Blvd., EPS, Suite 450, Rockville, MD 20892-9904; (301) 402-2466; Fax (301) 402-4741; (Internet E-mail: jaqui@helix.nih.gov).

Office of Disease Prevention and Health Promotion, National Health Information Center, Public Health Service, U.S. Dept. of Health and Human Services, P.O. Box 1133 Washington, DC 20013-1133; (800) 336-4797. Has computerized directory of health related organizations and many health promotion publications.

Physicians Committee for Responsible Medicine, P.O. Box 6322, Washington, DC 20015; (202) 686-2210. Interest in nutrition, preventive medicine, and questions the ethics of animal research. Publishes quarterly journal, *Good Medicine.*

Research Council for Complementary Medicine, Suite 1, 19a Cavendish Square, London W1M9AD, Telephone: 01-493-6930. Working to compile and promote quality scientific research in the fields of acupuncture, chiropractic, homeopathy, naturopathy, osteopathy, and others.

★Society for Orthomolecular Medicine, 2698 Pacific Ave., San Francisco, CA 94115; (415) 346-2500; Fax (415) 346-4991.

Society of Prospective Medicine, P.O. Box 55110, Indianapolis, IN 46205-0110; (317) 549-3600. Emphasizes preventive health care. Available from them is the book: *SPM Handbook of Health Risk Appraisals,* compiled by Kent Peterson and Sumner Hilles.

Tree Farm Communications, 23703 N.E. 4th St., Redmond, WA 98053, (206) 868-0464. Provide educational audiotapes of current conferences and seminars.

Whole Person Associates and Whole Person Press, 210 West Michigan, Duluth, MN 55802; (800) 247-6789; Fax (218) 727-0505. Their *Stress Management and Wellness Promotion Resources Catalog* contains many good programs that could be presented to a wide variety of individuals and groups.

★Wright/Gaby Nutrition Institute, P.O. Box 21535, Baltimore, MD 21208; (410) 486-5656. One of the best places to get an education in clinical nutrition. Doctors Wright and Gaby are two of the preeminent nutritionally-oriented physicians in the country.

## ★ *Medical Clinical Laboratories Specializing in Nutritional Diagnostics*

Doctor's Data Inc., P.O. Box 111, W. Chicago, IL 60185, (800) 323-2784.

Great Smokies Diagnostic Laboratory, 18 A Regent Park Blvd., Asheville, NC 28806; (800) 522-4762.

Immuno Laboratories, 1620 W. Oakland Park Blvd., Ft. Lauderdale, FL 33311; (800) 231-9197 nationally; in Florida—(800) 628-4300, (305) 486-4500; Fax (305) 739-6563.

Meridian Valley Clinical Laboratory, 515 W. Harrison St., Suite 9, Kent, WA 98032; (206) 859-8700; Drs. only line (800) 234-6825.

MetaMetrix Medical Laboratory, 5000 Peachtree Ind. Blvd., Suite 110, Norcross, GA 30071, (800) 221-4640; (404) 446-5483.

Monroe Medical Research Laboratory, Route 17, P.O. Box I, Southfields, NY 10975; (800) 831-3133; (914) 351-5134; Fax (914) 351-4295.

National BioTechnology Laboratory, 3212 NE 125th St., Seattle, WA 98125; (800) 846-6285; (206) 363-6606; Fax (206) 363-2025.

Serammune Physicians Laboratory, 1890 Preston White Drive, Suite 200, Reston, VA 22091; (800) 553-5472; (703) 758-0610; Fax (703) 758-0615.

*Whatever you can do, or dream you can, begin it.*
*Boldness has genius, power, and magic in it.*

**Goethe**

RESOURCES

# PART TWO

## Aspects of Holistic Health

# CHAPTER THREE

# PHYSICAL HEALTH

*Our body is our temple where we live and where we do the work of becoming enlightened.*

**Ram Dass**

There are many ways to define physical health. The model that will be most useful for this discussion looks at four basic parameters: biochemical balance, organ efficiency, neurological integrity and musculoskeletal function. What we are looking for is adaptability, integration, harmony, and high-level performance in these areas as criteria for physical health. These four parameters of physical health are influenced by many factors, such as the psychological aspects of our being, our external environment, and societal pressures. In turn, all aspects of our being are affected by the harmonious integration of these four parameters. If we can look more closely at these elements of physical health and their intimate relationships with other aspects of life, we can more effectively provide procedures which promote total health and wholeness.

By looking at the "Web of Influences for Physical Health" diagram on the next page we can get a picture of all these intertwining influences.

In any particular individual a different combination of influences will combine positively or negatively to determine dynamically, every second, biochemical homeostasis, organ efficiency, musculoskeletal function, and neurological integrity. In some individuals, at particular times, certain influences will have great impact, and others may have a negligible role. One of the keys to prioritizing health care is to determine which influences are having the greatest impact, for either better or

worse, so that efforts can be undertaken to accentuate the positive and minimize the negative. So even if our most predominant *apparent* problem is on the physical plane with physical symptoms, say digestive upset, the major contributing influences that can remedy that situation *and* improve overall health and wholeness may be in the area of environmental toxins, relationship conflict, and occupational dissatisfaction. In this instance taking medication to resolve the symptoms not only does not address the source of the problem, it allows the true problem to remain, intensify, and arise in different forms. The problem is not significantly helped by turning to "New Age" or natural approaches like homeopathy, visceral manipulation, or herbs. They might be of some benefit or great advantage in other situations at different times or with other people, but their use in this situation may not be wise if other, more significant elements are ignored.

Although we are emphasizing the importance of choosing the most effective areas in which to concentrate our health enhancement efforts, we have to remember the importance of tending to all of the aspects. Preventive attention to all areas of one's being pays back rewards in reducing the number of aspects of our life that we end up having to concentrate on in times of crisis.

Let us look more closely now at the different components of physical health and their two-way relationship with other aspects of our being.

## WEB OF INFLUENCES ON PHYSICAL HEALTH

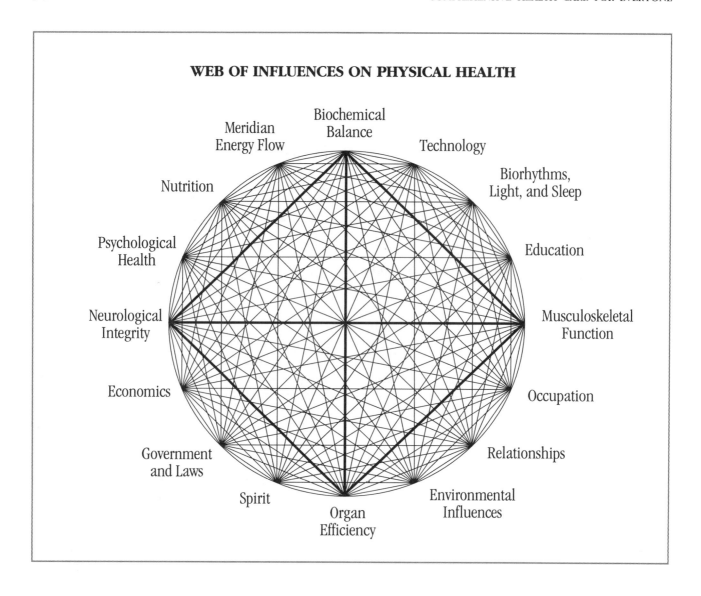

## BIOCHEMICAL BALANCE

The biochemical soup within our bodies is quite a complex concoction: not only for the number of various substances floating around, but in their moment-to-moment coordination—involving quantity, locale, and mixture—to supply our widely ranging needs. It is mind-boggling how hundreds of thousands of substances are produced, transferred, changed, used, recycled, and discarded in incredibly coordinated fashion every second. Vitamins, minerals, enzymes, trace elements, amino acids, neurotransmitters, fatty acids, glucose, glycogen, hormones, antibodies, dissolved gases, complex compounds . . . juggled masterfully by the intelligence of life striving towards harmony, health, wholeness, and Unity, all the while that it is interacting molecularly and energetically with the world outside of its container of skin.

In fact, as the science of nuclear physics advances, models of biochemistry are evolved based on molecular and atomic theories which substantiate an intimate intertwining of the energies of the universe. Quantum physics tells us that the physical barrier that separates us from the world, which we call skin, is much less of a true separation than it appears. It is more of an energetic transition zone of relatively dense energy wave patterns, substantial and delineated enough when compared to the surrounding air or other "relatively solid" materials. Skin and what it contains on the "inside" is intimately bound to, and interacts with, many seen and unseen energies on the "outside" where both inner and outer forces have more relationships than one realizes.

This is the complexity and intertwining nature of reality. The Web of Wholeness model was developed to bring this reality to health care.

What keeps this delicate balance within the narrow parameters necessary for ideal physical health? And how does biochemical harmony influence all the other aspects of health? There are two-way influences within the body and various influences from without. Some are direct and powerful, like nutrition. Some are indirect and powerful, like economic stability, which usually affects biochemical balance via other health aspects. Others are indirect and minor contributing agents. Some are powerful influences in one direction of a relationship and of only minor importance in its reciprocal action. For instance, laws and governmental programs may have a dramatic effect on a person's internal biochemistry through food safety laws, pesticide regulations, supermarket labeling regulations, governmental policies that regulate food distribution, the addition of fluoride in drinking water, government sponsored prenatal nutrition programs, and countless other avenues. But one person's internal biochemistry usually has minimal impact on government and laws. This is not to say that there are not significant collective influences when a disturbed biochemistry in millions of criminals in the U.S. alter criminal laws on a vast scale. Or when a very influential government official suffers some severe biochemical imbalance that drastically alters his capacity to do his job and thus dramatically affects many people.

## ORGAN EFFICIENCY

The stomach, thyroid, parathyroid, pituitary, pineal, adrenals, pancreas, small intestines, colon, liver, thymus, gall bladder, spleen, testicles, ovaries, bladder, heart, lungs—all these organs and glands must harmoniously interact with each other, all the chemical constituents of the body, the

nervous system, the musculoskeletal system, the psyche, spirit, and all the elements in the environment. Complex interrelationships indeed! And that is why organ function is a critical aspect to physical health. We will investigate examples of some of these relationships. For in-depth understanding, physiology texts would be good resources.

## NEUROLOGICAL INTEGRITY

The nervous system, consisting of the brain, spinal cord and all the peripheral nerves, regulates and coordinates the organs of the body and is the major intermediary between the individual and the environment, according to *Gray's Anatomy* and every other textbook on physiology. We will try to illustrate many examples of these relationships that determine health and wholeness. Again, referral to resources related to neurophysiology will provide an even greater understanding. Of particular interest might be the PBS series "The Mind" or Richard Restak's book, *The Brain,* published by Bantam in 1988.

The nervous system is the primary interface between our psychological selves and our physical being. Perceptions, cognition, emotional association, identity, response to the environment and other people, are all mediated by the nervous system and how it functions. Virtually all physical operations of the body are influenced by the psyche through the nerve system. Many times this is the avenue by which our psyche also alters biochemistry via nerve signaling.

## MUSCULOSKELETAL FUNCTION

Some experts in biological evolution argue that all the complex interactions between biochemicals, cells, tissues, organs, and systems in the human body have developed in support of the musculoskeletal system. For it is this aspect of ourselves, linked to the nervous system, that moves us through and actively engages us in our world. Not needing to enter fully into that evolutionary debate, we can nonetheless see the powerful two-way interconnections between our muscles, joints and bones, and all other aspects of our being. These contributions to health will be examined, and resources provided, to encourage the more curious to make further explorations.

A word needs to be said about levels of physical health assessment. We can evaluate physical performance, like how fast you can run two miles, or how close you can come to touching your toes. Another type of testing involves measuring one's lifestyle health habits that are known to either positively or negatively affect physical health, such as nutrient intake or cigarette smoking. In both there are tests spanning many degrees of depth, accuracy, and specificity. As always, the more elaborate and detailed your information about your health, the easier it is to match health building programs to that level of health. But cost-effectiveness, the availability of money, and risk versus benefit considerations have to be coordinated with immediate and long-term health goals to decide what testing is appropriate at any point in time. Close communication with an advising health professional who is well versed in the holistic approaches presented here is the best way to go.

This is particularly so since many physical health parameters cannot be readily evaluated by oneself, whether they be biochemical balance, organ efficiency, neurological integrity, or even musculoskeletal functioning. Laboratory tests, technical instrumentation, and professional examination are often at the baseline level of functional assessment. It's pretty hard for a person to "feel" whether his alkaline phosphatase level in the blood is normal, or whether his parathyroid gland is working optimally, let alone keep track of whether every one of the millions-per-second nerve impulses are getting to where they need to go.

We will try to outline self-testing methods when applicable, particularly in early detection situations, similar to our use of blood pressure monitoring to detect the beginning stages of hypertension in order to prevent a stroke.

Complex, intimate, health-giving relationships exist between our body's biochemistry, its organs, the musculoskeletal system, and the nerves. Some of these connections will be continually explored. But it is important that a good understanding of additional influences from other components of our wholeness be examined, for there are many important influences that go unrecognized. Because of this lack of awareness, our health suffers. We can also take as a general rule of thumb that when an external influence alters biochemistry, the organs, nerves, or locomotor system, it also affects the other parts of our being.

Some, particularly doctors of Oriental medicine and acupuncture, would include "meridian energy balance" as a major component of physical health, along with biochemical balance, organ efficiency, neurological integrity, and musculoskeletal function. This is a viable position. New research on the physiological effects of acupuncture under the watchful eyes of scientific instrumentation proves that energy flowing through the meridians of the body significantly affects these internal elements. Over thousands of years acupuncture techniques, herbalism, exercises, and lifestyle changes have been used in the Orient to manipulate this flow of energy to treat conditions of organ dysfunction, biochemical imbalance, neurological disorders, and musculoskeletal problems. In this discussion meridian energy flow has been put into a separate category only for organizational purposes. Referral to this section and its resources will help to put it into perspective with the other issues.

# SAFETY

*[No gift] is so important as the gift of safety, which is declared to be*
*the great gift among all gifts in this world.*

**Panchatantra**

Safety is a vital issue when discussing the survival and health of the physical body. Accidents are the third leading cause of death in the U.S., and the primary cause of death for those 1-45 years of age. Motor vehicle accidents make up the largest portion of fatalities, disabilities, and injuries. Burns, poisonings, suffocations, and electrocutions follow on this fatality list.

Safety touches many aspects of our health. If we glance at the Web of Influences on Physical Health we can see it entering into many of the strands—accidents involving technology (electricity, chainsaws, power tools, autos, planes . . .), accidents involving falling asleep and accidentally getting sunburned, accidents while playing sports, or on the job, accidents involving environmental poisonings like pesticide contamination. Overdoses of medication, or accidental reactions to medication, kill thousands every year. Observe how our courts are log-jammed with personal injury cases. Governmental laws that mandate the use of seat belts and motorcycle helmets save millions from injury and death. How many accidents occur because our minds are distracted by emotional turmoil? And there are even accidents with the nutritional aspects of our lives, either through accidental poisonings or by choking.

*Every year in the U.S. 500,000 people are*
*hospitalized with head injuries.*

## SAFETY PRECAUTIONS

*Nothing is as good as holding on to safety.*
**Euripides, 410 B.C.**

Obviously there are few areas that can offer more opportunities to enhance our health than safety precautions. Here are some general safety precautions with some specific examples:

Never use intoxicants! Alcoholics are seven times more likely to die in any accident than nondrinkers, with a five times greater risk of death in traffic accidents. Alcohol use has been indicted in at least 50% of all burn injuries with three times more deaths in cigarette fires. Problem drinkers have 2-3 times more industrial accidents than nondrinkers. Risk of dying due to a fall can be as much as 13 times greater with the excessive use of alcohol. One study showed that 83% of drowning victims used alcohol. That we are safely in control of our body and circumstances under the influence of even low to moderate amounts of alcohol or other intoxicants is one of the most costly lies we tell ourselves. Since we cannot accurately tell when our coordination is inhibited, or our reaction time is slowed, or our senses are dulled, or our judgment is fogged by some intoxicant, the safest rule of thumb is to never imbibe. If for some absurd reason you feel obligated to use intoxicants, at least do so in circumstances that would greatly reduce the risk of being involved in an accident. The use of intoxicants other than alcohol has been less studied but is no less dangerous.

Murders and suicides are greatly increased with the addition of intoxicants, and they are an alarming safety issue. The combination of deadly weapons and mind altering substances is not healthy. Firearms in themselves create many more injuries and deaths than they prevent. The number of accidental firearm deaths, and the number of homicides in the heat of passion between family members far surpasses the few instances in which citizens are saved by defending themselves with guns.

Be extremely careful with medications if you must take them in the first place. Be sure to read warnings and follow directions precisely. Half of all prescriptions are not taken as directed. Make sure your pharmacist *and* physician know all the medications, including herbs and over-the-counter medicines, that you take. Make sure they consult a drug-interaction computer program to verify safety, particularly when multiple medications are prescribed. They should also know about your use of alcohol, since this poses frequent problems with many medications. Often different drugs are prescribed by different doctors, each not knowing what the other is prescribing and thus unable to consider cross-reactions. Pharmacists are generally more knowledgeable than physicians about the potential hazards of mixing medications. Know if the medication package warns against driving or the operation of potentially dangerous equipment.

*I firmly believe that if the whole materia medica,*
*as now used, could be sunk*
*to the bottom of the sea, it would be all the better*
*for mankind—and all the worse for the fishes.*
**Oliver Wendell Holmes**

Be mindful and attentive to the task at hand. When performing any activity, do it with complete and undivided concentration. How many accidents occur when the body is trying to perform some function and the mind is off in another time and space thinking other thoughts, entrapped by emotions unrelated to the present task, reviewing past events or rehearsing future ones!

Be wary of hurry. A hectic pace causes so many accidents, with excessive traffic speeds probably heading the list. Our nervous system is capable of performing tasks at a certain optimal speed with a certain degree of accuracy. When we force the body and mind to operate faster, errors will increase. When too many tasks or thoughts are trying to be juggled at the same time, neurological overload ensues with incoordination as the result, and accidents soon to follow.

*Go placidly amid the noise and haste . . .*
**from "Desiderata"**

Become informed. Learn about safety at home, at work, in play, driving. Read all the warning labels on appliances, power tools, and electrical devices. An excellent book is *The Home Book: A Guide to Safety, Security, and Savings in the Home,* edited by Elizabeth Hax for Public Citizen. Take all the safety classes at work and encourage your employer and union to increase safety features and classes on the job. Know the risks of the sports you participate in and take advantage of all the safety gear available.

Drive safely designed, built, and maintained autos. Consumer magazines list classifications of the safest and most dangerous autos. Seat belts and shoulder harnesses should always be used, although automatic shoulder harnesses attached to the door should be replaced with safer models. Airbags are great. Drive within the speed limits. Encourage your legislators to enact safer driving regulations. Assume all other drivers on the road are idiots until proven otherwise.

*Every 10 seconds someone is injured*
*in an auto accident.*
*Every 11 minutes someone dies*
*in an auto accident.*

Avoid hazardous materials—at work, at home, at play. Children are particularly susceptible. Younger children cannot read warning labels. Older children do not have the good judgment to protect them from their curiosity. Refer to resources in the chapter on Ecological Health, particularly the section on "Sources of Environmentally Safe Products."

Avoid hazardous activities: firing weapons, risky sports, dangerous jobs, hazardous driving conditions, do-it-yourself construction (particularly electrical work). Children have to be closely supervised by responsible, knowledgeable adults in almost anything they do. They tend, unconsciously or consciously, to find risky activities and circumstances—and our modern world is full of them. Matches, bodies of water, power tools, farm implements, mechanical devices, anything that can be plugged in to an electrical socket, or the electrical socket itself.

Sports are areas where intelligent supervision is most critical for kids. Children should be guided away from the more risky collision and impact sports like boxing, wrestling, football, lacrosse, hockey, rodeo. Also, those sports like motorcycle racing, three wheeling, extreme skating and skateboarding should be replaced with safer play. Even sports which we consider to be relatively safe, like baseball and soccer, can be deadly when poor coaching or supervision allows children to participate without full protection from the most advanced protective devices. More than fifty children have died in the U.S., and many were seriously injured, from playing sandlot and organized baseball, primarily from not wearing adequately protective headgear and not using specially designed "soft" baseballs, which are mandatory in Japan. We assume a sport like soccer to be the ultimate in safety. But when unknowledgeable coaches allow young children to "head" soccer balls before their neck musculature is strongly developed (seldom before 16 years of age) they impose incalculable whiplash damage to thousands of children's spines. The symptoms and problems that result may not appear until months or years later. It is questionable whether the benefits of many of our "accepted" sports are worth the cumulative damage imposed on young bodies—particularly when there are so many noncompetitive, healthy, physical activities to participate in.

Infuse your life with a safety consciousness. Build safety mechanisms into all activities. Make safe choices when choices are available. Note and be particularly careful when the ego says, "Let's risk it for the adrenaline rush."

Use common sense. Put the lighter fluid on the charcoal before lighting the match. Unplug the toaster before sticking the knife in to get the stuck piece of toast. Don't set the plugged in record player on the edge of the tub while bathing. Don't dive into the lake without checking for depth and obstacles. As a safety exercise add 100 other examples to this list.

We will now move to more detailed analyses of factors which influence total health under the heading of Physical Health—nutrition, exercise, manipulative therapies, biological rhythms, sleep, light, Oriental medicine, biofeedback. Be sure to read the special section on Rating Health Enhancement Strategies. Other influences of physical health like economics, psychology, relationships, and spirit will be dealt with in their own chapters.

## SAFETY RESOURCES

★Denotes Best of the Best Resources

### Books and Catalogs

★Dadd-Redalia, Debra. *Sustaining the Earth: Choosing Consumer Products That Are Safe for You, Your Family, and the Earth*. Morrow & Co., 1994.

Hax, Elizabeth (ed.). *The Home Book: A Guide to Safety, Security, and Savings in the Home*. Public Citizen.

★Jacobson, Michael and Lefferts, Lisa. *Safe Food: Eating Wisely in a Risky World*. Living Planet Press, 1991.

Kirby, Andrew, ed. *Nothing to Fear*. U. of Arizona Press, 1990.

Kwitny, Jonathan. *Acceptable Risks*. Poseidon Press, 1992.

*The Safety Zone Catalog*, P.O. Box 19, Hanover, PA 19333-0019; (800) 999-3030. Catalog of products to make your life safer.

### Organizations

Center for Auto Safety, 2001 S St., N.W., Suite 410, Washington, DC 20009-1160; (202) 328-7700.

National Highway Traffic Safety Administration, 400 Seventh St. SW., NTS-13, Washington, DC 20590; (800) 424-9393 or (202) 366-0123.

National Injury Information Clearinghouse, 5401 Westbard Ave., Room 625, Washington, DC 20207; (301) 504-0424; Fax (301) 504-0124.

National Institute for Occupational Safety and Health, 200 Independence Ave. SW, Washington, DC 20201; (202) 472-7134 or (800) 356-4674. Other offices: 4676 Columbia Parkway, Cincinnati, OH 45226; (800) 35-NIOSH; (513) 533-8326; (513) 533-8287; Fax (513) 533-8573.

National Research Council, Transportation Research Board, 2101 Constitution Ave., NW, Washington, DC 20418; (202) 334-2936; Information (202) 334-2933; Publications (202) 334-3213 or (800) 424-9818.

National Safety Council, 444 North Michigan Ave., Chicago, IL 60611. Publishes *National Safety and Health News* and *Accident Facts*.

U.S. Consumer Product Safety Commission, 5401 Westbard Ave., Bethesda, MD (mailing address—Washington, DC 20207); (301) 504-0500; Information (301) 504-0580; Fax (301) 504-0399; Product Safety Hotline (800) 638-2772. Publishes *Product Summary Report* and other literature.

# NUTRITIONAL HEALTH

*Let thy food be thy medicine and thy medicine be thy food.*

**Hippocrates**

Balanced nutrition plays one of the most significant roles in providing health to the body. It is also one of the most influential determinants of psychological well-being. It is therefore one of the most powerful tools for self-care.

A simple Spectrum Analysis of Nutritional Health can be made by looking at the Basic Nutritional Health Enhancement Guidelines on page 63 to see how many of the guidelines are incorporated into your diet. More elaborate evaluations yield more accurate information on direct physiological relationships. For instance, there are numerous computer programs (of varying quality) that take dietary intake data and correlate it to information gained from laboratory testing of blood, urine, hair, feces, aerobic capacity, etc., to gain a better understanding of biochemical balance and organ function. Even blood tests for hidden food allergies can be incorporated as additional information to give a readout that will advise one on vitamin supplementation and menus, including recipes using allowable foods.

Whether these more involved types of nutritional evaluation might be needed in any particular individual situation is determined by a multitude of factors. The first of which is how your diet looks compared to the guidelines. If you are already abiding by most of the guidelines, and your physical health appears to be good, now may not be the time to invest a lot of money on more detailed testing. If your diet is obviously poor, it may be worthwhile to see if it is having a significant effect on organ function and biochemical balance. The testing might be applicable also if you are one of those who believes that the average American diet is OK, or that diet doesn't matter much, or that your diet is fine even though it differs drastically with the guidelines set forth here. This becomes particularly relevant as the number of symptoms, disease conditions, and physical or emotional health problems rise.

*Men dig their Graves with their own Teeth and die more by those fated Instruments than the Weapons of their Enemies.*

**"Health's Improvement"**
**Thomas Moffet, 1600 A.D.**

Cost, availability, and whether one is inclined to make dietary changes based on the findings, are other factors involved in deciding which level of testing is worthwhile. As always, consulting a health professional well versed with the professional resources at the end of this chapter is good advice if there is doubt about the necessity of further testing.

Consulting the average medical practitioner concerning these matters is probably worth as much as consulting a banana slug, so be forewarned about bringing up the subject of proper nutrition with just any health professional. Consulting a registered dietician for updated information on nutrition is usually not much more helpful.[1]

Another popular but highly flawed method for determining nutritional deficiencies and dietary advice is by an applied kinesiology type of muscle testing. The principle by which this is supposed to work is that the body knows its nutritional deficits and is willing and able to communicate this information via a mysterious mechanism by which nutritional supplements or food extracts are placed on the navel or in the "auric field" of the person being tested. Then a health professional supposedly trained in this complex methodology subjectively gauges the person's resistive response to a muscular strength challenge. The perceived strength or weakness of the muscular response indicates how much one needs the tested substance. Unfortunately all the available data on the validity of this technique points to its unreliability. Even the International College of Applied Kinesiology warns its practitioners to seek other means for verifying nutritional needs. See the resource section for professional nutritional referral information.

# BASIC NUTRITIONAL HEALTH ENHANCEMENT GUIDELINES

The following nutritional guidelines are general recommendations intended to assist average people on their journey towards optimal health. If there are particular health concerns that should vary from these general guidelines, a qualified nutritional expert should be consulted. These guidelines were meant to enhance all the other self improvement activities recommended in this book. Every individual is ultimately responsible for his or her nutritional intake. These guidelines are not an all-or-nothing proposition. The more of these suggestions one can incorporate into the daily diet the healthier that person will become. How rapidly do you want to become well? How healthy do you want to be?

---

**Let us begin with the poisons *not* to be put into our bodies:**

- alcohol, tobacco, caffeine, or other social drugs
- unnecessary medications
- foods fried in oil or fat, hydrogenated fats or trans-fatty acids, such as lard or margarine (fats should contribute only 10% of total calories)
- sugar, dextrose, corn syrup, saccharin, aspartame, or acesulfame-k
- refined white flour or products containing them
- refined, over-processed, or synthetic food
- artificial colors, sulfites, nitrates, nitrites, BHA, BHT, MSG

**Limit the following:**

- animal proteins and fat such as beef, pork, dairy, and Bambi Burgers.
- salt (beware of pickled foods . . . olives, pickles, etc.)
- honey, maple syrup, molasses (substitute fresh fruit)
- fish, fowl, and eggs (and buy organic)

Follow the above rules and half the battle is won!

**Let us look at how to eat:**

- Systematic under-eating is an important nutritional tip for most people.
- The diet should consist of substantial amounts of raw, whole, fresh, clean, nutrient-rich food that is in season. Organically grown produce is highly preferred over food grown with pesticides and herbicides.
- 75% of daily caloric intake should come from complex carbohydrates. Proteins should comprise approximately 15% and fats 10%. A wise blend of whole grains, legumes, beans, seeds and fresh vegetables should be the core of one's diet. This assures a high fiber diet also.
- Eat only when hungry.
- Eat slowly in a relaxed, unhurried atmosphere.
- Eat several small meals in preference to a few large meals.
- Chew food well.
- Never eat when in pain, mental or physical discomfort, when feverish, or working strenuously physically or mentally.
- Never eat 3-4 hours before bedtime.
- Drink plenty of pure water, particularly between meals. More is needed during lactation, exercise, and the hot summer months. Soda pop, Koolaid, etc. are unacceptable.
- Eat a diversity of foods. Do not eat the same foods or food families day in and day out.
- It is best to rotate specific foods to once every four days and food families to once every two days, particularly when allergies are present.
- Keep healthy snacks available (carrot, celery sticks, fruit, rice cakes, etc.).

The rationale behind the particular guidelines contained in this book can be found by referring to all of the resources at the end of this section. Approaches to nutrition occur in great variation and with much heated debate. The guidelines presented here are gleaned from the most reliable sources of progressive nutritional research. As general nutritional guidelines for the average person, they are suggestions which will most likely persist with time and become more reinforced as new research is done.

For instance, cardiovascular disease and cancer, the top two killers in civilized society, have diet as a major cause. The diet, supplementation recommendations, exercise, and ecological living guidelines suggested in this book are all designed to prevent these problems. They will even reverse many stages of the disease processes. The best rule of thumb is to use these guidelines and the nutritional resources referred to at the end of this section, until they are solidly proven ineffective. Also be sure to refer to the recommendations and resources in the chapter on Environmental Health for information related to allergies, since allergies have direct relevance to nutrition in many special circumstances.

*Leave your drugs in the chemist's pot*
*if you can heal the patient with food.*
**Hippocrates**

## NUTRITIONAL RELATIONSHIPS WITH OTHER HEALTH ASPECTS

*As food is necessary for the body,*
*prayer is necessary for the soul ...*
*No act of mine is done without prayer ...*
*I am not a man of learning,*
*but I humbly claim to be a man of prayer.*
**Mahatma Gandhi**

It is important to understand the scope and impact of nutritional influences on every aspect of our being so we can put it in proper perspective in our prioritization of health enhancement choices. We will now look at some examples of those

relationships for greater insight in how intimately this Web of Wholeness is woven. Nutrition influences health primarily by providing biochemical balance, proper organ function, and efficient electrochemical activity in nerve fibers. An interesting way to understand these relationships is to see nutrients as a form of energy. They are transformed into different bioelectric interactions which determine psychological function, interpersonal communication, educational endeavors, occupational and economic choices, relationships with the environment, and spiritual unfoldment.

### *Nutrition Affects Energy Flow in Acupuncture Meridians*

Oriental schools of thought use this energetic model in providing their own method of comprehensive, dynamic, health-restoring changes in a person. Traditional Oriental Medicine always looks at the energetic elements of food and herbs as they will most beneficially interact with *chi,* or life energy, through the meridians in acupuncture. See the section on Traditional Oriental Medicine and Acupuncture.

### *Nutritional Influences on Psychological Function*

*What a strange machine man is!*
*You fill him with bread, wine, fish, and radishes,*
*and out of him come sighs, laughter,*
*and dreams.*
**Zorba the Greek**

The fields of orthomolecular psychiatry and psychoneuroimmunology are both making great advancements in our understanding of the relationships between nutrition, the biochemical milieu of the body, neurological function and psychological well-being. Dramatic improvements of many psychological disorders by nutritional health enhancement strategies are coming into the forefront of research as interest in these correlations grows.[2] Depression, bipolar disorders, anxiety reactions, mood disorders, schizophrenia, and organic mental disorders have all shown improvement in well documented studies. Some of the most dramatic changes can be seen in work with hyperactive children. How many of the over 4,000,000 emotionally disturbed children in the U.S. could be significantly helped with nutritional improvements?

In simplified terms, nutrition affects our psychology in three ways:

1. it provides nutrients for brain function,

2. energy for brain function,

3. and influences our brain through toxicological or allergic reactions.

There are countless vitamins, minerals, trace elements, enzymes, coenzymes, hormones, fatty acids, amino acids, and polypeptides needed on a millisecond by millisecond basis for proper nerve transmission to take place in the brain. If they are not available, emotional centers and associated areas of the brain will not be able to function properly. This is why foods that have high nutritional content like vegetables, whole grains, and beans are to be preferred over nutrient poor foods such as processed foods, sweets, junk foods, fast foods, and fatty foods. Nutrient supplementation can help provide these essential components to psychological function. This may be particularly important in cases where the psychological problem is especially severe, persistent, and/or resistant to correction via other approaches.

The brain also needs its fuel—glucose, or blood sugar. Nerve tissue is very sensitive to the amount of this sugar in the blood. It must be maintained within certain narrow parameters for optimal function. Either too high or too low, and severe psychological, as well as physical disturbances, will occur. That is why the diet should contain mostly complex carbohydrates like vegetables, whole grains, and beans, because it is this type of food that releases a slow, steady flow of glucose into the blood stream for the brain's use. Eating small frequent meals low in fat also helps. Sweet foods or the use of stimulants like caffeine make the blood sugar skyrocket and plummet in a rollercoaster ride that takes our emotions along with it.

The brain's biochemistry can be disturbed by allergic reactions or sensitivities to the foods we eat, or to toxic contaminants in the food or drink. Often the body develops a reaction to foods in such a way that it does not present itself immediately or clearly as an allergy. Just as some substances we are allergic to make our eyes itch and nose run, other substances make our skin break out in hives. Still others make our stomach upset or produce intestinal gas. Some foods "irritate" our brain tissues instead of our intestines, skin, or eyes. These allergic or toxic inflammatory reactions of the brain have been known to cause every imaginable psychological disturbance. Reactions such as these also disturb blood sugar levels resulting in the same devastating psychological effects.

When there exists a psychological problem, using nutritional improvement as part of the solution is very wise.[3] The more severe the psychological problem, the more thorough the nutritional evaluation should be. The more physical symptoms accompany the psychological problem, the greater the likelihood that a nutritional approach will prove significant. For a referral to an orthomolecular psychiatrist or physician who can help identify the biochemical, nutritional aspects of psychological disturbances, contact the Well Mind Association, the Society for Orthomolecular Medicine, the Canadian Schizophrenia Association, or the American Association of Orthomolecular Medicine. They are listed in the Psychological Health resource section.

### Nourishing Relationships

It is not difficult to take the information on nutritional influences on psychological function and see how that in turn affects emotional interactions between people. Among the most obvious and pervasive nutritional problems that affect human interaction are the irritable mood swings that come about from erratic blood sugar changes, which are due in turn to poor dietary choices. People who eat according to the principles advocated in this book consume at regular intervals complex carbohydrates which keep blood sugar levels very even and within healthy ranges. Skipped meals, long intervals between meals, sweets, caffeine, tobacco, large meals, and allergenic foods tend to cause extreme fluctuations in blood sugar. This then makes the nervous system, including the nerves in the limbic centers of the brain that control emotions, excessively excitable, resulting in exaggerated behavior. Since we are classifying alcohol, tobacco and drugs as toxic agents, their effect on psychological function and interpersonal relationships will be discussed, along with allergies, in the chapter on Environmental Health.

## Food for Thought

Again, by looking at nutrition's influence on the nervous system, we can see its impact on intellect and educational aspirations. It has been estimated that 50% of a child's intelligence is determined by maternal nutrition while the child is in utero due to the nutritional needs of his rapidly growing nervous system. The influence hardly diminishes through childhood. As more studies are done, evidence accumulates substantiating the need for optimal nutrition for intellectual development. This can be dramatically illustrated with nutritional interventions to correct attention deficit disorders which affect over 5% of all children in the U.S. And don't think that adults cannot experience intellectual improvement by adopting nutritional health enhancement strategies. They can.

## Nutritional Influences on Occupational and Economic Health

Work performance, and thus economic well-being, are directly linked to nutrition. Job performance is adversely affected by poor concentration due to poor diet. Employee-employer and employee-employee relationships suffer from hypoglycemic induced mood swings due to bad diets. Look also at the staggering economic losses to individuals and businesses from absenteeism due to diet related illnesses, many involving vitamin C and A deficiencies. These weaken the immune system, resulting in upper respiratory tract infections like the common cold or the flu. There is even some suggestion that hostility increases with meat consumption. Premature deaths of executives by heart attack is a major concern for businesses because of the high cost of replacing these individuals, hundreds of thousands of dollars per death. In efforts to prevent these economic losses, businesses have adopted radical nutritional and exercise programs with great success. Note that a significant side benefit to this economic decision is that the executives become healthier, more productive, and live longer. Important resources related to these issues can be found in the chapter on Economic and Occupational Health.

## Nutritional Influences Related to Justice and Laws

The field of criminology is just beginning to acknowledge a previously unrecognized factor in criminal behavior—nutrition-related biochemical imbalance that generates adverse psycho-social behavior patterns via abnormal brain function. This goes far beyond the obvious correlations of alcohol and drug related crimes which account for up to 80% of all arrests. The close link between mental illness, criminal behavior, and the abnormal biochemical similarities of those two profiles is becoming better researched. From neurological lead poisoning to allergy-induced brain inflammations to neurotransmitter failure from lack of nutrients—the complexity and scope of the problem mounts. Over a decade ago books were written detailing these correlations.[4] *Ecologic-Biochemical Approaches to the Treatment of Delinquents and Criminals,* edited by Leonard Hippchen, is an admirable earlier work. Professional journals from a number of disciplines have articles on the subject.[5] The Web of Wholeness model needs to be used when addressing new models of criminal causation and rehabilitation. Criminal activity has many causes, and the only way to adequately deal with the ever-increasing problem of crime is to incorporate a holistic approach, with good nutrition as one of the major emphases.

### *Feeding the Spirit*

*The day that hunger is eradicated
from the earth there will be
the greatest spiritual explosion
the world has ever known.
Humanity cannot imagine the joy
that will burst into the world
on the day of that great revolution.*

**Frederico Lorca**

How can one hope to have the energy and clarity of mind to seek the higher aspirations of spirit when physically weakened from nutritional deficit?

## NUTRITION, DIETS, AND WEIGHT LOSS

It would be a gross omission not to discuss obesity, weight loss diets, and optimal nutrition. To put things into perspective, it is well to remember that health problems which the Web of Wholeness illustrates have many parts. Obesity and smoking are the two factors that increase morbidity and mortality in virtually every category of health statistics. Seventy to eighty million U. S. citizens are 2.3 billion pounds overweight.[6] Excess body fat is no small or simple problem. It is more accurate to look at it as a symptom of the problem of "lifestyle maladaptation." Look into the Web of Wholeness of any person suffering from overweight, and you will find many other health problems. Obviously, diet and nutrition have a major role to play in restoring normal body fat content. But look at the thousands of diet books on the market. Sure, they are filled with case histories and testimonials of those who have succeeded in losing weight, but the facts remain that these purely dietary approaches fail 95% of the time to keep weight off longer than one year. At any given time 48 million Americans are dieting. This in large part is due to failure to make substantial, permanent lifestyle changes to complement the dietary restrictions. These lifestyle changes bring into play the many other strands in the web of our being that establish good health.

To begin with, many of the popular weight loss diets do not have a sound nutritional basis. Secondly, they too often forget to emphasize the transition from the weight loss diet to optimal nutrition once ideal weight is achieved. Thirdly, elements of biochemical individuality must be considered in nearly all difficult cases. Many of these individuals have undiagnosed endocrinopathic obesity, which is to say that there is a substantial organ, glandular, and hormonal dysfunction that, if not addressed, will guarantee the failure of any diet. Just the incidence of unrecognized hypothyroidism (underfunctioning thyroid gland) contributing to unresolved weight problems is astronomical.[7]

Add to this the often omitted exercise, which is vital to good health.[8] Psychological and human relationship issues are large contributing factors to this biochemical distortion, which catches the eye on the surface as a weight problem. So if excess fatty tissue is part of the perceived problem, it is wiser not to focus exclusively on ridding oneself of the additional fat but to strive for wholeness on many fronts. Not only will ideal weight result by this healthier, safer process but many other dysfunctional body-mind-spirit relationships will be healed.

And from another perspective, it is interesting to note where we Americans put value by observing where we put our money. On one side of the scale, *$33 billion* for unsightly fat removal. On the other side, a fraction for the starving poor.

*During 1991 the U.S. gave the countries in Africa
$800 million in development aid.
During this same year citizens in the U.S. spent
$33 billion on weight loss programs
($400 million just on diet pills).*

## NUTRITIONAL SUPPLEMENTATION

Proper diet is the first and foremost element in nutritional health. Supplementation with nutritional factors such as vitamins, minerals, amino acids, fatty acids, friendly intestinal bacteria, herbs, and other botanical substances can also play an enormous role in both recovering from health problems and attaining optimal levels of performance and wholeness. It is an appealing, idealistic concept to think that we can get all our nutritional needs for optimal health by the foods in our diet alone. When realistic considerations are taken into account, supplementation provides many advantages. Let us look at some of the reasons.

1. High-quality, organically grown food produced in nutrient-rich soil is available and affordable for only a small number of individuals. Standard American agricultural foodstuffs, which most of us depend on, too often come from nutrient-poor soil and are contaminated by pesticides, herbicides, bacteria, hormones, and antibiotics. Foods imported from other countries can be even worse.

2. The large majority of foods available for consumption are processed and adulterated further, diminishing the nutrient quality per calorie.

3. Most people, even if they try hard to eat right, do not provide themselves or their families with a diet that has enough nutrients to accommodate basic nutritional needs.

4. Ninety percent of the population have special circumstances that increase their needs above those of the normal healthy adult—growing children, the elderly, pregnant and lactating women, the ill and infirm, those under stress at home or at work. . . .

5. Biochemical individuality demands that we recognize there are sometimes hundredfold differences in particular nutrient needs and utilization between any two people, depending on their particular circumstances at the time.

6. We would want to provide nutrients sufficient for optimal health, not just average existence.

If we choose higher levels of health than the average unhealthy American, then we need to find a system of supplementation that is cost effective for our individual health goals. Roughly speaking, our need for supplementation corresponds to our "spectrum of functioning" in biochemical balance, organ efficiency, and neurological integrity. Since these parameters are not easily tested by ourselves, we can use three simplified levels of supplementation.

The first level contains some basic supplements that nearly everyone can benefit from, no matter what their health status. No testing, no responsibility for designing an individualized program, and no further education on the subject are required. There are no adverse side effects. They are very inexpensive, but not very specific. This level is not suited for those individuals who have considerable nutritional deficits or particular needs. It is also not best suited for those who want optimal levels of health rather than just basic nutritional "insurance." Find the following in a reputable health food store and favor supplements from well-respected manufacturing companies with good track records:

- high potency multiple vitamin with 400 I.U. of vitamin E per day

- multiple mineral

- vitamin C—1-3 grams per day

- lactobacillus acidophilus (to be taken periodically)

The second level of supplementation follows the guidelines in either of these superb books: *Super Fitness—Beyond Vitamins: The Bible of Super Supplements* by Michael Rosenbaum and Dominick Bosco or *Staying Healthy with Nutrition* by Elson Haas. Both provide great, simple, prescriptive advice for many special needs and health goals without extensive testing. Dr. Haas' book is a must for every home.

The third level of supplementation is for those who have very demanding health problems, severely disturbed biochemistry, or who want maximum human performance. It involves advanced biochemical and physiological testing, followed by consultation with nutritional experts who can interpret these tests. To use this level of supplementation it is necessary to find a physician qualified to help. To do this contact the organizations listed in the professional resource section and ask for a referral to a physician in your area. If you are lucky, you might find a physician who belongs to several of these organizations, uses the best laboratories, and attends many of the cited educational programs. Since there are few of these progressive physicians in the U. S., it is difficult. The physicians are medical doctors, chiropractors, naturopaths, osteopaths, and even some dentists.

Generally, the determination of what combination of supplements or their dosage is best for you should *not* be made by a physician who does not specialize in nutrition, a dietician, a "nutritional consultant" who received a nutrition "certification" by mail order, a multilevel marketer selling supplements, a health food store worker, or your aunt Agnes. These people are unqualified or may be prejudiced.

## FOOD SAFETY

*Sixty to eighty million Americans suffer from food-borne illness every year. 9,000 die.[9]*

There can be many potentially harmful substances in the foods we eat: pesticides and herbicides from the farm, antibiotics and hormones fed to animals, environmental contaminants like lead and mercury, natural toxins like aflatoxins in peanuts, shellfish toxins, or bacteria from the meat processing plant or one's own kitchen. Using the guidelines previously outlined will greatly reduce the risk of food poisoning. A more detailed examination of this subject can be found in the book *Safe Food: Eating Wisely in a Risky World.*

*From 1980 to 1989 the USDA's Food Safety and Inspection Service reduced its poultry inspectors by 29%. During that same time Salmonella food poisoning increased by 42%.[9]*

## FASTING

Fasting has been used for centuries as a therapeutic device. With the correct, professionally supervised setting it can be a beneficial practice. There are two major reasons for its success. The first is that for the time of the fast the person is not consuming the junk food with which he normally was polluting his body. This in itself can explain many of the pronounced benefits of fasting. The second reason is that he is not consuming foods to which he was allergic, intolerant, or sensitive. Many of these are hidden food allergies. Now, add to this a diet with sufficient bulk to regularly cleanse the colon, and/or use periodic high enemas or colonics with oral acidophilus supplementation to insure healthy intestinal function, and you can minimize the need for expensively supervised fasting.

One of the more scientifically sound methods of modified fasting is to use a nutritionally balanced, non-allergic meal replacement supplement combined with an allergen elimination diet. This has several advantages: It does not stress the body with harmful allergic foods. It supplies the body with necessary nutrients for repair and recovery. It is simple to institute. It is inexpensive. A detailed description of this type of program can be found in the syllabus for Jeffrey Bland's seminar on "Metabolic Clearing Therapy" produced by Health-Comm.

Fasting for weight loss is not a recommended procedure except under qualified supervision using a modified protein-sparing fast with vitamin and mineral supplementation.

*A missionary was walking in Africa when he heard the ominous padding of a lion behind him. "Oh Lord," prayed the missionary, "grant in Thy goodness that the lion walking behind me is a good Christian lion." And then, in the silence that followed, the missionary heard the lion praying too: "Oh Lord," he prayed, "we thank Thee for the food which we are about to receive."*

**Cleveland Amory**

# NUTRITION RESOURCES

*Tell me what you eat and I will tell you who you are.*

**Anthelme Brilliat-Savarin**

★Denotes Best of the Best Resources

## *Books*

Balch, James and Phyllis. *Prescription for Nutritional Healing.* Avery, 1990.

Colgan. *Optimum Sports Nutrition: Your Competitive Edge.* Colgan Inst., 1993.

★Haas, Elson. *Staying Healthy with Nutrition.* Celestial Arts, 1991.

★Jacobson, Michael and Lefferts, Lisa. *Safe Food: Eating Wisely in a Risky World.* Living Planet Press, 1991. Available from Center for Science in the Public Interest.

*Nutrition and Mental Health.* U. S. Senate Select Committee on Nutrition and Human Needs, 1980.

Passwater, Richard. *The New Supernutrition Book.* Pocket Books, 1991.

Robbins, John. *Diet for a New America.* 1987. Stillpoint Publishing, Box 640, Walpole, NH 03608; (800) 847-4014. Excellent documentation and arguments for vegetarianism and ecologically conscious eating.

Robbins, John. *May All Be Fed.* Morrow, 1992. Sequel to *Diet for a New America.*

Rosenbaum, Michael and Bosco, Dominick. *Super Fitness Beyond Vitamins: The Bible of Super Supplements.* New American Library, 1987.

Sorenson, Marc. *Mega Health.* National Institute of Fitness, 1991. Good documentation for dietary guidelines.

Steinman, David. *Diet for a Poisoned Planet.* Random House, 1990.

Trenev, Natasha and Chaitow, Leon. *Probiotics: The Revolutionary "Friendly Bacteria" Way to Vital Health and Well-Being.* Thorsons Publishers Limited, 10 East 53rd St., New York, NY 10022.

Wurtman, Judith. *Managing Your Mind and Mood Through Food.* Rawson, 1986.

## *Periodicals*

*Health Counselor,* ImpaKt Communications, Inc., P.O. Box 12496, Green Bay, WI 54307-2496; (414) 499-2995.

*Let's Live,* 320 N. Larchmont Blvd., P.O. Box 74908, Los Angeles, CA 90004; Business Office—(213) 469-3901; Fax (213) 469-9597; Subscriptions—(800) 225-6473.

★*Nutrition Action Health Letter,* Center for Science in the Public Interest, 1875 Connecticut Ave., N.W. #300, Washington, DC 20009; (202) 667-7483; (202) 332-9110; Fax (202) 265-4954. This periodical has good information on proper diet but closed-minded, unhelpful information on how nutritional supplementation can help people's health.

*Vegetarian Times,* For subscriptions—P.O. Box 446, Mt. Morris, IL 61054; (800) 435-9610. For information—1140 Lake St., Suite 500, Oak Park, IL 60301; (708) 848-8100.

*Vegetarian Journal,* Vegetarian Resource Group, P.O. Box 1463, Baltimore, MD 21203; (410) 366-8343.

*In a desperate attempt to dupe the public into thinking cow flesh is good nutrition, Beef Industry spokesperson, James Garner, tells us on TV commercials that "Beef is Real Food for Real People." He doesn't tell us that he had multiple bypass surgeries to reroute his blood around fat-clogged arteries caused by that "real" food.*

## *Videos*

*Lower Your Cholesterol Now!* Available from the Center for Science in the Public Interest.

*Supermarket Savvy* by Leni Reed and available from the National Wellness Institute or the Center for Science in the Public Interest. Aisle by aisle nutrition label evaluation of foods.

Robbins, John. *Diet for a New America*

## *Consumer Computer Software for Nutritional Evaluation and Prescription and Computer Databases*

CAB: Human Nutrition—From CAB International. Extensive database on a wide variety of clinical nutritional subjects.

*CPdsk,* Clinical Pearls 1990-93 on disk. Available from ITServices, 3301 Alta Arden #3, Sacramento, CA 95825; (800) 422-9887; (916) 489-4400.

*Nutri-Calc,* Camde Corp., 449 E. Saratoga St., Gilbert, AZ 85234-7772; (602) 926-2632.

Pressman, Alan. *Clinical Assessment of Nutritional Status*. Williams & Wilkins, 1990. See Appendix for list of nutritional software.

## Organizations

Carl Pfieffer Treatment Center, 1804 Centre Point Drive, Suite 102, Naperville, IL 60563; (708) 505-0300. An outpatient treatment center focusing primarily on the nutritional and biochemical diagnosis and treatment of behavioral disorders.

★National Wellness Institute, Inc., 1045 Clark St., Stevens Point, WI 54481; (715) 342-2969; Fax (715) 342-2979. Books, video and audio tapes, computer software, workbooks, conferences.

Princeton Bio Center, 862 Route 518, Skillman, NJ 08558; (609) 924-8607. A biomedical research and treatment center that addresses the neurobiological and nutritional aspects of mental illness.

Price-Pottinger Nutrition Foundation, P.O. Box 2614, La Mesa, CA 91944-2614; (619) 574-7763; (619) 582-4168. Publishes the *PPNF Nutrition Journal*.

## PROFESSIONAL RESOURCES

### Books

Bland, Jeffrey. *Medical Applications of Clinical Nutrition*. Keats, 1983.

Bland, Jeffrey. *Advancement in Clinical Nutrition: New Protocols for Improving Health*. HealthComm, 1994. Workbook and/or audiotapes.

Braverman, Eric with Pfeiffer, Carl. *The Healing Nutrients Within: Facts, Findings, and New Research on Amino Acids*. Keats, 1987.

Frank, R. and Irving, H. *The Directory of Food and Nutrition Information for Professionals and Consumers*. Oryx Press, 1992.

Garrison, R. H. and Somer, E. *The Nutrition Desk Reference*. Keats, 1990.

Grabowski, Ronald. *Current Nutritional Therapy: A Clinical Reference*. Image Press, 1993.

★Hamilton, Kirk. *Clinical Pearls in Nutrition and Preventive Medicine*. ITServices, (annual from 1990-94).

Hippchen, Leonard. *Ecologic-Biochemical Approaches to Treatment of Delinquents and Criminals*. Van Nostrand Reinhold, 1978.

Hoffer, Abram. *Orthomolecular Medicine for Physicians*. Keats, 1989.

Pfeiffer, Carl. *Nutrition and Mental Illness: An Orthomolecular Approach to Balancing Body Chemistry*. Healing Arts Press, 1987.

Philpott, William and Kalita, Dwight. *Brain Allergies: The Psycho-Nutrient Connection*. Keats, 1980.

★Pizzorno, Joseph and Murray, Michael. *A Textbook of Natural Medicine*. Bastyr College Publications.

Pressman, Alan. *Clinical Assessment of Nutritional Status*. Williams & Wilkins, 1990.

★Werbach, Melvyn. *Nutritional Influences on Illness: A Sourcebook of Clinical Research*. Third Line Press, 1988. Third Line Press: 4751 Viviana Drive, Suite 204, Tarzana, CA 91356; (818) 996-0076.

★Werbach, Melvyn. *Nutritional Influences on Mental Illness: A Sourcebook of Clinical Research*. Third Line Press, 1991.

### Journals, Magazines, Conference Audiotapes, and Newsletters

*American Journal of Clinical Nutrition*, the Official Journal of the American Society for Clinical Nutrition, 428 E. Preston St., Baltimore, MD 21202-3923; (301) 530-7038; Fax (301) 571-8303.

Bastyr College's quarterly updates to Pizzorno's and Murray's *Textbook of Natural Medicine* provides a good source of up-to-date information on nutrition and natural health care approaches.

*Free Radical Research Communications*, International Publishing Distributors, P.O. Box 200029, River Front Plaza Station, Newark NJ 07102-0301; (201) 643-7500; (800) 545-8398.

★Hamilton, Kirk. *CP Currents*. Hundreds of monthly summaries and citations of research in nutrition and preventive medicine from hundreds of medical journals internationally. Indispensable method for progressive physicians to keep up-to-date with the rapid advancements in these fields. This is the source for Hamilton's abbreviated monthly report, *Clinical Pearls News* and the yearly *Clinical Pearls*. All of which can be obtained from ITServices, 3301 Alta Arden #3, Sacramento, CA 95825; (800) 422-9887; (916) 489-4400.

★Health Comm, Inc., 5800 Soundview Drive, #E-102, P.O. Box 1729, Gig Harbor, WA 98335; (800) 843-9660. Provides up-to-date information on advances in nutritional and preventive medicine for physicians in both audio and written form.

Insta-Tape, Inc., P.O. Box 1729, Monrovia, CA 91016-5729; (818) 303-2531. Provides educational audiotapes of current conferences and seminars.

*International Journal of Sport Nutrition,* Human Kinetic Publishers, P.O. Box 5076, Champaign, IL 61825-5076; (800) 747-4457; (217) 351-5076; In Canada—Human Kinetics, Box 224040, 1275 Walker Rd., Windsor, Ontario N8Y 4Y9; (519) 944-7774.

*Journal of Applied Nutrition,* The Official Journal of the International Academy of Nutrition and Preventive Medicine, P.O. Box 18433, Asheville, NC 28814; (704) 258-3243.

*Journal of Optimal Nutrition,* 2552 Regis Dr., Davis, CA 95616; (916) 756-3311; Fax (916) 758-7444. Research on nutritional supplementation.

★ *Journal of Orthomolecular Medicine,* Canadian Schizophrenia Association, 16 Florence Ave., New York, Ontario, Canada M2N 1E9; (416) 733-2117.

*Nutrition & Healing,* P.O. Box 84909, Phoenix, AZ 85071; (800) 528-0559. A monthly educational newsletter for nutritionally oriented physicians by the superb team of Jonathan Wright, M.D. and Alan Gaby, M.D.

★ *Quarterly Review of Natural Medicine,* Natural Product Research Consultants, 600 First Ave., Suite 205, Seattle, WA 98104; (206) 623-2520; Fax (206) 623-6340.

★ *Townsend Letter for Doctors,* 911 Tyler Street, Port Townsend, WA 98368, (206) 385-6021.

Tree Farm Communications, 23703 N.E. 4th St., Redmond, WA 98053, (206) 868-0464. Provide educational audio and video tapes of current conferences and seminars plus other educational information.

## *Professional Computer Software for Nutritional Evaluation and Prescription*

*Cooper Clinic Nutritional and Exercise Evaluation Program.* Available from the National Wellness Institute.

CP *dsk,* Clinical Pearls 1990-93 on disk. Available from ITServices, 3301 Alta Arden #3, Sacramento, CA 95825; (800) 422-9887; (916) 489-4400.

*Nutri-Calc,* Camde Corp., 449 E. Saratoga St., Gilbert, AZ 85234-7772; (602) 926-2632.

Pressman, Alan. *Clinical Assessment of Nutritional Status.* Williams & Wilkins, 1990. See Appendix for list of nutritional software.

## *Organizations*

★American Academy of Environmental Medicine, P.O. Box 116106, Denver, CO 80216, (303) 622-9755. Progressive group of physicians practicing "clinical ecology" who use the most updated methods for identifying and treating toxic and allergic reactions to the environment. They can provide a referral to a physician nearest you. Audio tapes of the Academy's Seminars and conferences are available from Insta-Tape, Inc., P.O. Box 2926-D, Pasadena, CA 91105.

★Canadian Schizophrenia Association, 16 Florence Ave., New York, Ontario, Canada M2N 1E9; (416) 733-2117. Publishes the *Journal of Orthomolecular Medicine,* and *Health and Nutrition Update* and *Nutrition and Mental Health.*

★Health Comm, Inc., 5800 Soundview Drive, #E-102, P.O. Box 1729, Gig Harbor, WA 98335; (800) 843-9660. One of the best places to get an education in clinical nutrition. Dr. Bland's organization offers seminars on different nutritional subjects; periodicals in written and audio format on medical nutrition, preventive medicine, and food science (*Preventive Medicine Update*), and books.

★International Academy of Nutrition and Preventive Medicine, P.O. Box 18433, Asheville, NC 28814, (704) 258-3243. Publishes the *Journal of Applied Nutrition.*

Olive W. Garvey Center for the Improvement of Human Functioning, Inc., 3100 N. Hillside Ave., Wichita, KS 67219; (316) 682-3100. Educational, research, and treatment facility.

Princeton Bio Center, 862 Route 518, Skillman, NJ 08558-9631; (609) 924-8607. Research organization for orthomolecular medicine.

Society for Orthomolecular Medicine, 2698 Pacific Ave., San Francisco, CA 94115; (415) 346-2500; Fax (415) 346-4991.

★Wright/Gaby Nutrition Institute, P.O. Box 21535, Baltimore, MD 21208; (410) 486-5656. One of the best places to get an education in clinical nutrition. Doctors Wright and Gaby are two of the preeminent nutritionally-oriented physicians in the country.

## ★ *Physician Laboratories Using Advanced Nutritional Testing*

Doctor's Data Inc., P.O. Box 111, 170 W. Roosevelt Rd., W. Chicago, IL 60185; (800) 323-2784.

Great Smokies Diagnostic Laboratory, 18 A Regent Park Blvd., Asheville, NC 28806; (800) 522-4762.

Immuno Laboratories, 1620 W. Oakland Park Blvd., Ft. Lauderdale, FL 33311; (800) 231-9197; in Florida—(800) 628-4300; (305) 486-4500; Fax (305) 739-6563.

Meridian Valley Clinical Laboratory, 515 W. Harrison St., Suite 9, Kent, WA 98032; (206) 859-8700; Drs. only line (800) 234-6825. A high-quality clinical lab providing an array of superb functional biochemical tests.

MetaMetrix Medical Laboratory, 5000 Peachtree Ind. Blvd., Suite 110 Norcross, GA 30071, (800) 221-4640; (404) 446-5483. Another excellent multi-service lab.

Monroe Medical Research Laboratory, Route 17, P. O. Box I, Southfields, NY 10975; (800) 831-3133; (914) 351-5134; Fax (914) 351-4295. Another excellent multi-service lab.

National BioTechnology Laboratory, 3212 NE 125th St., Seattle, WA 98125; (800) 846-6285 or (206) 363-6606; Fax (206) 363-2025. Another excellent multi-service lab.

Serammune Physicians Laboratory, 1890 Preston White Drive, Suite 200, Reston, VA 22091; (800) 553-5472; (703) 758-0610; Fax (703) 758-0615. This superb lab specializes in the most advanced type of immunological tests (ELISA/ACT™) to determine a person's reactivity to environmental agents, including food.

SpectraCell Laboratories, 515 Post Oak Blvd., Suite 830, Houston, TX 77027; (800) 227-5227; (713) 621-3101; Fax (713) 621-3234. Provides two specialty tests: Essential Metabolic Analysis (EMA), a functional nutrient status blood test and Spectrox, a functional antioxidant capacity blood test.

## Nutritional Supplement Wholesalers

Emerson Ecologics, 436 Great Road, Acton, MA 01720; (800) 654-4432; (508) 263-7238; Fax (508) 263-6051. Wholesaler for 50 different nutritional supplement suppliers.

Nu Biologics, Inc., 2470 Wisconsin, Ave., Downers Grove, IL 60515; (800) 332-3130 or (708) 969-7600; Fax (708) 969-6809.

NutriSupplies, 7901 79th Way, West Palm Beach, FL 33407; (800) 388-8808; (407) 640-7900; Fax (407) 640-2781.

Terrace International Distributors, Inc., P.O. Box 817, Forest Falls, CA 92339; (800) 824-2434; (714) 794-7674; Fax (909) 794-7674. Wholesaler for 40 different nutritional supplement suppliers.

Threshold Enterprises, Ltd., 23 Janis Way, Scotts Valley, CA 95066; (800)777-5677; Fax (408) 438-7410. Wholesaler to health food stores for approximately 150 different nutritional supplement manufacturers, and producer of Source Naturals line of supplements.

## Nutritional Supplement Companies

Allergy Research Group, 400 Preda St., San Leandro, CA 94577; (800) 545-9960; (510) 639-4572; Fax (510) 635-6730. Produce high quality hypo-allergenic nutritional supplements primarily for immune system repair and enhancement in individuals suffering from allergies, toxic reactions, and environmental illness. They provide excellent educational materials and workshops to professionals on these clinical issues.

Advanced Medical Nutrition, Inc. (AMNI), 2247 National Ave., P.O. Box 5012 Hayward, CA 94540-5012; (800) 437-8888; Fax (510) 783-8196.

BioSan Laboratories, P.O. Box 325, Derry, NH 03038; (800) 634-6342; (603) 432-5022; Fax (603) 434-4736.

Bio-Therapeutics / Phyto-Pharmica, 825 Challenger Dr., Green Bay, WI 54311; (800) 553-2370.

Biotics Research Corporation and Probiologics, Inc., 14714 NE 87th St., Redmond, WA 98052; (800) 678-8218.

DaVinci Laboratories, 20 New England Dr., Essex Junction, VT 05453; (800) 325-1776; Call collect from VT or AK (802) 878-5508; Fax (802) 878-0549.

Douglas Laboratories, 600 Boyce Rd., Pittsburgh, PA 15205; (800) 245-4440 or (412) 494-0122; Fax (412) 494-0155.

Ecological Formulas / Cardiovascular Research, 1061-B Shary Circle, Concord, CA 94518; (800) 888-4585; CA, AK, and Int'l (510) 827-2636.

KAL Vitamins, P.O. Box 4023, Woodland Hills, CA 91365; (818) 340-3035.

Key Company, 1313 W. Essex, St. Louis, MO 63122; (800) 325-9592 or in St. Louis (314) 965-6699; Fax (314) 965-7629.

Klaire Laboratories, Inc., 1573 W. Seminole St., San Marcos, CA 92069; (800) 533-7255; in CA (619) 744-9680.

Metagenics, 130 Ryan Court, Suite 200, San Ramon, CA 94583; (510) 838-7858; (800) 692-9400; Fax (510) 838-0482.

NF Formulas, Inc., 9775 SW Commerce Circle, Suite C5, Wilsonville, OR 97070-9602; (800) 547-4891; (503) 682-9755; Fax (503) 682-9529.

Progressive Laboratories, Inc., 1701 W. Walnut Hill Lane, Irving, TX 75038; (800) 527-9512; (214) 518-9660; Fax (214) 518-9665.

Pure Encapsulations, 490 Boston Post Road, Sudbury, MA 01776; (800) 753-2277; (508) 443-1999; Fax (508) 443-9664.

Schiff Products, 180 Moonachie Ave., Moonachie, NJ 07074; (800) 526-6251.

Solaray, 2815 Industrial Dr., Ogden, UT 84401; (800) 669-8877; (801) 621-5631.

Standard Process Laboratories, 12209 Locksley Lane, Suite 15, Auburn, CA 95603; (916) 888-1974; (800) 662-9134.

Thorne Research, Inc., Sand Point, ID 93964; (800) 228-1966.

Tyler Encapsulations, 2204-8 N.W. Birdsdale, Gresham, OR 97030; (800) 869-9705.

Vitamin Research Products, 3579 Hwy. 50 East, Carson City, NV 89701; (800) 877-2447; (702) 884-1300; Fax (800) 877-3292.

## REFERENCES

1. Anderson, Mark, from a letter to the editor of *Townsend Letter for Doctors* (April, 1991) 236-240. Good commentary on value of registered dieticians.

2. Jaffe, Russel, and Kruesi, Oscar, "The Biochemical-Immunological Window: A Molecular View of Psychiatric Case Management," *Journal of Applied Nutrition* 44:2 (1992) 26-42.

3. Schoenthaler, Stephen; Moody, Jeannie; Pankow, Lisa, "Applied Nutrition and Behavior," *Journal of Applied Nutrition* 43:1 (1991) 31-9.

4. Hippchen, Leonard, *Ecologic-Biochemical Approaches to Treatment of Delinquents and Criminals* (Van Nostrand Reinhold Company, 1978). And: Schauss, Alexander, *Diet, Crime, and Delinquency* (Parker House, 1980).

5. Walsh, William, "Biochemical Treatment of Behavior, Learning and Mental Disorders," *Townsend Letter* (Aug/Sep. 1992) 698-702. And: *Journal of Orthomolecular Medicine,* The Official Journal of the American Association of Orthomolecular Medicine, 7375 Kingsway, Burnaby, BC V3N 3B5 Canada.

6. Bland, Jeffrey, ed., *Medical Applications of Clinical Nutrition* (Keats, 1983) 99.

7. Langer, Stephen, and Scheer, James, *Solved: The Riddle of Illness* (Keats, 1984)

8. Bailey, Covert, *Fit or Fat? A New Way to Health and Fitness Through Nutrition and Aerobic Exercise* (Houghton Mifflin, 1978).

9. USDA and Centers for Disease Control.

## HEALTHY COOKBOOKS

*The discovery of a new dish does more for the happiness of mankind than the discovery of a star.*

**Anthelme Brilliat-Savarin**

Bland, Jeffrey. *Your Health Under Siege.* Greene, 1982.

Chiavetta, Janet. *Eat, Drink, and Be Healthy: A Guide to Healthy Eating & Weight Control.* Piedmont, 1993.

Cluff, Sheila and Brown, Eleanor. *The Ultimate Recipe for Fitness: Spa Cuisine . . .* Fitness Ojai, 1990.

D'Agostino, Joanne and D'Agostino, Frank. *Italian Cooking for a Healthy Heart.* Eagle Publishing, 1990.

Gerras, Charles. *Feasting on Raw Foods.* Rodale Press, 1980.

Guste, Roy. *Louisiana Light: Low fat, Low Calorie, Low Cholesterol, Low Salt Cajun and Creole Cookery.* Norton, 1989.

Hackett, Arlyn. *Health Smart Gourmet Cooking,* Hastings, 1992.

McDougall, John. *The McDougall Health Supporting Cookbook: Vol. 1.* New Century, 1984.

McDougall, John. *The McDougall Health Supporting Cookbook: Vol. II.* New Century, 1986.

McDougall, John and Mary. *The New McDougall Cookbook.* Penguin, 1993.

Ornish, Dean. *Eat More, Weigh Less.* HarperCollins, 1993.

Pickarski, Brother Ron. *Friendly Foods: Gourmet Vegetarian Cuisine.* Ten Speed Press, 1991.

Riccio, Dolores. *Super Foods: 300 Recipes for Foods that Heal Body & Mind.* Warner Bks., 1994.

Robertson, Laurel and Flanders, Carol and Ruppenthal, Brian. *The New Laurel's Kitchen.* Ten Speed Press, 1986.

Rose, Gloria. *Enjoying Good Health.* Herm Barr Pub., 1987.

Saltzman, Joanne. *Amazing Grains: Creating Vegetarian Main Dishes with Whole Grains.* H. J. Kramer, 1990.

Shulman, Martha Rose. *Fast Vegetarian Feasts.* Dolphin Books, 1987.

Thomas, Anna. *The Vegetarian Epicure.* Vintage Books, 1972.

Thomas, Anna. *The Vegetarian Epicure II.* Alfred A. Knopf, 1978.

Turner, Kristina. *The Self Healing Cookbook.* Earthtones Press, 1989.

Williams, Marcia. *More Healthy Cooking with No Apologies.* Crossing Press, 1991.

Wilson, Marie. *The Good-For-Your-Health, All-Asian Cookbook*. Tuttle, 1989.And: *The Healthy Heart Cookbook*, 1992.

Lakhani, Fatima. *Indian Recipes for a Healthy Heart*, Fahil Pub, 1992.

## COOKING SCHOOLS

*A good cook is the peculiar gift of the gods.*
*He must be a perfect creature*
*from the brain to the palate,*
*from the palate to the finger's end.*

**Walter Savage Landor**

Natural Gourmet Institute for Food and Health, The Natural Gourmet Cookery School, 48 W. 21st St., New York, NY 10010; (212) 645-5170.

School of Natural Cookery, 1520 Euclid, Boulder, CO 80302; (303) 444-8068.

### *Videos*

*I'm on a seafood diet. I see food and I eat it.*

**Unknown**

Colbin, Annemarie. *The Basics of Healthy Cooking*. The Natural Gourmet Cookery School, 48 W. 21st St., New York, NY 10010; (212) 645-5170.

*Anyone who eats three meals a day*
*should understand why cookbooks outsell*
*sex books three to one.*

**L. M. Boyd**

# EXERCISE

*Too much rest is rust.*

**Sir Walter Scott**

Proper, balanced exercise is one of the most important health enhancement strategies we have at our disposal. A wise integration of aerobic conditioning, flexibility exercise, strength training, activities that build neuromuscular coordination, and play, is at the heart of any true holistic lifestyle. The benefits span all realms of our being, not just our physical health.

Each of these elements of exercise supports each of the other elements. Choosing the right combination needs to be done in a systematic way. Selecting the right type of each of these elements is even more difficult. Hopefully the information that follows will help you choose the exercises best suited to you.

## AEROBIC CONDITIONING

Aerobic fitness is the biochemical, cardiopulmonary, and muscular capacity to generate useful energy for physical activity. It is a relative matter, in part determined by age, sex, heredity, disease, and circumstance. An eighty-year-old woman might be at her maximum aerobic fitness level, giving her the capability to do daily chores, work in the garden for short spells throughout the day, take the dog for a walk to the neighbors, and climb a few flights of stairs per day. An elite distance runner might be optimally fit when he runs a marathon in just over two hours after months of training at 100 miles of running per week.

In holistic health terms, aerobic fitness is related to a level of functioning that provides the highest level of benefits with the lowest level of disadvantages, consistent with a well-balanced lifestyle that supports the individual's life goals. That's different from maximal aerobic capacity or endurance.

*30-60% of Canadians and Americans engage in no leisure-time physical activity.[1]*

Bob always looked up to his father, a world class Olympic steeplechase runner. From a young age Bob was surrounded by his father's trophies and exciting tales of dramatic photo finishes. Bob wanted to be just like his father, in part because his dad never had time to pay too much attention to him. Bob needed that recognition early in life, never received enough parental acknowledgment, and always afterward strived to excel in an unconscious effort to finally win his father's long sought approval. Unfortunately, Bob didn't get his father's "athletic" genes. In fact, Bob was born prematurely and throughout his youngest years was quite sickly. But that did not deter him from working very hard to overcome these physical limitations. He succeeded well enough to at least make the school track team. He would work out twice as long and twice as hard as any of his teammates. But still he could not even place third in track meets. As the years passed, Bob continued to train almost exclusively for that elusive attainment of self-esteem masquerading as Olympic hopes. His grades suffered. He had no social life. He had no energy left for them. He lost many jobs and quit many others so that he could train.

For six years his best times in events never improved, no matter how he changed his training regimen. The harder he worked, the more injuries he suffered. The physical stress of training so hard depressed his immune system, and he was frequently ill with different infections. Obviously, he had reached his best aerobic development years earlier, and it was not going to improve, regardless of any change of technique or increase in effort. As with most human endeavors, there is a point of diminishing returns when added effort does not produce enough additional results to justify those efforts. This is particularly true when we are considering a *balanced* lifestyle that invests time and energy in different activities to build the health of the whole self, not just one part of it.

Bob might have been much better served if he had participated in exercise designed to improve his overall health. Then, instead of using a disproportionate amount of effort to achieve maximal performance over and above healthy fitness levels, he could have used all that wasted energy balancing out his life—using psychotherapy to resolve old issues of self-esteem left over from childhood, engaging in a healthy social life, focusing on education and right livelihood to bring inner fulfillment.

One of Bob's mistakes was to unknowingly use exercise to perform a task it was not best suited to achieve—psychotherapy. That is not to say that exercise in its many different forms does not have great benefits on mental health. There are many documented emotional and psychological benefits, particularly of aerobic training. It is just not specific for particular problems like Bob's. Many people use exercise in a maladaptive, unconscious fashion—avoidance of conflict, repression of hidden desires, transference of aggression, running from fear. This illustrates the benefits of a planned, prioritized, health enhancement program for each individual, like that which is advocated in this book.

**Bodily exercises are to be done discretely; not to be taken evenly and alike by all men.**
**Thomas à Kempis**

## The Health Benefits of Aerobic Exercise

So how should we use aerobic exercise to improve our entire well-being? Looking at how the body adapts to physical activity, and the documented health benefits it receives, will help us answer this question. A reasonable amount, frequency, duration, and intensity of aerobic exercise has been documented to do the following:

*It increases physical energy.* This means more energy to accomplish what we need or want to do on a daily basis. Heart and lung capacity and efficiency increase. The oxygen carrying capacity of the blood improves. There is a more efficient use of various energy pathways in the cells and tissues of the body, the muscles especially.

*There is an improvement in mental health with exercise.* Depression, anxiety, tension are all reduced. Intellectual functions and learning are enhanced. Multiple causes for these improvements have been researched and can be explained, in part, by increased blood flow to the brain, hormonal changes, alterations in neurotransmitters, the production of endogenous opiates (mood elevators within the brain), reduced stress due to better balance in the nervous system's autonomic functions, and the tranquilizing effects of increased body temperature. This does not even take into account the psychological benefits of achieving goals, discovering a sense of self-control, improving self-esteem, transforming one's self-image, or socializing with others.

*Longevity is increased.* This is due in part to physiological improvements, such as a decrease in blood pressure in those millions with hypertension, increases in blood vessel strength and size, decrease in body fat, decrease in blood cholesterol, an increase in heat acclimatization, more rapid recovery from illness, and delay of the aging process.

Other health benefits: lowering the risk of injury by strengthening the bones, ligaments, tendons, and muscles; improvements in work performance; regularity of bowel movements, thus reducing conditions such as toxic bowel syndrome, constipation, and hemorrhoids; improvements in liver and kidney function resulting in enhanced detoxification of the body's metabolites and poisons; better digestion, thus improvements in nutritional health; better menstrual function due to regulation of hormones and increased blood circulation; healthy child bearing; improvements in sleep patterns; reductions in skin infections, and less hunger.

*"10% of Americans and 25% of Canadians are regularly and vigorously active."* [1]

So how do we achieve these benefits? How do we determine the correct level and type of aerobic training? As usual, the first step is to assess the present level of fitness and then determine how much improvement is needed. Once again, there are multiple levels of fitness testing. On the lower end of the scale are submaximal aerobic exercise tests which measure one's ability to complete an aerobic task, like run a mile or run for about fifteen minutes in reasonable comfort.

A more precise calculation of this physiological limit can be made through maximal treadmill or cycle ergometer exercise. Monitoring of ventilatory capacity of the lungs with an evaluation of blood gases, blood pressure, heart rate, and ECG readings can all add more information. For most purposes it is unnecessary. There are also some risks in doing maximal testing on the old and the infirm. These more precise tests can be performed on the serious athlete if desired, or on people needing special care, such as those with high blood pressure, cardiovascular disease, and in rehabilitation programs.

For the most part, the submaximal fitness testing described in the recommended books, and readily available at YMCA exercise programs, is adequate for most peoples' health enhancement needs. If you are over forty and/or not accustomed to regular aerobic exercise, it is advised that you first consult with a health care professional specializing in sports medicine for a preliminary evaluation. This can be a chiropractor, physical therapist, exercise physiologist, naturopath, osteopath, or medical doctor. Contacting the American College of Sports Medicine for a referral to someone appropriate in your locale is a good approach. Otherwise, following the recommendations for gradual, progressive, aerobic conditioning in the resource books is usually sufficient.

It is important to know our target heart rate, regardless of what fitness activity we choose. This is the heart beats per minute that, if sustained during aerobic exercise, will give the best conditioning. Conditioning increases in proportion to intensity, duration, and frequency of exercise within this training zone, with diminishing returns at the maximal limits. Fitness improvement generally occurs when the heart is beating at 60-90% of its maximum capacity. (The elderly can elicit an improvement from training with as little as 40% of maximal heart rate.) To calculate the maximum heart rate, just subtract your age from 220 (there are more accurate measures for athletes with low resting heart rates). Adults with no symptoms of disease can achieve their best conditioning at 70-

85% of this figure. Patients on a cardiac recovery program generally start at 50-65% of maximal heart rate for their training zone. Elite athletes have to push the upper limits of this zone to see improvement. Pushing these upper limits in not only intensity but duration and frequency can result in diminished health from overtraining. The immune system can be depressed and energy reserves sapped. Fatigue and sickness often result.

*The dropout rate for supervised exercise programs is usually 40-50%.*[1]

Below is a list of the most effective and safe aerobic activities.

- cross-country skiing and quality indoor x-country ski machines such as Nordi-Trac
- swimming
- bicycling, including stationary bikes
- non-impact aerobics
- water aerobics
- stair climbing, including stair climbing machines
- power walking with hand-held weights or ski poles
- aerobic circuit training with weight training equipment
- aerobic backpacking and hiking
- skating
- running
- soccer
- basketball
- tennis
- handball, racquetball, squash
- aerobic sculling, paddling, or rowing
- rowing machines, including Health Rider types
- tantric sex (just checking to see if you're still awake)

**The only reason I'd take up jogging is because I'd want to hear heavy breathing again.**

**Erma Bombeck**

# FLEXIBILITY TRAINING

*When man is living, he is soft and flexible.*
*When he is dead, he becomes hard and rigid.*
*When a plant is living it is soft and tender.*
*When it is dead, it becomes withered and dry.*
*Hence, the hard and rigid keep company*
*with the dead,*
*The soft and supple keep company*
*with the alive.*

**Lao Tzu**

A supple, freely-moving body is a major asset to total health. When joints and soft tissues possess ideal flexibility, benefits are seen not only in the musculoskeletal system; the benefits ramify, mostly through improved neurological function, to virtually every organ and system of the body. The vast majority of people are not aware of the enormous impact that flexibility has on different aspects of our health, despite the praise hatha yoga practices have accumulated over thousands of years. Today stretching exercises get high praise from athletic trainers, sports medicine specialists, and athletes, because of their proven ability to prevent injury and increase performance.

Even with that high praise, few individuals engage in any significant stretching routines. Fewer still use them intelligently or frequently enough to even prevent injuries. And only a minuscule number practice a flexibility routine that is designed for their special needs and structural weaknesses. Even dedicated adherents of hatha yoga in many cases do not have sound routines for improving flexibility in the tighter areas while protecting and stabilizing excessively mobile regions.

## *The Physiology and Benefits of Flexibility*

When muscles, tendons and ligaments are too tight, they limit proper joint motion. This causes several unhealthy reactions in the body. Tightness in soft tissues generates excessive nerve impulses through much of the nervous system, altering functions in different parts of the body. Sometimes these excessive nerve transmissions interfere with normal nerve signals to internal organs, confusing them and causing them to malfunction. For instance, lower back and gluteal muscles, if too tight, can trigger excessive nerve firing and cause excessive uterine contractions in women, making their menstrual cycles more uncomfortable.

Another mechanism involves the classic stress syndrome of "fight or flight." This happens when an individual habitually learns to respond to stress by unconsciously tightening muscles that do not really need to be activated. This results in chronically tight, shortened muscle fibers, and even pain. Virtually every organ in the body is affected by this stress-generated muscle tension; it cascades neurologically and hormonally throughout the body, inflicting both short and long term damage.

Soft tissue tightness can also restrict joint motion enough to disrupt the flow of nerve impulses coming from the neurological bed of the joint itself. This causes the same confusion of nerve signals to internal organs, as described above. For example, abnormal nerve firing from improperly functioning joints in the thoracic spine can send abnormal rhythms to the heart or produce too much stomach acid.

When joints are restricted, other joints nearby usually become excessively mobile in an automatic effort to compensate. This creates even more abnormal nerve signaling. It is one of the prime causes of joint injury at work, in the home, or in athletic activities.

Proper stretching creates:

- muscles that are relaxed and at a normal length while at rest (this actually makes them stronger)

- soft tissues that have a strong tensile strength

- soft tissues that do not contribute extraneous nerve impulses into other systems of the body

- joints that move fully and freely through their designed range without producing abnormal nerve signals

For people with considerable muscle tightness, joint restrictions, and/or excessive mobility, restoring better, balanced flexibility will:

- reduce injuries to the musculoskeletal system
- diminish the "flight or fight" stress syndrome
- reduce muscle tension and alleviate many joint and muscle aches and pains
- reduce the symptoms and progressive deterioration of many types of arthritis
- improve sleep patterns
- improve athletic and work performance
- contribute to better posture
- allow for more efficient movement throughout the day
- decrease the frequency, duration, and intensity of headaches
- lower blood pressure
- reduce respiratory distress
- improve internal organ function

### Obstacles to Performance of Effective Stretching Exercises

With all those benefits, why do people not engage in good stretching programs? There are two reasons.

*One,* it is usually not a very fun exercise. Not only does it border on painful, the psychological rewards that come with other forms of exercise are missing. Somehow, gaining an extra inch of movement in a stretch after a couple weeks does not give the same joy as finishing a 10 K run in a personal best time. There is not a similar "endorphin high" that aerobic exercise induces. While there are running, triathalon, biking and swimming competitions and clubs, and social events that support those activities, stretching gets nowhere near the same support. Yoga classes are the closest one comes to camaraderie in this form of exercise. Yoga vacation retreats and workshops are available, but on a limited basis.

*Two,* stretching has failed to catch on because of the poor quality of current techniques. It is important to mention the two most serious offenders. The first is the bouncing stretches where a person stretches a muscle complex and joint to its maximum and then bounces it in an oscillatory

manner past that point repeatedly. This is a less painful stretch than the slow, steady-pressure maneuvers which are not as likely to cause tissue damage. Bouncing stretches will also give a sense of quick improvement for that moment. Unfortunately, with every bounce small tears occur in soft tissues; if done repeatedly, bounce stretches eventually end up producing rigid scars. There are therapeutic times when this type of stretching is used to break up joint adhesions, and in those situations it is effective if specifically and properly directed. But using a bounce-type stretch for general soft tissue elongation is not wise.

The other type of stretching that poses many problems for people is stretching joints or soft tissues that already are overstretched or hypermobile (excessively moving). This occurs when general stretching exercises are adopted by people without an accurate, preliminary assessment of which areas really do need increased flexibility and which might actually need to be stabilized and avoid excessive motion. Yoga classes and individual yoga practitioners frequently fall into the trap of doing a prepared routine that is generalized for everybody without recognizing the high number of individual needs that people have. All too often the problem comes from stretching a broad area that overall might be restricted, but individual joints or particular angles of motion are already too mobile. Instead of the stretching force going into elongating the shortened tissues, it impacts the excessively mobile segments.

A typical example is doing a back arch exercise, like the Bow or Cobra, in yoga terminology, to increase spinal extension motion. Well, in many people the thoracic spine, or mid-back, needs this type of stretch, but they also have an unstable lower lumbar spine that will be severely irritated by the same maneuver. Often it is difficult, at the time of the exercise, to distinguish between the pain of the stretch and the pain of injury. The standard precaution given in yoga instructions is that if it hurts afterwards, either be careful in repeating the exercise or omit that particular stretch altogether. Unfortunately, the damage has often been done already. It seems a much wiser approach to have a skilled professional carefully evaluate flexibility, both restrictions and excesses, then plan specific stretches for the areas of limitations and stabilization / strengthening exercises for the hypermobile, over-elongated areas.

## Undertaking Effective Flexibility Training

How can one find someone skilled in making this assessment and prescription? Good chiropractors and physical therapists who do a lot of sports injury work will often be the best people to ask. Some yoga instructors who have special relationships with these knowledgeable health professionals will be good at accommodating special needs. Once again, the more preliminary evaluations that are done in any aspect of our health, the more accurate the health enhancement procedures can be. This is particularly important in those individuals who have significant musculoskeletal problems already or have been injured in the past with residual weaknesses. Individuals who strive for optimal levels of athletic performance and push themselves to the limits should also seek out professional assistance. They are risking injury, not so much because of serious weaknesses, but because small biomechanical faults can pose an enormous risk when the body is challenged to the brink of its capacity.

These are also reasons for integrating a stretching program with strength training and manipulative therapy. After full assessment of flexibility, strength, and joint motion—stabilization training, stretching and joint manipulation can be combined to give benefits far superior to a stretching program alone. Often a person will stretch a restricted joint for months on his own with only minimal improvement and some overstretching of surrounding tissues. Then a therapist may introduce an effective joint manipulation taking a few milliseconds to accomplish what one had agonized over in hours of self-stretching.

It is also important to mention that there are different types of stretching ideally suited for various types of restrictions. Shortness and excessive tightness in muscle contractile fibers are best stretched and relaxed using techniques incorporating neurological inhibition mechanisms like proprioceptive neuromuscular facilitation (PNF). These involve stretching the tight muscle, then isometri-

cally contracting it for several seconds at full length, then contracting its antagonist muscle, and sometimes even incorporating different eye motions and breathing patterns—all in order to reflexively condition the nervous system to assist in the relaxation and stretching of the muscle group.

Stretching non-contractile fibers such as ligaments, tendons, and fascia utilize slow, prolonged stretching techniques. Joints can be stretched similarly, or manipulative techniques involving slow, rhythmic oscillations or quick movements can be used.

Elongation of any human tissues is enhanced with increased temperature. That is the reason why all stretching programs should be done only after the tissues are warmed. The usual way to accomplish this is by any gentle, safe, aerobic warm-up exercise for 10 minutes before stretching.

Many people have the misconception that they get enough flexibility exercise in the activities of daily living that they don't need extra programmed stretching. "I get plenty of stretching bending over picking up kids, my husband's dirty clothes, and working in the garden." Nothing could be further from the truth. There are scores of joints and muscles throughout the body that need regular stretching in *all* directions for optimal health. Providing it will reap many unseen benefits. Ignoring it will sow the seeds of future problems.

Since there are few people who would not benefit appreciably from a regular stretching routine, there are many who need to find some form that is suitable for their needs. For those seeking self-care through flexibility training without professional assistance, it is advised to use Evjenth and Hamberg's book, *Auto-Stretching*. The excellent illustrations show in superb detail how to isolate specific muscles and angles that are often overlooked by more generalized works.

## A Warning

There is little reason, in holistic health terms, to justify excessive efforts towards extreme flexibility. Two blatant examples of stretching excesses that have few advantages, if any, over what might be termed reasonable, healthy flexibility are gymnastics training in childhood and advanced yoga postures. Unless one thinks he or she can gain holistic health by being an Olympic gymnast or contortionist, these practices should be discouraged. Encouraging young children, particularly girls, to force their developing bodies into stressful positions and maneuvers their tissues were not meant to sustain is asking for tragic consequences in later years. Remember that holistic health connotes balance and moderation.

## STRENGTH TRAINING

*What is strength*
*without a double share of wisdom?*
**John Milton**

The strength of a muscle refers to how much force it can generate. There is also the factor of muscular endurance, which is the ability to perform low-intensity work over a sustained period of time. Power refers to performance of work per unit of time. This is calculated by multiplying force times velocity of motion. There is also tensile strength of tissues, which is the ability to resist tearing, or forces pulling apart. Resistance to compression forces in bone needs a certain type of strength, too. In nontechnical, holistic health terms, we want to be strong enough to engage in all the desired activities of daily living without fatigue or risk of injury.

Improvement of one's strength comes about by challenging the tissues to ever-increasing, graded exercise that stresses the tissues sufficiently to stimulate an adaptive response to the challenge—muscles grow in size, blood vessels expand to bring more oxygen and nutrients to the area, ligaments and tendons change their internal structure, and bone increases its matrix of living cells and minerals.

### *The Benefits of Strength*

Improving all these types of strength produces many health benefits. It can give us more livelihood, social and recreational opportunities, raise self-esteem, and provide more variety in our lifestyle.

Strength protects against injury and the process of aging. One of the most frequent causes of incapacitating back pain is weak muscles.

*Eighty percent of all adults will suffer back pain*
*at some time in their lives.*
*Twenty five percent of all worker compensation*
*claims are for industrial back injuries.*
*Ninety-eight percent of all people with*
*back problems have weak spinal musculature.*

Osteoporosis, or the demineralization and weakening of bones with age, can be greatly reduced by activities that promote strength. Any muscular effort stimulates bones that the muscles pull against to increase their mineral content and the substances that connect the minerals into strong shapes. So when we talk of strength training we refer primarily to the direct strengthening of muscles and the consequent strengthening of the bones.

*Twenty million Americans*
*suffer from osteoporosis.*
*Of the 1,300,000 fractures caused by osteoporosis*
*every year, 50,000 of our elders will die from*
*hip fractures and their complications.*

The elderly fall and break their hips and other bones because their leg muscles are weak from lack of proper exercise. Ninety-year-olds have three times less thigh muscle mass than they did at twenty years of age. Proper strength training exercise at 60, 70, 80, 90, or even 100 can produce important increases in strength. Not only is balance improved, but the increased muscle mass from strength training reduces the percentage of body fat.

### *Assessment of Strength*

The first level of strength assessment is just asking oneself "Am I a weenie?" If the answer is yes, then some sort of strength enhancement is recommended. There are more sophisticated tests than this, but if you fail this one, further testing will just determine degree, or "weenie factor," in technical terms. More detailed testing of strength is valuable in many individuals.

Sub-maximal testing with strength training equipment at gyms or at home can provide valid testing data for the average person to start a strength training regimen, periodically retest progress, and alter the training protocols accordingly for effective strength improvements. Self-motivated individuals can use the recommended resources to accomplish this. But there are, fortunately, sufficiently informed personnel at most gyms who are more than willing to assist those needing help in the proper use of strength training testing, equipment, and procedures. Some of the less knowledgeable personnel in gyms and spas convey improper information regarding strength training techniques. To guard against being misinformed, one can reconfirm procedures with the guidelines presented here and by using the recommended resources.

For a large segment of the population though, more careful and precise forms of strength testing are advised. People who should approach strength training from this avenue would include:

- people recovering from a significant musculoskeletal injury, particularly of the spine

- those who have had a long period of inactivity which might make them susceptible to injury due to lack of conditioning

- those with significant alterations in flexibility, either very restricted mobility or excessive mobility

- those with significant musculoskeletal handicaps

- elderly who are susceptible to osteoporosis, particularly inactive, postmenopausal women not using hormone replacement therapy

- those of any age whose athletic or work endeavors demand pushing their bodies to the limit of physical capabilities

There are a number of different facilities that do advanced strength and musculoskeletal testing. These facilities are equipped with a variety of instruments, many computerized. The best muscle and functional strength assessment equipment evaluates different types of strength in isolated muscles at all angles through which they work. They can identify certain types of weaknesses undetectable by more generalized and cruder mechanisms suitable for relatively healthy individuals. By finding these "hidden" weak points, special exercises can be prescribed to overcome them. Other instruments can evaluate bone density as a factor of strength.

They are supervised and operated by different combinations and quality of health professionals—chiropractors, physical therapists, exercise physiologists, and doctors specializing in physical medicine. One group that works for quality control in medical facilities is the Commission on Accreditation of Rehabilitation Facilities, 101 N. Wilmot Rd., Suite 500, Tuscon, AZ 85711; (602) 748-1212.

## *Principles of Holistic Strength Training*

When we speak of holistic strength training we are, in part, implying that there is a level of adequate strength and that this strength be balanced. We want to focus our priorities on how much strength we need to safely and efficiently carry out any of the day's activities. There is no need to engage in a regimen involving bench pressing 400 pounds if you are never going to require your body to even approach those levels of achievement on a day-to-day basis. Holistic strength training is designed to produce and maintain strength at a level which will support all the other aspects of life.

Too often people get carried away with one aspect of fitness improvement, and this distorts other aspects and priorities in their lives. Many bodybuilding enthusiasts display such an imbalance. There are some physical and many psychological reasons for enjoying ever-increasing strength and muscular bulk beyond what is holistically needed. That is why it is important to carefully and continually assess the goals of any self-improvement program if the overall goal is *holistic* health. Otherwise some minor priority like heightened sexual attractiveness might overtake and obscure the big picture.

Balance in strength can be looked at several ways. There is a balance between strength and flexibility which is very important. The excessively bulked-up body builder who lacks a proportionate flexibility is a typical example of this. In reality, high levels of strength training and muscular development can and should come about with *increased* flexibility. Proper pre- and post- stretching routines should complement strength training.

Balance can also refer to an equality of strength between left and right pairs of muscles. Many people engaged in irregularly balanced activities, either at work or at play, can develop left-right strength imbalances so significant they put them at risk of injury. Laborers, like carpenters or landscapers who are predominantly one-sided in their activities—hammering, sawing, raking, shoveling—in many cases have visibly larger muscles on that side. An accident is often just waiting to happen. Developing the weak-sided muscles assures better biomechanical function and improved neuromuscular coordination.

A less noticeable strength imbalance, but not less frequent, is that between muscles and their antagonists and/or stabilizers. Muscles that act as primary movers of a joint are termed just that, primary movers, or agonists. Muscles that stabilize the joint complex while the primary movers act to produce the desired motion are called stabilizers. Antagonist muscles are the muscles that counteract the force and motion of the primary movers. They must be neurologically signalled to relax at the same time the primary movers and stabilizers are signalled to contract. A confusion in nerve signalling, altered flexibility of the tissues or joints, or excessive tone or weakness of the antagonists, will cause problems.

There are now scientific calculations on specific muscle strength ratios that are healthiest—back extensors to abdominals, quadriceps to hamstrings, various shoulder girdle muscle ratios. There are even differences calculated for maximal performances in different sports—the quadriceps to hamstring ratios should be different between runners and cyclists, and rowers have different ideal strength ratios in the shoulder muscles than baseball pitchers.

### Elements of Proper Strength Training Techniques

Isokinetic and isotonic strength training exercises are superior to isometric types of training.

Isokinetic and isotonic exercises involve moving a joint against some resistance through the joint's entire range of motion. The resistance can be in many different forms: free weights (dumbbells and barbells), pulley system weights (Universal Gym, Isolator, and Nautilus type equipment), hydraulic systems (Unex and others), surgical rubber tubing, "the most cost-effective strength training system" (Lifeline Gym, Medi-Cordz, Theratubing, Xercise Tube, and Thera-Band), isokinetic machines (Cybex, Biodex, Lido, Kin-Com, and Fitnet), and using a partner to provide the resistance. These build the strength of muscle cells throughout the length of the muscle. Isometric exercise of a muscle means contracting it against resistance without moving the joint. Muscle cells are then stimulated to strengthen in only one portion of the muscle. Isotonic exercise involves keeping equal tension on the muscle throughout the entire range of movement. Isokinetic exercise involves moving the joint through an entire range of motion at a steady rate of speed while keeping maximum tension on the muscle.

Muscle strength can increase during both the contracting phase and the relaxing phase of resistive exercises. The contracting phase, when the muscle is shortening, is termed *concentric contraction*. It is usually the act of lifting a weight. *Eccentric contraction* is the term used when the muscle is lengthening. For holistic strength training purposes, concentric contractions are preferred over eccentric because there appears to be more tissue damage and muscle soreness from eccentric exercise. More rest time is also required between exercise sessions when doing eccentric exercise. Competitive athletes sometimes like to use eccentric exercises because these can sustain the greatest forces, thus stimulating maximal strength. Unfortunately, injuries increase with these escalating tensions.

Although some of the best strength gains come when taxing muscles to 90% of their maximal capacity for work, it is difficult to tell when 90% maximal effort is actually taking place. This encourages training to absolute fatigue. Unfortunately, it also threatens the health of the muscle. The likelihood of injury increases as greater tensions and weights accumulate, and also as fatigue sets in. Egotistical urges to push to the upper limits are not conducive to preventing injuries or obtaining holistic health.

*Slower is safer* is another rule of thumb that serves holistic strength training well. Rapid, ballistic maneuvers are known to produce power more than slow movements. In some sports-specific exercises, these quick, powerful contractions are needed to perform the desired activities (boxing punches and vertical leaps in volleyball are examples). Unfortunately, these quick, forceful bursts produce very small muscle tears every time they are performed. They can also lead to more serious tearing injury to the muscles and tendons. In resistive types of exercise it is wise to contract a muscle concentrically for a slow count of two and contract eccentrically for a slow count of four.

The number of repetitions needed to contract a muscle to 90% of its capacity for work varies, depending on the amount of resistance. The greater the resistance, the fewer repetitions needed to induce fatigue. For holistic strength training purposes it is wise never to use a resistance so great one cannot perform 8 repetitions. The forces and risk of injury become too great. Super fit athletes, body builders, power lifters, often use high resistance with as few as one repetition for maximal strength gains. Remember that maximal performance is different from optimal health. Upper body resistance exercises for strength usually require 8-12 repetitions for good improvement. For lower body and trunk, 12-20 repetitions is usual. For endurance gains, lighter resistance is used with higher repetitions in the 40-80 range. In one exercise session one muscle group can be contracted for the desired number of repetitions, and then after a short rest this can be repeated. This is termed "doing multiple sets" of an exercise. There are different opinions about the degree of benefit from doing multiple sets.

Sufficient rest time after each session of resistive training is a must. *Strength gains do not occur during exercise; they occur during the rest periods between exercises.* Some people need longer rest intervals than others. At least 48 hours of rest between successive bouts is mandatory. Some athletes will exercise different muscle groups on different days so that they can train on successive days. They might have 2, 3, or 4 different routines, each working different groups of muscles. They then rotate the routines in such a way that they give plenty of rest to muscles but also restimulate them in sufficient time to continue strength gains. A once-a-month visit to the gym to pump some iron won't cut it. In order to make significant improvements in strength, a six-week period of three exercise sessions per week is usually required. To maintain strength, challenging the muscles in two sessions per week is typically necessary.

There are an infinite number of different combinations of resistance, repetitions, sets, frequency, rest, and exercise equipment. In the arena of maximal performers such as competitive body builders and powerlifters, football players, and hammer throwers, there is much discussion of which combination is best. For those seeking well-balanced, optimal, holistic health, the debate over the details and nuances of strength training is irrelevant. Engaging in a strength training regimen within the recommended parameters set forth here is adequate. Remember though, that these recommendations include seeking qualified assistance when needed. And the importance of balancing strength training with aerobic conditioning, flexibility exercises (at least 10 minutes of stretching before and after a strength training session is absolutely necessary), and coordination activities, is essential.

## COORDINATION ENHANCEMENT

*The centipede was happy, quite*
*Until the frog in fun*
*Asked, "which leg comes after which?"*
*This set his mind in such a pitch*
*He lay distracted in a ditch*
*Figuring how to run.*

**Unknown**

Synchronized, efficient movement of the body is a result of proper neuromuscular signalling. This in turn is dependent upon full joint motion, tissue flexibility, strength, brain function, and learning. If joints do not move fully and freely, abnormal arcs of motion develop to accommodate the best movement possible. This abnormal motion disturbs proper signalling from the joint to the brain and spinal cord, and then these coordination centers send the wrong signals back to the muscles. These nerve signals generate more stress on the tissues involved and make one more vulnerable to injury, both frank injury and the repetitive motion stress of cumulative small insults over time.

If the soft tissues—muscles, ligaments, tendons—are not flexible enough, they disturb joint movement, and the same abnormal nerve signalling occurs. If muscles are not strong enough, abnormal motion results with similar neurological aberrations. Most locomotor functions are learned. There are some rudimentary, inborn movements like sucking, reaching, head turning, and crawling, but any sophisticated movement is basically a series of conditioned reflexes and responses. Some children are born with better brain function than others. Those whose nervous systems were damaged from fetal alcohol syndrome or maternal cocaine use or any other neurotoxin cannot be expected to have as efficient nerve signalling as those with healthy prenatal environments. Those infants who are blessed with an environment that encourages a wide diversity of movements and opportunities for learning proper locomotor skills will be more coordinated as adults, since that early childhood neuromuscular conditioning is repeated correctly millions of times before adulthood.

Even elements like proper nutrition are important aspects to keep in mind when addressing optimal coordination. Minerals like calcium and magnesium and B-complex vitamins are essential for proper control of movement. In one study it was shown that the fine muscle coordination needed to competitively shoot a rifle in Olympic biathalon events was dramatically improved if the athletes were given vitamin and mineral supplements in addition to a good diet.

Visual acuity, binocular coordination, and the accurate interpretation of visual data are vital to coordinated movement, since so much of our activities are visually dependent. If we are not getting accurate information into our brains about the world around us, it is very difficult to interact with that world in a coordinated, healthy fashion. Progressive factions of the optometric profession

have developed a number of important tests that go beyond the normal visual acuity tests needed to prescribe lenses. Tests are now available that more accurately assess how both eyes coordinate their movements to produce efficient stereoscopic vision. There are more sophisticated tests to determine how the brain interprets images. Those who find it difficult to comprehend the written word, who have always done poorly at school, and who refrain from reading, may be suffering from an undetected visual deficit rather than from being "stupid" or "lazy."

The same may be true of children and adults who are often seen as clumsy in athletics. It may be due to hidden visual disturbances not identified by standard optometric testing. Finding an optometrist trained in vision development may be helpful. Refer to the Vision section of the Special Subject Resources for more help.

*In the United States accidents are the leading cause of death for people in the 1-37 age group.*

### *Coordination Assessment*

Below is a short test that might reveal the subtle signs of incoordination. This test is not meant for those with serious neuromuscular impairment such as: cerebellar dysfunction, cerebral palsy, muscular dystrophies, multiple sclerosis, amyotrophic lateral sclerosis, seizure disorders, etc.

Are you always the last to be chosen for a pickup team sport?

Do people always offer to drive when they go somewhere with you, even if it's your car?

Do you find yourself spending an inordinate amount of time gluing things back together?

Does your spouse keep sharp objects where you can't find them?

Do you find yourself in hospital emergency rooms more often than all your friends?

Has your spouse suggested increasing your life insurance policy?

When you offer to fix something around the house, like changing a light bulb, does your spouse say, "No, maybe we should call a professional"?

If in answering these questions you have the feeling that improved coordination is needed in your life, it would be wise to take many of the recommendations that follow. Even if answering this small quiz gave you a feeling of confidence in your coordination, certain suggestions that follow might significantly improve the quality of your life and prevent injuries even in well-coordinated individuals.

We have tried to add a bit of humor to this discussion when addressing the average person. For those unfortunate individuals suffering serious coordination difficulties due to significant neurological disease or injury, incoordination is no laughing matter. It is important to mention that if there is any suspicion of serious incoordination, it could be a sign of a major health problem. Many advanced testing procedures to discover the root causes of serious coordination disturbances are available and should be sought out. Consulting with your family physician, chiropractor, naturopath, or physical therapist for possible referral to a neurologist with extensive testing capabilities, is advised.

But for the klutz who is all thumbs and who doesn't have the excuse of serious nerve damage to fall back on, and for the individual who just wants to function optimally, the question is, How do we become more coordinated and enhance living and our health?

## Tai Chi Chuan

Tai Chi Chuan exercises from China are extremely appropriate for anyone seeking better coordination—from the elite athlete honing his or her skills to those with serious clinical coordination problems. The repeated practice of moving the entire body in refined, flowing motions will condition and integrate one's body-consciousness. Balance and awareness is learned. We tune in to a more harmonious relationship with our environment.

Use the recommendations in the section on Traditional Oriental Medicine for finding instructors, books, and videos about Tai Chi.

## Proper Ergonomics

Ergonomics refers to energy-efficient, proper body motions. Learning how to move properly in relation to all the objects we interact with, and all the activities we engage in, is more important than we think. Our initial reaction is to just do something. Our bodies should know how. Yes, our bodies are quite remarkable. They will usually figure out a way to do what we ask. But the key word is *properly*. Optimal safe, efficient movement has many times to be better learned.

Proper lifting technique is an ideal example. Many people lift objects on the floor by bending over at the waist with knees straight or only slightly bent. This causes enormous strain on the low back—the muscles, ligaments, and discs of the spine. A more biomechanically sound method is to squat with the knees and keep the lumbar spine relatively straight.

Carrying objects close to the body rather than at arms length is another obvious example of efficient body movement. Pushing heavy objects to move them, rather than pulling them, is also more sound biomechanically.

Proper body positioning during relatively passive endeavors, like sitting while reading or typing, is important also. Having one's reading material or computer screen at an ideal height for relaxed eye movement and neck comfort can have a dramatic impact on physical health when these activities occupy many hours and days of our time. Just a few inches of variation in wrist position can make the difference between comfortable, healthy typing and the development of incapacitating carpal tunnel syndrome. Scott Donkin's *Sitting On the Job: How to Survive the Stresses of Sitting Down to Work—A Practical Handbook* is a good reference for practical steps towards better ergonomic coordination.

## Stabilization Exercises

Stabilization exercises are part coordination training, part strength training, and part ergonomic training. These exercises are done for the low back, particularly in people with unstable, hyper-mobile, lumbar (low back) spinal joint abnormalities or previous injuries as part of a rehabilitation program. The exercises strengthen weak trunk musculature in order to help stabilize the low back. They include coordination exercises which teach new movements that stabilize weak structures. And they include training in ergonomically sound performance of daily tasks. The San Francisco Spine Institute has put together some good videotapes and handouts for these procedures. Look for their address in the resource section. Consulting with a physical therapist or chiropractor who utilizes these programs is recommended when spinal problems threaten one's health.

## Sports Ergonomics

Nearly every sport has been ergonomically studied with slow motion photography and computer analysis of body mechanics to determine the optimal movements that will most efficiently maximize performance and enhance safety. Video, personal, and group instruction on sports-specific training techniques are available in almost every sport.

Places to look:

- libraries usually have large sections devoted to highly illustrated how-to books on individual sports;
- video stores are now carrying more sport instructional films;
- contact athletic associations specific to the sport;
- tennis clubs, swimming facilities, ski resorts and the like usually have appropriate personal and group instruction available.

The American College of Sports Medicine has a referral service and directory of exercise physiologists, athletic trainers, and human performance laboratories that can help individuals find the necessary ergonomic testing.

## Defensive Driving Courses

Many accidental injuries occur from driving automobiles, so efforts to improve coordinated, defensive driving skills may be an important health enhancement strategy. This may be particularly important for those who have frequent motor vehicle accidents or those who have to drive a good deal of the time in the midst of other uncoordinated drivers. Courses that focus on emergency and high speed maneuvering are particularly valuable to train these health and life saving responses into our biocomputer programs. Unfortunately, they are very expensive. Consulting your yellow pages for driving schools that provide such services is recommended. As mentioned before, refraining from intoxicating substances that adversely alter coordination while driving is essential. Mindfulness training while driving is also highly valuable. An interesting book on this subject is *Zen and the Art of Driving*.

## Summary of Elements Contributing to Coordination

- Maintain optimal flexibility of joints, muscles, tendons, and ligaments with regular stretching exercises and any necessary manipulative therapy.
- Maintain balanced strength of musculature.
- Provide optimal nutrition and supplementation for ideal nerve system function.
- Locomotor skill development, and opportunities for varied interactions with the world from a young age, are of the utmost importance.
- Identification and correction of any hidden visual deficits that might contribute to distorted sensory input to the central nervous system, and thus to altered psychomotor responses, might prove helpful in a large number of individuals.

- Mindfulness concentrates our attention to produce more precise action with fewer errors. Mindfulness training would enhance everyone's well-being, not only in the realm of coordination.

- Avoidance of intoxicants obviously improves coordination. There are also many prescriptive and over-the-counter pharmaceuticals that adversely affect the nervous system, causing incoordination significant enough to cause many accidents. Warning labels on medicines that advise against use while driving or operating dangerous equipment should be heeded.

- Tai Chi Chuan exercises are moving meditations that do much more than improve coordination. They are beneficial enough to recommend to everybody.

- Attending to proper ergonomic function in all of the day's activities is a key to healthy coordination.

- For those who have weakened or injured musculoskeletal functions, special stabilization exercises should be undertaken.

- For those active in athletics and sports, instruction on ideal biomechanics is valuable.

- For those in a higher risk category for motor vehicle accidents, high speed and emergency defensive driving schools might prove very valuable.

---

## EXERCISE RESOURCES

*Health is the vital principle of bliss,*
*And exercise of health.*

**James Thomson**

★Denotes Best of the Best Resources

### Aerobic Conditioning and Combined Fitness and Sports

#### Books

Bailey, Covert. *Fit or Fat?* Houghton Mifflin, 1978.

Cooper, Kenneth. *The New Aerobics.* Bantam, 1983.

Donkin, Scott W. *Sitting On the Job: How to Survive the Stresses of Sitting Down to Work—A Practical Handbook.* HM, 1989.

Getchell, Bud. *The Fitness Book.* Benchmark Press, 1987.

★Kisner, Carolyn and Colby, Lynn. *Therapeutic Exercise: Foundations & Techniques.* Davis, 1990. For exercise therapists but great for those wanting one source for excellent exercise protocols.

Peterson, James. *Conditioning For a Purpose.* Leisure Press, 1977.

Shephard, Roy. *Economic Benefits of Enhanced Fitness.* Human Kinetic Publishers, 1986.

Tinley, Scott and McAlpine, Ken. *Scott Tinley's Winning Guide to Sports Endurance.* Rodale, 1992.

★Yanker, Gary and Burton, Kathy. *Walking Medicine: The Lifetime Guide to Preventive & Therapeutic Exercisewalking Programs.* McGraw-Hill, 1990.

★Human Kinetic Publishers, P.O. Box 5076, Champaign, IL 61825-5076; (800) 747-4457; (217) 351-5076; In Canada: Human Kinetics, Box 224040, 1275 Walker Rd., Windsor, Ontario N8Y 4Y9; (519) 944-7774. Provides a wide array of books, journals, and software on every aspect of exercise.

#### Periodicals

*Bicycling,* Rodale Press, 33 E. Minor St., Emmaus, PA 18098; (215) 967-5171.

*Canoe,* P.O. Box 7011, Red Oak, IA 51591; (800) 678-5432.

*Runner's World,* Rodale Press, 33 E. Minor St., Emmaus, PA 18098; (215) 967-5171. Good fitness suggestions but with a competitive slant.

*Triathlete,* 1127 Hamilton St., Allentown, PA 18102; (215) 821-6864.

*The Walking Magazine,* Walking Inc., 9-11 Harcourt St., Boston, MA 02116; (617) 266-3322.

*Vital Signs: Instrumentation for Rehabilitation, Sports Medicine, and Physical Fitness.* Available from Country Technology, Inc., P.O. Box 87, Gays Mills, WI 54631-0028; (608) 735-4718; (608) 735-4859. Primarily a catalog for professionals, but it is also relevant to the average person.

RESOURCES

### Videos

Aerobics with Soul: Serengeti—(800) 423-9685.

*The Complete Guide to Exercise Videos,* Collage Video Specialties, 5390 Main St. NE, Minneapolis, MN 55421; (800) 433-6769.

Non-Impact Aerobics Videos, NIA Techniques, 6244 SW Burlingame Ave., Portland, OR 97201; (800) 762-5762; (503) 245-9886.

The Wave: Ecstatic Dance for Body & Soul—(800) 76-RAVEN.

### Computer Databases

SPORT—From Sport Information Resource Center, 1600 James Naismith Dr., Gloucester, Ontario, Canada K1B 5N4; (613) 748-5658. A wide variety of subjects and sources on sport and fitness.

### Organizations

ACSM Fit Society, P.O. Box 1440, Indianapolis, IN 46206-1440; (317) 637-9200. The American College of Sports Medicine's public outreach organization that promotes intelligent fitness activities.

Adventure Cycling, P.O. Box 8308, Missoula, MT 59807; (800) 721-1776. The largest cycling organization has created the National Bicycle Route Network consisting of 16,000 miles of cycling routes.

Aerobics and Fitness Association of America, 15250 Ventura Blvd., Suite 200, Sherman Oaks, CA 91403; (818) 905-0040. Publishes *American Fitness* magazine.

Aerobics and Fitness Foundation of America; (800) 233-4886. Provides information on safe and effective exercises.

American Running and Fitness Association, 4405 East-West Hwy., Suite 504, Bethesda, MD 20877; (301) 913-9517; (800) 776-2732.

League of American Bicyclists, 190 W. Astend St., Suite 120, Baltimore, MD 21230; (410) 539-3399. System of local bike clubs throughout the country.

President's Council on Physical Fitness and Sports, 701 Pennsylvania Ave. NW, Suite 250, Washington, DC 20004; (202) 272-3430; Fax (202) 504-2064. Many materials are available on the subject.

## Flexibility Exercise

### Books

★ Evjenth, Olaf and Hamberg, Jern. *Auto Stretching: The Complete Manual of Specific Stretching.* Alfta Rehab Forlag, 1989.

### Magazines

★ *Yoga Journal,* Yoga Teachers Association, 2054 University Ave., Berkeley, CA 94704; (510) 841-9200; (510) 644-3101; book and tape orders—(800) 359-9642; subscriptions—(800) 334-8152. This is the best place to keep up with the latest yoga books, videos, and retreats.

### Videos

*Autostretching Prevents Repetitive Stress Injuries.* Available from Orthopedic Physical Therapy Products.

Rudra Press, 541 NE 20th Ave., Suite 108, Portland, OR 97232; mailing address—P.O. Box 13390, Portland, OR 97213-0390; (800) 876-7798; (503) 235-0175. Offers a good selection of hatha yoga video tapes for varying skill levels including yoga during pregnancy.

*Yoga Journal's* "Yoga Practice Series." From Healing Arts, 2434 Main St., Suite 201, Santa Monica, CA 90405; (800) 722-7347.

### Organizations

Orthopedic Physical Therapy Products, 3700 Annapolis Lane, Suite 175, P.O. Box 47009, Minneapolis, MN 55447-0009; (612) 553-0452; (800) 367-7393; Fax (612) 553-9355. Many of the best books, videotapes and therapeutic aids relating to rehabilitative stretching and strengthening exercises are available through their catalog.

## Strength Training

### Books

★ Kisner, Carolyn and Colby, Lynn. *Therapeutic Exercise: Foundations & Techniques.* Davis, 1990. This is one of the best books on *all* aspects of exercise.

## *Periodicals*

It would be helpful if popular body building and strength training magazines promoted a more balanced health education. An almost devotional attitude to physique and strength seriously detracts from some of the informative, beneficial information. There is also quite a bit of excessive hype in the magazines' advertisements. All things considered, it is best to use Kisner and Colby's strength training recommendations combined with the advice from knowledgeable exercise physiologists or athletic trainers.

## *Videos*

San Francisco Spine Institute, 1850 Sullivan Ave., Suite 200, Daly City, CA 94015; (415) 991-6761. Available from the Institute is a good lumbar stabilization exercise video program that is helpful for specific strengthening of the low back for those recovering from injury or susceptible to it.

Williams and Wilkins Electronic Media, 428 East Preston Street, Baltimore, MD 21202; (800) 527-5597; (410) 528-4000. Distributes a shoulder rehabilitation video and one for knee rehab for instruction of patients.

## *Sources of Rubber Tubing Exercise Equipment*

Lifeline Gym. Lifeline International, Inc., 1421 South Park St., Madison, WI 53715; (800) 553-6633; Wisconsin (608) 251-4778; Fax (608) 251-1870.

Medi-Cordz. Available from Wahl and Associates, 1001 B Ave., Suite #212, Coronado, CA 92118; (619) 437-1422; (800) 266-7257.

Theraciser. Foot Levers, Inc., 518 Pocahontas Ave., N.E., P.O. Box 12611, Roanoke, VA 24027; (800) 553-4860; Canada (800) 344-4860; Fax (703) 345-0202.

Theraband. The Hygenic Corp., 1245 Home Ave., Akron, OH 44310-2575; (800) 321-2135; (216) 633-8460; Fax (216) 633-9359. Also available from Orthopedic Physical Therapy Products, 3700 Annapolis Lane, Suite 175, P.O. Box 47009, Minneapolis, MN 55447-0009; (612) 553-0452; (800) 367-7393; Fax (612) 553-9355.

Theraband, Theratubing, Xercise Tube, Xercise bands, and Can-Do-Bands. Available from Scrip, Inc., 101 South St., Peoria, IL 61602-1896; (800) 747-3488; (309) 674-3488; Fax (309) 674-3489.

Xercise Tube, Xercise bands, and Can-Do-Bands. SPRI Performance Systems, Inc., 111 Pfingsten Rd., Suite 318, Deerfield, IL 60015; (800) 488-SPRI; (708) 272-7211; Fax (708) 272-0402.

## Coordination Training

### *Videos*

*Feldenkrais Method: Basic Lessons in Awareness Through Movement,* Stephen Rosenholtz, Rosewood Publications, 2075 Pioneer Court, San Mateo, CA 94403; (415) 343-7288; Fax (415) 343-3346.

How-to Sport Videos at your local video store.

Tai Chi Chuan videos. See the resources in the section on Traditional Oriental Medicine.

San Francisco Spine Institute, 1850 Sullivan Ave., Suite 140, Daly City, CA 94015; (415) 991-6761. Available from the Institute is a good video program for learning coordinated movements to protect the lumbar spine.

### *Organizations*

Back Designs, 1045 Ashby Ave., Berkeley, CA 94710; (510) 849-1923. This company carries a wide selection of ergonomic aids for home and office. Their catalog of products is, in part, an instructional manual on proper body movement and posture.

Ergonomics Sciences Corporation, 2672 Bayshore Parkway, Mountain View, CA 94043; (415) 964-3135. This company carries top-of-the-line ergonomic devices for the workplace and will help custom-fit workstations that are ideal for proper body function. Their services are particularly helpful for those suffering from repetitive motion injuries.

Feldenkrais Guild, P.O. Box 11145, San Francisco, CA 94101; (415) 550-8708.

## PROFESSIONAL EXERCISE RESOURCES

## Aerobic Conditioning and Combined Fitness

### *Books*

★Kisner, Carolyn and Colby, Lynn. *Therapeutic Exercise: Foundations & Techniques.* Davis, 1990. This is one of the best books on *all* aspects of exercise. Every health care professional should have it, no matter what their specialty. Although it is technically written to convey valuable information to clinicians, a well educated lay person could gain a much deeper understanding of this important, broad field of health enhancement.

Bouchard, Claude, et al. *Exercise, Fitness and Health: A Consensus of Current Knowledge.* Human Kinetics Publishers, 1990. This is a comprehensive compilation from the Proceedings of the International Conference on Exercise, Fitness and Health. For anyone who wants to know the ramifications of exercise on any human function, if it's been studied, it can be found here.

★American College of Sports Medicine. *Exercise and Sport Sciences Review,* (annual). Macmillan or Williams and Wilkins, depending on the year.

Heyward, Vivian. *Advanced Fitness Assessment and Exercise Prescription.* Human Kinetic Publishers, 1991. This is a very practical book for health care workers who do fitness assessment and exercise prescription, from simple and effective techniques to complex ones.

Sharkey, Brian. *New Dimensions in Aerobic Fitness.* Human Kinetic Publishers, 1991.

McDougall, J.D.; Wenger, H.A.; Green, H.J., ed. *Physiological Testing of the High-Performance Athlete.* Human Kinetic Publishers, 1991.

The following publishers have a wide selection of books, journals, and software for the health professional.

★Human Kinetic Publishers, P.O. Box 5076, Champaign, IL 61825-5076; (800) 747-4457; (217) 351-5076. In Canada: Human Kinetics, Box 224040, 1275 Walker Rd., Windsor, Ontario N8Y 4Y9; (519) 944-7774.

★Brown & Benchmark, 2460 Kerper Blvd., Dubuque, IA 52001; (800) 338-5578; Fax (800) 346-2377.

## *Journals*

*Chiropractic Sports Medicine,* Official Journal of the American Chiropractic Association Council on Sports Injuries & Physical Fitness and The Federation Internationale de Chiropractique Sportive, published by Williams & Wilkins, 428 East Preston Street, Baltimore, MD 21202; (800) 527-5597; (410) 528-4000.

*International Journal of Sports Medicine,* Thieme Medical Publishers, 381 Park Ave. S., Suite 1501, New York, NY 10016; (212) 683-5088.

*Medicine and Science in Sports and Exercise.* Official journal of the American College of Sports Medicine, published by Williams and Wilkins, 428 East Preston Street, Baltimore, MD 21202; (800) 527-5597; (410) 528-4000.

*Physical Fitness/Sports Medicine Bibliography,* President's Council on Physical Fitness & Sports, 701 Pennsylvania Ave. NW, Suite 250, Washington, DC 20004; (202) 272-3421.

*Sports Medicine,* ADIS International, 940 Town Center Dr., Suite F-10, Langhorne, PA 19047; (215) 741-5200.

*Sports Medicine Digest,* Raven Press, 1185 Avenue of the Americas, New York, NY 10036; (800) 365-2468; (212) 930-9500.

## *Organizations*

★American College of Sports Medicine, 401 West Michigan Street, Indianapolis, IN 46202; (317) 637-9200.

Cooper Institute for Aerobics Research, 12330 Preston Road, Dallas, TX 75230; (800) 635-7050. Ken Cooper's fitness professional's training program.

Exercise Safety Association, 10151 University Blvd., Suite 138, Orlando, FL 32817. For orders only, (800) 622-7233; business office: (407) 677-9501. Fitness professionals trying to improve safety of exercising. Publishes *ESA Member Directory* and *Exer-Safety News,* which survey current scientific information on exercise.

Orthopedic Physical Therapy Products, 3700 Annapolis Lane, Suite 175, P.O. Box 47009, Minneapolis, MN 55447-0009; (612) 553-0452; (800) 367-7393; Fax (612) 553-9355. Many of the best books and videotapes on ergonomics and therapeutic exercise are available through their catalog.

Saunders Group, 4250 Norex Dr., Chaska, MN 55318-3047; (800) 456-1289; Fax (800) 375-1119. Excellent books, videos, and courses on therapuetic exercise and ergonomics.

## Flexibility Exercise

### *Books*

★Kisner, Carolyn and Colby, Lynn. *Therapeutic Exercise: Foundations & Techniques.* Davis, 1990.

★Evjenth, Olaf and Hamberg, Jern. *Muscle Stretching in Manual Therapy: A Clinical Manual.* (Two volumes, *Trunk* and *Extremities*) Afta Rehab Forlag, 1984. Available from the Education Division, Chattanoga Group, 4717 Adams Road, Hixson, TN 37343; (800) 592-7329; (615) 870-2281; Fax (800) CHAT-FAX.

## Strength Training

### *Books*

Davies, George. *A Compendium of Isokinetics in Clinical Usage and Rehabilitation Techniques.* S & S Publishers, 1985.

Jones, Arthur et al. *Safe, Specific Testing and Rehabilitative Exercise for the Muscles of the Lumbar Spine.* Sequoia Communications, 1988.

★Kisner, Carolyn and Colby, Lynn. *Therapeutic Exercise: Foundations & Techniques.* Davis, 1990. Oriented towards exercise therapists but great for well-educated individuals wanting one source for excellent exercise protocols.

### *Videos*

*Back Stabilization Exercises,* San Francisco Spine Institute.

### *Organizations*

Med X Corporation, 1401 NE 77th Street, Ocala, FL 34479; (800) 876-6339. This company has some of the most advanced back and neck strength training rehabilitation equipment available. It is backed by excellent research and professional training seminars.

San Francisco Spine Institute, 1850 Sullivan Ave., Suite 140, Daly City, CA 94015; (415) 991-6761. Available from the Institute is a good lumbar stabilization exercise video program.

Strive Enterprises, Inc., 849 Henderson Ave., Washington, PA 15301; (800) 368-6448; Fax (412) 222-8478.

Walker Fitness Systems, Inc., 12007 Sunrise Valley Dr., Reston, VA 22091; (800) 253-9797; (703) 648-0908; Fax (703) 648-0032. Their EXSYS Reconditioner is a computerized strength rehabilitation device.

## Coordination

### *Books*

Adrian, Marlene and Cooper, John. *The Biomechanics of Human Movement.* Brown and Benchmark, 1989.

Singleton, W. ed. *The Body at Work: Biological Ergonomics.* Cambridge University Press, 1982.

### *Journals*

*Applied Ergonomics. IPC* Business Press, 205 East 42 St., New York, NY 10017.

*Ergonomics.* Taylor & Francis, 1900 Frost Rd., Suite 101, Bristol, PA 19007; (215) 785-5800.

*Human Factors.* The Human Factors Society, Inc., Box 1369, Santa Monica, CA 90406; (310) 394-1811. Engineering and design geared to researchers and practitioners in the ergonomics field.

*Journal of Biomechanics.* Pergamon Press, Maxwell House, Fairview Park, Elmsford, NY 10523; (914) 592-7700.

### *Videos and Computer Software*

Maglischo, Cheryl. *BioMAChanics.* Brown and Benchmark, 1991. Provides computerized biomechanical analysis of videotaped athletic performances.

## REFERENCES

1. Dishman, Rod. "Determinants of Participation in Physical Activity" p. 75. In: Claude Bouchard, ed. *Exercise, Fitness, and Health.* Human Kinetics, 1990.

RESOURCES

# PLAY

*A happy heart acts like good medicine.*

**The Bible**

Recreation, sport, and leisure can have very important influences on health. There can also be negative impacts. Many factors need to be considered when evaluating how to integrate different playful activities into a health enhancing lifestyle.

## A BALANCE BETWEEN HIGH ENERGY AND LOW ENERGY ACTIVITIES

*Play is the exaltation of the possible.*

**Martin Buber**

A balance needs to be struck between active and passive leisure activities. Most of us are familiar with the extreme dominance of one over the other, as in the case of the compulsive, hyperactive amateur athlete who trains in the gym four nights a week, and runs and cycles five days a week, just to keep in shape for his sporting activities. All of his weekends are devoted to some high-energy, competitive event, whether in basketball, marathons, racquetball, triathalons, or tennis. Vacations are spent at a frantic pace using every possible moment skiing, rock climbing, windsurfing, or whitewater kayaking. Because of this obsessive drive, many injuries are sustained, and there is often physical burnout when the body reaches the limit of its abuse.

Contrary to this, but equally damaging, is the sedentary couch potato. It is identified in its extreme form by a combination of hobbies, none of which requires a maximum peak energy output greater than that needed to open the refrigerator door and snap open another can of beer. If watching old movies on the boob tube, stamp collecting, playing cards, and counting liver spots is the sum total of our recreational activities, efforts to increase more active leisure endeavors would prove useful.

This is not to say that there is no value in playful abandon. Tramping through puddles barefoot on a rainy day, building sandcastles that will wash away momentarily, or flying kites to pay homage to the wind spirits all have enormous value when they grace our lives in a timely fashion. Music too can be a unifying and healthy form of recreation. If it brings joy to the heart or meaning to the soul, its value is clear. If it shatters eardrums, throws the body into a frenzy, and provokes the mind with turmoil, it probably is not healthy recreation. In the resource section there will be some recommendations on where to find good, *whole*some music.

*Music attracts the angels in the Universe.*

**Bob Dylan**

## CONDITIONING BALANCE

Are we providing a balance of aerobic conditioning, flexibility and strength development, and coordination training, with more passive relaxing activities? Most people like to mix their health-promoting, physical-conditioning activities with some enjoyable sport. It seems that most of us stay with a regular exercise regimen if it is part of our play and is not just pounding our feet on a treadmill, lifting hunks of iron, and stretching to the tune of creaking joints. Finding a good combination of sport and play to be supplemented by more specific training endeavors is usually not difficult, and the variety increases the joy.

*Men do not quit playing because they grow old; they grow old because they quit playing.*

**Oliver Wendell Holmes**

Imagine this week of sport, play, exercise, relaxation, and socialization: relaxing but energizing moving meditation with Tai Chi three mornings per week, silent, seated meditation three mornings per week, and one session of group meditation, prayer, song, chanting, or other form of worship; a high energy walk in the park on one day, a mountain bike ride in the woods on another, a swim or some water aerobics on another, an aerobic rest day, a bicycle ride the next day, an aerobic strength training session with rubber tubing the following day, a volleyball, tennis, or racquetball game on the seventh day. During every energetic pastime a short period of pre- and post-stretching exercises is performed. Seven days a week are also filled with time to listen to relaxing music, dancing, singing, helping others, artistic expression, stimulating reading (often on health subjects, we hope).

Many of the above can be done alone or with friends and family. A balance needs to be found. Notice some items not included: hanging out at the mall, shopping for non-necessities and eating at the mall, drinking in the bars until the wee hours of the morning, stripping brain gears with mega-decibel heavy metal music listening, mud bog tractor pulls, sitting in a corner rocking for more than three hours straight, television watching, video game playing, thumb sucking, or nose picking.

Again this implies the wise use of priorities for overall happiness in life while traveling the paths to wholeness. The best use of time is a large factor when choosing types of recreation. That is why it is wise to find those activities that provide multiple health benefits where they are most needed in one's life. Finding sports that are fun, relaxing, energizing, mentally stimulating, and which also provide good opportunities for healthy interpersonal relationships, are valuable indeed. Choosing pastimes with the most health benefits and the least detrimental qualities is what we should strive for.

## APPROPRIATENESS OF SPORTS FOR THE HEALTH NEEDS OF THE BODY

Are the sports one participates in matched to one's physique and potential? Too often our athletic activities put too much stress on our tissue weaknesses, and injuries are the result. This happens at times when our egos tell us to push, against the good judgment of the body's feedback mecha-

nisms telling us to take it easy. Competition is a prime culprit in deceiving us to push our bodies past their limits. The endorphin/adrenaline high that comes with the excitement of competition often blocks good judgment of what is best for our bodies. Competition and striving for maximal performance involve pushing the body to the limit. It is a fine line which we often misjudge. The result of stepping over the line of tissue strength is injury.

> *Health and competition
> are mutually exclusive.*
> **Arnold Schwartzenegger**

It is even more tragic if parents push their children into sports, competition, or levels of performance not fully and freely chosen by the children—and just for the egoistic fulfillment of the parents. Untold physical and emotional tragedy occurs to children when they play, not for play's sake, but for some psychological emptiness in themselves or their parents. This increases in intensity in direct proportion to the level of competition.

## RISK

> *In our play we reveal
> what kind of people we are.*
> **Publius Ovidius Naso**

Consideration should also be given to the risks inherent in the sport relative to its benefits—risk of death, risk of serious injury, risk of cumulative injury, risk of minor injury. Statistics for college and high school athletics show that for categories of death, catastrophic injury, and serious injury, football far and away leads the list. Wrestling, basketball, and gymnastics follow. For non-collegiate sports high altitude mountain climbing may be one of the riskiest. This should be expected when a sport involves pushing oneself to the very limits of physical capacity in a hostile environment of enormous unpredictability. Boxing's inherent cumulative head trauma is also another sport one would find difficulty fitting into a balanced holistic health program.

## PSYCHOLOGICAL CONTRIBUTION OF PLAY

*I will not play at tug o' war,*
*I'd rather play at hug o' war,*
*Where everyone hugs*
*Instead of tugs,*
*Where everyone giggles*
*And rolls on the rug,*
*Where everyone kisses,*
*And everyone grins,*
*And everyone cuddles,*
*And everyone wins.*

**Shel Silverstein**

Attention needs to be focused on the psychological qualities reinforced by games. Are cooperation and improvement of self-esteem encouraged, or is ego-protecting competition the rule? It is often very educational to investigate the ulterior motives for participation in any athletic event. Is it a way of gaining acceptance, making friends, expressing hostility, frustration, anger, overcoming fear, displacing emotions, or battling perceived inferiority? If so, is the event an effective means for enhancing life, or should its ends even be questioned? So the issue is not so much does this or that recreation make us feel *good* emotionally, but rather does it feed our psychological growth or does it prey on our emotional weaknesses?

*The place of the dance is within the heart.*

**Tom Robbins**

## LEISURE AS A PART OF ALONE TIME AND INTERPERSONAL RELATIONSHIPS.

*It is a happy talent to know how to play.*

**Ralph Waldo Emerson**

How many activities are done alone and for what reasons? Healthy alone time is much needed in an increasingly hectic world. But an excessive compulsion to spend leisure time alone could indicate unfulfilled needs in other aspects of one's life. Likewise, a fear of being alone and always needing someone else's company could indicate problems. How much does a particular form of recreation improve interpersonal relationships? Is there a good balance between solitary recreation and participation with others?

## MIND PLAY

*Our minds need relaxation, and give way*
*Unless we mix with work a little play.*

**Moliere**

Is the leisure activity intellectually stimulating? A game of chess has more intellectual health benefits than watching a monster truck drag race, but feeding pigeons at the park is probably more stimulating to the brain than watching glorified internal combustion engines race from one end of a roadway to another. Physically active sports can also be intellectually challenging. Route finding with map and compass while backpacking, or creative choreography in dance, are examples.

## ECOLOGICAL CONCERNS OF RECREATION

*Hunting is a sport where your opponent*
*doesn't know he's playing.*

**Unknown**

How does the environmental setting influence health? Observe how the ear-shattering decibels of a rock concert differ in their impact on one's health from listening to a bubbling brook in a high mountain setting. Or imagine how an all-night poker game in a smoke-filled room adversely contributes to one's health. Also, how much of an impact does any particular recreational activity have on the environment? Could it be too damaging to be worthwhile? Compare the benefits of actively bicycling to automobile racing spectator events; or canoeing as opposed to high horse-power boating or boat racing.

## RECREATIONAL HEALTH ANALYSIS
Rate each hobby, sport, pastime, or recreational activity on a scale from
minus 5 (very health damaging) to plus 5 (very health enhancing).

| | -5 | -4 | -3 | -2 | -1 | 0 | 1 | 2 | 3 | 4 | 5 |
|---|---|---|---|---|---|---|---|---|---|---|---|
| **Enhances Physical Health** | | | | | | | | | | | |
| aerobically | -5 | -4 | -3 | -2 | -1 | 0 | 1 | 2 | 3 | 4 | 5 |
| flexibility | -5 | -4 | -3 | -2 | -1 | 0 | 1 | 2 | 3 | 4 | 5 |
| strength | -5 | -4 | -3 | -2 | -1 | 0 | 1 | 2 | 3 | 4 | 5 |
| coordination | -5 | -4 | -3 | -2 | -1 | 0 | 1 | 2 | 3 | 4 | 5 |
| **Risk Factors** | -5 | -4 | -3 | -2 | -1 | 0 | 1 | 2 | 3 | 4 | 5 |
| **Improves Psychological Development** | | | | | | | | | | | |
| nurtures self-esteem | -5 | -4 | -3 | -2 | -1 | 0 | 1 | 2 | 3 | 4 | 5 |
| emotionally satisfying participation | -5 | -4 | -3 | -2 | -1 | 0 | 1 | 2 | 3 | 4 | 5 |
| **Compulsive Activity Feeding Unresolved Needs** | -5 | -4 | -3 | -2 | -1 | 0 | 1 | 2 | 3 | 4 | 5 |
| **Intellectually Challenging** | | | | | | | | | | | |
| strategy | -5 | -4 | -3 | -2 | -1 | 0 | 1 | 2 | 3 | 4 | 5 |
| planning | -5 | -4 | -3 | -2 | -1 | 0 | 1 | 2 | 3 | 4 | 5 |
| quick thinking | -5 | -4 | -3 | -2 | -1 | 0 | 1 | 2 | 3 | 4 | 5 |
| intuition | -5 | -4 | -3 | -2 | -1 | 0 | 1 | 2 | 3 | 4 | 5 |
| creativity | -5 | -4 | -3 | -2 | -1 | 0 | 1 | 2 | 3 | 4 | 5 |
| memory | -5 | -4 | -3 | -2 | -1 | 0 | 1 | 2 | 3 | 4 | 5 |
| **Turns Brain to Goop** | -5 | -4 | -3 | -2 | -1 | 0 | 1 | 2 | 3 | 4 | 5 |
| **Develops Wholesome Interpersonal Relationships** | | | | | | | | | | | |
| emphasizes cooperation | -5 | -4 | -3 | -2 | -1 | 0 | 1 | 2 | 3 | 4 | 5 |
| builds healthy bonds | -5 | -4 | -3 | -2 | -1 | 0 | 1 | 2 | 3 | 4 | 5 |
| overly competitive | -5 | -4 | -3 | -2 | -1 | 0 | 1 | 2 | 3 | 4 | 5 |
| excessive solitary activity | -5 | -4 | -3 | -2 | -1 | 0 | 1 | 2 | 3 | 4 | 5 |
| **The Environmental Setting** | | | | | | | | | | | |
| conducive to personal health | -5 | -4 | -3 | -2 | -1 | 0 | 1 | 2 | 3 | 4 | 5 |
| damaging to personal health | -5 | -4 | -3 | -2 | -1 | 0 | 1 | 2 | 3 | 4 | 5 |
| **Ecological Impact of the Activity** | | | | | | | | | | | |
| beneficial | -5 | -4 | -3 | -2 | -1 | 0 | 1 | 2 | 3 | 4 | 5 |
| detrimental | -5 | -4 | -3 | -2 | -1 | 0 | 1 | 2 | 3 | 4 | 5 |
| **Cost-Benefit Ratio** | -5 | -4 | -3 | -2 | -1 | 0 | 1 | 2 | 3 | 4 | 5 |
| **Time-Benefit Ratio** | -5 | -4 | -3 | -2 | -1 | 0 | 1 | 2 | 3 | 4 | 5 |

## THE COST OF FUN

Cost of the play also enters into the calculations. It's most useful to look at the cost-benefit ratio in this regard. Some recreational activities, like a brisk hike in the woods, have both great benefits and low cost, making them ideal, particularly when they are available to so many people. On the other hand, high-altitude Himalayan mountaineering is extremely costly (not to mention extremely risky) in relation to its benefits for most people.

Using the "Recreational Health Analysis" work sheet on page 97, evaluate several present day recreational activities and several potential new modes of play which you might consider bringing to an integrated health enhancement program. Take each pastime and rate from minus 5 to zero those negative qualities that apply. Then rate from zero to plus 5 the advantages of each.

*He who laughs, lasts.*

**Mary Pettibone Poole**

---

## RECREATIONAL HEALTH RESOURCES

*The true object of all human life is play.*
*Earth is a task garden; heaven is a playground.*

**G.K. Chesterton**

### Books

Adams, Samuel; Adrian, Marlene; Bayless, Mary; ed. *Catastrophic Injuries in Sports: Avoidance Strategies.* Benchmark Press, 1987.

Buxbaum, Robert and Micheli, Lyle. *Sports for Life.* Beacon Press, 1979.

Fluegelman, Andrew, ed. *The New Games Book.* Doubleday, 1976.

Fluegelman, Andrew. *More New Games!* Doubleday, 1981.

Hodgson, Michael. *America's Secret Recreation Areas.* Foghorn Press, 1993.

Junghanns, Herbert. *Clinical Implications of Normal Biomechanical Stresses on Spinal Function.* Aspen, 1990. Contains the most detailed research on the implications of varying biomechanical spinal stresses of most sports and leisure activities.

Klein, Allen. *The Healing Power of Humor.* Tarcher, 1988.

Kohn, Alfie. *No Contest: The Case Against Competition—Why we lose in our race to win.* Houghton Mifflin, 1986.

Leonard, George. *The Ultimate Athlete.* North Atlantic, 1990.

Ludmer, Larry. *The Great American Wilderness: Touring America's National Parks.* Hunter Publishing, 1993.

McCullagh, James, ed. *Ways to Play: Recreational Alternatives.* Rodale Press, 1978.

McMenamin, Paul, ed. *The Ultimate Adventure Sourcebook.* Turner Publishing, 1992.

Orlick, Terry. *The Cooperative Sports and Games Book.* Pantheon, 1978.

Orlick, Terry. *The New Cooperative Sports and Games Book.* Pantheon, 1982.

Orlick, Terry. *Winning Through Cooperation—Competitive Insanity: Cooperative Alternatives.* Hawkins and Associates, 1978.

Paciorek, Michael and Jones, Jeffrey. *Sports and Recreation for the Disabled: A Resource Manual.* Benchmark Press, 1989. The most comprehensive resource manual on this subject.

San Diego Chapter of the Sierra Club. *Wilderness Basics: The Complete Handbook for Hikers and Backpackers.* The Mountaineers, 1993.

Webster, Harriet. *Great American Learning Adventures.* HarperPerennial, 1994.

### Periodicals

*Backpacker,* Rodale Press, 33 E. Minor St., Emmaus, PA 18098; (215) 967-5171.

*Bicycling,* Rodale Press, 33 E. Minor St., Emmaus, PA 18098; (215) 967-5171.

*Canoe,* P.O. Box 7011, Red Oak, IA 51591; (800) 678-5432.

*Great Expeditions,* P.O. Box 180036, Raleigh, NC 27619; (800) 743-3639.

*Outside,* Mariah Publications, 400 Market St., Santa Fe, NM 87501; (505) 989-7100; subscriptions—Box 5472, Boulder, CO 80322-4729; (800) 678-1131.

## Music

***My favorite piece of music
is the one we hear all the time if we are quiet.***

**John Cage**

*Alcazar*, P.O. Box 429, Waterbury, VT 05676, (800) 541-9904. Expansive catalogue with tunes from nearly every genre to put a song in one's heart.

*Heartbeats*, Backroads Distributors, 418 Tamal Plaza, Corte Madera, CA 94925, (800) 825-4848. Catalogue has approximately 3,000 titles of great music that can help one to wholeness.

*Creedence Cassettes*. P.O. Box 419491, Kansas City, MO 64141-6491; (800) 444-8910; (800) 333-7373. Large selection of music.

*Sounds True*. 735 Walnut St., Boulder, CO 80302; (800) 333-9185; (303) 449-6229. Music from many cultures.

## Organizations

***Laughter is the shortest distance
between two people.***

**Victor Borge**

Check with your local Parks and Recreation Department, community college, Sierra Club, bicycling club, or sporting goods store for healthy, fun activities nearby.

***Life is what happened to you while you were making other plans.***

**Unknown**

***We are always getting ready to live but never living.***

**Ralph Waldo Emerson**

RESOURCES

# MANIPULATIVE THERAPIES

Manual manipulation of the body for healing purposes has been documented for thousands of years. Clear descriptions and illustrations of manipulative techniques have been found in hieroglyphics on Egyptian pyramids and in papyrus scrolls of ancient China. Today, with the vast amounts of new research on the subject, we are beginning to discover the importance of manipulative techniques to all aspects of our overall well-being. It is no longer a field relegated to just the relief of minor pains. For two decades the medical description of manipulation has been the following:

> Manipulative therapy involves the application of accurately determined and specifically directed manual forces to the body. Its objective is to improve mobility in areas that are restricted, whether the restrictions are within joints, in connective tissues or in skeletal muscles. The consequences may be the improvement of posture and locomotion, the relief of pain and discomfort, the improvement of function elsewhere in the body and enhancement of the sense of well-being.[1]

For our purposes here, we will divide manipulative techniques into four categories: spinal and extremity joint manipulation, soft tissue manipulation, cranial manipulation, and visceral (organ) manipulation.

There are few low-level procedures for determining one's need for these techniques. Most depend upon a health professional performing examinations and probing the tissues of the body in certain ways to gain information. Except for symptomatic hints, an individual has few *accurate* means to determine his need for manipulative therapy. There are also some guidelines for when to seek preventive care in these areas or when to undertake early detection measures. We will also note ways to seek out wise counsel and referral to the best therapists.

## SPINAL AND EXTREMITY JOINT MANIPULATION

*Look well to the spine for the cause of disease*
**Hippocrates**

The bodies which we are entrusted to take care of for a lifetime were meant to move fully and freely. Some have suggested that our nervous system and organs evolved primarily to support the musculoskeletal system in its efforts to move and interact with the world around it for optimal survival. Others would add that the purpose of this development was to permit the nervous system to become aware of the unity of all things. Whatever our perspective, we acknowledge that a healthy, fully functioning musculoskeletal system enhances our well being. When restrictions on the proper movement of the bones, muscles, joints, tendons, and ligaments occur, abnormal nerve signals begin to emanate from these tissues. This abnormal neurological signaling not only perpetuates, complicates, and intensifies other musculoskeletal dysfunctions (somato-somato reflexes), it also abnormally signals internal organs to dysfunction (somato-visceral reflexes). John Bourdillon, M.D. documents in his book, *Spinal Manipulation*, the "dramatic and lasting" correction of deafness in a patient by thoracic spine manipulation. This mimics the event that heralded the birth of the chiropractic profession in 1895 when D. D. Palmer restored the hearing of his janitor by a similar maneuver.

It is a frequent occurrence for a person to seek joint manipulation for a neuro-musculoskeletal discomfort and to find, upon correction of the abnormality, that some other complaint resolves itself. A chiropractic manipulation is used to correct a "catch in the ribs" and the patient's peptic ulcer complaints disappear. An osteopathic manipulation is used to correct a patient's low back pain, and with the relief from back discomfort comes a resolution of a 15-year history of painful menstrual periods.

*After being blind for three months following a head injury, a patient received 11 chiropractic manipulations of the cervical spine over another three months, experiencing progressive improvement to normal vision.[2]*

As more research is done in all the fields related to this subject, we are discovering that nerve insults and joint movement abnormalities have a far greater impact on total health than we ever imagined. Exploring the professional resources at the end of this section should keep the most curious investigators busy with detailed research confirming the significance of manipulative therapy in a comprehensive health care program.

## The Cause of Joint Motion Abnormalities and the Resulting Nerve Interference

There are a number of causes for the most prevalent types of joint motion abnormalities. The most obvious is a trauma to the musculoskeletal structures—a fall, sprain, strain, broken bone, or joint dislocation. Upon such an occurrence, an altered motion is imposed on the joints. The surrounding soft tissues are injured and unable to respond normally. Protective muscle guarding then follows. As time heals the tissue damage, the body strives to restore normal motion to the joints. Unfortunately, tissues do not always heal normally. Frequently scar tissue forms, and tendons and ligaments shorten. Many times the musculature does not recover its full strength. Often the length of time in recovery conditions the nervous system to drive the muscles in uncoordinated patterns rather than directing them to move the body normally. These situations then ingrain movement abnormalities into the joints. This occurs most frequently when there is not enough rehabilitation following the injury. All too often people just "let things heal by themselves," with not even the slightest program for strength or flexibility retraining. This will always result in less than full recovery. What is worse is when an unskilled physician casts a broken bone or prescribes pain medication and an orthopedic support, then recommends no follow-up rehabilitation program. This falsely im-

plies to the patient that nothing else is needed. It reinforces the use of a quick fix for symptom alleviation without concern about the level of functional recovery afterwards.

The spinal trauma that occurs at birth has been highly suspected to cause joint motion abnormalities—particularly in the cervical spine because of the prevalence of joint restrictions there in children under the age of one. It is fairly easy to see how the frail neck of a newborn, with its undeveloped musculature, can be sprained during the ordeal of the birth process. The need to heal then goes unnoticed, and so does the need for some form of rehabilitation. The infant can't say, "Hey, my neck hurts. Get me to a chiropractor." The cries are interpreted as something else. The crisis passes. But residual joint restrictions and excessive areas of movement remain because the problem was never identified and rehabilitated properly. The child grows and develops with these abnormal patterns of motion ingrained, predisposing the area to the risk of future problems of greater severity. What unknown internal malfunction or disease process, distant from the injury site, will be initiated by this early, uncorrected trauma to the nervous system? Some suggest that Sudden Infant Death Syndrome, SIDS, has part of its origin here.

Micro-trauma also results in the same pathological processes as those detailed above in the illustration of an obviously noticeable injury. The difference is that micro-trauma injuries occur from unnoticed, or barely acknowledged, cumulative tissue stress. Since there are minimal warning signals of functional or pathological disturbances in the involved tissues until major damage occurs, no corrections are made until the problem is full blown. Repetitive motion stresses are frequently causes of micro-trauma injuries. Examples include: running too many miles, resulting in heel spurs, shin splints, and knee inflammations; excessive typing, resulting in carpal tunnel syndrome; and too much bending over while picking produce in farm work leads to degenerative, proliferative arthritis of the lumbar spine. Most people have early signs that these conditions are present and continuing but tend to ignore the slight early warning discomforts as "normal aches and pains." Regular use of over-the-counter pain medication to mask these early warning signals is prevalent. It keeps many conditions from being treated effectively in their early stages.

These repetitive stress syndromes occur more frequently when a learned pattern of *abnormal* movement affects the tissues. A typical example is repetitive stress injury to a pitcher's shoulder accentuated by a faulty throwing motion. The motion unduly strains and abrades delicate tendons. Poor posture also falls into this category.

Genetic or developmental structural abnormalities also cause poor joint motion. Then one has to deal with the wide range of ramifications stemming from the adapted neurological signaling. A frequent example is unequal leg length, where one leg is shorter than the other by an amount sufficient to cause distorted walking. An imbalanced neurological response occurs with each step, in addition to stresses on other structures that are trying to adapt. Scoliosis of the spine frequently results.

### *Prevention*

There are many ways to prevent joint motion abnormalities in the spine and extremities, beginning with good prenatal care. Good prenatal nutrition and low stress prevents many skeletal and neurological defects in the newborn. Natural childbirth programs also help provide a less traumatic birth process.

*In a study of infantile colic 94% of 316 infants showed improvement with chiropractic manipulation. This is far better than any other known treatment. Remember also that no placebo effect can occur with infants.[3]*

Reducing the incidence and severity of injuries is another way to prevent many joint problems from total health. Remember that there are approximately 9,000,000 accidental, disabling injuries every year in the U.S. Mindfulness while at home, work, play, or driving is a key. Look at all the safety precautions that can make enormous differences in ones's life while driving: defensive driving techniques, seat belts, shoulder harnesses,

head rests, child safety seats, airbags, anti-lock brakes, quality tires, good visibility. We can look at play also and see where we can assure more safety. Participation in non-collision sports helps enormously. Taking a step further—playing for fun rather than competition protects us from letting our egos override our body's caveats for moderation. Our minds often push our body tissues to their limits of failure trying to gain some psychological reward when the body is unable to comply.

Keeping aerobically fit, muscularly strong and flexible, are essential for preventing not only joint injuries, but soft tissue injuries also. Being well nourished in order to support those healthy tissues is not to be forgotten either. Proper ergonomics, or body movements and posture, are very helpful. Efficient, non-stressful ways of moving through the world of work, play, and daily activities can have enormous impact on structural health because of the strong forces that wrong movements can impose on tissues, even if they occur in small amounts over an extended period of time.

### *Early Detection*

When prevention fails, having good ways to detect joint abnormalities early assures that problems can be dealt with while they are still simple. Detecting early joint motion aberrations oneself is difficult. A skilled professional, well trained at detecting small "arthro-kinematic" faults by examination, will almost always find these early joint problems before they are noticed by the individual and long before physicians doing merely "range of motion" orthopedic testing.

There are some things everybody can do. One, don't ignore joint pain. Be suspicious of muscles that are frequently tight, achy, and sore. They are signs of either joint abnormalities or muscle tightness that eventually may cause joint motion problems. Beware of the chronic use of pain medication for constant or reoccurring discomforts. Be careful to observe limitations in flexibility when doing exercises, and find the cause of those limitations. Look for short legs and/or irregular curvatures in the spine, particularly in children. Often mothers notice a need to hem one pant leg more than another. Or family photos always show a child with one shoulder higher than the other.

Early detection by skilled professionals is the best bet. When should checkups be scheduled to assess early signs of problems before they cause more severe difficulties? No dependable statistics are available, and individual susceptibility to these problems varies greatly. Those individuals who take more preventive care of all aspects of their health are more likely to avoid accelerating problems. People who have a history of physical injury, whether from birth trauma or an incident later on in life, are more likely to develop a reccurrence of some past biomechanical fault. This is particularly so when insufficient rehabilitation was used in the correction of these past injuries. Lifestyles and work which unduly stress the musculoskeletal system also increase the need for early detection programs.

*When chiropractic pre-employment screening was instituted in a manufacturing setting, the incidence of back problems was reduced 80%.[4]*

Would an asymptomatic, well-nourished, non-stressed individual with no history of past injury who participates in a program of balanced exercise with aerobic conditioning, strength training, and stretching need periodic examinations for early detection of joint motion problems? Probably not, but then there might be only three people in the world who fit that description. For the rest of us, it is more relevant to use a guideline based on the assumption that most of us have some biomechanical faults which, if corrected, could contribute to our overall health. Determining the degree of impairment, and making cost-benefit evaluations for its correction, would best be made by consulting a trustworthy therapist skilled in manipulation.

Some conditions which respond well to spinal and/or extremity joint manipulation are: whiplash injuries, torticollis (wry neck), low back strains and sprains, sacroiliac problems, shoulder-arm-hand syndromes, numbness or tingling in the arms and legs, carpal tunnel syndromes, tennis and golfer's elbow, knee and hip pain, headaches, failed back surgery syndrome, infantile colic, asthma, and

childhood behavioral problems. Karel Lewit, M.D. documents in his book, *Manipulative Therapy in the Rehabilitation of the Locomotor System*, the successful use of chiropractic manipulation in conditions like respiratory problems, digestive disorders, migraine, vertigo, heart disease, tonsillitis, and menstrual disorders.

Individuals suffering from these problems would be well advised to consult a professional skilled in manipulation to determine whether they might have a joint motion abnormality.

### Choosing a Manipulative Therapist for Spine or Extremity Joint Motion Problems

*When back surgery is considered, it is important to remember that death rates due to anesthesia hover around 1 in 1000. In a thirty-year literature review during a time that saw billions of chiropractic manipulations given, there was one reported death by chiropractic adjustment and nine involving medical manipulation.[5]*

Chiropractors have by far the most extensive training in spinal manipulation and would thus have the greatest chance of providing high quality treatment. Physical therapists, osteopaths, and even naturopaths take some courses in manipulation while in school. A few medical doctors have also trained themselves in manipulative techniques. But there are far more chiropractors who are qualified to do good manipulation than all other kinds of therapists combined. Many chiropractors primarily use joint manipulation techniques that involve quick, short thrusts. Osteopaths are more known for their generalized multi-joint manipulations. Physical therapists most frequently utilize slow oscillatory mobilizations in the spine and extremities. A careful, discriminating combination of techniques utilizing the physical therapist's mobilization approaches and the chiropractor's specific, dynamic adjustments will elicit the best results.

As with any skill, or in any profession, there will be a wide range in quality from the best to the worst. Finding the best therapists and avoiding the worst is not always easy. Here are some tips which might help. First, call the Motion Palpation Institute listed in the resource section to find a chiropractor in your area who has taken post graduate courses in the high quality techniques this professional educational organization teaches. It will show you those who are at least trying to improve their techniques. If this does not produce any leads, start calling chiropractors from the phone book and ask them if they use examination and correction procedures like those advocated in some of the key resources found in this section:

- Schafer, Richard and Faye, Leonard. *Motion Palpation and Chiropractic Technique.* Motion Palpation Institute, 1990.

- Grieve, Gregory. *Common Vertebral Joint Problems.* Churchill Livingstone, 1981.

- Grieve, Gregory. *Modern Manual Therapy of the Vertebral Column.* Churchill, 1986.

- Kessler, Randolph and Hertling, Darlene. *Management of Common Musculoskeletal Disorders: Physical Therapy Principles and Methods.* Harper & Row, 1983.

- Dr. Faye's instructional videos on spinal and extremity joint manipulation.

If they are unfamiliar with these *bibles* of manipulative therapy, look elsewhere. There are a number of chiropractors who do not use these standardized, proven methods of correction. Some use experimental, unproven techniques. (See the section on Rating Therapies.) If your search for a satisfactory chiropractor is not fruitful, try the same questions with physical therapists. Therapists who specialize in athletic injury rehabilitation might be good to turn to next. There are many avenues for emphasis in clinical physical therapy practice. Not all physical therapists are skilled, hands-on manipulators. Some spend 99% of their time with exercise rehab.

Only ten percent of all osteopaths integrate manipulation into their practice, and when they do it is only with 10% of their clients. So finding ones that are well practiced is difficult in this day and age when most osteopaths tend toward surgical and medicinal approaches.

A very small number of M.D.'s, physiatrists, and physical medicine specialists actually do their own manipulation. Most just write prescriptive orders for physical therapists to do the hands-on work.

Once a good therapist is found, integrating his manipulative interventions with a well rounded program of soft tissue rehabilitation and exercise is the best approach to take.

## SOFT TISSUE MANIPULATION

For purposes of organization we have separated soft tissue manipulation from joint manipulation, but there are many times when it is difficult to make distinctions between the two. Whenever we mobilize the joints, we move and treat the surrounding soft tissues. When we use various techniques on the muscles, tendons, fascia, and ligaments of the body, we improve joint motion. Sometimes joint techniques cannot even be attempted before soft tissue methods are first used in preparation. Often soft tissue problems don't respond to direct techniques until regional joint manipulation is done to eliminate abnormal neurological signaling to those soft tissues. Joint manipulation, soft tissue techniques, and exercise rehabilitation procedures should be considered and integrated in almost every situation for the best results.

### Causes, Prevention, and Early Detection

The causes and prevention of soft tissue injuries are similar to those of joint problems. Some early detection measures can be taken without professional assistance. Weak muscles, excessively contracted muscles, tender trigger points, can be perceived by the average person in early stages of dysfunction. Even the help of an unskilled friend to probe painful trigger points in unreachable locales adds to some early warning capabilities. Muscles should not be tender to deep pressure.

Professional assessment provides added detail and locates many problems unrecognized by simple self-examination. The technology can get quite complex—computerized muscle strength and power curves calculated at every angle of movement in a joint, electromyographic evaluation of muscle electrical activity during rest and various activities, thermographic images of blood flow to soft tissues, and even biopsies to look inside the tissue structure and cellular components.

One of the better ways to begin using early self-detection and self-correction methods is to consult these books from the resource section of this chapter:

- *Myotherapy* by Bonnie Prudden
- *Spasm* by John Lowe

They will help you identify certain soft tissue functional faults and the residue of old injuries. They also offer instruction on how to correct some of the problems you may find. Some soft tissue problems include muscular weaknesses which need to be identified and corrected. Strength imbalances between agonist and antagonist muscles, or between right and left sides of a pair, can cause significant tissue injury. The risk increases with the stress that tissues might encounter, whether from large isolated incidents or small, cumulative, repetitive stress syndromes. This subject will be investigated further in the section on exercise.

Of course you may find yourself faced with problems that call for professional help. You should then consult with someone skilled at specific hands-on therapy, someone who is also able to integrate it with other procedures. Ideal functioning comes from such a comprehensive approach. As the severity and complexity of the problem increases, it becomes more difficult to put together such an approach.

Let us imagine a fairly ideal, inexpensive, but comprehensive procedure for treating a soft tissue problem. What do we have to begin with? We have a wide variety of individuals with different capacities and goals. On one side of this spectrum is the very healthy, self-motivated, regular exerciser who tears a hamstring muscle and simply needs some deep tissue massage. All other systems are unaffected. The person is quite capable and well-suited for self-directed, health enhancement measures. Why should he be burdened with the expense of extensive work-ups or excessive therapies?

On the other side of the spectrum is the person with multiple, serious tissue injuries and biomechanical problems. This person will need extensive, detailed pretesting in different areas. Soft tissues will need long-term treatment. Joints will have to be mobilized as the soft tissue recovers. A complete exercise rehabilitation program has to be coordinated with the other therapies. Medical and surgical interventions may be needed.

Then there are the masses of people who fall in between these extremes. Choosing the correct, cost-effective level of testing and correction is difficult for professionals to decide upon, much less the lay person. And those decisions are made more difficult by many factors: the health knowledge of patients limits what they can do for themselves and also impedes their own decisions concerning health goals. The medical profession has excellent technology and facilities to provide for a wide variety of problem solving, but finances may impose limits. Scientific research has given us good manipulative and other procedures for helping the body heal musculoskeletal problems, but many of those techniques are difficult to institute, particularly in a complementary fashion because of professional, political, and economic turf battles.

Medical doctors and hospitals have lots of money and great facilities, but they refuse access to chiropractors and force physical therapists to work by medical prescription. In concert with powerful insurance companies, the medical profession directs musculoskeletal rehabilitation away from multi-disciplinary, comprehensive programs towards a more limited agenda for maximum profit.

Osteopaths have been pressured to forsake excellence in manipulation in order to be accepted by the medical establishment. Chiropractors and physical therapists play off their own strong points, competing with one another rather than joining forces. Some professionals try to minimize their own hands-on work and build profits by bringing in assistants, nurses and massage therapists. Massage therapists, while complaining about lack of credibility and acceptance by other health professionals, resist more stringent educational and licensing arrangements to upgrade their profession. Occupational therapists have not been adequately integrated into therapy regimens. They seldom go beyond work hardening programs that condition clients in the demands of their job. They could do much more to help people improve their livelihood and lifestyle and create truly holistic transformations.

There are also some isolated manipulative techniques of value which are difficult to classify and could be parts of a thorough approach like that described above. Unfortunately, there is little documentation on how to best integrate them into a total health care program in a cost-effective way. Techniques like Feldenkrais, Hellerwork, and Structural Integration (Rolfing) have been valuable to certain individuals.

Hopefully, more research in these fields will yield guidelines for the best use of their techniques in an integrated health program. In part, it is up to the organizations who advocate and teach these methods to provide the scientific validation for their use. Their practitioners are paid for their services and should therefore have some responsibility for financially supporting scientific research. The established medical research community also has some responsibility for researching all potentially valid techniques, since they have amassed an incredibly vast network of resources and funding for such purposes. Even though the economic incentives drive that system to direct energies and finances elsewhere, enormous health benefits are waiting to be discovered and proven in the manipulative therapy sciences.

We have been discussing just an isolated musculoskeletal health improvement program and the difficulty in integrating its many aspects just in that field. We haven't even mentioned the full integration of this with other elements of a complete holistic health approach including nutrition, psychotherapy, spiritual practices, and so on.

## CRANIAL MANIPULATION

The skull is made up of a number of cranial and facial bones with many connecting joints called sutures. These structures are held together in large part by a complex system of fascial membranes that blend in with other structures of the body, such as the dura of the brain, spinal dural coverings, and the body's musculature. The intracranial system of skull bones, joints, and supporting structures were designed to protect the delicate brain tissues. The joints and membranous supports need to be rigid enough to protect, but just flexible enough to accommodate, the rhythmic fluctuations of cerebrospinal fluid that also protects and nourishes the brain. A close look at the structure of cranial and facial joints will show how it does this.

There are cyclic differences in the pressure of the cerebrospinal fluid that move the brain, its membranes, and the surrounding bones and joints. They occur at a rate between 8 and 14 pulses per minute in normal individuals. The cranial bones move in correspondence with these rhythms, although this motion is so small that we don't notice it; and it is difficult to detect by touch except by those trained and practiced in the necessary techniques. The electrical activity in the brain rises and falls with these changes in fluid pressure and structural movement.

As with any system of the body, problems can and will occur. Often they occur first with disturbances in the motion of the cranial sutures or other connective tissue structures which then alters the movement of the cerebrospinal fluid. This then influences the neurological transmission of brain signals. The result may be any number of physiological or psychological disturbances.

*Recurring headaches afflict
15,000,000 Americans who spend
$300,000,000 a year for pain relief medication
which only covers up the causes of the problem.*

Head trauma, whether from a difficult birth process or any significant blow to the head, seems to be a frequent cause of unnoticed joint motion abnormalities in the skull which then result in fluid alterations and neurological irritation. Strain in any significant portion of the muscle or fascial system of the body due to injury also seems to have a dramatic effect on the dural membranes of the spine and brain. Further investigation into the mechanisms of this normal physiological process and the pathological aberrations that can occur with it can be found by reading some of the excellent resources at the end of this section. It is important to present here, though, some guidelines so that the average individual can determine whether he needs to include cranial manipulation in his health enhancement regimen.

## Prevention

Prevention is always the first step. And in reference to this subject it obviously means preventing head injury.

*50,000 bicyclists suffer serious head injury every year. 1,300 die.*
*90% of these injuries could be prevented with the use of approved helmets.*

This involves a wide spectrum of preventive measures from natural childbirth, participation in non-contact, non-collision sports, the use of protective head gear with bicycles and motorcycles, and mindfulness in daily activities (like withdrawing your head fully from beneath the kitchen sink before rising up). All of the suggestions made in the previous section concerning prevention of musculoskeletal injury apply here also. Again, notice the interconnections between musculoskeletal health and health of the "craniosacral respiratory system," as it is sometimes called. Emotional stress transformed into muscular tension, particularly in the neck and jaw, should be prevented also, because the excessive, continuous, abnormal muscle pulling on the skull bone attachments distorts cranial joint motion.

## Early Detection

*For patients complaining of headaches at the base of the skull, 93% reported relief following chiropractic manipulations.[6]*

Other than suspicious looking symptoms, there are no reliable means for self-detection of cranial motion abnormalities. History of head injury, Temporomandibular joint (TMJ or jaw joint problems) problems, headaches, facial pain, difficult to diag-

nose nerve conditions, chronic, posttraumatic pain syndromes, ringing in the ears, childhood hyperactivity, learning disabilities, unresolved health problems that have a neuromuscular component, are all indications that might warrant a cranial evaluation. There is clinical evidence that other conditions are helped significantly when cranial distortions are corrected. They include: systemic infections, peptic ulcers, visual disturbances, asthma, cardiac arrhythmias, irritable bowel syndromes, rheumatoid arthritis, Raynaud's ischemia (causing cold or painful extremities), vertigo, and cerebral ischemic attacks (blood being cut off from the brain).

Finding a therapist skilled in cranial manipulation is not easy. Osteopaths and chiropractors were the first to develop systems for cranial manipulation decades ago. Most of the clinical investigation has stayed in these two professions with osteopathic research and documentation in the forefront. Cranial manipulation was not widely used in either profession. Only a small percentage of these physicians practice it. It is a very subtle palpatory skill. Much is still unknown about how cranial manipulation works or which techniques are best. This makes many physicians hesitate about adopting procedures until much more data is in.

Although the Southerland Cranial Teaching Foundation limits its cranial manipulation education exclusively to medical doctors, osteopaths, and dentists, the Upledger Institute has an extensive series of training courses open to professionals and nonprofessionals alike. Whereas the instructors of the Southerland Cranial Teaching Foundation feel that cranial manipulation is best left in the hands of certain doctors of their choosing, thereby limiting the availability of this valuable technique, Dr. Upledger and his colleagues feel that this new element of the health sciences is so valuable that its dissemination is best done on a broader scale. Since cranial techniques as taught by the Upledger Institute are extremely safe with little, if any, potential for adverse side effects, it is felt that any dedicated individual can learn, utilize, and help people with the procedures. Unfortunately, this leads to a great number of undertrained individuals who profess craniosacral manipulation skills but really lack sufficient knowledge to do a high quality job.

The best way to get referrals for cranial manipulation is to contact the Southerland Cranial Teaching Foundation or the Upledger Institute from the addresses and phone numbers at the end of this section. The chiropractic profession has several groups and individuals teaching their "brand" of cranial manipulation. Since there is little or no valuable research documentation about these types of cranial manipulation, it is probably wise to wait for some efficacy studies first. If these chiropractors are also trained sufficiently in osteopathic techniques such as Upledger's, then they might be excellent cranial manipulators, since chiropractic training in general requires extensive development of this subtle sense of touch.

## VISCERAL MANIPULATION

All of the body's viscera, or organs such as stomach, liver, or colon, are connected by a matrix of connective tissue. All of these organs move in response to the many movements of the body. This includes not only the usually recognized walking, bending, and twisting of the musculoskeletal system, but also the rhythmic pulse of respiration. There is an intrinsic motion within each organ, most noticeably seen in the peristaltic action of the digestive organs or the pulse of the heart, but also existing in structures like the kidneys and liver. Any disturbances in these movements have the potential for altering the internal workings of the organs. And nearly any physical or psychological disturbance can adversely alter organ movement—internal inflammatory processes, surgical adhesions, musculoskeletal problems, disturbances in neurological signaling, glandular and endocrine disorders, reactions to certain foods or allergic substances, environmental toxins, and psychological or emotional stresses.

Obviously prevention of the above situations is important. Early detection of these movement abnormalities of organs is not likely in self-evalua-

tion. Finding a skilled practitioner who can do an evaluation in early stages of dysfunction, before serious repercussions ensue, seems to be a good approach for those who might suspect these problems. Unfortunately, finding a skilled practitioner is not easy. Visceral manipulation has developed primarily with some osteopaths in France. Learning and using the techniques can be quite involved, requiring sensitive fingers. As we have mentioned, the Upledger Institute teaches these techniques to professionals and nonprofessionals alike. They have a referral service for locating qualified practitioners, who are few and far between.

Visceral manipulation should be considered if any of the following have been experienced or are presently health problems: lung, digestive tract, or urinary tract infections, neck and arm pain, back pain, rib pain, digestive discomfort or difficulty, bladder problems, weakened immune system, thoracic or abdominal cavity surgery, urogenital surgery.

## SUMMARY

The various types of manipulative therapies are rarely utilized in today's health care delivery system. There are many reasons for this. Interdisciplinary political and economic turf battles have prevented good research and inhibited professional cooperation and the development of clinical excellence. This has resulted in physicians, insurers, and the public being poorly informed about what is the best care available. Using the guidelines here will allow individuals to use these hands-on therapies more wisely. As more research is done to decide the best clinical techniques, practitioners will improve their skills. Patients will become better educated and demand high quality care. This will drive professionals to cooperate with each other for the benefit of the client. Prevention, early detection, and the best utilization of techniques will make health care less expensive at the same time that it makes people healthier. Everybody wins.

# MANIPULATIVE THERAPY RESOURCES

★Denotes Best of the Best Resources

## *Books*

Altman, Nathaniel. *Everybody's Guide to Chiropractic Health Care. Tarcher*, 1990.

Lowe, John C. *Spasm: Why Your Body Is Painfully Tight & How You Can Loosen It for Good*. McDowell Publishing, 1983.

Moore, Susan. *Chiropractic: The Illustrated Guide*. Harmony, 1988.

Prudden, Bonnie. *Myotherapy*. The Dial Press, 1984.

## *Newsletters*

*Staying Well*, FCER/Staying Well, 1701 Clarendon Blvd., Arlington, VA 22209-2723; (800) 637-6244. This is an informative newsletter available through the chiropractic profession. It deals with natural health care issues with a strong emphasis on spinal care.

## RESOURCES FOR PROFESSIONALS

The following resources are primarily geared for the health professionals specializing in these fields and those not working directly in these specialties but in need of learning how these domains of health services might relate to their own. Well educated lay individuals can learn much from many of these works to better help themselves. They can use the resources to challenge and educate their therapists to deliver a higher quality of care. The organizational resources can also be used by the lay person for referral services.

## Soft Tissue, Spinal, Extremity Manipulation; Sports Injury; and General Musculoskeletal Rehabilitation

### *Books*

Calliet, Rene. *Low Back Pain Syndrome*. F. A. Davis, 1981.

Calliet, Rene. *Soft Tissue Pain and Disability*. F. A. Davis, 1977.

Calliet, Rene. *Shoulder Pain*. F. A. Davis, 1981.

Calliet, Rene. *Knee Pain and Disability*. F. A. Davis, 1983.

Calliet, Rene. *Neck and Arm Pain*. F. A. Davis, 1981.

Calliet, Rene. *Foot and Ankle Pain*. F. A. Davis, 1983.

Calliet, Rene. *Hand Pain and Impairment*. F. A. Davis, 1982.

Cantu, Robert and Grodin, Alan. *Myofascial Manipulation: Theory and Clinical Application*. Aspen, 1992.

Cyriax, James and Coldham, Margaret. *Textbook of Orthopaedic Medicine: Treatment by Manipulation, Massage, & Injection*. Saunders, 1984.

Foreman, Steve and Croft, Arthur. *Whiplash Injuries: The Cervical Acceleration-Deceleration Syndrome*. Williams and Wilkins, 1988.

★Gould, James A. and Davies, George J. *Orthopaedic and Sports Physical Therapy*. C. V. Mosby, 1985.

Grieve, Gregory. *Common Vertebral Joint Problems*. Churchill Livingstone, 1981.

★Grieve, Gregory. *Modern Manual Therapy of the Vertebral Column*. Churchill, 1986.

Haldeman, Scott. *Modern Developments in the Principles and Practice of Chiropractic*. Appleton-Century-Crofts, 1980.

Hammer, Warren, ed. *Functional Soft Tissue Examination and Treatment By Manual Methods: The Extremities*. Aspen Publishers, 1990.

Jaskoviak, Paul and Schafer, R. C. *Applied Physiotherapy: Practical Clinical Applications with Emphasis on the Management of Pain and Related Syndromes*. The American Chiropractic Association, 1986. The American Chiropractic Association, 1701 Clarendon Blvd., Arlington, VA 22209; (703) 276-8800.

Junghanns, Herbert. *Clinical Implications of Normal Biomechanical Stresses on Spinal Function*. Aspen, 1990. Detailed research on spinal stresses in daily living.

★Kessler, Randolph and Hertling, Darlene. *Management of Common Musculoskeletal Disorders: Physical Therapy Principles and Methods*. Harper & Row, 1983.

Kirkaldy-Willis, W. H. *Managing Low Back Pain*. Churchill Livingstone, 1983.

Korr, Irvin M. *The Neurobiologic Mechanisms in Manipulative Therapy*. Plenum Press, 1977.

Lewit, Karol. *Manipulative Therapy in the Rehabilitation of the Motor System*. Butterworth, 1985.

Lawrence, Dana J., ed. *Fundamentals of Chiropractic Diagnosis and Management*. Williams and Wilkins, 1991.

Lawrence, Dana J., ed. *Advances in Chiropractic.* Mosby, 1994.

Lawrence, Dana J., ed. *The 1994 Year Book of Chiropractic.* Mosby, 1994.

Maitland, G. M. *Peripheral Manipulation.* Butterworths, 1977.

Mennell, John. *The Musculoskeletal System: Differential Diagnosis from Symptoms and Physical Signs.* Aspen Publishers, 1991.

★ Schafer, Richard and Faye, Leonard. *Motion Palpation and Chiropractic Technique.* Motion Palpation Institute, 1990.

Shands, Cely. *Chiropractic Rehabilitation.* Life At Its Peak, 1992.

Sweere, Joseph, ed. *Chiropractic Family Practice: A Clinical Manual.* Aspen Publishers, 1992.

★ Travell, Janet and Simons, David. *Myofascial Pain and Dysfunction: The Trigger Point Manual.* Vol I: *Upper Extremities.* Williams and Wilkins, 1983; Vol II: *Lower Extremities,* Williams and Wilkins, 1993.

## *Journals*

*Annals of the Swiss Chiropractic Association.* Available in the U.S. from the Motion Palpation Institute.

*The Backletter.* Available from the Motion Palpation Institute. Multidisciplinary review of research on spinal therapies.

*The Chiropractic Report,* 3080 Yonge St., Suite 3002, Toronto, Ontario M4N 3N1 Canada; (800) 506-2225; Fax (416) 484-9665. An international review of professional and research subjects published bi-monthly.

*Chiropractic Sports Medicine,* Official Journal of the American Chiropractic Association Council on Sports Injuries & Physical Fitness and The Federation Internationale de Chiropractique Sportive, by Williams & Wilkins, 428 E. Preston St., Baltimore, MD 21202; (410) 528-4000; (800) 527-5597; (800) 628-6423.

*Journal of Biomechanics,* Pergamon Press, Inc., Maxwell House, Fairview Park, Elmsford, NY 10523.

*Journal of the Canadian Chiropractic Association,* Canadian Chiropractic Association, 1396 Egliton Ave. W, Toronto, ON Canada M6C 2E4; (416) 781-5656; (800) 668-2076.

*Journal of Chiropractic Technique,* sponsored by National College of Chiropractic, published by Williams and Wilkins, 428 E. Preston St, Baltimore, MD 21202; (410) 528-4000; (800) 527-5597; (800) 638-6423.

*Journal of Manipulative and Physiological Therapeutics,* official journal of National College of Chiropractic, published by Williams and Wilkins, 428 E. Preston St, Baltimore, MD 21202; (410) 528-4000; (800) 527-5597; (800) 638-6423.

*Journal of Manual Medicine,* Springer-Verlag New York, Inc., Service Center Secaucus, 44 Hartz Way, Secaucus, NJ 07094.

*Journal of the Neuromuscular System,* Produced by the American Chiropractic Association.

*Journal of the Neuromusculoskeletal System,* an official journal of the American Chiropractic Association. Subscriptions: Data Trace Chiropractic Publishers, P.O. Box 1239, Brooklandville, MD 21022-9978; (800) 342-0454; (410) 294-4994; Fax (410) 494-0515.

*Journal of Orthopaedic and Sports Physical Therapy,* Williams and Wilkins, 428 E. Preston St, Baltimore, MD 21202; (410) 528-4000; (800) 527-5597; (800) 638-6423.

*Physical Fitness/Sports Medicine Bibliography,* President's Council on Physical Fitness & Sports, 701 Pennsylvania Ave. NW, Washington, DC 20004; (202) 272-3421.

*Physical Medicine & Rehabilitation Clinics of North America,* W.B. Saunders, Periodicals, 6277 Sea Harbor Dr., Orlando, FL 32887; (800) 654-2452.

*Physical Therapy,* American Physical Therapy Association, 1111 N. Fairfax St., Alexandria, VA 22314; (703) 684-2782.

*Selected Clinical Updates,* Australian Spinal Research Foundation, P.O. Box 1047, Springwood, Queensland, 4127 Australia; (617) 808-4098.

*Spinal Manipulation: A Review of the Current Literature,* Published quarterly by the Foundation for Chiropractic Education and Research (FCER), 1701 Clarendon Blvd., Arlington, VA 22209-2723; (800) 637-6244.

*Topics in Clinical Chiropractic,* Aspen Publishers; (800) 638-8437.

## *Videotapes*

★ L. John Faye has produced a series of instructional videotapes on spinal and extremity manipulation for professionals which is superb. It is available from the Motion Palpation Institute.

★ Travell, Janet and Daitz, Ben. *Myofascial Pain Syndromes: The Travell Trigger-Point Tapes.* Available from Williams and Wilkins, 428 Preston St., Baltimore, MD 21202; (800) 527-5597.

## *Organizations*

American Back Society, 2647 East 14th St., Suite 401, Oakland, CA 94601; (510) 536-9929. Multi-disciplinary professional organization that supports research and continuing education in spinal health care services.

American Massage Therapy Association, 820 Davis St., Suite 100, Evanston, IL 60201; (708) 864-0123.

Hellerwork, Inc., 406 Berry St., Mount Shasta, CA 96067; (800) 392-3900; (916) 926-2500; Fax (916) 926-6839.

★Motion Palpation Institute, P.O. Box 6100, Huntington Beach, CA 92615; (714) 960-6577. Chiropractic postgraduate educational organization and referral service. Attending their workshops does not guarantee a good technician skilled in manipulation, but it does seem to be one of the best chiropractic referral sources. There are also good chiropractors who have not attended MPI's educational course work. Many of the best books and journals on manipulative therapy are available through their bookstore; (800) 359-2289.

North American Academy of Musculoskeletal Medicine, 7611 Elmwood Ave., Suite 202, Middleton, WI 53562; (608) 831-9240. Small group of medical doctors advancing manipulative techniques. Affiliated with the Federation of Manipulative Medicine.

Orthopedic Physical Therapy Products, 3700 Annapolis Lane, Suite 175, P.O. Box 47009, Minneapolis, MN 55447-0009; (612) 553-0452; (800) 367-7393; Fax (612) 553-9355. Many of the best books and videotapes on manipulative therapy and therapeutic exercise are available through their catalog.

Rolf Institute, P.O. Box 1868, Boulder, CO 80306; (303) 449-5903. Teaches structural integration style of deep tissue massage.

San Francisco Spine Institute, 1850 Sullivan Ave., Suite 140, Daly City, CA 94015; (415) 991-6761. Available from the Institute is a good lumbar stabilization exercise video program.

Saunders Group, 4250 Norex Dr., Chaska, MN 55318-3047; (800) 456-1289; Fax (800) 375-1119. Excellent books, videos, and courses on manipulative therapies, therapeutic exercise, and ergonomics.

Somatics Society, 1516 Grant Ave., Novato, CA 94945; (415) 892-0617. Progressive body-centered therapists.

## Cranial Manipulation

### *Professional Books*

Upledger, John E. and Vredevoogd, Jon D. *Craniosacral Therapy*. Eastland Press, 1983. Eastland Press, P.O. Box 12689, Seattle, WA 89111. One of the better explanations of physiology, rationale, research and basic techniques.

Upledger, John E. *Craniosacral Therapy II: Beyond the Dura*. Eastland Press. Expansion on the first volume but less useful.

Gehin, Alan. *Atlas of Manipulative Techniques*. Eastland Press, 1985. Comprehensive, well illustrated guide to many of the most accepted cranial manipulative techniques. No commentary, physiology, research, or rationale.

Feely, Richard, ed. *Clinical Cranial Osteopathy: Selected Readings. Cranial* Academy, 1988.

Magoun, Harold. *Osteopathy in the Cranial Field*. Cranial Academy, 1976.

### *Organizations*

Cranial Academy, 3500 Depauw Blvd., #1080, Indianapolis, IN 46268-1136; (317) 879-0713.

Dennis Hertenstein, D.C., 4737 Sonoma Hwy, Santa Rosa, CA 95409; (707) 538-3554. Dr. Hertenstein teaches cranial manipulation to health care professionals.

Southerland Cranial Teaching Foundation, 4204 Billglade Road, Fort Worth, TX 76109; (917) 926-0737. Osteopathic cranial manipulation educational organization limited to MD's or DO's. The material presented is good, and referrals can be acquired through the organization.

★Upledger Institute, 1121 Prosperity Farms Road, Palm Beach Gardens, FL 33410; (800) 233-5880. Educational organization teaching cranial and visceral manipulation, among other related subjects, to health professionals and lay practitioners. These well organized and frequent courses are one of the few avenues for people other than MD's and DO's to gain the clinical skills of cranial manipulation. The organization also offers a referral service to advanced practitioners and runs a Brain and Spinal Cord Foundation for the treatment of severe neurological disorders.

## Visceral Manipulation

### *Books*

Barral, Jean Pierre and Mercer, Pierre. *Visceral Manipulation. Eastland* Press, 1988.

Barral, Jean Pierre. *Visceral Manipulation II.* Eastland Press, 1989.

### *Organizations*

Upledger Institute, 1121 Prosperity Farms Road, Palm Beach Gardens, FL 33410; (800) 233-5880. One of the few organizations that offer course work in this highly specialized field.

## REFERENCES

1.  M. Goldstein, *The Research Status of Spinal Manipulative Therapy,* monograph 15 (National Institute of Neurological and Communicative Disorders and Stroke, 1976).

2.  G. Gilman and J. Bergstrand, "Visual Recovery Following Chiropractic Manipulation," *Journal of Behavioral Optometry* 1:3 (Reprinted in *California Chiropractic Journal* 15:6, June 1990) 22-8.

3.  N. Klougart, N. Nilsson, and J. Jacobsen, "Infantile Colic Treated by Chiropractors: A Prospective Study of 316 Cases," *Journal of Manipulative and Physiological Therapeutics* 12 (1989) 281-8. Also: N. Nilsson, "Infantile Colic and Chiropractic," *European Journal of Chiropractic* 33 (1985) 624-65.

4.  "Industrial Health—Chiropractic Results," *The Chiropractic Report* 1:3 (March 1987) 1.

5.  Andries M. Kleynhans, "Complications of and Contraindications to Spinal Manipulative Therapy," in Haldeman, Scott, *Modern Developments in the Principles and Practice of Chiropractic* (Appleton-Century-Crofts, 1980).

6.  J. Droz and F. Crot, "Occipital Headaches," *Annals of the Swiss Chiropractors' Association* 8 (1985) 127-35.

*The closed mind, if closed long enough,
can be opened by nothing short of dynamite.*

**Gerald Johnson**

# TRADITIONAL ORIENTAL MEDICINE

*In order to contract,*
*It is first necessary to expand.*
*In order to weaken,*
*It is first necessary to strengthen.*
*In order to destroy,*
*It is first necessary to build.*
*In order to grasp,*
*It is first necessary to give.*

Lao Tzu

Traditional Oriental Medicine, also referred to as Traditional Chinese Medicine, is a 5000-year-old, holistic-oriented system of health care. Acupuncture and herbology are the two best known elements of this fairly comprehensive system.

There are other important aspects.

Tai Chi Chuan is a "meditation in movement" exercise system. Dietary counseling according to Oriental principles such as The Five Elements and the Balance of Yin & Yang has been a large part of Oriental medical practice. Most people in the West who are familiar with Oriental dietary guidelines know them as macrobiotics. But macrobiotics, as it has been presented to the West by George Ohsawa and Michio Kushi, is more than a diet. It is a practical philosophy of life that has as one of its predominant elements man's harmonious relationship with nature. Here the connection with food is a vital link. Holistic lifestyle counseling similar to that which is supported by macrobiotic advocates is an integral part of good traditional Oriental medicine. This holistic perspective arises from principles of Confucianism and Taoism, which deal with subjects like relationships, social responsibilities, psychological health, morality, livelihood, and humans blending with natural forces. Joint manipulation and muscular massage have been in use and documented for thousands of years in China.

Preventive health education is even strongly presented in traditional Chinese medicine. It comes in the form of Qigong exercises. Qigong means cultivation of life energy in its many manifestations. Through specific breathing exercises and lifestyle changes, plus vivid visualization practices, one learns to direct life energy for dramatic

transformations of health. Doing certain Qigong exercises to raise and mobilize life energy to heal physical ills has had clinical success. Doing other Qigong exercises to recruit life energy for the purpose of maturing spiritually can produce positive results.

As many suggest, it is wisest to use all the elements of traditional Chinese medicine as an integrated package. Problems can arise by extracting one aspect of the system from its network of synergistic partners. So too are there problems with using traditional Oriental medicine and ignoring modern advances in health care.

As an example, menstrual disorders such as PMS or dysmenorrhea (difficult periods) respond well to acupuncture alone. But that is not the whole picture. Many more women respond faster, better, and more completely when dietary indiscretions are corrected, lumbar spinal joint irritation is eliminated, herbal formulas are used, exercises are performed, and daily stresses are reduced. This would argue against using acupuncture alone and for using a more comprehensive, but still traditional, Oriental approach.

But modern holistic science would argue another way. There are some authorities who prefer electrical instrumentation or cold laser acupuncture over needles. Modern advances in nutritional evaluation and allergy assessment might be more effective for the heterogeneous mix of races in North America than ancient dietary laws developed by trial and error for Asians. Modern chiropractic manipulation and physical therapy procedures would seem to be more effective than the cruder "bonesetter" techniques of primitive China. Tai Chi Chuan provides many benefits as an exercise, not to mention its meditative value. But extensive modern research has provided a vast array of physiological assessments and therapeutic protocols that have the ability to more specifically tailor an exercise regimen to an individual's needs. The same can be said with regards to psychological testing and therapy.

So the question is not, should we use acupuncture outside the framework of its integrated partnership with the rest of traditional Oriental medicine? Nor is it, should we use traditional Oriental medicine *or* modern health enhancement strategies? A better question is, how can we integrate the best aspects of the old and new, East and West?

Part of the answer to that question is that more high-quality research needs to be done on the efficacy of different combinations of comprehensive health care approaches.

> *Being and non-being produce each other.*
> *Difficult and easy complete each other.*
> *Long and short contrast each other.*
> *High and low distinguish each other.*
> *Sound and voice harmonize each other*
> *Front and back follow each other.*
>
> **Lao Tzu**[2]

Different motives draw people to traditional Oriental medicine. People investigate Oriental dietary approaches, Taoism, or Confucianism for different reasons. Most people search these avenues because of a feeling that they need "something." Their life lacks something—wholeness, harmony, or health.

As we said before, using the entire system of holistic-oriented traditional Oriental medicine integrated with more modern advances might be one of the more ideal ways to utilize any of its elements. This is particularly so if we are lucky enough to find not only a practitioner well versed in putting all the components of the traditional approach together effectively, but also one who is open-minded, intelligent, and skilled enough to utilize more modern improvements of the old traditional system.

Depending on our level of wholeness already and what "piece of the puzzle" is being searched for, certain elements "stand alone" very well. For instance, Tai Chi Chuan exercises can benefit almost anyone at any age. As a "moving meditation" practice, it is superb. To enhance coordination it is excellent. To discover a new way of looking at the world from a perspective of harmonious energy flow, it is quite unique and helpful. But if you choose it as your sole way of getting aerobic exercise after a heart attack, you might do better to use other forms of proven exercise rehabilitation with it. The same mistake can be made by thinking that it will provide you with the same degree of flexibility improvements as other more documented approaches to stretching and joint mobility.

Through the use of such techniques as pulse diagnosis, examination of the tongue and eyes, electronic Ryodoraku or Akabane evaluation, otherwise unnoticed or unrecognized problems of disturbed energy flow in the meridians can be detected and corrected before serious problems arise.

But most people seek out acupuncture care once health problems have already arisen, and in many instances only after numerous other treatments have failed. These are some of the more common conditions that acupuncture can significantly help:

| | |
|---|---|
| acne | |
| alcoholism | headaches |
| allergies | high blood pressure |
| arthritis | insomnia |
| autism | Meniere's disease |
| back pain | menstrual disorders |
| bursitis | multiple sclerosis |
| cerebral palsy | obesity |
| depression | Parkinsonism |
| dizziness | schizophrenia |
| drug addiction | seizures |
| eczema | sinusitis |
| dyskinesia | tinnitus |
| extremity pain | |
| extremity numbness or tingling | |
| facial pain | |

Chinese herbs also have good documentation verifying their assistance with a large number of conditions—conditions described in traditional Oriental medicine terms and modern Western diagnoses. It is good to be reminded, though, of the preference for prevention and health enhancement lifestyles over dependence on therapeutic intervention herbally, even though it is preferable to turn to natural, whole plants that have several thousand years of use than the possibly more risky modern day pharmaceuticals.

As a philosophy of life, Taoism and Confucianism have much to offer in this modern age, no matter what religious preference one might have. Taoism, particularly, has a way of bringing us more in harmony with the natural world, our environment, and our relationships with others.

## ORIENTAL MEDICINE RESOURCES

### Self-Care

Self-care opportunities exist within the realm of traditional Oriental medicine, primarily with respect to lifestyle philosophy, macrobiotic style diet, and Tai Chi Chuan exercises. The acupuncture and herbalism elements are so complex they are best left in the hands of physicians specializing in these techniques.

### Philosophy and Diet

The following books should provide a good look at the Oriental philosophy behind the healing practices:

Kaptchuk, Ted. *The Web That Has No Weaver: Understanding Chinese Medicine.* Congdon & Weed, 1983.
Lao Tzu translated by Yu, Anthony C. *The Tao Te Ching: The Classic Book of Integrity and the Way.* Bantam, 1990. One of the best translations of this classic.
Wilhelm, Richard translated by Baynes, Cary. *I Ching— The Book of Changes* Bollingen Foundation, 1950.
Kushi, Michio. *The Book of Macrobiotics: The Universal Way of Health, Happiness, and Peace.* Japan Publications, 1986.

The last book is the best reference for understanding the macrobiotic dietary principles. Add to it the following cookbooks, and better health from this type of regimen can be achieved. It is advisable to modify these dietary principles, good though they may be, with the other nutritional recommendations and resources in this book. For instance, macrobiotic style overuses salt in the recipes and diminishes the use of raw foods. Kushi and his advocates also have an outdated view of nutritional supplementation which must be compensated for.

Kushi, Aveline with Esko, Wendy. *The Changing Seasons Macrobiotic Cookbook.* Avery Publishing, 1984.
Kushi, Aveline with Jack, Alex. *Aveline Kushi's Complete Guide to Macrobiotic Cooking for Health, Harmony, and Peace.* Warner Books, 1985.

### Tai Chi Chuan

*The Tao is like an empty bowl,*
*Which in being used can never be filled up.*
*Fathomless, it seems to be the origin of all things.*
*It blunts all sharp edges,*
*It unties all tangles,*
*It harmonizes all lights,*
*It unites the world into one whole.*
*Hidden in the deeps,*
*Yet it seems to exist forever.*
*I do not know whose child it is.*
*It seems to be a common ancestor of all,*
*The father [and mother] of all things.*

**Lao Tzu[2]**

A good introduction to Tai Chi Chuan is Al Huang's *Embrace Tiger, Return to Mountain*. Excellent video tapes can be a good way to learn and benefit from Tai Chi exercises when quality live group instruction is unavailable. There are many styles to choose from—long or short forms, expansive flowing ones, or conservative. Terry Dunn's *Tai Chi For Health: Yang Long Form* is excellent. Below are listed a few places to find good Tai Chi videos.

RESOURCES

★Wayfarer Publications, P.O. Box 26156, Los Angeles, CA 90026. To order: (800) 888-9119; Fax (213) 665-1627; for information: (213) 665-7773. They offer over 200 books and videos on Tai Chi.

Interarts / Tai Chi For Health, 279 South Beverly Dr., Suite 1037, Beverly Hills, CA 90212; (800) 777-9865.

Wishing Well Distributing: (800) 888-9355.

To find a Tai Chi instructor in your area, consult the telephone yellow pages. Frequently it is listed under martial arts. If none is listed, occasionally a martial arts studio will know of someone giving unadvertised small classes. As in all instruction, there are good teachers and bad. Some admirably convey the Taoist philosophy with the movement training. Others do not. On rare occasions I have seen accomplished karate instructors attempt to teach Tai Chi, only to make the class an extension of their self-defense course instruction rather than a moving meditation. Or their presentation of the movement instruction is flawless, but the harmonious ambience is lacking. Feel comfortable with the philosophy, style, attitude, and instructional skill of the teacher. Introductory or trial classes are good ways to get a good feel for the instructor as well as other students and the location of the classes. In many instances personal or group instruction can be splendidly supplemented by at home video instruction.

## Professional Diagnosis and Treatment

*Even when walking in a party*
*of no more than three*
*I can always be certain of learning*
*from those I am with.*
*There will be good qualities*
*that I can select for imitation*
*and bad ones that will teach me*
*what requires correction in myself.*

**Confucius**

Expect to find a wide range of skill levels in practitioners of traditional Oriental medicine. There are a few top-rated therapists who have had extensive traditional schooling supplemented with training in modern advances. They also practice a holistic approach including the wise integration of herbalism with acupuncture. There is a fairly well populated middle ground consisting primarily of acupuncturists with good reputations but only moderate to minimal integration of other elements of a holistic Oriental approach. There is also a large segment of therapists that have only the minimal skills necessary to gain certification or license in a state. They exist in such large numbers not as a testament to the overall level of skill required to meet the regulatory requirements, but as evidence of the public's lack of confidence in modern medicine, the public's new acceptance of alternatives to medicine and surgery, the salesmanship of the therapists, and the frequency and level of success that acupuncture has, even with minimal levels of knowledge and skill.

Contact the state licensing board for legally practicing therapists in your area. See if they will provide information on disciplinary action or malpractice claims. [Each state has vastly different regulations governing the practice of acupuncture, Oriental medicine and herbalism.]

Questions to ask when choosing a practitioner of Oriental medicine or acupuncture: How extensive was your schooling? Where did you train? Was it six years in China or several weekend seminars? How long have you been in practice? Remember, practice makes perfect.

If a particular condition is of concern, ask about the doctor's results and request that patients who have been successfully treated contact you to discuss their experience. Other points to ask about: For this condition do you generally use needles, laser, or electronic stimulation? You may have a hesitancy about needles. More studies in the future might indicate a preference of one over others. And: Do you use auriculo-therapy or body points or both? Which primarily? Auriculo-therapy is a system using the acupuncture points on the ear alone. A practitioner who uses both is probably preferable in most instances. Exclusive use of auriculo-therapy, though helpful, is probably less desirable.

Ask about fees, estimates of frequency, and duration of care.

## Qigong Practitioners

There is growing interest and research into those Oriental practitioners who have practiced Qigong exercises and have achieved such great mastery in manipulating the forces of life energy that they can perform extraordinary feats of healing. For those who have experienced or even witnessed these special practitioners, diagnosis without physical exam or history, manipulation of joints from across the room, or stimulation of meridian flow just by directing a finger towards the acupuncture point in order to induce a total anesthesia, makes the mind want to rethink what energy medicine is all about. These extraordinary practitioners are few and far between. Don't think that you will find many listed in the yellow pages.

What is more practical is utilizing the principles of Qigong practice for self-care. From the ancient texts on Qigong we know that there are certain lifestyle activities that deplete and disorganize Qi energy: overwork, poor diet, emotional turmoil, and undisciplined use of sexual energy. There are also those activities that generate, organize, and conserve Qi: right diet, specialized breathing, movement exercises like Tai Chi Chuan, meditation, and visualization practices.

The Qigong aspects of traditional Oriental medicine will undoubtedly gain greater acceptance and usage in the future as more research supports its clinical and lifestyle usage. Self health care in its many forms is the wave of the future.

*He who knows others is wise.*
*He who knows his true Self is enlightened.*

**Lao Tzu[2]**

## Qigong Resources

### *Books*

Chang, Stephen. *The Complete System of Self-Healing: Internal Exercises.* Tao Publishing, 1986.

Dong, Paul and Aristide, H. *Chi Kung: The Ancient Chinese Way to Health.* Paragon House, 1990.

Jahnke, Roger. *The Self-Applied Health Enhancement Methods.* Health Action Books, 1989.

Takahashi, Masaru. *Qigong for Health: Chinese Traditional Exercise for Cure and Prevention.* Japan Publications, 1986.

### *Periodicals*

*Qi: The Journal of Traditional Eastern Health and Fitness,* P.O. Box 221343, Chantilly, VA 22022; (800) 787-2600; (703) 378-3859; Fax (703) 378-0663.

### *Organizations*

The Healing Tao Center, P.O. Box 1194, Huntington, NY 11743; (516) 367-2701. Teaches classes throughout the world and also provides instructional videotapes.

Qigong Institute, East-West Academy of the Healing Arts, 450 Sutter St., Suite 2104, San Francisco, CA 94108; (415) 788-2227; Fax (415) 788-2242.

## Herbs

*Man masters nature not by force*
*but by understanding.*

**Jacob Bronowski**

Herbs have a limited but significant role in assisting the body's efforts to recover a normal state. Herbs can be helpful to a comprehensive, natural, recovery. Botanical medicines are most useful as a safe alternative to powerful, toxic pharmaceuticals. They also have a place in preventive health enhancement.

Prescription and nonprescription drugs usually have a narrow margin of safety between the dosage that will give a positive effect and that which will give an adverse effect. Herbs are safer in this respect for several reasons:

Particularly with regard to the use of Chinese herbs, there have been several thousand years of experience in prescribing them safely. Most pharmaceuticals used today have only a forty-year track record, and that record is not good.

In herbs, not only are the active ingredients of a low dosage, but they are synergistically linked to other buffering and assisting biochemicals which make interaction with human biochemical processes easier, safer, and more effective. Though drugs are often derived from plants, active ingredients are artificially isolated and extracted or synthesized, leaving them no natural buffers—so they act much more aggressively, particularly at the high dosages prescribed.

Finding a qualified physician who can integrate the prescription of herbs into a comprehensive health enhancement program, rather than use these plant substances as just another "magic bullet" cure of symptoms, may be a difficult matter. Do-it-yourself herbology is more complex than one may think, and most people using this methodology are again not using a comprehensive approach where herbs play only a small, isolated role to temporarily improve body physiology until other aspects of health building can take over.

Some of the wisest physicians who use herbs are traditional acupuncturists, particularly the ones who studied for six or more years overseas in traditional colleges of Oriental medicine. Modern day naturopaths are probably next in line for having the most training in the use of botanicals. Also, they have been exposed to not only the old Chinese texts on herbology but newer research. They are sometimes more holistic in their orientation, with broader knowledge, than the old-time acupuncturists who are unexposed to more modern approaches. Traditional acupuncturists usually get their herbs from wholesalers of imported Chinese herbs. Naturopaths have access to these suppliers but tend to also utilize the modern North American suppliers who provide them with updated research on better clinical usage.

A certain number of chiropractors compare with naturopaths and Oriental physicians in their qualifications, experience, and utilization of herbs. Again, one would hope that these chiropractors, as with the naturopaths and acupuncturists, would be comprehensive in their approach to health—not just using an herb as a "quick fix" cure of symptoms. A few M.D.'s and D.O.'s are also skilled in the use of herbs, but finding these practitioners is more difficult because of their low numbers.

We should be very wary of self-proclaimed herbalists, "certified nutritionists," or health food store personnel when seeking advice about bringing herbs into our health improvement program. Ninety-nine percent of these individuals are well-

intentioned and truly want to help. Often their recommendations can be somewhat helpful. They will all cite instances of other people they have helped with similar symptoms. And herbs are effective and relatively safe at altering body physiology. Here are the problems:

Most of the so-called nutritionists and herbalists received their degrees from mail order diploma mills. Or, after reading a few popular books and some promotional literature from some herb wholesalers, they proclaim themselves as "Master Herbalists" or "Certified Nutritionists" and start a "practice." If one of these herbalists wants to charge a person money for consulting about herbal approaches to health, or sell these herbs to people trying to get well, he has a responsibility to be truthful to his clients about his qualifications. How many years did it take to graduate from herbal college? Was it a correspondence course? Was there an extensive internship where many clients were treated under the supervision of qualified, experienced clinicians? Where is the scientific research validating the use of these herbs in my condition?

Unlicensed nutritionists, herbalists, or health food store personnel usually make their sole income, or most of it, from the sale of their products. They have a vested economic interest in persuading clients to purchase their products. This is a risky conflict of interest. If their argument is more "sales pitch" than presentation of convincing research data, beware. Physicians also sometimes sell what they prescribe and can fall prey to overprescribing for personal economic benefit. But the income gained by the sale of these products is not their only or predominant source of income; they have less of an imperative to push an item unnecessarily. Ideally, if you can find a physician who charges you for his interpretation of tests and consulting wisdom, then prescribes the needed herbal formulas for you to purchase at a place where there is no economic conflict of interest, you have the best solution.

*Heaven lasts long, and Earth abides.*
*What is the secret of their durability?*
*Is it not because they do not live for themselves*
*That they can live so long?*

**Lao Tzu**[1]

## PROFESSIONAL RESOURCES

★Denotes Best of the Best Resources

Finding an Oriental physician, acupuncturist, or herbalist who uses the resources below is at least assurance that he is exposed to reliable health information.

### Books

Bensky, Dan. *Chinese Herbal Medicine: Materia Medica.* Eastland Press, 1986.

Hoffmann, David. *Therapeutic Herbalism.* Viriditis, 1991.

Hoffmann, David. *The New Holistic Herbal.* Element Books, 1992.

Holmes, Peter. *The Energetics of Western Herbs: Integrating Western and Oriental Herbal Medicine Traditions.* 2 volumes Nat Trop Pub, 1990.

★O'Conner, John and Bensky, Daniel. *Acupuncture: A Comprehensive Text.* From the Shanghai College of Traditional Medicine, Eastland Press, 1981.

Oleson, Terry. *Auriculo-therapy Manual; Chinese and Western Systems of Ear Acupuncture.* 1990. Available from Health Care Alternatives, 8033 Sunset Blvd., Suite 2657, Los Angeles, CA 90046; (213) 656-2084.

Wang Deshen, *China Zhenjiuology,* A 15 part video series plus text from David and Davidson, Inc., 42-46 Kissena Blvd., #1A, Flushing, NY 11355-3213; (718) 359-7788 or 886-4431.

Wensel, Louise. *Acupuncture in Medical Practice.* Reston, 1980.

★Werbach, Melvyn and Murray, Michael. *Botanical Influences on Illness.* Third Line Press, 1994. Good research-supported use of botanical medicine.

### Journals and Newsletters

*American Journal of Acupuncture,* Box 610, Capitola, CA 95010-2513; (408) 475-1700; (408) 475-1439.

*American Journal of Chinese Medicine,* Institute for Advanced Research in Asian Science and Medicine, Box 124, 450 Clarkson Ave., Brooklyn, NY 11203; (718) 270-1629.

*Canadian Journal of Herbalism,* 181 Brookdale Ave., Toronto, Ontario, Canada M5M 1P4.

*HerbalGram,* American Botanical Council, P.O. Box 201660, Austin, TX 78720; (800) 373-7105; (512) 331-8868; Fax (512) 331-1924. One of the best herbal periodicals.

*Journal of Traditional Acupuncture,* Traditional Acupuncture Institute, American City Bldg. 100, Columbia, MD 20144; (301) 997-4888.

*Phytomedicine: International Journal of Phytotherapy and Phytopharmacology,* VCH Publishers, 303 NW 12th Ave., Deerfield Beach, FL 33442-1705.

*Planta Medica: Journal of Medicinal Plant Research,* Georg Thieme Verlag, Stuttgart & New York.

*Protocol Journal of Botanical Medicines*—(800) 852-6271. Peer-reviewed research publication on the therapeutic use of herbs.

*Quarterly Review of Natural Medicine,* Natural Product Research Consultants, 600 First Ave., Suite 205, Seattle, WA 98104; (206) 623-2520; Fax (206) 623-6340.

### Computer Software

*Globalherb,* Steve Blake, 5831 S. Highway 9, Felton, CA 95018; (408) 335-9011. Therapeutic herbal prescriptive assistance with extensive cross referencing for innumerable facts about 700+ herbs.

### Organizations

Acupuncture Society of America, 4140 Broadway, Kansas City, MO 64111; (816) 931-0287. Attempts to integrate oriental approaches with western advancements.

American Association of Acupuncture and Oriental Medicine, National Acupuncture Headquarters, Suite 601, 1424 18th Street, Washington, DC 20036; (202) 265-2287.

American Botanical Council, P.O. Box 201660, Austin, TX 78720; (800) 373-7105; (512) 331-8868; Fax (512) 331-1924. Nonprofit education and research organization that can provide accurate credible information on the healing qualities of herbs. It publishes a quarterly journal, *HerbalGram,* and operates an "HerbLine": (900) 226-4545.

American Foundation of Traditional Chinese Medicine, 505 Beach St., San Francisco, CA 94133; (415) 776-0502; Fax (415) 776-9053.

American Herbal Products Association, P.O. Box 2410, Austin, TX 78768; (512) 320-8555. This organization can provide a list of reputable herb suppliers.

American Herbalist Guild, P.O. Box 1683, Soquel, CA 95073; (408) 464-2441. They can provide information concerning herbal practitioners and educational programs.

Herb Research Foundation, 1007 Pearl St., Suite 200, Boulder, CO 80302; (800) 748-2617; (303) 449-2265; Fax (303) 449-7849. Closely associated with the American Botanical Council.

RESOURCES

National Accreditation Commission for Schools and Colleges of Acupuncture and Oriental Medicine, 1424 16th St. NW, Suite 501, Washington, DC 20036; (202) 265-3370.

*Thirty spokes converge upon a single hub.*
*It is on the hole in the center*
*that the use of the cart hinges.*
*We make a vessel from a lump of clay;*
*It is the empty space within the vessel*
*that makes it useful.*
*We make doors and windows for a room;*
*But it is these empty spaces*
*that make the room livable.*
*Thus, while the tangible has advantages,*
*It is the intangible that makes it useful.*

**Lao Tzu[1]**

## Acupuncture Suppliers

Boston Chinese Medicine, P.O. Box 5747, Boston, MA 02114; (617) 720-4448.

OMS—Oriental Medical Supplies, 1950 Washington St., Braintree, MA 02184; (800) 323-1839; (617) 331-3370; Fax (617) 335-5779.

## Herbal Suppliers

Abundant Life Seed Association, P.O. Box 772, Port Townsend, WA 98368; (206) 385-5660.

Arkopharma, Advanced Medical Nutrition, Inc., P.O. Box 5012 Hayward, CA 94540; (800) 437-8888.

Bio-Therapeutics Phyto-Pharmica, P.O. Box 1348, Green Bay, WI 54305; (800) 553-2370. Modern herbal formulas.

Blessed Herbs, 109 Barre Plains Rd., Oakham, MA 01068; (800) 489-4372; (508) 882-3839; Fax (508) 882-3755.

Eclectic Institute, 14385 SE Lusted Road, Sandy OR 97055; (800) 332-4372; (503) 668-4120; Fax (503) 668-3227. Large herbal supplier that also carries excellent textbooks on therapeutic herbalism.

Frontier Cooperative Herbs, Box 299, Norway, IA 52318; (800) 669-3275.

Herbal Education Center, 6 Crescent Rd., Burlington, VT 05401.

Herb Pharm, P.O. Box 116, Williams, OR 97544; (800) 348-4372; (503) 846-6262; Fax (503) 846-6112.

Herbs ETC., 1340 Rufina Circle, Santa Fe, NM 87501; (800) 634-3727.

Health Center for Better Living, 6189 Taylor Rd. Naples, FL 33942-1823; (813) 566-2611.

Murdock Pharmaceuticals, 1400 Mountain Springs Park, Springerville, UT 84663; (800) 962-8873.

Nature's Herbs, 600 East Quality Dr., American Fork, Utah 84003; (800) 437-2257; (801) 763-0700; Fax (801) 763-0789.

Nature's Way, (800) 234-4408.

Nu-Pro, P.O. Box 1405, Provo, UT 84601; (800) 453-1468.

Planetary Formulas, P.O. Box 533, Soquel, CA 95073; (800) 777-5677.

Traditional Chinese Botanicals, Metagenics, 971 Calle Negocio, San Clemente, CA 92672; (800) 692-9400.

## REFERENCES

1. Lao Tzu, *Tao Te Ching,* Translated by John C.H. Wu and edited by Paul K.T. Sih (New York: St. Johns University Press, New York, 1961).
2. Adapted from: *Tao Te Ching.*

*We can do no great things—only small things with great love.*

**Mother Teresa**

# BIOFEEDBACK

### *Know Thyself*

The human nervous system is the most complex communication system known to exist in the universe. It has more interconnections (synapses) than stars in the sky. It regulates, controls, and coordinates the moment-by-moment flux of thousands of chemicals in the body, organ functions, all our movements, our perceptions of the world, our intellect, thoughts, emotions, learning, interpersonal communication, and links us spiritually to the cosmos. Most of this activity happens unconsciously and automatically without our knowledge or effort. As with any complex communication system, signals can get confused, messages will go awry. In the human nervous system patterns of nerve transmission, if repeated often, become ingrained and habituated—even if they are not adaptive or healthy.

If we are frequently under stress, being excessively vigilant, constantly tensing more than necessary in a "fight or flight" type of response, our bodies and mind get used to this out-of-balance operation. In the animal world a fight or flight response to a dangerous situation had survival value. Stressful circumstances for humans today produce the same ancient brain and body responses, but they can have serious adverse results. Biochemical imbalances and high levels of stress become habitual. Patterns of behavior and emotional responses get inefficiently programmed. Spiritual development is shackled. The effects accumulate over time, and the body eventually treats them as normal.

It is then important to be able to monitor this nerve activity and its consequences. If there are abnormal patterns or unhealthy programs, they can be changed. The human nervous system is highly responsive to a change in programs. All that is needed is to recognize the old, unhealthy pattern, adopt a method for monitoring it, and bring it to one's awareness as it is happening. Then get the nervous system to relearn what "healthy" is.

Biofeedback, as defined in Mark Schwartz's *Biofeedback: A Practitioner's Guide,* is:

. . . (1) a group of therapeutic procedures that (2) utilizes electronic or electromechanical instruments (3) to accurately measure, process, and 'feed back' to persons (4) information with reinforcing properties (5) about their neuromuscular and autonomic activity, both normal and abnormal, (6) in the form of analog or binary, auditory and/or visual feedback signals. (7) Best achieved with a competent biofeedback professional, (8) the objectives are to help persons develop greater awareness and voluntary control over their physiological processes that are otherwise outside awareness and/or under less voluntary control, (9) by first controlling the external signal, (10) and then by the use of internal psychophysiological cues.

There is a growing number of instruments and physiological processes that can be monitored for biofeedback applications. Some of the more common applications are:

- electromyographic (EMG) instruments that monitor muscle tone, tension, and electrical activity
- skin temperature as an indicator of peripheral blood flow
- sweat gland activity as an assessment of autonomic nervous system function
- electroencephalographs (EEG) to measure brain wave function
- blood pressure
- heart rate and rhythm
- electrogastrography (EGG) to control stomach functions
- respiration rate, rhythm, and volume
- moisture sensors to alert bladder incontinence
- strain gauges to monitor penile erections
- and mechanisms to help control eye movements.

Instrumentation is not always needed. One of the most effective psychotherapeutic approaches,

Gendlin's "Focusing," is basically a matter of tuning into bodily signals for feedback about psychological states. "When angry I clench my jaws and fists." "When I am anxious my stomach gets fluttery and queasy." Research has found that feeling emotions clearly in the body is one of the best signs that psychotherapy will have a beneficial outcome.

Clinical biofeedback is used successfully to treat the following problems:

- anxiety
- mild depression
- epilepsy
- headaches
- poor concentration in education and meditation
- poor control of brain waves in spiritual development, achieving inner tranquility, or problems establishing dream control in psychotherapy
- musculoskeletal disorders involving chronic muscle tension
- failure in relaxation therapies
- unsuccessful stress management techniques
- awkward neuromuscular re-education of gait mechanics
- chronic pain syndromes
- high blood pressure
- asthma
- circulatory problems such as Raynaud's Disease
- temporomandibular joint (TMJ) syndrome, jaw pain, and dysfunction
- bruxism (teeth grinding, often at night)
- urinary incontinence (bedwetting, nocturnal enuresis, leaky bladder)
- fecal incontinence
- Attention Deficit Disorders.

If one or more areas on the above list is of prime concern, biofeedback might be one of the better approaches to healing. Again it is important to be reminded that, like any modality, it works best when integrated with other health care approaches.

## FINDING A QUALIFIED BIOFEEDBACK SPECIALIST

Whereas biofeedback processes can be self-administered, as with Focusing and self-scored learning programs, clinical biofeedback with instrumentation is reasonable only with assessment and instruction from a trained professional, at least initially. Then, when training programs are finished, there are usually many at-home, self learning skills to practice and improve on.

Many different specialists in the health care professions use biofeedback—clinical psychologists, neurologists, chiropractors, preventive medical specialists, urologists, and nurses. Contacting the specialty that seems most relevant to your needs, then inquiring about the clinician's use of biofeedback for that problem, is one approach. The other is to look in the yellow pages under "Biofeedback" to see if any of the relevant specialties are listed there. If there are just general listings for biofeedback services, it is then necessary to call and inquire if they accept clients with your requests. Most professionals working in the biofeedback field have only limited equipment, and their experience and inclinations drive them to address only specific types of conditions. With them or any other biofeedback trainer, it is good to use the guidelines for choosing a biofeedback therapist that Mark Schwartz details in his book *Biofeedback: A Practitioner's Guide* in the chapter on ". . . Assuring Competence."

Included in your inquiries should be: How many years experience have you had helping people with concerns like mine? What success rates do you get in similar conditions? Could some of your past clients with the same problem call and discuss their experience with me? Are you certified with the Biofeedback Certification Institute of America? Are you a member of any of the state or national biofeedback professional organizations? Do you attend their continuing educational programs frequently? Do you follow the *Application Standards and Guidelines for Providers of Biofeedback Services?* What are your fees? Do you work with other health professionals on integrative treatment plans for situations like mine?

## SUMMARY

Biofeedback methods in their many forms can provide numerous avenues for health enhancement—from neurological training in serious disease or injury conditions to enrichment of spiritual meditative disciplines. Biofeedback can help us to not only reduce or eliminate medications and surgery, alleviate suffering, provide insight into our inner workings, and give us more control of our lives, but to also help us towards wholeness in ways still unexplored.

---

## BIOFEEDBACK RESOURCES

★Denotes Best of the Best Resources

### Books

★ Gendin, Eugene. *Focusing.* Bantam, 1981.
Green, Alyce and Green Elmer. *Beyond Biofeedback.* Knoll Publishing, 1989.
★ Kabat-Zinn, Jon. *Full Catastrophe Living: Using the Wisdom of Your Body and Mind to Face Stress, Pain, and Illness.* Dell, 1990.
Pelletier, Ken. *Mind as Healer, Mind as Slayer.* Dell, 1977.

### Video

*Relax,* Capstone Media, San Anselmo, CA.

---

## PROFESSIONAL RESOURCES

### Books

Criswell, E. *Biofeedback and Somatics.* Freeperson Press, 1995.
Peper, E., Ancoli, S., and Quinn, M. *Mind/Body Integration: Essential Readings in Biofeedback.* Plenum.
Schwartz, Mark. *Biofeedback: A Practitioner's Guide.* Guilford Press, 1987.

### Periodicals

*American Journal of Clinical Biofeedback,* American Association of Biofeedback Clinicians, Plenum Publishing, 233 Spring St., New York, NY 10013-1522; (212) 620-8000.
*Biofeedback,* Association for Applied Psychophysiology and Biofeedback, 10200 West 44th Ave., Suite 304, Wheat Ridge, CO 80033; (303) 422-8436; (800) 477-8892; Fax (303) 422-8894.

*Biofeedback and Self Regulation,* Association for Applied Psychophysiology and Biofeedback, 10200 West 44th Ave., Suite 304, Wheat Ridge, CO 80033; (303) 422-8436; (800) 477-8892; Fax (303) 422-8894.
*Psychophysiology,* Society for Psychophysiological Research, 2101 Winchester Dr., Champaign, IL 61821-6311; (217) 398-6969.
*Psychosomatic Medicine,* Williams & Wilkins, 428 Preston St., Baltimore, MD 21202; (410) 528-4000; (800) 527-5597; (800) 638-6423.

### Organizations

Association for Applied Psychophysiology and Biofeedback, 10200 West 44th Ave., Suite 304, Wheat Ridge, CO 80033; (303) 422-8436; (800) 477-8892; Fax (303) 422-8894. Publishes the professional journal, *Biofeedback and Self Regulation,* professional guidelines, *Application Standards and Guidelines for Providers of Biofeedback Services,* and the quarterly newsmagazine, *Biofeedback.* It also sponsors the largest annual symposia on clinical biofeedback.
Association for the Advancement of Behavior Therapy, 15 W. 36th St., New York, NY 10018; (212) 279-7970.
Biofeedback Certification Institute of America, 10200 West 44th Ave., Suite 304, Wheatridge, CO 80033; (303) 420-2902; Fax (303) 422-8894. Publishes *Blueprint Tasks and Knowledge Statements* which outlines basics needed by practitioners and prepares them for certification exams.
Biofeedback Training and Research Institute, 331 East Cotati Ave., Cotati, CA 94931; (707) 795-2460. The director, Stephen Wall, M.A., developed an advanced, computerized biofeedback instrument called the Biointegrator. His monograph, *Biointegration: A Developmental Approach to Biofeedback Training,* details his innovative holistic perspective on how biofeedback can transform people's lives.

Institute for the Study of Human Knowledge, P.O. Box 381062, Boston, MA 02238-1062; (800) 222-4745. Publishes *Mental Medicine Update.*

National Institute for the Clinical Application of Behavioral Medicine, P.O. Box 577, 6 King Road, Storrs, CT 06268; (203) 429-7949.

Society of Behavioral Medicine, 103 S. Adams St., Rockville, MD 20850; (301) 251-2790. Publishes *Annals of Behavioral Medicine,* and *Behavioral Medicine Abstracts* which abstracts 200 scientific articles per quarter.

Stens Corporation, 6451 Oakwood Dr., Oakland, CA 94611; (800) 257-8367. This company carries the widest selection of biofeedback instrumentation and professional educational materials. They sponsor excellent biofeedback training programs for health care professionals and researchers.

*Make the best use of what is in your own power, and take the rest as it happens.*

**Epictetus**

# BIOLOGICAL RHYTHMS, LIGHT, AND SLEEP

*In the morn of life we are alert, we are heated in its noon,*
*and only in its decline do we repose.*

**Walter Savage Landor**

Driven by millions of years of evolutionary adaptation to the diurnal light and dark rhythms of the planet, our daily biological cycles are quite ingrained. Such well established, efficient body functions do not readily tolerate our modern day tampering.

The sun rises in the east. Our bodies stir from sleep. Not only from the increase in light penetrating our eyelids, but also because the body was already preparing to meet the sun. It has been conditioned for eons to know when the sun will rise today, whether cloudy or clear. The body prepares by making innumerable biochemical and neurological changes. Body temperature begins to rise from an early morning low. This comes from a complex neurohormonal interaction in the hypothalamus of the brain. The body needs these higher temperatures for more efficient enzymatic and biochemical operation during the day. Blood sugar also begins to elevate in order to provide for the increase in energy needs. Hormones fluctuate in concentration and activity. Fluid balance is altered. Both red and white blood cell counts change. The reticular activating system of the brain, the awareness control center, begins to let more sensory impulses into our awareness. Sometimes it does so slowly, with the pleasant remembrance and review of an early morning dream, and sometimes it is forced to activate more quickly by the gear-grinding noise of the alarm clock—BBBRRR-IIINNNNGGG.

As the morning comes into full swing, many things alter our physiological workings. The wavelength, intensity, position, and movement of light, whether natural or artificial, affect our internal, neurochemical fluctuations. What we are doing, and how intensely we do it, contributes to these internal regulatory mechanisms. The nutritional or non-nutritional substances we take in help determine how our biochemicals will be able to respond to the ancient imperatives of "standard morning operating procedures." Substances like caffeine severely and adversely alter our normal biological rhythms.

The afternoon intensity and position of the sun, coupled with our activities, stresses, dietary intake, and evolutionarily conditioned biorhythms, continue to change our internal neuro-biochemical workings. Sunlight and our ancestral programming drive our bodies to natural, healthy functioning. Our daily activities and lifestyle choices can either assist this healthy, pre-programmed operation, or foul it up.

The same is true as the sun sets in the west and our bodies start to wind down. The more we listen to our bodies and the rhythms of the natural world and attune ourselves to those healthy rhythms, the better we will function. Just as the body is driven into activity during the day by the sun and eons of biological conditioning, it is programmed into quiescence at dusk.

We so often tamper with these natural rhythms:

- of light and dark
- artificial light instead of sunlight
- rhythms of activity and sleep
- artificial stimulants to stay awake when our bodies' natural sense is to rest
- sedatives to confuse the nervous system to calm down when something else is driving it to vigilance

Ill health will inevitably ensue.

Some of these disturbances to normal biological rhythms are temporary, transient conditions like jet lag or one night of no sleep. The effects might be disruption of normal physiological functioning for a few days to a week before we recover fully. But many people suffer from multiple, daily, repetitive, cumulative assaults on healthy biorhythms. Everyone knows a classic example. The person who would sleep till noon if they could because of excesses the night before but instead is awakened at 6:00 a.m. after finally hearing 10 minutes worth

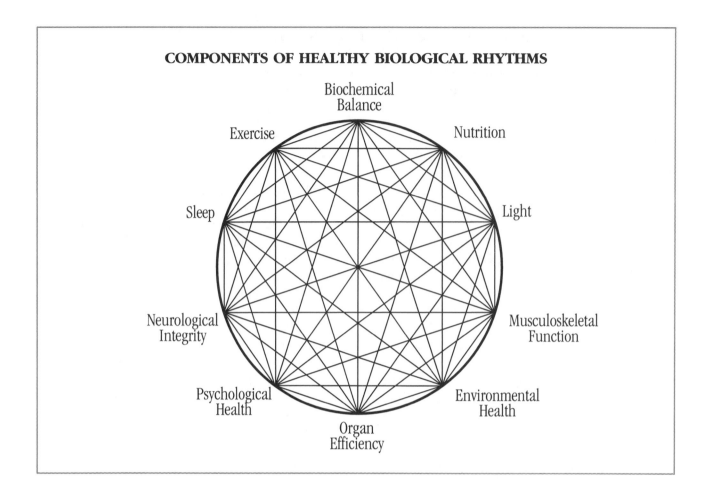

**COMPONENTS OF HEALTHY BIOLOGICAL RHYTHMS**

of ear-shattering alarm clock noise. The person is a vegetable until he can slug down several cups of caffeine with a sugary donut. Within a short period of time this substandard nutrition, virtually a biochemical fix, becomes sufficient to counteract the sleeping pills taken the night before and results in a rocketlike propulsion of activity. This activity swings up and down dramatically throughout the day, pushed and pulled by erratic blood sugar levels from poor dietary habits and content. Erratic emotions and hectic lifestyle demands further disrupt normal physiological functioning and the regularity of biological rhythms. Day-in, day-out, year-in and year-out, the effects accumulate, and with them comes an endless stream of symptoms, poor health, and lost human potential.

There are some rules of thumb for sustaining healthy biological rhythms. Some primary interrelationships are represented in the "Components of Healthy Biological Rhythms" chart.

To highlight some of the more significant and relevant elements that can be altered to improve biological rhythms, we will look at light, sleep, toxins, allergens, exercise, nutrition, psychological stressors, and their interrelations.

## ACTIVE BY DAY, RESTFUL BY NIGHT

First, we must respect the inborn cycles that all life on earth is controlled by—light and dark, day and night. Sometimes we humans think we are not bound by the same natural laws that affect all other life on the planet. This arrogance or lack of awareness proves to be very self-destructive. We should be active during the day. And this means *active*. Sedentary lifestyles are replete with problems of health, some of which are related to biological rhythms. High physical activity should be an element of most of the days of our lives. The proper amount of aerobic exercise tends to normalize energy levels so that we are not fatigued during the day but can rest well at night. Flexibility exercises tend to alleviate muscle tension and joint discomfort, which then allows for less internal irritation while trying to sleep, and reduces abnormal nerve signaling which could disturb proper organ function.

Altered musculoskeletal function and neurological irritation can disrupt biological rhythms by disturbing sleep and normal physiological function. If this factor is particularly bothersome, special efforts might be needed to make the individual more comfortable at night. This might include special pillow support for neck problems. Changing mattress firmness to something comfortable also helps. (Some people will do better with firm mattresses, others with softer ones. Waterbeds can be altered in firmness and seem to provide good support for many people.) Frequently, manipulative therapy improves restful sleep. When chronic muscle tension is ingrained, biofeedback can relax it at night as well as during the day. Psychotherapy may be needed if the underlying causes of muscle tension are in fact psychological.

*Sleep that knits up the ravelled sleeve of care,*
*The death of each day's life, sore labour's bath,*
*Balm of hurt minds,*
*great nature's second course,*
*Chief nourisher in life's feast.*
**Shakespeare**

We should sleep at night. Adults for eight hours. Less than ten per cent of adults can truly function healthfully on less than eight hours sleep every day. That also means that if you get five hours sleep one day of the week, sooner or later you will have to catch up on this sleep or else adverse health effects are likely, whether they are noticed or hidden. Teenagers need at least nine and one half hours of daily sleep.

It is natural for infants to sleep about 17 hours per day in two to four hour segments. From one year of age to the teen years, hours of sleep decrease from 14 to 10, and these hours congregate more at night with just short daytime nap periods. Anything that disturbs these patterns disturbs health.

There is a supreme absurdity in taking artificial stimulants to keep you up at night when your natural body rhythms are encouraging you to rest.

*There is more to life than increasing its speed.*
**Mahatma Gandhi**

Avoid night jobs. The economic benefits are seldom worth the adverse effect on one's health. Swing shifts are the worst. Even temporary nighttime wakefulness, like pulling "all-nighters" for school, has considerable disadvantages. Ability to concentrate, attention spans, thinking accuracy, are all adversely affected. Not to mention poor coordination leading to accidents, depressed immunity leading to infections, heightened emotional irritability leading to decreased performance in any endeavor.

*There are 500,000 motor vehicle accidents*
*with 8,000-10,000 deaths in the U.S. per year*
*caused by sleep deprivation.*

Sleep deprivation and biological rhythm disturbance can so adversely affect intellectual performance that it is infinitely wiser to plan a study schedule that respects biological laws. We should also mention silence as an aid to sleep. Any excessive noise, when the nervous system is already excessively irritable, has a greater chance of disturbing sleep. Providing a bedroom that is insulated from external background noise is usually helpful in sleeping more soundly. This can be more than a minor problem for those light sleepers who have partners who snore.

Overall, we seldom recognize that sleep is a major component of our total well-being.

*There cannot be a crisis next week.*
*My schedule is already full.*
**Henry Kissinger**

## LET THERE BE LIGHT

Closely linked with sleep is the influence of light on biological rhythms, biochemical balance, neurological integrity, and psychological functioning. Light enters the eye and strikes the retina. This structure in the back of the eye changes the light energy to nerve signals that differ in intensity and wave length. Most of these signals go via the optic nerve to the visual cortex in the back of the brain for interpretation and association with other sensory inputs and motor responses. A small portion of these signals is diverted before entering the visual cortex. It goes by another "energetic portion" of the optic nerve to the pineal and pituitary glands in the middle of the brain. Here the light-initiated nerve signals influence a wide array of neurohormonal functions throughout the body, in no small part because the pituitary gland is the "master gland" of the body and regulates many of the body's hormonal functions. Differences in the quantity, intensity, and wavelength of light create variances of neuro-biochemical responses throughout the entire body as mediated by this pineal-pituitary-hypothalamus nerve and hormone mechanism.

By doing research on biochemical and health differences between sighted individuals and the blind, and on people who lost sight with cataracts and then had their vision restored with surgery, we have discovered much about the potential impact that light has on biochemical balance, organ efficiency, neurological integrity, and even musculoskeletal function. A few examples: Blind individuals have a significantly more difficult time regulating internal body temperature than the sighted do because of light's effect on the hypothalamus—which modulates much of the body's temperature control. Degree of blindness has also been correlated to degrees of developmental skeletal deformities in part due to disturbed mineral balance. Electrolyte balance has been directly correlated to the quantity of light entering the eyes. This is mediated through the renin-angiotensin-aldosterone hormone system of the pituitary, kidney, and adrenals. Quantity and wavelength of light also have been shown to help the daily balance of red and white blood cell count, blood sugar levels, menstrual cycles, kidney clearance abilities, liver detoxification capacity, antibody levels, and so on. Much more documentation can be found in the resources for this section.

Since this light-nerve-hormone system formed over millions of years of evolutionary development, it responds best to natural sunlight. In fact, certain types of artificial light sources, because of differences in wavelength, intensity, movement, and position, cause a disruption of these nerve and hormone networks. It is therefore imperative to expose the eyes to large quantities of natural sunlight with minimal interference from wavelength altering filters or screens like those found in sunglasses, even regular glasses or windows, particularly tinted ones.

*If the doors of perception were cleansed, man would see things as they are, infinite.*

**William Blake**

Here are some rules of thumb to use to provide better health from light.

I. Avoid artificial light
  A. Use "full-spectrum" lighting fixtures instead of normal incandescent or fluorescent bulbs at home and work.
  B. Minimize watching television.
  C. Minimize use of computer monitors or get high quality screens and filters to eliminate hazardous electromagnetic radiations.

II. Expose eyes to more natural sunlight.
  A. Spend more time outdoors.
    1. When sunglasses are needed, be sure they block 95% or more of the UV rays, but minimize use of sunglasses as much as possible.
    2. Wear sunglasses at high altitudes and whenever there is significant snow or water glare in order to protect the eyes from the ill effects of intense UV rays.
    3. Use sunglasses if glare while driving impairs safety.
    4. Use contacts instead of glasses if possible. They distort light wavelength less.
    5. Cataract prone individuals, or people with cataracts or eye diseases such as macular degeneration or retinitis, have to be more careful about exposure to UV radiation but get sufficient sunlight.

## LIGHT DEFICIT DISORDERS

*We must be as courteous to a man*
*as we are to a picture,*
*which we are willing to give the advantage*
*of a good light.*

**Ralph Waldo Emerson**

Insufficient ocular exposure to light has been found to contribute to a number of disorders including: Seasonal Affective Disorder (SAD), also known as "winter blues," nonseasonal depression, other mood disorders, sleeping disorders like insomnia and delayed sleep phase syndrome, visual disturbances like too much sensitivity to light, and poor night vision, fatigue syndromes, fear and anxiety disorders, child and adult hyperactivity, attention deficit disorders and learning disabilities. Some of these problems are due to insufficient exposure to natural sunlight; some are due to excessive artificial lighting exposure. Some may be due to a newly theorized mechanism of abnormal nerve inhibition.

In this mechanism, if an individual experiences physical injury (particularly head or spinal column trauma to the nervous system), emotional trauma, accumulative effects of everyday stress, or even prolonged exposure to indoor lighting, the nervous system's defenses against pain or stress will often overreact by greatly inhibiting the flow of nerve impulses throughout the brain and peripheral nerves. This stops millions of sensory and motor nerve impulses that are needed by the body. Many times the brain, after the crisis is over, will somehow forget to reset the normal flow. Sometimes this incoordination involves the energetic portion of the optic nerve. When that happens, it can accentuate the health problems associated with circadian rhythm dysfunction. Even in instances where an individual is exposed to large amounts of sunlight, this neurological inhibition may be so great that insufficient stimulation of the pineal and pituitary glands still poses problems.

For problems such as Seasonal Affective Disorder, where the new treatment of choice involves exposure of the eyes to large banks of full-spectrum light for several minutes or hours every day in the winter months, correcting significant nerve inhibition improves the benefits. In many cases correction of the nerve inhibition eliminates the necessity for year-in-year-out, full-spectrum light therapy.

Neurosensory Development Training developed by an optometrist, John Downing, seems to be an effective correction for this inhibition of the energetic portion of the optic nerve. It involves viewing certain wavelengths of light flashed in the eyes for a duration and frequency sufficient to restore normal nerve transmission. Preliminary data suggests that it could be a viable, natural health enhancement protocol for many of the light deficit disorders previously mentioned—and then some. Another advantage is that there are some preliminary testing protocols which can measure the amount of photocurrent which the brain can process. This can then find hidden problems and tell who might most benefit from this form of neurological retraining. It can also provide follow-up comparison exams to check on a client's progress. Refer to the resource section for more information on this subject.

In natural light we can easily see the interconnections between the transpersonal elements of health. Sunlight from millions of miles away gives life to our planet. It provides food for the nourishment of body, mind, and spirit. It allows us to see and interact joyously with all around us. It stimulates our nervous system to more efficiently regulate functions of both the body and the mind.

*How do I know about the world? Inward light!*

**Lao Tzu**

## PSYCHOLOGICAL DISTURBANCES TO BODY RHYTHMS AND SLEEP

Psychological stresses can disrupt biological rhythms in a number of ways.

Unresolved psychological conflict being mulled over when trying to fall asleep is a prime cause of insomnia. The subject of the conflict can be anything sufficient to energize enough neurological irritation to engage the reticular activating system to maintain vigilance and wakefulness. Old psychological scars coming to the surface, interpersonal relationship problems, difficulties at work or with finances, are frequent causes.

Psychological conflict can depress energy levels during the day, thus disturbing biorhythms. Part of this might involve a neurological fatigue from repetitive cyclic firing of the same nerve pathways without rest or resolution.

There is also the effect of biochemical upset during emotional turmoil.

*This art of resting the mind and the power of dismissing from it all care and worry is probably one of the secrets of energy in our great men.*

**Captain J. A. Hadfield**

Much of what we have been discussing also involves psychological stress coming *from* biological rhythm disturbances, light deficit disorders, and sleeping problems. Once again the multidimensional interconnections of health appear.

## NUTRITION AND BIOLOGICAL RHYTHMS

Nutrition has a powerful impact on the body's biochemistry and thus on biorhythms. We will explore a few simple examples of those influences. The first is one which nearly everyone is familiar with—eating a big meal too close to bedtime. The blood sugar rises, activates nerve excitability, and you are either staring at the ceiling, pacing the hall, or screaming in some high-glucose induced nightmare.

One night of poor sleep might disturb biorhythms for a week. Related to this is poor dietary regulation during the day, leading to uneven blood sugar levels and roller coaster energy swings and moods. (Children are particularly affected by this.) A more specific example is insufficient magnesium and calcium, resulting in nighttime nerve hyperexcitability. This is characterized by difficulty sleeping, "nervous legs," and even "charlie horses" at night. Using the nutritional guidelines that are detailed in this book should make sure that nutritional influence on biological rhythms is benefiting and not damaging.

## ALLERGIES AND TOXINS

Linked with nutritional disturbances to biological rhythms are food and inhalant allergies or sensitivities. Hidden or obvious reactions can cause severe disturbances in biochemistry, organ function and nerve activity. Extreme fluctuations in energy levels can disrupt sleep/activity balances. Allergies are stimulated when normal substances contacting the body are perceived and reacted to as toxins. It is no surprise then that poisons and toxic substances will create similar disturbances. If you suspect allergies or environmental poisons are affecting your body's normal rhythms, refer to the advice and resources in the Ecological Health chapter.

## CRANIAL ELECTRICAL STIMULATION

Electrical stimulation of the brain with very safe, minute, and barely noticeable microamperage current can help reestablish normal neurotransmitter function when that is at the core of any biorhythm imbalance. Progressive physicians who prescribe Cranial Electrical Stimulation (CES) have successfully treated insomnia and other sleep disorders for decades. Magnetic therapy may also operate under similar principles when used as a remedy for disturbed sleep problems.

## MELATONIN SUPPLEMENTATION AS AN AID IN RESETTING NORMAL SLEEP PATTERNS

Melatonin is a hormone secreted by the pineal gland. It is significantly responsible for modulating our biological clocks. Melatonin is secreted by the pineal in diurnal rhythms dependent on light exposure. Blood levels are ten times higher at 2 A.M. than at the lowest part of the day. Often supplementation with melatonin at bedtime can reset a disturbed biological clock and thus correct insomnia or delayed sleep phase syndrome. Since our melatonin production decreases with age, supplementation is particularly helpful in sleep disorders of the elderly. Care needs to be taken with dosage since only very small quantities are needed to affect change, and too much can make one drowsy in the morning. It is also important to time the ingestion of melatonin to a regular, set schedule before retiring at night so that the peak functional levels are properly programmed to fall at the same time. As of the time of this publication, melatonin is available in health food stores. Using a natural substance is far safer and makes more sense than using potentially dangerous and addictive medicine.

It is fascinating to observe how the rhythms of Life flow along the strands in the Web of Wholeness. It is even more wondrous to *feel* the harmony that healthy interconnections can provide. Observe in yourself which strands are in most critical need of attention. Use all the resources necessary to attain this unity of "Life Energy" flow.

---

## BIOLOGICAL RHYTHMS, LIGHT, AND SLEEP RESOURCES

*Sing a song of seasons!*
*Something bright in all!*
*Flowers in Summer,*
*Fires in the Fall.*

**Robert Louis Stevenson**

\* denotes resources that are primarily oriented to health care and research professionals.

### Books

Binkley, Sue. *The Clockwork Sparrow: Time, Clocks, and Calendars in Biological Organisms.* Prentice Hall, 1989.

Borbely, Alexander. *Secrets of Sleep.* Basic, 1988.

\*Daan, Serge and Gwinner, Eberhard. *Biological Clocks and Environmental Time.* Guilford Press, 1989.

Hauri, Peter and Linde, Shirley. *No More Sleepless Nights.* Wiley, 1991.

\*Hollwich, F. *The Influence of Ocular Light Perception on Metabolism in Man and Animal.* Springer - Verlag.

Hyman, Jane. *The Light Book: How Natural and Artificial Light Affect Our Health, Mood, and Behavior.* Tarcher, 1990.

Kime, Zane. *Sunlight.* World Health Publications, 1980.

\*Kupfer, D.; Monk, T.; Barchas, J., eds. *Biological Rhythms and Mental Disorders.* Guilford Press, 1988.

Liberman, Jacob. *Light: Medicine of the Future.* Bear & Co., 1991.

\*Montplaisir, Jacques and Godbout, Roger, eds. *Sleep and Biological Rhythms.* Oxford University Press, 1990.

Moore, Martin; et al. *The Clocks That Time Us.* Harvard University Press, 1982.

Rose, K. *The Body in Time.* Wiley and Sons, 1988.

Rosenthal, N. *Seasons of the Mind.* Bantam, 1990.

\*Rosenthal, N. and Blehar, M., eds. *Seasonal Affective Disorders and Phototherapy.* Guilford Press, 1989.

Rosenthal, N. *Winter Blues: Seasonal Affective Disorder: What It Is and How to Overcome It.* (800) 538-2662.

\*Thompson, Chris and Silverstone, Trevor. *Seasonal Affective Disorder.* Clinical Neuroscience Publishers, 1990.

Wurtman, Richard; Baum, Michael; Potts, John. *The Medical and Biological Effects of Light.* New York Academy of Sciences, 1985.

### Journals

\**Journal of Biological Rhythms,* Guilford Publications, 72 Spring St., New York, NY 10012; (212) 431-9800.

### Miscellaneous

*Oh sleep! it is a gentle thing,*
*Beloved from pole to pole!*

**Samuel Taylor Coleridge**

Bower, B. *Bright-light therapy expands its horizons.* Science News, 5-26-1990.

Health Studies Collegium, *Information Handbook: Immune Enhancement Program.* Serammune Physicians Lab, 1990. Activity Appendix 4: "Photobiology: Trigger of Brain Rhythms" has instructions on the use of colored light therapy for immune enhancement and sources of these lights. Serammune Physicians Laboratory, 1890 Preston White Drive, Suite 200, Reston, VA 22091; (800) 553-5472; (703) 758-0610.

Toufexis, Anastasia, et al. *Drowsy America.* Time Magazine, 12-17-1990.

## *Organizations*

*That we are not much sicker and much madder*
*than we are is due exclusively to*
*that most blessed and blessing of all*
*natural graces, sleep.*

**Aldous Huxley**

*Association of Professional Sleep Societies, 1610 14th St. NW, Suite 300, Rochester, MN 55901; (507) 287-6006. Umbrella group for: Sleep Research Society, American Sleep Disorders Association, and the Association of Polysomnographic Technologists. The American Sleep Disorders Association sponsors a journal, *Sleep,* published by Allen Press; (800) 627-0629.

Center for Environmental Therapeutics, Box 532, Georgetown, CO 80444; (303) 569-0910. Researches alternative therapies for fatigue, diminished work performance, seasonal disorders, and insomnia.

John Downing, O.D., Ph.D.; (707) 525-4747. Can provide a referral to centers using Dr. Downing's Neurosensory Development Training protocols and Lumitron colored light device.

Light Therapy Information Service, New York Psychiatric Institute; (212) 960-5714. A clearinghouse for related information.

Lumitron Corporation, 2261 Market St., Suite 504, San Francisco, CA 94114; (404) 458-6509; Fax (404) 458-4109. Can provide a referral to centers doing Neurosensory Development Training and other protocols using the Lumitron colored light device.

*Society for Light Treatment and Biological Rhythms, P.O. Box 478, Wilsonville, OR 97070; (503) 694-2404. A professional research and educational organization that is a great resource for scientific information in this field. Publishes a monthly newsletter.

## *Cranial Electrical Stimulation Device Suppliers*

Cranial electrical stimulation (C.E.S.) equipment requires doctors' prescriptions. Chiropractors, naturopaths, acupuncturists, osteopaths, and medical doctors can prescribe these units to patients depending on differences in state laws. These companies also provide substantial compilations of data on the therapeutic benefits of C.E.S. These medical devices are approved by the FDA for depression, anxiety, and insomnia. They are being used successfully on a research basis for substance abuse withdrawal and dependency, cognitive dysfunction, attention deficit disorders, behavioral problems of childhood associated with hyperactivity, and phobic disorders.

*Alternative Electronics, P.O. Box 1941, Rogue River, OR 97537; (503) 582-2382.
*CES Labs, 11230 75th Ave. NE, Kirkland, WA 98034; (800) 237-7948.
*Robert Picker, M.D., Electro-Therapeutics, 1741 Geary Road, Walnut Creek, CA 94596; (800) 743-1457.

## *Full Spectrum and Therapeutic Lighting Suppliers*

Duro-Test Corporation, 2321 Kennedy Blvd. North Bergen, NJ 07047, (201) 808-1800.

Lighting and Energy Consultants, P.O. Box 427 Mediapolis, IA 52637; (800) 999-4027; (319) 394-3093.

Medic-Light, 34 Yacht Club Drive., Lake Hopatcong, NJ 07849; (800) LIGHT-25.

Ott Light Systems, Inc., 28 Parker Way, Santa Barbara, CA 93101, (800) 234-3724, (805) 564-3467. The best full spectrum lighting available.

The Sunbox Company, 19217 Orbit Dr., Gathersburg, MD 20879; (800) 548-3968; (301) 762-1786.

# ENERGY MEDICINE

*What is now proved was once only imagined.*

**William Blake**

"Energy medicine" is a term that will be used in this book to discuss healing methods in which so-called "subtle energies" are the attributed mechanism of operation. Although all healing techniques are in reality an alteration of energetic processes at different levels with varying forms of energy, Energy medicine describes methods in which the form of the energy is a bit elusive to find and define. Homeopathy, acupuncture, distant healing, therapeutic touch, aromatherapy, orgone, radionics, Qigong, sound, magnets, intuitive diagnosis, light, Zero Balancing, direction of energy techniques in craniosacral therapy, crystals, and chakra balancing are among the techniques that have been placed in this Energy medicine realm.

Although the reasons for placing acupuncture and various forms of light therapy in this category are understandable, this author feels that their mode of action is better explained by more conventional or well researched mechanisms. They are therefore taken out of this category for the sake of clarity in the organization of information for this book. Of the remaining methods, homeopathy may be the most widely used and a good place to investigate first.

## HOMEOPATHY

Homeopathy is a system that has been developed over 200 years using "remedies" prepared from minute doses or dilutions of substances. Traditionally, a lengthy initial interview provides a detailed list of the person's symptoms, and this list is used to choose a remedy that has been found experimentally in years past to produce the same symptoms when given to healthy individuals. Proponents of homeopathy have proposed a theory of like cures like, but how this works has not been adequately proven. Homeopathy is classed as a type of energy medicine because the remedies are made by diluting the remedy material so much that only a few molecules, if any, of the substance is left

in what the patient eventually takes. The explanation is that the carrier solution, usually alcohol and water or milk sugar, picks up the energetic essence of the remedy substance in a dramatically "potentiated" form. In fact, it is an accepted understanding among homeopaths that the more dilute preparations are the most powerful.

This section will try to separate the scientific facts and clinical reliability of homeopathy from the hype, advertising, unproven theory, placebo effects, and folklore so readers can better judge how to integrate homeopathy into their holistic health program.

## *Research Summary*

There have been approximately 100 clinical trials of homeopathy in the last 25 years that are available for review in the medical literature. Most of these studies have methodological problems that make reliable conclusions difficult to come by. Out of approximately a dozen of the better designed studies there is sufficient evidence to suggest that homeopathy can be of benefit in some conditions, including hay fever, influenza, some bacterial infections, migraines, abnormal labor during childbirth, some musculoskeletal pain syndromes and injuries, and varicose veins. There is suggestive evidence from clinical experience that other benefits might extend to post-operative surgical healing improvement, some psychological problems, other allergies, menstrual difficulties, minor dermatological conditions, pediatric problems, and digestive complaints.

So, faced with potential benefits from a natural therapeutic system, how does the average person use homeopathy wisely?

Much more quality research needs to be done. What conditions are *best* addressed with homeopathy? The research done so far just gives us hints to some of its potential. Which conditions are inappropriate for homeopathy? What system of determining remedy choice is best? Is the traditional, painstaking history-taking and matching to the symptoms best? Or are the newer, experimental systems, using applied kinesiology, acupuncture instrumentation, pendulums, radionics, or computer software more valid? One company even purports to transfer homeopathic remedies electronically onto audio cassettes so that you can just listen to a tape and not actually consume the remedies. No one has ever tested or compared any of these variations scientifically, yet many therapists treat with them. Their use is taught in seminars to homeopathic practitioners and lay persons alike with little solid justification. When are "shotgun" or general formulas for self-care appropriate? Where are homeopathy's prevention and early detection capabilities, if any?

Once research clearly defines homeopathy as a valid clinical science it can move out of its era of disrepute by:

- Establishing standards of clinical care and excellence.

- Developing a respected training, accreditation, and licensing program for homeopathic physicians. Now it is very difficult to know how to choose a good homeopath. Virtually anyone who wants to use the remedies can do so and think up their own diagnostic style.

- Warning the public about invalid diagnostic techniques and false product claims is essential. Many presently accept all systems and products as valuable, using advertising as the main method of propagating the health care approach rather than a scientific flow of information.

- Its methods must be integrated into a comprehensive holistic health care system.

So we ask again: how is the average person to wisely use homeopathy today, while this disorganized health care field sorts itself out over the coming years?

The first rule of thumb is to not get caught in the trap of perpetuating the "quick fix" offered by a brand of homeopathy which looks at symptoms and prescribes "remedies" for the perceived symptomatic "problems." We must not use homeopathy *instead* of holistic health enhancement and lifestyle measures. But when we develop symptoms or a condition and are already addressing the other aspects of our health that are either proven or are most likely to have a major impact, we can turn to this system as *one* of the helpful natural modalities. Again, however, we must keep priorities in mind.

For assistance with problems such as reducing the symptoms of hay fever or flu, trying over-the-counter general remedies available in health food stores is an inexpensive way to see what works. For more serious or involved symptoms or conditions one might want to consult with an experienced homeopath *in addition* to other health professionals in order to put together a more total approach. For any serious condition, avoid putting your primary health care choice into the hands of homeopathy until more research validates its effectiveness and the profession improves and agrees upon what acceptable clinical practice is.

To find a homeopath, one can ask for a referral from:

National Center for Homeopathy, 810 N. Fairfax #306, Alexandria, VA 22314.

Or for more information, contact:

Homeopathic Educational Services, 2124 Kittredge St., Berkeley, CA 94704; (510) 649-0294; for orders only: (800) 359-9051; Fax (510) 649-1955.

This will just provide you with someone who practices homeopathy. It is not a guarantee that they practice it skillfully or knowledgeably. Until more research proves otherwise, it is best to choose a homeopath who spends at least an hour on the first visit to take a thorough history in order to properly match symptoms with the traditional homeopathic prescriptions. During this initial visit the homeopath should ask you questions not only about your physical symptoms but about your psychological state of health, too. If he or she uses muscle testing, electronic acupuncture testing or other instruments to determine a correct remedy, be wary. Ask for the undisputed research proving this methodology over the more traditional means before making a commitment to the initial visit. As of this writing, such research does not exist. Traditionally, only one remedy is used at a time with follow-up visits to change prescriptions as needed. Occasionally multiple remedies are used, but this is sometimes a sign that the homeopath is not being specific and accurate enough in the history taking and prescription. Also be wary of the homeopath who wants you to stop all other forms of treatment such as nutritional supplementation, manipulative therapy, acupuncture, etc. There is strong value in interdisciplinary, multifaceted, integrated care.

Homeopathy has the potential to reduce the damaging effects of modern medicine's reliance on powerful drugs if replacement remedies can be found through good scientific inquiry. Until that time, consumers need to use caution, not so much to guard against any adverse side effects from homeopathy (for it has a good safety record), but more to prevent being taken in by the unscientific, non-holistic way in which homeopathy is sometimes practiced. This can lead to delay in proper treatment or to spending money on a homeopath who doesn't know what he is doing.

## OTHER ENERGY MEDICINE MODALITIES

*Every man takes the limits of his own field of vision for the limits of the world.*

**Arthur Schopenhauer**

Most open-minded scientists and health practitioners can provide a space in their minds for accepting that there are phenomena which occur in the energetic process of healing which we know nothing about. Over the centuries clinicians and lay individuals have experimented with this far edge of the unknown in health care. Sometimes amazing health transformations have occurred due to experiments in this outer realm of healing. Much fascination has surrounded this field of energy medicine because enough empirical data has amassed over the years, because some anecdotal experiences have been so significantly positive, and because some scientific research has validated either clinical results or mechanisms of action. Unfortunately this excitement has not brought with it any clear way by which people can avail themselves of its promise. Health professionals involved in energy medicine have not been able to speak in a unified voice with solid scientific support that educates people about how they can easily incor-

porate these varied techniques into their own comprehensive, holistic, health care program.

If you have the time and money, it is an alluring field to experiment with. For those who are doing every high priority health enhancement and corrective procedure recommended in this book already and still need more health improvement, this field might be investigated. But it is difficult to give clear guidance in a health care field with so little substantial evidence for its proper use. It seems wiser to provide resources where future developments might be more closely followed. The following resources will provide reasonably good objective analysis of continuing, updated information:

Center for Frontier Sciences, Temple University, Ritter Hall 003-00, Philadelphia, PA 19122; (215) 787-8487; Fax (215) 787-5553. A networking and educational exchange for scientific advances leading towards wholeness.

Committee for the Scientific Investigation of Claims of the Paranormal, P.O. Box 703, Amherst, NY 14226-0703; (800) 634-1610. Publishes the *Skeptical Inquirer,* a quarterly journal that counterbalances with reason, logic, conservatism, and science the many wild claims that pervade the field of energy medicine.

Institute of Noetic Sciences (IONS), P.O. Box 909, Sausalito, CA 94966-0909; (800) 383-1586; (800) 383-1394; (415) 331-5650..

International Society for the Study of Subtle Energies and Energy Medicine, 356 Goldco Circle, Golden, CO 80401; (303) 278-2228; Fax (303) 279-3539.

Society for the Study of Scientific Exploration, Stanford University, ERL 306, Stanford, CA 94305-4055: (415) 723-1439.

World Research Foundation, 15300 Ventura Blvd, Suite 405, Sherman Oaks, CA 94103; (818) 907-5483.

There are also a few books and journals that provide some research and empirical evidence in the field of energy medicine, with a glance at what might be possible.

Becker, Robert and Seldon, G. *The Body Electric: Electromagnetism and the Foundation of Life.* William Morrow & Co., 1985.

*Bridges: Journal of the International Society for the Study of Subtle Energies and Energy Medicine,* 356 Goldco Circle, Golden, CO 80401; (303) 278-2228; Fax (303) 279-3539.

Dossey, Larry. *Recovering the Soul: A Scientific and Spiritual Search*. Bantam, 1989.

*Frontier Perspectives*. A semiannual journal from Center for Frontier Science.

Gerber, Richard. *Vibrational Medicine: New Choices for Healing Ourselves*. Bear & Co., 1988.

*Journal of Scientific Exploration,* Stanford University, Center for Space Science and Astrophysics, Stanford, CA 94305-4055; (415) 723-439.

Krieger, Dolores. *Accepting Your Power to Heal: Personal Practice of Therapeutic Touch*. Bear & Co., 1993.

Krieger, Dolores. *Living the Therapeutic Touch: Healing as a Lifestyle*. Mead & Co., 1987.

Macrae, Janet. *Therapeutic Touch: A Practical Guide*. Knopf, 1988.

Philpott, William and Taplin, Sharon. *Biomagnetic Handbook: A Guide to Medical Magnetics—The Energy Medicine of Tomorrow*. Enviro-Tech. 1990. Available from Enviro-Tech Products, 17171 S.E. 29 Street, Choctaw, OK 73020, (405) 390-3499.

Rubik, Beverly ed. *The Interrelationship Between Mind and Matter*. Center for Frontier Science at Temple University, 1992.

*Skeptical Inquirer,* Committee for the Scientific Investigation of Claims of the Paranormal, P.O. Box 703, Amherst, NY 14226-0703; (800) 634-1610.

One practical piece of advice that can assist with any type of energy medicine has to do with the beneficial use of the powers of mind. The capacity of the mind to alter the way the body works is undeniable. Years of research in biofeedback, stress, and placebo effect can attest to it. What is less known is the research validating the ability of mind to alter someone else's body functions. Some of the resources listed above review that literature. It is sparse but impressive. It also provides a possible mechanism for the healing response in many instances.

Whenever a good caregiver engages in a therapeutic process, there is a compassionate and willful focus on a positive outcome. The mental energy invested in this often unconscious act of empathy has appreciable impact on the healing response of the body-mind-spirit of the patient, regardless of the tools or forms of care. It is reasonable to believe that in some situations this mental effect on healing can be more substantial than the actual health care technique.

*It is remarkable that one characteristic which seems to separate man from the allegedly lower animals is a recurring desire to escape from reality.*

**C.H.W. Horne & J.A.W. McCluskie**

Imagine a charismatic, innovative healer, Zambini, who has secretly developed an amazing Wellness Widget. By passing it over a patient's body in a particular pattern, the Widget is claimed to heal all kinds of ills. Zambini travels the world treating desperately sick people with his Widget. Remarkable healings occur. Many give glowing testimonials. Results seem unpredictable, though. Frequently people feel some initial benefit, but with time this is lost. A large number are not helped at all.

The demand for Zambini's services is so great he cannot keep up, so his shrewd public relations manager and business partner convince him to build a bunch of Widgets, give certification seminars on how to become a Wellness Widget Therapist, and with the workshops sell the Widgets with the seminars. This catches on like wildfire. Thousands of therapists are being certified and Widgeting tens of thousands of sick people.

At seminars experienced Widgetors stand up and give testimonials about dramatic cases that healed with just a few treatments with the Widget. Dynamic and enthusiastic Widgetors describe the bundles of money they have earned delivering this valuable health care service. Quiet, mild-mannered Widgetors listen with envy to all these success stories. They have seen some results and are convinced of the benefits but don't seem to get those really "good" cases. They take advanced courses to learn the detailed nuances of Widgeting.

Independent Widgetors set up their own seminars to teach their special kind of Widgeting which they intuitively "developed." There emerges Widgeting Kinesiology, Crystal Widgeting, and Computerized Homeopathic Widget Integration. Widgeting in all its forms becomes a multimillion dollar industry. Magazine articles and books are written about it. Television infomercials on Widgeting can be seen in millions of homes on Sunday morning.

Then after years of Widgeting frenzy a curious researcher sets up a double-blind, controlled, crossover experiment with the Widget. No health improvement is found. Widget advocates charge that it takes skill to Widget even though the device in itself is therapeutic and that the widgetors in the experiment were not properly trained.

The experimenters charge that any healing effects are not the result of the Widget but are caused by:

- the patients' mental imagery of healing—the placebo effect—plus

- the Widgetors' prayer-like mental efforts producing a non-contact healing effect

*A great many open minds*
*should be closed for repairs.*
**Toledo Blake**

How much of energy medicine's benefits come from the powers of the mind, regardless of the techniques used? Might it be that the value of some of the energy medicine techniques is that they offer a means by which we can more readily focus our mental attention on a beneficial outcome? We do know that visualization, prayer, loving-kindness meditations, and the evocation of positive emotions all have a beneficial impact on health. That is why all psychotherapies and spiritual guidelines encourage the affirmation and evocation of positive thoughts, emotions, speech, and behavior in addition to minimizing the internalization of negative qualities. We also know that when the agency for transformation is internal, great healing potency is captured. It might be most important to

research and investigate how we can most effectively utilize these mechanisms of mind rather than getting too caught up in the enthusiasm of exotic "healing machines" or unusual techniques done by therapists for profit. Important aspects of therapeutic relationships are emerging as we learn more about this field of energy medicine. As science and individuals discover the full ramifications of the interdependence of all life, and how the complex strands of the Web of Wholeness are woven, what is revealed is that our interconnections are more pervasive and vast than imagined. My thoughts not only impact myself but others, in powerful ways. Energy medicine may have more to teach us about human relationships than about unknown forms of energy.

It would be a tragedy if large amounts of human time, money, and energy were diverted away from nurturing healthy psycho-social-spiritual development in favor of creating, promoting, and selling some process that elicits *just* a small functional improvement of the body without knowing how that benefit came about.

The practical advice that might be most valuable then are the tried and true guidelines:

- Observe negative, destructive conditioning in yourself with moment-by-moment daily mindfulness, and understand its source.

- Allow positive, healthy actions to arise from the truthful insights gained.

- Disperse those positive qualities in thought, word and deed, with love, to all living beings.

*Let man overcome anger by love; evil by good;*
*greed by generosity; and lies by truth.*
**Buddha**

# CHAPTER FOUR

# ECONOMIC / OCCUPATIONAL HEALTH

*Why is there so much month left at the end of the money?*

**Unkown**

## ECONOMIC HEALTH

Economics has great impact on all aspects of life and health. Because of this, it is important to carefully analyze these relationships so that they can be optimized and harmonized. Looking at how economics affects specific health aspects will be the first order of business. Then it will be easier to observe how money impacts our total health. By following this procedure we will also be better able to prioritize our financial disbursements in the most healthy manner. Reevaluation of expenditures also affects decisions on income production. A new assessment can often be made about what we do to earn a living and how many hours we should devote to it.

*All progress is based upon a universal, innate desire on the part of every organism to live beyond its income.*

**Samuel Butler**

How do we evaluate our daily, monthly, and yearly expenditures for all categories of spending? Do we have an effective assessment of these spending proportions? (Joe Dominguez's program "Transforming Your Relationship with Money & Achieving Financial Independence" is an ideal program for making these monetary evaluations.) To reprioritize our spending in more wholesome ways, we must find out the truth about where all our money goes and integrate that with our necessary expenses. This will inspire dramatic behavioral changes.

*I have enough money to last me the rest of my life, unless I buy something.*

**Jackie Mason**

Ideally, it is best to start out with an accurate picture of where our money is spent. If we have that data available, we can use it to go into the next step of evaluating each aspect of our life to see how we wisely are spending money in that area. Are we spending it wisely? Have we provided for our necessities? Are we spending too much in certain places? Have we reached a level of spending in a particular category where more spending is not achieving greater gains in health or happiness? Have we achieved optimal health from what money could buy in a specific area?

If the data is not available, it is recommended that Dominguez's seminar or book, *Your Money or Your Life* be used to gain those insights. In the meantime rougher estimates can be used to continue evaluating how one's economic status is influencing the health of each aspect of our being.

*Too many people spend money they haven't earned, to buy things they don't want, to impress people they don't like.*

**Will Rogers**

As we proceed with the following exercises, let us remember that many people emphasize the economic aspects of life too much. People believe that money is the key to health and happiness and that great effort has to be exerted earning money before other enterprises are started in order to be healthy. This is not true, and we hope that the manner in which the spectrum analyses are arranged and worded does not support that belief.

## ADVERTISING'S INFLUENCE ON SPENDING AND BEHAVIOR

Corporations spent *$130 billion* in 1990 on thought control and behavior modification advertising in the U.S. Five hundred million dollars of that was targeted for children two to twelve years of age because children four to twelve spend *$8 billion* per year and influence their parents to spend another *$1 billion* per *week*. For those of you who say, "Oh, that advertising doesn't influence me. I'm a conscious shopper," think again. Big business is betting approximately *$130 billion,* year in and year out, that it does influence you. What is even worse is that advertising is also meant to sell and manipulate images of who we are, how we should feel, what values we should hold, how we should behave, and what goals in life we should have. Those who are concerned about this seductive invasion of our lives might consult the Center for the Study of Commercialism. (See page 357.)

Two excellent resources are: Elgin, Duane, *Voluntary Simplicity: Toward a Life That Is Outwardly Simple, Inwardly Rich,* William Morrow & Co., 1981; and St. James, Elaine, *Simplify Your Life,* Hyperion, 1994. Both are filled with practical, daily suggestions for improving the quality of life and everyone's health and unity, while keeping economics and materialism in proper perspective.

*Live simply, so others may simply live.*
**Mahatma Gandhi**

Let us not forget that economic hardship has its advantages in building beneficial life-coping qualities which end up contributing to overall health. Let us also remember that the more simple and healthy our lifestyles are, the less money we need. Being content with what we have is a fine, healthy virtue.

Also observe that at higher levels of economic health more resources are donated to others. That's economic *health,* not economic wealth. More precisely, middle income individuals donate a larger percentage of their income to charities than higher income individuals. Many middle income people choose not to focus enormous amounts of time and energy solely on earning money to be wealthy. They have a priority to distribute their life energy and activities in ways that are more diversely healthy. They can give money to those in need because they have a psycho-spiritual closeness to the disadvantaged unknown to many wealthy individuals who are immersed in an all-consuming attachment to money.

*The rich are the scum of the earth in every country.*
**G. K. Chesterton**

Wise earners are also more likely to realize that luxuries do not enhance their lives as much as charitable work. Others, however—many of the wealthy—believe that the earnest money of earlier years used to purchase necessities or simple, hard-earned comforts, will now offer the same happiness in buying luxuries. Instead, they face the law of diminishing emotional returns. Money spent more on superfluous items than on true needs or simple amenities gives no joy. What is the difference? Perhaps it is that middle income people are also not so far removed socially, educationally, and occupationally from the needy. Excessive wealth can intensify emotional separation from, and decrease empathy for, individuals of other economic classes. Ideal economic health should enhance self-development while deepening one's unity with all life.

*Luxury is more ruthless than war.*
**Unknown**

Let us now explore the concept of economic health and how it can enrich all aspects of our life and bring us closer to wholeness.

## MONEY → FOOD → HEALTH

How do we use finances to provide us with food for more optimal health? First use the spectrum analysis chart below to determine how money is used with regard to food. Remember that the descriptions for each level, 0-10, are just examples of rough estimates of how others might correlate actuality with numbers. After a numerical figure is chosen, we can look more closely at ways in which we might optimize our food budget. Then, once we look at the whole picture, we will reassess that budget amount in proportion to other aspects of health where money can be spent for other types of improvement.

Buying quality food is one of the best ways to optimize our food dollars. Following the Basic

Nutritional Health Enhancement Guidelines detailed in the nutrition section of the book is a good way to do this. Some of its elements that really save money are:

- buying nutrient dense foods with a high nutrient per cost ratio such as vegetables, whole grains, complex carbohydrates, low-fat proteins

- avoiding nutrient poor foods such as simple sugars, sodas, junk food, fast food, sugary cereals

- avoiding harmful groceries such as alcohol, tobacco, caffeine, salty foods, fats, most meats

- eating out less often and dining only on healthy fare.

### ECONOMIC SPECTRUM ANALYSIS — FOOD

10

Financially stable enough to buy the best organically grown food and quality vitamin and mineral supplementation.

Financial status is such that the best can't be bought, but good food is provided in sufficient quantities to feel acceptable.
Evaluations as to cost per unit of quality are always made when buying food and vitamin supplementation.

Finances dictate purchasing poorer quality food than what seems acceptable for adequate health.
Protein and caloric intake is only adequate.
Cheap vitamins are bought occasionally.

Food quality and quantity diminish prior to the next payday.
Marginal protein and caloric intake.
No vitamins or mineral supplements can be afforded.

Starving

0

Buying quality vitamin and mineral supplements is also a very cost effective way to provide essential nutrients which will save money long into the future because of the improved health that results in their wise use. More detailed information on optimal nutrient supplementation can be found in the section on Nutrition.

## ECONOMICS AND CLOTHING

*The reason it is so difficult to make ends meet is because someone is always moving the ends.*
**Unknown**

One of the best ways to optimize the dollars spent on clothes is to maintain a healthy psychological attitude toward apparel. Those with self-esteem issues, who require an excessive budget to keep up a certain appearance, may have warped priorities which will ultimately sabotage their health. True, certain jobs require more elaborate or special apparel. It is important to properly evaluate the difference between adequate dress for the circumstances and superfluous attire for the ego. If self-worth is high, items such as ties, designer clothes, the latest fashions, nylon stockings, high heel shoes, jewelry, and cosmetics could be virtually eliminated from the clothing budget and transferred to a more health enhancing area. High heel shoes, for example, should be banned for the millions of dollars in back disorders they cause. Cosmetics, particularly synthetically derived ones, could be excluded, with the result that you may cure many hidden allergy problems. Once again

## ECONOMIC SPECTRUM ANALYSIS — CLOTHING

10

Financial status is sufficient to buy all the necessary, comfortable clothes made from organically grown natural fibers.

Finances allow plenty of clothes but not of the best quality.

Clothes are adequate, but strict budgeting is necessary.

All clothes are bought on sale and at discount stores.

Warm enough but must buy all clothes at Salvation Army.
Job interviews are difficult because of the
quality of clothes that must be worn.
Socializing is embarrassing.
The children are made fun of at school
because of their clothes.

Just the rags on
my back.

0

use the spectrum analysis on page 141 to rate from 0-10 how finances affect clothes, keeping in mind that which is in different ways relevant to health.

*Our culture places more money and value on outer trappings than what is within one's heart.*
**Unknown**

If we buy good quality, durable, comfortable clothes of a type that is always in style rather than high priced fashions, a great deal of money can be saved. Purchasing clothes made of natural fibers not only reduces immunological stress from the avoidance of petro-chemically derived, synthetic fabrics, it also contributes to global ecological health by reducing demand on the use of fossil fuels. This in turn reduces carbon emissions, pollution, and global warming. Buying clothes pro-duced from cotton and wool grown closer to the point of purchase reduces transportation costs and stresses on the environment caused by long distance shipping. It also supports agricultural use of the land. Going one step further, demanding organically grown cotton is even more preferable for a healthy ecology, and it is sometimes essential to those individuals who are extremely sensitive to pesticide residues in their clothes.

One health promoting reason for buying foreign made clothes might be to support small Third World cottage industries. When our own financial health is rating a 9 or 10 on the spectrum analysis scale for clothing, we might choose to promote the health of those in lesser developed areas by purchasing clothing and accessories from the stores, co-ops, charities, and mail order marketplaces that specialize in these items.

## ECONOMIC SPECTRUM ANALYSIS — SHELTER

10

Wealthy enough to own without mortgage an ecologically designed home using no toxic products, and powered by alternative, renewable energy sources such as solar and wind. There is plenty of room for an organic garden and open space. It is untouched by pollution or the hectic pace of civilization.

Not the best ecological, mortgage free home, but a relatively safe, energy efficient, country home with a small garden and manageable mortgage

Comfortable, mass-produced, suburban tract home with high mortgage payments and energy costs.

City home with pollution, crime, and traffic as amenities; triple mortgaged up to the eyeballs.

Nice apartment with thin walls on a year lease.

Dilapidated apartment with thin walls, scraping up rent month-to-month.

Living with relatives or friends.

Cardboard box.

0

## BUDGETARY ALLOCATIONS FOR SHELTER

A man's castle, a mother's nest, a child's world, a roof over one's head—home has been defined many ways. The "optimal" description given on page 142 is not necessarily the only ideal. It is meant to illustrate how money *can* be used to optimize shelter in a healthy way if the financial budget for housing is high. For some, an ideal healthy shelter might be a teepee—if closeness to nature is deemed of highest priority for overall wholeness.

These decisions are highly personal. How much money should go for which type of housing to provide optimal health? If too much money is allocated for shelter, other areas of health will be sacrificed. If too little money is available for shelter,

a multitude of problems can arise in many different aspects of health. Home ownership seems to be more and more difficult for the average family. Shelter of any kind seems to be drawing a larger proportion of finances than we can sustain healthfully. Some of this has to do with macro-economics—global, national, and regional. Just the legal, governmental predisposition toward land use and land ownership has enormous impact on the economics of home ownership for the average family, in relation to land ownership and to rentals by real estate manipulators. Other aspects can be changed by individual action.

Owning or renting a home is really payment for the privilege of caring for that parcel of the planet with shelter during our short stay on Earth. This should be kept in mind with each rental or mortgage payment.

---

### ECONOMIC SPECTRUM ANALYSIS — HEALTH CARE

10

Any health enhancement program desired.

Excellent health insurance plus some discretionary out-of-pocket expenses for health enhancement programs not covered by insurance.

Good health insurance but only minimal extra cash available for special health care services not covered by insurance or the rare instance of health enhancement programs of great value.

Poor quality health insurance or HMO that limits services significantly and/or has high deductibles. No discretionary cash for health care expenditures beyond what the insurance will cover.

No insurance. Health care costs are all out-of pocket expenses. Can only afford care when absolutely necessary.

Must depend on inadequate, welfare based, health plans. Health suffers significantly because of this.

Prayer alone is all that can be afforded.

0

## FINANCES AVAILABLE FOR HEALTH CARE

Wise use of our resources to care for our health is what this book is all about. Allocation of financial resources for specific health care is what this section is about. The first question is: how does our economic health affect the money we devote to health care? This we can rate on the spectrum analysis scale on page 143. Other questions are concerned with how we can devote our money to the wise use of preventive and health enhancing programs. Are we putting our first resources towards inexpensive self-care with large cost-effective returns? Are we making wise use of professional assessments and health improvement in-

struction before turning to expensive medical treatment? Help with these questions are spread throughout the book in appropriate sections.

Other questions: How can we reprioritize all other expenditures so that more money can be made available for our health? The most cost-effective way to deal with a physical health problem might not be to spend money at the doctor's office, but rather to redirect energies and money toward other aspects of one's life—play, improving intimate relationships, or spiritual meditation. This too will be addressed in different parts of the book.

By doing the exercises in this book and adopting the health enhancement programs detailed in every chapter, more money should become available for the necessary health care procedures.

## ECONOMIC SPECTRUM ANALYSIS — EDUCATIONAL ASPIRATIONS

10

Wealthy enough to afford any educational opportunity.

Financial stability sufficient to afford priority educational opportunities.
A quality college education is not denied because of money.
Budget allows for purchase of significant books, journals, and classes to improve health.

Finances limit educational opportunities.
Can scrape money together for a mediocre college education.
Most sources of additional health-oriented education come from
libraries and inexpensive community classes.

Can't afford college but can scrimp sufficiently to attend
trade school. Must get all outside educational
materials from libraries.
Intellectual development is stifled.

Income low enough to force one to
work long hours.
No time, energy, or money is
left over for educational
advancement or
intellectual
stimulation.

0

## MONEY FOR THE MIND

Do we have enough money to satisfy educational aspirations that ultimately contribute to our overall health? How severely do financial difficulties impede educational opportunity? That is what we need to rate numerically on the Educational Aspirations Spectrum Analysis scale on page 144 and then transfer that rating to the Summary on page 154.

## ECONOMICS SUPPORTING PSYCHOLOGICAL HEALTH

As with other elements of our life, the more self-health care, prevention, and education we do, the less we have to participate in expensive interventions by professionals. But if we need professional assistance and cannot afford it, our total health can suffer greatly. Following the guidelines in the chapter on Psychological Health, and using the

### ECONOMIC SPECTRUM ANALYSIS — PSYCHOLOGICAL HEALTH

10

Wealthy enough to afford a wide variety of psychological self-improvement conferences. Insurance and/or available cash allows as much personal and group psychotherapy as needed. Psychological books and journals for personal growth and development are never denied because of finances.

Can only attend occasional, high priority psychological health workshops. Insurance will cover most of the psychotherapeutic interventions needed. Discretionary spending on other psychotherapy that is not covered by insurance is limited. Care is also taken with regards to purchase of psychological books and magazines.

Only rare, inexpensive, or essential psychotherapeutic seminars can be afforded. Insurance will cover only the most critical psychotherapeutic claims with less than the ideal protocols. Finding the extra money for additional personal or group psychotherapy sessions is difficult. Minimal purchases of books and magazines is all that can be afforded

Only free psychological counseling workshops or very inexpensive, community sponsored ones can be afforded. Insurance does not cover any worthwhile psycho-therapy. Total dependence on library for psychological health educational material.

Money, time, and energy are exhausted from working hard to survive. Money problems cause great emotional distress. No insurance.

0

resources identified there, will help greatly in affording one's needs in psychological health. There are many opportunities to improve psychological health. Some of these depend on money. It is time now to rate how budgetary restrictions impede psychological health on a 0-10 scale and make the appropriate entries on the charts.

## FINANCES AFFECTING INTIMATE RELATIONSHIPS

Individual differences in psychological security are reflected in our attitudes towards money. These very sensitive and core issues about security and money are often the primary trigger for discord in intimate relationships. Relationship conflict has a devastating effect on our health in a multitude of ways. Often money is linked to time. If we have to work so much, or if our job is so draining that we do not have time to build healthy intimate relationships, there can be tragic consequences. Also, money should be available for family counseling, couples workshops, or relationship books. The careful evaluation and use of the resources in this chapter will dramatically improve the connections between money, psychological security, and close personal relationships. Be sure to calculate, then mark in the appropriate spectrum analyses charts, how eco-

**ECONOMIC SPECTRUM ANALYSIS — INTIMATE RELATIONSHIPS**

10

Wealthy enough to have all the money needed to support healthy intimate relations. Couples workshops, marriage counseling, books, are readily available. The economic situation affords the time to spend building relationships.

Financially stable enough to afford priority couple workshops and a significant number of books on the subject. Insurance will pay for some marriage and family counseling. Economically stable enough to allow time to work on relationships.

Only rare, inexpensive, or essential couples seminars can be afforded. Insurance will pay for only minimal counseling. A limited number of books and time are available for at-home relationship work.

Only free counseling workshops or very inexpensive community sponsored ones can be afforded. Insurance does not cover any worthwhile relationship therapy sessions. Total dependence on library for relationship health educational material.

Money, time, and energy are exhausted from working hard to survive. Finances are a continual area of relationship conflict. No insurance.

0

nomics is presently affecting the health of your intimate relationships. This can be a first step towards deepening relationships; we will explore this further in later chapters.

## ECONOMIC STATUS AND SOCIAL HEALTH

A never-ending saga continues to be played out in infinite ways. "Keeping up with the Joneses" dominates our social lives with unhealthy results. So much of what we buy is for social image. If more social interaction centered around charitable efforts rather than conspicuous display of materialistic image-enhancers, everyone's health would ben-

efit. After evaluating how money affects healthy social relationships and marking the charts accordingly, ask, how can I turn my budget away from things to prop up my image and toward making worthwhile social contacts? Assistance with this question comes in the chapter on Relationship Health.

## MONEY AND THE LAW

How does our personal economic situation affect the legal aspects of our life? This is not only a reference to how much money we can spend on good legal advice; we also have to look at how our

---

### ECONOMIC SPECTRUM ANALYSIS — SOCIAL HEALTH

10

Wealthy enough that money provides many opportunities for broad socialization without any restrictions.

Affluent enough to benefit from social opportunities others are restricted from, but these are not unlimited advantages. No apparent adverse impact on overall health.

Certain social tiers are unavailable because of economic status. This begins to mildly impact overall health.

A wide range of social opportunities is denied because of economic position. Overall health is harmed in a multitude of ways.

Financial difficulties exclude most opportunities for healthy socialization. This is a major factor contributing to ill health.

Homeless outcast where most social contacts produce more problems.

0

financial position influences legislation which has a certain health impact.

Obviously certain aspects of our health can be determined by how much money we have to spend on quality legal work in business contracts, divorces, wills, tax law, trusts, etc. Evaluate this impact. Add it to an assessment of how laws affect personal health when our economic position determines how much we can influence those laws.

There are many laws that intentionally or unintentionally adversely affect the health of the disadvantaged. It is more difficult to change these inequitable laws when one's finances are shaky. In the world of legislative action money moves bills through to passage. Historically, the economically disadvantaged have always had a more difficult time supporting laws which assist in building their own health: civil rights, women's rights, protection and access for the handicapped, health care for the poor, progressive tax reform, food stamps, nutrition programs for poverty ridden mothers and infants, educational support from government assistance, job training, drug treatment programs— all struggle for continued legislative support because they are poor and have less influence on legislators. If your health is suffering because of these legislative inequities, factor this into the rating of the Spectrum Analysis on Legal Health.

## ECONOMIC SPECTRUM ANALYSIS — LEGAL HEALTH

10

Wealthy enough to hire the best lawyers. Employ lobbyists to influence legislation that improves personal health. Legal health is never jeopardized for lack of money.

Affluent enough to hire good legal counsel on priority issues. Lobbyists cannot be afforded, but time and money can be spent phoning legislative representatives when necessary.

Financially stable enough to hire attorneys when necessary, but must be cost conscious when choosing the lawyer and the situations. Can afford a rare phone call to legislative representatives, but mostly write letters when the issues seem important and directly affect personal health.

Monetarily forced to use do-it-yourself wills and divorces. Consult paralegals before writing own business contracts. Speak up at city council meetings only when issues have substantial personal impact.

Poverty forces unethical arrangements with sleazy lawyers and doctors in order to glean some pennies from an inequitable system. Much yelling and screaming about unjust laws, but no one hears.

0

## BUDGETING FOR OPTIMAL TECHNOLOGICAL ADVANTAGE

*The cost of a thing is the amount of what I call life which is required to be exchanged for it, immediately or in the long run.*

**Henry David Thoreau**

Make a list of how many technological advances you could use in daily life that cannot be afforded but would significantly contribute to overall health. The technology of simple sanitation, food preservation, basic health care, and plain, efficient transportation are foundations on which to start. Appropriate technology to fit one's needs is a valuable commodity. Unfortunately, many people have difficulty prioritizing what is wise technology.

How we wisely choose the technology that serves us on a daily basis determines how much money we have for a wide range of health costs. Some individuals, because of their health status, might require very expensive high technology, such as kidney dialysis. For them, this is wise use of technology, even though it is very expensive. A power-assisted toilet paper roller (if it is ever categorized as a health enhancing, appropriate technology) may be relatively inexpensive in comparison, but is the $19.95 justified when you don't have hot running water? Everybody knows some-

---

## ECONOMIC SPECTRUM ANALYSIS — TECHNOLOGICAL HEALTH

10

Wealth bestows the ability to purchase any technological device that will improve or maintain health.

Affluence affords many technological advances that help one's health.

Financial security allows some opportunities for technology to positively influence health.

Economic status dictates careful utilization of technology that affects health on priority basis only.

Monetary concerns significantly limit the opportunity to benefit from needed technological advances related to health matters.

Economic impoverishment severely denies opportunities to benefit from even modest health-oriented technology.

Significant health damage occurs due to economically-compelled reliance on ineffectual technology.

0

one who could greatly benefit from a complete brain transplant, but who is going to pay for that technological advancement?

When everything is considered, rate from 0-10 personal economic influences on how technology contributes to wholeness.

*I'm living so far beyond my income that we may almost be said to be living apart.*

e. e. cummings

## FINANCES AND TRANSPORTATION

At one end we have a poor, destitute person exposed to high risk hitchhiking and dangerous, smog-laden air. He is unable to hold or get jobs because of unreliable transportation; he is im-

peded from normal social contacts and cannot develop intimate relationships adequately, and he is even discouraged from regular worship because he can't get to it. A rating of 0 on the Transportation Spectrum Analysis scale would be appropriate here.

At the other end of the range, a 10 rating, there may be a millionaire who can arrange to work close enough to ride a bicycle on safe bike paths. On special trips he can afford to purchase a rare Volvo prototype car that gets 100 mpg. For long vacations he has the time to use his sailboat rather than fly far away.

Most will find themselves somewhere in between.

*To get back on your feet miss two car payments.*

Unknown

## ECONOMIC SPECTRUM ANALYSIS — TRANSPORTATION

10

Wealthy enough to afford ultra-modern, super fuel-efficient, environmentally clean, and safe modes of transportation with no limitations.

Affluence enables one to purchase transportation alternatives that assure high levels of health protection.

Economically secure enough to benefit from priority choices on different transportation options.

Financial constraints force use of transportation that imposes substantial risks and some negative health effects.

A very limited budget for transportation requires use of high risk transport that produces substantial health problems.

0

## ECONOMICS SUPPORTING ENVIRONMENTAL HEALTH

How do economics affect personal ecological health? Asking oneself the following questions might help calculate a rating for the Environmental Health Spectrum Analysis.

Do I have the financial capability to live in clean country air, or am I forced, by work, to live where urban pollution slowly takes its unknown toll on my health?

Do I have the money or superb insurance to afford the best allergy and toxicity tests and treatments by doctors of the American Academy of Environmental Medicine, or am I financially obliged to buy drug store quick fix antihistamines?

Can I afford safer dental fillings, or do I have to settle for the standard, cheap, toxic, mercury amalgams?

Can I afford organically grown produce, or am I lured into buying cheap pesticide, herbicide, and hormone-laden food?

Is the money available for top-quality home air filtration devices, or is breathing polluted indoor air a financially necessary reality?

Does my economic status allow me to use the best water purification systems, or am I left with drinking the questionable tap water?

Can I financially manage home testing for damaging agents like radon, electromagnetic radiation, and formaldehyde?

Am I able to surround myself with safe home construction materials like hardwoods, ceramic tile, earth, stone, and stainless steel, or am I

### ECONOMIC SPECTRUM ANALYSIS — ENVIRONMENTAL HEALTH

10

Wealth provides every conceivable protection from personal, adverse environmental impact. Money spent on ecological concerns improves one's own health and that of other living beings.

Affluence contributes to substantial ecological safety and assistance to others' environmental health.

Economic stability supplies some personal priority environmental protections.

Finances impose significant limits on discretionary environmental protection measures. Some obvious negative health effects result.

Poverty causes major, unavoidable toxic exposure that drastically influences personal health and the ecological health of others.

0

required to live with the immunological stress of paneling, particle board, plywood, foam, plastic, and synthetic carpets and fabrics?

Can I make an up-front investment in energy and resource conservation mechanisms like insulation, energy efficient light bulbs, refrigerators, furnaces, heat pumps, automobiles, water heaters, low-flow faucets, water-saving toilets? These will in the future pay me back many times over and contribute to global environmental health. Or am I financially forced to waste energy and resources because I don't have the money to invest in energy conservation?

Can I afford stainless steel cookware rather than cheap, toxic aluminum?

Can I afford organic, nontoxic cleaning agents?

## MONEY FOR PLAY

*Work hard and save your money, and when you are old you will be able to buy the things only the young can enjoy.*

**Unknown**

Wisely chosen play makes us happy and healthy. But do we allow enough time for wholesome recreation? "Time is money," and that is part of the problem. Many of us have to spend so much time earning the necessities of life that there is no time to "live" life. And when there is time, we are frequently too fatigued to really enjoy ourselves. Or we choose, often because of finances, types of recreation that do not promote healthy activity or

### ECONOMIC SPECTRUM ANALYSIS — RECREATION

10

No monetary or time restraints on recreational choices. This allows for significant health enhancement.

Recreational freedom plays an essential role in providing improved health. Options are not unlimited but substantial enough to have a significant positive health impact.

Recreational opportunities are frequent and substantial, but choices have to be carefully made because of budgetary constraints.
Health could be improved with more money and time available.

Play time is significantly reduced to occasions and circumstances that are essential.
Health is adversely affected by this situation.

Economic necessities have required continuous work for years without vacation. Weekends are not available for recreation either. Entertainment consists of a couple of beers on payday. Health suffers significantly.

0

exercise in the process. From the list below see if healthy fun can be distinguished from unhealthy fun:

- bicycling in the countryside
- wolfing down a couple of hot dogs and snorting a few beers at the tractor pull
- canoeing on a serene river
- lying on the couch all day watching soap operas while eating ice cream and candy
- backpacking in the mountains
- listening to ear-shattering music and dancing til the wee hours of the morning in a drug and alcohol induced brain fog
- swimming and windsurfing in a glistening lake.

- taking some brews to the woods and shredding some tin cans with the ole AK-47

The answers to this quiz are *not* at the end of the chapter. Don't forget to fill out the Recreation Spectrum Analysis and mark the Economic Health Summary.

## FINANCES AND SPIRITUAL FULFILLMENT

Observe the two extremes: 1.) One has too much cash not to be caught up in the drunkenness of materialism and sensuality that blind a person to the subtle inner urgings of spirit. 2.) One has so little money that stealing, cheating, lying, and otherwise corrupt personal behavior are forced for the sake of survival. This conflict between oneself

**ECONOMIC SPECTRUM ANALYSIS — SPIRITUAL FULFILLMENT**

10

Economic status fully supports spiritual aspirations without any inhibitions.

Monetary situation significantly assists spiritual endeavors.

Financial security provides no major economic detriment to spiritual development.

Fiscal constraints adversely impact spiritual efforts.

Money problems cause significant moral and spiritual degradation.

Poverty seriously degrades personal morality and has a major adverse impact on others' spiritual health.

0

and the world overrides the spiritual drives toward unity.

Between these two extremes lie the many degrees of influence that money imposes on spiritual development. How does money affect personal spiritual growth and fulfillment? Not enough money to partake in needed spiritual classes? So much money that it keeps me immersed in worldly desires and my self and away from the unknown All? Evaluate for yourself and choose an appropriate rating from 0-10.

*It is not wealth that stands in the way of liberation but the attachment to wealth.*

**E. F. Schumacher**

The individual Economic Health Spectrum Analyses should now be completed. We should now transfer the individual ratings to the Economic Health Spectrum Analysis Summary below. This gives us more of a comprehensive look at how money affects different aspects of our life and health. Ultimately, we want to direct our income to those aspects of our health that are in the greatest need of promotion and financial support. Some areas might need time and effort but not be significantly affected by more money.

Let us say we discover that we are spending a disproportionate amount of income on junk food, luxury fashions, and expensive cars. We also realize that these items are not providing the happiness

## ECONOMIC HEALTH
## SPECTRUM ANALYSIS SUMMARY

| How one's economic status influences degrees of contribution to each aspect of health. | poor | average | acceptable | optimal |
|---|---|---|---|---|
| | 0 | 5 | | 10 |

Food |⸺⸺⸺⸺⸺⸺⸺⸺⸺⸺|

Clothing |⸺⸺⸺⸺⸺⸺⸺⸺⸺⸺|

Shelter |⸺⸺⸺⸺⸺⸺⸺⸺⸺⸺|

Health Care |⸺⸺⸺⸺⸺⸺⸺⸺⸺⸺|

Educational Aspirations |⸺⸺⸺⸺⸺⸺⸺⸺⸺⸺|

Psychological Health |⸺⸺⸺⸺⸺⸺⸺⸺⸺⸺|

Intimate Relationships |⸺⸺⸺⸺⸺⸺⸺⸺⸺⸺|

Social Health |⸺⸺⸺⸺⸺⸺⸺⸺⸺⸺|

Legal Health |⸺⸺⸺⸺⸺⸺⸺⸺⸺⸺|

Technological Health |⸺⸺⸺⸺⸺⸺⸺⸺⸺⸺|

Transportation |⸺⸺⸺⸺⸺⸺⸺⸺⸺⸺|

Environmental Health |⸺⸺⸺⸺⸺⸺⸺⸺⸺⸺|

Recreation |⸺⸺⸺⸺⸺⸺⸺⸺⸺⸺|

Spiritual Fulfillment |⸺⸺⸺⸺⸺⸺⸺⸺⸺⸺|

or wholeness that we want. We also conclude that we have problems that might be helped considerably by spending more on healthy food, healthy, exercise-related recreation, and family counseling. By looking closely at ourselves in this way, we uncover a truer sense of where our values lie. This allows us to better coordinate our expenditures with our values. A more logical redistribution of finances will provide a more integrated wholeness and thus greater health and happiness.

**SUCCESS**
*To laugh often and much; to win the respect of intelligent people and affection of children; to earn the appreciation of honest critics and endure the betrayal of false friends; to appreciate beauty, to find the best in others; to leave the world a bit better, a garden patch or a redeemed social condition; to know even one life has breathed easier because you have lived. This is to have succeeded.*

**Ralph Waldo Emerson**

---

# OCCUPATIONAL HEALTH

*The trouble with the rat race is that, even if you win, you're still a rat.*

**Lily Tomlin**

We toil away at a job that is emotionally dissatisfying, economically marginal, intellectually suffocating, and spiritually stifling for decades just to put food on the table, a roof overhead, clothes on our back, and pull a few weeks of "vacation" every year. What is wrong with this ethic? Those might be minimal standards for survival, but when we want to look at the wholeness of our Being and see where economics and livelihood play a role in our overall health, we must look at more.

We will look at three alternatives to the work ethic described above. All three have significant advantages over what most people are engaged in. We will also present a careful spectrum analysis of how occupation affects each aspect of our health so that we can reassess how we might change important elements of this arena of life. We will also provide resources for more in-depth investigation of career choices.

In many cultures, and in the past of our own, the prime determinant of career choice was someone other than oneself. Depending on locale, women were, and are today, expected to have mothering as their primary career. Not much choice in most places. Men follow in the footsteps of their fathers by learning their trade or taking over the family business. Sometimes the state, by testing, design, need, or randomness determines job tracks. Sometimes military conscription determines to a large degree one's occupational description. In some cultures church or parents choose a young child for a religious career.

As the world changes, democracy spreads, new ways of behaving are adopted, specific skills are needed, and the uniqueness of individuals is discovered. People are making more independent choices about livelihood. This is a beneficial trend. It tends to break old ingrained patterns of behavior and adopts more thoughtful analysis of present circumstances. Yes, it will generate some conflict between old and new, but that is to be expected with any transition.

Also in the past, occupations were often seen as jobs of survival, occupations that supplied families with the necessities of life. This should be distinguished from actual livelihoods, a term which means more than just a survival income for time and effort spent. "Livelihood" connotes a greater contribution to one's total life. Since we are investigating how each aspect of our life affects our overall health, we certainly want to deal with all that "livelihood" signifies.

## WORK FOR JOY, NOT MONEY

Marsha Sinetar, in her book *Do What You Love, The Money Will Follow: Discovering Your Right Livelihood,* expounds eloquently on a fuller definition of right livelihood. Sinetar proposes a vision of work that takes its rightful place in our lives—as a major determinant of self. It shapes psychological growth, societal contribution, and spiritual development. If it factors in so powerfully with so many elements of our being over such an expanse of time, livelihood choice should be evaluated as much from the heart as from the pocketbook or from others' old programming. Our continually transforming values, insights, capabilities, expressive desires, sense of responsibility, and needs should weigh in along with monetary factors.

*Profit should be a by-product of serving others.*
                                                                    **Unknown**

## BUDDHIST RIGHT LIVELIHOOD

Sinetar's analysis is similar to a Buddhist work ethic that has been in existence for millennia. Four criteria determine "right livelihood," according to Buddhist precepts. They are listed here in descending order of importance.

1. The work should allow for the spiritual development of the participant.

2. It should help humanity.

3. It should do no harm to living beings.

4. And purposely last, it should provide for the family's needs but not its greed.

We will expand and detail these two outlooks more when we do a spectrum analysis of the effect of occupation on various aspects of our life. But, we want to touch upon another philosophy which was mentioned earlier in the context of economic health.

## TAKE THE MONEY AND RUN . . . TOWARDS GOOD DEEDS

The New Road Map Foundation distributes an audiotape seminar, *Transforming Your Relationship With Money & Achieving Financial Independence.* This guide proposes that the most effective way to live is to divorce those activities devoted to making a lot of money. The premise: the acquisition of money will always warp on-the-job decisions concerning values, aspirations, free expression, and spiritual conviction.

How do we avoid this conflict?

1. Energy is directed first towards earning money in the most diligent way possible, within the boundaries of our values.

2. Save much of our earnings for a quick retirement nest egg to be invested wisely.

3. Then live within the bounds of our personal definition of "voluntary simplicity."

4. Then we are free to participate in whatever kind of personal growth or "right works" is ideal, totally unshackled by monetary concerns.

Thus, the freedom of right livelihood from monetary lust creates a more authentic expression of our innermost drive towards unity. Who benefits from this program? Those who have a well paying but unfulfilling job and are considering a career change or early retirement to satisfy deeper feelings and drives.

*First secure an independent income,*
*then practice virtue.*
                                                                    **Greek proverb**

The question of right livelihood is clarified by a closer evaluation of how the work environment—past, present, or future—affects other parts of our life. A spectrum analysis of these relationships will provide more valuable information on which to base those decisions. We will look at nine influences, then try to integrate all of them into a personal occupational health summary.

But what of the unemployed? They include job seekers, those in retirement, and those taking a purposeful leave of absence from employment.

They may include full-time housewives and mothers—depending on how they define themselves. All of these individuals can proceed with the following evaluations and spectrum analyses, but the slant of the questions will be a bit different. Instead of answering how one's employment affects each aspect of health, the question deals with one's *un*employment and its influence on these various aspects of our being. Full-time mothers can answer from both perspectives—how does full time employment as a mother influence these different parts of oneself *and* how does not being employed outside of the home affect those same elements?

*A Johns Hopkins University study for
the Joint Congressional Economic Committee
found that when a 1% rise in unemployment
was sustained for six years,
the social stress of this occupational and
economic crisis for the one million workers
and their families could be seen vividly
in health statistics: 36,887 more deaths,
20,240 from heart and vascular problems,
495 from cirrhosis of the liver, 920 from suicides.
648 additional murders accompanied that
magnitude of work-related stress,
along with 3,340 more people going to prison
for other crimes.
There were also 4,227 added admissions
to psychiatric institutions.*

## LIVELIHOOD'S EFFECT ON PHYSICAL HEALTH

The first occupational influence we want to observe is the physical effects our job has on us. We can observe simple things. Do we arise in the morning greeting the sun, the birdsong, and work with joyful, energetic aliveness, or do we have to drag a numb, tired, weak carcass from bed to job site in the haze of half-closed eyes? How many cups of coffee does it take to keep functioning with some semblance of alertness throughout the workday? How many pain relievers or antacids are consumed in a week at work? How much energy is left for activities after work and on weekends? How

many on-the-job accidents are occurring? Is there high absenteeism among co-workers?

*"Between 75 and 85 % of all industrial accidents
are stress related."* [1]

Or a more complex analysis can be made. Upon careful examination by the appropriate health care professional: Is your blood pressure too high from stress at work? Is the level of nutrition in your blood deficient because of hectic eating habits at work? Is stress elevating your cholesterol? Are there high levels of toxic contaminants in the body due to exposure to harmful substances at work? Is aerobic fitness suffering because of a sedentary lifestyle? Are the physical demands of the job progressively damaging muscles, ligaments, tendons, joints, and nerves?

What are the risks of being killed on the job? What are the risks of being severely injured? What are the risks of long term exposure to your working environment?

*9,000,000 American workers are injured
every year due to on-the-job injuries.
70,000 are permanently disabled.
11,000 die.*

*Most Dangerous Occupations*

| | | | |
|---|---|---|---|
| 1. | Agricultural | 1500 deaths/year | 48/100,000 |
| 2. | Construction | 2200 deaths/year | 34/100,000 |
| 3. | Mining | 200 deaths/year | 25/100,000 |

Work satisfaction is a good statistical predictor of absenteeism, illness risk, and longevity. Conflict on the job can make one much more susceptible to minor physical stresses from the work than when job satisfaction accompanies these stresses. Having a sense of control on the job, as in managerial positions, protects one from high stress.

Evaluate as much information as you can gather concerning this relationship between work and physical well-being. Then choose a number on a scale of one to ten representing the safety of the job. A 0-2 rating should indicate that the job is severely damaging to physical health. Use a rating of 3-4 to show significant negative physical effects. A 5-6 rating might have both negative and positive physical health effects. When there are more advantages for physical health and only some minor disadvantages, use 7-8. Use 9-10 to signify an occupational environment that greatly enhances physical health. When a representative figure is chosen, transfer it to the appropriate scale on the Spectrum Analysis Summary on page 154.

Obviously, the more tests of one's physical condition, the more accurate the overall rating and evaluation will be. Remember that serious dysfunction and tissue damage may often be occurring unnoticed, and that physiological tests can reveal early signs of serious health problems. This point is particularly important in those individuals who in any way are at high risk, either because of their health, the circumstances they work under, or both.

## INFLUENCES ON PSYCHOLOGICAL FUNCTIONING

Turning to the psychological effects of our job, we can use the same method of inquiry, from simple to complex assessment. Because of the intimate, intertwining bond between body and psyche, even some of the same questions can be asked. In the section above when answering the question, "Do we arise in the morning greeting the sun, the birdsong, and work with joyful, energetic aliveness?" the reply can tell us as much about our emotional attitude concerning work as the physical effects.

Do we look forward to work each day? What parts of the work day do we enjoy? Which do we dread? Does our job increase our self-esteem or weaken it? Is a hectic pace, impatience, and hurriedness doing us harm? What emotions generated at work are brought home—joy and excitement, or are there unresolved negative feelings adversely impacting home life?

There are psychological inventories that can be taken to get a clearer description of our psychological state. These might be used if problems at work are significantly troublesome. If the psychological effects of the job are severe, closer reading of the chapter and resources on Psychological Health may help clarify the relationship between health on the job and emotional well-being.

## INTELLECTUAL STIMULATION AND EDUCATIONAL OPPORTUNITY

Does the job stimulate creativity and allow for its free expression? Does it encourage the wise use of logic? Or is it a mindless wasteland with repetitive tasks that turn the brain into mush? On the other hand, does it demand fatiguing mental work that leaves you drained? Are your colleagues intellectually stimulating or do they inspire images of brain-damaged crustaceans? Are there opportunities for educational advancement? Again, rate these influences on a scale from one to ten, then transfer that figure to the Occupational Health Spectrum Analysis Summary on page 161.

## OCCUPATION'S PROVISION FOR ECONOMIC SECURITY

After proceeding through the evaluations earlier in this chapter, you should have the beginning of a more accurate picture of your livelihood's effect on other aspects of your health. Now the task is to assess how much your business contributes to economic security. Is it impeding your vital needs? Or is it providing just your needs with few comforts? At the upper end of the scale is it providing every conceivable economic advantage?

One of the economic aspects to consider is how our job provides for health care or health insurance, since every man, woman, and child in America spends about $3,760 per year on health care costs. It is also wise at this juncture to see how the money which work provides gives you the ability to help other aspects of your life. But what we are specifically looking at in this section is how the job itself contributes to these health aspects.

## CONTRIBUTIONS OF WORK TO ENHANCING SOCIAL RELATIONSHIPS

How do we get along with our colleagues? Everyone knows from personal experience how enjoyable or how stressful these relationships can be. And studies have verified the positive and negative results of on-the-job interactions, whether they be in reference to co-workers or the employer. Our livelihood sometimes provides one of the most substantial opportunities for health enhancing human relationships. On-the-job contacts with colleagues might produce very enriching experiences and turn into fulfilling, off-the-job friendships. There may be opportunities to expand our social network beyond its present bounds into classes above and below our own and thereby augment our wholeness in many ways.

The same can be said for other people we meet in the course of our employment, like customers and clients. But all these relationships could be detrimental in nature also. We only have to imagine the stresses that could beset a manager in charge of customer complaints or an undercover police officer dealing on a daily basis with only the dregs of the earth.

Rate from 0-10 how livelihood contributes to social health with this in mind.

## EFFECT OF WORK ON PERSONAL RELATIONSHIPS AT HOME

How does my job affect my intimate relationships and family life? This often consumes time, money, and emotions. Does my job give me time to spend with my loved ones? Do the economic circumstances surrounding my employment affect my home relationships beneficially or adversely? How does the way work makes me feel carry over to how I relate to others outside of work?

## SOCIETAL VALUE OF THE JOB

*Unless life is lived for others,*
*it is not worthwhile.*
**Mother Teresa**

Our sense of societal obligation has much to do with how fulfilling our livelihood is. Many people have quit otherwise lucrative jobs because they perceived little positive benefit to humanity—or perhaps an actual detriment. How much we value this aspect of our occupation is a gauge of how expanded the person's sense of self is. People with

the attitude of "Hey, it's good money. It's not my concern how my job affects others" have a very egocentric perspective on the world. People in the alcohol, tobacco, and illicit drug businesses are typical examples of this stance. One can just see, smell, and taste the separateness that permeates this attitude, distancing oneself from unity, wholeness, and health.

Others have a sense of self so all-encompassing that what they do for themselves is almost indistinguishable from what they do for others. All decisions take in the ramifications of their actions for everyone else. This means more responsibility, but it also carries a deeper sense of fulfillment.

Again, use the 0 to 10 rating scale to evaluate how your livelihood contributes to humanity. When the entire Occupational Health Spectrum Analysis Summary is completed, an additional evaluation can be made of how much this aspect is important to your personal occupational health.

*I slept and dreamt that life was joy,*
*I woke and saw that life was service,*
*I acted and behold, service was joy.*
**Rabindranath Tagore**

## PERSONAL ENVIRONMENTAL SAFETY

Rating our job with respect to how well it protects workers from harmful environmental contaminants is often overlooked. We will be taking a deeper look at personal environmental safety in a later chapter, but we want to begin the investigation here with the work environment.

*Approximately 20,000 workers die each year*
*because of carcinogen exposure*
*at their place of employment.*

For some individuals, like those who work with toxic pesticides and herbicide or industrial chemicals, environmentally caused illness may be the most significant agent affecting their entire health. And others may work in environmental conditions that actually enhance health, like park rangers and organic farmers. Listed below are some items in the workplace to be wary of as possible causes of environmental illness. The chapter on Environmental Health will provide additional resources about other possible offensive agents as well as early warning signs and symptoms of contamination—which can be psychological as well as physical.

Beware of:

- secondhand cigarette smoke
- synthetic cleaning agents and solvents
- air fresheners
- products containing formaldehyde (plywood, particle board, paneling, foam)
- plastics
- vinyl chloride
- pesticides
- herbicide
- treated lumber
- heavy metals like lead, mercury, and cadmium
- asbestos
- petroleum based chemicals
- radioactive substances or ionizing radiation devices
- burned fuel by-products—soot, carbon monoxide, sulphur dioxide, nitrogen dioxide.

If you are suspicious that there are environmental contaminants in your work place or that you are suffering adverse health effects, it is important to work closely with a physician from the American Academy of Environmental Medicine, the Occupational Health and Safety Administration, or the Environmental Protection Agency. Use the resources in the chapter on Environmental Health.

## COMMUNITY AND PLANETARY ECOLOGICAL CONTRIBUTION

With the increasing awareness of environmental responsibility, the impact of our livelihood on community and/or global ecological health becomes a part of our evaluation of occupational health. There is a great upsurge in the number of people seeking employment in companies that treat the environment kindly. People are also more hesitant to work for businesses known for their polluting ways. Even greater is the number of individuals who see ecological harm being done by their employers and choose to creatively remedy those offenses for the benefit of the environment and the company. Many businesses are seeing great savings, significant profit gains, and better public relations by adopting energy and resource conservation methods. Many companies are being forced by public opinion and employee pressure to adopt cleaner methods of operation, which often make them more cost effective in the marketplace.

When a person's sense of self is larger than what is encased in his body he will usually want his job, if it is going to be contributing to holistic health, to benefit, or at least not harm, the environment. So rate how *your* job satisfies *your* environmental concerns.

## OPPORTUNITY FOR SPIRITUAL DEVELOPMENT

Here are some questions which will help you rate how your job contributes to your spiritual growth and fulfillment:

Does your job help humanity, animals, and plants to flourish, blossom, and express their true nature without suffering?

Do you have the opportunity to care for others with your skills?

Does your livelihood give you a deep, inner joy?

Does it provide an opportunity to practice concentration and mindfulness that ultimately can benefit spiritual awareness?

Does your occupation help put ego in proper perspective with spirit? Or does your work build up the ego disproportionately, thus stifling your spiritual Self? Or does your job so degrade the ego that it produces self-esteem with such a weak foundation that the spiritual Self has nothing to build on?

Does your job give you the opportunity to dedicate your daily efforts to the Unity of all Beings?

## A COMPREHENSIVE VIEW OF OCCUPATIONAL HEALTH

Now that we have investigated individual aspects of occupational health, we can gather together all that information, integrate it, and use it to make any necessary changes in livelihood that will enhance our total health. Now it must be remembered that action in this area will be influenced by further evaluations in later chapters. Right now we may have a multitude of agendas to remedy. Many may be work-related health problems. But as we investigate different aspects of our being, these agendas may be altered in importance or character. It is hoped that by the end of the book an all-inclusive perspective can be built that will allow for the most effective choice of priority health enhancement strategies; changes of livelihood are just one part of this.

For now what can be done with the information in this section is to

1. realize how important occupational influences are on so many different aspects of our health;

2. begin to see what aspects of livelihood can be altered to improve overall health;

3. start using the resources at the end of this chapter to further investigate important elements of occupational health that might need priority attention, once a comprehensive health enhancement program is started;

4. begin some occupational health changes that are certainly and definitely needed now.

For instance, you may now realize more clearly that one aspect of your livelihood is in serious need of alteration, but other areas are quite acceptable. This might tell you that a change of career is not

## OCCUPATIONAL HEALTH
## SPECTRUM ANALYSIS SUMMARY

| How one's occupation influences each aspect of health. | poor | average | acceptable | optimal |
|---|---|---|---|---|
| | 0 | 5 | | 10 |

***************************************************************************************************

| | |
|---|---|
| Physical Health | |———————————————————| |
| Psychological Well-being | |———————————————| |
| Intellectual Stimulation and Educational Opportunity | |———————————————————| |
| Economic Security | |———————————————————————| |
| Social Relationships | |———————————————————————| |
| Personal Relationships at Home | |———————————————————————| |
| Societal Value of the Job | |———————————————————————| |
| Personal Environmental Safety | |———————————————————| |
| Community and Planetary Ecological Contribution | |———————————————————————| |
| Opportnity for Spiritual Development | |———————————————————————| |

necessary, but something specific must be done, and that particular resources in the book must be consulted to best determine what actions will be most appropriate.

Or you may realize that your job has so many detriments that it is a major cause of ill health—so much so that a complete change of career is needed. Look at the career change resources and continue on through the book to see what other areas might need attention.

*Why should we be in such desperate haste to succeed, and in such desperate enterprises?*
*If a man does not keep pace*
*with his companions,*
*perhaps it is because he hears*
*a different drummer.*
*Let him step to the music which he hears,*
*however measured or far away.*

**Henry David Thoreau**

---

## ECONOMIC / OCCUPATIONAL HEALTH RESOURCES

*Ultimate success will depend on your commitment to honesty, peace, and love for your planet home.*

**Lawrence J. Peter**

★Denotes Best of the Best Resources

### *Books*

Bolles, Richard. *What Color Is Your Parachute?* Ten Speed Press, 1993.

Bolles, Richard. *The Three Boxes of Life—and How to Get Out of Them.* Ten Speed Press, 1981.

Bolles, Richard. *How to Create Your Ideal Job or Next Career.* Ten Speed Press, 1989.

★Breton, Denise and Largent, Christopher. *The Soul of Economies: Spiritual Evolution Goes to the Marketplace.* Idea House Publishing Company.

Dail, Hilda. *The Lotus and the Pool.* Shambhala, 1985. Using the wisdom of the unconscious self for career development.

★Dominguez, Joseph R. *Transforming Your Relationship with Money & Achieving Financial Independence. 1986.* Excellent audiotape seminar and workbook produced and distributed by The New Road Map Foundation.

★Dominguez, Joe and Robin, Vicki. *Your Money or Your Life.* Viking, 1992.

Durning, Alan. *How Much Is Enough? The Consumer Society and the Future of the Earth.* W.W. Norton, 1993.

★Elgin, Duane. *Voluntary Simplicity: Toward a Life That Is Outwardly Simple, Inwardly Rich.* William Morrow & Co., 1981.

Fassel, Diane. *Working Ourselves to Death.* Harper/San Francisco, 1990.

Fox, Mathew. *The Reinvention of Work: A New Vision of Livelihood for Our Time.* HarperSan Francisco, 1994.

*Good Works.* Dembner Books, 1994. Available from the Essential Information, P.O. Box 19405 Washington, DC 20036; (202) 387-8030. Where to find work that helps humanity.

Gruenfeld, Donald and Gruenfeld, Deborah. *Stress in the American Workplace: Alternatives for the Working Wounded.* LRP Publications.

Harman, Willis and Horman, John. *Creative Work: The Constructive Role of Business in a Transforming Society.* Knowledge Systems, Inc., 1990.

★Hawkins, Paul. *The Ecology of Commerce; A Declaration of Sustainability.* HarperCollins, 1993.

Hawkins, Paul. *The Next Economy.* Balantine, 1984.

★Hwoschinsky, Paul. *True Wealth.* Ten Speed Press, 1990. Systematic evaluation of one's true values and how to live them with money being just a tool.

★Karasek, Robert and Theorell, Tores. *Healthy Work: Stress, Productivity, and the Reconstruction of Working Life.* Basic, 1990.

Kassiola, Joel. *The Death of Industrial Civilization: The Limits to Economic Growth and the Repoliticization of Advanced Industrial Society.* SUNY Press, 1990.

Lacey, Dan. *Your Rights in the Workplace.* Nolo Press, 1991.

Makower, Joel. *Office Hazards: How Your Job Can Make You Sick.* Tilden Press, 1981.

Nader, Ralph and Smith, W.J. *The Frugal Shopper.* Available for $10 from P.O. Box 19367, Washington, DC 20036.

Needleman, Jacob. *Money and the Meaning of Life.* Doubleday, 1991.

Porter, Michael. *The Competitive Advantage of Nations.* Free Press, 1990.

Repa, Barbara Kate. *Your Rights in the Workplace*. Nolo Press, 1993.

Robinson, Bryan. *Work Addiction*. Health Communications, 1989. (800) 851-9100.

★ St. James, Elaine. *Simplify Your Life*. Hyperion, 1994. Great suggestions!

Schor, Juliet. *The Overworked American: The Unexpected Decline of Leisure*. Basic Books, 1991.

★ Schumacher, E. F. *Small Is Beautiful: Economics as if People Mattered*. Harper Collins, 1989.

Schumacher, E. F. *Good Work*. Harper Row, 1979.

Sinetar, Marsha. *Do What You Love, The Money Will Follow: Discovering Your Right Livelihood*. Paulist Press, 1987.

Smith, Devon, ed. *Great Careers*. Garrett Park Press, 1990. Garrett Park Press, P.O. Box 190B, Garrett Park, MD 20896. Where to find right livelihood.

Tulku, Tarthang *Skillful Means*. Dharma Publishing, 1978.

Wachtel, Paul. *The Poverty of Affluence: A Psychological Portrait of the American Way of Life*. New Society Publishers, 1988.

Weisbord, Marvin. *Productive Workplaces: Organizing and Managing Dignity, Meaning, and Community*. Jossey-Bass, 1991.

★ Whitmire, Claude, ed. *Mindfulness and Meaningful Work: Explorations in Right Livelihood*. Parallax Press, 1994.

## *Organizations*

*Most men would feel insulted if it were proposed to employ them in throwing stones over a wall, and then in throwing them back, merely that they might earn their wages. But many are no more worthily employed now.*

**Henry David Thoreau**

Institute for Consumer Responsibility, Box 95770, Seattle WA 98145; (206) 526-8662. Publishes the *National Boycott Newsletter*.

★ The New Road Map Foundation, P.O. Box 15981, Seattle, WA 98115; (206) 527-0437; (206) 527-5114. Helps people lower their consumption of "things" while improving the quality of life on the planet.

The Rockport Institute, 10124 Lakewood, Rockville, MD 20850, (301) 279-2383. Offers a mail order Career Choice Program that evaluates aptitudes, personalities, interests, values, lifestyles, and spiritual orientation to help individuals better choose right livelihood.

## *Career Workshops*

*Nature will not forgive those who fail to fulfill the law of their being.*
*The law of human beings is wisdom and goodness, not unlimited acquisition.*

**Robert M. Hutchins**

*Life/Work Planning: Practicality and Spirituality*. Annual two-week workshop presented by Richard Bolles, P.O. Box 379, Walnut Creek, CA 94597; (510) 935-1865.

## Socially Responsible Spending, Investing, and Doing Business

*If ignorance paid dividends most Americans could make a fortune out of what they don't know about economics.*

**Luther Hodges**

## *Books*

Brill, Jack and Reder, Alan. *Investing from the Heart: The Guide to Socially Responsible Investments and Money Management*. Crown, 1993.

Domini, Amy and Kinder, Peter. *Ethical Investing*. Addison-Wesley, 1984.

Lowry, Ritchie. *Good Money: A Guide to Profitable Social Investing in the 90's*. W.W. Norton, 1991.

Makower, Joel. *The E Factor*. Random House, 1993. Business environmentalism.

Reder, Alan and Brill, Jack. *Investing from the Heart*. Crown, 1992.

## *Periodicals*

*Good Money* and *Netback* are two newsletters about socially responsible investing from Box 363, Calais Stage Road, Worcester, VT 05682; (800) 535-3551.

## *Organizations*

Center for Economic Democracy, P.O. Box 64, Olympia, WA 98507.

Center for the Study of Commercialism, 1875 Connecticut Ave., N.W., Suite 300, Washington, DC 20009-5728; (202) 332-9110.

★ Co-op America, 1850 M St. NW, Suite 700, Washington, DC 20036; (202) 872-5307. Non-profit organization with discount catalog of useful products from so-

RESOURCES

cially responsible businesses. They also publish four other periodicals: *The Socially Responsible Financial Planning Guide, Co-Op America Quarterly* magazine, *Boycott Action News,* and *Co-Op America's National Green Pages,* a directory of businesses that are environmentally and socially responsible.

Council on Economic Priorities, 30 Irving Place, New York, NY 10003; (800) 822-6435. Publishes *Shopping for a Better World.*

New Road Map Foundation, P.O. Box 15981, Seattle, WA 98115. Distributes the audiotape seminar *Transforming Your Relationship with Money and Achieving Financial Independence,* which is also in book form—*Your Money or Your Life* by Joe Dominguez and Vicki Robin.

Social Investment Forum, P.O. Box 57216, Washington, DC 20037; (202) 833-5522; (617) 723-7171; (612) 333-8338. Publishes a quarterly newsletter and investment guide to socially responsible financial professionals.

---

## PROFESSIONAL RESOURCES

*There are four steps to accomplishment:*
*Plan Purposefully.*
*Prepare Prayerfully.*
*Proceed Positively.*
*Pursue Persistently.*

**Unknown**

### Books

Chenoweth, David. *Planning Health Promotion at the Worksite.* Benchmark Press, 1987.

Jacobs, Martin and Sweere, Joseph. "The Role of the Chiropractic Physician in Occupational Health." Sweere, Joseph, ed. *Chiropractic Family Practice: A Clinical Manual.* Aspen Publishers, 1992.

Klarreich, S. Editor *Health and Fitness in the Workplace.* Praeger, 1987.

Parmeggiani, Luigi, ed. *Encyclopedia of Occupational Health and Safety.* 3rd edition, 2 volumes. International Labour Organization, CH—1211, Geneva 22, Switzerland.

Pheasant, Stephen. *Ergonomics, Work, and Health.* Aspen, 1991.

O'Donnell, Michael, ed. *Health Promotion in the Workplace.* Delmar, 1984.

Scofield, M., ed. *Worksite Health Promotion.* Hanley and Belfus, 1990.

Tibbs, Hardin. *Industrial Ecology: An Environmental Agenda for Industry.* Global Business Network, 1993.

### Periodicals

*American Industrial Hygiene Association Journal,* American Industrial Hygiene Association, 345 White Pond Dr., Akron, OH 44311; (216) 873-2442.

*At Work: Stories of Tomorrow's Workplace,* Berrett-Koehler Publishers, Inc., 155 Montgomery St., San Francisco, CA 94104-4109; (800) 929-2929. How-to stories of integrating empowerment, democracy, community involvement, global responsibility, and personal values into the workplace.

*Business Ethics,* P.O. Box 14748, Dayton, OH 45413; (612) 962-4700. Journal of business ethics, social responsibility, environmental consciousness, and community involvement.

*The Green Business Letter,* Tilden Press, 1519 Connecticut Ave., Washington, DC 20036; (800) 955-GREEN; Fax (202) 332-3028. Environmentally sound business practices.

*In Business,* Magna Publications, 2718 Dryden Dr., Madison, WI 53704; (608) 249-2455; Fax (608) 249-0355. Lots of environmental tips for businesses.

*Occupational Hazards,* Penton Publishing, 1100 Superior Ave., Cleveland, OH 44114; (216) 696-7000.

*Pollution Prevention Review,* Executive Enterprises Publications, 22 W. 21st St., New York, NY 10010-6904; (800) 332-8804. Primarily oriented to large companies trying to reduce waste and pollution.

*Professional Safety,* Official Journal of the American Society of Safety Engineers, 1800 E. Oakton St., Des Plaines, IL 60018; (708) 692-4121.

*Safety and Health Magazine,* National Safety Council, P.O. Box 558, Itasda, IL 60143-0558; (800) 621-7619.

*World Business Academy Perspectives,* Berrett-Koehler Publishers, Inc., 155 Montgomery St., San Francisco, CA 94104-4109; (800) 929-2929. Dedicated to transforming the workplace with creativity, social and environmental responsibility, and personal growth to create a better world.

### Organizations

*The Gods only laugh when people*
*pray to them for wealth.*

**Japanese saying**

American Industrial Hygiene Association, 475 Wolfe Ledges Parkway, Akron, OH 44311; (216) 762-4566.

American Society of Safety Engineers, 1800 East Oakton St., Des Plaines, IL 60018-2187; (708) 692-4121.

Bureau of Labor Statistics, Safety, Health, & Working Conditions, 601 D St., NW, Washington, DC 20212; (202) 501-6467.

Department of Occupational Health, Northwestern College of Chiropractic, 2501 West 84th St., Bloomington, MN 55431; (612) 888-4777.

Global Business Network, P.O. Box 8395, Emeryville, CA 94662; (510) 547-6822; Fax (510) 547-8510. Explores healthier business practices of the future.

International Academy of Chiropractic Occupational Health Consultants, 930 Crestview Lane, Owatonna, MN 55060-2116; (507) 455-2524.

International Health Awareness Center, 350 East Michigan Ave., Suite 301, Kalamazoo, MI 49007-3851; (800) 334-4094. Publishes health related brochures, newsletters, booklets, and videos.

National Institutes for Occupational Safety and Health, U.S. Department of Health and Human Services, Public Health Service, Centers for Disease Control, 4676 Columbia Parkway, Cincinnati, OH 45226; (800) 35-NIOSH; (513) 533-8326; Fax (513) 533-8573. Other offices: 200 Independence Ave. SW, Washington, DC 20201; (202) 472-7134; (800) 356-4674.

National Resource Center for Worksite Health Promotion, Washington Business Group on Health, 777 North Capitol St., NE, #800, Washington, DC 20002; (202) 408-9320.

Parlay International, Box 8817, Emeryville CA 94662-0817; (800) 457-2752; (510) 601-1000; Fax (510) 601-1008. Publishes a wide variety of employer, employee, and family health education information, including many safety training programs and OSHA compliance resources.

Washington Business Group on Health, 777 N. Capitol St. NE, Suite 800, Washington, DC 20002; (202) 408-9320; TDD: (202) 408-9333; Fax (202) 408-9332. Provides some valuable information on worksite health promotion.

## REFERENCES

1. Gruenfeld, Donald and Deborah. *Stress in the American Workplace: Alternatives for the Working Wounded.* LRP Publications, 1990.

*Humanity, let us say, is like people packed in an automobile which is traveling downhill without lights at a terrific speed and driven by a four-year-old child. The signposts along the way are all marked "progress."*

**Lord Dunsany**

RESOURCES

# CHAPTER FIVE

# INTELLECTUAL / EDUCATIONAL HEALTH

*Wisdom cherishes only that which makes for the development of the highest potentialities of Man. . . .*
*Only with courage and wisdom can mankind deal with ignorance, with folly, with greed, with violence.*

**Ralph Borsodi**

Pop quiz time!

We will now see how our education is contributing to our wholeness or detracting from it. Although this is obviously an open book test, no reading ahead is allowed to find the "right" answers. Scoring will be on the honor system anyway.

## SECTION 1

***The only reason some people get lost in thought is because it is unfamiliar territory.***

**Paul Fix**

You have 10 x's to disperse amongst the following publications proportional to the amount of time you spend reading them.

_____ Publications listed in this book as resource materials

_____ Books in health food stores and the psychology, self-help, nutrition, exercise, environment, and spirituality sections of bookstores

_____ Daily newspapers, weekly and monthly magazines

_____ Comics

_____ Romance novels, westerns

_____ Porno magazines

_____ Tabloid press

## SECTION 2

***The difference between genius and stupidity is that genius has its limits.***

**Unknown**

You have 10 x's to disperse amongst the following resources proportional to the amount of time you spend on them to better your health.

_____ Resources listed in this book

_____ Similar high quality books and journals not listed

_____ Investigative journalism, news reports, and PBS specials on TV

_____ Medical school textbooks

_____ Popular magazines—*Cosmopolitan, Family Circle* . . .

_____ Pamphlets from the hospital, drug store, or doctor's office

_____ Tabloid press

_____ Advertisements—TV, print, point-of-purchase, radio, billboards

_____ "General Hospital"

## SECTION 3

*When a book and a head collide and there is*
*a hollow sound, is it always from the book?*
**Georg Christoph Lichtenberg**

You have 10 x's to disperse amongst the following resources proportional to the amount you use them as sources for learning about the world.

_____ Active participation in a broad spectrum of endeavors

_____ Resources described in this book

_____ Quality books, journals, PBS programs, how-to videos . . .

_____ Daily newspapers, weekly and monthly magazines

_____ Standard TV programming

_____ Pulp magazines and books

_____ "Who needs more edukashun. I gradutated from high skool."

In each of the three sections above note how high up the x's seemed to congregate. The higher the better. There is no scoring. Everybody passes as long as there is the realization that the more we expose ourselves to quality educational experiences, the closer we move towards wholeness. Those who want A's and B's in the course have to take that realization and act on it in broad fields of human experience by eliminating exposure to garbage inputs and maximizing exposure to the highest quality educational resources.

## SECTION 4

*The two most common things in the Universe are*
*hydrogen and stupidity.*
**Harlan Ellison**

Rate from -10 to +10 how your present knowledge and learning experience detracts from or enhances different aspects of your health.

_____ Physical health
   lifestyle behaviors—stress, accident prevention, risk reduction
   nutritional status
   exercise level and types

_____ Health care choices

_____ Economic status

_____ Occupational opportunities, including degrees and certifications needed

_____ Psychological well-being, including intuition

_____ Relationships
   interpersonal communications
   conflict resolution
   expression of feelings
   learning to love

_____ Ecological safety and responsibility

_____ Spiritual fulfillment and values clarification

Note the areas that need more educational exposure in order to balance your Web of Wholeness.

*The aim of the game is true awakening,*
*full development of the powers latent in man.*
*The game can be played only by people*
*whose observations of themselves and others*
*have led them to a certain conclusion, namely,*
*that man's ordinary state of consciousness,*
*his so-called waking state, is not the highest level*
*of consciousness of which he is capable.*
*In fact, this state is so far from real awakening*
*that it could appropriately be called a form of*
*somnambulism, a condition of "waking sleep."*
**Robert S. DeRopp**

Are we providing ourselves with holistic education to tap all the potentialities of the mind? Or are we muddling through with knowledge and relevant skills insufficient to provide ourselves with even the foundations for a reasonably integrated wholeness?

The human brain is a marvelous system—a grand sending and receiving switchboard and networking center. It receives information from innumerable sources, along many channels of communication (sight, smell, touch, etc.), accommodating countless energy wave forms (light, sound, heat, etc.). Some of these sources, channels, and energy are well known, and many are unknown and unidentified. The ability to integrate all this information in a way that makes us happy, functional human beings is truly amazing.

*Aristotle was famous for knowing everything. He taught that the brain exists merely to cool the blood and is not involved in the process of thinking. This is true only of certain persons.*

**Will Cuppy**

What is even more remarkable is that the brain is merely our mechanism for tapping an infinite Mind, a non-local field of energy, awareness, and meaning not bound by time.

We are blessed with only a few short years on this wondrous planet in these miraculous bodies to discover unimaginable adventures with the senses and even more spectacular explorations into the inner recesses of our being. It is a tragedy to waste the time we have by not using and training our brains to experience life more fully.

What powers of mind and qualities of intellectual performance do we have to cultivate to become more whole, more healthy?

1. One-pointed concentration

2. Moment-to-moment mindfulness

3. Deductive reasoning

4. Inductive reasoning

5. Data storage and information retrieval

6. Logical analysis

7. Abstraction

8. Development of skills and qualifications to provide a living and the necessities of life

9. Intuition

10. Creativity

11. Recognition, expression, and integration of emotions with one's thought processes

12. Keen perception through all of the senses

13. Linguistics

14. Interpersonal communications

15. Values clarification

16. Empathy—blending the wisdom of the mind with the compassion of the heart

17. Development of skills to help others

18. Body knowing
    a. integration of body sensations with emotions
    b. coordination of body movement patterns

19. Adaptive behavioral learning
    a. letting go of bad habits
    b. adopting new, life-enhancing programs
    c. becoming flexible enough to change

20. Learning to integrate one's life with the ecological balance of nature

21. Spiritual insight and wisdom

*We must humble ourselves and acknowledge that despite our intellectual sophistication our actual awareness of mind is primitive.*

**Chogyam Trungpa Rinpoche**

A helpful way to better understand these elements is to illustrate them in an Educational Web of Wholeness.

*Life is a teacher that keeps giving you new problems before you've solved the old ones.*

**Unknown**

Note what qualities need to be worked on to have a balanced Educational Web of Wholeness. Making a commitment to improve these aspects of mind and capacities of the brain will provide many rewards.

A good way to start is to eliminate things that dull our senses and thought processes: standard TV programming, tabloid press, pulp magazines and books, violent, mindless movies.

For more penetrating self-analysis on many aspects of health education, with exercises for improvement, see Denis Postle's *The Mind Gymnasium.*

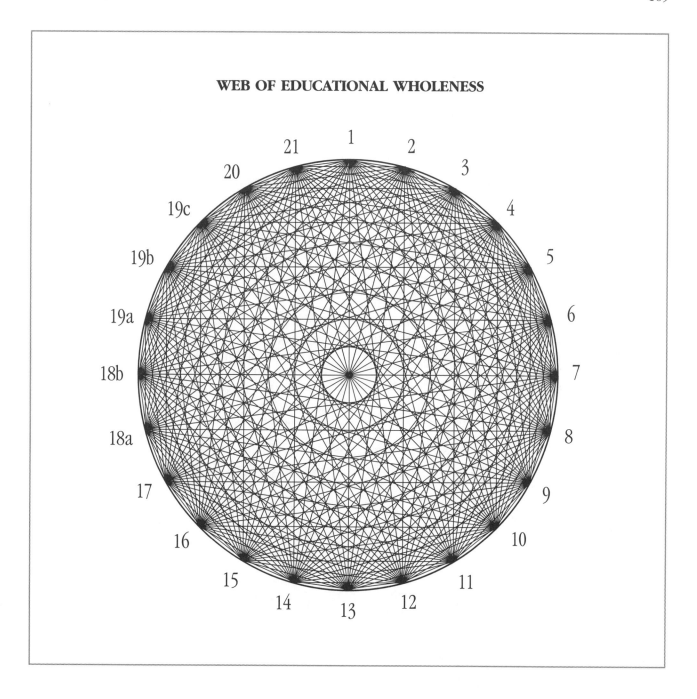

**WEB OF EDUCATIONAL WHOLENESS**

The next step is to start exposing yourself to the Best of the Best Resources to gain more general knowledge of different aspects of health. At the same time look at the more specific resources at the ends of particular sections that are most relevant to you. There is no aspect of health that cannot be improved with better education. It is truly one of the most important avenues to total health enhancement.

*Failures are divided into two classes: those who thought and never did, and those who did and never thought.*

**Salak**

# EDUCATIONAL RESOURCES

*Without an integrated understanding of life, our individual and collective problems
will only deepen and extend. The purpose of education is not to produce
mere scholars, technicians, and job hunters, but integrated men and women who are free of fear;
for only between such human beings can there be enduring peace.*

**J. Krishnamurti**

★Denotes Best of the Best Resources

## *Books*

Anderson, Marianne and Savary, Louis. *Passages: A Guide for Pilgrims of the Mind.* Harper and Row, 1973.

Botkin, James; Elmandjra, Mahdi; and Mircea, Malitza. *No Limits to Learning.* Permagon Press, 1987.

Campbell, Bruce, et al. *LearningWorks: Teaching and Learning Through Multiple Intelligences. 1991.*

Chafetz, Michael. *Smart for Life: How to Improve Your Brain Power at Any Age.* Penguin, 1992.

Clark, Barbara. *Optimizing Learning.* Charles Merrill, 1988.

*Common Boundary Graduate Education Guide,* Common Boundary, 1994. Common Boundary, 5272 River Rd., Suite 650, Bethesda, MD 20816; (301) 652-9495.

Cornell, Judith. *Drawing the Light From Within: Keys to Awaken Your Creative Power.* Prentice-Hall, 1990.

Decker, L. *Community Education: Building Learning Communities.* National Community Education Association, 1990.

Fiske, Edward. *Smart Schools, Smart Kids: Why Do Some Schools Work?* Touchstone, 1991.

Fobes, Richard. *The Creative Problem Solver's Toolbox: A Complete Course in the Art of Creating Solutions to Problems of Any Kind.* Solutions Through Innovation, 1993. Available from Solutions Through Innovation, P.O. Box 1327, Corvallis, OR 97339-1327; (800) 247-6553.

Gibbs, J.J. *Dancing with Your Books: The Zen Way of Studying.* Plume, 1990.

Gross, Ronald. *Peak Learning: A Master Course in Learning How to Learn.* Tarcher, 1991.

Harman, Willis and Rheingold, Howard. *Higher Creativity: Liberating the Unconscious for Breakthrough Insights.* Jeremy P. Tarcher, 1984.

Hoffer, Abram and Walker, Morton. *Smart Nutrients: A Guide to Nutrients That Can Prevent and Reverse Senility.* Avery, 1994.

Kozol, Jonathan. *Illiterate America.* Anchor Press / Doubleday, 1985.

Kozol, Jonathan. *Savage Inequalities: Children in America's Schools. Crown,* 1991.

Mark, Vernon H. and Mark, Jeffrey P. *Brain Power: A Neurosurgeon's Complete Program to Maintain and Enhance Brain Fitness Throughout Your Life.* Houghton Mifflin, 1989.

★ Miller, John. *The Holistic Curriculum.* Ontario Institute for Studies in Education, 1988. Available from Scholarly Book Services, 77 Mowat Ave., Suite 403, Toronto, Ontario, M6K 3E3 Canada.

★ Miller, Ron. *Guide to Resources in Holistic Education.* Holistic Education Press.

★ Miller, Ron, ed. *New Directions in Education: Selections from Holistic Education Review.* Holistic Education Press, 1991.

Miller, Ron. *Renewal of Meaning in Education: Responses to the Cultural & Ecological Crisis of Our Time.* Holistic Education Press, 1993.

Miller, Ron. *What Are Schools For?* Holistic Education Press, 1992.

Mintz, Jerry. *Handbook of Alternative Education.* MacMillan, 1994.

Neville, Bernie. *Educating Psyche: Emotion, Imagination and the Unconscious in Learning.* Collins Dove, 1989.

Novak, Joseph and Gowin, Bob. *Learning How to Learn.* Cambridge University Press, 1984.

Ostrander, Sheila and Schroeder, Lynn. *Super-Memory.* Carroll & Graf, 1991.

Postle, Denis. *The Mind Gymnasium: A New Age Guide to Self-realization.* McGraw Hill, 1989.

Reed, Donn. *The Home School Source Book.* Brook Farm Books, 1991.

Vaughan, Frances. *Awakening Intuition.* Doubleday, 1979.

West, Thomas. *In the Mind's Eye.* Prometheus Books, 1991.

Wood, George. *Schools That Work: America's Most Innovative Public Education Programs.* Plume, 1992.

Wujec, Tom. *Pumping Ions: A Guide to Mental exercise.* Doubleday, 1988.

## Catalogs, Reviews, Indexes, Newsletters, Databases, Software, etc. Food for the Holistic Mind

*The recipe for perpetual ignorance is to be satisfied with your opinions and content with your knowledge.*

**Elbert Hubbard**

*Adult and Continuing Education Today,* P.O. Box 1425, Manhattan, KS 66502.

★ *Alternative Press Index,* Alternative Press Center, P.O. Box 33109, Baltimore, MD 21218; (410) 243-2471. Encourage your local library to carry this rather expensive but valuable reader's guide to alternative publications.

*The Brain-Based Education Networker,* 449 Desnoyer, St Paul, MN 55104. Contains innovative learning techniques.

*Brain/Mind: Bulletin of Breakthroughs,* Interface Press, P.O. Box 42211, Los Angeles, CA 90042.

Educational Resources Information Center (ERIC), One Dupont Circle NW, Suite 610, Washington, DC 20036-1186; (202) 293-2450; Fax (202) 457-8095. Over a half million citations from a vast number of sources on a wide variety of educational subjects.

★ *Holistic Education Review,* Holistic Education Press, P.O. Box 328, 39 Pearl St., Brandon, VT 05733-0328; (802) 247-8312; (800) 639-4122.

*The Learning Bulletin,* National Learning Laboratory, 8417 Bradley Blvd., Bethesda, MD 20817. Newsletter containing progressive learning techniques.

Mindware, 1803 Mission St. Suite 414, Santa Cruz, CA 95060; (408) 427-9455; Fax (408) 429-5302. Affordable software for improved intellectual and psychological health.

*The New Leaf Catalog of Books for Growth and Change.* This wholesale catalog can be obtained from local bookstores.

*On the Beam,* New Horizons for Learning, 4649 Sunnyside North, Seattle, WA 98103; (206) 547-7936; Fax (206) 547-0328. Newsletter of progressive teaching and learning approaches.

*Possibilities Catalog.* New York State Education Department, Office of Instruction and Program Development, Room 1076-EBA, Albany, NY 12234. Wondrous collection of educational possibilities.

*Rethinking Schools,* 1001 E. Keefe Av., Milwaukee, WI 53212; (414) 964-9646. A quarterly journal of progressive education transformation.

Williams, Martha *Computer-Readable Data Bases: A Directory and Sourcebook.* American Society for Information Science. Where to find the titles and originators of 700+ databases.

*Yes! Bookshop Catalog,* 1035 31st St. NW, Washington, DC 20007; (800) YES-1516; (202) 338-7874; Fax (202) 338-8150. Excellent retail catalogue of progressive books, tapes, and videos in personal development on a wide variety of subjects.

## Audiotapes and Videos

*All human beings, by nature, desire to know.*

**Aristotle**

Audio Forum, 96 Broad St., Guilford, CT 06437; (800) 243-1234; (203) 453-9794. Educational audiotapes.

Audio Literature, P.O. Box 7123, Berkeley, CA 94707; (800) 841-2665. Educational audiotapes.

Big Sur Tapes, P.O. Box 4, Tiburon, CA 94920; (415) 435-5511. Educational audiotapes.

*Educational Film and Video Locator of the Consortium of College and University Media Centers and R. R. Bowker,* 4th Edition. 2 volumes. R.R. Bowker, 1990.

Mystic Fire Video, P.O. Box 2249, Levonia, MI 48150; (800) 727-8433. More progressive video food for the mind.

New Dimensions Tapes, P.O. Box 410510, San Francisco, CA 94141; (800) 935-8273; (415) 563-8899. Hundreds of audiotapes of every imaginable progressive thinker of our time from the nationally syndicated radio program.

Pacifica Radio Archive, 3729 Cahuenga Blvd. W, North Hollywood, CA 91604; mailing address—P.O. Box 8092, Universal City, CA 91608; (800) 735-0230. 20,000+ progressive, thought-provoking radio programs to choose from.

PBS Video: (800) 328-PBS-1; (800) PBS-VIDEO. Some of the best educational television.

Pyramid Film and Video, P.O. Box 1048, Santa Monica, CA 90406; (800) 421-2304; (310) 828-7577. A wide variety of health educational videos—parenting, nutrition, safety, drug rehab. . . .

Sounds True, 735 Walnut St., Boulder, CO 80302; (800) 333-9185; (303) 449-6229. Select health-oriented audiotapes of conferences, workshops, and interviews.

Thinking Allowed, 2560 Ninth St., Suite 123, Berkeley, CA 94701; (800) 999-4415; (510) 548-4415; Fax (510) 548-4275. Videotape interviews with top-notch, progressive intellectuals on a wide variety of subjects.

RESOURCES

Wishing Well Distributing, P.O. Box 1008, Silver Lake, WI 53170; (800) 888-9355. Lots of videos.

## Organizations

*An education's purpose is to replace
an empty mind with an open one.*

**Malcolm S. Forbes**

Accelerated Learning Systems, 3028 Emerson Ave. S., Minneapolis, MN 55408; (612) 827-4856.

★ Global Education Associates, 475 Riverside Drive, Suite 1848, New York, NY 10115; (212) 870-3290. Non-profit research and educational institution that focuses on issues of peace, sane economic development, ecological balance, and human rights.

★ Institute of Noetic Sciences (IONS), P.O. Box 909, Sausalito, CA 94966-0909; (800) 383-1394; (800) 383-1586. A non-profit, public foundation for broadening knowledge of the nature and potentials of mind and consciousness, and to apply that knowledge to the enhancement of the quality of life on the planet. It gives grants for scientific and scholarly research. Some of this work has been involved in: the inner mechanisms of the healing response, exceptional human abilities, emerging paradigms in science and society, and altruism. It publishes books, a journal, a newsletter, special reports, and sponsors a national public television series *Thinking Allowed*.

New Horizons for Learning, 4649 Sunnyside Ave. N., Seattle, WA 98103; (206) 547-7936. An international network of education innovators.

Rudolf Steiner College, 9200 Fair Oaks Blvd., Fair Oaks, CA 95628; (916) 961-8727. Waldorf Teacher Training facility.

The Teaching Company, P.O. Box 96870, Washington, DC 20090-6870; (800) TEACH12. Provides high quality video and audiotape college courses by mail.

The Waldorf Institute, 260 Hungry Hollow Road, Spring Valley, NY 10977; (914) 425-0055.

## Sources of Statistical Information on Education in America

*Enthusiasm without knowledge is like
running in the dark.*

**Unknown**

High/Scope Educational Research Foundation, 600 N. River St., Ypsilanti, MI 48198; (313) 485-2000; (313) 485-8000.

National Assessment of Education Progress, Educational Testing Service, P.O. Box 6710 Princeton, NJ 08541-6710; (609) 734-1624; (800) 223-0267; Fax (609) 734 1878.

National Center for Education Statistics, 555 New Jersey Ave. NW, Washington, DC 20208; (202) 219-1651; (800) 424-1616; Fax (202) 219-1970.

*How much has this nation lost because there are men walking around today
with invisible chains?*

**Ralph Nader**

# CHAPTER SIX

# PSYCHOLOGICAL HEALTH

*It is an illusion to think that more comfort means more happiness.*
*Happiness comes of the capacity to feel deeply, to enjoy simply, to think freely,*
*to risk life, to be needed.*

Storm Jameson

New information and scientific research indicates the enormous effects our psyches have on physical health, work productivity, educational attainment, economic prosperity, relationship harmony, and spiritual development.

## PSYCHOLOGICAL INFLUENCES ON PHYSICAL HEALTH

*Life is an endless process of self-discovery.*
John Gardner

Psychological stress as measured by a simple health survey has strong predictive value concerning mortality.

Individuals who are very impatient and hostile have a higher incidence of heart attacks.

People who have internal, stable, and universal assumptions about the causes of their problems have a greater chance of illness. This means that a negative event such as an illness, accident, loss of a job, or a defeat in a sporting event invokes hopelessness. They think: "It has always been this way and always will. This will ruin everything else in my life." These people with self-critical attributions do not heal as rapidly or completely as people with more positive self-images.

Individuals who score higher in hopelessness, emotional suppression, and depression on psy-

chological inventories have a greater risk of developing and dying from cancer. Specific immune system biochemical differences can be detected, such as a decrease in natural killer cell activity.

Having a sense of purpose or meaning in life will alter biochemistry beneficially and lead to improved physical well-being.

The cumulative stress from dramatic life changes (divorce, marriage, loss of job, promotion, death in family, a birth, etc.) is statistically correlated to risk of illness and loss of longevity. When one's ability to cope with these changes is calculated into the equation, the correlations become even stronger. The more difficult it is for a person to cope with a changing environment, whether that change is positive or negative, the greater the negative impact on physical health.

Low serotonin levels in the brain are associated with higher incidence of violent suicide.

Cognitive Therapy, changing the way we think about ourselves, is often more effective for people with depression than powerful drug therapy. Part of the mechanism involved in the success of this talk therapy lies in its ability to alter brain biochemistry.

Guided imagery, hypnosis, and relaxation protocols have all been found to activate specific biochemical improvements in immune system functions, resulting in improved physical health.

Faith, caring, belief, laughter, a sense of control, affirmations, visualizations of positive attributes, and healing imagery have all been found to be statistically significant modulators of physical health.

People put in psychologically stressful circumstances will show abnormally higher EMG readings indicating excessive muscle tightness. Different muscle groups will tighten in different people. Someone "who holds his tongue" and does not express negative feelings verbally often are those with TMJ (temporomandibular, or jaw, joint) pain and dysfunction that are the most difficult to resolve. It is an interesting inquiry to ask people with cervical spine pain what or who in their life is a "pain in the neck." Physicians who deal with many orthopedic problems invariably see numerous examples of chronic trapezius trigger point pain (excessive tightness of the upper shoulder muscles) in individuals who psychologically are "carrying the burden of the world on their shoulders."

Stress can contribute to the cause or perpetuation of ulcers, arthritis, asthma, hay fever, fatigue, impotence, acne, diabetes, heart arrhythmias, irritable bowel syndrome, frigidity, strokes, eczema, colitis, infections, insomnia, high blood pressure, obesity, etc.

Fear can cause one to tremble, cower, or defecate.

Psychological trauma of a sexual nature, when unresolved, can lead to pelvic muscle or organ pain, dysfunction, and/or disease.

Chronic pain from injury is often perpetuated by a repetitively firing nerve loop linked to unresolved emotions existing at the time of the injury. Until that emotion is expressed and the psychological process resolved, the pain will continue.

A typical example is the football player who can't recover from a knee injury after years of surgery and physical therapy and then dramatically heals during a Somato-Emotional Release session when he deals with the anger towards the guy who took a "cheap shot" at his knee from the blind side. Or the woman who was in a car accident that took her mother's life and has suffered years of excruciating chest pain afterwards, even though she had only a minor bruise of the chest bone. The pain completely resolved only after the woman, during Integrative Body Psychotherapy sessions, had ex-

tensive psychotherapeutic dialogue with her deceased mother—asking forgiveness, expressing anger, talking about "matters of the heart," saying things that never got said . . . like "good-bye."

It is amazing how many "accidents" are caused by a split-second loss of awareness that springs out of attention diverted momentarily to a strong emotion rather than the task at hand, like driving, skiing, or cycling. So profound are these psychological links that future physical therapy rehabilitation centers dealing with chronic pain will offer psychological assessment and therapy side-by-side with their body-centered techniques.

## THE PSYCHE'S INFLUENCE ON LIVELIHOOD

*Always leave enough time in your life*
*to do something that makes you happy,*
*satisfied, or even joyous.*
*That has more of an effect on economic*
*well-being than any other single factor.*
**Paul Hawken**

Psychological stress on the job is the fastest growing health problem in worker compensation claims.

Not only does psychological stress cause physical health problems which lead in turn to absenteeism and lost productivity, but emotional and mental turmoil leads directly to inefficiency, mistakes, and decreased desire to be productive.

## EMOTIONS AND LEARNING

*It is the mark of intelligence, no matter what*
*you are doing, to have a good time doing it.*
**Unknown**

Psychological stress in school or other learning environments restrains educational attainment in a profound way that also negatively affects physical health. It is difficult to learn, not only when absent from class, but also when ill or in pain.

Psychological stress directly interferes with learning neurologically by increasing errors, decreasing memory, speed, efficiency, attention span, concentration, decisiveness, and motivation for excellence.

Psychological stress alters brain substances, such as enkephalins, which restrict learning and memory.

## OUR MIND'S LINK WITH OTHERS

*Even as radio waves are picked up wherever*
*a set is tuned in to their wave-length,*
*so the thoughts which each of us think*
*each moment of the day go forth into the world*
*to influence for good or bad*
*each other human mind.*

**Christmas Humphreys**

Our psychological health or lack of it directly affects every human interaction and relationship we have. There is no way that a disturbed psyche can be prevented from negatively affecting our relationships. Fear erupts as anger at others. Many of the international conflicts that take such an enormous toll in human life and suffering are not caused so much by disagreements over borders, economics, politics, race, or culture, but by personal psychological disharmony and fear which is then multiplied by many people.

*If we could read the secret history of our*
*enemies, we should find in each man's life*
*sorrow and suffering enough*
*to disarm all hostility.*

**Longfellow**

Our own unfulfilled emotional needs interfere with how much we are willing or able to give to others. Most neurotic disturbances will eventually become projected unconsciously onto those around us, whether they are our intimate friends and family or whole classes and races of people. Similarly, good emotional health disperses far and wide to touch all those who are fortunate enough to relate to emotionally healthy people. These people can often be recognized in a room by the positive feelings other people have when around them.

## PSYCHOLOGICAL IMPACT ON GOVERNMENT AND LAWS

Emotions of the masses are often the catalysts, if not the driving forces, behind most dramatic changes in government. That is why our individual psychological health is so important for the health of government. People vote and overthrow regimes based on the strength of their hearts as much as what is in their minds. Look at the examples:

- the emotional landslide election of Ronald Reagan
- the overthrow of the communist governments of Eastern Europe and USSR
- the election of Corozon Aquino in the Philippines
- the civil war in Bosnia and Rwanda

Observe also how the psychological health of criminals affects how laws must be made and enforced to protect citizens from criminal psychopathology. In all these instances the effect was a change in some aspect of many people's health, for better or worse.

*Wanting good government in their states, they*
*first established order in their own families;*
*wanting order at home,*
*they first disciplined themselves.*

**Confucius**

It should not be forgotten that the psychological health of political leaders plays pivotal roles in governmental actions. These problems are more prominent in dictatorships. History is replete with instances where the insanity of one person in a position of ultimate authority overrode whatever sanity was around him—Adolph Hitler, Idi Amin, the Duvaliers, and Saddam Hussein.

The same is true about how laws are changed. Look at the burning political issues of our time and peoples' emotional commitment to influencing lawmaking:

- abortion
- environmental protection
- civil rights
- gun control
- drugs
- violent crime
- the right to die
- the death penalty

All these subjects are extremely emotional.

## PSYCHOLOGICAL HEALTH—SPIRITUAL HEALTH: ONE AND THE SAME? TRANSPERSONAL PSYCHOLOGY

*To be what we are, and to become what we are capable of becoming, is the only end of life.*
**Robert Louis Stevenson**

Since the humanistic branch of psychology with Maslow, Rogers, and Assagioli appeared, there has been a growing respect for both psyche and spirit in theories of human behavior and in the practical use of psychotherapy. We will be using these transpersonal and humanistic models of psycho-spiritual function in the following discussions and recommendations because they prove to be the most helpful in building holistic health. Simply put, the more factors of healthy psychological development we have working for us, the better our spiritual development. Psychological disturbances of any kind fragment our personalities and keep us from both personal and spiritual oneness. And conversely: the more effectively our everyday spiritual practices bring us to a closer Union with all living beings, the greater psychological integration is possible. For a clearer description of the link between psychological development and spiritual growth, refer to the following resources:

★Denotes Best of the Best Resources

★Almaas, A. H. *The Pearl Beyond Price: Integration of Personality into Being.* Diamond Books, 1988. Diamond Books, P.O. Box 10114, Berkeley, CA 94709.
★*Journal of Transpersonal Psychology,* The Association for Transpersonal Psychology, P.O. Box 3049, Stanford, CA 94309.

Wilber, Ken. *The Spectrum of Consciousness.* A Quest Book, 1977.
★Wilber, Ken. *No Boundary: Eastern and Western Approaches to Personal Growth.* Shambhala, 1985.
Wilber, Ken; Engler, Jack; and Brown, Daniel. *Transformations of Consciousness: Conventional and Contemplative Perspectives on Development.* Shambhala, 1986.

*Our normal waking consciousness,
rational consciousness as we call it,
is but one special type of consciousness,
whilst all about it, parted from it by
the filmiest of screens, there lie potential forms
of consciousness entirely different. . . .
No account of the universe in its totality can be
final which leaves these other forms
of consciousness quite disregarded . . .
they forbid a premature closing of
our accounts with reality.*
**William James**

### More Resources

*The young man who has not wept is a savage,
and the old man who will not laugh is a fool.*
**George Santayana**

If you should doubt the effect that your psyche plays in your overall health, please refer to the following resources that will more than convince you:

Cousins, Norman. *Head First—The Biology of Hope.* E. P. Dutton, 1989. Describes the scientific evidence linking positive emotions to physiologic events and their impact on health and disease.
★Goleman, Daniel and Gurin, Joel (eds.). *Mind Body Medicine: How to Use Your Mind for Better Health.* Consumer Reports Books, 1993. Contains many excellent resources.
Justice, Blair. *Who Gets Sick: How Beliefs, Moods, and Thoughts Affect Your Health.* Jeremy P. Tarcher, 1988.
Keleman, Stanley. *Your Body Speaks Its Mind.* Center Press, 1975.
Locke, Steven and Colligan, Douglas. *The Healer Within: The New Medicine of Mind and Body.* New American Library, 1987.

★The Newsletter of the American Institute of Stress, The American Institute of Stress, 124 Park Ave., Yonkers, NY 10703, (914) 963-1200.

Rossi, Ernest L. *The Psychobiology of Mind-Body Healing*. W. W. Norton, 1986.

Upledger, John. *SomatoEmotional Release and Beyond*. Upledger Institute, 1991.

*Anger is never without reason,*
*but seldom with a good one.*

**Ben Franklin**

Let us see how all this information can be arranged in usable forms.

To begin with, everyone can benefit significantly from appropriate psychological programs. Choosing which to engage in at any particular point in time is the only question. Why everyone can benefit from psychotherapy at all stages of life can be understood better if we bring in a model of psychological health different from most medical doctors, psychiatrists, and insurance companies

**PSYCHOLOGICAL HEALTH SPECTRUM**

10

Last stage of Enlightenment

Third stage of Enlightenment

Second stage of Enlightenment

First Enlightenment experience

The seventeen stages of psycho-spiritual growth leading to the first spiritual Enlightenment

Transpersonal realms of psycho-spiritual growth

Healthy ego structure and function with no psychological symptoms of significance

Mild neuroses with psychological and relational conflict

Hidden psychological distress of significant proportions masked by an acceptable personality in everyday life. Physical symptoms are a component.

Non-hospitalized but significant overt, psychological suffering—outpatient

Hospitalized with severe psychological disturbances— schizophrenia, psychosis

Suicide

0

RESOURCES

recognize. Their model views psychological health in three tiers:

- those who are not having symptoms serious enough to present their problems to doctors or police (even though they might have significant psychological problems)
- those who have symptoms deemed treatable in outpatient programs using drugs and talk therapy
- those more severe cases who are treated with drugs, electroconvulsive therapy and/ or talk therapy in a hospital setting.

A more accurate and useful model is one that includes an entire psycho-spiritual spectrum of functioning somewhat like what is seen on page 177.

## PSYCHOLOGICAL TRAITS

*Every belief is a limit to be examined and transcended.*
**John C. Lilly**

There is an infinite assortment of psychological qualities and processes affecting our lives from day to day, so even this Psychological Health Spectrum graph is a crude overview. For more detailed understanding and application, survey Table 1 for qualities of psychological health and determine which characteristics are strongly expressed in your life and which need greater expression. Note how many of these qualities can be associated with "spiritual" virtues. Then survey Table 2 for qualities of psychological dysfunction. Which characteristics are negatively affecting your life? Notice how many of these qualities, good and not so good, arise, pass away and are replaced by others from one moment to another. Be particularly observant how some keep repeating.

## ELEMENTS FOR PSYCHOLOGICAL HEALTH ENHANCEMENT AND DISRUPTION

*After twelve years of therapy my psychiatrist said something that brought tears to my eyes. He said, "No hablo ingles."*
**Ronnie Shakes**

Looking at the Elements for Psychological Health Enhancement on page 180 and the Elements That Disturb Psychological Health on page 181 will help us see what is needed for psychological growth. The more positive elements, and the fewer negative ones we incorporate into our lives, the more our total health will be enhanced.

*When one door of happiness closes, another opens; but often we look so long at the closed door that we do not see the one which has been opened for us.*
**Helen Keller**

## TABLE 1
## QUALITIES OF PSYCHOLOGICAL HEALTH

Mood—happy, but free to express difficult emotions when they arise: enthusiasm, playfulness, humor, joy, cheerfulness

Self-Esteem—self-confidence, self-worth, courage

Communication—free expression of feelings, good listener, openness

Body Integration—relaxed, efficient body posture and functioning; respect for the body

Identity—full integration of various identities or subpersonalities into a healthy being, recognition and incorporation of a personal essence that transcends ego

Relationships—fulfilling, close relationships; compassion, non-judgment, effective conflict resolution skills, ability to give and receive love, generosity, cooperativeness; inclusiveness, patience, empathy, friendliness, sensitivity, openness, affectionate nature

Other Qualities—mindfulness, decisiveness, creativity, comfortable with sexual expression, responsible for self and others' well-being, constructive stress-coping ability, equanimity, will power, clarity, sense of wonder, willingness to risk, truthfulness, perceptiveness, sincerity, humility, modesty, trustworthiness, autonomy, non-dependence, tolerance, flexibility/adaptability, spontaneity

## TABLE 2
## QUALITIES OF PSYCHOLOGICAL DYSFUNCTION

Mood—depression, sadness, inability to express emotions, irritability, anger, humorlessness

Self-Esteem—self-hate, fear, non-assertiveness

Communication—argumentative, opinionated, confrontational

Body Integration—tense, disrespectful of the body

Identity—fragmented subpersonalities, no recognition of an essence beyond the ego

Relationships—conflict in close relationships, coldheartedness, judgmental, inability to love or be loved, unapproachable, greedy, overly competitive, exclusive, impatient, unfriendly, insensitive, violent, demanding

Other Qualities—indecisive, repressive or aggressively dysfunctional sexually, irresponsible, poor stress coping ability, lack of will power, dull, untruthful, untrustworthy, insincere, boastful, excessively dependent on others, worrisome, secretive, intolerant, rigid/reactive

*"Come, come to the Edge." He encouraged.*
*"No, no, we will fall." They replied.*
*"Come, come to the Edge." He repeated.*
*So they went to the Edge. And he pushed them.*
*And they flew.*

**Unknown**

## ELEMENTS FOR PSYCHOLOGICAL HEALTH ENHANCEMENT

1. Provisions for physiological needs
   A. Ideal diet with supplementation
   B. Non-toxic environment
   C. Adequately clothed
   D. Adequate housing
   E. Quality health care access

2. Safe environment that elicits feelings of security but with sufficient challenges to prevent stagnation

3. Love of family and friends with good social supports

4. Adherence to moral, lawful code of behavior

5. Good communication skills

6. Quality, relevant, holistic education

7. Regular exposure to plenty of natural sunlight and full spectrum lighting

8. Spending time in nature

9. Mindfulness of body feelings, emotions, thought, speech, actions

10. Daily periods of silent meditation and contemplation

11. Positive childhood programming that instills love, self-worth, and service to others

12. Moderate, achievable challenges in everyday life

13. Recognition, acceptance, and integration of different "subpersonalities" into one's being (recognition of the constant flux of emotions, mindstates, thoughts, motivations, preferences arising and passing away)

14. Fulfilling work
    A. Providing a good, stable, secure standard of living
    B. Contributing to self-worth
    C. Helping others and the environment
    D. Intellectually stimulating

15. Protective, life-enhancing social milieu

16. Regular, enjoyable physical activity
    A. Aerobic fitness
    B. Relaxed musculature from proper flexibility exercises
    C. Play

17. A nervous system free from irritating or aberrant stimuli
    A. Proper muscle tone
    B. Proper joint mobility
    C. Proper organ function
    D. Proper neurotransmitter function

18. Balance of energy, *chi*, through acupuncture meridians of the body

---

*As long as we have what we have inside, the capacity to love, to work, to hear music, to see a flower, to look at the world as it is, nothing can stop us from being happy ... but one thing you must take seriously. You must get rid of the "ifs" of life. Many people tell you, "I would be happy— if I had a certain job, or if I were better looking, or if a certain person would marry me." There isn't any such thing. You must live your life unconditionally, without ifs.*

**Artur Rubinstein**

# ELEMENTS THAT DISTURB PSYCHOLOGICAL HEALTH

1. The struggle to meet physiological needs
   A. Hunger, malnutrition, junk food, contaminated food, food allergies, thirst, dehydration
   B. Insufficient clothes for protection from elements or to contribute to self-worth
   C. Unreliable, inadequate housing
   D. Poor health care access
   E. Toxic physical environment, allergies

2. Risk of illness, injury, or death

3. Conflict, anger, hate, fear generated by family and friends. No effective social support system for psychological growth

4. Participation in immoral, unethical, lawless behavior

5. Poor communication skills

6. Poor education

7. Malillumination
   A. Lack of exposure to natural sunlight
   B. Excessive exposure to artificial (non-full spectrum) light sources that have adverse neurobiological reactions— fluorescent, TVs, VDTs

8. Insufficient time in nature; too much time in urban environments

9. Mindlessness—"running on automatic"

10. Busy, busy mind in a hectic daily routine

11. Negative childhood programming and conditioning that limits psychological freedom with fear, hate, and delusion

12. Stresses and life changes that overtax one's ability to respond to those challenges healthfully.

13. Conflict and fragmentation of various aspects of personality

14. Unemployment or undesirable employment
    A. Lack of income for needs
    B. Harmful to self or others
    C. Boring
    D. Damaging to self-esteem

15. Life-threatening or health-threatening social or political conditions—totalitarianism, repression, crime, injustice

16. Inactivity leading to lethargy and abnormal muscle contracture

17. Physical irritants, pain, illness or neurotransmitter imbalance impacting emotional centers in the brain

18. Disturbance of acupuncture meridian energy balance

*That the birds of worry fly over your head, this you cannot change, but that they build their nests in your hair, this you can prevent.*
**Chinese proverb**

## COMMENTARY ON ENHANCEMENTS AND DISTURBANCES TO PSYCHOLOGICAL HEALTH

*Rule # 1 is, don't sweat the small stuff.*
*Rule # 2 is, it's all small stuff.*
*And if you can't fight and you can't flee, flow.*

**Robert Eliot, M.D.**

There are many aspects to psychological health, many approaches for assessment of psychological problems, many techniques for correction of emotional problems, many avenues for enhancement of psychological well-being. As you read the following commentary on psychological health enhancement measures, note those that are relevant to your situation. Note neglected areas which might now contribute greatly to psychological development and thus to your total health. Sometimes we will be drawn intuitively towards paths that are particularly helpful at this stage in our journey. But often, the dysfunctionally protective defense mechanisms of the injured human psyche deviously sabotage investigation into precisely those enterprises that will most dramatically challenge us to grow. Is there reluctance then to look deeper into that resistance? If necessary, ask for wise counsel on the appropriateness of these approaches from a qualified mental health professional.

Remember also: holistic health is not just choosing one or two magic bullets that will "cure a problem" from a smorgasbord of techniques. We are trying to encompass many lifestyle approaches, lifelong health enhancement efforts, and natural therapeutic methods into an intertwining network that provides for the highest expression of humanness as we walk the entire path of life from birth to death and beyond. So, as you look at the Web of Psychological Wholeness, do not think of which few strands of the web need the most work with the *exclusion* of the others, but rather think of how you might improve all the strands, even if just a little bit. This will lead to better progress. You can even assign percentages. Each facet of health enhancement will claim at least a small percent of your attention; others are designated a greater role, so that the sum is 100%.

## *Psychological Health Assessments*

*The archer strikes the target, partly by pulling, partly by letting go.*

**Unknown**

With each aspect of our health there are many different levels and kinds of evaluations that give us more detailed descriptions of our state of health. Having better maps of the terrain where we are and have been allows us to proceed more safely, efficiently, and joyously on our journey to a fuller life. Tests relevant to our psychological health are very numerous.

There are specific pen and paper tests to identify precise psychodynamic glitches. There is specialized electronic instrumentation like EEG, or medical imaging techniques like MRI, PET, and BEAM scans that test for neurophysiological faults in the brain which might alter perception, cognitive function, or behavior. Generalized tests like the Minnesota Multiphasic Personality Inventory and its offsprings and cousins offer important insights into the psyche. Personality profiles such as the Myers-Briggs Type Indicator and its short form, or the Million-Illinois Self Report Scale, allow us to look at our personalities in an organized way that assists growth. The book *Mindscapes* by Pino Gilioli is filled with interesting personality self analyses. The Holmes and Rahe Social Readjustment Rating Scale, and the Stress and Coping Inventory, provide a way of looking at life stress indicators as they relate to our overall health. Denis Postle's *The Mind Gymnasium* is filled with a variety of excellent self-assessment exercises for different facets of our psychological selves.

Other simple written tests provide accurate indications of neurophysiological faults which might distort our psychological health. The Hoffer Osmond Diagnostic (HOD) and the Experiential World Inventory (EWI) are two such tests with specific indicators for early differential diagnosis of schizophrenia. The Stress Audit and the Psychophysiological Stress Assessment have both been proven to be useful tools for evaluating different aspects of how stress disrupts function. Stress-Check is a diagnostic computer program designed for supervised patient use in the evaluation of stress-related illness.

In areas indirectly related to psychological function there are other tests which can be very helpful for our emotional well-being. Food allergy tests such as ELISA/ACT™ immunological tests can be *the* most important tests for helping our psychological health if hidden brain allergies are a primary cause of the disturbances. RAST tests for inhalant allergies are very helpful. Hair analysis can detect some toxic heavy metal contamination. The following is a list of just a few of the substances that we generally come in contact with daily that can have adverse effects on our psychological health: pollens, molds, mildew, pesticides, herbicides, household cleaning agents, petroleum products, cosmetics, animal dander, toxic heavy metals such as lead, mercury, cadmium, recreational drugs, medications, industrial pollutants, electromagnetic radiations, ozone, and electrostatic charges. They can cause any of the following psychological disturbances or combinations of problems: agitation, rage, lethargy, paranoia, melancholy, delusions, depression, fear, anxiety, confusion, attention deficits, reduced comprehension, or hallucinations.

Specialized orthopedic tests that reveal the hidden, correctable causes of chronic pain at the source of an intractable depression may be an invaluable aid to our psychological growth.

The first step in evaluating priorities for testing is to look into the problem areas that are most puzzling, or the most obvious sticking points. Then if self testing via the resources available can provide the answers, use those. Many of the recommended books in each section have valuable self-testing tools in them. If the problems are too significant or confusing to handle alone, consult the appropriate health care professional to assist you in determining which tests would be most cost-beneficial.

## Physiological Needs

*They laughed at Edison and Einstein, but somehow I still feel uncomfortable when they laugh at me.*

**Ashleigh Brilliant**

Physiological needs are at the foundation of Maslow's hierarchy of needs for psychological well-being. How could it be otherwise? Plagued by hunger, thirst, and the assaults of the elements of nature, how can any human achieve a reasonable degree of psychological balance? But the holistic model used in this book goes a bit farther. It says that we need the basics of sufficient food, water, clothing, and housing to avert psychological crisis. But what if we supply more than just essential physiological needs? Not just full bellies, but *optimal* nutrition; not superfluous clothing but apparel that enhances self-esteem; not just housing but a home that can be proudly owned; access to quality health care without the stressful risk of having no insurance. Such factors contribute to higher levels of psychological wellness.

At least one third of America's one million homeless are mentally ill. All are under extreme psychological stress. Imagine how disturbed the brain's biochemistry must become with insufficient caloric intake, erratic blood sugar levels, contaminated water, toxic fumes, and only coffee, cigarettes, and junk food to consume. Subsequent depression of immune function and increased infections and other illnesses result. Then there is the lack of adequate health care services. Imagine just the psychological stress of the streets: worrying about the next meal, the fear of death because no hospital will accept you, the continual presence of crime, or even the stress of finding a place to relieve your bladder. How are all these people expected to struggle out of this black hole of desperate, unfulfilled needs with the limited social programs available? Such programs do not offer holistic correction of their problems.

Let us not even use such an extreme example to illustrate how many of us are not providing basic physiological needs sufficient to support even good, let alone optimal, psychological function.

George works for a small company in the city. He and his family can't afford housing in town, so George commutes from a housing project in a neighboring town. Their living quarters are cramped, dirty, and in a crime ridden neighborhood. The commute to work is an hour each way in rush hour traffic. The urban air quality, particularly during the commute, is very disruptive to George's biochemistry. Because of poor nutrition his body has great difficulty fending off this type of pollution.

His company is small and cannot afford health insurance for its employees. George cannot afford health insurance on his own because the premiums are too high. He and his family forego many preventive health care procedures. They delay proper health care until a severe problem forces them into the emergency room.

Nutritionally, George and his family are equally stressed. They have enough food to survive but not to thrive. Their budget is less of a problem than their nutritional education. They eat many processed foods, high in fats, sugars, contaminants, preservatives, artificial ingredients, low in vitamins and minerals, which disrupt proper nerve function of emotional centers in the brain. George eats breakfasts and lunches at fast food outlets. Unknowingly, George is allergic to many of these foods, neurologically reacting in a way that further affects his mood and behavior and thus his work performance and his family interactions.

Although George and his family have the basics of food, drink, housing, clothing, and income, they lack good psychological health. Millions of Americans have a similar experience. The resources in this book are designed to help with these physiological needs. For anyone with significant psychological disturbance that has warranted long term therapy, medication, and/or hospitalization, nutritional, ecological, toxicological, and allergic approaches are essential. Also, the chapter on economics should help to provide a more stable livelihood that can lessen these physiological needs.

## Physically Safe Environment

*We blame fate for other accidents, but we feel personally responsible when we make a hole in one.*

**Unknown Golfer**

Obviously the overt risk of illness, injury, and imminent death are not conducive to optimal psychological well being. A safe, secure, stable living environment can contribute greatly to emotional health. Individuals are in part responsible for providing a low risk environment by choosing safe behaviors, working at safe jobs, and living in locations that do not pose great risks. But society, government, and business too, are partly responsible for educating people about safe and dangerous activities, protecting the workplace from hazards, keeping crime in check, and providing mechanisms for quality health care access. Using the varied resources in this book should help individuals toward a safer lifestyle.

## Social Support

*The love for my own self is inseparably connected with love for any other being.*

**Erich Fromm**

Loving relationships with family, friends, and even pets, contribute greatly to psychological health and in turn to physical and spiritual health. Strong social support structures are invaluable foundations for psychological well-being, just as conflict, anger, hate, and fear generated by our social contacts deteriorate our emotional and total health. If this element of our life is not enhancing our psychological well-being, we must change these relationships. Sometimes physical separation from toxic relationships is necessary. Finding new friends, divorcing abusive spouses, or creating safe distances between family members can help. But more often, the key is learning new tools for interpersonal relationships by reading some of the resource materials on relationships from Chapter 7 or books on transactional analysis. Workshops and classes in these areas are also available. It may be wise or necessary to consult a marriage and family counselor or therapist specializing in these issues. If this aspect of your life is not in order, psychological well-being will be impossible to attain and push total health out of reach.

## Morality

*O Lord, help me to be pure, but not yet.*

**St. Augustine**

Adherence to a moral, lawful code of behavior can be psychologically liberating. Unethical, immoral, or lawless behavior, on the other hand, can be highly stressful. Evading the law, constantly looking over your shoulder, lying, trying to remember which lies you told, being secretive, not being able to trust those close to you, and conflicts of conscience play heavily on the emotions. The five precepts of Buddhism, the Ten Commandments of Judaism and Christianity, and all the guidelines of morality in all other religions exist in part because of the recognition that they play instrumental roles in contributing to the psychological, as well as the social and spiritual, development of their followers. There are some psychotherapists who regularly use "contracts" of moral behavior as part of the therapeutic process with their clients. Obviously, psychological health in itself leads to morality and ethical behavior. For more information on working with this aspect of health, refer to the chapter and resources on spiritual health.

## Communication

*Communication, when it succeeds, is one of man's greatest assets, and when it fails it is his worst enemy.*

**John C. Lilly**

Expression of our emotional selves, particularly communicating our feelings to others, is a key to psychological well-being. Undereducated individuals with poor linguistic skills have great difficulty adequately communicating their feelings to friends and loved ones. This in itself is very taxing emotionally. At times of emotional stress or interpersonal crisis, individuals who cannot express themselves adequately will in frustration resort to extremes in behavior to get their point across—consciously or unconsciously, and all too often with violence or disruptive, inappropriate behavior. This negatively affects psychological health even more. Improving our education, language repertoire, communication skills, ability to express feelings, and interpersonal conflict resolution skills, will contribute greatly to psychological health. Use the appropriate resources to help in this aspect of development.

## Education

*The greatest discovery of my generation is that human beings may alter their lives by altering their attitude of mind.*

**William James**

Quality holistic education, relevant to individual development, provides the foundation of a healthy psyche. Proper education has to include all the aspects of human development, including nutrition that supports psychological as well as physiological excellence—safety, morality, communications, interpersonal relations, appropriate expression of emotions, right livelihood, mindfulness, values clarification, creativity, how to be of service to others, how to love, how to improve health with exercise, etc. We cannot guarantee these positive qualities by teaching them, but we also can't expect them to arise if we don't teach them. Again, each of us must examine his own life and evaluate the need for improved education. Education leading to psychological health is usually paid back many times over.

## Light

**No one is a light unto himself, not even the sun.**
**Antonio Porchia**

Light has a dramatic impact on psychological well-being. Optimum quantity and quality of full-spectrum light, preferably from natural sunlight, can be enormously supportive of psychological health. Conversely, insufficient light in quality or quantity can have devastating effects on the mind via abnormal brain function. If an individual is suffering from mood disorders like mild depression, particularly Seasonal Affective Disorder ("winter blues") or phobic reactions (fear or anxiety disorders), a light-deficit disorder might be a significant contributing cause. Becoming more informed with the information resources in that section referring to light therapy will be helpful, page 131.

## Nature

**Those who flow as life flows feel no wear,**
**feel no tear, need no mending, no repair.**
**Lao Tzu**

Nature heals. Being exposed to beautiful, peaceful, natural surroundings has enormous therapeutic advantages. The elements of nature are symbolic archetypes of positive psycho-spiritual traits and qualities: freedom of the wind, flowingness of water, constant change of cycles and rhythms, strength of mountains, interdependence of ecological health, groundedness of the earth, inspiration of birds soaring in flight, joy of rainbows, new beginnings of sunrises, a sense of wonder in it all.

Being out in natural surroundings encourages non-judgmental attitudes in two ways. We can be relaxed in nature because we know that the stars, sun, moon, wind, rain, rivers, mountains, clouds, rainbows, plants, and animals are totally non-judgmental. They expect nothing. They ask little. They give unconditionally. This is seldom seen in the work-a-day world of our daily lives. Nature is difficult to criticize. Should the grass be greener,

the sky bluer, the birdsong a different tune? Nature is what it is—perfect. Taking a rest from critics, suspending judgmental attitudes, and loving unconditionally, are valuable lessons to be learned from nature.

On a more physiological level, sunshine, non-polluted air, and high negative ion concentrations can have strong positive physiological effects on psychological well-being. Usually when we retreat to natural settings, a non-hectic pace encouraged by the intrinsic qualities of nature contributes to emotional renewal, also.

Some would say there is a centering process that also occurs from being put in natural environments. Evolutionary memories of a return to the roots of our species' existence are triggered. If that is too much of a stretch for some, another aspect of the transpersonal realm of psychological health might seem more relevant. Nature tends to encourage a unity consciousness which makes the lines of separation between "things" less concrete. It encourages an integration of fragmented personalities within oneself and a more harmonizing attitude with others.

For more information on how to use nature to enhance psychological well-being, look to the sections on light, play, spiritual health, and ecology.

## Mindfulness

**If any man seeks for greatness, let him**
**forget greatness and ask for truth**
**and he will find both.**
**Thomas Mann**

We can only alter unwanted or harmful psychological processes within us by being aware of them in the first place and seeing how they disrupt our lives and make us unhappy. So much of our lives is "run on automatic"—just following and perpetuating our conditioning, no matter how helpful, harmful, adaptive, or disruptive it is. Daily moment-by-moment observation of body feelings, emotions, thoughts, speech, and actions reveals so much that normally slips by us that we are able to gain a new perspective on who we really are. Most often there are great discrepancies between how our bodies feel, the emotions we express, our thoughts that ramble on, what we say and how we behave. We don't tell people our true emotions, yet our actions betray them. Our bodies are in revolt against the repression of emotions.

Mindfulness is the great balancer that brings truth to our being and allows us to integrate our incongruities. Mindfulness practices can be found in the resource section in the chapter on spiritual health. Biofeedback training can be a valuable tool in learning how to tune into what our bodies have to tell us about our health. It can also help us learn to decondition harmful, unconscious reactions and develop more skillful responses to life's challenges. Refer to the section on Biofeedback for more resources.

*To become a spectator of one's own life is to escape the suffering of life.*

**Oscar Wilde**

## Silence

*Man's great misfortune is that he has no organ, no kind of eyelid or brake, to mask or block a thought, or all thoughts, when he wants to.*

**Paul-Toussaint-Jules Valery**

Silence is one of the greatest aids to mindfulness and peace of mind. Not only outward silence but more importantly, inner silence, a respite from the continual onslaught of thought. In periods of silence we can hear much more clearly what our body feelings, emotions, thoughts, speech, and actions are really telling us. Setting aside at least a half hour twice a day for silent meditation or contemplation is one of the most powerful tools for psycho-spiritual growth.

*The mad mind does not halt. If it halts, it is enlightenment.*

**Zen saying**

## Childhood Programming

*In the Indian way, everything is for the children. They learn respect because we show respect for them; we let them be free, but at the same time, there is always someone there to teach them how to act, the right way to treat people. When we get our land back, the first thing we will do is to make places for spiritual things and for the children, places where the children can learn the right way to live, to be generous, to be respectful, and to love all the living things. We believe in the Great Hoop: the Great Circle of Life; everything comes back to where it started.*

**Matthew King**

Being born to well integrated, conscious, knowledgeable, loving parents is one of the best psychological health enhancement strategies known. The major flaw of the strategy is that the choice is in the laws of karma or God or some other process we have no particular conscious control of. Much of our entire psychological self is basically formed before we reach first grade. The love, attention, and contact with the world we experience from birth through the first few years of life can be the foundation of a grand, psychologically well-balanced, adult life. But the converse is all too often the case.

Many of the psychological problems that plague us in adult life are the result of early childhood scripts written by our experiences at those earlier times. These negative programs were then reinforced innumerable times over the years, resulting in a conditioned pattern of maladaptive behavior very resistant to change. The more severe the psychological insult was in youth, the more impact it may have in adult life. That is not to say that seemingly minor psychological stress in earlier life can't have devastating effects when combined with certain other circumstances and conditions.

Very early childhood trauma, particularly those events that are difficult to remember, seem to be very resistant to resolution. But psychotherapeutic techniques can make dramatic improvements. There is nothing we can do to change the past. But there are many techniques that can provide insight into the past conditioning of our present maladaptive behavior and unhappiness. There are also many techniques available to decondition this programming and build new, more adaptive, healthier behaviors. For those self-motivated individuals who do not have severe psychological problems, there are plenty of resources for self-care. *Transforming Childhood* by Strephon Kaplan-Williams is one such book. See the resource section for many others. Some individuals who have moderately severe psychological disturbances, but are still capable and willing to do a significant amount of therapeutic work for themselves, should be able to find excellent psychotherapists who are good facilitators, using the formal in-office therapy session as a springboard for the more important and extensive "homework" done by the client independently.

### *Great is the man who does not lose his child's heart.*

**Mencius**

Those with serious psychological problems like psychosis, schizophrenia, or severe depression, or those at risk of hurting themselves or others, need close professional supervision. In many of these cases licensed psychotherapists, particularly clinical psychologists, can be of great help. But since many of these conditions have a significant biochemical component, a physician who can perform the necessary laboratory tests and work with correcting these biochemical imbalances in the brain is also essential. Unfortunately, there are few "orthomolecular psychiatrists" in practice. They use predominantly nutritional corrective measures rather than pharmacological approaches, thus trying to avoid the drugs' inherent toxicity and dangerous adverse side effects. The International Academy of Nutrition and Preventive Medicine, the Society for Orthomolecular Medicine, or the American Association of Orthomolecular Medicine can provide a referral to orthomolecular oriented physicians. Before any traditional psychiatrist prescribes a long-term course of psychotropic medication, a second opinion should be sought out from

an orthomolecular physician. In addition, other measures such as Neurosensory Development Training, full spectrum light therapy, exercise, acupuncture, and cranial electrical stimulation should be incorporated into the therapy, since these are approaches that could make significant improvements yet have very little or no risk of serious adverse reactions.

Be sure to use the information in the section on Rating Therapies as well as resources in the chapters on Relationships and Spiritual Health.

### *Show me a sane man and I will cure him for you.*

**C. G. Jung**

## *Challenges in Life*

### *Stress is an integral part of life. We set our whole pattern of life by our stress end-point. If we hit it exactly, we live dynamic, purposeful, useful, happy lives. If we go over, we break. If we stay too far under, we vegetate.*

**Howard A. Rusk**

Our daily life should be filled with achievable challenges that stress our adaptive skills in beneficial ways but do not exert pressures which overtax our ability to recover. Finding that line Rusk speaks about is not always easy. But all the multifaceted strategies suggested in this book are designed to improve our power to adapt to challenges so that the buffer zone of safety can become larger. One way to view stress in everyday life is through the metaphor of a rain barrel. A rain barrel can hold only so much water until it overflows. Life is like this. Our lives can accommodate only so much activity, so much stress. If we surpass our ability to cope with stress, if we take on more responsibilities and tasks than we can efficiently handle, then we overflow, make a mess, and become unable to do well. There are three basic strategies for coping with thunderstorms: *one,* build a bigger rain barrel; *two,* take water out of the rain barrel before it overflows; or *three,* let it overflow and make a mess.

The same is true about stress in daily life. We can reduce the stress with stress reduction techniques, which means altering our lifestyles to perform at less of a hectic pace with fewer responsibilities, or we can learn stress management skills so that, metaphorically, our container is bigger. The third option is one which too many of us choose by default—we overstress ourselves and make a mess of our lives—with ruined marriages, failed businesses, dysfunctional family relations, poor physical health, and an early death.

*Don't tell me that worry doesn't do any good.
I know better.
The things I worry about don't happen!*
**The Watchman-Examiner**

Stress reduction techniques include:

- Make fewer commitments which you have difficulty meeting.

- Live more simply, reduce superfluous spending so excessive economic pressures are lessened.

- Change to a less stressful job.

- Reduce techno-stress and information overload by moderating the high speed influence which car phones, telephone answering machines, next day mail service, fax machines, call waiting, call forwarding, impose.

- Spend more time playing and laughing, more time in nature, more time enjoying family and friends.

- Don't stress the body with unhealthy junk food or drugs, especially tobacco, alcohol, caffeine.

- Get sufficient sleep every night and be properly rested.

*Reality is the leading cause of stress amongst
those in touch with it.*
**Jane Wagner**

Stress management techniques are internal changes to cope better with the negative stresses we can't change. These are very important methods for dealing with stress. They are ways to make us more whole as human beings. Regular, daily meditation or programmed relaxation time is one of the most useful tools. There are many relaxation audio tapes that can. Biofeedback can be used for this purpose with excellent results. One of the more simple but effective tranquility induction methods that has been used for centuries is just to focus attention on virtually anything—a candle flame, a mantra, a neutral word, or a peaceful phrase. Doing this for thirty minutes, twice per day, is enormously rewarding.

Spiritual values and a spiritual focus in life can have enormous stress managing capabilities. This should be sharply distinguished from the guilt and blame, shoulds and shouldn'ts, of religious dogma that create intrapersonal and interpersonal divisiveness and conflict, and thus even more stress.

*If you are patient in one moment of anger,
you will escape a hundred days of sorrow.*
**Chinese proverb**

Since much of our stress-coping ability depends on how we have been programmed to view ourselves and the world, and how we interact in the world, psychological techniques for changing our programming are essential for good stress management. We have to learn to be more adaptive. We have to change our view of ourselves to be more integrated, more inclusive. We have to change our behavior with others to be more cooperative and use better communication skills. There are many self-help psychological techniques that will assist with this. Psychotherapists can help those who need more than what can be accomplished alone. Refer to the resource section for more information.

Regular, balanced, enjoyable exercise can be considered a powerful stress management tool. In moderate amounts, wisely performed, many physical activities can lower stress. Stretching and play can help us relax. Aerobic exercise can increase endorphins which elevate our mood. It can also improve our energy levels, our immune system, and enable us to adapt to stress physically.

## Integration

### LISTEN

*If you are*
*in conflict*
*within your self,*
*have the*
*different parts*
*talk out loud*
*to one another.*
*Listen*
*to what they*
*have to say*
*to each other.*
*Feel, find out*
*what they/you*
*really want*
*to do.*

**Bernard Gunther**

At one moment we can seethe with rage, at another moment soar with joy, vacillate under some circumstances, be decisive in others, be truthful one minute, and lie the next. We can fluctuate from deep analytical thought to starry-eyed fantasy in a millisecond, play the role of loving parent one moment and with a phone call from work be immediately transformed into a demanding employer. There is a continual, split-second flux of emotions, feelings, mindstates, thoughts, motivations, and identities arising and passing away throughout our waking life and, during much of our sleeptime, as dreams. Being able to recognize and accept all the elements of this melodrama allows us to integrate all the disparate parts into a symphonic whole that makes us healthy and happy.

The problem is that many of the more trouble-some portions of our being are quite secretive, elusive, and devious, hiding deep in the inner reaches of our unconscious. The trick is to find methods to ferret out these hidden aspects of our being so we can consciously choose to own them or discard them. Shining the light of attentive mindfulness on them is very helpful, for they like to hide in the dark recesses of the mind. Slowing the hectic pace of life helps this process because a fast-paced life means letting the unconscious mind run the day—being "on automatic." This conditions us not to listen to the hidden whispers of the unconscious that push and pull us without our awareness. That's when the problems arise or perpetuate themselves. Silence, too, complements a slower, more deliberate lifestyle.

Many of the psychotherapeutic modalities are aimed at this discovery and integration process. Refer to the First Priority Strategies for Psychological Health on page 44 and the resources section in this chapter on Psychological Health for assistance in this part of the journey to awakening. Pay particular attention to the Psychosynthesis resources and the works of Assagioli and Ferucci.

## Right Livelihood

*Work and Love—these are the basics.*
*Without them there is neurosis.*

**Theodore Reik**

There are many ways in which right livelihood influences our psychological health. Providing for our physiological needs of food, drink, clothing, and shelter is the foundation. If our standard of living is stable and secure, it also helps our psychological well-being. Economics, as well as how we are treated at work, contributes greatly to our self worth. For many of us, our whole identity is wrapped up in our vocation. Physical, biochemical, and emotional stresses on the job have powerful influences on the psyche, whether they be exhaustive physical labor, pollution effects on brain biochemistry, or an emotionally demanding, hectic pace.

There are also psychological influences associated with how we perceive that our job helps others and the environment. To some, a job that harms others or contributes to the destruction of the environment is very stressful.

The intellectual stimulation of the job can be either enhancing or disruptive of psychological health. Without enough intellectual stimulation, boredom plagues the emotions. Too much intellectual strain overtaxes the emotions.

See the chapter on Occupational Health for more resources about how to get the most from right livelihood.

## Societal Influence

*I believe I've found the missing link*
*between animal and civilized man.*
*It is us.*

**Konrad Lorenz**

Imagine a close-knit, prosperous community where no one locks his doors, and everyone is free to pursue a truly fruitful life without restrictions. Then observe the lives of people oppressed by totalitarian regimes, or terrorized by urban crime, or shackled by the injustice of apartheid. Influences of culture, government, and the social milieu cannot be ignored when considering factors that influence psychological health. Three avenues exist for reversing the negative impact of society on this aspect of our health. Either transform the social conditions, escape to a healthier environment, or insulate these effects by building up other factors of psychological health. Using combinations of all three strategies seems to be the most advisable. Be sure to use the chapter on relationships as an aid to psychological well-being. It is indispensable.

## Enjoyable, Fitness-Producing Activities

*To keep the body in good health is a duty ...*
*otherwise we shall not be able to keep our mind*
*strong and clear.*

**Buddha**

Because there is an inseparable link between brain and body, psyche and soma, mind and matter, activities that produce a fit body with endurance, quickness, energy, and strength tend to evoke those same psychological qualities. Stretching exercises will help create a flexible attitude toward life. Allowing the physical body to play and enjoy movement creates happiness in the heart. Inactivity, weakness, or stiffness of the body breeds similar psychological disturbance—lethargy, fragility, inflexibility, lack of enthusiasm for life.

## Neurological Integrity

*It is more important to know what sort of*
*person has a disease than to know what sort of*
*disease a person has.*

**Hippocrates**

Irritating, abnormal, or disharmonious nerve stimuli from excessive muscle tone, restricted or hypermobile joint mechanics, organ dysfunction, tissue damage, illness, or neurotransmitter imbalance can negatively impact the emotional centers of the brain. Simply put—when we are in pain, when our bodies are not functioning properly, or we are ill, there is psychological stress. However we say it, we are reminded of the intertwining nature of our physical and psychological selves. It tells us that whenever we feel emotionally down, or irritated or blocked or confused, there is wise counsel in looking to the body to see if healing efforts there might not elicit improvements in the psyche.

Many psychotherapies are now much more active in using the body not only for insights into the psyche, but as an avenue for direct intervention and healing. Integrative Body Psychotherapy, Bioenergetics, Somato-Emotional Release Work, and deep tissue massage techniques such as Structural Integration, are some of many.

At least 30% of those individuals presenting psychological problems to psychotherapists and psychiatrists have physical symptoms as part of their major complaints. It is important to address these physical problems adequately for proper resolution of their emotional difficulties. All too often the physical symptoms are ignored as being psychosomatic or are dealt with in only a symptomatic way with drug prescriptions. Using the natural therapies mentioned in the section on Rating Physical Health Enhancement Strategies is a key to dealing with this aspect of mind-body interdependence.

The value of certain therapies in this regard should not be overlooked. Manipulative therapies in conjunction with other physical therapy modalities have a powerful effect in eliminating the tremendous neurological irritation that comes from excessive muscle tightness, fascial restrictions, trigger points, abnormal organ function, and abnormal joint mobility in the spine, extremities and cranium. Cranial Electrical Stimulation (CES) can correct imbalanced neurotransmitter function and contribute to a dramatic improvement in cases of depression, anxiety, phobias, and behavioral problems associated with hyperactivity. It can often eliminate or reduce the need for medication used for a similar effect.

Acupuncture too, whether acting through neurological mechanisms or by the process of balancing *chi* through the meridians of the body, has profound impact on healing processes. And acupuncture has been used successfully with direct intervention in a wide variety of psychodynamic disturbances.

## POWERFUL PSYCHOLOGICAL HEALERS

The following are some of the most powerful psychological health enhancers that every one should be incorporating into his life:

- Proper nutrition with supplementation
- Regular exercise—aerobic, flexibility, and play
- Daily meditation and mindfulness exercises
- Stress reduction and management efforts
- Improved social support activities with family, friends, and colleagues
- Regular self-psychotherapy practices
- Right livelihood.

## PSYCHOLOGICAL HEALTH RESOURCES

*Out of clutter find simplicity. From discord make harmony.*
*In the middle of difficulty lies opportunity.*

**Albert Einstein**

★Denotes Best of the Best Resources

### *Books*

Abrams, Jeremiah, ed. *Reclaiming the Inner Child*. Tarcher, 1990.

Andersen, Marianne S. and Savary, Louis M. *Passages: A Guide for Pilgrims of the Mind*. Harper and Row, 1973.

Assagioli, Roberto. *Psychosynthesis: A Manual of Principles and Techniques*. Penguin, 1976.

Assagioli, Roberto. *The Act of Will*. Penguin, 1974.

Bradshaw, John. *The Family: A Revolutionary Way of Self Discovery*. Health Communications, 1988.

Bradshaw, John. *Healing the Shame that Binds You*. Health Communications, 1988.

Bradshaw, John. *Homecoming: Reclaiming and Championing your Inner Child*. Bantam, 1990.

Brown, Molly Young. *Growing Whole: Exploring the Wilderness Within—An Audio and Guided Journal for Discovering Your Strength, Creativity, and Wisdom*. Hazelden, 1993.

Csikszentmihalyi, Mihaly. *Flow: The Psychology of Optimal Experience . . . Steps Toward Enhancing the Quality of Life*. Harper & Row, 1989.

★Ferrucci, Piero. *What We May Be: Techniques for Psychological and Spiritual Growth*. Tarcher, 1982.

Friedman, Howard. *The Self-Healing Personality: Why Some People Achieve Health and Others Succumb to Illness*. NAL-Dutton, 1992.

★Gendlin, Eugene T. *Focusing*. Bantam, 1978.

Gilioli, Pino. *Mindscapes: Psychological Mazes for Personality Insight*. Macmillan, 1984.

Hippchen, Leonard. *Ecologic—Biochemical Approaches to Treatment of Delinquents and Criminals*. Van Nostrand Reinhold, 1978.

★Kabat-Zinn, Jon. *Full Catastrophe Living: Using the Wisdom of Your Body and Mind to Face Stress, Pain, and Illness*. Dell, 1990.

Keirsey, David and Bates, Marilyn. *Please Understand Me: Character and Temperament Types*. Prometheus Memesis, 1984.

*Nutrition and Mental Health*. U. S. Senate Select Committee on Nutrition and Human Needs, 1980.

★Palmer, Helen. *The Enneagram in Love and Work: Understanding Your Intimate and Business Relationships*. HarperSanFrancisco, 1995.

Peper, Erik and Holt, Catherine. *Creating Wholeness: A Self-Healing Workbook Using Dynamic Relaxation, Images, And Thoughts*. Plenum, 1993.

★Pfieffer, Carl. *Nutrition and Mental Illness: An Ortho-molecular Approach to Balancing Body Chemistry.* Healing Arts Press, 1987.

Philpott, William and Kalita, Dwight. *Brain Allergies: The Psycho-Nutrient Connection.* Keats, 1980.

Postle, Denis. *The Mind Gymnasium: A New Age Guide to Self-Realization.* McGraw Hill, 1989.

Progoff, Ira. *At a Journal Workshop: The basic text and guide for using the Intensive Journal process.* Dialogue House Library, 1977.

Randolph, Theron and Moss, Ralph. *An Alternative Approach to Allergies—The New Field of Clinical Ecology Unravels the Environmental Causes of Mental and Physical Ills.* Lippincott and Crowell, 1980.

Walsh, Roger and Vaughan, Francis. *Paths Beyond Ego: The Transpersonal Vision.* Tarcher, 1993.

Wurtman, Judith. *Managing Your Mind and Mood Through Food.* Rawson, 1986.

## Periodicals

*If one advances confidently in the direction of his dreams, and endeavors to live the life which he has imagined, he will meet with a success unexpected in common hours.*

**Henry David Thoreau**

*Brain/Mind: Bulletin of Breakthroughs,* Interface Press, P.O. Box 42211, Los Angeles, CA 90042. Newsletter documenting latest information on psycho-physical health connections.

*Journal of Humanistic Psychology,* The Association for Humanistic Psychology, 1772 Vallejo St., San Francisco, CA 94123-9816; (415) 346-7929. For subscription: Sage Periodicals Press, 2455 Teller Rd., Newbury Park, CA 91320; (805) 499-0721.

*Journal of Transpersonal Psychology,* The Association for Transpersonal Psychology, Transpersonal Institute, P.O. Box 3049, Stanford, CA 94309; (415) 327-2066.

★The Newsletter of the American Institute of Stress, The American Institute of Stress, 124 Park Ave., Yonkers, NY 10703; (800) 24-RELAX. One of the better resources for abstracts of up-to-date research and information about mind-body interconnectedness and health.

*Psychology Today,* P.O. Box 51844, Boulder, CO 80321-1844; (303) 447-9330.

## Videotapes

*The best and most beautiful things in the world cannot be seen or even touched. They must be felt with the heart.*

**Helen Keller**

Hartley Film Foundation, 59 Cat Rock Road, Cos Cob, CT 06807; (203) 869-1818; (800) 937-1819; Fax (203) 869-1905.

## Audiotapes

*I fear my inner guru may be senile. He offers contradictory advice.*

**Sam Keen**

*Health Journeys—Guided Imagery Cassette Series,* Health Journeys, Image Paths, Inc., P.O. Box 5714, Cleveland, OH 44101-0714; (216) 623-4680.

*Multi-Evocation Hypnotic Cassettes,* The Changeworks Catalog, P.O. Box 10616, Portland, OR 97210-0616; (800) 937-7771. A series of high-quality, innovative Ericksonian hypnosis audio tapes for self improvement.

Source Cassette Learning Systems, Inc., P.O. Box W, Stanford, CA 94309; (800) 52-TAPES. Some of the best tapes available.

## Organizations

*The optimist expects his dreams to come true, a pessimist expects his nightmares to.*

**Unknown**

The Mental Health Crisis Line: (800) 222-8220.

National Alcohol and Drug Abuse Hotline: (800) 252-6465.

RESOURCES

## HEALTH PRACTITIONER RESOURCES

*I've got good judgment.*
*Good judgment comes from experience.*
*And experience—well,*
*that comes from having bad judgment.*

**Peter De Vries**

### Books

★ Almaas, A. H. *The Pearl Beyond Price—Integration of Personality into Being: An Object Relations Approach*. Diamond Books, 1988.

Dickey, Lawrence, ed. *Clinical Ecology*. Charles C. Thomas Publisher, 1976.

Fried, Robert with Grimaldi, Joseph. *The Psychology and Physiology of Breathing In Behavioral Medicine, Clinical Pathology, and Psychiatry*. Plenum, 1993.

Hersen, M. and Bellack, A. S., ed. *Dictionary of Behavioral Assessment Techniques*. Pergamon, 1989.

Hippchen, Leonard. *Ecologic-Biochemical Approaches to Treatment of Delinquents and Criminals*. Van Nostrand Reinhold, 1978.

★ Hoffer, Abram. *Orthomolecular Medicine for Physicians*. Keats, 1989.

Hyman, S.E. and Nestler, E.J. *The Molecular Foundation of Psychiatry*. American Psychiatric Press, 1993. Good examination of the neurochemistry of mental illness.

Krug, Samuel, ed. *Psychware: A Reference Guide to Computer-Based Products for Behavioral Assessment in Psychology, Education, and Business*. Test Corp. of America, 1984. Westport Publishers, 330 W. 47th St. Kansas City, MO 64112.

Kurtz, Ron. *Body-Centered Psychotherapy: The Hakomi Method*. LifeRhythm, 1990. Available from Life-Rhythm, P.O. Box 806, Mendocino, CA 95460; (707) 937-1825.

Pauley, J. and Peiser, H., ed. *Psychological Managements for Psychosomatic Disorders*. Springer-Verlag, 1989.

Pfieffer, Carl; Mailloux, Richard; and Forsythe, Linda. *The Schizophrenias: Ours to Conquer*. Bio-Communications Press, 1988. Available from Bio-Communications Press, 3100 North Hillside Ave., Wichita, KS 67219.

★ Rea, William. *Chemical Sensitivity* Vol. 4. Lewis, 1994.

Richardson, Mary Ann. *Amino Acids in Psychiatric Disease*. American Psychiatric Press, 1990.

Stricker, George and Gold, Jerold. *Comprehensive Handbook of Psychotherapy Integration*. Plenum, 1993.

Sweetland, Richard and Keyser, Daniel, ed. *Tests: A Comprehensive Reference for Assessments in Psychology, Education, and Business*. PRO-ED, 1991.

★ Werbach, Melvyn. *Nutritional Influences on Mental Illness: A Sourcebook of Clinical Research*. Third Line Press, 1991.

Wilber, Ken; Engler, Jack; and Brown, Daniel. *Transformations of Consciousness: Conventional and Contemplative Perspectives on Development*. Shambhala, 1986.

Zeig, Jeffrey and Munion, W. Michael. *What Is Psychotherapy?* Jossey-Bass, 1990. Resource for practitioners to compare different types of therapy.

### Periodicals

*The Six Mistakes of Man*
*1. The delusion that personal gain is made*
*by crushing others.*
*2. The tendency to worry about things that*
*cannot be changed or corrected.*
*3. Insisting that a thing is impossible because*
*we cannot accomplish it.*
*4. Refusing to set aside trivial preferences.*
*5. Neglecting development of the mind and*
*not reading.*
*6. Attempting to compel others to believe and*
*live as we do.*

**Cicero**

Bland, Jeffrey. "A Functional Approach to Mental Illness" *Townsend Letter for Doctors* (Dec. 1994): 1335-41.

★ Jaffe, Russel and Kruesi, Oscar. "The Biochemical-Immunological Window: A Molecular View of Psychiatric Case Management." *Journal of Applied Nutrition* 44:2 (1992) 26-42.

★ Johnston, G. A. "Megavitamins and Psychotherapy: Effective, Economical and Time-Saving Treatment—A Three Year Study" *Journal of Orthomolecular Medicine* 8:2 (1993): 104-20.

*Journal of Analytical Psychology*, Routledge Publications, ITPS Ltd., Dept. J., Cheriton House, North Way, Andover, SP10 5BE, UK; phone: 0264 332424; Fax 0264 364418. International Jungian Journal.

*Journal of Contemplative Psychotherapy*, The Naropa Institute, 2130 Arapahoe Avenue, Boulder, CO 80302; (303) 444-0202.

★ *Journal of Humanistic Psychology,* The official Journal of the Association for Humanistic Psychology, 1772 Vallejo St., San Francisco, CA 94123-9816; (415) 346-7929. Published by Sage Periodicals Press, 2455 Teller Rd., Newbury Park, CA 91320; (805) 499-0721.

★ *Journal of Orthomolecular Medicine,* American Association of Orthomolecular Medicine Publication Office, 16 Florence Ave., Toronto, Ontario M2N 1E9 Canada.

★ *Journal of Transpersonal Psychology,* Association for Transpersonal Psychology, Transpersonal Institute, P.O. Box 4437, Stanford, CA 94309; (415) 327-2066.

*Integrative Physiological and Behavioral Science Journal,* Transaction Publishers, Rutgers University, New Brunswick, NJ 08903; (908) 932-2280.

*The Newsletter of the American Institute of Stress,* The American Institute of Stress, 124 Park Ave., Yonkers, NY 10703; (800) 24-RELAX. One of the better resources for abstracts of up-to-date research and information about mind-body interconnectedness and health.

*Psychosynthesis Digest,* P.O. Box 18559, Irvine, CA 92713.

Schoenthaler, Stephen; Moody, Jeannie; Pankow, Lisa. "Applied Nutrition and Behavior," *Journal of Applied Nutrition,* 43:1 (1991): 31-9.

★ Walsh, William. "Biochemical Treatment of Behavior, Learning and Mental Disorders." *Townsend Letter* (Aug/Sep 1992): 698-702.

## Computer Databases and Software

*We are not primarily put on this earth*
*to see through one another,*
*but to see one another through.*

**Peter De Vries**

Interactive Health Systems, 525 Broadway, Suite 210, Santa Monica, CA 90401; (310) 451-8111. They produce client oriented software such as: "Personal Stress Survey," "Therapeutic Learning Program," which is a counsellor assisted ten-session computer program of brief psychotherapy, "StressCheck," "Moods, Foods, and Willpower," and "Reality," a counselling system for schools, grades 6-12.

PsycINFO. From the American Psychological Association. Covers thousands of journal articles and reports dating back to 1967 on every conceivable issue relating to psychological health.

## Organizations

*Brains are like hearts,*
*they go where they are appreciated.*

**Robert McNamara**

*Note: Many of these organizations hold annual conferences and/or smaller workshops throughout the year. Contact them for on-going educational programs.

The Academy for Guided Imagery, P.O. Box 2070, Mill Valley, CA 94942; (800) 726-2070; Fax (415) 389-9342.

American Academy of Environmental Medicine, P.O. Box 116106, Denver, CO 80216; (303) 622-9755. Progressive group of physicians practicing "clinical ecology" who would be most likely to use the most up-dated methods for identifying and treating toxic and allergic reactions to the environment. They can provide a referral to a physician nearest you. Audio tapes of the Academy's Seminars and conferences are available from Insta-Tape, Inc., P.O. Box 2926-D, Pasadena, CA 91105.

American Association for Marriage and Family Therapy, 1100 17th St. NW, Tenth Floor, Washington, DC 20006; (202) 452-0109. For a therapist referral: (800) 374-2638; (800) 792-1970.

American Counseling Association, 5999 Stevenson Ave., Alexandria, VA 22304; (703) 823-9800.

American Dance Therapy Association, 2000 Century Plaza, Suite 108, Columbia, MD 21044; (410) 997-4040. Publishes the *Journal of Dance Therapy.*

American Group Psychotherapy Association, 25 E. 21st St., 6th Floor, New York, NY 10010; (212) 477-2677. Publishes consumer guide to group psychotherapy.

American Institute of Stress, 124 Park Ave., Yonkers, NY 10703; (914) 963-1200. A clearing house and educational center for information on stress-related physical and psychological elements of daily life.

Association for Holotropic Breathwork International, c/o Laurie Weaver, 250 Annis Rd., Brisbane, CA 94005; (415) 468-6930.

★ Association for Humanistic Psychology, 1772 Vallejo St., San Francisco, CA 94123-9816; (415) 346-7929.

Association for Psychological Type, 9140 Ward Pkwy., Kansas City, MO 64114; (816) 444-3500. Focus is on Myers-Briggs psychological typing.

Association for the Study of Dreams, P.O. Box 1600, Vienna, VA 22183; (703) 242-8888.

RESOURCES

★Association for Transpersonal Psychology, Transpersonal Institute, P.O. Box 3049, Stanford, CA 94309; (415) 327-2066. Publishes a yearly directory of transpersonal psychology schools and programs and the *Journal of Transpersonal Psychology*.

C.G. Jung Foundation for Analytical Psychology, 28 E. 39th St., New York, NY 10016; (212) 697-6430. Publishes *Quadrant* journal.

Canadian Schizophrenia Association, 16 Florence Ave., Toronto, Ontario, Canada M2N 1E9; (416) 733-2117. Publishes the *Journal of Orthomolecular Medicine, Health and Nutrition Update*, and *Nutrition and Mental Health*.

Carl Pfieffer Treatment Center, 1804 Centre Point Drive, Suite 102, Naperville, IL 60563; (708) 505-0300. A treatment center primarily focusing on the nutritional and biochemical diagnosis and treatment of behavioral disorders.

Center for Mind/Body Studies, 5225 Connecticut Ave., Suite 414, Washington, DC 20015; (202) 966-7338. A multidisciplinary, professional organization that actively engages in integrating multidimensional health promotion programs.

Common Boundary, 5272 River Rd., Suite 650, Bethesda, MD 20814; (301) 652-9495. A non-profit organization for health care professionals exploring the connections between psychotherapy and spirituality.

The Focusing Institute, 29 S. La Salle, Suite 1195, Chicago, IL 60605; (312) 629-0500. Teaches Dr. Gendlin's Focusing techniques in workshops as well as publishing a journal and assisting with referrals.

Institute for Rational-Emotive Therapy, 45 E. 65th St., New York, NY 10021; (212) 535-0822. Publishes the *Journal of Rational-Emotive & Cognitive Behavior Therapy*.

International Institute for Bioenergetic Analysis, 144 E. 36th St., New York, NY 10016; (212) 532-7742. Publishes the journal *Bioenergetic Analysis*.

International Transactional Analysis Association, 1772 Vallejo St., San Francisco, CA 94123; (415) 885-5992.

The International Transpersonal Association, 20 Sunnyside Ave., A-257, Mill Valley, CA 94941; (415) 383-8819; (415) 383-7788.

★National Institute for the Clinical Application of Behavioral Medicine, P.O. Box 523, 6D Ledgebrook Dr., Mansfield, CT 06250; (800) 743-2226; (203) 456-1153; Fax (203) 423-4512. Publishes *The Psychology of Health, Immunity and Disease Workbooks*.

NLP Comprehensive: Neuro-Linguistic Programming, 2897 Valmont, Road, Boulder, CO 80301; (800) 233-1657; Fax (303) 442-0609.

NLP Institute of California, P.O. Box 12, Felton, CA 95018; (800) 767-6756; (408) 335-3858.

Princeton Bio Center, 862 Route 518, Skillman, NJ 08558-9631; (609) 924-8607. A biomedical research and treatment center that addresses the neurobiological and nutritional aspects of mental illness.

Process-Oriented Psychology: Contact the Process Work Center of Portland, 733 NW Everett, Box 11, Portland, OR 97209; (503) 223-8188; Fax (503) 227-7003.

Progoff Intensive Journal Workshops, Dialogue House, 80 E. 11th St., New York, NY 10003; (800) 221-5844; (212) 673-5880. Teaches organized method of journal keeping for psycho-spiritual growth. Excellent!

For independent Psychosynthesis centers throughout the world see Piero Ferrucci's *What We May Be*, pages 241-3.

Rosenberg-Rand Institute of Integrative Body Psychotherapy, 1551 Ocean Ave., Suite 230, Santa Monica, CA 90401; (310) 394-0147. Trains psychotherapists in their highly effective techniques and provides the public with referrals to qualified practitioners.

★Society for Orthomolecular Medicine, 2698 Pacific Ave., San Francisco, CA 94115; (415) 346-2500; Fax (415) 346-4991.

The Synthesis Center, Box 575, Amherst, MA 01004; (413) 256-0772. Psychosynthesis Counselor Training Program.

Well Mind Association, 4649 Sunnyside Ave. N., Seattle, WA 98103; (206) 547-6167.

*Before you realize who you are, it is not possible for you to go your own direction.*

**Shunryu Suzuki**

# CHAPTER SEVEN

# RELATIONSHIP / SOCIAL HEALTH

*There is a destiny that makes us brothers,*
*None goes his way alone—*
*All that we send into the lives of others*
*Comes back into our own.*

**Unknown**

Man is not an island unto himself. Humans are social animals. A large part of our being is intertwined with others. We must recognize this when addressing health as holistic. Really, there is no such thing as individual health separate from the health of others or separate from interconnectedness with others. The most dominant way in which relationship health affects our total well-being is through its interconnections with our psycho-spiritual wholeness.

*The greatest challenge of the day is:*
*how to bring about a revolution of the heart,*
*a revolution which has to start*
*with each one of us.*

**Dorothy Day**

Remember the qualities present in healthy relationships, as seen in the preceding chapter on Psychological Health. (Here again it is difficult to separate psychological health from relationship health.)

Compassion, generosity, free expression of feelings, empathy, openness, truthfulness, trustworthiness, good communication including conflict resolution skills, patience, non-judgment, empathetic listening, free flow of love, giving and receiving, cooperativeness, sensitivity, tolerance, sincerity, sympathetic joy (rejoicing in others' good fortune and happiness), non-dependence—these and other qualities create positive ramifications in other aspects of health.

And the qualities present in disharmonious relationships can be compared:

Selfishness, greed, and exploitation; separateness and aloofness; an argumentative, opinionated, and confrontational style of communication; competitiveness; coldheartedness; judgmental attitudes; an inability to love or be loved, plus difficulty giving and receiving; impatience; insensitivity; intolerance; secretiveness; distrust; insincerity; fear; violence. These and other negative psychological attributes create negative ramifications in other aspects of our health.

*It is perfectly monstrous*
*the way people go about nowadays*
*saying things against one,*
*behind one's back, that are absolutely*
*and entirely true.*

**Oscar Wilde**

## RELATIONSHIP INFLUENCES ON OTHER ASPECTS OF HEALTH

*Love is friendship that has caught fire.*
*It is quiet understanding, mutual confidence,*
*sharing and forgiving. It is loyalty through good*
*times and bad. It settles for less than perfection*
*and makes allowances for human weaknesses.*
*Love is content with the present, it hopes for*
*the future and it doesn't brood over the past.*
*It's the day-in-and-day-out chronicles of*
*irritations, problems, compromises,*
*small disappointments, big victories and*
*common goals.*
*If you have love in your life, it can make up for a*
*great many things you lack. If you don't have it,*
*no matter what else there is, it's not enough.*

**Unknown**

Following will be some examples of how these qualities, good and bad, affect our physical health, work productivity, educational attainment, economic prosperity, and spiritual development.

### *Relationship and Physical Health*

*I shall pass through this world but once.*
*Any good that I can do, or any kindness that*
*I can show any human being,*
*let me do it now and not defer it.*
*For I shall not pass this way again.*

**Stephen Grellet**

People who describe themselves as happily married have fewer illnesses and greater longevity than single, divorced, or unhappily married people.

Individuals with more social contacts have less illness and greater longevity than people with few social contacts.

People who have a sense of purpose and contribution to the community live longer than those who believe they have nothing to give.

Those with pets recover from illness sooner, and live longer, than non-pet owners.

Interpersonal violence leads to injury in addition to the psychophysical stress dynamics.

### *Relationship and Livelihood*

*I arise in the morning torn between a desire*
*to improve (or save) the world and a desire*
*to enjoy (or savor) it.*
*This makes it hard to plan the day.*

**E. B. White**

Productivity increases when workers are integrated into a team management program where they have a mutual working relationship with supervisors in which their suggestions will be heard and they sense some control over their workplace and the quality of their work. This works better than a unilateral relationship where "orders" come down from above to be "obeyed" without discussion.

One of the largest reasons for lost productivity is employer-employee interpersonal conflicts. Employee-employee conflict also reduces work productivity.

One of the most frequent causes of employee absenteeism and work inefficiency is relationship problems at home.

Cooperation in business leads to more cost-effective benefits than competitiveness does.

### *Relationship and Education*

*The simple realization that there are other*
*points of view is the beginning of wisdom.*
*Understanding what they are is a great step.*
*The final test is understanding*
*why they are held.*

**Charles M. Campbell**

Educational performance is directly linked with family harmony, classmate relationships, and instructor/student rapport. When there are problems in the home, school grades drop, from kindergarten through college. Tensions before, during, and after school with classmates dramatically affect learning performance. Students learn better from instructors they have a good relationship with, as opposed to teachers who are aloof and just convey facts.

There are studies of the ideal class size which indicate that a number small enough for significant interpersonal communication is the most effective.

Where will a person learn more, in an atmosphere of fear—or love?

### *Relationship and Spiritual Fulfillment*

*If we could share this world below,*
*If we could learn to love . . .*
*If we could share this world below,*
*We'd need no world above.*

**Ray Faraday Nelson**

Relationship enhancement is one of the most powerful avenues to spiritual unfoldment. If we can see our oneness with our fellow humans, it is much easier to see our oneness with the rest of the Universe, with God. Review the qualities of healthy relating. Note that they are also the qualities that our great spiritual leaders embodied and encouraged us to adopt. It can be seen in the compassionate acts of Jesus, the life of service for Karma Yogis, the nonviolent activism of Gandhi, the Dances of Universal Peace in Sufism, or the Buddhist Bodhisattva goals of liberating all beings from suffering.

## THE RELATIONSHIP SPECTRUM

*The purpose of life is a warm heart.*
*Think of other people.*
*Serve other people sincerely.*

**The Dalai Lama**

A spectrum of functioning can illustrate the wide variance in relationship health. Most of us can identify with qualities in the middle section of the graph appearing daily in our lives. Too large a

---

**RELATIONSHIP SPECTRUM OF FUNCTIONING**

Buddha, Jesus, or Similar Beings

Ability to embrace more living beings in love, generosity, and unity, leaving behind the vestiges of separateness.

Mastering many elements to relationship health.

Overcoming dysfunctional programming and difficult circumstances with new, healthy skills and behaviors.

Striving for better relationships but programming and circumstances still reinforce maladaptive interactions.

Win-lose attitudes, verbal conflict, psychological abuse, dysfunctional communication, and economic competition are the predominant characteristics of interaction.

Violent Conflict!

percentage of individuals experience a predominance of relationship interactions on the lower end of the scale. And few of us spend enough time in the upper echelons of idealized relationship, as represented by the higher levels on the graph. Putting relationships in this perspective helps us view this aspect of health in relation to other parts of our lives.

## ANALYSIS OF RELATIONSHIPS

*There is a single magic, a single power,*
*a single salvation, and a single happiness,*
*and that is called loving.*

**Herman Hesse**

Since relationships are dynamic and we all have many, analyzing each relationship is helpful before we can know where and how effort needs to be expended on building greater harmony. Use the following chart to rate how each relationship contributes to overall health—emotionally, physically, economically, spiritually. Take each positive and negative quality of relationship which was listed earlier to see how dominant each attribute is in that relationship. How can we reduce the difficult

tensions in the relationship? How can we learn to enhance the positive qualities? How much satisfaction is there in this relationship? How much do I benefit? How much do I give? Is the way we relate balanced? Do I benefit and not the other? Or does the other benefit to my detriment? How do I make new relationships? How do I improve my present relationships? What are the specific problem areas? How can more truthful, clear communication resolve these problems? Take a lot of time to do a thorough evaluation.

It must also be remembered that each relationship is to be weighted differently. A marriage carries more importance than a relationship with a pet—or at least it should. So although your rapport with your dog might get a +5 and you rate your relationship with your spouse +3 because of conflicts in interest and poor communications, that does not mean that Fido is more beneficial to your overall health than your marriage. It just means that your relationship with your dog is mutually beneficial with no problem areas that need work. This difference in weighting relationships in proportion to their importance in your life becomes valuable when it comes to deciding where efforts to build strong relationships need to be directed.

## RELATIONSHIP SPECTRUM ANALYSIS

|  |  | -5 | -4 | -3 | -2 | -1 | 0 | 1 | 2 | 3 | 4 | +5 |
|---|---|---|---|---|---|---|---|---|---|---|---|---|

Spouse
Ex-spouse
Child    1._____
       2._____
       3._____
Mother
Father
Mother-in-law
Father-in-law
Grandmother    1._____
       2._____
Grandfather    1._____
       2._____

## RELATIONSHIP SPECTRUM ANALYSIS (Cont.)

| | | -5 | -4 | -3 | -2 | -1 | 0 | 1 | 2 | 3 | 4 | +5 |
|---|---|---|---|---|---|---|---|---|---|---|---|---|

Siblings
1._____
2._____
3._____

Leaders and members of your spiritual affiliation
1._____
2._____
3._____
4._____

Friends
1._____
2._____
3._____
4._____
5._____
6._____

Co-worker
1._____
2._____
3._____

Boss
1._____

Neighbor
1._____
2._____
3._____

Health practitioner
1._____
2._____
3._____

Pet
1._____
2._____

Social or athletic club
1._____
2._____
3._____

Volunteer organization
1._____
2._____

The poor
1._____

Other races
1._____
2._____

## FORMULA FOR RELATIONSHIP WHOLENESS

*The vision of humanity as one enormous family,
one objective tribe may once have been utopian.
Now it is a practical necessity.*

**Oscar Ichazo**

So let's look at the major elements that contribute to healthy relationships. These factors seem to be quite universal. They work just as well with family, friends, co-workers, and pets.

We see from the diagram that the two great wings of the heart of a relationship are psychological and spiritual integration, and the center is composed of unconditional love. Closely linked to the spiritual cornerstone is mindfulness, and to the psychological one is communication skills. Obviously it is very difficult to separate these factors, since they are so closely interdependent—as indi-

cated by dotted rather than solid lines. But in order to present these concepts in an organized fashion, we will discuss how each influences relationships, whether with friends, family, intimate partners, co-workers, neighbors, elected representatives, strangers, enemies, or those who are impoverished, disadvantaged, or suffering.

### *Physical Health*

*Love is life in all of its aspects.
And if you miss love, you miss life. Please don't.*

**Leo Buscaglia**

How well our bodies function influences how we relate to others. If our physical selves are operating efficiently and healthfully, it will have a positive impact on those we come in contact with. Whenever we feel good we radiate the fact to

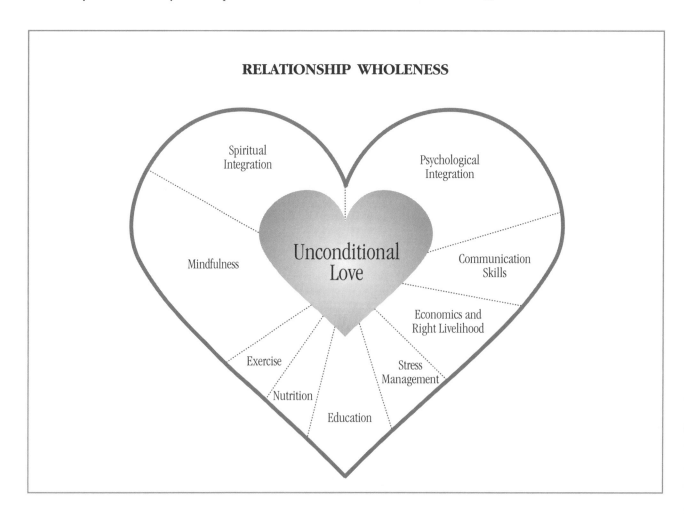

**RELATIONSHIP WHOLENESS**

others. We have more energy to give to them. But when our bodies are ill, it pulls our mood down, and that also rubs off on others. We need more from others at times of sickness and are able to contribute less to friends, family, and society.

Review the chapter on physical health and note what priority areas need to be addressed in order to work directly at improving that aspect of being. Balanced nutrition and exercise are two of the most important elements of self-care that enormously affect relational health.

## Education

*It's not what we don't know that hurts,
it's what we know that ain't so.*

**Will Rogers**

Understanding dynamics of human relationships is essential in order to attain higher levels of relationship health. Family relationship dynamics, parent-child interactions, small group dynamics, communication skills, principles of conflict resolution, have all been thoroughly studied and written about so that greater harmony can be enjoyed. There are also many seminars, workshops, classes, and professional assistance available to learn these skills. The time and effort spent in this arena of wholeness is always rewarded many times over because of its effect on the transformation of so many areas of life. Be sure to see the sources at the end of this chapter for more information.

*A mind is like a parachute,
it only works when it is open.*

**Unknown**

Educating ourselves about social issues and other peoples' problems, as well as different cultures, perspectives, religions, philosophies, and the suffering in the world, opens us up to the truth of the human condition with all of its possibilities for improvement. There are so many opportunities to practice generosity, if only we become informed and open our eyes to the suffering of humanity. As we learn more about other people, we begin to see our commonness and differences fade in impor-

tance. This brings about a tolerance and harmony that could not exist with ignorance.

*Resolve to be tender with the young, compassionate to the aged, sympathetic with the striving, and tolerant of the weak and wrong. Sometime in life you will have been all of these yourself.*

**Unknown**

## Stress Management and Reduction

*It is easy to love a person because they are wonderful, but the whole test of love is to love a person despite the fact that they do not live up to what one sees in them.*

**Pir Vilayat Inayat Khan**

When relationship difficulties arise, the last thing we need is more stress in other areas of our life. Reducing the number of stressful circumstances and incidents, even minor hassles, can play a large part in improving relationships. What helps even more are stress management techniques for dealing with the stresses we cannot reduce or eliminate. The chapter on Psychological Health has information and resources on stress. See also the section on Biofeedback.

## Right Livelihood

*Find out where you can render a service, then render it. The rest is up to the Lord.*

**S.S. Kresge**

Through right livelihood we have many powerful ways to advance human relations. Economic stability eliminates fear of insecurity. Money problems are one of the most frequent causes of marital discord. Children cannot be given what they need when money is tight. When there is tight budgeting, our relationship with the people who benefit from our charitable donations is adversely affected. We tend to participate less in social activities if there is little money to spend on them. Wars are fought over economic insecurity, which is personal fear multiplied by an entire population.

*Work is love made visible.*
**Kahlil Gibran**

When right livelihood provides a stable income there are fewer points of conflict. Children are not deprived. Money is charitably given. The success of right livelihood provides substantial psychological rewards and positively affects relationships. When it provides for one's spiritual development, here again positive relationship benefits are realized. If we are working in a job that fulfills the Buddhist definition of right livelihood, then we are causing no harm to living things, and in fact we should be aiding their well-being. Many choose a livelihood in service to others. What better way to improve relationship health and contribute to total well-being?

## Communication Skills

*Lord, when we are wrong, make us willing to change. And when we are right, make us easy to live with.*
**Peter Marshall**

Communication skills, like conflict resolution techniques, linguistic accuracy, listening, small group effectiveness, and negotiating skills, can make or break a relationship, whether it be with our most intimate friend or our most potent enemy. Many of these communication skills require that we learn how the human psyche functions as it interacts with others. There is usually no more interesting way to discover the inner workings of the mind than by examining how we communicate to others. A number of the resources in this section are specifically devoted to this subject.

## Psychological Integration

*God is discussing with His angels where He should place the secret of life so that it would be most difficult to find. One suggested the bowels of the earth, another the bottom of the sea, a third the highest mountain. A fourth angel objected: "Men will eventually search out all these places. The only place is within man himself. He will never dream of looking there."*
**Unknown**

At the foundation of all relationships is personal psychological health. In our interactions, what goes out is only a reflection of what is within us. If our psychological selves are well integrated, then we engage with others in a harmonious way. But a fragmented personality is projected outward and disrupts every relationship we have. If we are psychologically needy, then we unconsciously set up others to fulfill those needs. If we are filled with fear, we withdraw from others or defensively throw anger outward, most often hitting those closest to us. If we are experiencing relationship problems, the first place to look to find the source of the problem is not in the other person, the most frequent apparent cause. Look inward instead.

*The lover who leans upon the beloved's response, his love is like the flame that needs oil to live; but the lover who stands on his own two feet is like the lantern of the sun that burns without oil.*
**Hazrat Inayat Khan**

## Mindfulness

*It might turn out that exploring the far-out spaces of human consciousness is the fastest way to social transformation.*
**John C. Lilly**

This inward observation is a moment-by-moment attention to bodily sensations, feelings, thoughts, states of mind, speech, body "language," and behavior. Are they congruent? Or are we saying things we don't feel? Do our actions betray our thoughts? Does the body want to say "yes" and the mind "no"? Does our guilt drive us to give while our greed counteracts with stinginess? Knowing ourselves is the foundation of spiritual unfoldment. It is looking at who we really are. Only that which we truly are, not some spiritual ideal, can enter into a relationship with another.

## Spiritual Integration

*When the practice of nonviolence
becomes universal,
God will reign on earth as He does in heaven.*
**Mahatma Gandhi**

At the foundations of all religions there is a moral code that provides guidelines for interpersonal relations. Spirit is that most intimate essence which we all have in common. It binds us in a Unity that spans differences in language, borders, race, age, sex, and time. It is a relationship of Oneness, and at its heart is unconditional love. Spiritual integration involves a skillful blending of this unconditional love of the spirit with the conditioned realities of living in this world. We balance how much we can give to others and how much we need to give to ourselves.

*It is better to give and receive.*
**Bernard Gunther**

## Generosity

*Love in your heart wasn't put there to stay.
Love isn't love 'til you give it away.*
**Oscar Hammerstein**

Acts of generosity are some of the most powerful transformative processes one can engage in, in order to improve any relationship. There is a whole range of giving, from the most tentative to the unconditional. When we express our self-centeredness, holding back on what we give to others, it adversely affects our relationships. This tentative giving of only that which we can easily part with displays psychological insecurity and spiritual stinginess. There is a type of giving which on the surface looks like generosity but is really "calculated trading." A typical example is an oil company which "gives" a few pennies to some ecological cause that has good public relations appeal. It puts out a television ad in which it saves a cute, fluffy, baby owl whose nest was found on an oil rig, so that it may be associated with compassion for earth's little creatures rather than with its obscene profits from raping and desecrating the land. Often this same type of giving is seen with couples in discord. "I give her some flowers and jewelry every once in a while, and she does what I want." The highest form of generosity is giving with joy that which is most valuable to one's personal self, because in that there is the realization that there is no difference between self and other.

*If I truly love one person I love all persons,
I love the world, I love life.*
**Erich Fromm**

## SOME ADVICE ON SPECIAL RELATIONSHIPS

### Intimate Relationships

*True love is like two deep rivers that meet
and merge, intertwining completely into one,
then flowing on together.
The joys, happiness, and sorrows of each
become the joys, happiness, and sorrows
of the other. True love cannot be hurried;
but once unselfishly rooted, it will grow forever.*
**Unknown**

Intimate relationships can provide the opportunity for unparalleled happiness or a powerful spiritual path with great rewards beyond earthly happiness. They can also be nightmares from hell. To make intimate partnerships into beneficial paths to wholeness, the resources in this chapter provide excellent touchstones for further growth, in books, journals, workshops and organizations.

Because sexuality is a powerful modulator of behavior in intimate relationships, it requires special care and sensitivity. This is particularly important in American culture where we overemphasize sexuality. Communicable diseases make it no less important.

*Love does not consist in gazing at each other but in looking forward together in the same direction.*

**Antoine De Saint-Exupery**

## Family Relationships

*If the family were a container, it would be a nest, an enduring nest, loosely woven, expansive, and open. If the family were a fruit, it would be an orange, a circle of sections, held together but separable— each segment distinct. If the family were a boat, it would be a canoe that makes no progress unless everyone paddles.*

**Letty Cottin Pogrebin**

The family as a basic structure in human development is so important that most good psychotherapists use family dynamics models in at least a part of their diagnostic and treatment programs, no matter what the complaint might be. The family is where we learn the fundamental processes for all future relationships. When there are discordant relationships, it is often due to dysfunctional family patterns learned in childhood. These maladaptive patterns persist into adulthood, following us around like hidden saboteurs of happiness and health. Anyone seeking improved relationships, or just interested in psychological growth, would not go astray by using the resources at the end of the chapter on family therapy and the Satir Model approaches to psychotherapy or counseling. Therapists skilled in these approaches can help us effectively weed out these old, counterproductive story lines in our lives and reprogram new, nourishing scripts for a better life.

## Parent and Child

*I was a friendly cloud that floated across my children's lives.*

**Unknown**

The parent-child relationship is the most important relationship of our lives. Because of that importance, all parents are advised to utilize as many of the resources as possible in the special appendix on Parenting and Children. An entire book needs to be written on holistic health care for children, and thus an adequate, comprehensive presentation cannot be given within these pages. But the Appendix contains some of the more significant resources that can put readers on the right path.

## Friends

*A friend is one to whom you can pour out your entire heart, both chaff and grain, knowing that the most gentle of hands will take and sift it, keep what is valuable, and with a breath of kindness blow the rest away.*

**Ancient Arab saying**

Where would we be without friends? It is important to appreciate their value in our daily lives. One way to show that appreciation is to use the resources in this chapter to learn more about ourselves and communication with others.

## Employer-Employee

*Those who bring sunshine to the lives of others cannot keep it from themselves.*

**Sir James Barrie**

Most businesses are beginning to understand the importance of improved employer-employee relations for economic well-being. If they cannot or will not open their eyes to the business advantages, it is hoped that they would improve relationships with their employees simply for the sake of everyone's sanity.

## Teacher-Student

*A [teacher] is like fire. If you get too close, you get burned. If you stay too far away, you don't get enough heat. A sensible moderation is recommended.*

**Tibetan Proverb**

In life we are all teachers and all students, giving and learning all the time. More gets accomplished if we continually realize this lesson and accommodate its truth.

## Client and Health Practitioner

*People who think they know everything are very irritating to those of us who do.*

**Unknown**

The health practitioner is there for the benefit of the client's healing transformation and acts as a facilitator in his or her growth. Health practitioners should be open to opportunities for their own psychological, educational, and spiritual growth in every professional interaction. But if there is a conscious or unconscious, egotistical agenda that takes precedence over the health of the client, problems arise. Money, sex, power, prestige, often have a way of seeping into a wholesome "doctor-patient" relationship and distorting it. But health care consumers have a responsibility to be on guard and assert their rights. One of the most important ways of doing this is by taking responsibility for self-care and to become well-informed about health issues like those discussed in this volume.

## Rich and Poor

*Civilization is just a slow process of learning to be kind.*

**Charles L. Lucas**

There are many interconnections that bind all humans as sisters and brothers, whether we are aware of those bonds or not. We are all dependent on each other. The more we realize the depth of these links, the more we build a sense of responsible social interaction. When we truly realize that we are our brother's keeper, we are less apt to act in egotistical ways that separate and divide us. When we are not attentive to our bonds with a poor Third World peasant we are more apt to become involved in some pattern of selfish, conspicuous consumption at home rather than volunteer relief efforts. Our hearts open with generosity when we deeply feel our connection with those who are disadvantaged or infirm. It is thus necessary to keep our eyes open to the truth of the suffering that surrounds us. We must not isolate ourselves from knowing that part of our larger Self also needs healing.

## Enemy versus Enemy

*Hatred does not cease by hatred, but only by love. If anyone has hurt me or harmed me, knowingly or unknowingly, in thought, word, or deed, I freely forgive them. And I too ask forgiveness if I have hurt anyone or harmed anyone, knowingly or unknowingly, in thought, word, or deed. May all beings be Happy May all beings be Peaceful May all beings be Free.*

**Buddhist Lovingkindness Meditation**

*Love may not make the world go around, but it sure makes the trip worthwhile.*

**Unknown**

## RELATIONSHIP HEALTH RESOURCES

★Denotes Best of the Best Resources

## Couples

### *Books*

*Eating an artichoke is like
getting to know someone really well.*
**Willi Hastings**

Branden, Nathaniel. *The Psychology of Romantic Love.* Bantam, 1980.

Campbell, Susan, M. *The Couple's Journey: Intimacy as a Path to Wholeness.* 1980. Impact Publishers, P.O. Box 1094, San Luis Obispo, CA 93406.

Ferguson, Bill. *How to Heal a Painful Relationship.* 1990. Return to the Heart, Box 541813, Houston, TX 77254.

Keyes, Ken, Jr. *A Conscious Person's Guide to Relationships.* 1979. Love Line Books, 700 Commercial Ave., Coos Bay, OR 97420.

Leonard, George. *Adventures in Monogamy: Exploring the Creative Possibilities of Love, Sexuality, and Commitment.* Tarcher, 1988.

★Levine, Stephen and Ondrea. *Embracing the Beloved: Relationship as a Path of Awakening.* Doubleday, 1995.

Mandel, Bob. *Two Hearts Are Better Than One: A Handbook on Creating and Maintaining a Lasting and Loving Relationship.* Celestial Arts, 1986.

McCann, Eileen. *The Two Step: The Dance Toward Intimacy.* Grove Press, 1985.

Prather, Hugh and Prather, Gayle. *A Book for Couples.* Doubleday, 1988.

Prather, Hugh and Prather, Gayle. *Notes to Each Other.* Sills, Judith. *A Fine Romance.* Jeremy P. Tarcher, 1987.

★Welwood, John. *Challenge of the Heart—Love, Sex, and Intimacy in Changing Times.* Shambhala, 1985. Great to read and discuss with a loved one.

★Welwood, John. *The Journey of the Heart: Intimate Relationship and the Path of Love.* HarperCollins, 1990. Great to read and discuss with a loved one.

### *Periodicals*

*Journal of Couples Therapy,* Haworth Press, 10 Alice St., Binghamton, NY 13904; (607) 722-5857; (800) 342-9678. Editorial office—3500 St. Charles Avenue, New Orleans, LA 70115; (504) 891-1200.

## Beyond the Pair— Family, Friends, and Colleagues

*A loving heart is the truest wisdom.*
**Charles Dickens**

### *Books*

Andreas, Steve. *Virginia Satir: The Patterns of Her Magic.* Science & Behavior, 1991.

Banmen, John. *The Satir Model: Family Therapy and Beyond.* Science & Behavior, 1991.

Crum, Thomas. *The Magic of Conflict: Personal Guidance System.* Aiki Works, 1989. Includes book, tapes, and workbook.

Eisler, Riane and Loye, David. *The Partnership Way: New Tools for Living and Learning, Healing Our Families, Our Communities, and Our World.* Harper Collins, 1990.

Fisher, Roger and Brown, Scott. *Getting Together: Building a Relationship That Gets to Yes.* Penguin, 1989. Good models of relationship building with friends, family, business, and governments.

Keyes, Ken, Jr. *The Power of Unconditional Love: 21 Guidelines for Beginning, Improving, and Changing Your Most Meaningful Relationships.* Love Line Books, 1990. Love Line Books, 700 Commercial Ave., Coos Bay, OR 97420.

Paul, Margaret and Paul, Jordan. *From Conflict to Caring, A Program for Creating Loving Relationships.* Bantam, 1989.

Pennebaker, James. *Opening Up: The Healing Power of Confiding in Others.* Morrow, 1990.

Vissel, B. and Vissel, J. *The Shared Heart.* Ramira Publishing, 1984. Ramira Publishing, P.O. Box 1707, Aptos, CA 95001. Spirituality in intimate and family relationships.

### *Professional Periodicals*

*American Journal of Family Therapy,* Brunner/Mazel, Inc., 19 Union Square W, 8th Floor, New York, NY 10003; (212) 924-3344.

*Contemporary Family Therapy,* Human Sciences Press, 233 Spring St., New York, NY 10013; (212) 620-8000.

*Family Therapy Networker,* 8528 Bradford Rd. Silver Spring, MD 20901.

## *Workshops*

*He is the happiest, be he king or peasant,*
*who finds peace in his home.*

**Johann Wolfgang von Goethe**

*Practical Application of Intimate Relationship Skills,* The PAIRS Foundation, 3705 S. George Mason Dr., Suite C3S, Falls Church, VA 22041; (703) 998-5550. Sixteen week course for couples and singles touching many subjects related to having healthy intimate relationships.

Journey of the Heart Seminars, 3315 Sacramento St., #317, San Francisco, CA 94118; (415) 381-6077. Excellent Workshop led by John Welwood, author of *Challenge of the Heart,* and his wife.

Weekend retreats and local meetings sponsored by The Association of Couples and Marriage Enrichment. A newsletter is also published. Contact: Marriage Enrichment, 502 N. Broad St., P.O. Box 10596, Winston-Salem, NC 27108; (800) 634-8325; (910) 724-1526.

## *Professional Organizations*

American Association for Marriage and Family Therapy, 1100 17 St. NW, 10th Floor, Washington, DC 20036; (202) 452-0109; (800) 374-2638. Publishes *Family Therapy News* and *Journal of Marital and Family Therapy.*

American Counseling Association, 5999 Stevenson Ave., Alexandria, VA 22304-3300; (703) 823-9800.

National Association of Social Workers, 750 1st St. NE, Suite 700, Washington, DC 20002; (202) 408-8600.

## *Healthy Sexuality*

*Love is the only game that is not called*
*on account of darkness.*

**M. Hirschfield**

The Sexuality Library, Open Enterprises, 938 Howard Ave., San Francisco, CA 94110; (415) 974-8985. This mail order company provides hundreds of resources (books, videos, magazines) on the subject of healthy sexuality. Below are a few select items.

Anand, Margo. *The Art of Sexual Ecstasy: The Path of Sacred Sexuality for Western Lovers.* Jeremy P. Tarcher, 1989.

Comfort, Alex. *The Joy of Sex.* PB, 1987.

Comfort, Alex. *More Joy of Sex.* PB, 1987.

Douglas, Nik and Slinger Penny. *Sexual Secrets: The Alchemy of Ecstasy.* Destiny Books, 1989.

Henderson, Julie. *The Lover Within: Opening to Energy in Sexual Practice.* Station Hill, 1987.

## *Games for Intimacy*

*An Enchanted Evening,* Games Partnership, Ltd., Inc., 116 New Montgomery St., Suite 500, San Francisco, CA 94105; (415) 495-4411. For couples who want to rediscover a loving relationship.

# Social Health

## *Books*

***The Seven Social Sins***
*1. Politics without principles.*
*2. Wealth without work.*
*3. Pleasure without conscience.*
*4. Knowledge without character.*
*5. Business without morality.*
*6. Science without humanity.*
*7. Worship without sacrifice.*

**Unknown**

Adams, Tom. *Grass Roots: How Ordinary People Are Changing America.* Carol Pub., 1991. How to be an effective social activist.

Addo, Herb. *Development as Social Transformation.* Westview Press, 1986.

Benjamin, Medea and Freedman, Andrea. *Bridging the Global Gap.* 1989. A guide to getting involved with global interconnectedness.

Bobo, Kim and Kendall, Jackie. *Organizing for Social Change: A Manual for Activists in the 90's.* Seven Locks Press, 1991.

Crum, Thomas. *The Magic of Conflict: Turning a Life of Work Into a Work of Art.* Touchstone, 1988.

Eppsteiner, Fred, ed. *The Path of Compassion: Writings of Socially Engaged Buddhism.* Parallax Press, 1988.

★ Etzioni, Amitai. *The Spirit of Community: Rights, Responsibilities, and the Communitarian Agenda.* Crown, 1993.

Etzioni, Amitai. *New Communitarian Thinking: Virtues, Persons, Institutions, and Communities.* U. Press of Virginia, 1995.

RESOURCES

Hollender, Jeffrey. *How to Make the World a Better Place: A Guide to Doing Good*. Quill, 1990.

Hunt, Morton. *The Compassionate Beast: What Science is Discovering About the Humane Side of Human-kind*. Morrow, 1990.

Ingram, Cathrine. *In the Footsteps of Gandhi: Conversations with Spiritual Social Activists*. Parallax Press, 1990.

Kohn, Alfie. *No Contest: The Case Against Competition— Why we lose in our race to win*. Houghton Mifflin, 1986.

★ Luks, Allan with Payne, Peggy. *The Healing Power of Doing Good: The Health and Spiritual Benefits of Helping Others*. Fawcett Columbine, 1992.

Marks, Linda. *Living with Vision: Reclaiming the Power of the Heart*. Knowledge Systems, Inc., 1989.

Mindell, Arnold. *The Year 1: Global Process Work*. Arkana/Penguin, 1990.

Moorehouse, Ward. *Building Sustainable Communities: Tools and Concepts for Self-Reliant Economic Change*. Bootstrap Press, 1989.

Oliner, Samuel and Oliner, Pearl. *Altruistic Personality: Rescuers of Jews in Nazi Europe*. Free Press, 1988.

Olson, Anette, ed. *Alternatives to the Peace Corps: A Directory of Third World & U.S. Volunteer Organizations*. Institute for Food and Development Policy, 1994.

★ Pilisuk, Marc and Parks, Susan Hillier. *The Healing Web: Social Networks and Human Survival*. University Press of New England, 1986. Linking relationships with physical and emotional health.

★ Ram Dass and Goleman, Daniel. *How Can I Help? Stories and Reflections on Service*. Knopf, 1985.

Ram Dass and Bush, Mirabai. *Compassion in Action: Setting Out on the Path of Service*. Bell Tower / Harmony Books, 1992.

Theobald, Robert. *The Rapids of Change: Social Entrepreneurship in Turbulent Times*. Knowledge Systems, 1987. A good resource book for help in navigating the rapids of a changing world.

Zimmerman, Richard. *What Can I Do to Make a Difference? A Positive Action Sourcebook*. Plume, 1991.

## *Periodicals*

***If you wish to be happy yourself,
you must resign yourself to seeing others
also happy.***

**Bertrand Russell**

*Communities Magazine,* 1118 Round Butte Dr., Fort Collins, CO 80524; (303) 224-9080.

*Fellowship,* Fellowship for Reconciliation, Box 271, 523 N. Broadway, Nyack, NY 10960; (914) 358-4601. Magazine on non-violent change.

Fellowship for Intentional Community Staff, eds. *Directory of Intentional Communities,* Fellowship for Intentional Community, 1992. Fellowship for Intentional Community, RR1, Box 155, Sand Hill Farm, Rutledge, MO 63563; (816) 883-5545.

*The Neighborhood Works,* Center for Neighborhood Technology, 2125 W. North Av. Chicago, IL 60647; (312) 278-4800. Practical community improvement.

*Peacework,* American Friends Service Committee, 2161 Massachusetts Ave., Cambridge, MA 02140.

*The Responsive Community,* 2020 Pennsylvania Ave. NW, Suite 282, Washington, DC 20006; (800) 245-7460; (202) 994-8142. Journal of the communitarian movement.

★*Who Cares: A Journal of Service and Action,* 1511 K St. NW, Suite 1042, Washington, DC 20005.

## *Community Computer Databases and Networks*

***The end of all political effort must be
the well-being of the individual in a life
of safety and freedom.***

**Dag Hammarskjold**

Center for Civic Networking, P.O. Box 65272, Washington, DC 20035; (202) 362-3831; (Internet: rciville@ civicnet.org).

Civic Information and Techniques Exchange (CIVITEX), National Civics League, 1445 Market St., Suite 300, Denver, CO 80202-1728; (800) 223-6004. Computerized indexing of innovative community solutions to local problems.

Community Action Network, American Values, 211 E. 43rd St., Suite 1203, New York, NY 10017; (212) 818-1360. Thousands of examples of efforts to solve social problems.

Community Information Exchange, 1029 Vermont Ave. NW, Suite 710, Washington, DC 20005; (202) 628-2981. Hundreds of community development projects are described, and assistance is available to implement them.

Livability Clearinghouse, Partners for Communities, 1429 21st St. NW, Washington, DC 20036; (202) 887-5990. Information source and assistance for a variety of community development projects.

National Public Telecomputing Network, 34555 Chagrin Blvd., Moreland Hills, OH 44022; (216) 247-5800; (216) 247-3328; Internet: info@nptn.org. Non-profit public information network.

The most important resource in this field may be:

★Rheingold, Howard. "Civic Networking" *Whole Earth Review,* Vol. 82, Spring 1994; pp. 26-27 which lists over thirty very valuable resources.

## *Organizations*

*It is one of the most beautiful compensations of this life that no man can sincerely try to help another without helping himself.*

**Ralph Waldo Emerson**

★American Alliance for Rights and Responsibilities, 1146 19th St. NW, Suite 250, Washington, DC 20036-3703; (202) 785-7844. A non-profit communitarian organization.

Amnesty International, 322 8th Ave., New York, NY 10001; (212) 807-8400. Publishes the annual *Report on Human Rights Around the World. The Amnesty International Handbook* is available from Hunter House, P.O. Box 2914, Alameda, CA 94501; (510) 865-5282.

Center for Partnership Studies, P.O. Box 51936, Pacific Grove, CA 93950. Riane Eisler's organization to study and teach cooperative methods of human interaction.

★Communitarian Network, 2130 H St. NW, Suite 714J, Washington, DC 20052; (202) 994-7997.

Foundation for Community Encouragement, 109 Danbury Rd., Suite 8, Ridgefield, CT 06877; (203) 431-9484; Fax (203) 431-9349. Teaches community building skills.

★Global Education Associates, Suite 456, 475 Riverside Drive, New York, NY 10115; (212) 870-3290 / (212) 870-3291. An international research and educational network advancing world peace and security, cooperative economic development, human rights, and ecological healing.

Refer to the white pages in your telephone directory for volunteer centers in your locale, or contact any environmental, peace, or service organization which would be interested in your volunteer services.

*When there is too much individualistic spirit, then everybody becomes concerned with his own self, his own interest, and as a result, the welfare of the people, and eventually the world suffers.*

**Haridas Chaudhuri**

# CHAPTER EIGHT

# GOVERNMENT / LEGAL

# HEALTH

*Injustice anywhere is a threat to justice everywhere.*

**Martin Luther King, Jr.**

Governments protect and serve their citizens (or at least should). In preserving order in society, unity of the individual parts is enhanced. The large size of government causes inefficiency and lowered ability to respond to local needs. The structure of government is of key importance. Having checks, balances and safeguards to protect against corruption, prejudice, and the abuse of power is necessary. Parliamentary democracies tend to provide the best outcomes for creating harmony. The more that citizens participate in government, the greater the likelihood that consensus and harmony will result.

On the one hand, America's Constitution, and the democratic structure it supports, are very beneficial to the health of most citizens of this country. But the way in which self-interest groups have manipulated government institutions for their own ends at the expense of the less powerful and the disadvantaged has eroded the health of many in this country to below that of many Third World countries.

Most of us have a daily awareness of how things like nutrition, exercise, stress, and relationships play important roles in our health. Few of us, though, realize the enormous impact government has on our moment to moment health. From the national level to the local, legislation influences every aspect of our lives. The administrative branches of these different levels of government enforce these laws, codes, and regulations. The courts interpret the laws of the land and settle disputes by means of them.

Try to go through a normal day's activities and find some aspect of your health and life that *isn't* influenced by government. The morning wake-up alarm rings. The electricity that runs the clock is regulated in many ways, from environmental laws that govern utilities to the rates they charge. The safety of the wiring in your home was approved by a government building inspector. The clock was made according to government regulated safety specifications and was sold according to fair and truthful advertising laws. The water in your shower must meet government standards of purity. The clothes you put on are not allowed to contain harmful dyes. The breakfast food you eat had to pass certain agricultural safety inspections and was labeled according to specific governmental guidelines to help insure healthy consumption. The car you drive to work was made under governmental guidelines for passenger safety and environmental protection, inadequate though they may be. The streets and signs along the way have to meet necessary safety standards.

## OCCUPATION AND ECONOMICS

*A government which robs Peter to pay Paul*
*can always depend on the support of Paul.*
**George Bernard Shaw**

Your workplace is governed by innumerable laws which affect wages, taxes, work standards, civil rights laws, employee safety, pension funds, employee-employer relations, health insurance coverage, environmental pollution, legal business practices. This profoundly affects not only your economic health, but all other aspects of health. In addition, governmental policies affect our individual financial well-being. Legislative budget priorities, pork barrel provisions, inefficient regulatory mechanisms, judicial inequities, governmental budget deficits, Federal Reserve interest rates, disproportionate military expenditures, inadequate oversight, administrative foot-dragging, all these and more compound themselves in powerful ways to influence personal health.

Since governments are in many cases the single largest employers in regions and nations, the character and emphasis of those governments determines to a powerful extent what jobs are available or how much unemployment exists. Many jobs in particular locales are decided by large government projects that dominate a region, like those assigned to a large defense contractor or military base. Governmental spending can have powerful influences on everyone's economic status.

## EDUCATION

*A people who mean to be their own governors*
*must arm themselves with the power*
*knowledge gives. A popular government without*
*popular information or the means of*
*acquiring it is but a prologue to a farce*
*or a tragedy, or perhaps both.*
**James Madison**

How well we are educated, or conversely how influenced we are by the education system, the media, the church, or our families, can all be linked in one way or another with governmental influence over these institutions.

Government officials with high intellect have the capacity to craft good laws, but this pure intelligence also needs to be influenced by high morals and healthy emotions, human understanding, and wisdom. There are many well-crafted laws drawn up with ruthless repression and heartless greed the goal and result. High intellect might not have as significant an effect on healthy laws as a mind expanded by broad exposure to ideas, people, and values.

*Those who are too smart to engage in politics*
*are punished by being governed by those*
*who are dumber.*
**Plato**

A more informed population created by a healthy education system tends toward more representative, fair, and functional government. Populations that are highly educated (in the true sense of higher education) lean toward democracies. Heavily propagandized populations are more accepting of authoritarian and totalitarian regimes. But even in democracies the quality of those freedoms is severely compromised by poor education. Sixteen million adult Americans are functionally illiterate. How would the landscape of American politics change if only a fraction of those illiterates could voice educated opinions to their representatives?

*What luck for rulers that men do not think.*
**Adolph Hitler**

When government controls what one learns in school, the health of the government (and remember that inherent in the definition of health is unity with all) has tremendous influence on the health of the children. Are they indoctrinated to think, act, and feel in a certain political, cultural, or religious way? Just how much a government spends on education determines, to some degree, the health of the education system. The United States government spends less than two dollars per year on teaching every illiterate adult basic skills.

Observe also how specific laws affect educational health. For example, note how laws that support racial segregation adversely affect educational standards. Or look at the inequities in funding poor and wealthy school districts.

## PSYCHOLOGICAL HEALTH

*I'm in favor of activism and politics*
*wherever possible purified of resentment,*
*anger, aggression, and pride.*

**Allen Ginsberg**

The effectiveness and fairness of government have a dramatic impact on confidence, motivation, and the general psychological health of individuals. This can nowhere be more clearly seen than in the transformation of Eastern European governments. The relief that is felt emotionally from the fall of dictatorships is enormous.

Look at the devastating, long-term psychological impact that laws of apartheid have had on black South Africans. Not only has it had a powerful impact on individual psychological health, it has devastated everyone's physical, economic, ecological, and spiritual health as well.

## RELATIONSHIPS

*"... a tooth for a tooth*
*... an eye for an eye.*
*What good is that?*
*That way the whole world will soon be*
*blind and toothless!*

**from *Fiddler on the Roof***

Governments and laws can have a large impact on socialization patterns, group psychology, interpersonal communications, and thus one's overall health. It is sometimes easier to see these relationships when observing very corrupt or dysfunctional governments. What is then noticed is the cultivation of social patterns which are dysfunctional and unhealthy. Most of us cannot imagine the complex relationship nightmares that are generated by strict authoritarian regimes that have friends and families spying on one another with dire consequences.

How governments enforce laws against violent crimes like child abuse, rape, assault, and murder, influence group behavior more than most realize. Having laws against child abuse does less to alter that behavior than does the performance of gov-

ernmental programs established to prevent and solve the problem.

Specific laws, too, influence the health of interpersonal relationships and thus our total health. Observe how apartheid laws adversely affect group psychology between races. Laws governing sexual conduct between consenting adults have been a controversial issue for ages. Laws regulating freedom of speech and assembly modify interpersonal relationships for good or ill. Legal restrictions on violence limit damaging interpersonal relationships. Some countries, like Brazil, have legal mechanisms which condone men murdering women if there was "justification in preserving the honor of the man."

## ECOLOGICAL HEALTH

*Man is not himself only ...*
*He is all that he sees;*
*all that flows to him from a thousand sources ...*
*He is the land, the lift of its mountain lines,*
*the reach of its valleys.*

**Mary Austin**

There are thousands of government agencies, laws, regulations and ordinances from national to local levels that directly address ecological harmony: the Environmental Protection Agency, the U.S. Forest Service, the Bureau of Land Management, The Fish and Game Department, the National Park Service, Water Resource Management Districts, the Clean Air Act, the Wild and Scenic Rivers Act, the Wilderness Act, etc. Thousands more indirectly impact the environment for better or worse. Governmental and legal mechanisms, money, time, manpower, and energy play a significant role in determining the local and global health of ecosystems. Governmental purchases have great impact on the environment. Government agencies could be instructed to buy only energy efficient light bulbs and energy conserving or nonpolluting vehicles. This would save billions of dollars and dramatically clean up the environment.

Much of the time, the state of the environment initiates governmental and legal action. In times of extreme ecological crisis or environmental damage, the sheer cost of remedial governmental efforts can put a strain on funding for other needed services. If governments around the world were to spend the money to clean up the parts of the earth that have been fouled, plus fund the maintenance and preventive steps that would really protect our home, planet Earth, not much money would be left over for other agendas with present tax rates. We may not like having to pay for these abuses of the past, but they are necessary expenses. Will we ask our children to deal with it instead?

## SPIRITUAL HEALTH

*I have no objections to churches so long as they do not interfere with God's work.*

**Brooks Atkinson**

People in Western democracies are fortunate in that they are provided with considerable freedom to worship without interference. The United States with its definitive separation of church and state affords some of the strongest protections for the pursuit of spiritual fulfillment. Other countries are not so lucky. And it is just those governments that restrict religious expression and practice that are themselves adversely affected by not having the benefits of the morality, cohesion, selfless service, nonviolence, and responsibility which spirituality advances.

It must also be remembered that many of today's man-made laws are descendants of ancient spiritual precepts.

## PLAY

*To the art of working well a civilized race would add the art of playing well.*

**George Santayana**

The laws of this nation allow much freedom of activity, joining of organizations, freedom of speech, and freedom of travel, and countless recreational areas are provided, all dramatically influencing individual and collective health.

## GOVERNMENT AND LAWS FROM BIRTH TO DEATH

*The divine science of government is the science of social happiness ...*

**John Adams**

From birth to death government influences our lives through, for example, laws governing abortion and the right to die in cases of extreme disability. Genetic, physical factors causing homosexual orientation interact with one's legal options. Because of the predetermined physical parameters governing sexual orientation, homosexuals have certain legal entanglements that heterosexuals do not. This has to do with the right to marry, work, divorce, have access to government employment (most notably the military), to be afforded common insurance guarantees with same sex spouses, and disperse property upon death, to name a few.

If one is physically handicapped or alternatively-abled ("disabled" in accustomed terminology) then one's legal status, as it relates to day-to-day life with regards to access, opportunity, discrimination, etc., is quite different from that of the average person.

## LEGAL HEALTH ENHANCEMENT

*I know no safe depository of the ultimate powers of the society but the people themselves; and if we think them not enlightened enough to exercise their control with a wholesome discretion, the remedy is not to take it from them, but to inform their discretion by education.*

**Thomas Jefferson**

There are two essential strategies for enhancing our health through the legal system. One is to be informed. The other is to take action.

There are two primary levels on which these strategies can take place. One is the personal level. The other is on a broader level. For organizational convenience the personal front is defined as those activities which address specific personal legal issues. The broader area that can be addressed concerns those issues that try to change local, state, national, or international laws which will benefit the health of not only oneself, but many others.

*Chance never helps those*
*who do not help themselves.*

**Sophocles**

On the personal level it is helpful to be informed and deal effectively with such legal issues as wills, divorces, tax laws, estate planning, durable power of attorney, living trusts, legal rights of health insurance policies, particularly worker compensation law and personal accident insurance, and contract law in business transactions. All of which can have a profound impact on one's overall health.

*The great end of life is not knowledge*
*but action.*

**Thomas Henry Huxley**

On the broader level, individual participation in our democratic government may at times seem insignificant, but it is collectively very important for everyone's health. Once one is informed of important health issues by reading the periodicals recommended in the resource sections of this book, two important activities can have dramatic impact on everyone's health:

1. Write your elected representatives (or attend public hearings and town meetings) encouraging them to act appropriately.

*Truth is not only violated by falsehood;*
*it may be equally outraged by silence.*

**Henri Frederic Amiel**

2. Vote.

*Too bad the only people who know how to*
*run the country are busy driving cabs*
*and cutting hair.*

**George Burns**

Below are some examples of legal issues that could be better addressed and which would benefit everyone's health.

Institute a national health insurance system similar to Canada's but with better provisions for services like preventive care, health education and promotion, prenatal care, natural childbirth, parenting classes, nutritional evaluations and prescriptions, chiropractic, and naturopathy.

More stringent auto and highway safety laws are needed.

Ban cigarette and alcohol advertising, and include heavy taxes to reduce consumption and eliminate any favorable agricultural subsides for the production of these substances.

Attack the root causes of crime with better education services, job training, drug rehabilitation, and with criminal rehabilitation instead of punishment for those who can and want to be rehabilitated. Assure isolation of those criminals dangerous to society who cannot be rehabilitated, support restitution instead of retribution, promote urban renewal, better community mental health services, housing subsidization, stringent gun control. . . .

More grants need to be made available for research in disease prevention and natural, noninvasive, holistic health care services.

Environmental protection laws need to be stronger. Taxes on energy and pollution will help. More stringent auto emission standards can be immediately instituted. Mandatory energy conservation measures can be established. Mass transit can be supported more. Toxic waste dumps can be cleaned up better and faster. More stringent controls can be created to limit the production and release of toxics. More research and development needs to be done on renewable energy sources like solar power.

National Parks, Wilderness Areas, Wildlife Refuges, Wetlands need to be expanded and better protected.

Occupational safety laws need to be strengthened and better enforced.

The Food and Drug Administration and the Agriculture Department need to better coordinate their efforts at protecting America's food supply, water, and the consumer. More inspectors are needed to insure safety. Legislation needs to be stricter, and enforcement needs to be stepped up. Improved food labeling laws can better inform citizens so they can choose a healthier diet. The FDA has to more rigorously question the safety of health care products such as mercury dental amalgams and silicone breast implants rather than waiting decades for research to filter in about their dangers. At the same time the FDA could greatly enhance public health by ending its irrational persecution of natural health products, such as nutritional supplements.

Our schools and libraries need better governmental support—a complete overhaul of financial issues and curriculum.

Political campaign finance reform at all levels of government needs to be instituted in order to protect the democratic process from being corrupted by economic special interests. The political process has to be changed in a way that will encourage a long term view rather than policy decisions made to please the voters in the next election.

There should be a taxation system that would decrease the gross inequities between rich and poor.

*We don't necessarily need less governmental intervention in our lives. We need a smarter government, more responsive to the needs of the people.*

**Thomas M. Colllins**

# GOVERNMENTAL AND LEGAL HEALTH RESOURCES

*In the long run every government is the exact symbol of its people, with their wisdom and unwisdom.*

**Thomas Carlyle**

★Denotes Best of the Best Resources

## *Books*

Bartlett, Donald & Steele, James. *America: Who Really Pays the Taxes.*

Bellah, Robert; et al. *The Good Society.* Knopf, 1991.

Belli, Melvin and Wilkinson, Allen. *Everybody's Guide to the Law.* Harper Collins, 1987.

Gross, Martin. *The Government Racket: Washington Waste from A to Z.* Bantam, 1992.

*National Health Directory,* Aspen, 1994. 688 pages of governmental health officials.

Porritt, Jonathon. *Seeing Green: The Politics of Ecology Explained.* Blackwell, 1985.

Public Citizen Litigation Group Staff & Lasson, Kenneth. *Representing Yourself: What You Can Do Without a Lawyer.* Public Citizen, 1987.

★Rifkin, Jeremy. *Biosphere Politics.* Harper SF, 1992.

Rifkin, Jeremy. *Voting Green.* Doubleday, 1992.

Tokar, Brian. *The Green Alternative: Creating an Ecological Future.* R. & E. Miles, 1987.

## *Periodicals*

*I don't make jokes. I just watch the government and report the facts.*

**Will Rogers**

Both Common Cause and Public Citizen have regular periodicals which keep subscribers informed about present legislative initiatives affecting health. Other environmental periodicals such as Wordwatch, Sierra, and Greenpeace keep abreast of new legislative action on the environmental health issues.

The Consumer Information Center, 18th & F St. NW, Room G142, Washington, DC 20405; (202) 501-1794. Or Consumer Information Center, P.O. Box 100, Pueblo, CO 81002; (719) 948-9724; (719) 948-3334. They distribute dozens of free and low-cost government publications for healthier living, including a pamphlet, *A Home Buyer's Guide to*

*Environmental Hazards,* which has good legal advice about obtaining an environmental audit before purchasing a home or other property which might be unknowingly contaminated by toxic substances.

*Mother Jones,* Foundation for National Progress, 1663 Mission St., 2nd Floor, San Francisco, CA 94103; (415) 357-0509. Investigative journalism magazine.

★*Nolo News,* Nolo Press, 950 Parker St., Berkeley, CA 94710; (800) 992-6656; (510) 549-1976. A catalog of legal self-help books.

## *Computer Databases, and Networks*

Local Exchange (LEX), National League of Cities, 1301 Pennsylvania Ave. NW, Washington, DC 20004; (202) 626-3180. Large database of progressive local government programs, problem-solving databases, and *Urban Affairs Abstract.*

Login Information Services (LOGIN), 125 SE Main St., Suite 341, St. Paul, MN 55414; (800) 328-1921. Enormous database of 70,000+ listings regarding local governments and other agencies.

## *Organizations*

**Ninety-eight percent of the adults in this country are decent, hard-working, honest Americans. It's the other lousy two percent that get all the publicity. But then—we elected them.**

**Lily Tomlin**

Center for National Independence in Politics, 129 N.W. 4th St., Suite 204, Corvallis, OR 97330; (503) 754-2746. Strives to improve democracy through better public education of our political process. They sponsor "Project Vote Smart," a national initiative to empower the electorate with the dissemination of important information about political candidates and the issues. CNIP does this by several means:
1. an electoral hotline for people to call to get up-to-date information about any congressional, gubernatorial, or presidential candidate
2. a Voter's Self-Defense Manual detailing all relevant information about electoral candidates, their positions, and even manipulative campaign strategies
3. a National Political Awareness Test given to candidates to identify their actual stands on specific issues
4. a Reporter's Resource Center that gives 5,000 political reporters instant access to information

and key knowledgeable experts so they can report on reliable data rather than use non-credible dis-information spread by election campaigns
5. designing curricula materials for classrooms in order to educate children about using information to make democracy work better.

★Center for Study of Responsive Law, P.O. Box 19367, Washington, DC 20036; (202) 382-8030. Ralph Nader's legal eagles.

★Common Cause, 2030 M St., NW, Washington, DC 20036; (202) 833-1200. A non-profit citizen's lobby trying to make national and state governments work better for the common good.

Innovations in State and Local Governments, John F. Kennedy School of Government, Harvard University, 79 JFK St., Cambridge, MA 02138; (617) 495-0557. Investigates and awards money to progressive, successful state and government programs. It publishes the details of these efforts and also makes available video cassettes illustrating how they work.

Management Information Service (MIS), International City Management Association, 777 N. Capitol St. NE, Washington, DC 20002-4201; (202) 962-3639. Has thousands of examples on how to help local governments.

★OMB Watch, 1742 Connecticut Ave., NW, Washington, DC 20009-1171; (202) 234-8494; Fax (202) 234-8584; E-Mail: ombwatch@rtknet.org. Provide technical and educational assistance in dealing with government agencies. They publish a general information quarterly newsletter, *OMB Watcher,* a bimonthly magazine on federal regulatory and information action, *Government Information Insider,* and a newsletter related to their RTK (Right To Know) environmental computer database network, *Online.*

★Public Citizen, 2000 P St., NW, Washington, DC 20036. A non-profit citizen watchdog group that does research, lobbying, and legal work to protect consumer rights. It works for safe products, a healthy environment, plus corporate and government accountability.

Social Services Organizations listed in your local Yellow Pages telephone directory offer numerous resources for legal assistance in many different fields.

★World Policy Institute, 65 5th Ave., Suite 413, New York, NY 10003; (212) 229-5808.

**A government job is an occasion for public service, not special privilege.**

**Jerry Brown**

# CHAPTER NINE

# ENVIRONMENTAL HEALTH

*This we know: The earth does not belong to man; man belongs to the earth.*
*All things are connected like the blood which unites one family.*
*Whatever befalls the earth befalls the sons of the earth.*
*Man did not weave the web of life; he is merely a strand in it.*
*Whatever he does to the web, he does to himself.*

**Chief Seattle, 1854**

One of the most useful models of wholeness and health to be envisioned is the Gaia Principle. This concept looks at Spaceship Earth as a living organism—the planet's biosphere as a complex, intertwining network of living systems, matter and energy, pulsing with the energy of their unity. When we as individuals become more whole, our sense of self expands. We can identify more with the beauty and wonder of all life. We become aware of our ecological selves and protect and nourish these larger aspects of our being. And just as with any other of the strands in the Web of Wholeness, as we enhance our ecological health it improves all other aspects. Those that offer us the wisdom of "deep ecology" see that at the root of all ecological devastation man has caused is this artificial separation we produce between our individual selves and all that surrounds us. This is displayed in our attitudes and actions.

Let us briefly survey how our environment can affect, adversely or beneficially, the various aspects of our health.

## PHYSICAL HEALTH

Our industrialized society produces a thousand new chemical compounds each year. Many of these are released into the environment without adequate testing for any damaging health effects. To understand the magnitude of the problem this poses to our physical health, peruse *Chemical Sensitivity Volume II* by Dr. Rea. It details the chemicals known to have deleterious health effects and lists them along with conditions they are known to cause. For a more condensed version of the common compounds which we are most likely to come in contact with in our daily lives, refer to Debra Dadd-Redalia's books on ecological living.

It is also quite noticeable to people who have allergies, whether airborne inhalants or foods. When they are able to avoid these elements of the environment that cause them to react in physically adverse ways, their health is much improved.

On the positive side of the ledger, it is quite easy to understand how a community that is lush with greenery is healthier because of the way trees and plants cleanse pollution, muffle noise, and add oxygen to the air.

## PSYCHOLOGICAL

Because the damaging effects of harmful environmental substances often impact the central nervous system, psychological aberrations can result. An entire array of psychopathological symptoms can be elicited by either toxic substances or allergens.

There are few people who cannot recognize the uplifting qualities of a beautiful natural setting, unspoiled by pollution or the impact of man. Even natural sunlight or full spectrum lighting in offices has noticeable effects, as does spaciousness and greenery.

## ECONOMIC / OCCUPATIONAL

A healthy environment contributes to economic well-being in many ways. When we have a clean environment we can be physically and psychologically healthier—which means we have to spend less money on health care.

From another perspective, if we look at those industries that pollute the environment the most and consume energy at the highest rates, we find that they are also the segments of our economy that employ the fewest workers per productive output—oil refining and coal products, chemicals, primary metals, and paper. Whereas jobs in energy conservation, renewable energy alternatives, recycling, environmental protection, and land stewardship are more labor intensive, less capital intensive, healthier, and thus can provide more people with better, more stable livelihoods than polluting industries will.

When businesses increase their energy conservation, they can save enormous amounts of money in getting their goods and services to consumers. This benefits businesses, consumers, and the communities in which these savings occur.

Energy conservation standing alone, on a personal level, is significantly beneficial to economic health.

## INTELLECTUAL

One of the most tragic illustrations of the damage that environmental pollution inflicts on the mind is children who are severely retarded due to toxic exposure to some environmental poison—whether it be prenatal maternal smoking, lead dust from car fumes settling in urban sand-

boxes, or chemical contamination of our water or food.

*Twenty-five percent of U.S. school age children have excessive toxic metal contamination in their bodies.*
*250,000 children will have neurological damage sufficient to cause an irreversible drop in intelligence.*

Alternatively, nutritional enhancement with diet and supplementation has been found to have appreciable benefits on intelligence prenatally, in infancy and throughout childhood education.

## SPIRITUAL

*Any religion which is not based on a respect for life is not a true religion. . . . Until he extends his circle of compassion to all living things, man will not himself find peace.*
**Albert Schweitzer**

The beauties of the natural world inspire a reverence for creation, life, and the Unity that binds these wonders together. In all religions there is a tradition of retreating to nature for renewal. Today we are also seeing a reaffirmation of this valuable asset—Nature—in the priorities of religious service work. More and more church groups are working hand in hand with environmentalists to save pristine, natural areas, in part, for their spiritually uplifting qualities.

*Nature is too thin a screen; the glory of the Omnipresent God bursts through everywhere.*
**Ralph Waldo Emerson**

For the purposes of this book we will divide this interconnected whole—the ecological system in which all life on Earth exists—into two parts: those things we can do for the planet as a whole, whether locally or globally, and those things we can do to protect our own ecological safety, even though when we take protective action on any part of the ecosystem, it should help all other parts.

# PERSONAL ECOLOGICAL APPROACHES

How do we interact with the environmental components of the Earth so that all life will benefit to the greatest degree? What is our right relationship with each animal and plant, the water and air, the wind and sun? How we answer these questions from a personal perspective should be no different than how we answer these questions collectively. We may nevertheless have to perform different actions on a personal level than on a global level.

On a personal level we have an immune system made up of various components that help us interact safely with our environment. It functions on a molecular-biochemical level, cellular level, and an organ level. This occurs without our conscious effort, although the immune system can be modulated and influenced by conscious intent. Protective substances guard our own tissues from damage from outside toxins. White blood cells eat harmful bacteria before they can cause us harm. The liver functions as a major detoxifying organ for metabolizing unwanted agents from outside the body.

These complex systems are designed to protect us from different types of invasive harm. There are different mechanisms designed to identify, tag, and eliminate naturally occurring toxic substances like lead, cadmium, mercury. These mechanisms can only handle small amounts of these toxic agents. In our industrialized societies we are exposed to very large quantities which then burdens our immune capabilities, thus requiring assistance to the immune system and extra efforts to avoid contamination.

Similar mechanisms are designed to protect us from man-made toxic substances.

*Every year U.S. industries pump approximately 3 billion pounds of chemicals into our air.[1]*

Our immune systems have very little tolerance for many of these toxic substances. Here too, efforts need to be made to enhance immune function and limit exposure.

Our immune system also protects us from microbial invasion—bacteria, protozoa, viruses, fungi.

In all these cases certain people have stronger immune systems than others. Some have weakened immunity because of too many accumulated foreign substances. In others there may be a weakness due to a genetic lack of certain enzymes that facilitate detoxification. In still others there may be psycho-social stresses or undernourishment that will also impede the immune system.

So when we talk of improving our personal relationship with the environment, we are talking about a multifaceted approach.

1. The first order of business is to become informed and educated. Environmental health is a new science. Few members of the medical community are at the forefront of these issues, so self-knowledge to combat professional ignorance is a great asset.

2. We have to reduce our exposure to harmful substances. Testing the water we drink, the air we breathe, the food we eat, and the electromagnetic fields that surround us may all be part of the process of identifying hazards. Reducing exposure might involve buying a home water purification system until one's environmental activism can help clean up the water supply. Or it might involve removing the mercury dental amalgams from one's own mouth until political activism convinces the FDA to ban the substance from dental offices. Each of us might do home radon or formaldehyde testing.

3. We have to reduce the toxic burden which our bodies have already accumulated. Testing our blood, urine, hair, metabolic pathways, immune system, and our ability to respond to toxins, might be necessary for a comprehensive picture of our personal internal milieu. Then we can engage in biochemical extracting procedures most accurately. This can entail:

   a. nutrient supplementation that absorbs harmful substances so they can be excreted or that detoxifies them

   b. physician administered I.V. chelation therapy with EDTA or Penacillamine to help heavy metal contamination be excreted from the body

   c. anti-microbial agents to fight infections and boost immunity:

      (1) herbs: Artemesia annua, Astragalus root, Echinacea, Goldenseal root, Licorice

root, Mistletoe, Shitaake Mushroom (refer to Serammune Physicians Lab in the resources; their immune enhancement handbook has more details)

(2) fatty acids

(3) Lactobacillus acidophilus supplementation (beneficial intestinal bacteria)

(4) medications

(5) vaccines

d. hyperthermia with exercise and saunas. (Refer to the BioToxic Reduction Program information under the heading *Detoxification* in the Special Subject Resource Section in the Appendix.)

4. Nutrient support is essential to establish and maintain vital immune system metabolic pathways. This involves a non-allergenic, nutritious diet with herbal and nutrient supplementation additions.

Often alkaline diets and proper food combinations can significantly aid the immune system. For more information on this subject refer to the immune enhancement handbook published by Serammune Physicians Laboratory, 1890 Preston White Drive, Suite 200, Reston, VA 22091; (800) 553-5472; (703) 758-0610; Fax (703) 758-0615.

5. Get moderate, regular, balanced exercise.

6. Psycho-spiritual support and stress management, psychotherapy, relaxation training, biofeedback, meditation, service to others, and social support of family and friends are very helpful.

7. Natural sunlight, Neurosensory Development Training, and/or 20 minutes per day viewing the light of a green Par 38 Dichromatic 150 watt bulb at five feet distance (refer to the Biological Rhythms, Light, and Sleep resource section for more information) are also useful.

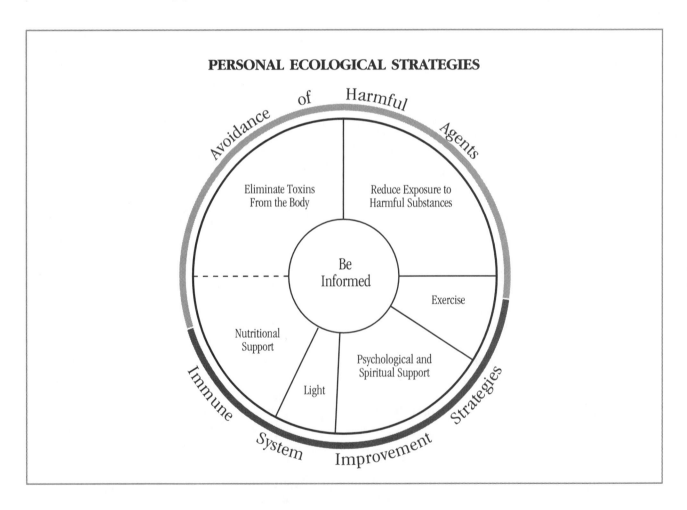

**PERSONAL ECOLOGICAL STRATEGIES**

Avoidance of Harmful Agents

Eliminate Toxins From the Body

Reduce Exposure to Harmful Substances

Be Informed

Exercise

Nutritional Support

Psychological and Spiritual Support

Light

Immune System Improvement Strategies

## PRIORITIZING PERSONAL ECOLOGICAL HEALTH ENHANCEMENT STRATEGIES

In our modern industrialized world we are assaulted from many fronts by things that disrupt a healthy relationship with Nature. Where do we start to correct these problems?

First, follow the flow chart on the next page to help you act in an informed, systematic manner. Use the help of specialists, if you need to.

It must be remembered that environmental assaults are often cumulative in their effect, so it is wise to diminish as many sources of potential harm as possible. But there are priorities with regard to which agents produce the most devastating risks. When using the above flow chart keep in mind the relative risk and the potential impact of various environmental hazards. Follow the Environmental Dangers Priority List for help here.

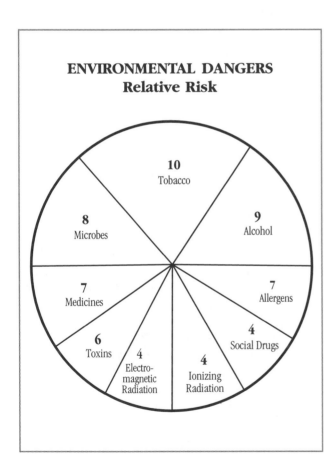

## ENVIRONMENTAL DANGERS PRIORITY LIST

### *TOBACCO*

Risk of Dysfunction, Disease, or Death
on a scale of 1–10
10

*Cigarette smoking causes 390,000 premature deaths per year in the U.S.
Every day 3,000 teenagers start smoking.
Children consume approximately 1,000,000,000 packs of cigarettes a year.*

*"Cigarette smoking causes more premature deaths each year than all of the following combined: AIDS, cocaine, heroin, alcohol, fire, car accidents, homicide, and suicide."*

**Stephen R. Yarnell, M.D.**

By far, the most obvious and significant environmental avoidance strategy we can undertake is to eliminate exposure to tobacco, particularly the smoke. Several facts make this the most powerful environmental risk.

1. It is pervasive in our society. Twenty-eight percent of our population uses tobacco products.
2. Tobacco's contents include hundreds of harmful substances, individually dangerous in themselves, and much more so in combination.
3. Exposure is repetitive on a daily basis over years of time, which compounds the cumulative effects.
4. The nicotine is many times more addictive than heroin. Ninety percent of first time users of tobacco are addicted.
5. It is a legal, accepted, highly-marketed product. The tobacco industry spends *$3 billion* per year promoting this form of suicide.
6. Even if you are not a smoker, secondary tobacco smoke is very dangerous, particularly to young children.

# PERSONAL ENVIRONMENTAL PROTECTION PROTOCOL

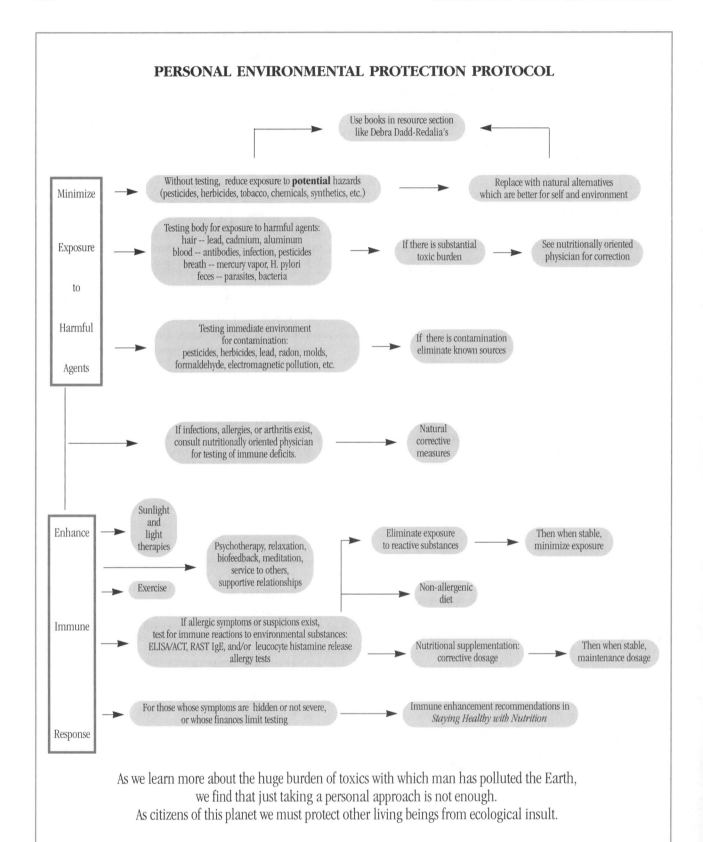

As we learn more about the huge burden of toxics with which man has polluted the Earth,
we find that just taking a personal approach is not enough.
As citizens of this planet we must protect other living beings from ecological insult.

*53,000 American nonsmokers die each year from exposure to secondhand cigarette smoke.*

## Avoidance Strategy

Don't start. If you smoke or use other tobacco products, quit immediately. Although 90% of people who successfully quit smoking do so on their own, there are a number of different aids and assistance programs. Consult your local Yellow Pages phone directory for "Smoking Treatment" centers, or contact the American Lung Association for more information. If you have unsuccessfully tried to quit in the past with one or more of these programs, a multifaceted approach may be necessary. This program might include acupuncture, hypnotherapy, homeopathy, herbs, vitamin C, allergy control, stress management, and addictive behavior modification, all working in concert.

Secondhand smoke is also difficult to avoid, but the tide is rightfully turning in favor of nonsmokers' rights to healthy air. Hopefully more legislation will continue to advance the progress of health protection.

## ALCOHOL

Risk of Dysfunction, Disease, or Death
on a scale of 1–10
9

*Two hundred thousand Americans die every year because of alcohol consumption.*

*Eight million teens use alcohol at least once per week; 4,600,000 have an alcohol abuse problem. U.S. teenagers consumed 1,100,000,000 cans of beer in 1990.[2]*

Several facts make this a powerful environmental risk factor.
1. It is pervasive in our society.
2. Alcohol harms the body and mind in many ways. It:
    a. damages the liver
    b. increases cancer risks, particularly in women
    c. disturbs metabolism
    d. interfers with proper nutrition
    e. contributes to excess calories
    f. alters behavior adversely and thereby increases relationship conflicts
    g. distorts perception and coordination and thereby increases accidents
    h. disturbs judgment and reduces inhibition and thus increases crime
    i. causes severe birth defects when taken even in small quantities
    j. decreases intellectual performance
    k. interferes with work productivity
    l. impairs sexual function
    m. aggravates personality aberrations
    n. damages heart muscle
3. Exposure is repetitive for millions of people.
4. Alcohol is addictive, particularly to that 10% of the population which has a genetic, metabolic predisposition for alcoholism, and those who suffer from addictive food allergy symptoms that perpetuate the craving.
5. It is a legal, accepted, highly-marketed product. The alcohol beverage industries spend *2 billion* dollars every year promoting this form of health abuse.

Even if you are a nondrinker, your health is diminished, and your life is put at risk by those around you who drink in excess. Health and auto insurance rates are higher for us all because of alcohol's impact on a certain segment of the population. Most violent crime is committed under the influence of alcohol. Every year 500,000 college students discontinue their academic training because of alcohol abuse. How many millions of broken homes are the result of alcohol abuse?

*Forty percent of all traffic accidents are alcohol related.*
*Drunk drivers kill 26,000 Americans per year.*

## Avoidance and Recovery Strategies

There are several groups of people who should have ZERO alcohol consumption:
1. pregnant women or those at risk of pregnancy

2. those diagnosed as having the disease of alcoholism
3. those with a family history of alcoholism
4. those who are noted to be problem drinkers by friends and family
5. those who have health problems which their doctors say will be aggravated by alcohol consumption
6. those who are taking medication which adversely interacts with alcohol.

Others should restrict or eliminate alcohol consumption for general health enhancement even if they are not at apparent high risk. As little as one glass of wine per week can have deleterious health effects in apparently symptom-free women. Avoiding others who drink, and places of inebriation, also reduces risk of indirect harm—as does avoiding night time driving when more alcohol related accidents occur.

If you are trying to quit, there are many different programs available. Most use some variation of Alcoholics Anonymous' Twelve-Step Program. The AA program is in every community, has a good track record, and is free. There are many medically supervised residential and outpatient programs which may be appropriate for those who have severe health problems and/or those who have insurance or the money to pay for these expensive treatment programs. Psychotherapy and behavior modification approaches are sometimes needed for long-term success. Cranial electrical stimulation has been proving to be an important adjunct to reduce craving and dependency, in addition to improving brain biochemistry in people with substance abuse problems. Biofeedback has also proven to be an important adjunct to treatment.

One approach that *everyone* with an alcohol problem should incorporate into their recovery program is nutritional/biochemical enhancement. The four resources most helpful here are these books:

Beasley, Joseph, *Wrong Diagnosis, Wrong Treatment: The Plight of the Alcoholic in America*, Random House, 1987.
Blum, Kenneth with Payne, James, *Alcohol and the Addictive Brain: New Hope for Alcoholics from Biogenic Research*, Macmillan Free Press, 1991.

Ketcham, Katherine and Mueller, L. Ann, *Eating Right to Live Sober*, Madrona Publishers.
Larson, Joan, *Alcoholism—The Biochemical Connection: A Biomedical Regimen for Recovery*, Villard/ Random House, 1992.

These authors discuss many biochemical and nutritional enhancement treatments that go hand-in-hand with spiritual and psychological approaches. Some of the key elements needed to correct many of these biochemical disturbances that perpetuate the addictive process are summarized below:

1. replenishing nutrient reserves and improving digestive efficiency
2. correcting low blood sugar calorie cravings and mood swings
3. identifying and correcting food allergy addictions that perpetuate cravings
4. restoring neurotransmitter balance with better amino acid nutrition, cranial electrical stimulation, and light therapy
5. improving prostaglandin metabolism with needed fatty acids (prostaglandins are hormones that seem to prevent alcohol toxicity and addiction)

## OTHER SOCIAL DRUGS— MARIJUANA, COCAINE, HEROIN, LSD, PCP . . .

Risk Probability of Dysfunction, Disease, or Death on a scale of 1–10

4

*There are approximately 750,000 drug arrests made in the U.S. every year.*

The relative low risk applied to this genre of harmful agents has more to do with their unavailability, illegality, and limited usage rather than their potency for body-mind damage. The relatively small segment of the population which abuses these drugs has a high risk of a variety of health problems. But even these individuals have psychosocial and economic problems that are of far greater risk to their health than simply drug abuse.

## Avoidance Strategies

Effective avoidance must center on correcting the root psychological causes for turning to this form of mind numbing. Economic hopelessness, low self-esteem, and an inadequate educational system are fundamental problems. Psychotherapy is only available to a few, but it should be utilized by all. As in the case of alcohol withdrawal, cranial electrical stimulation can be very helpful with abstinence from other social drugs. Similarly, nutritional enhancement and acupuncture can correct some of the biochemical aspects of addiction, but unfortunately it is available to only a small number of all those needing help. Most of the mechanisms for change lie with government, business, and community transformations. Personal strategies can be summed up as: get whatever help you can from friends, family, professionals, and social programs, but ultimately—avoid all these substances and find lifestyles that are healthier.

## INFECTIOUS AGENTS

Risk of Dysfunction, Disease, or Death
on a scale of 1–10
8

*If thy heart were right,
then every creature would be a mirror of life
and a book of holy doctrine.
There is no creature so small and abject
but it reflects the goodness of God.*
**Thomas á Kempis**

Our world is full of infectious agents: Bacteria, viruses, parasites, fungi, ricketsia—causing chlamydia, strep throat, pneumonia, anthrax, diptheria, salmonella, cholera, plague, tuberculosis, leprosy, candidiasis, histoplasmosis, typhus, lyme disease, Rocky Mountain Spotted Fever, measles, chickenpox, smallpox, mumps, CMV, EBV, AIDS, herpes, common cold, influenza, polio, rabies, malaria, dystentery. . . .

Risk of mortality is relatively low for infectious disease in the United States when compared to less developed countries or when compared to America

in the first half of this century. The most important reason for the reduced risk of death by infection is that we have adopted rigid public health standards for food and water purity. Public health education has played an important role, as does public assistance to those in poverty suffering from malnutrition. Antibiotics have also had some impact in reducing mortality and morbidity.

Because of these improvements, many of the infectious killers of the past pose less of a death threat. But serious disability and lost productivity from infectious environmental agents are still a problem for everyone's immune system, not only because of the primary infection and the endotoxins that are produced, but also because an allergic hypersensitivity to microbes can occur.

*Candida albicans yeast infection places an immunological burden on approximately 20,000,000 Americans.*

*One million Americans are infected with the intestinal roundworm Ascaris lumbricoides.*

*Ten million people in the United States are infected with the intestinal ameoba Entameba histolytica, and 9,000,000 with Giardia lamblia.*

*Approximately 25,000,000 Americans are infected with the parasite Enterobius vermicularis.*

Added to the picture are new forms of lethal microbes that wreak havoc on body and mind. Super strains of microbes which are resistant to drug therapy have started to appear, in large part due to the overuse of antibiotic therapy. Some of the most lethal strains of these "superbugs" are found in hospitals.

*Hospital acquired infections cause at least 50,000 deaths per year.
AIDS kills more than 10,000 Americans per year.*

Reducing exposure is the first key to reducing risk, next is building immune system strength and fighting the infections.

Reducing exposure to infections today involves both governmental policy and individual protective action. Government agencies assure a clean water supply, protect the quality of our food and inspect it for safety; the Centers for Disease Control monitor infectious disease throughout the country to accommodate changes in public policy that might be necessary to insure greater protection. How *well* these government agencies operate often determines our health risk.

Personal responsibility is also important. Safe sexual practices, clean food preparation, good nutrition, and stress management, all play important roles. Since the 33,000,000 cases of food-borne illness in the U.S. come primarily from meat, the two important strategies of vegetarianism and safe food preparation practices can help greatly.

Electing officials who have strong consumer protection records is also a prime individual responsibility. If you vote for the alluring concept of "less government for lower taxes," remember that you are most likely also voting for fewer food inspectors and less watchdogging of unscrupulous business practices that put us all at risk.

Fighting hidden infections often requires finding a progressive, well-read physician who can utilize innovative and advanced forms of testing along with nutritional and herbal treatments.

## PRESCRIPTION AND OVER-THE-COUNTER MEDICATIONS

Risk of Dysfunction, Disease, or Death
on a scale of 1–10
7

*Medicine is a collection of uncertain prescriptions the results of which, taken collectively, are more fatal than useful to mankind.*

**Napoleon**

*One billion six hundred million prescriptions for medicines are prescribed each year in the U. S.*
*Approximately 6,000,000 adverse drug reactions occur nationwide each year.*
*Almost half of these require hospitalization.*
*As many as 160,000 might die.*

Millions of people become ill, and thousands die, from the medicines that are supposed to be making them better. The problems are many.

First, drugs *all* have adverse side effects. Some medications have more serious complications. Some pharmacological agents have more numerous problems. For some drugs the problems come from the primary active ingredients; for others, it is the supposed "inert" ingredients—excipients, binders, fillers, colors, preservatives, carrier ingredients, and other additives.

Millions of people suffer today from yeast and fungal infections, or antibiotic-resistant strains of bacteria, because years ago there was an over-utilization of antibiotics and steroids, both in humans and animal agriculture. Approximately 11,000,000 pounds of antibiotics are given to live-stock animals in the United States every year. This made the people receiving these drugs, often unknowingly in their animal food products, more susceptible to other kinds of infection in several ways:

- The drugs, however they might have entered the person's body, could have caused bacteria to mutate and become antibiotic-resistant "superbugs."

- The pharmaceuticals could have killed beneficial intestinal microbes, which normally competed with bad bacteria, fungi, and yeasts. Without the competition these harmful microbes could then grow unchecked.

- Drugs of any kind put a stressful burden on the body. This, in itself, can decrease our resistance to infection.

Only as time goes on, with increasing numbers of people becoming ill and dying of medications, do we discover how harmful both prescriptive and non-prescriptive drugs are. Trying to externally manipulate the complex internal biochemistry of the human body with powerful man-made substances displays the arrogance of physicians with their limited knowledge. It is asking for trouble. (For more details see: Wolfe, Sidney; Hope, Rose-Ellen; and Public Citizen Health Research Group, *Worst Pills, Best Pills: The Older Adults' Guide to Avoiding Drug Induced Death or Illness*. Public Citizen, 1993.)

*One hundred twenty-five thousand Americans
call poison control centers every year
after adverse reactions to over-the-counter
cold medications.*

Second, hundreds of medications have never been proven effective.

*One billion dollars worth of cold medications
are sold in the U. S. per year.
After numerous studies, many experts have
concluded that most are not only ineffective at
reducing the severity or duration of symptoms but
may be more of a harm because of the
complications arising from the ingredients,
most notably the antihistamines.*

Third, even with drugs that are proven effective, patients are notorious for *not* following doctor's orders on how to take medication properly. Less than 50% of patients follow the directions given them. Many use medications that are out of date or were prescribed to other individuals. Tragically, thousands of people attempt suicide by medication overdose. Some succeed. All too frequently medications are used illicitly and sold on the streets to drug addicts.

*Over 1,000,000 people in the U.S. abuse
anabolic steroids;
500,000 teenagers use anabolic steroids without
proper medical supervision.*

Fourth, patients take more than one medication at a time, which causes disruptive drug interactions and complications. This is compounded when more than one doctor is prescribing medicines for different conditions without knowledge of the other medications being taken. It is further complicated when the patient is also self-medicating with over-the-counter drugs. The subject of adverse drug interactions is so complex that elaborate computer programs have been created to organize the volumes of data and to assist physicians and pharmacists with at least the *known* problems. For people taking more than one drug of any kind it is important to find a physician or pharmacist using one of these drug interact programs. Unfortu-

nately, there is much that is unknown about drug interactions which will not be put into these computer programs until more people get sick and die.

Fifth, many drugs destroy, inactivate, or increase the need for nutrients. If medications must be taken, nutritional supplementation is almost essential to prevent depletion, which is usually a problem already because of the condition the person is being treated for. Alan Pressman, in his book *Clinical Assessment of Nutritional Status,* has an excellent 15-page chapter, "Drug-Nutrient Interactions" which details these problems specifically.

Sixth, mistakes are made. When you play with fire expect to get burned. Many drugs are packaged in such a way that they make administration errors commonplace—and deadly!

*Ten people die every day in American hospitals
from the 56,000 medications that are
mistakenly administered. Oooops.
Unknown are the similar deaths and injuries
that occur in doctor offices or at home.*

Possibly the most harmful element of medication as a deleterious environmental agent is that it ingrains the misconception that "popping a pill gives us health." For doctors, pharmacists, and patients it seems an alluring, easy method of reducing unwanted symptoms rather than learning to deal with all the complex, multifaceted causes of dysfunction. The perpetuation of this "quick fix" philosophy prevents the adoption of more preventive, health enhancing activities. Pharmaceutical companies are more than willing to encourage these unhealthy attitudes so their high profits are sustained. A more judicious use of medications must be practiced by physicians and lay people alike. First priority should go to health improvement practices. Medications should only be used when there are no other better or safer alternatives.

*Drug companies spend $10 billion every year
trying to persuade doctors and consumers to take
their medication "quick fix."*

## A SPECIAL NOTE:
## COMPULSORY MASS MEDICATION

A particularly disturbing aspect of medication usage is the dominance of the orthodox medical community in manipulating governments to force individuals to take medication against their will, without informed consent, when it can be harmful to their health. Vaccinations and water fluoridation are the two most potentially harmful circumstances.

### *Fluoridation*

Fluoride is added to drinking water in some communities to reduce the incidence of dental caries. Although some early studies support these benefits, more recent research seems to indicate that the benefits are minimal if they exist at all. Even if the evidence was incontrovertible, the potential adverse side effects might outweigh the benefits. Tooth mottling is the most obvious problem that occurs with excessive fluoride intake. Although just a cosmetic defect, it can be emotionally troublesome and costly to remedy. Less frequent but more devastating is the problem of skeletal fluorosis, a potentially crippling buildup of bony spurs. Millions of people with kidney disease who have difficulty excreting fluoride are at risk.

Some epidemiological studies have estimated that water fluoridation might cause as many as 10,000 extra cancer deaths per year.

More and more communities are voting down referendums on community water fluoridation. This seems reasonable since fluoride tooth pastes, mouthwashes, and prescriptive drugs are readily available to supplement normal dietary sources to those individuals that feel the need (after close consultation with their physician and/or dentist about risks and benefits) to restrain the growth of dental caries with this medication. Why impose mass medication when the subject is scientifically questionable and popularly objectionable? For more information on this subject contact the Center for Health Action, P.O. Box 270, Forest Park Station, Springfield, MA 01108; (413) 782-2115 or (800) 869-9610.

### *Vaccinations*

*Approximately 11,000 children are damaged per year and 800 die from being vaccinated with pertussis vaccine.*
*Four thasand claims have been filed with the National Vaccine Injury Compensation Program paying claimants $103,900,000.*

Vaccinations have been hailed as medical miracles saving humanity from dreaded diseases—smallpox, polio, whooping cough, diptheria, etc. But a closer epidemiological examination will show that some of these diseases were on a dramatic, natural, cyclic decline long before vaccinations for their cure were introduced. Some of these diseases show a stronger correlation for prevention with nutritional status and degree of public hygiene than with vaccination rates.

Five factors have to be considered when evaluating vaccination as a preventive health care procedure:

1. the risk of contracting the disease
2. the seriousness of the disease
3. the effectiveness of the vaccine
4. the potential risks of the vaccine itself
5. alternative methods of protection.

The resources at the end of this chapter will help in evaluating these factors with the addition of alternative perspectives on standardized vaccination protocols. Upon closer scrutiny, some vaccinations appear more dangerous than what they can prevent. Others can be given at different schedules or not combined with still others to reduce risks and increase effectiveness. Sometimes health problems that occur from vaccinations are due to just one production batch of the drug. *Many immunizations are obviously helpful.* Final decisions of benefit and risk lie with a fully informed health care consumer in close consultation with an open-minded physician who is not rigidly bound by standards of care which may not be in the best interest of the patient.

## ALLERGIES, INTOLERANCES, AND SENSITIVITIES TO FOODS OR INHALANTS

Risk of Dysfunction, Disease, or Death
on a scale of 1–10
7

*Ninety to ninety-five percent of the population is allergic or biochemically intolerant to one or more foods.*
*The National Institutes of Health estimate that thirty-one million Americans have significant allergic disorders.*

### Foods

Abnormal biochemical and neurological reactions to foods can come in the form of specific immune system disturbances. Or abnormal reactions can be the result of weak or missing enzymes such as a lactase deficiency creating an intolerance to milk sugar. There are numerous biochemical mechanisms that can be involved in these unhealthy reactions. Every organ system in the body can be adversely affected, often without overt symptoms. Food allergies, intolerances, and sensitivities are involved and unrecognized as contributors to many of the illnesses that plague us today—asthma, arthritis, cardiac arhythmias, atherosclerosis, colitis, otitis media, dermatitis, depression, emotional disturbances, hyperactivity, dyspepsia, hearing loss, behavioral problems, autism, alcoholism, sinusitis, incontinence, anxiety, stomach ulcers, kidney disease, obesity, headaches, fatigue, bursitis, seizures, learning disabilities, insomnia, bronchitis, respiratory failure, myalgia, neuralgia, cystitis, constipation, eczema, gallbladder disease, psychosis, delusions, hallucinations, and others.

Only through adequate testing can we discover *how* important its role might be in any specific individual case. If economics is critical, and the individual is diligent at self-care, at-home elimination and reintroduction of foods can reveal many food allergies. But if the person's condition is severe, or self-testing is unfeasible, a certain type of immunological allergy test, called ELISA/ACT™ blood tests, can be performed.

Once the offending foods are identified, eliminating them from the diet rapidly improves health. Prolonged abstinence from the offending foods frequently allows the body a chance to recover immunologically, and these substances can be reintroduced in moderation after several months.

Nutritional supplementation with antioxidants, vitamins, minerals, acidophilus, and trace elements also has enormous recuperative benefits. Guidelines can be found in: Murray, Michael, and Pizzorno, Joseph, *Encyclopedia of Natural Medicine,* Prima Publishing, 1991, and in Werbach, Melvyn, *Nutritional Influences on Illness: A Sourcebook of Clinical Research,* Third Line Press, 1988. Specially-designed hypo-allergenic supplementation can be purchased from a number of reputable companies. See the list in the professional resource section at the end of the chapter.

A certain percentage of severe allergies might be helped by a controversially effective but safe treatment called serial dilution desensitization. Doctors of environmental medicine use this technique to slowly introduce allergic substances into the body in very small doses in order to reduce the person's reaction to the irritating agents. A small percentage of food allergies is "fixed" with little chance of reintroduction without problems. For professional help in evaluation and treatment, contact the American Academy of Environmental Medicine for a physician nearest you. Sometimes food allergies are secondary to hidden infections. Finding a physician who is skilled at using the latest laboratory tests, such as comprehensive stool analysis, immune function profiles, and antibody titer levels of infectious agents (which might find hidden infections) may be quite helpful. Contacting the physician laboratories listed at the end of this chapter, or the other physician groups in the resource section of the Holistic Health chapter, will assist you in finding the best health professional for your needs.

## Inhalants

Pollens, dust, molds, animal dander, fragrances, and petrochemicals can cause numerous biochemical and neurological reactions that affect health adversely, much like foods. Here, too, any organ can be affected via diverse physiological pathways. Inhalant allergies contribute to the same wide array of diseases that foods do.

Identification of these allergies can be very accurately assessed with immune system allergy blood tests called RAST IgE. Avoidance can be more difficult. Extra cleaning diligence with natural products is often needed. Special HEPA air filtration systems are often helpful but add to the expense of treatment. Particular care is often needed in furnishing one's home to avoid offending substances. Serial dilution desensitization can also be used for inhalants much the same way as with foods. Nutritional supplementation and immune enhancement are again effective strategies. Use the same resources previously detailed in the above section on food allergies, and look into the resources at the end of this chapter.

## MAN-MADE CHEMICALS AND TOXIC ELEMENTS

Risk of Dysfunction, Disease, or Death
on a scale of 1–10
7

*Five hundred million tons of hazardous waste are produced in the U.S. per year. The largest source of this waste is the U.S. military, contributing 500,000 tons annually.[3]*

*There are approximately 50,000 chemicals used in North America with the introduction of about 1,000 new man-made substances per year.*

Pesticides, herbicides, formaldehyde (carpets, fiberboard, plywood, paneling, room deodorants, cosmetics), asbestos (roofing, flooring, brakes), arsenic (paints, dyes, wood preservatives, leather), benzene (inks, paints, rubber, drugs), DDT, oven cleaners, photographic supplies, glues, shoe polishes, spot removers, Dioxin, EDB (gasoline, food), hair dyes, PCB (transformers, hydraulic fluids, sealants), vinyl chloride (plastics, flooring, toluene (varnishes, solvents), acrylonitrile (food packaging, plastics, synthetic fibers), acetone (nail polish remover), butylated hydroxytoluene (lipstick, cosmetics, soap, body oils), coal tar (cosmetics, soaps, shampoos), polyvinylpyrrolidone (cosmetics), chlorine, fluoride (drinking water, toothpaste, mouthwash), lead (leaded crystal, gasoline, newsprint, paint, drinking water), mercury (dental mercury amalgams), aluminum (aluminum cookware, antacids), and cadmium (household batteries, cigarette smoke) are a few of the thousands of toxic substances that disrupt body-mind function and rob us of health.

Everyone is at risk. Every part of the body and mind can be affected. Disease, disability and death are more frequently caused by these agents than is imaginable. This is primarily true because we are assaulted by such a relentless, cumulative burden of these harmful substances, most often in the name of "progress" and "civilization."

*The National Academy of Sciences has estimated that 15% of the U.S. population is adversely affected by chemical hypersensitivity.*

Reducing the additive burden of potential toxins is a worthwhile endeavor. Replacing many man-made, synthetic, household and workplace articles with safe, natural alternatives is a primary health enhancement technique. Not only does it improve personal health, but choosing natural products helps the environment.

Some testing can be done to identify exposure risk, immunological/allergic reaction, or body burden. Examples of such tests are listed below.

Hair analysis will give reliable data on long-term exposure to lead, aluminum, cadmium.

Functional Liver Detoxification Capacity can assess the liver's reserve ability to detoxify poisons.

Immunological profiles (IgG, IgE, IgM antibody formation; ELISA/ACT™ testing; B and T cell enumeration; T-4 helper and T-8 suppressor ratio; complement C-3 and C-4 . . .) can determine assaults on specific parts of the immune system by particular poisonous agents, chemicals, and microbial toxins.

Functional antioxidant blood tests, such as Spectrox, can evaluate the body's ability to handle free radicals.

Twenty-four hour urine samples can detect mercury exposure, as can oral mercury gas analyzers. A small group of progressive dentists can be found to do this testing and replace toxic silver-mercury dental fillings with safer substitutes. No one should have new fillings placed in their mouths that contain mercury.

Lead test kits are available to test household items. Water and soil samples can be sent to laboratories for analysis.

Tap water testing is available that will identify bacteria, heavy metals, fluoride, dissolved solids, salt, other minerals, organic compounds such as pesticides, industrial pollutants, and herbicides.

Home formaldehyde tests can be purchased to identify this indoor air contaminant.

Since the fumes from gas stoves, furnaces, and water heaters are the most significant culprits triggering adverse reactions in the chemically sensitive, these sources should be checked for leaks and clean burning, if not eliminated from the home environment totally.

Pesticides and herbicides are also frequent culprits in triggering adverse reactions in the chemically sensitive due to their powerful ability to damage metabolic pathways in the body. Tests can be run to detect levels of these substances in the home. Also ELISA/ACT™ tests can be done on blood samples to determine a person's reactions to these substances.

Nutritional supplementation is essential when environmental toxins damage the complex biochemical, metabolic processes of the body. Use the same resources listed in the previous section on food allergies.

Use the resources at the end of the chapter for assistance in dealing with these issues. For more information on Dr. Gard's BioToxic Reduction Program for the medically supervised elimination of toxic substances from the body (recreational drugs, medicines, industrial pollutants, pesticides),

contact him at : Zane R. Gard, M.D., P.O. Box 1791 Beaverton, OR 97075-1791. Some members of the American Academy of Environmental Medicine use similar elimination protocols.

## ELECTROMAGNETIC RADIATION

Risk of Dysfunction, Disease, or Death
on a scale of 1–10
4

High tension electrical lines, electric blankets, televisions, video display terminals, hair dryers, appliances, home wiring, are all sources of electromagnetic radiation leakage which has deleterious effects on human and animal physiology. Not enough research has been done in this area to date. More research and guidelines are needed for safe use of electrical currents in everyday life. What research has been done has suggested that there is a consistent pattern of leukemia, neurological cancers, lymphoma, and birth defects associated with electromagnetic field exposure in humans. Animal studies suggest even more problems.

Testing for electromagnetic leakage at home and at work can be done with a gaussmeter available from catalogs listed in the resource section. Without testing there are some wise general rules: Do not sleep with an electric sleeping blanket turned on. Do not sleep with an electric clock close to your head. Stay six feet from viewing a television or older video display terminal or use an electromagnetic screen to filter out the energy field. Newer, "low radiation" computer monitors are now made so that sitting closer is safe. Use a towel instead of a hair dryer.

## IONIZING RADIATION

Risk of Dysfunction, Disease, or Death
on a scale of 1–10
4

*According to EPA estimates in 1990 21% of U.S. homes have health-threatening levels of radon.*

*The Department of Energy estimates that the cost of cleaning up nuclear contamination from nuclear power plants and weapon facilities will be at least $200 billion and take thirty years to complete. The worst news is that science has yet to find any safe method of disposal.*

Medical x-rays, nuclear medicine, radon gas and cigarette smoke in the home, leakage from nuclear power and weapons facilities, are all sources of low-dose ionizing radiation. Everyone on the planet is exposed to a background level of this form of radiation. Higher cumulative doses become a problem over time. That is why it is important to reduce any added sources of exposure. Some of the conditions known to be caused by prolonged, low-dose exposure include the following: amenorrhea; infertility; blood conditions such as anemia, leukopenia, thrombocytopenia; leukemia; cataracts; hair loss; thickening, atrophy, and ulceration of the skin; kidney dysfunction; cancer; birth defects.

Personnel who work with or near sources of ionizing radiation should have their exposure monitored by a reputable company. Sources of radiation like hospital x-ray machines should be inspected regularly for leakage. Health care facilities are frequently found to be operating outside the standards of safety in some states. If your doctor wants to take x-rays, ask if they are absolutely necessary. Do not hesitate to express your concerns. If x-rays are a must, request the fewest number of pictures needed rather than an entire "series," some of which could be taken later if, after viewing the primary films, more information is required. Question your doctor's use of "routine" films, or repeated follow-up x-rays. Pre-employment x-rays may be illegal if there are no signs of disease indicating the necessity for diagnostic x-rays. Pre-hospital admission x-rays are now being frowned upon except when absolutely necessary. Fewer dental x-rays are being used as dentists become more sensitive to the new found dangers of low-dose exposure. There are also few, if any, good reasons for full spine chiropractic x-rays. Smaller localized pictures of isolated regions of the spine provide better quality films with less radiation.

Doing an at-home radon test (available from catalogs in the resource section) might be advisable if you live in a geographical area that has high radon emissions from the ground. Your regional Environmental Protection Agency should have that information available. Since high levels of radon are found in cigarette smoke, everyone has another good reason to avoid this contaminant.

## THE MAJOR AVENUES OF POLLUTION—AIR, WATER, FOOD

Three avenues of pollution transmission to individuals need to be particularly addressed—air, water, and food. Does the air we breathe, the water we drink, and the food we eat support or harm health? How much are we contributing to the problem? How much are we helping? What is each of us doing to encourage legislators and businesses to clean and protect these aspects of our environment and health?

### AIR POLLUTION

*I shot an arrow into the air, and it stuck.*
**L.A. graffiti**

### Outdoor air pollution

There are a number of primary outdoor air pollutants that are of great concern.

1. Suspended particulates—ash, smoke, soot, dust, liquid droplets. These are produced by burning fuels, industrial processes, or agricultural and forest fires.

*The American Lung Association estimates that approximately 3% of all deaths in the United States are caused by suspended particulates in the air.*

2. Smog—nitrogen oxide, ozone, and volatile organic compounds. Smog is created by burning fuels, gasoline fumes, and industrial chemicals.

*In 1988 approximately 19.8 million metric tons of nitrogen dioxide and 18.6 million metric tons of ozone were released into the air in the U.S.*

3. Sulfur dioxide—acid rain. This acidification of the air and water comes from burning coal and oil.

*"At present, power plants in the United States release about 20 million tons of sulfur dioxide into the atmosphere each year."[4]*

4. Carbon monoxide. This harmful compound is the result of burned fuels also. Carbon monoxide prevents oxygen from being carried by your blood.

*At low levels it can cause chest pains, headaches, dizziness, and incoordination. At higher levels it can* kill.

5. Toxic air pollutants. These are hazardous chemicals released by manufacturing plants, refineries, chemical plants, dry cleaning companies, and automobiles.

*"In 1988, 2.7 billion pounds of toxic air pollutants were released in the United States."[5]*

### The Solution

One of the most effective, short-term, personal solutions to the problem of outdoor air pollution is to live far from polluted areas. But not all of us have the luxury of living in a pristine mountain setting. If living in a polluted city is a must because of other compelling personal circumstances, care must be taken to breathe the worst air as infrequently as possible. Drive with your car's vents closed in heavy traffic. Don't exercise near heavy traffic or on days when the pollution is particularly bad. Spending much of your time indoors in an air conditioned environment is protective. Purchasing effective air filtration systems for the home is expensive but helps with both outdoor and indoor pollution. They are sometimes essential when a member of the family suffers from a respiratory condition which is aggravated by air pollution. See the resource section at the end of the chapter for help in finding the right air filtration system for your needs.

Ultimately, the actions that will be most effective at eliminating outdoor air pollution are the individual acts that are multiplied by millions:

1. conserving energy
2. recycling
3. mass transit
4. fuel efficient autos
5. alternative fuel cars—natural gas, electric
6. use of natural products rather than synthetics
7. citizens forcing politicians to pass, administrations to enforce, and businesses to comply with, more stringent environmental protection laws.

### Indoor Air Pollution

*Indoor air pollution appears to be more of a health threat than outdoor air pollution.*

There are several factors that make indoor air pollution so health damaging:

1. Lack of adequate air circulation concentrates pollutants to levels that can be 100 times those found outdoors.
2. The number of indoor air pollutants is staggering.
3. We spend most of our time indoors.
4. Public awareness of the problem is minimal. If you don't know a problem exists, you can't correct it.

## *The Problem*

### Radon Gas

*Radon may contribute to as much as 15%
of all lung cancers.*

The extent of this problem is enormous when we consider that the Environmental Protection Agency believes that one fifth of American homes is plagued with dangerous levels of this form of radioactivity. Certain types of geology emit high quantities of radon. If you build over these geological structures, the gas can filter up into the home and concentrate there, depending on the building's construction.

### Secondhand Tobacco Smoke

*Tens of thousands of people die, and millions
become ill every year, due to secondary tobacco
smoke. Children are the most vulnerable.*

**Formaldehyde**—foam insulation, plywood, particle board, panelling, wood glue

*The Consumer Product Safety Commission has
thousands of health complaints on file related to
formaldehyde fumes emitted from home building
products and furnishings.*

**Synthetic Chemicals**—plastics, synthetic fibers, chemical cleaning agents, mothballs, air fresheners, solvents, polishes, paints, foam upholstery, aerosols, disinfectants, dry-cleaned clothes, pesticides, refrigerants, perfumes, etc. The cumulative toxic burden of all these substances concentrated in an indoor environment is unknown. But additional research continues to reveal more and more health damaging effects.

### Asbestos

*Asbestos exists in over 300 consumer products
and has more than 3,000 industrial
applications.[6]*

**Burned Fuel By-products**—carbon monoxide, nitrogen dioxide, suspended particulates from kerosene, wood, or gas stoves, ovens, heaters, and fireplaces.

*There is a greater incidence of respiratory
problems in homes with these sources
of burned fuels.*

**Biological Pollutants**—molds, mildew, bacteria, viruses, pollen, dust mites, animal dander, and bad breath from cockroaches (just checking to see if you're paying attention).

*Along with chemical contaminants,
biological pollutants are the two primary sources
of "sick building syndrome."*

## *The Solution*

1. Replace synthetic products with natural alternatives.
2. Insure good ventilation.
3. House plants clean the air, particularly spider plants, English ivy, golden pothos, marginatas, peace lilies, potted mums, and warneckiis.
4. Have your house tested for radon in highly susceptible locales. If levels are high, hire a professional to correct the problem. It can be expensive.
5. Use electric, solar, or wind power rather than combustible fuels. If necessary, well-ventilated, properly-maintained natural gas stoves, ovens, and heaters can be used. Wood stoves should be newer, more efficient EPA approved stoves for fewest emissions. Fireplaces and kerosene heaters are the most problematic.
6. Never use chemical pesticides or herbicides, particularly indoors!
7. Keep indoors clean and dry (30-50% humidity). Hardwood floors are healthier than carpets. If carpets must be used, purchase natural fiber throw rugs that can be cleaned more readily. Clean all bedding regularly.

8. Some people who are particularly sensitized to inhalant contaminants may need to purchase HEPA (high efficiency particulate attenuating) vacuum cleaners and air filtration systems.
9. DON'T SMOKE!

## WATER POLLUTION

*The Environmental Protection Agency has estimated that 11 million gallons of gasoline leak into ground water aquifers each year.*

### The Problem

#### Microorganisms

Bacteria—Edwardsiella, E. coli, Salmonella, Shigella, Vibrio cholerae, Yersinia.

Viruses—Adenovirus, Coxsakie, Echo, Hepatitis A, Norwalk, Polio, Reovirus, Rotavirus.

Parasites—Giardia

*According to the Centers for Disease Control 20,000 people were reported ill from water-borne infections in 1983 alone. Unreported cases are much higher.*

**Toxic Minerals and Metals**—aluminum, arsenic, asbestos, barium, cadmium, chromium, copper, fluoride, lead, mercury, nitrate, nitrite, selenium, silver.

*Ninety percent of U.S. rivers have the same or more pollution today as twenty years ago. Is this environmental progress?*

#### Organic Chemicals

*Seventy percent of the country's 400,000 landfills and waste lagoons lack liners to prevent toxic chemicals from leaching into the groundwater. U.S. industries release 9.7 billion pounds of chemicals into surface streams each year. Over 700 organic chemical contaminants have been found in U.S. drinking water; 50,000,000 Americans are now at risk of consuming pesticide contaminated water.*

**Radioactive Substances**—Radium 226 and 228, uranium 234 and 238, and radon 222.

*Approximately 500 water systems in the United States exceed the maximum contaminant level for radium 226.*

**Additives**—chlorine, fluoride, flocculents

*Because of studies linking fluoridation to cancer, public outrage has forced most municipal water authorities to stop medicating the water in this way.*

*Chlorine, when combined with chemical contaminants in water, produces substances called trihalomethanes that can pose serious health threats.*
*If you think your water is "safe," think about who determines whether it is safe: the Environmental Protection Agency. They think that a safe level of trihalomethane is 100 parts per million in tap water. The European Economic Community's Environmental Council says 1 part per million is safe. Which standard do you want to risk your life and health on, particularly when reflecting on the political influence that tarnishes so many of the EPA's policies?*

### The Solution

If you must drink tap water, let the water run for at least 30 seconds to flush out any heavy metals that may have leached out into the standing water in the pipes. Do not use hot tap water for internal consumption. Water that has been stored in plastic containers for any length of time will absorb plastic particles from the container. If water must be stored, use clean glass containers. The longer any stored water sits, the greater the chance of microbial contamination.

See the resources at the end of the chapter for places to buy environmentally sound products like water filters and distillers. The best water purifiers seem to be combination filters with reverse osmosis membranes. For information refer to Ingram, Colin. *The Drinking Water Book: A Complete Guide to Safe Drinking Water.* Ten Speed Press, 1991.

## *FOOD POLLUTION*

### Microbes and their toxins

*Microbes in food make 80 million Americans ill and kill 9,000 every year.*[7]

Go vegetarian, learn wise food preparation techniques (buy fresh, keep it cold, cook it thoroughly). The book, *Safe Food,* should be in every kitchen.

**Agricultural Chemicals**—herbicides, pesticides, fungicides, antibiotics, hormones

*American agribusiness uses 2,000,000,000 pounds of pesticides every year;*
*99% of these toxic chemicals never reach the insects they are meant for.*
*All too often they do reach, and adversely affect, humans through food and water contamination. Seventy-eight percent of the pesticide residue found in the American diet comes from meat and dairy; 25,000 cancer deaths per year are attributed to pesticide exposure.*

Buy organic. If this is difficult, use the book *Diet for a Poisoned Planet* to choose the safest foods. The book *Safe Food* is also a helpful guide here.

**Industrial Contaminants**—mercury and PCBs in fish

Know what fish are least or most likely to be contaminated. See the book *Safe Food.*

**Food Additives**—preservatives, colors, flavor enhancers, waxes, contaminants from plastic wraps.

*"The average American consumes about five pounds of food additives per year."*[8]

Buy vegetables, whole grains, and fruits at organic grocers. Refrain from consuming processed foods.

### Food Irradiation

Avoid it until long term studies can prove its safety. Support legislation to ban it until then.

## SUMMARY OF PERSONAL ENVIRONMENTAL PROTECTION STRATEGIES

1. Do not smoke. Avoid secondhand smoke.
2. Do not drink alcohol. Avoid people who abuse it.
3. Take precautions to prevent infection. Practice safe sex. If there is a suspicion of hidden infection, consult a progressive, nutritionally oriented physician skilled at interpreting the newer immunological laboratory tests.
4. Do not take medications unless absolutely necessary and other health enhancement endeavors are activated on first priority. Know what adverse side effects might be elicited by your medications. Find out if your medication depletes particular nutrients from the body or creates a greater need for their utilization. Supplement accordingly. If more than one medication is being taken, consult a drug interact computer program.
5. If allergies to food or inhalants might be a significant health problem, be tested for them in the most cost-effective, accurate manner. Then engage in a program to nutritionally correct the problem.
6. Reduce exposure to as many man-made chemicals and toxic elements as feasible— pesticides, herbicides, chemical cleansers, petroleum based products, plastics, synthetics, industrial pollutants, lead, mercury, cadmium, aluminum, etc.
7. Test home and workplace for excessive electromagnetic radiation, and reduce any excessive exposure.

8. Avoid excessive radiation from medical and dental x-rays, radon gas in the home, and nuclear power and weapons facilities.
9. Choose uncontaminated foods and prepare them safely.
10. Be active and vocal in your support of legislation to protect the environment, the consumer, and the workplace from toxic substances.
11. Engage in an immune enhancement program.

We cannot separate our personal physical, psychological, intellectual, and spiritual health from the health of our surrounding environment.

---

## GLOBAL ECOLOGICAL ACTIVISM
## *THINK GLOBALLY, ACT LOCALLY*

*I tremble for my species when I reflect that God is just.*

**Thomas Jefferson**

Resource depletion, ozone destruction, global warming, dead seas, deforestation, toxic pollution, radiation contamination, species extinction, are all life and death problems for which science has no answers. We may exterminate ourselves if we do not solve these problems in *this* generation.

We have an opportunity which no other people in the history of humankind has ever had—the opportunity to save our species from extinction and save the lives of many, many living beings. Are we up to this, the greatest challenge humanity has ever known? What will you do for your part? Will you daily think, can I do more to actively cherish this home, my earth—to revere my fellow living organisms, the four-legged, feathered, finned, and leafed?

When the forces of destruction are so powerful and pervasive, the task of ecological restoration sometimes seems too overwhelming for one person to make any difference.

*What you do to help others may seem insignificant, but that you do it is very important.*

**Mahatma Gandhi**

How to help:

Become informed: read the recommended resources, particularly the magazines, for updated information.

Become active: vote, write representatives, attend town meetings, join and support environmental protection groups, boycott companies that destroy the environment.

Be responsible in your own actions: conserve resources like fuel and water; be careful about excessive consumption of commercial products; recycle; buy locally produced products; cultivate an organic garden, no matter how small; act more as a integral part and guardian of Mother Earth rather than a separate, ego-centered entity designed for self gratification at the expense of other living beings; spend time in natural settings to fully appreciate its gifts. The Global Ecological Health resource section at the end of this chapter has numerous aids to help anyone be more ecologically responsible.

*The world now stands on the brink of the final abyss. Let us all resolve to take all possible steps to ensure that we do not, through our own folly, go over the edge.*

**Earl Mountbatten**

## ENVIRONMENTAL HEALTH RESOURCES

★Denotes Best of the Best Resources

## Personal Environmental Health— Toxics and Allergy

*When we try to pick out anything by itself,
we find it hitched to everything else
in the universe.*

**John Muir**

### *Books*

Berthold-Bond, Annie. *Clean & Green: The Complete Guide to Nontoxic and Environmentally Safe Housekeeping.* Ceres Press, 1990.

Bower, John. *The Healthy House.* Carol Communications, 1989.

★Dadd, Debra Lynn. *The Non-Toxic Home & Office.* Tarcher, 1992.

★Dadd-Redalia, Debra. *Sustaining the Earth: Choosing Consumer Products That Are Safe for You, Your Family, and the Earth.* Morrow & Co., 1994.

*Everyone's Guide to Toxics in the Home.* Available from Greenpeace USA, 1436 U St. NW, Washington DC 20009; (202) 462-1177; (202) 319-2444.

*Fighting Toxics: A Manual for Protecting Your Family, Community, and Workplace.* Island Press, 1990. Available from National Toxics Campaign, 1168 Commonwealth Ave., Boston, MA 02134; (617) 232-0327.

Goldman, Benjamin. *The Truth About Where You Live: An Atlas for Action on Toxins and Mortality.* Random House, 1991.

★Golos, Natalie and Golos, Francis. *Coping With Your Allergies.* Simon and Schuster, 1979.

*A Guide to Hazardous Products Around the Home,* Household Hazardous Waste Project, 1989. Available from Household Hazardous Waste Project, 1031 E. Battlefield, Suite 214, Springfield, MO 65807; (417) 889-5000.

Harte, John et al. *Toxics from A to Z: A Guide to Everyday Pollution Hazards.* 1991.

Lawson, Lynn. *Staying Well in a Toxic World.* Noble Press, 1994.

Makower, Joel; Elkington, John; and Hailes, Julia. *The Green Consumer.* Penguin, 1993.

★Philpott, William and Kalita, Dwight. *Brain Allergies: The Psycho-Nutrient Connection.* Keats, 1980.

Randolph, Theron and Moss, Ralph. *An Alternative Approach to Allergies—The New Field of Clinical Ecology Unravels the Environmental Causes of Mental and Physical Ills.* Lippincott and Crowell, 1980.

Rogers, Sherry. *The E. I. Syndrome: "Are You Allergic to the 21st Century?" An Rx for Environmental Illness.* Prestige Publishing, P.O. Box 3161, Syracuse, NY 13220; (315) 455-7862; (800) 846-ONUS.

### *Periodicals*

*Allergy Connections,* P.O. Box 154, Pewaaukee, WI 53072; (414) 691-0960. Excellent newsletter resource for those with allergies and environmental sensitivities.

*Earth Island Journal,* 300 Broadway, Suite 28, San Francisco, CA 94133-3312.

*The Ecologist,* MIT Press Journals, 55 Hayward St. Cambridge, MA 02142; (617) 253-2889; Fax (617) 258-6779.

*E Magazine,* P.O. Box 6667, Syracuse, NY 13217-7934.

*\*Firmament: The Quarterly of Christian Ecology* and *Earthkeeping,* North American Conference on Christianity and Ecology, P.O. Box 14305, San Francisco, CA 94114; (415) 626-6064.

*Friends of the Earth,* 218 D St., SE, Washington, DC 20003; (202) 783-7400.

*Garbage,* Dovetale Publishers, 2 Main St., Gloucester, MA 01930-9941; (800) 274-9909.

*Green Alternatives,* 38 Montgomery St., Rhinebeck, NY 12572; (914) 876-6525. Ecological consumer products and ways to live more environmentally safe.

*The Green Consumer Letter,* 1519 Connecticut Ave. NW, Washington, DC 20036; (202) 332-1700; (800) 955-GREEN; Fax (202) 332-3028. Keeps track of what products and services are environmentally sound.

*Greenpeace Magazine,* Greenpeace USA, 1436 U St. NW, Washington, DC 20009.

*Mother Earth News,* P.O. Box 56302, Boulder, CO 80322-6302; (303) 447-9330.

*Plain: The Magazine of Life, Land, and Spirit.* Center for Plain Living, P.O. Box 200, Burton, OH.

*Sierra,* Sierra Club, 730 Polk Street, San Francisco, CA 94109.

*\*Voice of the Trees,* Keepers of the Earth: (215) 844-8150.

*The Wary Canary,* P.O. Box 2204, Fort Collins, CO 80522; (303) 224-0083. Helpful newsletter for people with multiple chemical sensitivities.

*World Watch,* Worldwatch Institute, 1776 Massachusetts Ave., NW, Washington, D.C. 20036; (202) 452-1999. Fax: (202) 296-7365. E-mail: Worldwatch@igc.apc.org. One of the best, most scientifically substantiated, comprehensive environmental magazines. Its contributors do a superb job of defining problems in their complexity, and more important, propose excellent solutions.

## *Organizations*

★American Environmental Health Foundation, 8345 Walnut Hill Lane, Suite 225, Dallas, TX 75231; (214) 361-9515 or (800) 428-2343. Non-profit educational and research organization. Sponsors international research and symposia for professionals in environmental medicine. Provides resources and products for the environmentally sensitive.

Citizen's Clearinghouse for Hazardous Waste, P.O. Box 6806, Falls Church, VA 22040; (703) 237-2249. Publishes *Environmental Health Monthly* and *Everyone's Backyard* journal.

Environmental Protection Agency Public Information Center, 401 M St. SW, Washington, DC 20460; (202) 260-2080; Fax (202) 260-6257. EPA Pollution Prevention Hotline and Information Clearinghouse— (202) 260-1023; Fax (202) 260-0178; E-mail: ppic@ epamail.epa.gov. A great source of free information on how to protect oneself and others from environmental contaminants.

★Human Ecology Action League (HEAL), Box 49126, Atlanta, GA 30359-1126; (404) 248-1898. Information network and support group for patients with environmental illness and allergies. Publishes the *Human Ecologist* quarterly.

National Lead Information—(800) LEAD-FYI (Hotline); (800) 424-LEAD (Clearinghouse); (800) 526-5456 (TDD).

National Pesticide Telecommunications Network— (800) 858-7378; M-F, 8 AM-6 PM Central Time. Answers a wide range of questions on nearly every aspect of pesticides and health.

Pesticide Education Center, P.O. Box 420870, San Francisco, CA 94142-0870; (415) 391-8511. Educates the public about the dangers of pesticides.

Practical Allergy Research Foundation, P.O. Box 60, Buffalo, NY 14223; (716) 875-5578. Patient education organization that, in part, emphasizes pediatric allergy and chemical sensitivity.

Toxic Substances Hot Line—(202) 554-1404.

## Special Subject Resources

### *AIR*

"Air Filters: Selecting the Right Device to Clean Your Indoor Air", Bower, John, *EastWest: The Journal of Natural Health and Living,* Sept/Oct 1992; p. 28.

Anderson, Bruce, ed. *Ecologue: The Environmental Catalogue and Consumers Guide for a Safe Earth.* Prentice Hall, 1990: 138-9.

E.L. Foust Company, Box 105, Elmhurst, IL 60126; (800) 225-9549. Well respected air filtration manufacturer.

Indoor Air Quality Information Clearinghouse, P.O. Box 37133, Washington, DC 20013-7133; (800) 438-4318; (301) 585-9020; Fax (301) 588-3408.

Radon Information Hotline, (800) 767-7236; (800) 526-5456 (TDD).

### *ALCOHOL*

### *Books*

Allen, Tom. *EEG Biofeedback Foundation: Relevant Articles, Protocols, and Procedures.* This is a workbook for teaching biofeedback technicians protocols that are helpful for a number of conditions, including addiction recovery. It is published by a biofeedback equipment supplier, the Stens Corporation, (800) 257-8367.

★Beasley, Joseph. *Wrong Diagnosis, Wrong Treatment: The Plight of the Alcoholic in America.* Random House, 1987. Discusses the role of hidden food allergy to alcohol addiction and prescribes a detailed nutritional correction procedure.

★Blum, Kenneth with Payne, James. *Alcohol and the Addictive Brain: New Hope for Alcoholics from Biogenic Research.* Macmillan Free Press, 1991.

Dorsman, Jerry. *How I Quit Drinking Without A.A.: A Complete Self-Help Guide.* New Dawn, 1991.

*Drug, Alcohol, and Other Addictions: A Directory of Treatment Centers and Prevention Programs Nationwide.* Oryx Press, 1989.

★Ketcham, Katherine and Mueller, L. Ann. *Eating Right to Live Sober.* Madrona Publishers.

★Larson, Joan. *Alcoholism—The Biochemical Connection: A Biomedical Regimen for Recovery.* Villard/ Random House, 1992.

Milam, James and Ketcham, Katherine. *Under the Influence.* Madrona, 1981.

Moore, Jean, ed. *Road to Recovery: A National Directory of Alcohol and Drug Addiction Treatment Centers.* Collier Books, 1985.

Williams, Roger. *Alcoholism: The Nutritional Approach.* Texas Press, 1978.

### *Periodicals*

*Sober Times,* (206) 523-8005.

### *Organizations*

Alcoholics Anonymous—(212) 870-3400; or look in your local Yellow Pages Directory.

Center for Science in the Public Interest, Alcohol Policies Project, 1875 Connecticut Ave., NW, Suite 300, Washington, DC 20009; (202) 332-9110.

National Clearinghouse for Alcohol Information, P.O. Box 2345, Rockville, MD 20852; (301) 468-2600; (800) 729-6686; (800) 487-4889 (TTY/TDD); (301) 230-2867 (TTY/TDD); Fax (301) 468-6433.

National Clearinghouse for Alcohol and Drug Information and Hotline, P.O. Box 2345, Rockville, MD 20852; (800) SAY-NO-TO; (301) 468-2600.

National Council on Alcoholism and Drug Dependence, 12 West 21st St., New York, NY 10010; (212) 206-6770.

National Council on Alcoholism Hotline, (800) 622-2255; in NY, (212) 206-6770.

### *Holistic-styled Alcohol Treatment Programs*

Comprehensive Medical Care, 149 Broadway Place, Amityville, NY 11701; (516) 598-2960.

Health Recovery Center, 3255 Hennepin Ave., South, Minneapolis, MN 55408; (612) 827-7800.

Milam Recovery Program for adults, 14500 Juanita Dr. NE, Bothell, WA 98011; (206) 823-3116.

Milam Recovery Program for adolescents, 12845 Ambaum Blvd., SW, Seattle, WA 98146; (206) 241-0890.

### *Alcohol-Free Vacations*

Celebrate Life Tours, Jack Wilbur and Sharon Relihan, Professional Travel Corp. P.O. Box 662, Windsor, CT 06095; (800) 825-4782; (203) 246-1614.

Sober Vacations International, 2365 Westwood Blvd., Suite 21, Los Angeles, CA 90064; (213) 470-0606.

## *ELECTROMAGNETIC RADIATION*

### *Books*

Banta, John and Banta Trish. *Current Switch: The Video—How to Reduce or Eliminate Electromagnetic Pollution in the Home & Office.* Available from Tools for Exploration and Real Goods.

Becker, Robert O. *Cross Currents: The Perils of Electropollution, The Promise of Electromedicine.* Jeremy P. Tarcher, 1990.

Brodeur, Paul. *Currents of Death: Powerlines, Computer Terminals, and the Attempt to Cover Up Their Threat to Your Health.* Simon and Schuster, 1989.

Davis, Albert and Rawls, Walter. *Magnetism and Its Effects on Living Systems.* Acres USA, 1993.

Lee, Lita. *Radiation Protection Manual.* 1990. Grassroots Network, 2061 Hampton Ave., Redwood City, CA 94061. Makes nutritional as well as other recommendations.

Smith, Cyril W. and Best, Simon. *Electromagnetic Man: Health and Hazard in the Electrical Environment.* St. Martin's Press, 1989.

Sugarman, Ellen. *Warning: The Electricity Around You May Be Hazardous to Your Health.* Simon and Schuster, 1992.

### *Periodicals*

*BEMI Currents—Journal of the Bio-Electro-Magnetics Institute,* 2490 West Moana Lane, Reno, NV 89509-3936; (702) 827-9099.

## *FOOD*

### *Books*

Garland, Anne. *For Our Kids' Sake.* Sierra Club Books, 1989. Action guide to protect children from pesticide contaminated food.

★ Golos, Natalie and Golos, Francis. *Coping With Your Allergies.* Simon and Schuster, 1979.

★ Jacobson, Michael and Lefferts, Lisa. *Safe Food: Eating Wisely in a Risky World.* Living Planet Press, 1991. Available from Center for Science in the Public Interest.

Robbins, John. *Diet for a New America.* 1987. Stillpoint Publishing, Box 640, Walpole, NH 03608; (800) 847-4014. Excellent documentation and arguments for vegetarianism and ecologically conscious eating.

Steinman, David. *Diet for a Poisoned Planet.* Random House, 1990.

## Videos

Robbins, John. *Diet for a New America.*

## Organizations

Americans for Safe Food, a branch of Center for Science in the Public Interest, 1875 Connecticut Ave., NW, Suite 300, Washington, DC 20009; (202) 332-9110.

Center for Sustainable Agriculture, 2318 Bree Lane, Davis CA 95616; (916) 756-7177.

Eden Acres, Organic Network, 12100 Lima Center Rd., Clinton, MI 49236-9618; (517) 456-4288. Publishes an international directory of organically grown food.

Institute for Alternative Agriculture, 9200 Edmonston Rd., Suite 117, Greenbelt, MD 20770; (301) 441-8777.

National Coalition Against the Misuse of Pesticides, 701 E St., SE, Suite 200, Washington, DC 20003; (202) 543-5450.

National Pesticide Telecommunications Network, (800) 858-7378. Will answer questions about the use, misuse, and disposal of pesticides.

Organic Trade Association of North America, P.O. Box 1078, 23 Ames St., Greenfield, MA 01301; (413) 774-7511; Fax (413) 774-6432.

Public Voice for Food and Health Policy, 1101 14th St., NW, Suite 710, Washington, DC 20005; (202) 371-1840.

## INFECTIOUS AGENTS

Citizens Alliance for VD Awareness, P.O. Box 1073, Chicago, IL 60648. Clearinghouse for information on sexually transmitted disease.

National AIDS Hotline (CDC), (800) 342-AIDS. Answers questions about AIDS.

National STD Hotline, (800) 227-8922. Answers questions and provides written material about sexually transmitted diseases.

Enby, Eric; Gosch, Peter; Sheehan, Michael. *Hidden Killers.* Available from World Research Foundation, 15300 Ventura Blvd., Suite 405, Sherman Oaks, CA 91403; (818) 907-5483.

## MEDICATIONS

*The art of medicine consistes of amusing the patient while nature cures the disease.*

**Voltaire**

### Books

Illich, Ivan. *Medical Nemesis: The Exploration of Health.* Pantheon, 1982.

Mendlesohn, Robert S. *Confessions of a Medical Heretic.* Contemporary Books, 1979.

### Newsletters

★ *Health Letter,* Public Citizen Health Research Group, 2000 P Street, N.W., Washington, D.C. 20036.

*The Peoples' Doctor,* P.O. Box 982, Evanston, IL 60204.

## MERCURY DENTAL AMALGAMS

*One hundred million people have toxic mercury dental amalgams in their mouths.*

### Books

Fasciana, Guy. *Are Your Dental Fillings Poisoning You? The Hazards of Mercury in Your Mouth.* Keats, 1986.

Huggins, Hal. *It's All in Your Head: Diseases Caused by Silver-Mercury Fillings* Life Sciences Press, 1989.

Queen, H.L. *Chronic Mercury Toxicity: New Hope Against an Endemic Disease.* 1988. Queen and Company, Colorado Springs, CO 80919-9938.

Ziff, Sam and Michael. *Dental Mercury Detoxification.* Bio-Probe, 1993.

Ziff, Sam and Michael. *Dentistry Without Mercury.* Bio-Probe, 1993.

### Periodicals

Danscher, Gorm, et al. "Traces of Mercury in Organs From Primates With Amalgam Fillings." *Experimental and Molecular Pathology* 52 (1990): 291-9.

Denton, Sandra. "The Mercury Cover-up: Controversies in Dentistry." *Townsend Letter for Doctors* (July 1990): 488-91.

Eggleston, David. "Effect of Dental Amalgam and Nickel Alloys on T-Lymphocytes: Preliminary Report." *The Journal of Prosthetic Dentistry* (May 1984): 617-23.

RESOURCES

Eggleston, David, and Nylander, Magnus. "Correlation of Dental Amalgam With Mercury in Brain Tissue." *The Journal of Prosthetic Dentistry,* 58:6 (Dec. 1987): 704-7.

Glantz, Per-Olof. "On Amalgam Toxicity." *International Journal of Technology Assessment and Health Care* 6 (1990): 363-8.

Hanson, M. and Pleva, J. "The Dental Amalgam Issue. A Review." *Experientia* 47 (1991): 9-22.

Kennedy, David. "Sweden Bans Amalgam After 1991." *Health Consciousness* (Feb. 1990): 49-54.

Lorscheider, Fritz. "A Source of Mercury Exposure Revealed by Whole-Body Image Scan and Tissue Analysis" *Townsend Letter For Doctors* (Dec. 1990): 840-1.

Lorscheider, F. L. and Vimy, M. J. "Mercury From Dental Amalgams." *The Lancet* (Dec. 22/29, 1990): 1578-9.

Lorscheider, Fritz and Vimy, Murray. "Mercury Exposure From 'Silver' Fillings." *The Lancet* 337 (May 4, 1991): 110.

Siblerud, Robert L. "The Relationship Between Mercury from Amalgam and Mental Health." *American Journal of Psychotherapy* 18:4 (October 1989) 575-87.

Siblerud, Robert. "Relationship Between Mercury from Dental Amalgam and Oral Cavity Health." *Annals of Dentistry* (Winter, 1990).

### *Organizations*

American Academy of Biological Dentistry, P.O. Box 856, Carmel Valley, CA 93924; (408) 659-5385; Fax (408) 659-2417. Professional association which goes beyond just the promotion of non-toxic dental procedures. It publishes *Focus* quarterly.

Environmental Dental Association, 9974 Scripps Ranch Blvd., Suite 36, San Diego, CA 92131; (800) 388-8124; (619) 586-1208. Excellent resource for information on, and referral to, progressive dental practices.

Huggins Diagnostic Center, 5080 List Dr., Colorado Springs, CO 80919; (800) 331-2303; (719) 548-1600. Provides educational materials and mercury-free dental referrals to the public, plus training and diagnostic services to professionals.

## *SMOKING*

### *Books*

Krough, David. *Smoking: The Artificial Passion.* W.H. Freeman & Co., 1991.

### *Organizations*

Action on Smoking and Health, 2013 H St., N.W., Washington, DC 20006; (202) 659-4310.

American Lung Association, 1740 Broadway, New York, NY 10019; (800) LUNG-USA; (212) 315-8700.

U.S. Dept. of Health and Human Services, Office of Smoking and Health, 5600 Fishers Lane, Rockville, MD 20857; (202) 443-1575. Or the Atlanta office: 4770 Buford Highway NE., MS K50, Atlanta, GA 30341; (404) 488-5708; Fax (404) 488-5939.

## *VACCINATIONS*

### *Books*

Buttram, Harold and Hoffman, Chriss. *Vaccinations and Immune Malfunction.* Quakertown, PA 18951: Humanitarian Publishing.

Finn, Tom. *Dangers of Compulsory Immunization: How to Avoid Them Legally.* New Port Richey, FL 33552: Family Fitness Press, P.O. Box 1658A.

James, Walene. *Immunization: The Reality Behind The Myth.* Greenwood, 1988.

Mendelsohn, Robert. *The Risks of Immunizations and How to Avoid Them.* Available from "The People's Doctor." 1578 Sherman Ave., Suite 318, Evanston, IL 60201.

Neustaedter, Randall. *The Immunization Decision: A Guide for Parents.* North Atlantic Books, 1990. North Atlantic Books, 2800 Woolsey St., Berkeley, CA 94705.

### *Organizations*

Alternatives in Mothering, Inc., 629 Brick Blvd., Suite #439, Brick, NJ 08723. A resource center for information regarding vaccinations and alternatives.

Dissatisfied Parents Together (DPT), c/o Barbara Fisher, Box 563, 1377 K St., N.W., Washington, DC 20005. Activist parents who have seen some of the damage that vaccinations can cause and are trying to remedy the situation.

National Vaccine Information Center, 512 W. Maple, Vienna, VA 22180; (800) 909-SHOT; (703) 938-DPT3; (900) 288-1222; Fax (703) 938-5768.

## WATER

### Books

Gabler, Raymond, ed. *Is Your Water Safe to Drink?* Consumer Reports Books, 1989.

★Ingram, Colin. *The Drinking Water Book: A Complete Guide to Safe Drinking Water.* Ten Speed Press, 1991.

Stewart, John. *Drinking Water Hazards.* Envirographics, 1990.

### Water Testing Organizations

CHEMetrics, Inc., Route 28, Calverton, VA 22016; (800) 356-3072; (703) 788-9026.

EPA Safe Drinking Water Hotline, (800) 426-4791.

National Testing Laboratories, Inc., 6555 Wilson Mills Road, Cleveland, OH 44143; (800) 458-3330; (800) 426-8378; (216) 449-2525.

Spectrum Laboratories, Inc., 301 West County Road, New Brighton, MN 55112.

Suburban Water Testing Laboratories, (800) 433-6595.

## SOURCES OF ENVIRONMENTALLY SAFE PRODUCTS AND TESTING KITS

Allergy Resources, P.O. Box 888, Palmer Lake, CO 80133; (800) USE-FLAX. Products for the environmentally sensitive.

American Industrial Hygiene Association; (216) 873-2442. Will provide a list of labs that do radon testing for the home.

Auro Natural Plant Chemistry, P.O. Box 857, Davis, CA 95617-0857; (916) 753-3104. Source of non-toxic home supplies.

CHEMetrics, Inc., Route 28, Calverton, VA 22016; (800) 356-3072. They can provide do-it-yourself sulfite test kits for those individuals who have severe allergic reactions to sulfites in food and wine.

Conservatree Paper Co., 10 Lombard St., Suite 250, San Francisco, CA 94111; 800 522-9200. Recycled paper supplier.

★Co-op America, 2100 M St., Suite 403, Washington, DC 20036; (202) 223-1881. Has catalog of environmentally safe and socially responsible products.

★Cutting Edge Catalog, Befit Enterprises Ltd., P.O. Box 5034, Southampton, NY 11969; (800) 497-9516. They carry a variety of excellent products and testing kits.

Dust Free Mold Test Kit, from Dust Free, Box 519 Royse City, TX 75189; (214) 635-9565. To test for excessive levels of molds and fungi in home or workplace, a major cause of allergic reactions.

Earth Care, Ukiah, CA 95482; (800) 347-0070. Green products.

Earth Options, P.O. Box 1542, Sebastopol, CA 95473. For ordering information, (800) 269-1300. For technical assistance, (707) 829-4554.

EcoSource, Atlanta, GA; (404) 350-7200; (800) 688-8345. Their catalog is another great resource of products and information.

Enviro-Clean, 30 Walnut Ave., Floral Park, NY 11001; (800) 466-1425. Environmentally sound cleaning products.

Environmentally Sound Products, 8845 Orchard Tree Lane, Towson, MD 21286; (800) 886-5432.

Frandon Lead Alert Kit, Pace Environs, 120 W. Beaver Creek Rd., Unit #16, Richmond Hill, Ontario, Canada L4B 1L2; orders (800) 359-9000; (905) 709-1996.

Healthful Hardware, P.O. Box 3217, Prescott, AZ 86302; (602) 445-8225. Natural building materials.

Heart of Vermont, P.O. Box 183, Sharon, VT 05065; (800) 639-4123.

Hendricksen Naturlich, P.O. Box 1677, Sebastopol, CA 95473-1677; (707) 824-0914. Natural building materials.

Jade Mountain, P.O. Box 4616, Boulder, CO 80306; (800) 442-1972.

LeadCheck Swabs, HybriVet Systems, Inc., P.O. Box 1210, Framingham, MA 01701; (800) 262-LEAD. Source of home lead tests.

Lehman's Hardware, One Lehman Circle, Kidron, OH 44636; (216) 857-5757. Non-electric tools.

Livos Non-Toxic Home Products, 1365 Rufina Circle, Santa Fe, NM 87501; (505) 438-3448.

★National Ecological and Environmental Delivery System, 527 Charles Ave., 12A, Syracuse, NY 13209; (800) 634-1380. "One of the largest suppliers of products for the chemically sensitive and environmentally aware."

Natural Choice, 1365 Rufina Circle, Sante Fe, NM 87501; (800) 621-2591; (505) 438-3448.

Natural Lifestyles Supplies, 16 Lookout Drive, Ashville, NC 28804; (800) 752-2775; (704) 254-9606.

★Real Goods, 966 Mazzoni Street, Ukiah, CA 95482; (800) 762-7325. The largest and the best mail order resource for alternative energy and environmentally safe products. Publishes the *Alternative Energy Sourcebook,* a *must* catalog.

Real Recycled, 1541 Adrian Rd., Burlingame, CA 94010-2107; (800) 233-5335. Recycled consumer products.

★ Seventh Generation, 49 Hercules Dr., Colchester, VT 05446-1672; (800) 456-1177.

Save Energy Company—A Planetary Store, 2410 Harrison Street, San Francisco, CA 94110; (800) 326-2120.

Sinan Company: Natural Building Materials, P.O. Box 857, Davis, CA 95617-0857; (916) 753-3104. Natural glues, paints, lacquers, waxes, polishes.

Sunelco—The Sun Electric Company, 100 Skeels St., P.O. Box 1499, Hamilton, MT 59840; (800) 338-6844.

WorldWise, 341 Third St., Suite 201, San Rafael, CA 94901; (415) 485-2882. Ecologically safe home products.

## RESOURCES FOR THE ENVIRONMENTAL HEALTH PROFESSIONAL

**Growth for growth sake is the ideology of the cancer cell.**

Edward Abbey

### Books

Dickey, Lawrence, ed. *Clinical Ecology.* Charles C. Thomas, Publisher, 1976.

Hippchen, Leonard. *Ecologic—Biochemical Approaches to Treatment of Delinquents and Criminals.* Van Nostrand Reinhold, 1978.

Levine, Stephen and Kidd, Parris. *Antioxidant Adaptation: Its Role in Free Radical Pathology.* Allergy Research Group, 1986. Contains excellent guidelines for nutritional supplementation in the correction of allergies.

Pfeiffer, Guy and Nikel, Casimir, ed. *The Household Environment and ·Chronic Illness: Guidelines for Constructing and Maintaining a Less Polluted Residence.* Charles C. Thomas, Publisher, 1980.

★ Rea, William. *Chemical Sensitivity 1-4.* Lewis, 1994-6.

*Note: Lewis Publishers, 2000 Corporate Blvd., N.W., Boca Raton, FL 33431; (800) 272-7737. Provides a wide array of publications (books, journals, software....) on environmental health issues.

### Journals

*Archives of Environmental Health,* Heldref Publications, 1319 18th St. NW, Washington, DC 20036; (202) 296-6267; (202) 362-6445.

*Bulletin of Environmental Contamination and Toxicology,* Springer-Verlag, 175 5th Ave., New York, NY 10010; (212) 460-1500.

*Environmental Periodicals Bibliography,* International Academy at Santa Barbara, 800 Garden St., Suite D, Santa Barbara, CA 93101-1552; (805) 965-5010.

*Journal of Environmental Health,* National Environmental Health Association, 720 S. Colorado Blvd. Suite 970, South Tower, Denver, CO 80222; (303) 756-9090.

*Toxicology Abstracts,* Cambridge Scientific Abstracts, 7200 Wisconsin Ave. Suite 601, Bethesda, MD 20814; (800) 843-7751; (301) 961-6700.

### Organizations

**Disease is the retribution of outraged Nature.**

Hosea Ballou

Agency for Toxic Substances and Disease Registry, Division of Toxicology, 1600 Clifton Rd., NE, MailStop E28, Atlanta, GA 30333.

★ American Academy of Environmental Medicine, P.O. Box 16106, Denver, CO 80216; (303) 622-9755. Progressive group of physicians practicing "clinical ecology" who would be most likely to use the most updated methods for identifying and treating toxic and allergic reactions to the environment. They can provide a referral to a physician nearest you. Audio tapes of the Academy's Seminars and conferences are available from Insta-Tape, Inc., P.O. Box 2926-D, Pasadena, CA 91105.

★ American Environmental Health Foundation, 8345 Walnut Hill Lane, Suite 225, Dallas, TX 75231; (214) 361-9515 or (800) 428-2343. Non-profit educational and research organization. Sponsors international research and symposia for professionals in environmental medicine. Provides resources and products for the environmentally sensitive.

Huggins Diagnostic Center, 5080 List Dr., Colorado Springs, CO 80919; (800) 331-2303; (719) 548-1600. Professional training center for dentists who want to use less toxic and reactive substances on their patients, a referral center for these physicians and ones that might be able to test for oral mercury vapor, and a diagnostic center.

★ National Center for Environmental Health Strategies, c/o Mary Lamielle, 1100 Rural Ave., Voorhees, NJ 08043; (609) 429-5358. Publishes the quarterly, *The Delicate Balance,* and provides other excellent publications on environmental health.

Pan American Allergy Society, P.O. Box 947, Fredricksburg, TX 78624; (210) 997-9853.

## *Professional Suppliers*

★ Allergy Research Group, 400 Preda St., San Leandro, CA 94577; (800) 545-9960; (510) 639-4572; Fax (510) 635-6730. Produces high quality hypo-allergenic nutritional supplements primarily for immune system repair and enhancement in individuals suffering from allergies, toxic reactions, and environmental illness. They provide excellent educational materials and workshops to professionals on these clinical issues.

## ★ *Physician Laboratories Using Advanced Allergy, Nutritional, Toxicological or Immunological Testing*

Doctor's Data Inc., P.O. Box 111, 170 W. Roosevelt Rd., W. Chicago, IL 60185; (800) 323-2784.

Great Smokies Diagnostic Laboratory, 18 A Regent Park Blvd., Asheville, NC 28806; (800) 522-4762.

Immuno Laboratories, 1620 W. Oakland Park Blvd., Ft. Lauderdale, FL 33311; (800) 231-9197 nationally; in Florida, (800) 628-4300; (305) 486-4500; Fax (305) 739-6563.

Meridian Valley Clinical Laboratory, 515 W. Harrison St., Suite 9, Kent, WA 98032; (206) 859-8700; Drs. only line (800) 234-6825. One of the most progressive, high-quality clinical labs in the country on the leading edge providing an array of functional biochemical tests to determine nutritional needs and environmental response. They also sponsor educational programs for physicians, upgrading their ability to use advanced testing.

MetaMetrix Medical Laboratory, 5000 Peachtree Ind. Blvd., Suite 110, Norcross, GA 30071, (800) 221-4640; (404) 446-5483. Another excellent multi-service lab.

Monroe Medical Research Laboratory, Route 17, P.O. Box 1, Southfields, NY 10975; (800) 831-3133; (914) 351-5134; Fax (914) 351-4295. Another excellent multi-service lab.

National BioTechnology Laboratory, 3212 NE 125th St., Seattle, WA 98125; (800) 846-6285; (206) 363-6606; Fax (206) 363-2025. Another excellent multi-service lab.

Serammune Physicians Laboratory, 1890 Preston White Drive, Suite 200, Reston, VA 22091; (800) 553-5472; (703) 758-0610; Fax (703) 758-0615. This superb lab specializes in the most advanced type of immunological tests (ELISA/ACT™) to determine a person's reactivity to environmental agents including food. This lab publishes a very helpful, multi-faceted, immune enhancement handbook compiled by the Health Studies Collegium.

SpectraCell Laboratories, 515 Post Oak Blvd., Suite 830, Houston, TX 77027; (800) 227-5227; (713) 621-3101; Fax (713) 621-3234. Provides two specialty tests: Essential Metabolic Analysis (EMA), a functional nutrient status blood test and Spectrox, a functional antioxidant capacity blood test.

*Note: If testing is needed to discover specific human environmental contamination in puzzling cases of toxic exposure the following two labs can analyze the broadest spectrum of chemicals in body tissues:

Accu-Chem Laboratories, 990 North Bowser Rd., Suite 800, Richardson, TX 75081; (800) 451-0116; in TX, (214) 234-5412.

Pacific Toxicology, 1545 Pontius Ave., Los Angeles, CA 90025; (310) 479-4911.

*Note: If close monitoring or hospitalization for difficult cases of environmental illness is necessary, contact the American Academy of Environmental Medicine for a list of specialized, environmental isolation facilities staffed by well-trained physicians. Below are two of the best:

Environmental Health Center, 8345 Walnut Hill Lane, Suite 205, Dallas, TX 75231; (214) 368-4132. Outpatient clinic doing the most progressive testing and multifaceted treatment for the chemically sensitive.

Environmental Control Unit, Tri-Cities Hospital, 7525 Scyene Road, Dallas, TX 75227; (214) 275-1430; (214) 381-7171. Has specialized environmentally controlled isolation rooms for testing extremely sensitive and seriously ill people with toxic and allergic problems.

## Global Ecological Health

*Mindfulness Prayer To Be Done*
*While Washing Hands:*
*Water flows over these hands.*
*May I use them skillfully*
*to preserve our precious planet.*
**Thich Nhat Hanh**

Note: An * denotes a resource that draws a close link between spirituality and ecology.

### *Books*

Anderson, Bruce, ed. *Ecologue: The Environmental Catalogue and Consumer's Guide for a Safe Earth.* Prentice Hall, 1990.

American Council for an Energy-Efficient Economy. *A Consumer Guide to Home Savings: Listings of the Most Efficient Products You Can Buy.* 1990.

*Badiner, Allan. *Dharma Gaia: A Harvest of Essays in Buddhism and Ecology.* Parallax Press, 1990.

*Berry, Thomas. *The Dream of the Earth.* Nature & Natural Philosophy Library, 1990.

Bill, David. *Practical Home Energy Savings.* Rocky Mountain Institute, 1991.

Brown, Lester and Kane, Hal and Ayres, Ed. *Vital Signs 1993: The Trends That Are Shaping Our Future.* Wordwatch Institute, 1993.

Corson, Ben, et al. *Shopping for a Better World.* 1989.

Earth Works Group. *50 Simple Things You Can Do to Save the Earth.* Earthworks Press, 1989.

Earth Works Group. *Recycler's Handbook: Everything You Need to make Recycling a Part of Your Life.* Earthworks Press, 1990.

*Easwaran, Eknath. *The Compassionate Universe: The Power of the Individual to Heal the Environment.* Nilgiri Press, 1989.

Elkington, John; Hailes, Julia; Makower, Joel. *The Green Consumer.* Viking/Penguin, 1990.

Global Tomorrow Coalition. *The Global Ecology Handbook: What You Can Do About the Environmental Crisis.* Beacon Press, 1990.

Greenline, Stewart. *Environmental Directory: Products, Technologies, Services, Organizations.* Available from Real Goods.

Keller, Hans, ed. *Who Is Who in Service to the Earth.* VisionLink Education Foundation, 1991. Extensive environmental resource guide available from Vision-Link Education Foundation, 47 Calhoun Rd., Waynesville, NC 28786; (704) 926-2200; Fax (704) 926-9041.

MacEachern, Diane. *Save Our Planet.* 1990.

*Macy, Joanna. *World as Lover, World as Self.* Parallax Press, 1991.

*Macy, Joanna; Seed, John; Fleming, Pat; Naess, Arne. *Thinking Like a Mountain: Toward a Council of All Beings.* New Society Publishers, 1988.

*McDonagh, Sean. *To Care for the Earth: A Call to a New Theology.* Bear & Co., 1986. The book examines some theological aspects to environmentalism.

Media Network, 39 W. 14th St., Suite 403, New York, NY 10011; (212) 929-2663; (212) 929-2732. Sells a media guide, *Safe Planet: The Guide to Environmental Film and Video.*

Milbrath, Lester. *Envisioning a Sustainable Society: Learning Our Way Out.* SUNY Press, 1989.

Naar, John. *Design for a Livable Planet: How You Can Help Clean Up the Environment.* Harper and Row, 1990.

National Wildlife Federation, *1994 Conservation Directory.* National Wildlife Federation, 8925 Leesburg Pike, Vienna, VA 22184; (800) 432-6564. Extensive listing of private and governmental groups and resources.

Porritt, Jonathon. *Save the Earth.* Turner Publishing, 1991.

Porter, Gareth and Brown, Janet. *Global Environmental Politics.* Westview Press, 1991.

Rich, Bruce. *Mortgaging the Earth: The World Bank, Environmental Improvement, and the Crisis of Development.* Beacon Press, 1993.

Rifkin, Jeremy. *The Green Lifestyle Handbook: 1001 Ways You Can Heal the Earth.* Henry Holt and Company, 1990.

Roszak, Theodore. *The Voice of the Earth.* Simon and Schuster, 1992.

Wilson, Alex. *Consumer Guide to Home Energy Savings.* 1990, American Council for an Energy-Efficient Economy, 1001 Connecticut Ave. N.W., Suite 535, Washington D.C. 20036.

Seymour, John and Giradet, Herbert. *Blueprint for a Green Planet: Your Practical Guide to Restoring the World's Environment.* Prentice Hall, 1987.

World Resource Institute. *Environmental Almanac,* Houghton Mifflin (annual). An extensive compendium of useful facts and information regarding environmental issues.

# Environmental Organizations

*Be like a tree in pursuit of your cause.*
*Stand firm, grip hard, thrust upward,*
*bend to the winds of heaven,*
*and learn tranquility.*

Dedication to
Richard St. Barbe Baker,
Father of the Trees

African Wildlife Foundation, 1717 Massachusetts Ave. NW, Suite 602, Washington, DC 20036; (202) 265-8393; Fax (202) 543-6142.

American Rivers, 801 Pennsylvania Ave. SE, Suite 303, Washington, DC 20003; (202) 547-6900. Tries to protect wild and scenic rivers.

Citizen's Clearinghouse for Hazardous Waste, P.O. Box 926, Arlington, VA 22216.

Conservation and Renewable Energy Inquiry and Referral Service, Renewable Energy Information, P.O. Box 3048, Merrifield, VA 22116; (800) 523-2929.

Conservation International, 1015 18th St. NW, Suite 1000, Washington, DC 20036; (202) 429-5660.

Defenders of Wildlife, 1101 14th St., Washington, DC 20005; (202) 682-9400.

Ecopsychology Institute, California State University at Hayward. Publishes *Ecopsychology Newsletter,* P.O. Box 7487, Berkeley, CA 94707-0487; (415) 455-5957. Important articles on how psychological health interacts with ecological health.

Elmwood Institute, P.O. Box 5765, Berkeley, CA 94705; (415) 845-4595. A clearinghouse for information on ecological restoration projects.

Emergency Planning and Community Right-to-Know Act Hotline and Superfund Hotline, Environmental Protection Agency, OS -120, 401 M St., S.W. Washington, DC 20460; (800) 535-0202.

Energy Efficiency and Renewable Energy Clearinghouse, P.O. Box 3048, Merrifield, VA 22116; (800) DOE-EREC. Provides fact sheets on various energy conservation subjects and handles telephone inquiries, whether technical or general.

★Greenpeace, (U.S. Headquarters) 1436 U St., NW, Washington, DC 20009; (202) 462-1177; Fax (202) 462-4507; Chicago office, 847 West Jackson Blvd., Chicago, IL 60607; (312) 563-6060; Seattle office, 4649 Sunnyside Ave., N., Seattle, WA 98103; (206) 632-4326; San Francisco office, 139 Townsend St., San Francisco, CA 94107; (415) 512-9025; New York office, 462 Broadway, New York, NY 10013; (212) 941-0994.

Institute for Global Communications, 18 DeBoom St., First Floor, San Francisco, CA 94107; (415) 442-0220. Operates EcoNet, an on-line computer conference and bulletin board for environmental activism, as well as PeaceNet, ConflictNet, and Global Action Net.

International Union for the Conservation of Nature, 1400 16th St., NW, Washington, DC 20036; (202) 797-5454.

*Keepers of the Earth, 5500 Wissahickon, Suite 804C, Philadelphia, PA 19144; (215) 844-8150. Jewish spiritual ecology organization. It develops school programs and publishes *Voice of the Trees.*

National Recycling Coalition, 1101 30th street, NW, Suite 305, Washington, DC 20006.

Natural Resources Defense Council, 40 W. 20th St., New York, NY 10011; (212) 727-2700. Attorneys and scientists trying to do what the Environmental Protection Agency should be doing.

*North American Conference on Christianity and Ecology, P.O. Box 14305, San Francisco, CA 94114; (415) 626-6064. A Christian organization trying to rediscover a spiritual stewardship of the Earth. It has established the Green Cross, similar to the International Red Cross, but orienting its work to saving endangered ecosystems. It also publishes the quarterly, *Firmament: The Quarterly of Christian Ecology* and the bimonthly, *Earthkeeping.*

Rainforest Action Network; (800) 989-7246.

Rainforest Alliance; (212) 677-1900.

★Rocky Mountain Institute, 1739 Snowmass Creek Road, Old Snowmass, CO 81654-9199; (303) 927-3851; Fax (303) 927-4178. Top-notch research, educational, and consulting organization with emphasis on energy conservation and alternatives.

★Sierra Club, 730 Polk St., San Francisco, CA 94109; (415) 665-9008; Fax (415) 776-0350; Washington, DC office; (202) 547-1141.

Sierra Club Legal Defense Fund, 180 Montgomery, San Francisco, CA 94105-4209; (415) 627-7600. Aggressive attorneys who sue polluters.

Society for Ecological Restoration and Management, University of Wisconsin Arboretum, 1207 Seminole Hwy., Madison, WI 53711; (608) 262-9547. Publishes *Restoration & Management Notes* and *Restoration Ecology.*

Solid Waste Information Clearinghouse, Environmental Protection Agency, (800) 67-SWICH.

Toxic Release Inventory User Support Service, Environmental Protection Agency, Office of Pollution Prevention and Toxics, OPPT Library (7407), 401 M St., S.W. Washington, DC 20460; (202) 260-1531.

RESOURCES

*United Nations' Environment Programme—International Coordinating Committee on Religion and the Earth plus the Environmental Sabbath, UNEP, DC-803, United Nations, New York, NY 10017; (212) 963-8094.

★ Wilderness Society, P.O. Box 296, Federalsburg, MD 21632-1296; (212) 833-2300.

Wildlife Conservation International, New York Zoological Society, 185th St. and South Blvd., Bldg. A, New York, NY 10460; (212) 220-5155.

★ Worldwatch Institute, 1776 Massachusetts Ave., NW, Washington, D.C. 20036; (202) 452-1999. Think tank and research organization involved with increasing public awareness of global environmental issues while also advocating local activism. A cost-effective place to put some of your environmental donation dollars.

## Computer Games

*Balance of the Planet*—Environmental education game.
*SimEarth*—Ecological survival game based on the Gaia hypothesis

## Computer Networks and Software

*Awakening Technology,* Awakening Technology, 695 Fifth St., Lake Oswego, OR 97034, (503) 635-2615. Computer conference seminars to unlock human potential. Some related to ecology like "Earth and Spirit."

*EcoNet,* Institute for Global Communications, 18 DeBoom St., San Francisco, CA 94107; (415) 442-0220. Largest global environmental computer conferencing system.

*EnviroNet,* 139 Townsend St., 4th Floor, San Francisco, CA 94107. Another computer conference network.

Rittner, Dan. *Ecolinking: Everyone's Guide to Online Environmental Information.* Peachpoint Press, 1992. A guidebook to environmental computer networking.

*RTK Net,* OMB Watch, 1742 Connecticut Ave., NW, Washington, DC 20009-1171; (202) 234-8494; Fax (202) 234-8584; E-Mail: ombwatch@rtknet.org. Non-profit computer network that has a free environmental database.

*TOXNET,* National Library of Medicine, Bethesda, MD. Computer database that contains the EPA's Toxics Release Inventory.

## Videos

Bullfrog Films, P.O. Box 149, Oley, PA 19547; (800) 543-3764. Wide selection of environmental films.

## REFERENCES

*Facts do not cease to exist*
*because they are ignored.*

**Aldous Huxley**

1. Bruce Anderson, ed., *Ecologue: The Environmental Catalogue and Consumers Guide for a Safe Earth* (Prentice Hall, 1990).
2. National Institute on Alcohol Abuse and Alcoholism, and the Office for Substance Abuse Prevention.
3. Michael Renner, "War on Nature," *Wordwatch* (May-June, 1991) 20.
4. John Wright, ed. *The Universal Almanac* (Andrews and McMeel, 1990) 535.
5. World Resources Institute, *Environmental Almanac* (Houghton Mifflin, 1991) 151.
6. Albert Fritsch, ed., *The Household Pollutants Guide* (Anchor Press, 1978) 58.
7. Michael Jacobson and Lisa Lefferts, *Safe Food: Eating Wisely in a Risky World* (Living Planet Press, 1991) 14.
8. Jacobson and Lefferts, *Safe Food,* 150.

*My heart is tuned to the quietness that the stillness of nature inspires.*

**Hazrat Inayat Khan**

# CHAPTER TEN

# SPIRITUAL HEALTH

*Know that, by nature, every creature seeks to become like God.*

Meister Eckhart

*Being one with the universe, one with God—that is what we wish for most, whether we know it or not.*

Fritz Kunkel

Holistic health is, in a paradoxical way, really ours already. It exists for us here and now just as we are. There are intertwining threads to the Web of Life that make us whole because our essence is not a personal self but rather the Universe in its totality. Spirit, Unity, God, the Universe, whatever one wants to call it, is all-encompassing. It is non-dualistic. It contains the good and the bad, joy and sorrow, thriving and suffering. We are all One at the core, not separate. The Universe is one seamless whole of matter, energy and meaning. As individuals, we are all interdependently arising with everything in the universe, whether or not we realize it or acknowledge it.

If we realize it deeply, some call this enlightenment. And there have been throughout history, in different esoteric branches of religions, systematic descriptions of different levels of *realization* of this Reality or Truth. These descriptions are quite similar regardless of religious persuasion. The *Mahamudra* is an excellent, representative text that details the stages of Understanding or consciousness evolution from a Buddhist perspective and also recommends particular spiritual practices helpful at each stage. But there is a big difference between the reality of our true Oneness and the different depths of realization of that reality. Most people have simply an intellectual conception of

this, if they even believe in a Universality of Spirit or Essence at all. Most people still hold on to religious beliefs that encourage exclusiveness and separation. Primarily, we will be discussing in this chapter, and providing resources for, authentic spiritual approaches to the direct experience of this Oneness rather than intellectualization about it.

A true, deep appreciation of this all-encompassing Current that intertwines the Universe tells us that we are that part of God that has the ability to be aware of Itself. It's as if God or the Universe were a body, and an individual was the eye that could look into a mirror and realize it is not just an eye but rather a part of a larger whole. Our brain gives us this ability to tap the Mind-at-Large and be the eye that perceives the grander whole.

*Every individual is an expression of the whole realm of nature, a unique action of the total universe.*

Alan Watts

This *acknowledgment* of Oneness evokes an expression of an inherent responsibility of the individual to care for all the parts of the Universe, including the personal self, to the best of one's ability. Not for the sake of our personal desires and private goals, but to augment our capacity to embrace and love more of the Universe.

The greater the realization of Unity, the more it drives us outside of our personal skin to make efforts in the world-at-large—to help others less fortunate and the biosphere which supports life. When we have this expansive level of consciousness, we can comprehend our True Identity and not be deceived into thinking that we are merely a bag of bones, fluid, and thoughts.

The greater this *awareness* of Unity the more we can see the common goals and meaning of different religions and philosophies, and the less we dwell on highlighting differences. An admirable documentation of the basic similarities of the major religions of man is Aldous Huxley's *The Perennial Philosophy*. For those who might think that there is only one way of experiencing spiritual insight or only one valid religious belief system, Piero Ferrucci's *Inevitable Grace* shows how some 200 famous men and women realized spiritual insight while traveling different spiritual paths.

For scientists, men and women of logic, and atheists, an intriguing exploration is Ken Wilbur's *Quantum Questions*. It is an investigation of what the world's great physicists thought about esoteric mysticism and how their own spiritual views arose.

*The most beautiful and most profound emotion*
*we can experience is the sensation*
*of the mystical. It is the sower of all true science.*
*He to whom this emotion is a stranger,*
*who can no longer stand in awe*
*is as good as dead.*
*That deeply emotional conviction of the presence*
*of a superior reasoning power, which is*
*revealed in the incomprehensible universe,*
*forms my idea of God.*
**Albert Einstein**

Intense scientific inquiry into the essence of natural phenomena can elicit spiritual insight. Does this arise out of long-term concentration, curiosity, the search for truth—all outer-directed, thus expanding consciousness and programming an identification with something other than the personal self? The mystical bent of the 20th century's most famous physicists is an interesting phenomenon to explore.

We all need to translate the basic principles presented here into the spiritual or "non-spiritual" language and constructs with which we are most comfortable. It is hoped that the resources provided will allow many to expand their horizons and gain that which is offered by other, possibly unfamiliar, spiritual practices.

Although every effort was made to draw from varied religious experiences, a predominance of Buddhist references and views might be perceived. There are several reasons for this. These are the spiritual practices and writings with which the author is most familiar. But more importantly, Buddhism, unlike any other major religion, strongly cautions against dogma, religious authority, and exclusiveness. The Buddha's *Kalama Sutra* has very deliberate warnings not to believe anything just on hearsay, the word of a religious teacher, scriptures, or even the Buddha himself. The instructions are to listen carefully to spiritual teachings, observe and analyze everything in life, evaluate all questions from a foundation of personal experience, feel internally what is right for the benefit of all living beings, and only then, when you feel it is in concert with heart and mind, live by that.

Buddhism is also the only major world religion that you can take parts of and integrate into your life without having to "adopt Buddhism" as your religion. It is perfectly acceptable and workable to take certain practices, like any of its various meditative techniques or mindfulness exercises, and use them in complementary harmony with your own religious practices or incorporate them into your life without religious overtones. There are no efforts to "convert" people to a certain belief. Also, the esoteric discipline of Buddhism has been very well organized and systematized over the centuries and therefore provides easy-to-follow guidelines and well marked pitfalls of practice.

## DIFFERENT TYPES OF SPIRITUAL PRACTICES

With respect to esoteric disciplines for the direct realization of Unity (as opposed to exoteric teachings—beliefs about reality) different types of spiritual practices have been developed over the centuries to enhance this awareness beyond the state of a mere idea or belief.

*Going to church or temple doesn't make you spiritual any more than going to the garage makes you an automobile.*

**Unknown**

Most of these practices involve altering normal consciousness and changing one's identification away from personal selfhood to an "extended Self." We will investigate these avenues individually, but it must be remembered that none of them excludes the others. In fact, the more of these practices that can be judiciously incorporated into daily life, the better.

## TREAT YOUR BODY AS A TEMPLE OR INSTRUMENT OF GOD. DO NOT DEFILE IT WITH TOXIC SUBSTANCES OR HARMFUL ACTIVITIES. PROTECT AND NURTURE IT WITH GREAT CARE.

*Remember, the body is just a rental unit wherein Life resides and the Universe expresses itself.*
*From the moment we are given this body no one knows when the rental agreement expires.*
*The body should thus be treated as a Temple of God and be cared for as such.*
*Not so much with irrelevant primping and perfuming or excessive indulgences,*
*but meaningful care, and with an attitude of non-attachment.*
*For all temples crumble, whether built of stone or flesh.*
*They are built anew . . . in another time and another place.*
*The Life Energy of the Universe continues its unfoldment.*

**Thomas M. Collins**

It is tragic to see the many people who hold high spiritual values but abuse the body. Often it is just a lack of knowledge or effort in caring for the body. But sometimes it is a matter of insane rationalization or abrogation of personal responsibility, as if God did not give us the power of reasoning and choice: "God will take me when He decides, whether I smoke and drink or not." Or, "The body is just an illusion anyway." Or my favorite, "We don't need medicines or doctors, faith in God is all that cures."

*The strongest principles of growth lie in human choice.*

**George Eliot**

There is significant documented evidence of physical healings due to spiritual transformations, prayer, and lovingkindness guided imagery. But it is a far stretch to force that data to the conclusion

that we needn't pay attention to all the other aspects of our being. Yes, spirit can be referred to as the thread that binds us all together as one—definitely a powerful force—but not the thread that mends all ills at all levels.

It is also important to see how our spiritual lives cannot be fully expressed if the body and mind do not work properly. Religious institutions could do much more to assist people through this kind of spiritual growth. Churches and other religious organizations possess untold potential for improving physical and mental well-being and thus advancing spiritual values.

It is no longer sufficient for churches to simply and dogmatically dictate "Just Say No to Drugs and Alcohol!" In this day and age it is necessary to be more scientific in our understanding of why people turn to intoxicants and harmful lifestyles. We can be more sophisticated in how we help them live without being so destructive.

## REGULARLY EXPOSE THE MIND TO READING SPIRITUAL WRITINGS.

*Man's mind, once stretched by a new idea, never regains its original dimensions.*

**Oliver Wendell Holmes**

In the same vein as "you are what you eat," we are what influences our mind. Exposure to the ideas and values of spiritual leaders from many different religions brings a thoughtfulness about universal values. Contemplation of diversity in views breeds tolerance. Conversely, cluttering the mind with "entertainment" reading or viewing can be detrimental to our psycho-spiritual health. This is particularly so when our mind is assaulted by violence, greed, vanity, fear, and hatred.

It is not necessary to have high intellectual knowledge of religious scriptures, or even the ability to read, to have deep spiritual insights, attain enlightenment, or reach heaven. It might even be argued that infants and young children have a deeper spiritual sense that is inborn, uncontaminated by conditioning or the beliefs of others. But for many people, an education that penetrates deeply into matters of spiritual philosophy and practice is very spiritually fulfilling. Repetitive exposure to media that emphasize violence, greed, hatred, and fear, without counterbalanced programming of compassion, generosity, love, courage and other spiritual virtues, spells disaster.

It is also true that too many "religious" teachings, possibly better termed as indoctrinations, affect true spiritual development adversely. Called into question here is any aspect of religious thought, belief, or action that encourages any form of separation, either between one person and another, one nation and another, one religion and another, or even between man and God. Many people have deeply felt, spiritually unifying, experiences or alterations in consciousness. These dramatic changes in life perspective are often referred to as being born-again, or as enlightenment, depending on one's culture and religious background. Often the people who have these powerful spiritual awakenings make the error of trying to interpret their meaning through the distortions of a narrow or biased religious context, thus diluting or even erasing the potential benefits of these experiences.

Since true spiritual development implies an embrace of the entire Universe, it involves an expansion of the mind and consciousness to know deeply about everything. This is an inner knowledge that is experienced and not found in books. By the most respected accounts, it is far superior to academic learning of religious beliefs.

But still, it is disturbing to know that 30,000,000 Americans couldn't read any religious scriptures even if they wanted to, because of rampant illiteracy.

*The [human] brain ... is the only example of evolution providing a species with an organ which it does not know how to use.*

**Arthur Koestler**

## REGULARLY SIT IN MEDITATIVE OR CONTEMPLATIVE SILENCE.

*Our normal waking consciousness, rational consciousness as we call it, is but one special type
of consciousness, whilst all about it, parted from it by the filmiest of screens,
there lie potential forms of consciousness entirely different....
No account of the universe in its totality can be final which leaves these other forms
of consciousness quite disregarded ... they forbid a premature closing of our accounts with reality.*

**William James**

There are spiritual practices that use predominantly mental exercises like concentration practices, introspection, mindfulness activities, contemplative prayer, affirmations, and rituals. Every religion uses some of these practices because of its power to alter consciousness in a way that de-emphasizes attachment to a personal agenda and refocuses attention to our "higher spiritual Being."

It is amazing to witness the transformations that occur when the automatic babbling of the mind is allowed to stop. The whispers of spirit are much more easily heard with a silent mind.

### *We are caught in a traffic jam of discursive thought.*

**Chogyam Trungpa Rinpoche**

Spiritual teachers from long ago to the present have realized the effect of one-pointed concentration exercises—tranquility—a quality essential for spiritual insight. It also provides a necessary prelude to deep introspection.

For millennia the sacramental application of drugs has been used to achieve similar states of inner illumination by *drastically* altering consciousness. In primitive cultures this has taken the form of shamanistic rituals using botanicals such as peyote, mescaline, and cannabis. In modern times hallucinogens like LSD, or empathogenic chemicals like MDA and MDMA, have been used in transpersonal psychotherapeutic settings to expand one's sense of self. Needless to say, these are approaches that require extreme caution, expert supervision, and are appropriate for only a select type of spiritual aspirant.

Contemplative prayer, mindfulness exercises, rituals and affirmations, can act as powerful reminders of a more important agenda than our own personal melodrama.

Affirmations, or reflection on positive qualities of the soul, can help some individuals who have a very weak cultivation of certain spiritual virtues develop these qualities—joy, love, courage, strength, tolerance, truthfulness, gratitude....

### *I was going to buy a copy of* **The Power of Positive Thinking,** *and then I thought: What the hell good would that do?*

**Ronnie Shakes**

A misuse of affirmations is the unconscious application of this technique to deny or mask actual negative feelings or behaviors, thus not living with the truth of the here and now. Everyone knows smiley-faced, positive thinkers who are inwardly seething with anger, shivering in fear, hoarding greedily, or confused and uncertain. Not admitting the truth prevents correction of the problems. Affirmations have to be used very judiciously, preferably with the guidance of a respected spiritual teacher.

Petitionary prayer can sabotage spiritual growth. "Please God, let our team win this ball game." If it creates a separation between the individual and the world, or the personal self and God, there are serious problems. If you are relegating responsibility for actions to an outer agency, rather than the God within yourself, problems arise.

### *Practical Prayer is harder on the soles of your shoes than on the knees of your trousers.*

**Austin O'Malley**

Contemplative prayer is not asking some outer agency for something that the personal self wants but is more a deep introspection or internal embodiment of God, or spirit, or spiritual virtues. If we do it on a regular basis, we begin to tune into these qualities within that Self which is *both* personal and universal.

When healing prayer is directed with unconditional love and compassion, scientific research has found that it can play a dramatic role in improving physical health. Larry Dossey, M.D., in his two books, *Recovering the Soul* and *Meaning and Medicine,* documents the power of the spirit on physical health.

Mindfulness practices also act as repetitive reminders that we are something more than what our personal melodramas seem to display. These are on-going, moment-by-moment efforts at altering consciousness.

Rituals are more formalized forms of mindfulness practices. They can also be more deliberate and powerful acts to change consciousness—the whirling dances or repetitive movements of zikr in Sufism, Tibetan and Hindu chanting, Native American fasting and vision quests, and so on.

There are spiritual practices which center around devotion and surrender—devoting one's life to a teacher or teaching, surrendering the personal ego to higher authority. As an example, students of Sufism and Advaita Vedanta legitimately use this approach effectively with benefits for their practitioners, as do others. In some aberrant forms, without organized and vigilant checks and balances, there is the risk that devotional types of practice can degenerate into cultish, mindless, devotion to corrupt or unskilled teachers, causing severe disservice to one's development.

## SERVE OTHERS, PRACTICE GENEROSITY.
## DO NOT AVERT YOUR EYES FROM THE SUFFERING OF OTHERS.

### THE GOLDEN RULE

*No one of you is a believer until he desires for his brother
that which he desires for himself.*

**The Hadith of Islam**

*What is hateful to you, do not to your fellow man.
That is the entire Law, all the rest is commentary.*

**The Talmud of Judaism**

*Do not to others which if done to you would cause pain.*

**The Mahabharata of Hinduism**

*That nature only is good when it shall not do unto another
whatever is not good for its own self.*

**Dadistan-i-Dinik of Zoroastrianism**

*Hurt not others with that which pains yourself.*

**Udana-Varqa of Buddhism**

*All things whatsoever ye would that men should do to you,
do ye even so to them, for this is the law and the prophets.*

**The Bible of Christianity**

The Golden Rule, from whatever religion or culture, in whatever language, is a spiritual influence on interpersonal relationships throughout all of humanity. The degree to which it is followed dictates spiritual development. In all major religions of man there is an element of Karma Yoga, or service to others in the name of spirit. Even monks in solitary hermitage have a significant spiritual relationship with all other people on the planet. Spirituality and interpersonal relationships influence each other strongly. The health of one determines in part the health of the other.

The way of service expands our sense of self to others. In a way it is like surrendering the personal ego, not to a higher authority, but to a cause or those in need, whether it be the family or the underprivileged. There are many examples: Albert Schweitzer, Florence Nightengale, the millions of devoted mothers who get rich spiritual fulfillment from nurturing their children and family ties, and all those participating in the many service organizations for the disadvantaged.

Sometimes our livelihood is our primary mode of giving to humanity. Others dedicate a certain amount of time, effort, and money per year in volunteer services. In whatever form seems best to the individual, sharing our life energy with others can be the most spiritually uplifting acts we can do. And it is not without personal rewards. It is a well-known, documented phenomenon that helping others improves the helper's health, physically as well as emotionally and spiritually.

There are pitfalls too in this type of service. Again, it sometimes comes from blind, mindless devotion to the service without adequately looking at its potential adverse results. There are examples of religious aid organizations bringing so much relief food to an area that it ruined the local farming economy. How many millions have died in holy wars fought to save the souls of nonbelievers? On a personal level there are those who have wrapped themselves up so much in service to others they neglected their own well-being (the typical co-dependent personality) and became ill or died an early death because of it. Everyone should read *How Can I Help?* by Ram Dass and Dan Goleman, and *Compassion in Action* by Ram Dass and Mirabai Bush. They are the best books about wisely giving to others.

*In our era, the road to holiness necessarily passes through the world of action.*

**Dag Hammarskjold**

## REDUCE MATERIALISTIC CONSUMERISM.

*Superfluous wealth can buy superfluities only. Money is not required to buy one necessity of the soul.*

**Henry David Thoreau**

In many spiritual approaches there is the practice of generosity, or giving of oneself, to others or God. Again this is another way to let go of personal desires and expand the sense of self. By no means is this practice of generosity a method of purchasing enlightenment or buying our way into heaven. There is no evidence of a direct correlation between the quantity of dispersed wealth and assurance of spiritual advancement. Rather, the importance lies in the psychological quality of self renunciation for a larger vision. As economic well-being moves from sustenance to comfort, and then even more so from comfort to luxury, our tendency to identify ourselves with the material world can draw us toward ego-centeredness and the separation of self from others. This can pull us away from egoless identification with the spiritual unity of all things, if care is not taken.

*It is easier for a camel to go through the eye of a needle, than for a rich man to enter into the kingdom of God.*

**Jesus of Nazareth**

## PRACTICE A LIVELIHOOD WHICH IS BENEFICIAL TO ALL BEINGS.

*Work as if everything depends on work. Pray as if everything depends on prayer.*

**G. I. Gurdjieff**

Throughout all cultures and all religions there has been commentary concerning what is spiritually right livelihood. We do not have to work for the church to find a job that is spiritually fulfilling. Work in service of others in need has always provided an avenue for our spiritual expression of caring. So too has work with the land. In ancient times the earth was considered the sustainer of life. And today we are rediscovering this relationship with increased awareness of ecology. Jobs in this field are now seen as valuable paths to bring spirit into the realm of work.

Obviously there are also occupations that inhibit spiritual attainment. Each person's list will differ depending on culture, religion, and personal conditioning. Included in that list might be the following: interrogators who use torture; violent criminals; executioners; jobs involved with weapons, tobacco, alcohol, drugs; or in polluting businesses.

*Certain professions are more or less completely
incompatible with the achievement of
man's final end; and there are certain ways
of making a living which do so much moral,
intellectual and spiritual harm that,
even if they could be practised in a non-attached
spirit (which is generally impossible),
they would still have to be eschewed by
anyone dedicated to the task of
liberating, not only himself, but others.*

**Aldous Huxley**

*Every kind of work can be a pleasure.
Even simple household tasks can be an
opportunity to exercise and expand our caring,
our effectiveness, our responsiveness.
As we respond with caring and vision to all
work, we develop our capacity to respond fully
to all of life. Every action generates positive
energy which can be shared with others.
These qualities of caring and responsiveness are
the greatest gift we can offer.*

**Tarthang Tulku**

Spirituality's effect on our economic state is probably more complex than the most simplistic assumptions gathered from the famous quote:

*Seek first the Kingdom of Heaven
and all things will be added unto you.*

**Jesus**

Those who greedily believe in "prosperity consciousness" generally translate this quote to mean "put efforts into spiritual thoughts, words, and deeds, and you will personally grow rich with the luxuries of your prayers." Those who are more sophisticated and spiritually enlightened interpret the biblical meaning to be closer to: "As your spiritual endeavors bring greater awareness of the nature of reality, you will discover that what you identify as 'I' encompasses *all* and thus eliminates the need to acquire that which you already are." Contentment with our material possessions, no matter how meager, and loss of the need for material aggrandizement seems to accompany spiritual fulfillment.

Spirituality's effect upon our jobs, even our household tasks, can be enormous contributors to our overall health, not to mention our productivity.

This mindfulness in daily life, of which work is usually a significant part, affects all aspects of our being. Its impact on work performance can be best illustrated by the following story: A passerby noticed a bricklayer working on a new construction sight and asked what it was he was building. "A wall," the laborer replied gruffly without looking up, as he lumbered through the motions of placing additional mortar in a joint. As the passerby rounded the next corner, he noticed another bricklayer working on an adjacent wall at about the same pace as the first laborer and asked what he was erecting. "A building," the man said in a tone only slightly more pleasant than the first. Well, as the still curious passerby came to the far side of the construction site he found yet another mason. This one seemed hard at work, apparently accomplishing far more than the other two workmen put together. "What are you building?" asked the man for the third time. "Oh," exclaimed this worker, looking up with bright eyes. "This is a grand cathedral." He explained with an enthusiastic voice and animated gestures. "I am building a temple for God."

*Work is love made visible.*

**Kahlil Gibran**

## SURROUND YOURSELF WITH OTHERS WHO STRIVE TO LIVE A SPIRITUAL LIFE. AVOID VIOLENT, BITTER, DIVISIVE, AND EGOTISTICAL INDIVIDUALS.

*The traditional greeting in India is "Namaste" which translated means
"I honor the place in you in which the entire universe dwells. I honor the place in you
which is of love, of truth, of light and of peace. When you are in that place in you
and I am in that place in me, We are One."*

**Unknown**

All religions promote the activities of a cohesive spiritual community, or *sangha*. Finding support from friends and family in living a spiritual life helps at times of need. When we are in psycho-spiritual crisis there are those around us who will understand and assist. When we act too egotistically there are living reminders close by that life is meant to be lived for others. Surrounding ourselves with others who are making efforts at positive psycho-spiritual growth protects us from being overly influenced by negative individuals.

Spiritual community can be too closed, though. Congregations or spiritual communities run the risk of developing cult-like qualities if they are particularly isolated from outside influences, or lack critical self-analysis or open discussions of problems. If their religious leaders are not properly supervised by outside agencies or ethics committees, this too can pose problems. A close, supportive community of spiritual friends values truth over conformity, open communication over limits of freedom of expression, reaching out to help others rather than isolation.

## RENEW YOURSELF IN NATURE FREQUENTLY AND LEARN HER LESSONS. ATTENTIVELY PROTECT EVERYTHING IN NATURE.

*O these vast, calm, measureless mountain days ... days in whose light everything seems equally divine,
opening a thousand windows to show us God.*

**John Muir**

Inspiration from the vast beauty of Nature can be so powerful that it elicits a deep penetration into the wisdom of the Universe. All religions have noted this.

*Every part of the Earth is sacred to my people.
Every shining pine needle, every sandy shore,
every mist in the dark woods, every clearing
and humming insect is holy in the memory
and experience of my people.
The sap which courses through the trees
carries the memories of the red man.
We are part of the earth and it is part of us.
The perfumed flowers are our sisters;
the deer, the horse, the great eagle,*

*these are our brothers.
The rocky crests, the juices in the meadows,
the body heat of the pony, and man—
all belong to the same family.
One thing we know,
which the white man may one day discover—
our God is the same God.
You may think that you own Him
as you wish to own our land; but you cannot.
He is the God of man, and His compassion is
equal for the red man and the white.
The Earth is precious to Him,
and to harm the earth is to heap contempt
on its Creator ...*

**Chief Seattle**

Ecology and spirituality have some very common principles. Among them, the interconnectedness of the universe and respect for all living things. In spiritual writings of every religion and every culture, nature and natural beauty have always been associated with the evocation of spiritual insight. Spiritual development and insights also bring about a feeling, a knowing, of oneness with the natural world.

This breaks down the boundaries and hierarchies between man and other species. There is more respect and less exploitation of other sentient beings. Old, harmful interpretations of scriptures that call man to take domination over other living things are being replaced by a better understanding of both ecosystem health and spiritual unity.

> *You may never get to touch the Master,*
> *but you can tickle his creatures.*
>
> **Thomas Pynchon**

# WORK DILIGENTLY AT YOUR OWN PSYCHOLOGICAL DEVELOPMENT.

> *A little common sense, a little tolerance, a little good humor,*
> *and you don't know how comfortable you can make yourself on this planet.*
>
> **Somerset Maugham**

Modern transpersonal psychotherapies have tried to draw on a multitude of methods to systematically achieve psycho-spiritual integration. By carefully evaluating our psycho-spiritual development, specific approaches can be engaged to take advantage of our strengths or to correct psychodynamic weaknesses which prevent spiritual fulfillment.

This can help to eliminate the frequent pitfalls of spiritual activities which end up magnifying psychological problems. Often people are drawn to certain modes of spiritual engagement or practice because of strong underlying strengths. Some very outer-directed, energetic individuals are very well suited for service work. Some scientists with great powers of concentration, and a powerful drive to investigate mysteries, are graced with epiphanies because of their work in this realm. But conversely, people can be drawn toward various spiritual practices out of self centeredness or a drive to protect maladaptive, ego-defense mechanisms.

For instance, many individuals have been so emotionally or physically traumatized in youth that they have deep, ingrained emotional patterns which cut them off from their own bodies and feelings. Many have learned to escape to the comfort of the mind and thoughts at times when emotional conflict starts to be felt in the body. These individuals are frequently attracted to spiritual disciplines that center around mental exercises, which they are often quite good at. But spiritual maturity, integration, and wholeness are sabotaged, because what these individuals need most is precisely what they are avoiding—intimate contact with their bodies and emotional soul. They probably do *not* need any more reinforcement of patterns that stimulate mental activity.

Sometimes individuals who have a vivid imagination and a fantasizing mind are ill served by certain meditative practices that encourage spaciousness and expansiveness of being; these practices can further blur the person's discrimination of what is real and what is merely a creation of thoughts. More appropriate exercises might be ones that are more grounding, that center on physical sensations and active engagement in the here and now.

Some individuals who never achieved a strong, healthy sense of self might get caught up in devotional practices and have great difficulty perceiving what healthy boundaries are needed in life in the real world. The sense of one's personal self often becomes confused with that of a deity or teacher. This leads in many cases to blind obedience by followers to unskilled or corrupt religious leaders in a cult where physical, sexual, and emotional abuse occurs.

One particularly powerful psychological poison that damages spiritual development is judgments. They can be in the form of internalized parental superego attacks, self criticisms, perfectionism, or self hatred. They might also show up as judgments projected onto others or our environment, or as continual nonproductive comparisons of self and other. The damage arises from the engagement of different psychological mechanisms which obscure our true identity. When an ego is attacked by judgments it is triggered into defending a perspective in which it is a separate self, apart from others and the rest of the Universe. Self criticism also blocks trust that the Universe is unfolding perfectly as it is. Judgments obscure acceptance of reality as it *is*. When we can't accept the here and now, we are forced to act like a separate individual who needs to *do* something rather than to let his Being unfold in harmony with the Universe.

Therefore an important aid to psycho-spiritual unfoldment is careful awareness of our daily judgments and comparisons, along with a contemplative investigation into the limited self images and identities that spawn them.

With a resurgence of spiritual practices that focus on direct experience of the Spirit (whether that be a direct relationship with God as in born-again Christianity or a direct experience of enlightenment, kensho, or insight of Eastern esoteric disciplines) there seems to be a growing number of individuals who have difficulty integrating this powerful spiritual emergence into the framework of their daily lives. Transpersonal psychologists have worked with this phenomenon of spiritual emergence that becomes a spiritual *emergency*. These psycho-spiritual crises can also come during other stages of spiritual unfoldment and have been documented in all of the world's spiritual traditions. The experiential phenomena are often depicted with symptoms similar to severe psychological disturbance, emotional conflict, and mental dysfunction. People experiencing such spiritual transformations are frequently in altered states of consciousness, are disoriented by their surroundings, have difficulty relating to others, and are frightened by very unusual bodily sensations. They can think that they are possessed by the devil, going crazy, spoken to by God, undergoing a "dark night of the soul," or being assaulted by psychic forces. By looking at the experience as a difficult phase in psycho-spiritual development, professionals working at the Spiritual Emergence Network help these individuals understand and integrate their experience into the whole of their lives.

*Fear less, hope more; eat less, chew more; whine less, breathe more; talk less, say more; hate less, love more; and all good things are yours.*

**Swedish proverb**

# SPEAK KINDLY AND TRUTHFULLY.

*O' Great Spirit*
*help me always to speak the truth quietly, to listen with an open mind when others speak,*
*and to remember the peace that may be found in silence.*

**Cherokee Prayer**

*I believe that unarmed truth and unconditional love will have the final word in reality.*

**Martin Luther King, Jr.**

The truth is often agonizing, but it always leads to the here and now, which is where we need to start solving any painful situation. When we speak to others about what we think to be true, it is important to speak in a respectful, calm manner. Our truth is sometimes different from *the* truth and often different from someone else's truth. When another's perception of truth differs from ours, we sometimes get caught up in trying to prove our perspective rather than discovering the truth together. Confrontational positions can lead to stronger attachment to *our* stance. Words can turn harsh, and schisms can result. Since truth should lead us to Unity, divisive speech is not helpful. If we speak to everyone as if a saint is before us, truth will emerge and innumerable benefits will follow.

The resources at the end of the chapter will provide an excellent set of approaches to explore our spiritual wholeness.

*Men occasionally stumble across the truth,*
*but most of them pick themselves up and hurry off as if nothing had happened.*

**Winston Churchill**

# SPIRITUAL HEALTH RESOURCES

*Millions long for immortality*
*who do not know what to do with themselves on a rainy Sunday afternoon.*

**Susan Ertz**

★Denotes Best of the Best Resources

★ Almaas, A. H. *The Elixir of Enlightenment.* Samuel Weiser, 1984.

★ Almaas, A. H. *Essence.* Samuel Weiser, 1986.

★ Almaas, A. H. *Elements of the Real Man,* Diamond Books, 1987.

★ Almaas, A. H. *The Freedom to Be,* Diamond Books, 1989.

★ Almaas, A. H. *Being and the Meaning of Life,* Diamond Books, 1990.

Bragdon, Emma. *The Call for Spiritual Emergency: From Personal Crisis to Personal Transformation.* Harper/San Francisco, 1990.

Booth, Leo. *When God Becomes a Drug: Breaking the Chains of Religious Addiction & Abuse.* Tarcher, 1991.

Campbell, Joseph. *Hero with a Thousand Faces.* Princeton University Press, 1990.

Campbell, Joseph. *Inner Reaches of Outer Space.* Harper Row, 1988.

Campbell, Joseph. *The Masks of God.* Penguin, 1970-76.

Campbell, Joseph. *Myths to Live By.* Bantam, 1984.

Chittick, William. *Sufi Path of Love: The Spiritual Teaching of Rumi.* SUNY, 1984.

Cotner, June. *Graces: Prayers and Poems for Everyday Meals and Special Occasions.* HarperSanFrancisco, 1994.

Dhiravamsa, V. R. *The Way of Non-Attachment: The Practice of Insight Meditation.* Turnstone Press, 1984. Available from Blue Dolphin Publishing, Inc., P.O. Box 1908, Nevada City, CA 95959; (916) 265-6925.

Dossey, Larry. *Recovering the Soul: A Scientific and Spiritual Search.* Bantam, 1989.

Feldman, Christina and Kornfield, Jack. *Stories of the Spirit, Stories of the Heart: Parables of the Spiritual Path from Around the World.* HarperCollins, 1991.

Ferrucci, Piero. *Inevitable Grace—Breakthroughs in the Lives of Great Men and Women: Guides to your Self Realization.* Tarcher, 1990.

Fox, Mathew. *Creation Spirituality: Liberating Gifts for the Peoples of the Earth.* HarperSF, 1991.

★ Goldstein, Joseph. *The Experience of Insight: A Simple and Direct Guide to Buddhist Meditation.* Shambhala, 1983.

★ Goldstein, Joseph. *Insight Meditations: The Practice of Freedom.* Shambhala, 1993.

★ Goldstein, Joseph and Kornfield, Jack. *Seeking the Heart of Wisdom: The Path of Insight Meditation.* Shambhala, 1987.

Grof, Christina and Grof, Stanislav. *The Stormy Search for Self: A Guide to Personal Growth Through Transformational Crisis.* Tarcher, 1990.

Grof, Stanislav and Grof, Christina. *Spiritual Emergency: When Personal Transformation Becomes a Crisis.* Tarcher, 1989.

Huxley, Aldous. *The Perennial Philosophy.* Harper & Row, 1970.

Johanson, Greg and Kurtz, Ron. *Grace Unfolding: Psychotherapy in the Spirit of the Tao-te Ching.* Bell Tower, 1991.

Kaplan, Aryeh. *Jewish Meditation.* Schocken Books, 1985.

Kapleau, Philip. *The Three Pillars of Zen: Teaching, Practice, and Enlightenment.* Doubleday, 1989.

★ Kornfield, Jack. *A Path with Heart: A Guide Through the Perils and Promises of Spiritual Life.* Bantam, 1993.

Kramer, Joel & Alstad, Diana. *The Guru Papers: Masks of Authoritarian Power.* North Atlantic, 1993. A "buyer beware" guide for choosing a spiritual path.

Lao Tzu translated by Yu, Anthony C. *The Tao Te Ching: The Classic Book of Integrity and the Way.* Bantam, 1990. Out of the many translations of this classic, this is one of the best.

Lerner, Michael. *Jewish Renewal: A Path of Healing and Transformation.* Putnam, 1994.

Levine, Stephen. *Guided Meditations, Explorations and Healings.* Doubleday, 1991.

Metzner, Ralph. *Opening to Inner Light: The Transformation of Human Nature and Consciousness.* Tarcher, 1986.

Roberts, Elizabeth and Amidon, Elias ed. *Earth Prayers from Around the World: 365 Prayers, Poems and Invocations for Honoring the Earth.* Harper Collins, 1991.

Ryan, M. J. *A Grateful Heart: Daily Blessings for the Evening Meal from Buddha to the Beatles.* Conari Press, 1994.

Shah, Idries. *The Sufis.* Doubleday, 1971.

Sheinkin, David. *Path of the Kabbalah.* Paragon House, 1986. Judaic meditative practices.

Solè-Leris, Amadeo. *Tranquility and Insight: An Intro-duction to the Oldest Form of Buddhist Meditation.* Shambhala, 1986.

Tart, Charles T. *Waking Up: Overcoming Obstacles to Human Potential.* Shambhala, 1986.

Thich Nhat Hanh. *The Miracle of Mindfulness.* Beacon Press, 1987.

Thich Nhat Hanh. *The Sun My Heart.* Parallax Press, 1988.

Thich Nhat Hanh. *A Guide to Walking Meditation.* Fellowship Publications, 1985. Fellowship Publications, Nyack, NY 10960.

Thich Nhat Hanh. *Present Moment Wonderful Moment.* Parallax Press, 1990.

★ Thich Nhat Hanh. *Interbeing.* Parallax Press, 1987.

Walsh, Roger and Vaughan, Francis. *Paths Beyond Ego: The Transpersonal Vision.* Tarcher, 1993.

White, John. *What Is Enlightenment? Exploring the Goal of the Spiritual Path.* Tarcher, 1984.

★ Wilber, Ken. *No Boundary: Eastern and Western Ap-proaches to Personal Growth.* Shambhala, 1985.

Wilber, Ken; Anthony, Dick; and Ecker, Bruce, ed. *Spiritual Choices: The Problem of Recognizing Au-thentic Paths to Inner Transformation.* Paragon House, 1987.

## ★ Periodicals

### Just to be is a blessing. Just to live is holy.
**Rabbi Abraham Heschel**

*Buddhism Now,* Sharpham North, Ashprington, Totnes, Devon, TQ9 7UT, England. Bimonthly journal con-taining articles, translations, poetry and book re-views.

*Common Boundary,* 4304 East West Hwy., Bethesda, MD 20814; (301) 652-9495.

*Creation Spirituality,* Institute of Culture and Creation Spirituality, Holy Names College, 3500 Mountain Blvd., Oakland, CA 94619; (510) 436-1046; (510) 547-8073.

*The Empty Vessel: A Journal of Contemporary Taoism,* The Abode of the Eternal Tao, 1991 Garfield, Eu-gene, OR 97405.

*Gnosis,* Box 14217, San Francisco, CA 94114.

*Inquiring Mind,* P.O. Box 9999, North Berkeley Station, Berkeley, CA 94709. Bi-annual journal of the Ameri-can Vipassana Community in tabloid format con-taining articles, poetry, letters, book reviews, and spiritual retreat schedules throughout the world.

*Journal of the Order of Buddhist Contemplatives,* Shasta Abbey, P.O. Box 199, Mt. Shasta, CA 96067; (916)

926-4208. Quarterly journal with articles on Bud-dhist training and events sponsored by the Abbey and affiliated groups.

*Karuna: A Journal of Buddhist Meditation,* P.O. Box 24468, Stn. C, Vancouver, B.C. V5T 4M5 Canada.

*The Quest,* The Quest Subscriptions, P.O. Box 3000, Denville, NJ 07834-3000. This is a publication of the Theosophical Society of America; (708) 665-0130.

*ReVision: The Journal of Consciousness and Change,* Heldref Publications, 1319 18th St. NW, Washing-ton, DC 20036; (202) 296-6267; (202) 362-6445.

*Shambhala Sun,* 1345 Spruce St., Boulder, CO 80302-4886; (902) 422-8404.

*Sufi Review,* PIR Publications, 256 Post Rd. E., Westport, CT 06880.

*Tikkun,* P.O. Box 460926, Escondido, CA 92046; (800) 846-8575.

*Tricycle: The Buddhist Review,* P.O. Box 3000, Denville, NJ 07834-9897; (212) 645-1143.

*Turning Wheel: Journal of the Buddhist Peace Fellow-ship,* BPF, P.O. Box 4650, Berkeley, CA 94704; (510) 525-8596.

*Values and Visions: A Resource Companion for Spiritual Journeys;* (800) 929-4857.

## Videotapes

### Religion is a candle inside a multicolor lantern. Everyone looks through a particular color, but the candle is always there.
**Mohammed Naguib**

Hartley Film Foundation, 59 Cat Rock Road, Cos Cob, CT 06807; (203) 869-1818; (800) 937-1819; Fax (203) 869-1905. The Foundation's catalog of over 50 films encompasses many subjects relevant to holistic health. Here are a few of the most dynamic videos on spirituality:
*Voices of the New Age*
*Art of Meditation* with Alan Watts
*Islamic Mysticism: The Sufi Way* with Huston Smith
*Requiem for a Faith*
*Buddhism Comes to America*
*The Way to Baba*
These films are also available from the Institute of Noetic Sciences, 475 Gate Five Road, P.O. Box 909, Sausalito, CA 94966-0909; (415) 331-5650; (800) 383-1394.

*The Roots of Consciousness.* with Joseph Campbell, Huston Smith, Arthur Young, and Stanislav Grof from Thinking Allowed, PBS TV, and the Institute for Noetic Sciences

RESOURCES

*The Power of Myth* with Joseph Campbell and Bill Moyers. Six part series on video or audio tapes from PBS TV or the Institute of Noetic Sciences

Meridian Trust, 330 Harrow Road, London W9 2HP, UK. Has a wide selection of spiritually-oriented films, particularly on Buddhist teachings.

Mystic Fire Video, P.O. Box 2249, Levonia, MI 48150; (800) 727-8433.

Warm Rock Tapes, P.O. Box 108, Chamisal, NM 87521. Video and audio tapes of Stephen and Ondrea Levine.

## Spiritual Music and Audiotapes

### You cannot perceive beauty
### but with a serene mind.
**Henry David Thoreau**

Audio Literature, P.O. Box 7123, Berkeley, CA 94707; (800) 841-2665. Spiritual literature on tape.

Creedence Cassettes, P.O. Box 419491, Kansas City, MO 64141-6491; (800) 444-8910; (800) 333-7373. Large selection of lectures and music.

*Global Meditation* is a four volume set of multi-denominational spiritual music.

Sacred Spiritual Music, Box 1030D, Shaker Rd., New Lebanon, NY 12125; (518)794-7860.

Sounds True, 735 Walnut St., Boulder, CO 80302; (800) 333-9185; (303) 449-6229. Talks and music from many disciplines and cultures.

## Spiritual Health Organizations

### There is only one religion,
### though there are a hundred versions of it.
**George Bernard Shaw**

The Association for Transpersonal Psychology, Transpersonal Institute, P.O. Box 3049, Stanford, CA 94309; (415) 327-2066. Publishes a *Listing of Professional Members* that can be used as a referral directory when seeking a psychotherapist who incorporates a spiritual perspective in practice.

Buddhist Peace Fellowship, P.O. Box 4650, Berkeley, CA 94704; (510) 525-8596. Works for peace, environmental issues, social volunteer projects from a Buddhist perspective.

Cambridge Insight Meditation Center, 331 Broadway, Cambridge, MA 02139; (617) 491-5070.

Center for the Dances of Universal Peace, P.O. Box 626, Fairfax, CA 94978.

★ DHAT Institute, Ridhwan School, and Ridhwan Foundation, P.O. Box 10114, Berkeley, CA 94709; (510) 287-8900. The psycho-spiritual process which these organizations support comes from the work of Hameed Ali who writes under the pen name A. H. Almaas. It may be one of the best integrated programs for methodical psycho-spiritual awakening.

Insight Meditation Society, Pleasant St., Barre, MA 01005; (508) 355-4378.

Institute of Culture and Creation Spirituality, Holy Names College, 3500 Mountain Blvd., Oakland, CA 94619; (510) 436-1046.

International Association of Sufism, P.O. Box 2382, San Rafael, CA 94912; (415) 472-6959; Fax (415) 472-6221.

Spirit Rock Meditation Center, P.O. Box 909, Woodacre, CA 949733; (415) 488-0164.

Spiritual Emergence Network, 603 Mission St., Santa Cruz, CA 95060; (408) 426-0921. A hot-line for psycho-spiritual crises and referral service to psychotherapists, physicians, and spiritual practitioners who recognize the need to nurture one's psycho-spiritual transformations during apparent emergencies.

Sufi Order in the West, P.O. Box 574, Lebanon Springs, NY 12114. Non-profit educational organization providing information, publications, home study courses, and spiritual retreats.

Refer to the white pages in your telephone directory for volunteer centers in your locale or contact any environmental, peace, or service organization which would be interested in your volunteer services.

## SPIRITUAL HEALTH RESOURCES FOR THE PROFESSIONAL

*The true laws of God are the laws of
our own well-being.*

**Samuel Butler**

Following are a few texts that might have special interest to professionals. These resources have a depth and complexity which are best appreciated by those highly knowledgeable in the field of psycho-spiritual development.

★Almaas, A. H. *The Pearl Beyond Price—Integration of Personality into Being: An Object Relations Approach*. Diamond Books, 1988.

★Bragdon, Emma. *A Sourcebook for Helping People in Spiritual Emergency*. Lightening Up Press, 1988.

Namgyal, Takpo Tashi (translated by Lobsang P. Lhalungpa). *Mahamudra: The Quintessence of Mind and Meditation*. Shambhala, 1986.

Shapiro, Deane and Walsh, Roger; ed. *Meditation: Classic and Contemporary Perspectives*. 1984. Aldine Publishing Co., 200 Saw Mill River Road, Hawthorne, NY 10532.

Wilber, Ken; Engler, Jack; Brown, Daniel P. *Transformations of Consciousness: Conventional and Contemplative Perspectives on Development*. Shambhala, 1986.

## *Journals*

*I count religion but a childish toy,
And hold there is no sin but ignorance.*

**Christopher Marlowe**

*Journal of Consciousness Studies,* Jonathan Shear, Dept. of Philosophy, Virginia Commonwealth University, Richmond, VA 23284-2025; Fax (804) 282-2119.

*Journal of Transpersonal Psychology,* Association for Transpersonal Psychology, Transpersonal Institute, P.O. Box 4437, Stanford, CA 94309; (415) 327-2066.

*It is necessary, if I would truly realize the oneness of all things,
for me to live also in such a way as constantly to affirm this oneness—
by my kindness towards all beings, by compassion, by love.*

**J. Donald Walters**

RESOURCES

# PART THREE

## From Here to There:
### Starting from Known Dysfunction
### to Ideal Health

# FROM HERE TO THERE

*The greatest happiness is to know the source of unhappiness.*

Fyodor Dostoevsky

Remember those important aids in our journey toward wholeness—knowing where we are at present, how we got here, where we want to go with our life, and good roads to take us there? We obtain a good base for a new understanding when we evaluate the present and the conditions that may have led up to this point. This, combined with resources, leads us to the goal—a vision about wholeness as a goal to work toward. We presented many avenues for self-care and professional intervention in all aspects of health, ways to prioritize health care efforts and choose qualified practitioners.

Health enhancement programs presented in this book are best undertaken before dysfunction and illness arise. But since many people begin this journey with significant health problems, it is important to show how to proceed to higher levels of wellness from there.

In this chapter, we will look at the causes of several common health problems, estimate the extent to which they contribute to our ill health, then assign a multifaceted corrective procedure which will first deal with the most critical elements of the problem, then carry us to the roots of wholeness.

Pie charts are used in the next section in order to more clearly illustrate two very important principles of health: first, that physical, psychological, and social illness have many causes, and second, that the most effective correction is a multifaceted health enhancement strategy incorporating all the different aspects of our being. Often in modern medicine there is such a one-pointed focus on symptom relief that the big picture is not seen. This leads to premature termination of health services once symptoms are no longer seen. There is seldom a deep investigation into the many causes of the problem or the interdisciplinary correction of all the contributing aspects in one's life. These pie charts will also show, indirectly, but quite clearly, how inappropriate our "modern" medical-surgical disease care system is for over 90% of our health problems.

Let us say that a Circle of Illness Causation pie chart is divided into nine major contributing factors which are known to be causes for a condition. In any given individual, one of those causes might contribute 50% of the dysfunction, while another known cause contributes only 1% or zero. In another individual there might be a more even distribution of causes, with perhaps nine factors, all contributing about 11% to the development and perpetuation of the disease.

A Circle of Health Enhancement pie chart for the same illness might have ten possible, natural, corrective procedures—all contributing varying degrees of potential benefit in different individuals. For any given illness with ten corrective measures, one individual might find the therapies helping him equally, while another person might get 90% correction from just two. In one individual it might be necessary to actively engage in seven out of ten of the programs for health enhancement

## CHRONIC FATIGUE
## SUSAN

**Circle of Illness Causation**

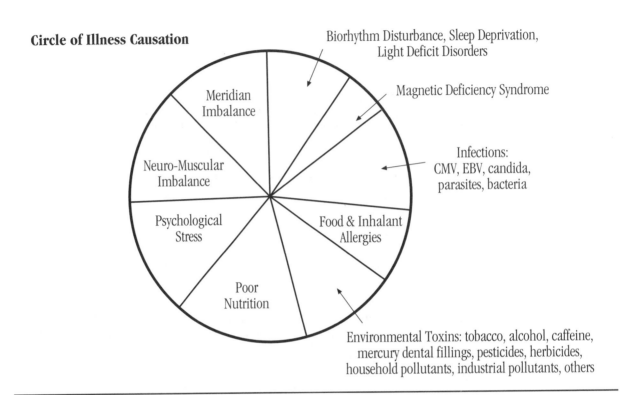

Biorhythm Disturbance, Sleep Deprivation,
Light Deficit Disorders

Magnetic Deficiency Syndrome

Infections:
CMV, EBV, candida,
parasites, bacteria

Meridian
Imbalance

Neuro-Muscular
Imbalance

Psychological
Stress

Food & Inhalant
Allergies

Poor
Nutrition

Environmental Toxins: tobacco, alcohol, caffeine,
mercury dental fillings, pesticides, herbicides,
household pollutants, industrial pollutants, others

**Circle of Health Enhancement**

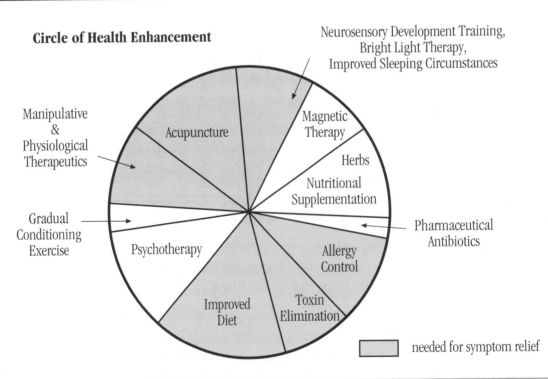

Neurosensory Development Training,
Bright Light Therapy,
Improved Sleeping Circumstances

Manipulative
&
Physiological
Therapeutics

Acupuncture

Magnetic
Therapy

Herbs

Nutritional
Supplementation

Gradual
Conditioning
Exercise

Psychotherapy

Allergy
Control

Pharmaceutical
Antibiotics

Improved
Diet

Toxin
Elimination

needed for symptom relief

## CHRONIC FATIGUE
## ANDREA

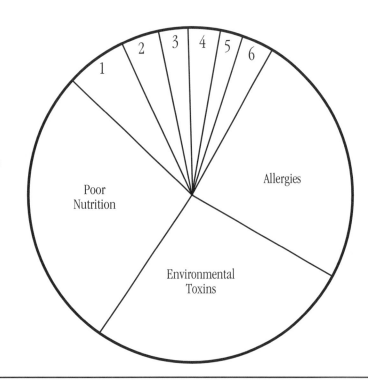

**Circle of Illness
Causation**

1. Psychological Stress
2. Neuro-muscular Imbalance
3. Meridian Imbalance
4. Biorhythm Disturbance
   Sleep Deprivation
   Light Deficit Disorder
5. Magnetic Deficiency
6. Infection

**Circle of Health
Enhancement**

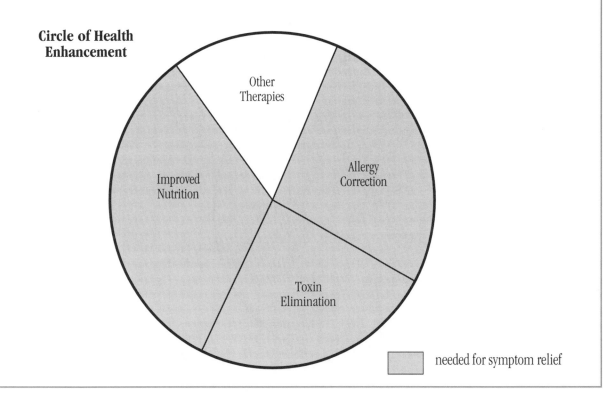

needed for symptom relief

**CHRONIC FATIGUE
TONY**

**Circle of Illness Causation**

1. Neuro-muscular Imbalance
2. Meridian Imbalance
3. Biorhythm Disturbance,
   Sleep Deprivation,
   Light Deficit Disorder
4. Magnetic Deficiency
5. Allergies
6. Environmental Toxins
7. Poor Nutrition

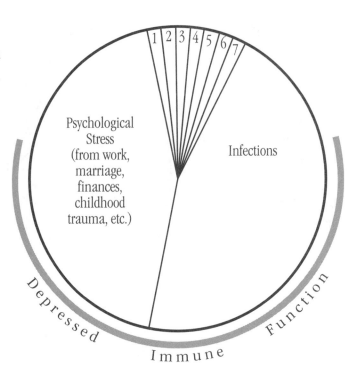

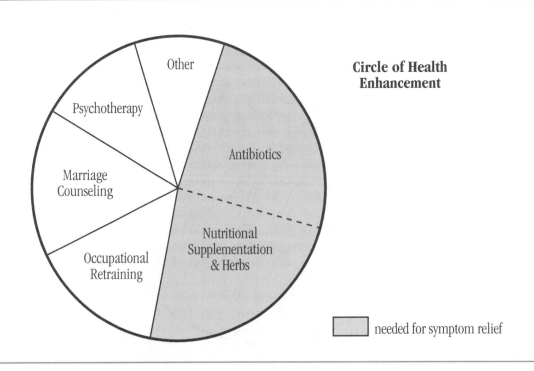

**Circle of Health
Enhancement**

needed for symptom relief

before symptom improvement is seen. Whereas another individual might start on two health enhancement programs and get total and immediate symptom improvement. This is why different therapies claim a certain percentage of success with the same condition when used in isolation rather than as part of a multidimensional, comprehensive program.

These variations are seen in the cases of Susan, Andrea, and Tony, all of whom suffered from chronic fatigue.

In the illness causation and health enhancement charts that follow, the examples given are average estimates. For any individual, these estimates may differ greatly. More research might improve upon these "guestimate" percentages, but exact percentages can never be calculated because too many factors are involved. They don't need to be completely accurate, though, if we remember some basic principles.

- Statistical, epidemiological averages are not as important as the biological diversity of individuals.

- If you strive for wellness, illness prevention will be yours, along with illness correction. If you just look at symptom or illness correction as a goal, you will miss true health, which is the wholeness and integration of all parts of your being. If you just look at illness correction as the quick fix through the eyes of "modern" medicine and use their disease care methods, the chances are great that you will not even get satisfactory symptom relief or illness correction. The problems will often worsen, and you will waste enormous amounts of money on high tech futility in the process.

- When you are on a horse ranch and hear the sounds of hooves behind you, don't expect to turn around and see a zebra. In other words, when a pie chart shows only a thin sliver don't first jump to the conclusion that your problem is caused by some rare, exotic condition or put all your hopes and dreams on that single "magic bullet" cure.

## A NOTE

These pie charts, both for cause and correction, are designed to show the *major* natural health care approaches. Occasionally medical and surgical interventions are noted when particularly important in severe cases. At other times, medical and surgical options are not listed. That does not mean they do not exist or should not be considered. Other lesser known health approaches, particularly those with little research available, are not listed but might prove valuable. Also, it is important to remember our Web of Wholeness model and realize that no matter what health difficulty a person may be experiencing, all the aspects of being are involved. Often in the pie charts education about these health alternatives—awareness enhancement, optimal sleep, governmental influences, or spiritual practices—are not mentioned. These basics help form the foundation of our health enhancement practices. For simplicity, the major elements are the only ones emphasized in the pie charts.

*A thousand ills require a thousand cures.*
**Publius Ovidius Naso**

The question is often asked: "How long will it take to get well, Doc?"

With the health enhancement suggestions that are outlined in the book, personal health recovery can be generally determined by using the following self-scoring test. The more we can place ourselves to the left of the scales, the faster and more complete the recovery. The more factors that are to the right of the scale, the slower and less complete recovery will be. Remember also not to fall into the trap of thinking that relief of symptoms is synonymous with health. Holistic health is a never-ending dance of discovery on the Path of Life.

# DETERMINATION OF RATE AND EXTENT OF HEALTH RECOVERY

## *Health Status Starting Point*

Optimal health                                    symptoms                    very sick    hospitalized
|_____|_____|_____|

## *Number of Systems Involved/Complexity of the Problem*

simple                                                                          multifacted
|_____|_____|

## *Ongoing, Adverse Stress Levels*

no stress                                                                       high stress
|_____|_____|

## *Degree of Participation in Health Enhancement Endeavors*

full participation                    mediocre cooperation          no efforts to improve
|_____|_____|

## *Number and Extent of Necessary Resources Used*

extensive use                                              a few easy, quick fixes
|_____|_____|

## *Nutritional Status*

excellent                                      average American diet          very poor
|_____|_____|

# DETERMINATION OF RATE AND EXTENT OF HEALTH RECOVERY (Cont.)

## *Fitness Level*

excellent                                          average American                    very poor
|_____|_____|_____|

## *Age*

0                                                50                                          100
|_____|_____|

## *Open-Mindedness to Holistic Health Care Approaches*

optimistic, enthusistic                          neutral            skeptical      adversarial
|_____|_____|_____|_____|

## *Family, Peer, Employer, and Social Support for Your Health Endeavors*

everyone helping                          some support          antagonistic negation of efforts
|_____|_____|

## *Financial Commitment to Total Health*

insurance and economic                                                    severely limited
position excellent                                                      economic resources
|_____|_____|

## *Quality and Open-Mindedness of Physicians and Therapists Helping You*

excellent                                     average                                   poor
|_____|_____|

# ACNE

**Beauty is truth, truth beauty . . .**

**John Keats**

Note that the pie chart illustrating the causes of acne does not include a blood deficiency of antibiotics such as tetracycline or erythromycin. Nor does the pie diagram that illustrates health enhancement measures include recommendations for their use. But millions of these prescriptions are ordered, filled, and taken without adequately addressing fundamental causes or using safer natural methods.

*Three hundred million dollars worth of over-the-counter acne medication is bought in the U.S. per year.*

Disturbances and fluctuations in the body's biochemistry cause acne. But what causes the disturbances? Remember that the body is not some lone, separate entity operating on its own, independent of mind, emotions, food, water, family, friends, sunlight, environmental toxins, etc.

For acne, "modern medicine" (read "outdated, disease care") chooses to focus on killing germs in those small, localized, inflammatory reactions in the skin while ignoring the big picture. Millions of Americans accept this narrow-minded, health-damaging approach.

There is a better way. We must look at acne as more of a symptom of a deeper dysfunction beyond the skin. Acne occurs when excessive oils are produced by the skin under the influence of hormones. The various skin changes, combined with weakened immune function, will cause a buildup of these oils and waxes in the pores, along with an overgrowth of bacteria which infect and inflame these sites.

Here is how to get excellent results in the correction of acne and in the same process make improvements in a number of aspects of our overall health:

- Correct the cause of excessive oil in the skin. Don't just try to wash the oil away once it is there.
- Reduce inflammatory reactions throughout the body, not just in a few pores.
- Improve the body's defenses against infection with a reduced reliance on pharmacologic antibiotics.
- Moderate the hormone changes which trigger acne.

## UNDERLYING CAUSES

The biochemical imbalances that lead to acne and are accentuated by hormonal changes, particularly around puberty, usually arise in many combinations. Nutritional imbalances are some of the most powerful and prevalent problems setting the stage for abnormal skin changes. Dietary indiscretion can lead to a toxic bowel syndrome. Poisonous substances in the small intestines and colon can alter biochemistry in such a dramatic way that it affects the health of the skin. This is particularly so when antibiotics are used to control skin infection. In the process of killing bacteria on the skin to make a temporary improvement of the acne, the antibiotics kill the beneficial bacteria of the intestines, and that in turn allows for the overgrowth of harmful bacteria—often leading to a long-term worsening of the acne, along with other adverse side effects from the medication.

A high fat diet also leads to more acne problems. Excessive sugar or sweets in the diet will cause erratic blood sugar changes which encourage bacterial growth on the skin. Hidden food allergies also contribute to this erratic blood sugar problem and increase inflammation of the skin. All this burdens the immune system, making it more difficult to fight infection. Typical culprits in food allergy which contribute to acne are dairy, chocolate, and beef.

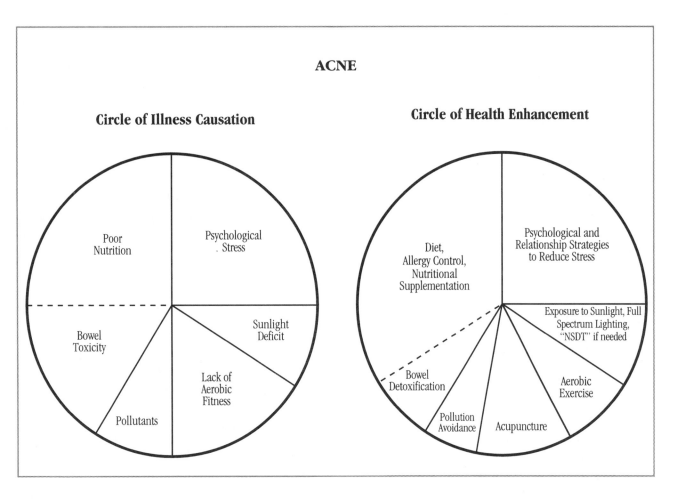

**ACNE**

**Circle of Illness Causation**

- Poor Nutrition
- Psychological Stress
- Sunlight Deficit
- Lack of Aerobic Fitness
- Pollutants
- Bowel Toxicity

**Circle of Health Enhancement**

- Diet, Allergy Control, Nutritional Supplementation
- Psychological and Relationship Strategies to Reduce Stress
- Exposure to Sunlight, Full Spectrum Lighting, "NSDT" if needed
- Aerobic Exercise
- Acupuncture
- Pollution Avoidance
- Bowel Detoxification

Allergic or toxic reactions to environmental agents also can cause acne, sometimes in its most severe form. Industrial pollutants, coal tar compounds, chlorinated hydrocarbons like Agent Orange, and other pesticides or herbicides, are among the many agents known to cause acne-type skin reactions. Smoking tobacco, or breathing secondhand smoke, is the most prevalent toxic cause of acne.

Vitamin and mineral deficiencies are major contributors to acne. Many of the biochemical defences against acne have key vitamin and mineral components; if they are missing or in low quantities, the body cannot recover well.

Insufficient sunlight leads to more acne. Not only does sunlight dry the skin in a helpful way, it is also antibacterial. Sunlight entering the eyes also has a biochemical balancing effect. It balances hormone levels, blood sugar levels, blood cell counts, and enhances immune capabilities.

Aerobic exercise also has a biochemical balancing effect that improves the skin condition. Better blood flow and tissue oxygenation comes from the forced perspiration. Other effects come from various biochemical adaptations to physical activity, not to mention the psychological and stress management benefits of exercise.

Stress, which takes many forms in daily life, is another major cause of the biochemical disturbances leading to acne. And when is there a more stressful time than puberty? The psychological stresses of our own maladaptive behavioral patterns, life transitions, relationship tensions, school worries, and work pressures create many waves of biochemical changes that alter health and set up the conditions for acne. Steroid hormones are produced in response to stress. Biochemically, they make fertile ground for skin dysfunction.

## CORRECTION

Here is a multifaceted program for preventing and/or correcting the causes of acne.

The diet should follow the one outlined in the section on Nutritional Health. It should be particularly low in fat, sugar and allergenic foods. It should contain plenty of water and fiber with complex carbohydrates supplied in adequate quantities at regular intervals throughout the day in order to maintain stable blood sugar levels.

This should also reduce most bowel toxicity syndromes. Although in difficult situations, particularly when antibiotics have destroyed the beneficial intestinal flora, professional colonic irrigation, or at-home enemas followed by ingestion of a high quality lactobacillus acidophilus and bifidobacterium culture, may be necessary to fully restore proper function to the small and large intestines.

Vitamin and mineral supplements are often very helpful. Below are listed therapeutic doses of nutrients found to successfully improve acne:

- B-complex vitamins—25-75 mg per day of the major B vitamins. Folic acid in doses up to 2 mg per day may be particularly helpful. High therapeutic doses up to 10 mg per day have proven very successful but need to be supervised by a knowledgeable health care professional.

- Vitamin A—50,000-300,000 I.U. per day—has proven to be effective. Toxic reactions can occur at these higher doses and require supervision by a knowledgeable physician. A portion of this dosage may be provided by the beta carotene form of the vitamin, since it is less toxic.

- Vitamin C—1-3 grams per day or to a bowel tolerance level (the dose just below that which will cause loose stools). A pH neutral ascorbate form with 5-10% bioflavonoids is most often best to use.

- Vitamin E—400 I.U. per day

- Selenium—200 micrograms per day.

- Zinc—45-135 mg per day. Higher doses over a prolonged time can pose problems, particularly by interfering with copper utilization. Copper supplementation to counteract this effect may be needed. Supervision is advised at higher levels of supplementation. The benefits far outweigh the risks, considering that some studies have found zinc to be more effective than the antibiotic tetracycline, which has many more serious adverse side effects than zinc.

- Chromium—200 micrograms per day.

Avoid pollutants by following the guidelines and using the resources in the chapter on Environmental Health.

Provide yourself with regular aerobic exercise.

Expose eyes and skin to sunlight every day, if possible, but avoid excessive exposure or burning. When natural sunlight is unavailable, or while you are indoors, use full spectrum lighting. Neurosensory Development Training (NSDT) may be indicated if a light deficit disorder is present. Refer back to the chapter on Biological Rhythms, Light and Sleep, for more information.

The psychological component cannot be ignored in acne. Often it is one of the major factors. Utilizing all the relevant suggestions and resources in the chapters on Psychological and Relationship Health will insure the best results.

Acupuncture and botanical preparations have proven to be natural approaches of significant value in the treatment of acne. They can help in liver detoxification, hormonal balancing, immune system improvement, and emotional stabilization. Herbal supplementation can include: Echinacea, Goldenseal, Dandelion, and Milk thistle (or its active ingredient silymarin).

As with all holistic approaches, all aspects of health should improve, not just some isolated set of symptoms.

## REFERENCES

1. Michael Murray and Joseph Pizzorno. *Encyclopedia of Natural Medicine*. (Prima Publishing, 1991) 103-9.
2. Melvyn Werbach. *Nutritional Influences on Illness: A Sourcebook of Clinical Research*. (Third Line Press, 1988) 3-10.

# BACK AND NECK PAIN

Eighty per cent of all people will suffer incapacitating back pain at some time in their lives. At any given time approximately 7% of the adult population in America is suffering from a prolonged bout of back pain. Once one is injured, there is a four times greater risk of subsequent spinal injury. It is the second leading reason for consulting a physician. Back pain is one of the top two causes of worker absenteeism—costing more than *$16 billion* in lost wages per year in the U.S. When all costs are considered, Americans lose approximately *$100 billion* a year because of spinal pain. For those disabled by back pain for more than six months, only half will ever return to work. The leading cause of employee disability is back injury, with more than 500,000 permanently disabled each year. Just in America, 250,000 back surgeries are performed every year. Only 10% of those are necessary. Within 18 months following back surgery, 20-45% of the cases end up being classified as Failed Back Surgical Syndrome. Successful back surgery is categorized such when the patient has 50% less pain than prior to surgery.

So what are the causes of spinal pain, and what are better routes to the correction of this condition while on the path to greater wholeness?

## CAUSES

### *Injury*

Spinal trauma at work, at home, during sporting activity, in an auto accident. This does not have to involve strictly a one incident trauma. Cumulative tissue stress from repetitive motion can also be categorized as an injury. A typical example is the worker who has been loading sacks of concrete on trucks for ten years and one day is incapacitated with low back pain. X-rays reveal that there had been a progressive degeneration of the discs that went unnoticed over the years until finally "the straw that broke the camels back" was loaded.

Initial trauma can occur years before and be neglected. There are frequent incidents of birth trauma occurring to the cervical spine; never corrected adequately in infancy, it becomes chronic later on in life.

### *Cumulative Postural Stress*

The office worker who continually has her head turned to view a computer screen, that is not in the best location for proper ergonomics, or the one who has the phone receiver held in place by a severe contortion of the neck and raising of the non-dominant shoulder to produce a cradle for four hours a day, or the person who has his head bent over a desk with rounded shoulders for six hours a day. These habitual structural patterns painfully stress tissues, but they also often lead to injuries by predisposing the spine to weaknesses and abnormal movements.

### *Lack of Fitness*

Weak muscles, excessively mobile joints, restricted flexibility, poor endurance conditioning, excessive weight, and lack of coordination can each cause spinal discomfort or pain in its own right. But each is also a very dominant contributor in setting the stage for injury, whether by repetitive motion stress or frank trauma. That is why preventive fitness programs reduce the incidence and severity of back pain and accelerate recovery when injury does occur. Regular exercise also contributes to bone strength. This is important for the elderly, particularly women, who are most vulnerable to osteoporosis. Osteoporosis causes back pain and compression fractures. Lack of strength, altered joint mobility, and poor fitness contribute to distorted body movements, which then also lead to injury. As an example, look at the sedentary businessman who has weak back muscles and severely reduced flexibility from lack of exercise. Then during a weekend golf game he bends over to pick up a tiny golf ball and falls to the ground in excruciating pain. Was the golf ball too heavy?

Probably not. More a matter of a lack of fitness combined with poor biomechanics producing a body ripe for injury.

## Poor Biomechanics

Uncoordinated movement patterns—whether learned or ingrained from weak muscles, distorted joint flexibility or poor posture—will cause undue stress on tissues, resulting in pain or possibly predisposing the spine to injury or repetitive motion tissue degeneration.

## Psycho-Social Distress

The two mechanisms most likely to cause musculoskeletal problems in this category are chronic, abnormal muscle tension, which then alters movement and predisposes the spine to injury, and other mechanical stresses or distressing circumstances which distract the mind at the wrong moment and cause injury. Other intricate, complex, or indirect mechanisms can also be contributors. A hectic, stressful pace at work can cause a person to have an ulcer. This then causes thoracic spine muscles to contract abnormally, and the ensuing problems. It could also cause improper nutrition, which then weakens the spinal structures.

## Inadequate Nutrition

Poor nutrition weakens body tissues and makes them more susceptible to stress and injury. Healing is delayed, and recoveries from trauma are less complete. When damaged vertebral discs were examined after surgery and compared to normal discs, they were found to contain substantially less vitamin C, manganese, magnesium, and calcium. How are damaged tissues expected to heal rapidly if nutritional building blocks are not available? A deficiency of minerals such as calcium and magnesium also contribute to osteoporosis. Also, hidden food allergies can cause persistent or periodic joint inflammations of the spine.

## Smoking

People who smoke have a greater incidence of back pain than nonsmokers. Possibly the smoking depletes nutrients and leads to weakness. Ninety percent or more of smokers are allergic to nicotine. This could also be causing an unnoticed low level inflammatory reaction in the joints, resulting in progressive degeneration of spinal structures. There also seems to be a peculiar reflex that distorts cervical motion whenever there is lung irritation. This may be one reason why many physicians who treat cervical spine problems notice slower and less complete recoveries in smokers as opposed to nonsmokers.

## Indirect Causes

We must also consider many indirect causes of injury. Occupational stresses, both physical and psychological, contribute to many back injuries, and continued adverse working conditions often drastically slow or prevent recovery. Governmental consumer protection laws play a role in spinal injury. When good laws are enacted before problems arise, much human suffering is averted. But when laws are not in effect to protect the consumers, tragedy is the frequent result. We only have to look at labor practices laws, highway and auto safety, to see dramatic examples.

Economic issues should not be ignored either. Economic stress will force individuals to take on jobs they are not suited to perform, make them work past the point of fatigue, possibly resulting in injury. People under economic stress tend to purchase cheaper, less nourishing food. This lack of good nutritional support undermines their ability to withstand their stressful life.

## HEALTH ENHANCEMENT MEASURES

So if these are the causes, what are the most logical ways to correct them? Let's look at the traditional, modern medical standard of care first. Initially, it involves either waiting forever to get an appointment with the family physician or waiting

# BACK AND NECK PAIN

## Circle of Illness Causation

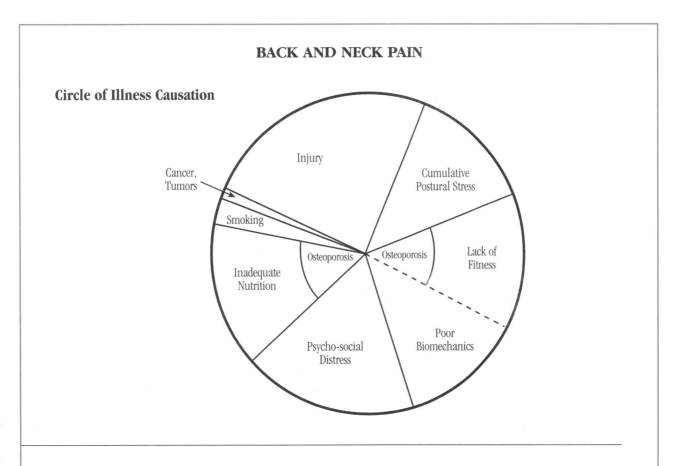

## Circle of Health Enhancement

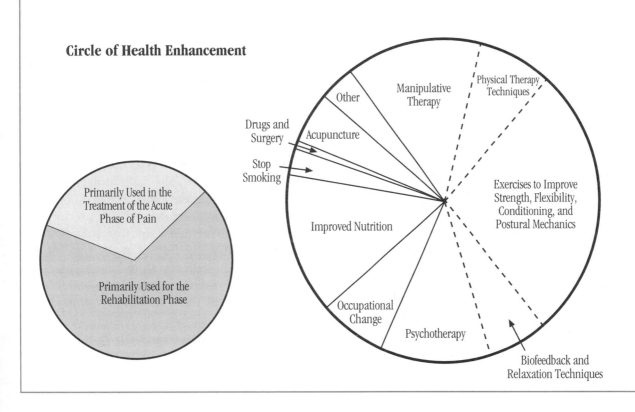

an interminable time at the emergency room in the most tortuous chairs filling out reams of paperwork. Then after a cursory exam, the general practitioner, who usually doesn't have a clue as to the mechanisms surrounding musculoskeletal injury and effective correction, will write a prescription for muscle relaxants, anti-inflammatories, and/or pain relievers (thinking that there must be a blood deficiency of these substances?), tell you to rest in bed (which has been found to be one of the most damaging approaches to take), and quickly point you in the direction of the billing office. There the nurse tells you that if satisfactory results aren't realized in several weeks, you can be referred to a surgeon for his opinion.

There are ways that have been documented over the years to be much more effective at the correction of a wide variety of different types of back and neck pain. They involve less expensive care with fewer adverse side effects. In the acute phases of pain, ice applied locally can be almost as effective as anti-inflammatory drugs. It will have no adverse side effects, particularly if other natural anti-inflammatory agents are included:

- protein digesting enzymes—approximately 400 mg—four times per day away from meals (bromelain, pancreatin, and trypsin are the most popular)

- quercetin, a bioflavonoid nutrient—approximately 400 mg—four times per day away from meals

- the herbs, tumeric and hawthorn—approximately 100 mg—four times per day away from meals

- vitamin B-6—50-150 mg per day or 25-75 mg of pyridoxal 5' phosphate (a form of B-6 which is easier for the body to use)

Manipulative therapies are very successful in both the acute and sub-acute phase of pain and disability management—soft tissue massage techniques, joint mobilization and manipulation, traction, ultrasound, diathermy, electrical stimulation, acupuncture, all have proven to be extremely helpful in correcting the initial tissue damage,

controlling pain and inflammation, and beginning the process of rehabilitation. Even when there is no frank trauma, and when spinal pain or discomfort comes from deranged biomechanics of the spine or extremities, manipulative and physiological therapeutics is the treatment of choice. How are drugs and bed rest going to improve faults in spinal motion?

After the acute pain phase of the problem is resolved, standard medical care usually ignores any follow-up. Whereas, from the Circle of Health Enhancement diagram, we can see that the predominant portion of correction comes in the rehabilitation phase. Here exercises are performed to strengthen not only structures weakened by injury but also any structures that were weak prior to injury and which contributed to the trauma in the first place. Flexibility exercises are performed to restore normal motion to areas that have been restricted by the injury and also to those areas which were restricted prior to injury. The tissues are conditioned to resist fatigue so that they can be better able to withstand the daily stresses imposed on them. Back school classes help re-coordinate efficient, safe movements and postures into the tasks of daily life and work. These participatory, instructional programs teach people with injured backs, or those at risk of injury, exercises and guidelines which will protect their spines from future trauma. Biofeedback and relaxation techniques can be used to retrain chronically tight musculature to respond in a healthier, more efficient manner.

Psychotherapy can be used in many ways in the rehabilitation process. It often helps resolve the emotional stresses that led up to the injury. Often, psychotherapy is used to also help individuals deal emotionally with their disability in more constructive ways. Frequently, injured tissues cannot heal adequately because there are unresolved emotional issues that were present at the time of the injury; these neurologically slow healing and irritate the nerves. Using psychotherapeutic techniques to resolve the emotional components makes for faster and more complete healing. This can be particularly so in cases that do not respond adequately with other modalities or in cases where the patient is experiencing a lot of emotional conflict.

How many times are workers injured on a job that they are physically ill-suited for and after recovery go right back to the same old tasks and re-injure themselves? Or how often does a psychologically stressful job inhibit physical healing of a spinal injury? Occupational therapy and a change of job are frequently among the most important rehabilitation efforts.

Good nutrition is essential in correcting musculoskeletal problems, particularly injuries. Often large doses of vitamin and mineral supplements accelerate healing. Avoiding allergenic food often helps recovery. It also helps reduce inflammation.

Stopping smoking helps *all* health conditions!

So what does this tell us about seeking wholeness from a situation involving back pain? And why do most people consult medical personnel more frequently than chiropractors and physical therapists, when the facts dramatically show much better success with manipulative and physiologic therapies than with medical care? Well, it has to do with education, both public and professional. People with lower educational levels will choose medical care more frequently. College educated individuals who are more exposed to the facts about proper care, and are also more able to critically evaluate differences in quality of care, choose chiropractic care and physical therapists with higher frequency. Closed-minded, "old school" medical doctors who do not keep up with the scientific literature outside their own narrow focus of medicine and surgery are less likely to recom-

mend interdisciplinary health care approaches and work with nonmedical health professionals than are their younger, more open-minded colleagues.

So the smart health care consumer prevents back pain by utilizing the health enhancement programs most directly linked to musculoskeletal health:

- maintenance of well balanced fitness, strength, flexibility, coordination
- good body mechanics and good posture
- stress management activities
- good nutrition
- periodic early detection tests for joint motion abnormalities at a chiropractic office, and manipulation if needed
- no smoking.

If injury or spinal pain arises, the smart health care consumer first consults with a chiropractor who is the most highly qualified and extensively trained specialist for spinal disorders. The chiropractor can refer to a medical or surgical specialist if necessary, but he will be best able to diagnose the problem and inexpensively correct it if surgery is not necessary. Whereas going to medical personnel first virtually eliminates the possibility that effective, conservative methods like manipulative therapy and proper rehabilitation will be used to prevent a surgical option. The smart, holistic health care consumer with back pain will also see to it that as many of the elements in the Circle of Health Enhancement will be utilized for best results.

More resources are available in the chapter on Manipulative Therapies.

# BENIGN PROSTATIC HYPERPLASIA (BPH)

More than 60% of men over 40 years of age have an enlarged prostate gland. Symptoms include progressive urinary frequency and urgency, particularly noticed at night. There is often hesitancy and intermittent changes in the force and quantity of urinary stream flow. Incomplete emptying, dribbling, and overflow incontinence can occur also.

When these symptoms exist, digital rectal examination of the prostate to determine enlargement is indicated. Since prostate specific antigen is elevated in 30-50% of men with BPH, having this laboratory test performed is helpful in confirming diagnosis.

## CAUSES AND CORRECTION

Hormonal changes that come with age are a primary cause. Trophic disturbances of the prostate gland related to neurological insult from spinal degenerative changes and other lumbar spine problems also seem to contribute.

Since lifestyle has the most significant impact on some of these hormonal changes, that is where most of the efforts at health enhancement need to be focused. Some of the hormonal changes which favor development of BPH are related to the normal process of aging. So aging healthfully is a skillful health enhancement strategy.

Alcohol, smoking, pesticide exposure, heavy metal contamination, and some medications have been implicated in the development of BPH. In the light of this, avoidance of these substances seems important. Detoxification procedures may need to be instituted if contamination is excessive. For instance, farmers exposed to high amounts of pesticides, or home owners who use significant quantities of pesticides and herbicides on their lawn and in their home, may need to be tested for pesticide contamination. If evidence exists that there is substantial body burden or a strong immunological reaction to these harmful substances, nutritional detoxification and hyperthermia treatments may be necessary.

Pesticide contamination is also a reason for consuming organically grown or pesticide free foods. Organically grown foods have a higher nutrient content. In order to lessen any immunological reactivity, only non-allergenic foods should be consumed. If there is a suspicion of food allergy, elimination diets with food challenges can help to identify problem substances. This involves eliminating suspected foods from the diet for a period of time ranging from a week to several months. This gives the body a bit of a rest from them. Often symptoms disappear with this avoidance. Then, the suspected foods are reintroduced as a "challenge." If the symptoms reappear, the test is positive and shows that the person reacts adversely to that food. ELISA/ACT™ immunological sensitivity tests can also be performed to identify delayed reactions to food.

A high complex carbohydrate and high fibre diet is recommended.

Zinc and vitamin B-6 are two of the more important nutrients related to a healthy prostate. Supplementation with zinc picolinate and B-complex vitamins is an essential part of natural therapy for BPH.

Essential fatty acids are important in the treatment of BPH. They can be attained with approximately a teaspoon per day of either flax, evening primrose, canola, sunflower, or soy oil.

A low cholesterol, low simple sugar diet with adequate aerobic exercise—and other strategies to decrease blood cholesterol levels—helps this condition.

Supplementation with the amino acids glycine, glutamic acid, and alanine has been found to be very therapeutic.

The herb *Seronoa repens* (Saw palmetto berries) is highly effective in treating BPH. The active ingredient, LSE seronoa, appears to be much more cost-effective and safer than the most popular prescriptive medication (Proscar) with a similar mode of action. The herbs, *Pygeum africanus, Equisetum arvense* (horsetail), *Hydrangea arborescens,* and ginseng have been used successfully in the treatment of BPH also.

*Note: There are a number of nutritional supplement companies that combine the above nutri-

# BENIGN PROSTATIC HYPERPLASIA

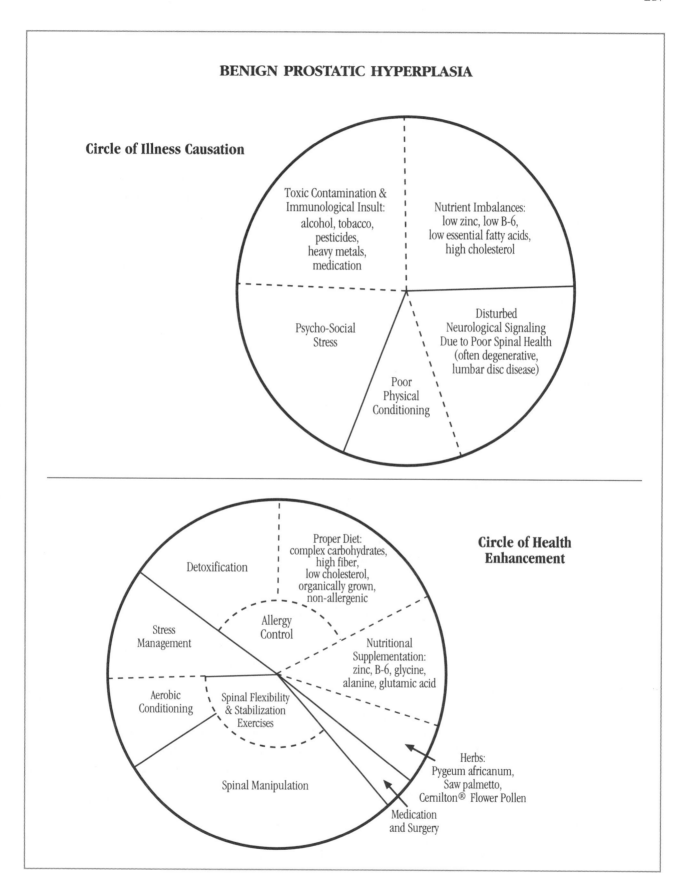

**Circle of Illness Causation**

Toxic Contamination &
Immunological Insult:
alcohol, tobacco,
pesticides,
heavy metals,
medication

Nutrient Imbalances:
low zinc, low B-6,
low essential fatty acids,
high cholesterol

Psycho-Social
Stress

Disturbed
Neurological Signaling
Due to Poor Spinal Health
(often degenerative,
lumbar disc disease)

Poor
Physical
Conditioning

**Circle of Health
Enhancement**

Detoxification

Proper Diet:
complex carbohydrates,
high fiber,
low cholesterol,
organically grown,
non-allergenic

Stress
Management

Allergy
Control

Nutritional
Supplementation:
zinc, B-6, glycine,
alanine, glutamic acid

Aerobic
Conditioning

Spinal Flexibility
& Stabilization
Exercises

Spinal Manipulation

Herbs:
Pygeum africanum,
Saw palmetto,
Cernilton® Flower Pollen

Medication
and Surgery

tional factors into one product specifically for prostate health.

Neurological innervation of the prostate is essential to its health. The most frequent cause of insult to the nerves of the prostate is lower lumbar spinal mechanical deficits. Continual low back instability can cause neurological irritation and progressive degenerative changes of the lumbar discs.

Proper spinal mechanics are dependent on:

- well-conditioned, strong, coordinated muscles of the trunk and lower extremities
- muscle and joint flexibility in the spine and lower extremities

To insure proper spinal mechanics and neurological integrity, several things can be done:

- aerobic, strength training, and coordination exercises for the trunk and lower extremities
- flexibility exercises for the trunk and lower extremities
- spinal and lower extremity joint manipulation

Aerobic conditioning, in general, helps this condition by other physiological mechanisms also. Improved oxygen flow to the tissues, improved blood flow generally, restored hormonal balance, and dissipation of emotional stress, among others, have their positive impact.

Stress management is important in keeping the body healthy. Aspects of this can include stress reduction, stress avoidance, better time management, occupational changes, biofeedback, relaxation training, meditation, psychotherapy, social support, and play.

A multifaceted, natural approach to health enhancement specific to individuals with prostatic enlargement seems far more cost effective than medical, standard-of-care pharmaceuticals. It is far, far better than surgical intervention, since there is a high rate of severe complications from this radical intervention, including impotence and incontinence. The natural approach is also designed to greatly reduce the incidence of prostatic cancer which often follows BPH.

# CRIME

*Great crimes come never singly; they are linked*
*To sins that went before.*

**Jean Racine**

Crime can be seen as a symptom of social ill health. It can also be viewed as individual aberrant behavior, which is also illness. If one is to comprehensively analyze crime, it has to be viewed from a perspective of many interconnected causes. Simple models do not do the subject justice.

Criminal behavior is due to many interlinked causes. It is insufficient to just say, "Some people are just born evil," or "Everybody has to make choices in life, and they made the wrong choice," or "They should just pick themselves up by the bootstraps and improve their life," or "I know people born into poverty and unwholesome conditions, and they worked hard and made something of themselves without resorting to crime. If

they did it, why can't these criminals?" or "Just lock 'em up and throw away the key."

Not many people have a full understanding of the various forces which act upon individuals to mold their behavior. If we look at these in detail, it is easier to see how conditioned patterns of behavior develop in aberrant ways.

It is highly questionable that there are truly people who are born evil. "Evil" is a word that fearful, frustrated, confused, angry individuals use when they do not fully understand the totality of causes for painful events. It is much more likely that "evil" appearing behaviors have logical but complex, sometimes mysterious, but understandable causes.

Looking at some facts about incarcerated individuals we find:

Most were born into a family situation that was far from wholesome (the first three years of life form the foundation of our adult personality).

Many children who entered a life of crime were conceived, not in an atmosphere of loving intention, but as an accidental, unwanted result of ignorance, neediness, carelessness, drunkenness, and other ills.

Many criminals spent nine months of inter-uterine life under siege from the disturbed biochemistry of a mother who was consumed by negative feelings, drugs, illness, and poor nutrition. (Some experts feel that 50% or more of a child's intelligence is a result of maternal nutrition while the child is in the womb.)

Infancy is not usually a nurturing environment for criminals. Often there are poverty, environmental toxins, poor nutrition, illness, insecurity, and pain in combinations and proportions far more damaging than in the general population. Their parents are either physically or emotionally absent, unskillful, or downright abusive. In the first three years of life a child needs to learn trust and love from his primary care providers. If he or she does not learn these lessons well, all future relationships will be severely and adversely affected.

In childhood their peers are in the same sad state of affairs, so there are few opportunities for learning wholesome friendship building.

Children can be seen as "consumers" of their environment in early formative years. They take all the air, water, food, sights, sounds, tastes, and feelings into their bodies, psyches, and souls. What goes in, comes out. Look at what goes in: a combination of environmental toxins (lead contamination may be responsible for lower I.Q. in 25% of urban children), violence in the streets, violence in the home, violence on television, violence in the movies, violence in sports, and violence in music; add feelings of being unwanted by parents, successful individuals, people of other races, and society in general. They get little or no spiritual support, a substandard education, reinforcement at every turn to be competitive, greedy, and self-centered. They are exposed to alcohol and street drugs, concrete, police sirens, traffic, noise,

no hope of an encouraging job market, and no hope of much of any type of a good life.

Can we expect that anything other than disturbed behavior will be the result? It is not amazing to discover that the history of a large percentage of criminals includes so many of the above harmful elements. Now some individuals can have many hardships stacked against them, but live exemplary lives because of very powerful positive elements that countered the negative ones. It only takes a few damaging factors at the "wrong" time to elicit severe criminal behavior (nutritional biochemists can predict with an 85% accuracy rate which criminals will be violent, just from blood tests). This does not negate responsibility for his behavior on the part of the criminal, but it does point to societal and parental culpability and accountability.

So how does this type of understanding help us with health enhancement endeavors when our society suffers from the ill health of crime?

## PREVENTION RATHER THAN CRISIS INTERVENTION

*Men and nations behave wisely once they have exhausted all the other alternatives.*
**Abba Eban**

The first principle of holistic health we can apply is that an ounce of prevention is worth a pound of cure. More time, effort, and money needs to be invested before problems arise so that higher costs and more traumas do not occur. This means more:

- parent effectiveness training for *all* parents
- cleaner environment
- good prenatal and childhood nutrition programs
- upgraded, holistic education systems
- job training programs
- livable communities
- spiritual support
- improved mental health care services.

# THE TANGLE OF CRIMINAL CAUSATION

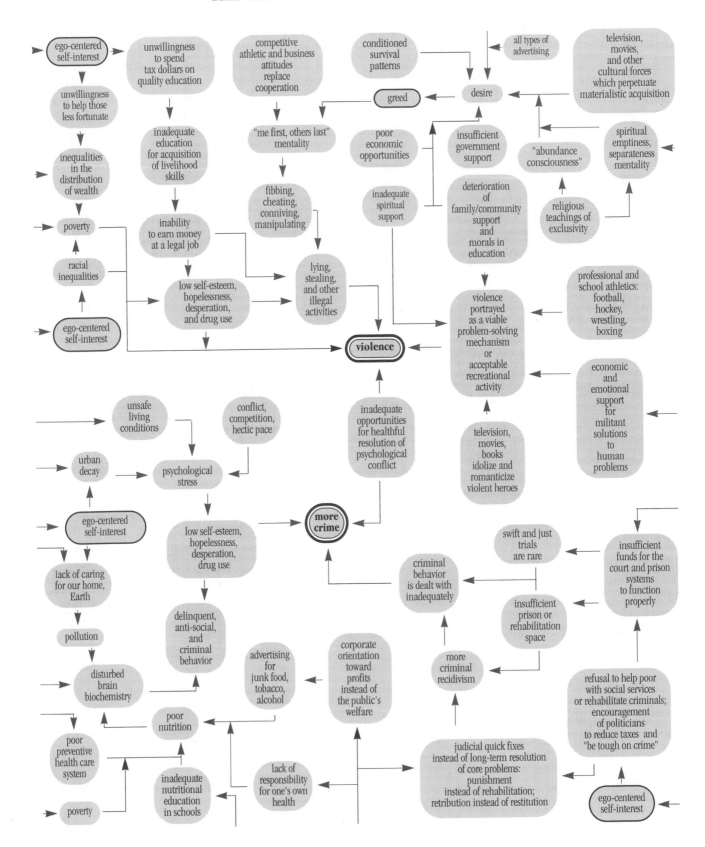

# THE INTERCONNECTED ELEMENTS IN CORRECTING CRIMINAL BEHAVIOR

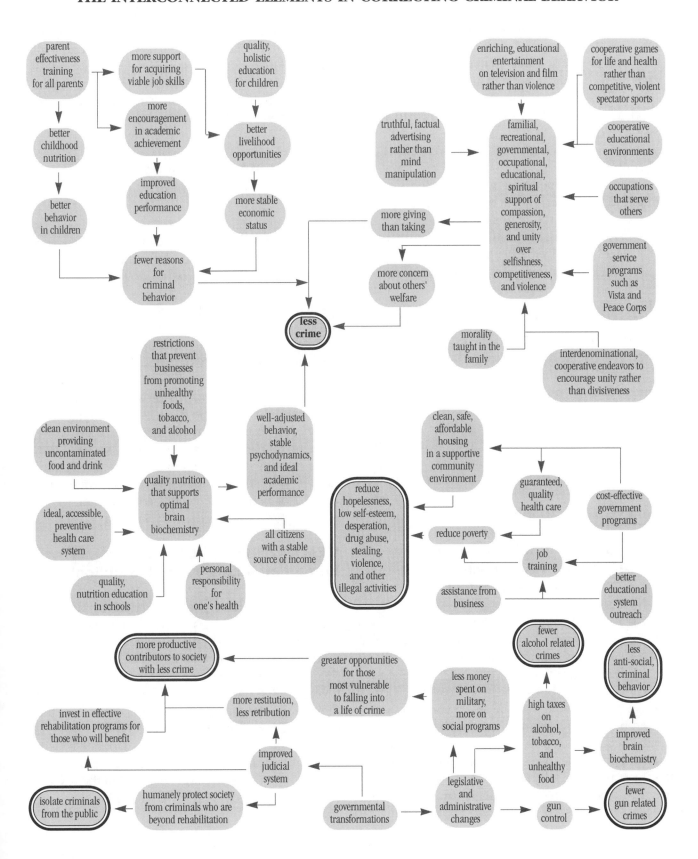

Once criminal events occur, we also have to look at how best to heal the damage done. We have to consider how to heal the immediate victims. Society at large needs healing too, for we are all victims of every crime that is committed, no matter how distant it is from us. And often we forget that the perpetrator of crime needs to be healed as well, in the instances in which that is possible. For as we have seen, there is usually a severe sickness in the criminal of the body, psyche, and soul.

In the age of medicine when all illness was thought to be caused by microbes, our treatments focused on killing the germs. It was only after a better understanding arrived that we could realize that we had to build the health of the body with good nutrition and proper lifestyle in order to resist infection. So too with crime.

In more ignorant times in human history, we believed that criminal behavior was due to the invasion of "evil spirits," and the body had to be burned at the stake to rid it of evil. Or at other times when we thought that punishment was effective, torture would be used "to teach people a lesson" and "act as a deterrent." It is only now, with new knowledge of human behavior and the interconnection of bodies, minds, souls, and environment, that we can embrace a more helpful perspective.

## HEALING THE CRIMINAL

### Effective Rehabilitation Rather Than Programming More Maladaptive Behaviors

When rehabilitation is possible and cost-effective in society's eyes, it proves more beneficial to everyone than prison environments that have no rehabilitation efforts or uplifting influences. Through advanced biochemical and psychological testing science is able, with increasing accuracy, to determine which criminals can and cannot be rehabilitated. If the court system looked at criminal behavior from the perspective of holistic health, this information could be used at sentencing. In this way a more equitable judgment can be handed

down—one that considers restitution to victims and the best protection for society. Often the best protection for society is effective, comprehensive rehabilitation for the criminal, since most criminals are back on the street at some time. It's only logical that those criminals we know are going to be released should be prepared to fit into a law-abiding community.

### When Rehabilitation Is Not Appropriate

Some criminals are too severely "ill" to ever be allowed release into society. Just as a hospital patient with a contagious infection needs to be isolated from others in order to protect them, so do serial rapists and mass murderers need to be permanently isolated from society—not only for society's good but so that the criminal can also benefit from not having the opportunity to continue his violent behavior. Some hospital patients have terminal illnesses where there is no reasonable hope for recovery. In those cases, humane comfort care is given. So too with the criminal who can never be trusted to interact with society. We need to humanely isolate him from society. That does not negate his responsibility to pay restitution. It only limits him to doing so within the context of permanent, secure confinement.

## HEALING THE VICTIMS
## Restitution Rather Than Retribution

How often have we been told by spiritual leaders from all religions, "Revenge is the poison of the soul," or "Love and forgiveness heal all wounds." Retribution will not make victims whole. Victims may temporarily feel better with a taste of revenge. But understanding from the heart and mind is the only medicine that will really heal the damage caused by the illness of crime.

Compensatory restitution, when possible, is a just and logical portion of the healing process for the perpetrator, victim, and society. But the restitution has to encompass a life-affirming process.

Imposing treble damages in cases such as fraud, and community service for nonviolent offenders, has many advantages over incarceration.

Often no adequate restitution can be gained for the more serious violent crimes. That doesn't mean that in those situations retribution can take its place. It just means that a lifetime of restitution may need to be imposed and that it will never be compensation enough.

## HEALING SOCIETY
## Protecting Society Rather Than Punishment

*All punishment is mischief.*
*All punishment in itself is evil.*
**Jeremy Bentham**

Healing society after a crime has been committed follows the same principles as healing the direct victims of a crime. Society can benefit from criminals paying restitution. But it does not seem to help society as a whole to punish criminals, particularly if it comes out of a sense of retribution or revenge. Punishment has a tendency to create a more bitter criminal upon release who will be more inclined to continue the cycle of revenge by perpetrating more crimes. It is helpful to society to rehabilitate those criminals who can be rehabilitated and who will ultimately be released from confinement. But it also helps to protect society from future crime by identifying those criminals who are too "ill" to ever be rehabilitated. That is the role of long term incarceration. Not as punishment, for that helps few people. Punishment is not very cost-effective as either a rehabilitative device or as a deterrent.

## A HOLISTIC HEALTH JUSTICE SYSTEM AND A MULTI-TIERED PRISON SYSTEM

Instead of having an adversarial, punishment-based justice and prison system which deals with convicted criminals in very limited ways, what may be more rational and cost effective is a multifac-eted, holistic health-based approach. In this new, progressive system of judicial problem-solving, crime would be seen as a health issue where there has to be healing of the immediate victims of the crime, healing of society, and healing of the criminal. For accused perpetrators who wanted to try to prove their innocence, the old adversarial trial system would be there for them as usual.

Plea bargains would be different, though. They would be based on the confessed criminal entering into a different "restitution-rehabilitation" program. It would begin with psychological and biochemical testing to identify the likelihood of rehabilitation. For those who are unlikely to respond to rehabilitation, humane confinement for the upper time limits of an incarceration, with opportunity for restitution within prison confines, would be available. For those who are likely to respond to rehabilitation, those programs would be instituted with provisions for restitution.

In order to encourage accused criminals to avoid costly trials to prove their guilt, there would be the incentive of better rehabilitation facilities, if rehabilitation were possible. And if not, better quality facilities to perform restitution, and possibly less stringent restitution payback terms. Accused criminals intent on using the adversarial system to "beat a rap," if convicted, would be subjected to longer prison times, more restitution, poorer facilities.

The goal of this type of system would be long term cost-effectiveness at reducing crime and protecting society.

## MULTI-DIMENSIONAL HEALING

Bringing to our justice system the principles of whole systems—interconnectedness, prevention, comprehensive functional assessment, multi-disciplinary analysis, win-win problem solving, true justice, common sense, and compassionate understanding from the mind and heart—will make us all healthier.

**CRIME**

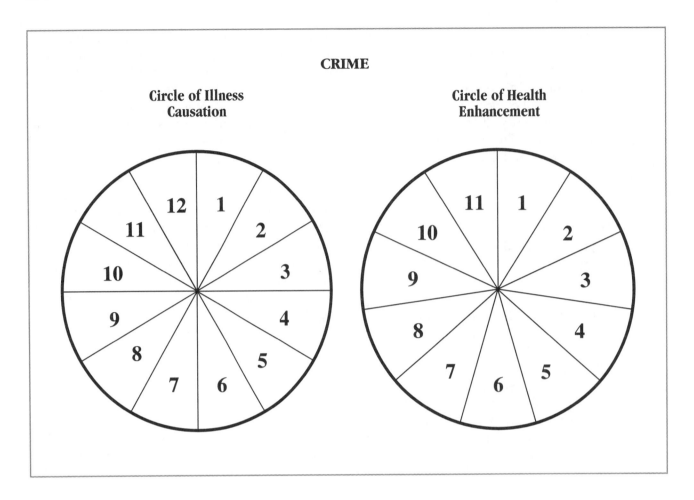

Circle of Illness Causation

Circle of Health Enhancement

## Crime
## Circle of Illness Causation

*As a single leaf turns not yellow*
*but with the silent knowledge of the whole tree,*
*so the wrong-doer cannot do wrong*
*without the hidden will of you all.*

**Kahlil Gibran**

Many of these factors contribute to the downward spiral of low self-esteem, hopelessness, desperation, drug use, and crime.

1. Personal, greedy, egotistical attitudes that isolate the individual from society leading to, and reinforced by, governmental policies and business goals.
2. Poverty—inequities in the distribution of the nation's wealth.
3. Racial inequalities and prejudice—separateness mentality.
4. Poor educational system.
5. Urban decay—unsafe living conditions, conflict and competition at every turn, pollution, hectic pace, and so on.
6. Inadequate social supports—no sense of community or family.
7. Inadequate spiritual influences.
8. Inadequate governmental support.
9. Lack of opportunities to right livelihood for all.
10. Upside-down focus on judicial quick fixes rather than cause-correction; punishment instead of rehabilitation, retribution instead of restitution.
11. Inadequate mental health care services.
12. People not spending enough time in nature to tap its healing power.

## Crime
## Circle of Health Enhancement

1. Transformation of personal, egotistical attitudes of greed and separateness into compassion and generosity. Spend more time giving to others than taking for oneself.
2. Uniting the differences which divide. Efforts at developing our unity rather than focusing on differences.
3. Parent effectiveness training for *all* parents.
4. Upgraded holistic education system.
5. Build livable communities from the urban rubble.
6. Knit the social supports into a web of mutual generosity, helping everyone to grow into the full use of his capabilities.
7. Adopt spiritual practices that encourage unity and a personal experience with all that binds us as One.
8. Reform governmental practices.
   a. Campaign finance reform
   b. Less defense spending and more social programs that work to solve the causes of problems
   c. Higher taxes on alcohol, tobacco, unhealthy food, energy, and pollution
   d. Gun control
   e. Job training in areas that help others and the environment
9. Improve the justice system.
   a. Humane protection of society from criminals who are beyond rehabilitation
   b. Effective rehabilitation programs for those who will benefit
   c. Restitution rather than retribution
10. Improve mental health care services.
    a. Access for everyone needing care
    b. Effective early detection methods
    c. Useful diagnostic testing
    d. Quality, multi-disciplinary psychotherapeutic and social services including neurochemical approaches: optimal nutrition for everyone, allergy, toxicology, bright light therapy, Neurosensory Development Training, cranial electrical stimulation, acupuncture, etc.
11. Value more exposure to the healing qualities of Nature.

---

## RESOURCES

### *Books and Journal Articles*

Hippchen, Leonard. *Ecologic-Biochemical Approaches to Treatment of Delinquents and Criminals.* Van Nostrand Reinhold, 1978.

Walsh, William. "Biochemical Treatment of Behavior, Learning and Mental Disorders." *Townsend Letter for Doctors* (Aug. 1992): 698-702.

Werbach, Melvin. "Nutritional Influences on Aggressive Behavior." *Journal of Orthomolecular Medicine* 7:1 (First Quarter 1992): 45-51.

Werbach, Melvyn. *Nutritional Influences on Mental Illness: A Sourcebook of Clinical Research* Third Line Press, 1991.

### *Organizations*

American Correctional Health Services Association, P.O. Box 2307, Dayton, OH 45401-2307; (513) 223-9630. A group interested in improving correctional health services.

Center on Juvenile and Criminal Justice; (415) 621-5661. Advocates for alternatives to incarceration.

# DEPRESSION

*Is there anything men take more pains about than to render themselves unhappy?*

**Benjamin Franklin**

*Depression affects approximately 27 million Americans, or 10% of the population.*

There are two basic and overlapping causes for depression—brain biochemistry abnormalities and psychological stress. The more deeply and profoundly that we can improve these two precursors to depression, the more complete and long-lasting will be its correction, along with an enhancement of other health aspects.

The death of a loved one, the loss of a job, a serious physical illness, and countless other psychological stresses, can trigger or accentuate a depressive episode in one's life. The damaging effects can be more profound if the person is already emotionally fragile from past psychological trauma, even dating back to early childhood. When depression is brought on solely by tragic circumstances and not complicated by severe psychological problems, most people recover in a reasonable amount of time. If prior psychological problems compound the difficulty, psychotherapy is often necessary. Various forms of psychometric testing can help identify the extent and characteristics of psychological dysfunction, relational conflict, and lifestyle stresses that need to be addressed.

The real problem arises when there are brain biochemistry abnormalities which inhibit the nervous system from responding normally to psychotherapy intervention, or when there are no apparent circumstantial or psychological reasons for the depression.

## CAUSES FOR BRAIN BIOCHEMISTRY ABNORMALITIES

There does seem to be some genetic predisposition for depression. In the future, new forms of DNA testing might be able to forewarn those individuals who might be predisposed. But at this time not much help of this kind is available.

A number of vitamin and mineral imbalances are known to cause depression, most notably deficiencies of vitamins B1, B2, B6, B12, C, biotin, folic acid, and minerals calcium, iron, magnesium, and potassium. Excesses of magnesium and vanadium have also been noted to be related to depression. Nutritional supplementation with amino acids phenylalanine, tryptophan, and tyrosine have helped correct depression because these nutrients are precursors to brain neurotransmitters.

Diet plays an important role in depression, not only because of its supply of the above nutrients, but also because a poor diet can cause hypoglycemia, low blood sugar, which is a known cause of fluctuating depression. Food allergy, as well as other allergies, can cause hypoglycemia but also induce depression by other biochemical and neurological mechanisms.

Light deficit disorders are documented causes of depression, nonseasonal as well as seasonal, unipolar (just depression) as well as bipolar (depression intermixed with bouts of mania).

## CORRECTION AND ENHANCEMENT OF BRAIN BIOCHEMISTRY

Psychotherapy, stress reduction, and social support assistance have their role in indirectly improving brain chemistry. Other measures focused more specifically in that direction can yield impressive results, particularly when combined in an integrated, comprehensive program. Use the resource section in the chapter on Psychological Health for more assistance.

Aerobic exercise is well documented in its ability to help overcome depression. There are many mechanisms by which this can occur. Exercise stimulates endorphin and enkephalin release within the brain as well as other biochemical changes. This same phenomenon is responsible, in part, for the so called "runner's high." Aerobic

**DEPRESSION**

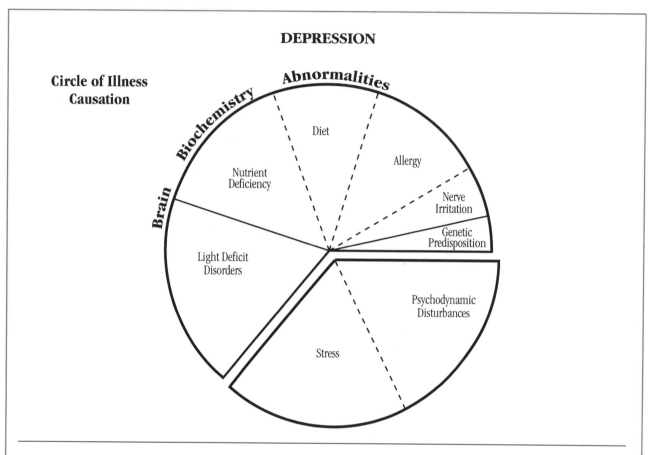

**Circle of Illness Causation**

Abnormalities

Biochemistry

Brain

Diet

Allergy

Nutrient Deficiency

Nerve Irritation

Genetic Predisposition

Light Deficit Disorders

Psychodynamic Disturbances

Stress

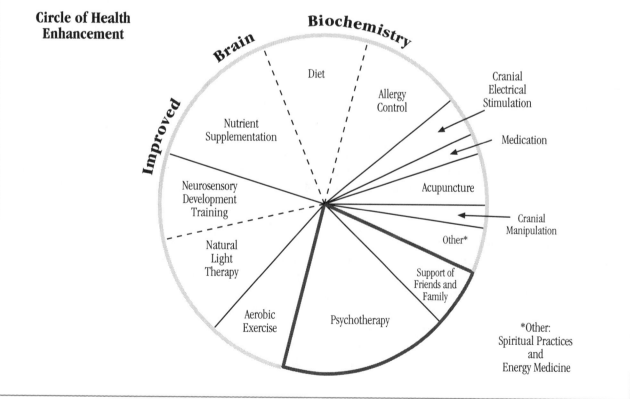

**Circle of Health Enhancement**

Brain

Biochemistry

Improved

Diet

Allergy Control

Cranial Electrical Stimulation

Nutrient Supplementation

Medication

Neurosensory Development Training

Acupuncture

Cranial Manipulation

Natural Light Therapy

Other*

Aerobic Exercise

Psychotherapy

Support of Friends and Family

*Other:
Spiritual Practices
and
Energy Medicine

exercise also tends to stabilize blood sugar levels and would thus improve any hypoglycemia-induced depression. Exercise also breaks the conditioned pattern of low energy reserves, reduced activity, withdrawn body posture, indoor confinement, deadened body sensations. It encourages energized vitality and an opening up of the body structure. No matter what level of conditioning the depressed individual is in, there can be a beneficial exercise regimen that is appropriate. Some may be able to use the resources in the earlier section on exercise. Others may need the advice, pretesting, and monitoring which an exercise physiologist can provide. The same resource section can help you locate professional assistance.

*One cloud is enough to eclipse all the sun.*
**Thomas Fuller, M.D.**

Natural light and full spectrum artificial light produce some of the most dramatic, non-invasive improvements of depressive states. For those who are depressed and spend a great deal of time indoors exposed to artificial light, and particularly to video display terminals and televisions, and for those who frequently wear sunglasses when outdoors because of light sensitivity, and those who live in northern latitudes or environments with many overcast days and low light levels, a therapeutic trial of high intensity full spectrum lighting may be very valuable. Neurosensory Development Training also helps when there is a light deficit disorder associated with the depression. Pretesting with the Downing protocols can help determine if a depressed individual will be a likely candidate for this form of neurohormonal balancing. Refer to the earlier section of the book on Biological Rhythms for resources.

Nutrient supplementation helps relieve depression dramatically when there are nutrient deficiencies in the individual. Diet diaries can be inexpensively interpreted by computer nutrition software as a screening device to identify potential nutrient imbalances. Even more simply, an individual can just see how closely he or she abides by the general nutritional guidelines set forth in the section on Nutritional Health. Sometimes nutrient supplementation at basic, generalized levels is enough to

get a positive change. For a large number of cases, some testing, prescription, and monitoring by a skilled professional is necessary because of the significant imbalances that can exist.

Improved diet can eliminate depression caused, or accentuated, by food allergies or hypoglycemia. Refer to the sections on Nutrition and the chapter on Environmental Health for resources and guidelines regarding diet and allergy. Other allergy correction measures can help correct nonfood sources of allergic reactions.

Cranial electrical stimulation (the use of microamperage, TENS-like units with stick-on electrodes) is an old technology, recently rediscovered, that reestablishes normal brain function in depressed patients. Clinical trials have shown impressive results as of this writing. Since it has no known adverse side effects, using it as an alternative to antidepressant medication is highly valuable.

Acupuncture has been used for centuries to successfully help those with depression. Consultation with a qualified doctor of Oriental medicine who has experience treating psychological problems might be an integral part of a complete, successful program of care.

Those who are skilled in cranial manipulation have noted significant improvement with cases of depression. Consulting with a qualified practitioner may be of help. See the resource section on Manipulative Therapies.

Spiritual practices, from affirmations to meditation, have proven to be worthwhile endeavors for those depressed. Not only have guided imageries and meditative practices been found to alter brain biochemistry, they assist in psycho-spiritual development. It is important not to neglect the spiritual aspect of ourselves when psychological ill health is predominant. There are closer ties here than what many of us think. It is also helpful to have the guidance of an experienced, skilled, compassionate spiritual teacher in times of depression. Sometimes depression is a sign of difficult spiritual transformation. Many on the path of spiritual awakening experience a "dark night of the soul." Assistance during those times of transition can be very helpful. Finding a spiritual teacher who also has a deep knowledge of transpersonal psychotherapy helps in integrating these two aspects of our lives. Use the resources in the chapter on Spiritual Health if needed.

Energy medicine in the form of magnet therapy and aromatherapy may yet prove to be helpful in the treatment of depression. More research into these arenas of neuropsychological treatments needs to be done.

Allopathic anti-depressive drug therapy, such as Prozac, has produced dramatic improvements in many people. They should not be discarded outright. But there are big questions when resorting to this form of therapy. Is it eliciting a quick fix and thus encouraging people to ignore proper diet, exercise, light exposure, allergy control, stress reduction, and psychological integration? Will this then cause further dysfunction in other ways in the future? Let us also not forget that while the natural therapies listed here have few or mild side effects, antidepressant drugs can have numerous, serious side effects. If well integrated, comprehensive, holistic health enhancement programs were developed and carried out by depressed individuals and their interdisciplinary network of health practitioners, would antidepressant drug therapy be needed?

*When man has lost all happiness, he is not alive. Call him a breathing corpse.*

**Sophocles**

---

# DIABETES

Approximately 10,000,000 Americans suffer from various forms of diabetes. Ten to fifteen percent of these cases are insulin dependent (type I diabetes mellitus). These involve 90% or greater destruction of pancreatic beta-cells which almost always occurs before the age of thirty. Childhood diabetes is most frequently of this type. It requires lifelong insulin medication to replace the inability of the pancreas to produce it internally.

## SYMPTOMS AND DIAGNOSIS

Excessive thirst, hunger, and urination are the classic signs of diabetes. In type I, weight loss is also frequently seen, whereas in type II obesity is the general rule. The diagnosis is made on the basis of two separate blood glucose tests which register greater than 139 mg/dl; each test must follow overnight fasting. If these tests are negative, and symptoms still suggest diabetes, an oral glucose tolerance test can be performed.

Most diabetes is adult onset (type II) which develops after age thirty and is more responsive to non-pharmaceutical interventions for complete correction.

Both types have a genetic predisposition. This hereditary influence most often affects pancreatic weakness in type I and insulin responsiveness of tissues in type II. Type I seems to be often influenced by pancreatic autoimmunity, possibly of viral origin. Consistently high blood sugar levels in the mother during gestation also seem to have a severe adverse effect on predisposing the infant to diabetes mellitus.

Type II diabetes mellitus is activated by a combination of poor diet, lack of exercise, obesity, and immunological insult. And those are the areas that need to be primarily addressed to enhance health in both type I and type II diabetes. Complete correction can often take place with an effective natural protocol for type II. Greatly reducing insulin requirements and complications of the disease can be attained by a similar program in type I cases.

## NUTRITION

A high complex carbohydrate, high fibre, low sugar, non-allergenic, vegetarian diet is one of the most important aspects of a health regimen for all types of diabetes.

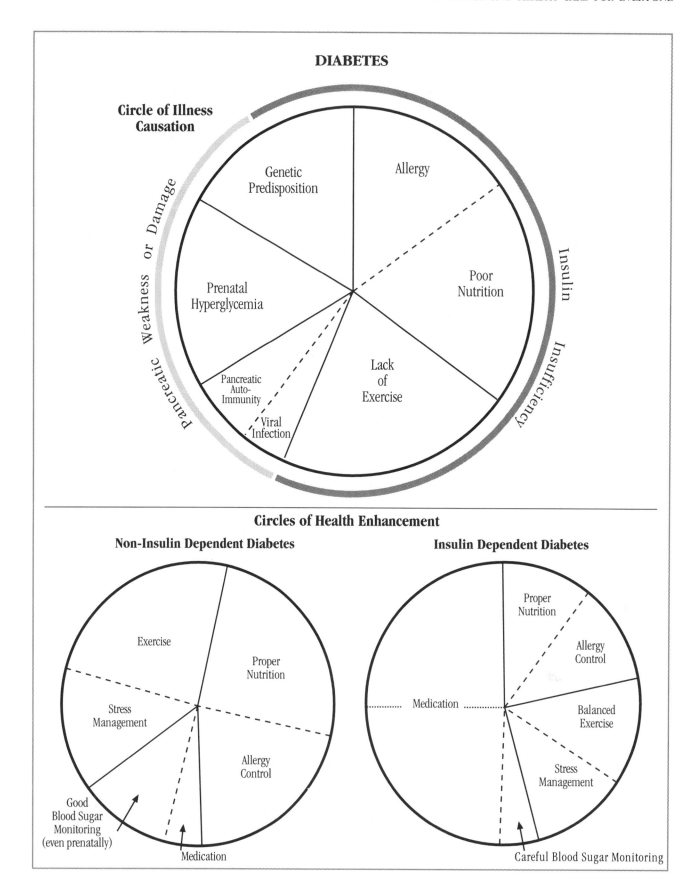

Supplementation can include those items below which have been found by research to help glucose tolerance and some of the complications of the disease:

- B-complex vitamins—25-50 mg per day. B-6, B-12, niacin, thiamine, inositol, and biotin seem to be particularly important in different metabolic pathways.

- Bioflavonoids containing 1-2 grams per day of Quercitin

- Vitamin C—1-3 grams per day or to a bowel tolerance dose. A pH neutral ascorbate form seems to be best in nearly all circumstances.

- Vitamin E—400-800 I.U. per day.

- Magnesium—400 mg per day.

- Chromium—200 micrograms per day.

- Coenzyme $Q_{10}$—30-100 mg per day.

- Cysteine—500 mg twice per day.

- Pectin—up to 7 grams 10 minutes before meals. Guar gum has been used similarly as an added hydrophilic fibre source to meet suggested requirements of 40 grams of total fibre per day.

- Manganese, zinc, copper, potassium, and carnitine may be deficient and need supplementation. Small daily supplemental doses might be taken, but it is often wise to test for deficiencies first and supplement accordingly.

- Hydrochloric acid may need to be supplemented for those with low stomach HCL levels. It is necessary for digestion and absorption of nutrients.

- Bitter melon, onion, fenugreek, garlic, and Gymnema sylvestre (200-400 mg three times per day with meals) are herbal aids to diabetes. Significant research validates their efficacy.

## ALLERGY

Dwight Kalita and William Philpott in their book *Victory over Diabetes* make a strong argument for identifying and correcting food allergies as a major help for diabetics. Using elimination diets with food challenges to determine offending agents is useful. For hidden, delayed immunological reactivity ELISA/ACT™ blood testing can be performed.

## EXERCISE

A safe, effective aerobic conditioning program is very helpful in both type I and type II diabetes. Use the resources in this book, and professional consultation, to select an appropriate exercise regimen to fit your needs.

## REGULAR BLOOD SUGAR MONITORING

Close monitoring of blood sugar levels for more careful administration of insulin can have a dramatic effect in reducing many of the complications of insulin medication and erratic blood sugar fluctuations in type I diabetes. The regular use of at-home blood sugar monitoring devices helps enormously.

## A MULTIDIMENSIONAL APPROACH

A multifaceted, integrated program specific to the individual will produce much better results in either type I or type II diabetes than standard allopathic care centered around drug therapy. Do not ignore all the other primary health enhancement factors listed in the section on Rating Therapies. Items like getting sufficient sleep and light can have an important effect.

## RESOURCES

Kalita, Dwight and Philpott, William. *Victory over Diabetes*. Keats, 1983.

Murray, Michael and Pizzorno, Joseph. *Encyclopedia of Natural Medicine*. Prima Publishing, 1991; pp. 269-85.

Rosenbaum, Michael and Bosco, Dominick. *Super Fitness Beyond Vitamins: The Bible of Super Supplements*. New American Library, 1987.

Rubin, Richard. *Psyching Out Diabetes: A Positive Approach to Your Negative Emotions*. Lowell House, 1992.

Werbach, Melvyn. *Nutritional Influences on Illness: A Sourcebook of Clinical Research*. Third Line Press, 1988; pp. 166-82.

Whitaker, Julian. *Reversing Diabetes*. Warner Books, 1987.

National Diabetes Information Clearinghouse, Box NDIC, 9000 Rockville Pike, Bethesda, MD 20892; (301) 654-3327; Fax (301) 907-8906.

---

# HEADACHES

Forty-two million Americans consult physicians for headache relief each year. Tens of millions more seek remedies outside the doctor's office. Over 250,000,000 work days, and $25,000,000,000 are lost in job productivity due to headaches.[1]

Headaches, like most other pain syndromes, are not so much problems that need simply to be relieved but warning signals identifying dysfunction in one or more of our health aspects. Probably less than 5% of headache cases that reach a physician's attention are caused by serious brain lesions such as tumors, aneurysms, or infections. So, approximately 98% of all headaches are the result of problems that are best dealt with outside the arena of medical/surgical care.

This is reflected in the Circle of Illness Causation for Headaches seen on page 303.

The two major causes of headache are biochemical abnormalities and neuro-musculo-skeletal dysfunction. They overlap, as in the case of headaches caused by hypertension when part of the elevated blood pressure is due to too much salt in the diet and a *tense* lifestyle causing constricted blood vessels. Of all the causes listed in these diagrams, most people experience headaches when several of these factors come into play. Remember, there is seldom ever just one cause to any health problem. The interrelatedness of life dictates that cause and effect relationships are usually complex.

So what do you do if you have a headache? Mindlessly mask these warning signals like the television ads and pharmaceutical companies want you to?

*Two hundred thousand to three hundred thousand cases of gastrointestinal bleeding occur each year, causing an estimated 10,000 to 20,000 deaths due to the use of nonsteroidal, anti-inflammatory pain medication like aspirin, acetaminophen, and ibuprofen.[2]*

Or rush off to a general practitioner's office fearing a brain tumor?

A wise, holistically-minded health care consumer will intelligently investigate the root causes and build a health enhancement program to address those parts of his life which are the most likely origin of the symptoms.

## HEADACHES AS SIGNS OF SERIOUS EMERGENCIES

To be safe, we can prioritize those headaches that might need urgent medical attention by certain characteristics:

Head injury with or without loss of consciousness, plus any of the following symptoms several days after the injury: temperature elevated over 100 degrees F, double or blurred vision with dilated or unequally sized pupils, nausea, vomiting, confusion, convulsions, incoordination, loss of bladder or bowel control, excessive drowsiness, or ear

# HEADACHES

**Circle of Illness Causation**

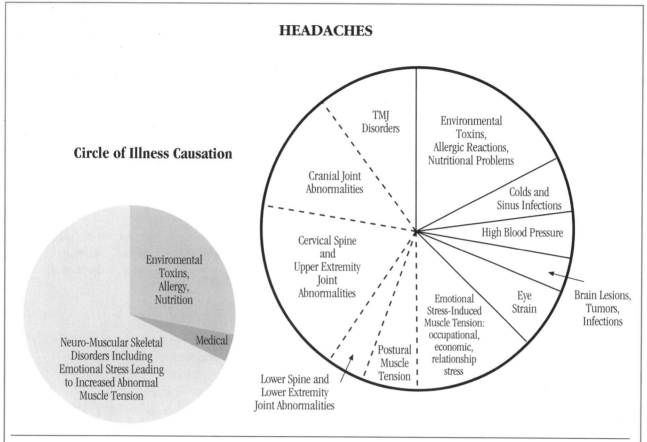

**Circle of Health Enhancement**

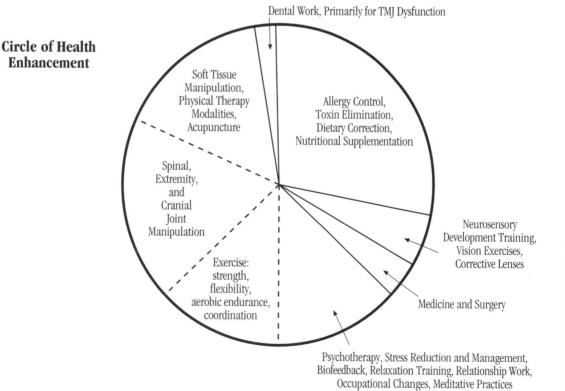

buzzing and ringing that is not brought about by high aspirin consumption. Contacting a physician or emergency room immediately is advised.

The headache began two to twenty-four weeks ago and has increased in intensity. It may be a fairly rapidly developing space occupying lesion or other medical emergency. If the severe pain of the same recent onset is accompanied by neck rigidity, it could be a serious subarachnoid hemorrhage; or if there is a fever, it could be meningitis. If the pain is in one eye with blurred vision and halos around lights, it could be acute glaucoma that needs immediate care. If you are over the age of 50 with a painful, tender temple accompanied by malaise, fever, inability to eat, and difficulty chewing there is the possibility of temporal arteritis which should be evaluated by your physician.

## NON-EMERGENCY CARE

For moderate headaches or periodic recurrent ones like those of migraine, tension, post-concussion syndrome, stress, biochemical imbalance, high blood pressure, mild infections, or eye strain, which account for 98% of all headaches, approaches other than standard medical disease care are more likely to help.

Tension headaches are the most predominant type of head pain. For the problems of muscle tension that create these symptoms, it is not only important to alleviate the muscle tightness and the neurological disruption that accompanies it, but also to address the perpetuating factors that drive the muscle into recurrent spasm. This can be seen as a twofold approach—one working on the neuromuscular structure and function, the other on the lifestyle stress.

Everyone has to evaluate and prioritize how much effort, time, and money needs to be spent on the different elements of lifestyle change involved in getting to the roots of these disturbances. Psychotherapy, biofeedback training, relaxation exercises, relationship work, occupational changes, and meditative practices have all proven to be valuable in the comprehensive treatment of headache. This is because of the powerful impact these factors can have on muscle tension levels.

Post-concussion syndrome (persistent headache, fatigue, personality aberrations, difficulty sleeping, memory and concentration deficits), that follows head injury or neck whiplash, robs at least two million people of their normal function and health every year in the U.S. Motor vehicle accidents are by far the most common cause. Manipulative and physiotherapy rehabilitation is essential for complete recovery.

### Neuro-musculo-skeletal Correction

Concerning the more immediate approaches to direct correction of the neuro-musculo-skeletal elements of the problem, many approaches are valuable:

1. Soft Tissue Manipulation
   a. Deep Tissue Massage
   b. Transverse Friction Massage
   c. Spray and Stretch Technique
   c. Proprioceptive Neuromuscular Facilitation Technique (PNF)
      Key muscles—Posterior cervical, scalenes, trapezius, sterno-cleidomastoid, masseter, anterior temporalis, sub-occipital
2. Joint Manipulation
   a. Spinal (particularly the neck)
   b. Cranial
   c. Extremity (occasionally shoulder restrictions)
3. Physical Therapy Modalities
   a. Electrical Muscle Stimulation
   b. Ultrasound
4. Meridian Therapy
   a. Acupuncture
   b. Micro-current stimulation of meridian points
   c. Auriculo-therapy

Which combination of the above modalities is best suited for any particular individual is probably best decided in close consultation with quality, trusted, health care providers who deliver such services—chiropractors, physical therapists, acupuncturists, in that order. During this process of neuro-musculo-skeletal rehabilitation, exercise can play a key role in recovery as well as overall health enhancement. Strength, flexibility, aerobic conditioning, and coordination assist in muscular integrity that diminishes the chances of headaches arising out of these tissues.

Sometimes the skill of a dentist who specializes in temporomandibular joint problems is called for when the above approaches are not sufficient to deal with them. When eye strain is part of the cause for the headache, an optometrist skilled in diagnostic techniques to identify stereoscopic tracking incoordination, and one skilled in prescribing visual exercise might be best to consult with. Sometimes corrective lenses are in order.

## Biochemical Causes

1. Allergy
   a. pollens, dust, molds, dander
   b. inhalant chemicals, "sick building syndrome"
   c. food, MSG, aspartame
2. Toxic Substances
   a. formaldehyde
   b. mercury dental amalgam
   c. toxic bowel syndrome
   d. chemical exposure (ie. pesticides, industrial solvents . . . )
3. Dietary Indiscretion
   a. caffeine intake and withdrawal
   b. hypoglycemia (low blood sugar)
   c. vasoactive amine consumption—(ie. tyramine, phenylethylamine, chocolate, cheese, alcohol . . . )
4. Nutritional Imbalance
   a. hypocalcemia (low calcium in the blood)
   b. deficiency of vitamins B1, B2, B3, or magnesium
   c. excessive vitamin A, D, or zinc
5. Biochemical abnormalities that can be corrected without drugs or surgery
   a. hypothyroidism (low thyroid function)
   b. anemia
   c. mild infections such as sinusitis, colds
   d. premenstrual syndrome
   e. brain neurotransmitter imbalances

These are some of the more frequent biochemical causes of headache.[3] If there is a suspicion that recurrent headaches occur in a pattern due to exposure to different foods or are related to certain environments or seasons, more detailed testing should be done to verify this likelihood. The simplest are symptom diaries that one can then correlate to food consumption or location. These are usually difficult and inaccurate, for allergic reactions can occur as much as seventy-two hours after exposure. Elimination diets are a bit more accurate but still involve inconvenience and interpretive grey areas. IgE RAST testing for inhalants of all kinds, and ELISA/ACT™ testing for foods, is the most accurate and cost effective method of allergy testing to date.

Exposure to toxic substances is almost unavoidable in modern society. Minimizing exposure and building up our body's defenses are the best we can do. Check living and working areas and eliminate potential hazards using Debra Dadd-Redalia's book, *Sustaining the Earth: Choosing Consumer Products That Are Safe for You, Your Family, and the Earth*. If there are significant mercury amalgam dental fillings to be concerned about, you can be tested for oral mercury vapor levels by contacting the Huggins Diagnostic Center (800) 331-2303; (719) 548-1600 for a referral.

Toxic bowel syndrome might be suspected if malodorous stools and flatulence is a problem. Testing can be done at a holistic physician's office who uses a comprehensive stool and digestive analysis or a similar diagnostic panel. Correction usually involves bowel detoxification, improved diet, and nutritional supplements which include healthy forms of *Lactobacillus acidophilus* and *Bifidobacterium*.

Caffeine intake and withdrawal are well known causes of headaches. Simple solution—no caffeine. Erratic blood sugar levels from poor dietary practices is also a very frequent cause of headaches. Using the nutritional guidelines in the section on Nutrition will solve most hypoglycemic (low blood sugar) problems. Allergies also cause hypoglycemia, so that has to be considered in addition, particularly food allergies. Some people react to vasoactive amines like phenylethylamine that is found in chocolate. Some professionals consider this to be an allergic reaction or food intolerance. By whatever name they go by, or by whatever method of identification is needed, find these irritative substances and eliminate them from the diet.

Nutrient levels can cause headaches also. On rare occasions excessively large and prolonged intake of supplemental A, D, or zinc can elicit a headache. A simple test and simple solution—a trial vacation from these supplements will bring quick relief. Much more frequent, though, is nutrient deficiency, particularly magnesium deficiency in cases of migraine headache. Since testing for nutrient deficiency is expensive and has variable reliability, often a more cost-effective approach is to take a high potency multivitamin and multimineral supplement for a six month trial period.

Neurotransmitter imbalance within the brain can be corrected with cranial electrical stimulation from a battery operated TENS-like device. This can frequently eliminate the need for medication.

There is a wide variety of biochemical abnormalities which can cause headaches. The vast majority can be dealt with by natural holistic approaches, not medical or surgical ones. Finding a good holistic physician to help might be indicated, but much can be done with self-care if the resources in this book are consulted.

## REFERENCES

1. Craig Nelson and Patrick Boline, "A Consensus on the Assessment and Treatment of Headache," *Chiropractic Technique* 3:4 (November 1991), 151.
2. Food and Drug Administration.
3. Charles Theisler, *Migraine Headache Disease: Diagnostic and Management Strategies* (Aspen Publishers, 1990).

---

## HYPERTENSION—HIGH BLOOD PRESSURE

Over 50,000,000 Americans have a repeatable blood pressure of 140/90 or greater. Millions of these individuals have dangerously high blood pressure (HBP) without knowing it because they have not been tested.

Approximately 10% of hypertension is caused by some other underlying disease such as kidney disease or heart disease. It is important to rule out these causative factors when HBP is discovered. When HBP is not secondary to some other organ disease, it can most often be managed well using nutritional and lifestyle changes, with medication being unnecessary. There are inherited factors which predispose individuals to HBP. These people usually have to be more diligent in maintaining their health.

The multidimensional Circle of Health Enhancement shows the details of effective lifestyle changes which can dramatically control HBP and provide better overall health in many other ways.

## NUTRITIONAL FACTORS

A major portion of the program will involve nutritional elements. Quite a bit of research supports the recommendations given here. A high-fibre, high-potassium, low-salt, low-fat, low-sugar, non-allergenic vegetarian diet is at the core of the nutritional considerations. Identifying food allergies is not always easy. Elimination diets with food challenges can find some offending substances. Other agents causing delayed immunological reactions and biochemical imbalance can be determined with an ELISA/ACT™ blood test.

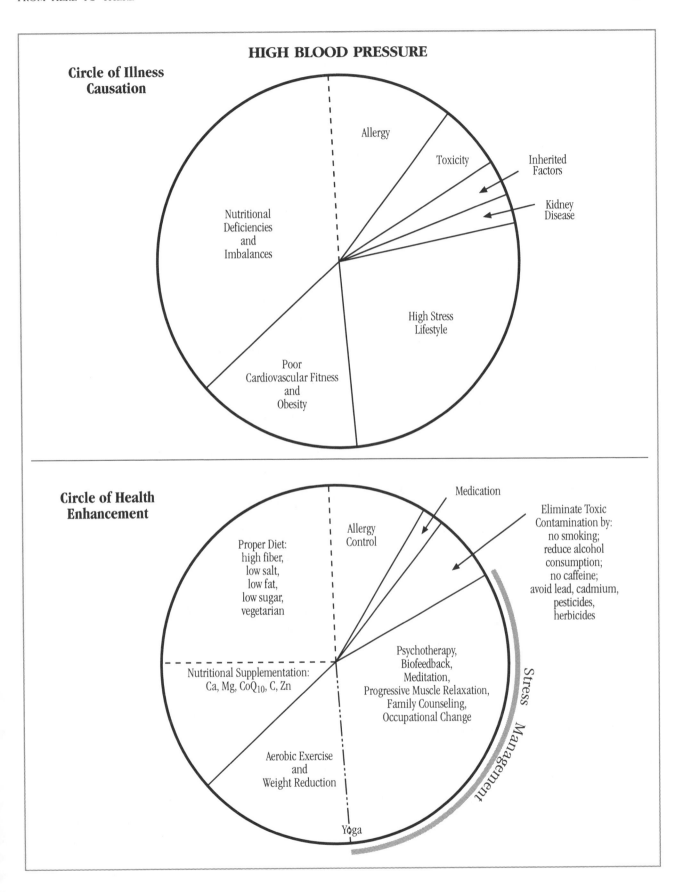

**HIGH BLOOD PRESSURE**

**Circle of Illness Causation**

Allergy

Toxicity

Inherited Factors

Kidney Disease

Nutritional Deficiencies and Imbalances

High Stress Lifestyle

Poor Cardiovascular Fitness and Obesity

**Circle of Health Enhancement**

Medication

Eliminate Toxic Contamination by: no smoking; reduce alcohol consumption; no caffeine; avoid lead, cadmium, pesticides, herbicides

Allergy Control

Proper Diet: high fiber, low salt, low fat, low sugar, vegetarian

Psychotherapy, Biofeedback, Meditation, Progressive Muscle Relaxation, Family Counseling, Occupational Change

Nutritional Supplementation: Ca, Mg, CoQ$_{10}$, C, Zn

Stress Management

Aerobic Exercise and Weight Reduction

Yoga

Nutritional supplementation which has been researched has fallen in the ranges indicated below:

- B-complex vitamins—25-75 mg per day of the major B vitamins.

- Beta carotene—10,000-25,000 I.U. per day.

- Vitamin C—1-3 grams per day or to a bowel tolerance dose. A pH neutral ascorbate form with 5-10% bioflavonoids seems to be best in nearly all circumstances.

- Vitamin D—is essential for mineral metabolism. Exposure to sunshine is usually sufficient to provide adequate amounts. If outdoor activity is limiting this nutrient 400 I.U. per day is a helpful supplemental dosage.

- Calcium—1-2 grams per day.

- Magnesium—300-800 mg per day. This mineral goes hand-in-hand with calcium.

- Potassium—500-2,000 mg per day. Although increased potassium intake is usually accomplished with the change to a vegetarian diet, often potassium supplementation can be helpful. For approximately 50% of hypertensives who are salt sensitive, lowering salt intake is also very important. Maintaining an ideal potassium to sodium ratio can be a key factor in controlling HBP.

- Coenzyme $Q_{10}$—60 mg per day.

- Essential fatty acids—10-16 grams per day of either Omega-3 or Omega-6 fatty acids in the form of fish liver oil, flaxseed oil, or evening primrose oil.

- Zinc—Supplementation can be used to counteract excessive cadmium levels.

## TOXIC FACTORS

Smoking is probably the most problematic and prevalent factor. Some of this may come from the heavy metal cadmium. A hair mineral analysis can identify body burden of this toxic element. Zinc supplementation can help counteract its effect. Lead has also been shown to be correlated with HBP and can be identified in a hair mineral analysis. Stopping smoking is a major part of the corrective measures needed.

Reducing alcohol consumption is another major health enhancement effort that will bring many rewards. Restricting caffeine consumption will also help. Pesticide and herbicide contamination may be contributing causes, also.

## EXERCISE AND WEIGHT REDUCTION

Because obesity is a major factor in HBP, any safe and effective weight reduction program is helpful. Part of that involves a vegetarian diet. Another major factor is regular aerobic exercise. It tends to relieve stress at the same time that it improves the cardiovascular function. Proper exercise prescription and professional monitoring is advisable for individuals with HBP.

Other exercise programs can work side-by-side with an aerobic protocol. Yoga stretching exercises are relaxing, in addition to helping condition the muscles and joints so that injuries are less frequent and severe. Progressive muscle relaxation exercises can relieve ingrained patterns of stress.

## STRESS MANAGEMENT

Stress management is important in managing hypertension. Aspects of this can include stress reduction, stress avoidance, lessening time urgency, occupational changes, biofeedback, hypnosis, relaxation training, meditation, psychotherapy, social support, and play.

## SUMMARY

When the proper combination of lifestyle changes is adopted, not only can blood pressure be controlled to normal limits, but our overall health can improve in many ways. When individuals do not want to take responsibility for these lifestyle changes, or on occasions of severe HBP, medication may be necessary, since this disease can be life threatening, even without symptoms.

## RESOURCES

Bennett, Cleave and Cameron, Charles. *Lower Your Blood Pressure Without Drugs!* Doubleday, 1986.

Kerman, Ariel with Trubo, Richard. *The H.A.R.T. Program: Lower Blood Pressure Without Drugs.* Harper-Collins, 1992.

Moore, Richard. *The High Blood Pressure Solution: Natural Prevention and Cure with the 'K' Factor.* Healing Arts Press, 1993.

Murray, Michael and Pizzorno, Joseph. *Encyclopedia of Natural Medicine.* Prima Publishing, 1991: 378-85.

Perlmutter, David. "Gaining Control of Hypertension." *Townsend Letter for Doctors* (June, 1994): 575-6.

Werbach, Melvyn. *Nutritional Influences on Illness: A Sourcebook of Clinical Research.* Third Line Press, 1988: 227-40.

---

# HYPERACTIVITY, ATTENTION DEFICIT DISORDERS, LEARNING DISABILITIES, AND SENSORY INTEGRATION DYSFUNCTION

*Children today are tyrants.*
*They contradict their parents, gobble their food, and tyrannize their teachers.*

**Socrates**

Various experts like to classify health problems of this genre in a multitude of different ways, depending on how each views their causes and the different combinations of manifestations. What name we attach to these related problems is less important than a comprehensive assessment of the various dysfunctional elements in all aspects of one's life. If we see these problems as multi-causal over a broad band of physical, psychological, educational, social, and ecological considerations, we will do much better at resolving these problems.

Basically we are looking at dysfunctional elements such as:

- Inability to concentrate, lack of one-pointed attention, doesn't complete tasks

- Impulsiveness

- Low stress tolerance and short temper, which disrupt relationships

- Poor time management

- Excessive mood swings—from hyperactivity to depression

- Slow in learning or achievement

- Not a systematic problem solver

- Visual complaints

Some have tried to simplify the causes, saying it is either genetic, brain damage during gestation, poor parenting practice, or a combination of the three. Whether these problems occur in the child or the adult, a more useful way to view the possible causative contributions is to consider all of those elements identified in the chart, Circle of Illness Causation.

A multitude of different assessment tools need to be applied in each segment of the Circle of Illness to determine how much each aspect is contributing to the problem. Often in evaluation of learning disabilities, conduct disorders, ADD, or hyperactivity, certain standardized psychometric and cognitive tests are performed to establish a diagnosis and acquire some baseline for performance in those areas. The Bender Visual-Motor Gestalt Test, Stanford-Binet, Halstead Reitan, Luria-Johnson Test of Cognition and Achievement, and the Weschler Intelligence Scale for Children are often used. But other forms of testing are ignored, thus blinding professionals, patients, and their families from pursuing important types of care.

In any given individual diagnosed as having learning disabilities, attention deficits, hyperactivity, or sensory integration dysfunction, different ratios of contributing elements will combine to

# HYPERACTIVITY, ATTENTION DEFICIT DISORDERS, LEARNING DISABILITIES, AND SENSORY INTEGRATION DYSFUNCTION

**Circle of Illness Causation**

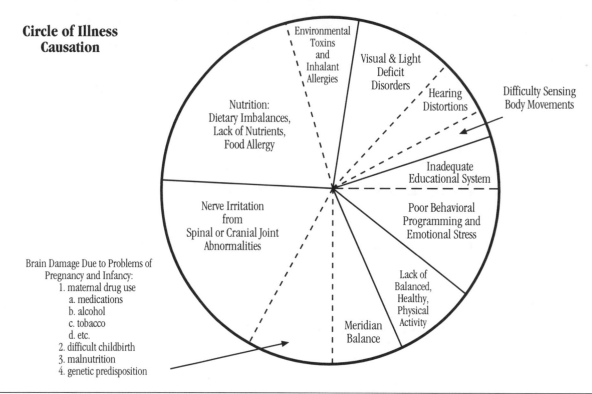

**Circle of Health Enhancement**

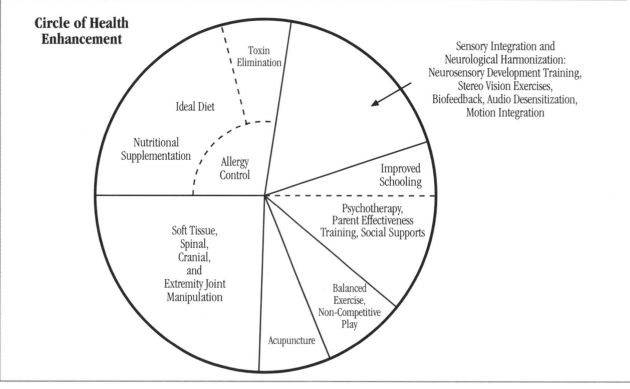

form their particular constellation of symptoms. No one will have a single cause. Most will have significant contributions from five or six areas, all of which might need some therapeutic intervention. Many patients will have substantial residual problems if just one area is left untreated—thus the importance of multi-disciplinary assessment and treatment.

## GENETIC PREDISPOSITION

Scientific research has identified some genetic influence in problems like dyslexia, but genetic testing for carriers of the markers is still in the future. Further into the future is any possible genetic correction of the problem.

## BRAIN DAMAGE AND NEUROLOGICAL INSULT

A thorough multigenerational history can give clues to genetic predisposition, maternal health practices during pregnancy, difficulties in delivery or infant care, and any dysfunctional family dynamics. This can lead to more detailed examination of increased nutritional needs later in life due to biochemical imbalance in those early formative periods. Or more attention might be given to identifying possible residual neurological damage due to a difficult birth. This might include tests not usually performed, such as chiropractic cervical spinal joint testing to identify hidden neurological irritations to structures like the reticular activating system. This nerve center at the top of the neck functions as our awareness center, which prioritizes nerve signals coming from the body to the brain. Osteopathic evaluations of the cranium can also prove valuable in identifying nerve irritants which are at the root of many of these diagnoses. Cervical spine and cranial joint abnormalities are so prevalent in these individuals that these problems should never go without treatment.

There is also evidence that abnormal behavior caused by unbalanced neurotransmitter function can be corrected with cranial electrical stimulation.

This involves placing stick-on electrodes to the surface of the head. Then through a battery pack electrical current (so small it can be barely felt) signals nerves to function better. This seems to stimulate normalization of the brain without any adverse side effects and can eliminate the need for medications.

## NUTRITION

Lack of sound nutrition can account for many of the symptoms. All cases should have multilevel nutritional evaluations done. Dietary indiscretions can create erratic blood sugar changes which can elicit most of the behavioral, cognitive, intellectual, emotional, and interactive problems associated with these conditions. Glucose tolerance tests can verify this type of abnormality. What is often a more valuable, less stressful, less expensive, and more simplified glucose monitoring method is the one which diabetics are using with increasing benefits. It involves periodic blood glucose testing throughout the day at home with advanced medical gadgetry that accurately assesses blood sugar levels from just a finger pinprick of blood.

The most obvious culprits in these instances are caffeine, simple sugars, and artificial additives. Large meals or extended spacing between meals are prominent offenders also. Sometimes the most significant offense is eating foods to which one has an intolerance, allergy, or hypersensitivity. This can cause an actual inflammation of the brain tissues or contribute significantly to erratic blood sugar levels or altered neurotransmitter function.

Elimination of the offending foods can bring dramatic results, as can various other forms of allergy control like orthomolecular (literally means "correct amount") nutritional supplementation to improve the immune response, or sometimes serial dilution desensitization (a technique which doctors of environmental medicine use to desensitize people to their allergens). If a thorough symptom diary reveals a hint of food allergy, or any addictive craving for certain foods, or only a certain small number of foods are eaten repetitively, more detailed ELISA/ACT™ food allergy testing can be done.

Because of these dietary indiscretions, or for other reasons, there are often too few vitamins, minerals, trace elements, or amino acids. Sometimes certain individuals have an increased need for certain nutrients even though they seem to be getting amounts that keep others healthy. A number of research studies show a direct correlation between nutrient levels and educational performance, and between nutrient levels and behavioral problems.

Biochemical testing for nutritional deficiencies and excesses is difficult. Many of the tests are inaccurate. The ones that are accurate are often expensive. Often the wisest approach is to take the recommendations in the section on Nutritional Health in the Physical Health chapter.

## ENVIRONMENTAL CONCERNS

Adverse neurological reactions to environmental agents are frequent and significant contributing causes to these conditions, and they need to be evaluated for in most cases. People can have abnormal reactions to normally-occurring natural substances like pollen or molds, or to unnatural pervasive substances like air pollution, perfume, synthetic products that emit chemicals which do not obviously elicit pronounced symptoms in most people; or to artificial colors, flavors and food preservatives, or to obvious toxins like lead, cadmium, aluminum, or mercury poisoning.

Lead, aluminum, and cadmium levels should be checked by hair analysis on all children and most adults with these diagnoses. Those with mercury dental amalgams should be analyzed for mercury vapor excesses in the oral cavity. Often removal of mercury dental amalgams, and replacement with less reactive materials, is recommended. It is not recommended that any new fillings containing mercury be added. High levels of toxic metals can be chelated out of the system with I.V. infusions of EDTA by physicians trained and certified by the American Board of Chelation Therapy. For those with less contamination and who can't afford this treatment, some extraction of these harmful substances can be obtained with:

- vitamins C, E, A
- calcium
- sulfhydral amino acids—lysine, methionine, cystine
- alginate
- pectin

Those with known or suspected inhalant allergies should be comprehensively tested with IgE RAST blood analysis.

## VISUAL AND LIGHT DEFICIT DISORDERS

Visual problems are prevalent in the learning disabled. New optometric testing to find slight abnormalities of stereoscopic coordination can help many of these problems. Computerized visual training programs have been designed to remedy many of these visual aberrations. An optometrist who is certified by the College of Optometrists in Vision Development (P.O. Box 285, Chula Vista, CA 91912; (619) 425-6191) could provide the proper testing and treatment for these abnormalities.

Light deficit disorders plague not only the learning disabled but also those with attention deficits, hyperactivity, and emotional components. Nerve signals going from the eyes to various portions of the brain influence many essential brain functions. Defects in this signaling can be corrected, but only if they are tested for. Contact John Downing, O.D., Ph.D. at (707) 525-4747 or Lumitron Corporation, mailing address—2261 Market St., Suite 504, San Francisco, CA 94114; (404) 458-6509; Fax (404) 458-4109 for a testing and treatment facility near you. Low light levels, prolonged exposure to artificial indoor light, heavy television or VDT watching, and inadequate exposure to direct sunlight are causes of light deficit disorders. Correction can come with repeated exposure to colored lights. Even if this is not readily available, simply increase exposure to natural light and use "full spectrum" lighting. Decrease exposure to unnatural wavelength frequencies which are emitted by normal fluorescent and incandescent bulbs.

## OTHER DISTURBANCES OF SENSORY INPUT

A significant percentage of children with learning disabilities have hearing problems which can in themselves create difficulties. But they also often combine with visual aberrations and motion perception difficulties. Often when an audiograph is done on a learning disabled child, certain sound frequencies are found to be hypersensitively perceived and interpreted differently in each ear. This can be very confusing to the nervous system.

An entire method of auditory retraining called the Berard Method has been developed to correct this problem. Once the hypersensitive frequencies are found through testing with an audiologist, a special audio enhancing device plays music to the children with these frequencies filtered out. This improves hearing and seems to make a profound difference in how efficiently the brain processes information.

One innovative way to correct multiple sensory integration problems is to use the Berard Method for auditory retraining, but at the same time expose the children to a particular sequence of colored light which helps harmonize the nervous system. This technique also incorporates body movement by having the child experience this sensory input while on a platform moving in a circular pattern. Excellent results have transpired. More research in this field needs to be done to discover the best protocols for optimal sensory training.

## INADEQUATE EDUCATION SYSTEM

*I took a course in speed reading and was able to read* War and Peace *in twenty minutes.*
*It's about Russia.*

**Woody Allen**

How are children affected by being forced to sit at desks in neat rows for prolonged periods of time when their bodies are telling them to run, play, dance, or escape the boredom and confusion? Individualized curriculum planning along with upgraded testing, placement, and teaching methods can serve our children's varying needs in a more productive way. It is possible to keep the causes of these problems from arising out of the school system itself. Furthermore, cutbacks in funds for schools harm the most disadvantaged children.

Educational counselors and tutors exist in nearly all communities who can help with the testing, diagnosis, and creation of special curricula to correct some of these problems.

Presently, relaxation training, concentration exercises, and biofeedback protocols are producing impressive results. New, more sophisticated, biofeedback training protocols are being successfully developed. Some include a multidimensional approach utilizing:

1. EMG training (to calm down excessive muscular activity)
2. EEG Sensorimotor Rhythm and Beta (13-25 Hz) enhancement (which stimulates cognitive function) combined with cognitive skills rehabilitation training
3. EEG Theta (4-7 Hz) suppression (which suppresses daydreaming-like mental activity)
4. Family systems counseling to correct dysfunction in the family.

## THE FAMILY'S INFLUENCE

*A torn jacket is soon mended;*
*but hard words bruise the heart of a child.*

**Henry Wadsworth Longfellow**

Psychological stresses in the home, such as poor behavioral programming, can contribute significantly to these problems, particularly when other problems have already taken their toll. Analyzing how the family works helps expose these contributing problems. When family counseling results in a more harmonious family life, it leads to enormous improvements in intellectual performance.

## PHYSICAL ACTIVITY

Balanced, healthy physical activity, in the adult and child, help the body maintain all of its different functions, especially neurologic coordination, maintenance of biochemical balance, and even the dissipation or expression of emotional energy.

## LIFE ENERGY

Practitioners of traditional Oriental medicine might say that many of the symptoms present in these conditions are the result of an imbalanced flow of *chi*, or life energy. Because acupuncture does make dramatic improvements in many of these cases, checking for meridian balance may be an important consideration.

## SUMMARY

Multidimensional approaches to learning disabilities, attention deficit disorders, hyperactivity, conduct disorders, and sensory integration dysfunction will be the standard of care in the future. The elements we have touched on here will be at the core of these protocols, but new procedures will emerge as investigation continues.

## RESOURCES

★Denotes Best of the Best Resources

### *Books*

Barkley, Russell. *Attention Deficit Hyperactivity Disorder: A Handbook for Diagnosis and Treatment.* Guilford Press, 1991.

Berard, Guy. *Hearing Equals Behavior.* Keats, 1993.

★Crook, William. *Help for the Hyperactive Child.* Professional Books, 1991.

Crook, William and Stevens, Laura. *Solving the Puzzle of Your Hard-to-Raise Child.* Random House, 1987.

Galland, Leo with Buchman, Dian. *Superimmunity for Kids.* Delta, 1988.

Hicks, Barbara. *Uncharted Waters: Parenting an Attachment Disordered Child.* Available from The Attachment Disorder Parents' Network of Massachusetts, 2 Bogren Lane, Wayland, MA 01778; (508) 655-3461. For severely violent behavioral disturbances.

★Hippchen, Leonard. *Ecologic-Biochemical Approaches to Treatment of Delinquents and Criminals.* Van Nostrand Reinhold, 1978: 61-74, 111-13, 206-28, 254-68, 328-40.

Humphrey, J.H. and Humphrey, J.N., ed. *Controlling Stress in Children.* Charles C. Thomas, 1988.

Liberman, Jacob. *Light: Medicine of the Future.* Bear & Co., 1991: 81-106.

*The Non-Toxic Baby,* from Natural Choices, 204 N. El Camino Real, Suite E214, Encinitas, CA 92024; (619) 632-1335.

Pizzorno, Joseph and Murray, Michael. *Encyclopedia of Natural Medicine.* Prima Publishing, 1991: 372-77.

★Rapp, Doris. *Is This Your Child? Discovering and Treating Unrecognized Allergies.* William Morrow and Co., 1991.

Rapp, Doris and Bamberg, Dorothy. *The Impossible Child in School, at Home: A Guide for Caring Teachers and Parents.* Practical Allergy, 1988.

Reynolds, Cecil and Kamphaus, Randy, eds. *Handbook of Psychological and Educational Assessment of Children: Personality, Behavior, and Context.* Guilford, 1990.

Rosenbaum, Lilian. *Biofeedback Frontiers.* AMS Press, 1989: 200-8.

Upledger, John E. and Vredevoogd, Jon D. *Craniosacral Therapy.* Eastland Press, 1983: 260-61.

Wender, Paul. *The Hyperactive Child, Adolescent, and Adult: Attention Deficit Disorder Through The Lifespan.* Oxford University Press, 1987.

Werbach, Melvyn. *Nutritional Influences on Mental Illness: A Sourcebook of Clinical Research* Third Line Press, 1991: 56-74, 177-91.

West, Thomas. *In the Mind's Eye.* Prometheus Books, 1991.

### *Journal Articles*

Buttram, Harold. "Protecting Children from Toxic Environmental Chemicals" *Townsend Letter for Doctors* (April, 1993): 312-15.

★ Buttram, Harold. "Volatile Organic Compounds: Contributory Causes of Learning Disabilities and Behavioral Problems in Children." *Townsend Letter for Doctors* (May, 1994): 473-75. Also: "Contaminated Classrooms: When Learning Becomes Lethal." *Townsend Letter for Doctors* (Jan, 1993): 114-18.

See—Liberman, Jacob. *Light: Medicine of the Future.* Bear & Co., 1991: 231-32.

Lubar, Joel. "Discourse on the Development of EEG Diagnostics and Biofeedback for Attention-Deficit/ Hyperactivity Disorders." *Biofeedback and Self-Regulation* 16:3 (1991): 201-25.

Torisky, Danielle, et al. "The NAC Pilot Project: A Model for Nutrition Screening and Intervention for Developmentally Disabled Children with Behavior Disorders." *Journal of Orthomolecular Medicine* 8:1 (1993): 25-42.

### *Computerized Biofeedback Training*

*Autogenic A620 EEG Neurofeedback System for ADD/ADHD,* Autogenics Physiological Monitoring and Feedback, 620 Wheat Lane, Wood Dale, IL 60191; (708) 860-9700.

"Clinical Applications of EEG: Alcohol & Drug Addictions, Attention Deficit Disorders (ADD/ADHD)." A two day course for clinicians with instructor Tom Allen, sponsored by the Stens Corporation, 6451 Oakwood Dr. Oakland, CA 94611-1350; (800) 257-8367; (510) 339-9053; Fax (510) 339-2222.

"Neurotherapy EEG Training Program for Intermediate or Advanced Practitioners." A three day course for clinicians with instructors Joel Lubar and Judith Lubar, sponsored by the Stens Corporation.

### *Organizations*

Learning Disabilities Association of America, 4156 Library Road, Pittsburgh, PA 15234; (412) 341-1515; Fax (412) 344-0224. Provides an extensive resource center for hundreds of publications on the subject.

The Georgiana Organization, P.O. Box 2607, Westport, CT O6880; (203) 454-1221. A clearinghouse for information on the Berard Method of auditory retraining.

The Orton Dyslexia Society; (800) 222-3123; (410) 296-0232 (in Maryland). A clearinghouse for information on testing, tutoring, and computer assisted aids.

# INFECTIONS

Upper respiratory infections, the common cold, the flu, and other microbial infections are the most frequent causes of worker and student absenteeism, the most prevalent reasons for seeing a general practitioner, and the causes of billions of dollars in lost earnings, productivity, and taxes.

Infections are such a pervasive problem not so much because of all the bad germs flying around everywhere, as because of all the assaults we impose on our bodies and minds. This weakens the immune system, which fights infections.

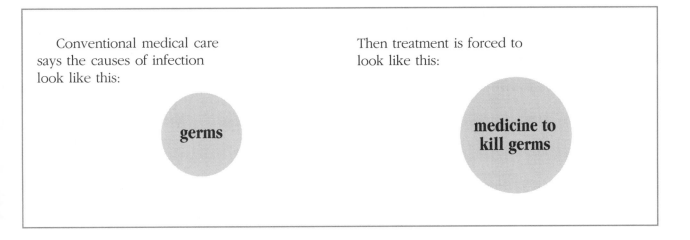

Conventional medical care says the causes of infection look like this:

germs

Then treatment is forced to look like this:

medicine to kill germs

Which, if we are lucky, leads to:

**same person,
same malfunctioning organs,
same weak immune system,
same dysfunctional lifestyle,
but with dead germ carcasses
floating in the body**

Or, if we are unlucky, like hundreds of thousands of people who react inadequately or adversely to antibiotics:

**sicker than before**    or    **hospitalized with a super infection**    or    **dead**

But if we look at the varied aspects of our life and how each one might weaken our immune system so that microbes have a fertile ground to run rampant, the "multi-causal" picture of infection looks more like this:

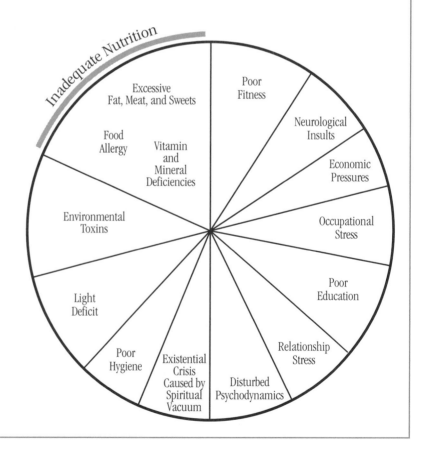

Which then makes immediate crisis intervention with natural, safe methods look like this:

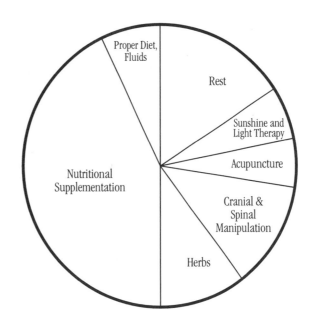

And true, natural enhancement of the immune system looks like this:

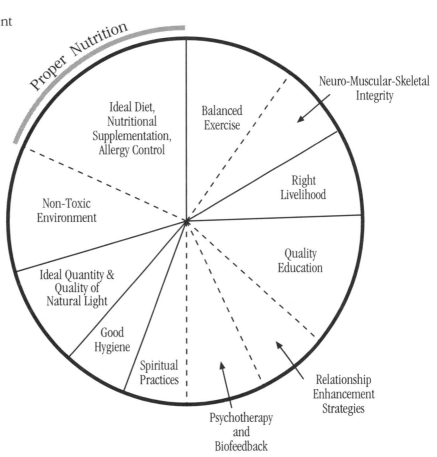

The result should then be:

**A transformed individual with optimally functioning body and mind, with minimal risk of infection, working productively at a livelihood that helps humanity and provides a good standard of living for the family. An individual who relates well to others and the environment in a way that provides wholeness and integration to all life.**

## IMMUNE ENHANCEMENT RESOURCES

★Denotes Best of the Best Resources

Enby, Eric; Gosch, Peter; Sheehan, Michael. *Hidden Killers.* Available from World Research Foundation, 15300 Ventura Blvd., Suite 405, Sherman Oaks, CA 91403; (818) 907-5483.

★Galland, Leo. *Superimmunity for Kids.* Copestone Press, 1988.

★Haas, Elson. *Staying Healthy with Nutrition.* Celestial Arts, 1991: 789-99.

★Health Studies Collegium. *Information Handbook: Immune Enhancement Program.* Health Studies Collegium, 1990. Available from Serammune Physicians Lab, 1890 Preston White Dr., Suite 200, Reston, VA 22091; (703) 758-0610; (800) 553-5472.

Murray, Michael and Pizzorno, Joseph. *Encyclopedia of Natural Medicine.* Prima Publishing, 1991: 57-68.

Schindler, Lydia W. *Understanding the Immune System.* NIH, 1991. (NIH pub. no. 92-529.)

Schmidt, Michael; Sehnert, Keith; Smith, Lendon. *Beyond Antibiotics: 50 (or so) Ways to Boost Immunity and Avoid Antibiotics.*

### PROFESSIONAL RESOURCES

Ader, R; Felten, D; and Cohen, N. eds. *Psychoneuroimmunology.* Academic Press, 1990.

★Bland, Jeffrey. *Immune Modulation: The Prevention of Immunosenescence.* HealthComm, 1989.

Kiecolt-Glaser, J.K. and Glaser, R. "Stress and the Immune System: Human Studies." *Annual Review of Psychiatry* 11(American Psychiatric Press, 1991): 169-80.

Levine, Stephen and Kidd, Parris. *Antioxidant Adaptation: Its Role in Free Radical Pathology.* Allergy Research Group, 1986.

Locke, Steven. *Psychological and Behavioral Treatments for Disorders Associated with the Immune System: An Annotated Bibliography.* Available from the Fetzer Institute, 9292 W. KL Ave., Kalamazoo, MI 49009; (616) 375-2000.

Werbach, Melvyn. *Nutritional Influences on Illness: A Sourcebook of Clinical Research.* Third Line Press, 1988: 252-62.

# PREMENSTRUAL SYNDROME

All menstruating women will experience some symptoms of Premenstrual Syndrome (PMS) at some time. Often the sensations are so mild they go unnoticed. For a large number of women the symptoms can be debilitating. The physical, emotional, and mental changes are the result of hormonal and biochemical fluctuations which normally occur at this stage in the menstrual cycle. Why is one woman's experience insignificant and another's devastating?

All living organisms have many ways to adapt to the stresses imposed upon them by their environment. In normal times when stress is moderate, these psychophysiological mechanisms can maintain a relatively healthy state. Add too much stress from the environment, and it can overtax the organism, bringing out symptoms and illness. Or if the internal physiological or psychological mechanisms are too damaged, weak, or ineffective, even normal amounts of stress cannot be tolerated without a breakdown.

Hormones are intimately involved in PMS. They are very potent modifiers of biochemistry. Any abnormal fluctuation in hormone levels can cause dramatic and erratic alterations in physiology. One is particularly vulnerable when external stresses or underlying nutritional deficiencies intensify hormonal imbalance.

So one of the wisest ways for a woman to pursue natural health enhancement is to understand some of the powerful sources of stress that distort hormone balance and upset so much of her physiology.

If we look at the Circle of Illness Causation for Premenstrual Syndrome, we see a number of important problems:

1. nutrient imbalances
2. toxic contamination and immunological insult
3. spinal nerve irritation
4. poor physical conditioning
5. psycho-social stress
6. altered biological rhythms

The more of these that operate in a woman, the greater is the likelihood that more significant symptoms will be present. Some women may be affected only by a few. In other women, all might be powerfully at work.

Let's turn to the multidimensional Circle of Health Enhancement for Premenstrual Syndrome and investigate each section of the circle separately.

## PROPER DIET AND NUTRIENT SUPPLEMENTATION

It is well documented that many nutritional factors play a role in PMS. From this scientific and clinical evidence we can make certain recommendations:

The diet should be one high in complex carbohydrates, vegetable proteins such as legumes, and green leafy vegetables. It should be low in refined sugars, cabbage, Brussels sprouts, cauliflower, dairy products, salt, coffee, tea, chocolate, or other sources of caffeine. Animal fats, saturated fats, trans-fatty acids (margarine) should be entirely replaced with a small quantity of vegetable oils such as flax, canola, olive, and sunflower, which are rich in essential fatty acids. Only organically grown meat should be consumed to avoid artificial veterinary hormone contamination. If there is evidence of food allergy, an elimination diet with food challenges may be necessary to avoid foods that are stressful to one's biochemistry. ELISA/ACT™ immune system sensitivity testing can be used to identify delayed food reactions.

Even with a good diet, supplementation can be helpful and in many cases essential. Scientific research supports the following therapeutic dosages when women are suffering from PMS:

- Beta carotene—50,000-300,000 I.U. per day for the two weeks prior to onset of menstruation. (Since the higher dosage ranges can have some toxic effects, supervision by a knowledgeable health care professional is recommended.)

- B-Complex vitamins—25-75 mg per day of the major B vitamins.

# PREMENSTRUAL SYNDROME

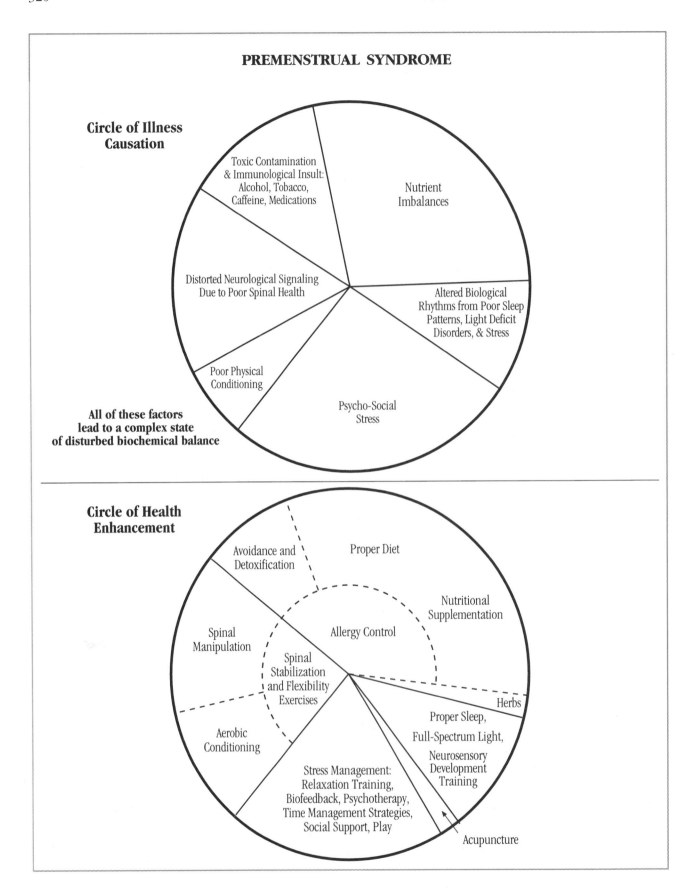

**Circle of Illness Causation**

Toxic Contamination & Immunological Insult: Alcohol, Tobacco, Caffeine, Medications

Nutrient Imbalances

Distorted Neurological Signaling Due to Poor Spinal Health

Altered Biological Rhythms from Poor Sleep Patterns, Light Deficit Disorders, & Stress

Poor Physical Conditioning

Psycho-Social Stress

**All of these factors lead to a complex state of disturbed biochemical balance**

**Circle of Health Enhancement**

Avoidance and Detoxification

Proper Diet

Nutritional Supplementation

Spinal Manipulation

Allergy Control

Spinal Stabilization and Flexibility Exercises

Herbs

Aerobic Conditioning

Proper Sleep, Full-Spectrum Light, Neurosensory Development Training

Stress Management: Relaxation Training, Biofeedback, Psychotherapy, Time Management Strategies, Social Support, Play

Acupuncture

- Vitamin B-6—100-500 mg per day, especially during the ten days prior to the onset of menstruation. (Long term doses of 200 mg per day and higher can cause sensory neurological damage. Early stage symptoms include tingling and numbness of the extremities. These adverse changes can most often be avoided with the use of a particular form of the vitamin, pyridoxal-5-phosphate.)

- Vitamin C—1-3 grams or to a bowel tolerance level. A pH neutral ascorbate form with at least 5% bioflavonoids is most often best.

- Vitamin E—400-800 I.U. per day.

- Magnesium—400-800 mg per day.

- Zinc—15-30 mg per day.

- Omega-6 fatty acids—1-2 grams per day from evening primrose or flax oil.

- Lactobacillus acidophilus—one dosage per day in either liquid, powder, or capsule form.

- Sometimes a multivitamin and a multi-mineral supplement can provide many of the above nutrients.

- For women who have as a major part of their symptom complex depression, memory loss, crying, insomnia, and confusion, the amino acid tyrosine at 300 mg per day may be particularly helpful.

- Women with symptoms of anxiety, nervousness, mood swings, and insomnia might benefit from extra bioflavonoids, about 1 gram per day.

- For women who have fluid retention as a significant complaint, the botanical, licorice (Glycyrrhiza glabra) can help at 1-2 grams per day in three divided doses.

- For women who suffer from excessive uterine cramping, Bromelain—100 mg four times per day between meals—can be helpful for its prostaglandin balancing action. An active ingredient in the herb, Black haw, is also a uterine relaxant.

## DEALING WITH A TOXIC ENVIRONMENT

Chemical sensitivity and toxic contamination can have a severe impact on women with PMS. Part of the reason is that hormonal balance is very easily influenced by these factors. For instance, pesticides and heavy metal contamination can linger in body tissues for decades and dramatically interfere with estrogen metabolism. But tobacco and alcohol are the two most prevalent toxic mediators in PMS and should be avoided.

Even non-toxic substances in our environment and food may be very disruptive in women who are particularly sensitive to them.

Sometimes we can recognize when a substance is irritating to our organism because of the immediate symptoms that arise when we contact the offending agent. But often it is difficult to pinpoint what might be troublesome. In such a case it is necessary to either test for body burden of toxics or use an immunological sensitivity test like ELISA/ACT™. This can identify delayed reactions and test for things we might not have thought could pose problems.

One strategy is to avoid known potential dangers. Use the chapter on Environmental Health as a guide. If one is tested and has specific agents to watch out for, this can be helpful.

Once our bodies have been contaminated, efforts at detoxification need to be made. Different methods are needed for different types of contamination. For instance, pesticide contamination responds well to a protocol involving hyperthermia and nutritional changes. Lead can be extracted with EDTA I.V. chelation therapy. A member of the American Academy of Environmental Medicine can be most helpful here. See the resource section in the chapter on Environmental Health for more assistance.

Often, avoidance and detoxification strategies are not enough; metabolic pathways and biological systems are too severely damaged by environmental hazards. In these instances extra nutritional support is necessary to help the body recover. This can take a good bit of time.

## SPINAL HEALTH

Spinal nerve irritation often plays a major role in PMS, particularly when low back pain and uterine cramping are part of the picture. The best treatment involves a combination of spinal manipulation by a chiropractor, spinal stabilization and flexibility exercises, and aerobic conditioning and coordination exercises. Remember, aerobic conditioning, in itself, can be a powerful influence for good health. Both the section on Manipulative Therapies and the one on Exercise can provide additional information in this area.

## STRESS MANAGEMENT

Effective stress management plays an important role in every health enhancement program. It is particularly important for women with PMS. Stress reduction, stress avoidance, better time management, occupational changes, biofeedback, relaxation training, meditation, psychotherapy, social support, and play can all have their place in restoring our health. Use the resources in the Psychological Health chapter and the Biofeedback section for more information.

## ACUPUNCTURE

Acupuncture has been used for centuries to help deal with the many varied symptoms and metabolic problems associated with PMS. It can be a powerful tool in a comprehensive program for better health. Refer to the section on Traditional Oriental Medicine for more help.

## BALANCED BIOLOGICAL RHYTHMS

A woman's menstrual cycle is a perfect example of biological rhythm. If there are disturbances in this rhythm there are often alterations in other body rhythms. It is helpful to look at major sources of balance and regularity in our biological rhythms. Sleep is one, light is another.

Insufficient or irregular sleep can greatly disturb hormonal cycles; so getting adequate, sound, regular, sleep at night is important for those with PMS. Using full-spectrum light can also be important. For those with light deficit disorders, Neurosensory Development Training may be needed to reestablish normal neurohormonal function. The section on Biological Rhythms, Light, and Sleep can contribute more advice.

## A COMPREHENSIVE APPROACH IS THE KEY

When a multifaceted program of health enhancement is instituted, the best results can be expected—it is far better than depending on medications which just treat the symptoms.

---

## RESOURCES

Boston Women's Health Book Collective Staff. *The New Our Bodies, Ourselves.* Touchstone, 1992.

*Journal of Women's Health,* Mary Ann Liebert, Inc., 1651 Third Ave., New York, NY 10130-0060; (212) 289-2300.

Lark, Susan. *Premenstrual Syndrome Self-Help Book.* Celestial Arts, 1993.

Murray, Michael and Pizzorno, Joseph. *Encyclopedia of Natural Medicine.* Prima Publishing, 1991.

National Women's Health Network, 1325 G St. NW, Washington, DC 20005; (202) 347-1140. Women's Health clearinghouse that provides health educational material and publishes a newsletter.

Werbach, Melvyn. *Nutritional Influences on Illness: A Sourcebook of Clinical Research.* Third Line Press, 1988.

# ADDENDUM

What follows are guidelines in outline form for some other problem conditions which are highly responsive to multifaceted health care measures. You and your health care practitioner can discuss these recommendations and create a cost-effective plan which suits your needs.

## AGGRESSIVE BEHAVIOR

[A] = high priority, [B] = second order priority, [C] = third order priority

## Helpful Functional Tests that Assist Treatment

- [A] Psychological assessment
- [A] Diet/symptom diary to help determine food sensitivities, intolerances, and allergic reactions.
- [A] ELISA/ACT™ blood tests for immunological reactivity to foods, inhalants, environmental agents, chemical pollutants, etc.
- [A] Hair analysis to determine aluminum, cadmium, and lead toxicity
- [B] serum ferritin to determine iron deficiency
- [B] serum lithium levels to determine deficiency
- [B] RBC superoxide dismutase and to a less reliable degree hair copper to determine copper levels
- [B] whole blood, lymphocyte, or hair manganese levels can identify deficiency or excess
- [B] Serum and urine tryptophan to identify deficiency
- [C] Glucose tolerance test to determine reactive hypoglycemia which is contributory to poor impulse control

- [C] RBC thiamine diphosphate or RBC transketolase activity to verify thiamine deficiency
- [C] 24 hour urinary excretion of magnesium as a screen for magnesium utilization or a magnesium challenge test for determining body stores

## Diet

- [A] Vegetarian, void of allergenic foods, low fat, low in simple sugars (sweets), infrequent dairy, high fiber.
- [B] Foods high in tryptophan: wheat germ, oats, egg, pork, avocado

## Nutritional Supplementation

### Vitamins

- [A] Multivitamin (high potency)—daily with meals
- [A] Vitamin C (best in ascorbate form with 5-10% bioflavonoids)—3,000 mg or more per day
- [A] Vitamin B-1 (Thiamine)—150-300 mg per day

### Minerals

- Mineral supplementation should follow blood, urine, and hair testing for deficiencies and excesses

### Amino Acids

- [C] L-Tryptophan—1-6 grams per day. Testing serum and urine amino acid levels as well as neurotransmitter levels allows for a more accurate determination of appropriate tryptophan supplementation.

## Other Helpful Aids

- [A] No tobacco, alcohol, or other recreational drugs
- [A] Psychotherapy
- [B] Cranial electrical stimulation
- [B] Chelation therapy if toxic levels of aluminum, cadmium, or lead exist
- [B] Biofeedback
- [B] Spiritual, contemplative, meditative practices

## Experimental Possibilities

- Neurosensory Development Training
- Acupuncture

## ATHLETIC PERFORMANCE

[A] = high priority, [B] = second order priority, [C] = third order priority

## Helpful Functional Tests that Assist Treatment

- [A] Diet/symptom diary to help determine food sensitivities, intolerances, and allergic reactions
- [A] ELISA/ACT™ blood tests for immunological reactivity to foods, inhalants, environmental agents, chemical pollutants, etc.
- [A] Lifestyle Stress Inventory to assess the sources and effects of stress in order to make lifestyle changes. Physiological assessment to see if biofeedback may be of benefit can be a part of the stress inventory, as can a psychotherapeutic interview.
- [A] Chiropractic examination to determine if joint fixations or trigger points are contributing factors that can be addressed with manipulation and therapeutic massage

- [A] Physiological examination of endurance, strength, flexibility and coordination can be made at the appropriate level relative to the person's needs.
- [B] Traditional Oriental Diagnosis to determine if acupuncture might be of significant assistance
- [B] Comprehensive stool analysis can show disturbances in intestinal flora, parasitic infection, toxic bowel contaminants, and digestive dysfunction.
- [B] Therapeutic trial of Betaine HCL to produce digestive ease or [C] Hiedelberg capsule gastric analysis can be done to verify degree of HCL deficiency, if suspected.
- [C] Fatty acid analysis of blood can help identify disturbances in fatty acid metabolism.
- [C] Amino acid analysis of blood can help identify disturbances in amino acid metabolism.
- [C] 24 hour urine mercury or methyl mercury gas analysis of breath to identify mercury toxicity.

## Diet

- [A] Vegetarian, organic, high fiber, moderate protein, low fat diet void of allergenic foods, simple sugars, and chemical contaminants
- [A] Plenty of clean water intake
- [B] Carbohydrate replenishment soon after workouts can replenish glycogen stores so energy reserves will be available for the next day's workout.
- [B] Carbohydrate loading prior to competition requiring large energy expenditure can be helpful. On the fourth and fifth day before a competition reduce carbohydrate consumption to 40-50% of total calories. On the second and third day prior to competition increase complex carbohydrates to 70-80% of calories.

## Nutritional Supplementation

### Vitamins

- [A] Multivitamin (high potency)—daily with meals. B-12 (1,000 mcg sublingual per day), E (400-800 I.U. per day), and folic acid (400 mcg per day) are particularly important.

- [A] Vitamin C (best in ascorbate form with 5-10% bioflavonoids)—3,000 mg or more per day

### Minerals

- [A] Multi-mineral supplements may be an adequate method of insuring base levels of mineral nutrition

- [A] Potassium—2 grams per day

- [B] Magnesium—400-800 mg per day if deficient (magnesium malate is particularly helpful)

- [C] Chromium—200 mcg per day if deficient

### Enzymes and Digestive Aids

- [B] Friendly Intestinal Bacterial Flora (primarily Lactobacillus acidophilus and Bifidobacterium strains)

- [B] Pancreatin—used with protein meals for better digestion

- [B] Betaine HCL—300-1200 mg per protein meal in those individuals who are deficient in gastric HCL

### Amino Acids

- Easily digestible form of protein (either free form amino acids or rice protein concentrate) if dietary source of protein is difficult to obtain. If large muscle mass is being trained for, 150-200 grams of total protein intake may be necessary.

- [B] L-carnitine—1-2 grams per day during intensive training periods

- [B] L-arginine—2-3 grams per day during intensive training periods

- [B] L-lysine—1 gram per day during intensive training periods

- [B] L-ornithine—2-3 grams per day during intensive training periods

- [B] Leucine, isoleucine, and valine—1-3 grams of each of these branched chain amino acids 30-60 minutes before a workout with 50 mg of vitamin B-6 or 25 mg of pyridoxal-5-phosphate

### Other Nutrients

- [B] Coenzyme $Q_{10}$—30-100 mg per day for a healthy heart

- [B] Inosine—300-500 mg per day for energy efficiency

- [C] Omega-3 Fatty Acids ("MaxEPA" or Eicosapentaenoic acid)—1-2 grams per day

- [C] Omega-6 Fatty Acids (gamma linoenic acid as found in evening primrose oil, borage seed oil, and flax seed oil)—1-3 grams per day

- [C] Octacosanol—15 mg per day for stamina

- [C] Dimethylglycine (DMG)—for better oxygenation of tissues

### Herbs

- [B] Korean Ginseng (Panax ginseng) 4-6 grams of dried root per day for 15-20 days cycled with a 14 day rest period

- [B] Siberian Ginseng (Eleutherococcus senticosus) 100-200 mg three times per day of a 1% eleutheroside E concentration per day for 60 days cycled with a 2-3 week rest period

Note that infrequently there can be some mild side effects from taking maximal doses of any ginseng over long periods of time. These include insomnia, irritability, anxiety, nervousness, high blood pressure, headaches, melancholy, and menstrual irregularities.

- [B] Procyanidolic oligomers (pycnogenol)—150-300 mg per day as an antioxidant and builder of connective tissue

## Other Therapeutic Aids

- [A] Avoidance of environmental contaminants, chemical pollutants, inhalant allergens, and toxic agents by using natural products at home and at work. If necessary, use HEPA air filters and replace mercury dental amalgams with less reactive alternatives. No alcohol or tobacco products.

- [A] Stress management including plenty of sound sleep and sufficient rest. Biofeedback can be an important part of stress management and also concentration development. Meditation can act in a similar fashion.

- [A] Chiropractic manipulation and therapeutic massage can increase the efficiency of muscle and joint function plus prevent injuries.

- [A] A training regimen should include a balance of aerobic conditioning, strength training, flexibility exercise, and coordination practices that are specific to the individual's needs. Excessive aerobic training can depress the immune system and make an athlete susceptible to infections.

- [B] Acupuncture

- [C] Avoid steroids, antibiotics, antacids, nonsteroidal anti-inflammatory drugs such as ibuprofen, acetaminophen, aspirin, and naprosyn unless specifically prescribed by a physician who is familiar with the protocols set forth here.

## BRONCHIAL ASTHMA

[A] = high priority, [B] = second order priority, [C] = third order priority

## Helpful Functional Tests that Assist Treatment

- [A] Diet/symptom diary to help avoid food sensitivities, intolerances, and allergic reactions

- [A] ELISA/ACT™ blood tests for immunological reactivity to foods, inhalants, environmental agents, chemical pollutants, etc.

- [A] Chiropractic examination to determine if joint fixations or trigger points are contributing factors that can be addressed with manipulation and therapeutic massage

- [A] Lifestyle Stress Inventory may be used to assess the sources and effects of stress in order to make lifestyle changes to correct this element of the problem; physiological assessment to see if biofeedback may be of benefit can be a part of the stress inventory, as can a psychotherapeutic interview.

- [A] Therapeutic trial of Betaine HCL to produce digestive ease or [C] Hiedelberg capsule gastric analysis can be done to verify degree of HCL deficiency.

- [B] Comprehensive stool analysis can show disturbances in intestinal flora, parasitic infection, toxic bowel contaminants, and digestive dysfunction.

## Diet

- [A] Vegetarian diet, low in fat and void of allergenic foods

- [C] Consumption of onions seems to be helpful.

## Nutritional Supplementation

### Vitamins

- [A] Multivitamin (high potency)—daily with meals. B-6, B-12, and folic acid are particularly important.

- [A] Vitamin C (best in ascorbate form with 5-10% bioflavonoids)—3,000 mg or more per day increasing to as high as 12 grams during reactions

## Minerals

- [A] Magnesium—maintain 400 mg per day, increasing to 800 mg per day during attacks.

## Enzymes and Digestive Aids

- [B] Betaine HCL—300-1200 mg per protein meal in those individuals who are deficient in gastric HCL to decrease allergenicity of consumed food

- [B] Pancreatin—used with protein meals for decreased allergenicity.

- [B] Friendly Intestinal Bacterial Flora (primarily Lactobacillus acidophilus and Bifidobacterium strains) daily

## Other Nutrients

- [B] Omega-3 Fatty Acids ("MaxEPA" or Eicosapentaenoic acid)—2-3 grams per day

- [B] N-acetyl cysteine—500 mg twice daily

- [C] Omega-6 Fatty Acids (gamma linoenic acid as found in evening primrose oil, borage seed oil, and flax seed oil)—2-3 grams twice daily

## Herbs

- [B] Aloe vera—5 ml of 20% solution of Aloe extract twice daily

- [B] Coleus forskohlii—1-10 mg of forskolin, the active therapeutic ingredient, per day

- [B] Ginko biloba—2.4 mg of inhaled or 240 mg of ingested ginkgolides A, B, and C, the active therapeutic ingredients

- [B] Tylophora asthmatica—200 mg of dried leaves twice daily or 40 mg of dry extract daily

- [C] Khella (Amni visnaga)—dosage fluctuates depending on khellin and visnagin content. These are the active therapeutic ingredients. If the khellin concentration is 70-80 % and the visnagin concentration 20-30%, doses of 120 mg per day are accompanied by mild side effects.

## Other Therapeutic Aids

- [A] Chiropractic manipulation

- [A] Stress management including biofeedback and psychotherapy, if indicated

- [A] Avoidance of environmental contaminants, chemical pollutants, inhalant allergens, and toxic agents by using natural products at home and at work. If necessary, use HEPA air filters and replace mercury dental amalgams with less reactive alternatives. Chlorinated swimming pools and jacuzzis may be particularly aggravating. No smoking is a must!

- [B] Use of beta-II agonists only infrequently in acute flair-ups, if at all. Regular use of standard doses for long time periods may perpetuate the condition.

## DIGESTIVE DISORDERS

[A] = high priority, [B] = second order priority, [C] = third order priority

## Differential Diagnosis

The major considerations:

1. Food allergy, sensitivity, or intolerance
2. Hypochlorhydria
3. Gastric or duodenal ulcer
4. Leaky gut syndrome
5. Irritable bowel syndrome
6. Gall bladder inflammation or gallstones
7. Infectious gastroenteritis including candidiasis
8. Esophageal reflux with or without hiatal hernia

A physician can help rule out more serious pathology such as pancreatitis, ulcerative colitis, Crohn's disease, food contamination, chemical contamination, adverse reactions to medication, inflammatory bowel disease, malignancy.

Some of these eight can coexist together. Health enhancement consists of four major elements:

1. Stop harmful actions on digestive tract (i.e. alcohol, nonsteroidal anti-inflammatory drugs, excessive consumption of harmful foods, etc.).

2. Provide digestive aids which the body cannot provide until healed (i.e. betaine HCL, lactase, pancreatic enzymes, etc.).

3. Reestablish normal intestinal flora by killing harmful intestinal microbes (using preferably botanical agents but on occasion pharmaceuticals) and replacing them with friendly intestinal microflora (predominantly bifidobacteria and lactobacillus).

4. Reestablish healthy intestinal lining, biochemical balance, nutriture, and organ functional capacities with lifestyle change, dietary alterations, nutrient supplementation, stress reduction.

## Diagnostic Aids

- [A] Detailed history of the character, onset, and course of the symptoms

- [A] Diet/symptom diary to help determine food sensitivities, intolerances, and allergic reactions

- [A] ELISA/ACT™ blood tests for immunological reactivity to foods, inhalants, environmental agents, chemical pollutants, etc.

- [A] Comprehensive stool analysis can show disturbances in intestinal flora, parasitic infection, toxic bowel contaminants, and digestive dysfunction.

- [A] Therapeutic trial of Betaine HCL to produce digestive ease or [C] Hiedelberg capsule gastric analysis can be done to verify degree of HCL deficiency, if suspected.

- [B] Gas analysis of breath or antibody test for evidence of Heliobacter pylori

- [B] Elevated serum bilirubin and alkaline phosphatase with symptoms of extrahepatic obstruction (jaundice, abdominal pain, chills and fever) point to cholecystitis, 95% of the time also accompanied by cholelithiasis. Diagnostic ultrasound can confirm with a high degree of accuracy.

- [C] Fatty acid analysis of blood can help identify disturbances in fatty acid metabolism.

- [C] Amino acid analysis of blood can help identify disturbances in amino acid metabolism.

- [C] 24-hour urine mercury or methyl mercury gas analysis of breath

- [C] Hiatal hernia can be visualized by x-ray.

## Helpful Functional Tests that Assist Treatment

- [A] Lifestyle Stress Inventory to assess the sources and effects of stress in order to make lifestyle changes to correct this element of the problem. Physiological assessment to see if biofeedback may be of benefit can be a part of the stress inventory, as can a psychotherapeutic interview.

- [B] Chiropractic examination to determine if joint fixations or trigger points are contributing factors that can be addressed with manipulation and therapeutic massage

- [B] Traditional Oriental Diagnosis to determine if acupuncture might be of significant assistance

## Diet

- [A] Vegetarian, organic, high fiber, low fat diet void of allergenic foods, simple sugars, and chemical contaminants

- [A] Plenty of clean water intake

## Nutritional Supplementation

### *Vitamins*

- [A] Multivitamin (high potency)—daily with meals; B-1, B-3, B-6, B-12, E, and folic acid are particularly important.

- [A] Vitamin C (best in ascorbate form with 5-10% bioflavonoids)—3,000 mg or more per day

- [B] Vitamin B-3—1000-2000 mg per day for inhibition of enterotoxin induced secretory activity of the intestines in cases of diarrhea

- [C] Calcium pantothenate—25-100 mg per day (particularly helpful in diarrheal irritable bowel syndrome)

### *Minerals*

- [B] Zinc—15-60 mg per day (picolinate or methionate forms may be best)

### *Enzymes and Digestive Aids*

- [B] Friendly Intestinal Bacterial Flora (primarily Lactobacillus acidophilus and Bifidobacterium strains)

- [B] Pancreatin—used with protein meals for decreased allergenicity

- [B] Betaine HCL—300-1200 mg per protein meal in those individuals who are deficient in gastric HCL

### *Amino Acids*

- Easily digestible form of protein (either free form amino acids or rice protein concentrate)

- L-glutamine—1-2 grams per day to nourish damaged intestinal cells

### *Other Nutrients*

- [B] Omega-3 Fatty Acids ("MaxEPA" or Eicosapentaenoic acid)—4-6 grams per day

- [B] Omega-6 Fatty Acids (gamma linoenic acid as found in evening primrose oil, borage seed oil, and flax seed oil)—1 gram four times per day

- [B] Fructo-oligosaccharides (FOS)—taken with beneficial intestinal flora supplements to enhance their survival

### *Herbs*

- [B] Deglycyrrhizinated Licorice—760-1520 mg between meals for 8-16 weeks for the treatment of peptic and duodenal ulcers

- [B] Rhubarb has been found to reduce bleeding in ulcers.

- [B] S-methylmethionine as found in raw cabbage juice—1 liter of raw cabbage juice per day helps heal duodenal and peptic ulcers.

- [C] Bilberry (Vaccinium myrtillus)—80-160 mg three times per day if anthocyanidin content is 25%, to help heal gastric ulcers

- [B] Artemesia annua—800 mg per day, helpful in eliminating parasitic infections

- [B] Citrus seed concentrate—100-400 mg per day between meals as an antiparasitic, antibacterial agent

- [B] Echinacea angustifolia—325-1000 mg per day of dried form in cases of gastrointestinal infection

- [B] Goldenseal (Hydrastis canadensis)—250-500 mg three times per day if the extract has a 5% hydrastine content in cases of gastrointestinal infection

- [B] Garlic (Allium sativum)—8 mg of the active ingredient, allicin per day in cases of gastrointestinal infection

- [B] Psyllium (Plantago ovata) to supplement dietary fiber

- [B] Flax seed powder to supplement dietary fiber

- [C] Turmeric (Curcumin longa)—250-500 mg of the active ingredient, curcumin three times per day. For the prevention and treatment of gallstones, it increases bile solubility.

- [C] Silymarin (Silybum marianum)—300-420 mg per day in the prevention and treatment of gallstones to increase bile solubility.

- [C] Plant terpenes (see *Botanical Influences on Illness* by Werbach and Murray for more specifics on this form of herbal assistance in the dissolving of gallstones)

- [C] Peppermint oil—.2-.4 ml in enteric coated capsules three times daily between meals to help soothe irritable bowel syndrome.

- [C] Ginger (Zingiber officinale)—1 gram of powdered root per day as an anti-nausea agent

## Other Therapeutic Aids

- [A] Avoidance of environmental contaminants, chemical pollutants, inhalant allergens, and toxic agents by using natural products at home and at work; if necessary, use HEPA air filters and replace mercury dental amalgams with less reactive alternatives. No alcohol or tobacco products.

- [A] Stress management including plenty of sound sleep and sufficient rest

- [A] Avoid steroids, antibiotics, antacids, nonsteroidal anti-inflammatory drugs such as ibuprofen, acetaminophen, aspirin, and naprosyn unless specifically prescribed by a physician who is familiar with the protocols set forth here.

- [B] Chiropractic manipulation

- [B] Graduated, moderate, conditioning exercise

- [B] Acupuncture

- [B] For esophageal reflux, small meals and weight loss are two important elements.

## EAR INFECTIONS (OTITIS MEDIA)

[A] = high priority, [B] = second order priority, [C] = third order priority

## Helpful Functional Tests that Assist Treatment

- [A] Diet/symptom diary to help avoid food sensitivities, intolerances, and allergic reactions

- [A] ELISA/ACT™ blood tests for immunological reactivity to foods, inhalants, environmental agents, chemical pollutants, etc.

- [B] Chiropractic examination to determine if joint fixations or trigger points are contributing factors that can be addressed with manipulation and therapeutic massage

- [C] Blood and hair analysis can help identify disturbances in mineral metabolism and deficiency or excess. This is particularly important with respect to copper, zinc, selenium, iron, and the toxic heavy metals.

## Diet

- [A] Breast feeding for first six months of life. If ear infections occur while breast feeding, the mother should eliminate her intake of allergenic foods, particularly dairy products.

- [A] Predominantly vegetarian diet, low in fat, low in saturated fat, low in simple sugars (sweets), high fiber, void of allergenic foods, artificial colors, flavors, preservatives

## Nutritional Supplementation

### *Vitamins*

- [A] Multivitamin (high potency)—daily with meals

- [A] Beta-carotene—5,000-100,000 I.U. per day depending on age

- [A] Vitamin C (best in ascorbate form with 5-10% bioflavonoids)—1,000 mg or more per day, preferably to a bowel tolerance level (dosage just prior to eliciting loose stools)

## Minerals

- [B] Zinc—4-10 mg per day (since zinc and copper are antagonists biochemically, it is sometimes difficult to maintain a good balance of these two minerals; a periodic hair and/or blood analysis may be helpful)

## Other Nutrients

- [B] Omega-6 Fatty Acids (gamma linoenic acid as found in evening primrose oil, borage seed oil, and flax seed oil)—1 gram per day for each year of life.
- [C] Thymus raw glandular extract—50 mg per day for each year of life

## Herbs

The dosage of herbal preparations varies greatly depending on

- the stage of the illness
- the age and weight of the patient
- what form the herb is in—dried, freeze-dried, powdered, fluid extract, or tincture
- what the potency of the active ingredients is in the herb.

Because of this, consultation with a respected physician who uses herbs is highly advised when using this element of the health enhancement protocol.

- [B] Echinacea angustiflolia
- [B] Garlic (Allium sativum)
- [B] Goldenseal (Hydrastis canadensis)
- [B] Licorice (Glycyrrhiza glabra)

## Other Therapeutic Aids

- [A] Avoidance of environmental contaminants, chemical pollutants, inhalant allergens, and toxic agents by using natural products at home and at work; if necessary, use HEPA air filters and replace mercury dental amalgams with less reactive alternatives.
- [B] Chiropractic manipulation

## FIBROMYALGIA

[A] = high priority, [B] = second order priority, [C] = third order priority

## Diagnosis

There must be at least a 3 month history of widespread pain including both right and left side of the body, above and below the waist; the trunk must be involved. Pain, not just tenderness, upon digital palpation of approximately 4 kilograms of force in 11 of 18 bilateral locations: occiput, lower neck, trapezius, supraspinatus, second costochondral junction, lateral epicondyl of elbow, buttocks, posterior greater trochanter, medial proximal knee.

Associated symptoms include: headache, depression, paresthesias, bowel and bladder disturbances, Raynaud's syndrome, bruxism, bursitis, sciatica, TMJ pain, allergies, and sleep disorders.

## Helpful Functional Tests that Assist Treatment

- [A] Diet/symptom diary to help avoid food sensitivities, intolerances, and allergic reactions.
- [A] ELISA/ACT™ blood tests for immunological reactivity to foods, inhalants, environmental agents, chemical pollutants, etc.

- [A] Chiropractic examination to determine if joint fixations or trigger points are contributing factors that can be addressed with manipulation and therapeutic massage

- [A] Therapeutic trial of Betaine HCL to produce digestive ease or [C] Hiedelberg capsule gastric analysis can be done to verify degree of HCL deficiency.

- [B] Comprehensive stool analysis can show disturbances in intestinal flora, parasitic infection, toxic bowel contaminants, and digestive dysfunction.

- [B] Thyroid function tests may be helpful to sufferers that have thyroid dysfunction. The Barnes morning basal temperature test may be more helpful than standard blood tests for identifying borderline cases.

- [B] Blood and hair analysis can help identify disturbances in mineral metabolism and deficiency or excess. This is particularly important with respect to copper, zinc, selenium, iron, and the toxic heavy metals.

- [B] Traditional Oriental Diagnosis to determine if acupuncture might be of significant assistance

- [C] Fatty acid analysis of blood can help identify disturbances in fatty acid metabolism.

- [C] Amino acid analysis of blood can help identify disturbances in amino acid metabolism.

## Diet

- [A] Vegetarian, organic, high fiber, low fat diet void of allergenic foods and chemical contaminants

## Nutritional Supplementation

### Vitamins

- [A] Multivitamin (high potency)—daily with meals; B-1, B-6, B-12, E, and folic acid are particularly important.

- [A] Vitamin C (best in ascorbate form with 5-10% bioflavonoids)—3,000 mg or more per day

### Minerals

- [A] Magnesium—maintain 400-800 mg per day (magnesium malate may be the most effective form of magnesium for this condition; fumarate, aspartate, and orotate forms are also effective)

### Enzymes and Digestive Aids

- [B] Friendly Intestinal Bacterial Flora (primarily Acidophilus and Bifidobacterium strains)

- [B] Pancreatin—used with protein meals for decreased allergenicity

- [B] Betaine HCL—300-1200 mg per protein meal in those individuals who are deficient in gastric HCL

### Amino Acids

- [B] S-adenosyl-L-methionine—500 mg twice daily

- [B] 5-hydroxytryptophan—100 mg three times per day (in some cases this may increase pain)

- [B] glutamine—1 gram three times per day, away from meals

- [B] N-acetyl cysteine—500 mg twice daily

### Other Nutrients

- [B] Omega-3 Fatty Acids ("MaxEPA" or Eicosapentaenoic acid)—4-6 grams per day

- [B] Omega-6 Fatty Acids (gamma linoenic acid as found in evening primrose oil, borage seed oil, and flax seed oil)—1 gram four times per day
- [B] Co-enzyme $Q_{10}$—60-120 mg per day

## *Herbs*

- [C] Capsaicin (the active, therapeutic ingredient in cayenne pepper, Capsicum frutescens)—topical application of .025-.075 % ointment to affected areas

## Other Therapeutic Aids

- [A] Chiropractic manipulation
- [A] Avoidance of environmental contaminants, chemical pollutants, inhalant allergens, and toxic agents by using natural products at home and at work; if necessary, use HEPA air filters and replace mercury dental amalgams with less reactive alternatives
- [A] Therapeutic massage of the involved areas 1-2 times per week
- [A] Stress management including plenty of sound sleep and sufficient rest
- [A] Avoid steroids, antibiotics, antacids, nonsteroidal anti-inflammatory drugs such as ibuprophen, actaminophen, aspirin, and naprosyn unless specifically prescribed by a physician who is familiar with the protocols set forth here.
- [B] Graduated, moderate, conditioning exercise
- [B] Acupuncture

## Resources

Fibromyalgia Network, 5700 Stockdale Hwy., Suite 100, Bakersfield, CA 93309.

Seattle Fibromyalgia Association, P.O. Box 77373, Seattle, WA 98177-0373; (206) 362-2310.

## LUPUS

[A] = high priority, [B] = second order priority, [C] = third order priority

## Helpful Functional Tests that Assist Treatment

- [A] Diet/symptom diary to help avoid food sensitivities, intolerances, and allergic reactions
- [A] ELISA/ACT™ blood tests for immunological reactivity to foods, inhalants, environmental agents, chemical pollutants, etc.
- [A] Lifestyle Stress Inventory to assess the sources and effects of stress in order to make lifestyle changes to correct this element of the problem; physiological assessment to see if biofeedback may be of benefit can be a part of the stress inventory, as can a psychotherapeutic interview.
- [A] Therapeutic trial of Betaine HCL to produce digestive ease or [C] Hiedelberg capsule gastric analysis can be done to verify degree of HCL deficiency.
- [C] Chiropractic examination to determine if joint fixations or trigger points are contributing factors that can be addressed with manipulation and therapeutic massage

## Diet

- [A] Vegetarian diet void of allergenic foods, low in calories, low in fats, and low in proteins which have large proportions of phenylalanine and tyrosine, such as beef and dairy
- WARNING: Do not eat alfalfa seeds or sprouts. They contain canavanine sulfate which aggravates systemic lupus erythematosus.

## Nutritional Supplementation

### Vitamins

- [A] Multivitamin (high potency)—daily with meals.
- [B] Beta Carotene—50 mg three times daily
- [B] Calcium pantothenate—2-4 grams daily
- [B] B-12—1000 mcg sublingual per day with 400 mcg of folic acid
- [B] Vitamin E—1200-1600 I.U. per day
- [C] Vitamin C (best in ascorbate form with 5-10% bioflavonoids)—3,000 mg or more per day increasing to as high as 12 grams during reactions

### Minerals

- [C] Selenium—200 mcg per day

### Enzymes and Digestive Aids

- [B] Betaine HCL—300-1200 mg per protein meal in those individuals who are deficient in gastric HCL to decrease allergenicity of consumed food
- [B] Pancreatin—used with protein meals for decreased allergenicity

### Other Nutrients

- [C] Omega-3 Fatty Acids ("MaxEPA" or Eicosapentaenoic acid)—2-3 grams per day
- [C] Omega-6 Fatty Acids (gamma linoenic acid as found in evening primrose oil, borage seed oil, and flax seed oil)—2-3 grams twice daily

### Herbs

- [B] Tripterygium wilfordi—30-60 grams per day in divided doses for 2-4 weeks

### Other Therapeutic Aids

- [A] Stress management including biofeedback and psychotherapy if indicated

- [A] Avoidance of environmental contaminants, chemical pollutants, inhalant allergens, and toxic agents by using natural products at home and at work; if necessary, use HEPA air filters and replace mercury dental amalgams with less reactive alternatives.
- [C] Chiropractic manipulation

## MENOPAUSAL SYMPTOMS

[A] = high priority, [B] = second order priority, [C] = third order priority

### Helpful Functional Tests that Assist Treatment

- [A] Diet/symptom diary to help avoid food sensitivities, intolerances, and allergic reactions
- [A] Chiropractic examination to determine if joint fixations or trigger points are contributing factors that can be addressed with manipulation and therapeutic massage
- [A] Lifestyle Stress Inventory to assess the sources and effects of stress in order to make lifestyle changes to correct this element of the problem. Physiological assessment to see if biofeedback may be of benefit can be a part of the stress inventory, as can a psychotherapeutic interview.
- [B] ELISA/ACT™ blood tests for immunological reactivity to foods, inhalants, environmental agents, chemical pollutants, etc.

### Diet

- [A] Vegetarian diet void of allergenic foods, very low in saturated fats, and *trans*-fatty acids, high in phytoestrogens from soy, nuts, seeds, fennel, celery, parsley, and clover sprouts, high in foods containing tryptophan—wheat germ, oats, egg, pork, avocado, cottage cheese, chicken, turkey, duck, and wild game

## Nutritional Supplementation

### Vitamins

- [A] Multivitamin (high potency)—daily with meals; B-6, B-12, and folic acid are particularly important.
- [A] Vitamin C (best in ascorbate form)—1-3 grams or more per day
- [A] Bioflavonoids—100-1000 mg per day
- [A] Vitamin E—100-400 I.U. per day

### Minerals

- One effect of the hormonal changes of menopause is an increased susceptibility to osteoporosis. Adequate mineral intake in women's 20s, 30s, and 40s has preventive protective effects in this regard. After menopause a woman should consume 1200-1500 mg of calcium and 600-1000 mg of magnesium per day.

### Other Nutrients

- [A] Omega-6 Fatty Acids (gamma linoenic acid as found in evening primrose oil, borage seed oil, and flax seed oil)—2-3 grams daily
- [B] Omega-3 Fatty Acids ("MaxEPA" or Eicosapentaenoic acid)—1 capsule three times per day

### Herbs

- [B] Black Cohosh (Cimicifuga racemosa)—8 mg per day
- [B] Dong Quai (Angelica sinensis)—1-2 grams of dried root three times daily. Overexposure to sunlight should be avoided while taking this herb.
- [B] Licorice Root (Glycyrrhiza glabra)—1-2 grams of powdered root three times daily or 380-760 mg of deglycyrrhizinated licorice 20 minutes before meals
- [B] Korean Ginseng (Panax ginseng) 4-6 grams of dried root per day for 15-20 days cycled with a 14 day rest period

- [C] Unicorn root (Aletris farinosa)
- [C] False Unicorn root (Helonias opulus)
- [C] Fennel seed (Foeniculum vulgare)

## Other Therapeutic Aids

- [A] Chiropractic manipulation
- [A] Stress management including biofeedback and psychotherapy, if indicated
- [A] Avoidance of environmental contaminants, chemical pollutants, inhalant allergens, and toxic agents by using natural products at home and at work; if necessary, use HEPA air filters and replace mercury dental amalgams with less reactive alternatives.
- [A] Physical exercise

## MULTIPLE SCLEROSIS

[A] = high priority, [B] = second order priority, [C] = third order priority

## Helpful Functional Tests that Assist Treatment

- [A] Diet/symptom diary to help avoid food sensitivities, intolerances, and allergic reactions
- [A] ELISA/ACT™ blood tests for immunological reactivity to foods, inhalants, environmental agents, chemical pollutants, etc.
- [A] Chiropractic examination to determine if joint fixations or trigger points can be addressed with manipulation and therapeutic massage in order to ease the stress on the nervous system
- [A] Lifestyle Stress Inventory to assess the sources and effects of stress in order to make lifestyle changes to correct this element of the problem; physiological assessment to see if biofeedback may be of benefit can be a part of the stress inventory, as can a psychotherapeutic interview.

## Diet

- [A] Vegetarian diet void of allergenic foods, very low in saturated fats, and *trans*-fatty acids with fish three times per week.

## Nutritional Supplementation

### Vitamins

- [A] Multivitamin (high potency)—daily with meals. B-6, B-12, and folic acid are particularly important.
- [A] Vitamin C (best in ascorbate form with 5-10% bioflavonoids)—3,000 mg or more per day
- [B] Vitamin D—400 I.U. per day or adequate sunshine
- [B] Vitamin E—400-800 I.U. per day

### Minerals

- [C] Selenium—200 mcg per day, if deficient

### Enzymes and Digestive Aids

- [B] Betaine HCL—300-1200 mg per protein meal in those individuals who are deficient in gastric HCL to decrease allergenicity of consumed food
- [B] Pancreatin—used with protein meals for decreased allergenicity

### Other Nutrients

- [A] Omega-6 Fatty Acids (gamma linoenic acid as found in evening primrose oil, borage seed oil, and flax seed oil)—2-3 grams twice daily
- [B] Omega-3 Fatty Acids ("MaxEPA" or Eicosapentaenoic acid)—3 capsules three times per day
- [B] D-phenylalanine—1-6 grams per day

### Herbs

- Padma 28 (Tibetan herbal combination)—2 tablets three times daily

## Other Therapeutic Aids

- [A] Chiropractic manipulation
- [A] Stress management including biofeedback and psychotherapy, if indicated
- [A] Avoidance of environmental contaminants, chemical pollutants, inhalant allergens, and toxic agents by using natural products at home and at work; if necessary, use HEPA air filters and replace mercury dental amalgams with less reactive alternatives.
- [B] Mild physical exercise
- [C] Hyperbaric Oxygen

## RESOURCE

Swank, Roy and Duggan, Barbara. *The Multiple Sclerosis Diet Book*. Doubleday, 1987.

## OSTEOARTHRITIS

[A] = high priority, [B] = second order priority, [C] = third order priority

## Helpful Functional Tests that Assist Treatment

- [A] Diet/symptom diary to help avoid food sensitivities, intolerances, and allergic reactions
- [A] ELISA/ACT™ blood tests for immunological reactivity to foods, inhalants, environmental agents, chemical pollutants, etc.
- [A] Therapeutic trial of Betaine HCL to produce digestive ease or [C] Hiedelberg capsule gastric analysis can be done to verify degree of HCL deficiency.
- [A] Chiropractic examination to determine if joint fixations or trigger points are contributing factors that can be addressed with manipulation and therapeutic massage

- [B] Traditional Oriental Diagnosis to determine if acupuncture may be of benefit
- [C] Lifestyle Stress Inventory to assess the sources and effects of stress in order to make lifestyle changes to correct this element of the problem; physiological assessment to see if biofeedback may be of benefit can be a part of the stress inventory, as can a psychotherapeutic interview.
- [C] Comprehensive stool analysis can show disturbances in intestinal flora, toxic bowel contaminants, and digestive dysfunction.

## Diet

- [A] Vegetarian, low fat, low saturated fat, low in simple sugars (sweets), high fiber void of allergenic foods
- [C] Increase foods containing sulfur—Choose from eggs, beans, fish, Brussels sprouts, onions, garlic, cabbage, brewer's yeast, and nuts.

## Nutritional Supplementation

### Vitamins

- [A] Multivitamin (high potency—100 mg of the major B vitamins) daily with meals
- [A] Vitamin B-12—1,000 mcg per day, sublingual
- [A] Folic acid—6,400 mcg per day
- [A] Niacinamide—Begin with 500 mg twice per day and increase to 1 gram three times per day, then decrease to the lowest effective dose.
- [A] Vitamin C (best in ascorbate form with 5-10% bioflavonoids)—3,000 mg or more per day
- [A] Pantothenic Acid—begin with 500 mg calcium pantothenate per day and over 2 weeks increase to 500 mg four times per day.
- [B] Vitamin E—900 I.U. per day

### Enzymes and Digestive Aids

- [B] Pancreatin—1400 mg three times per day away from meals
- [B] Betaine HCL—300-1200 mg per protein meal in those individuals who are deficient in gastric HCL
- [C] Bromelain—250-1000 mg (or 150-600 G.D.U.) three times per day away from meals
- [C] Friendly Intestinal Bacterial Flora (primarily Acidophilus and Bifidobacterium strains)

### Other Nutrients

- [B] Glycosaminoglycans—1-3 grams three times per day
- [B] Omega-3 Fatty Acids ("MaxEPA" or Eicosapentaenoic acid)—4-20 grams per day
- [B] Omega-6 Fatty Acids (gamma linoenic acid as found in evening primrose oil, borage seed oil, and flax seed oil)—1 gram four times per day
- [C] Bioflavonoids (primarily Quercitin and Catechin)—1000 mg or more taken with vitamin C
- [C] Shark cartilage—9 grams per day in divided doses

### Herbs

- [C] Articulin-F (a formula of Bostwellia serrata stem, Curcuma longa rhizome, Withanias somnifera root, and zinc)
- [C] Capsaicin (the active, therapeutic ingredient in cayenne pepper, Capsicum frutescens)—topical application of .025-.075 % ointment to affected areas
- [C] Devils claw (Harpoagophytum procumbens)—1.5 grams daily
- [C] Ginger (Zingiber officianale)—500-2,000 mg per day
- [C] Yucca Saponin extract

## Other Therapeutic Aids

- [A] Avoidance of environmental contaminants, chemical pollutants, inhalant allergens, and toxic agents by using natural products at home and at work; if necessary, use HEPA air filters and replace mercury dental amalgams with less reactive alternatives.

- [A] Moderate exercise—swimming or pool exercise, walking, etc.

- [A] Weight management in order to keep at an ideal weight

- [A] Chiropractic manipulation (not of acutely inflamed or unstable joints, though)

- [B] Acupuncture

- [C] Stress management

- [C] Pulsed electromagnetic fields—30 minutes every other day

## PEPTIC OR DUODENAL ULCERS

[A] = high priority, [B] = second order priority, [C] = third order priority

## Diagnostic Aids

- [A] Detailed history of the character, onset, and course of the symptoms

- [B] Gas analysis of breath or antibody test for evidence of Heliobacter pylori

- [C] Endoscopy

- [C] Barium x-ray study

## Helpful Functional Tests that Assist Treatment

- [A] Lifestyle Stress Inventory to assess the sources and effects of stress in order to make lifestyle changes to correct this element of the problem; physiological assessment to see if biofeedback may be of benefit can be a part of the stress inventory, as can a psychotherapeutic interview.

- [A] Diet/symptom diary to help determine food sensitivities, intolerances, and allergic reactions

- [A] ELISA/ACT™ blood tests for immunological reactivity to foods, inhalants, environmental agents, chemical pollutants, etc.

- [A] Comprehensive stool analysis can show disturbances in intestinal flora, parasitic infection, toxic bowel contaminants, and digestive dysfunction.

- [A] Therapeutic trial of Betaine HCL to produce digestive ease or [C] Hiedelberg capsule gastric analysis can be done to verify degree of HCL deficiency, if suspected.

- [B] Chiropractic examination to determine if joint fixations or trigger points are contributing factors that can be addressed with manipulation and therapeutic massage

- [B] Traditional Oriental Diagnosis to determine if acupuncture might be of significant assistance

- [C] Fatty acid analysis of blood can help identify disturbances in fatty acid metabolism.

- [C] Amino acid analysis of blood can help identify disturbances in amino acid metabolism.

- [C] 24-hour urine mercury or methyl mercury gas analysis of breath

## Health Enhancement

Health enhancement consists of four major elements:

1. Stop harmful actions on digestive tract (i.e. alcohol, nonsteroidal anti-inflammatory drugs, excessive consumption of harmful foods, etc.).

2. Provide digestive aids which the body cannot provide until healed (i.e. betaine HCL, lactase, pancreatic enzymes, etc.).

3. Reestablish normal intestinal flora by killing harmful intestinal microbes (using preferably botanical agents but on occasion pharmaceuticals) and replacing them with friendly intestinal microflora (predominantly bifidobacteria and lactobacillus).

4. Reestablish healthy intestinal lining, biochemical balance, nutriture, and organ functional capacities with lifestyle change, dietary alterations, nutrient supplementation, stress reduction.

## Diet

- [A] Vegetarian, organic, high fiber, low fat diet void of allergenic foods, simple sugars, and chemical contaminants
- [A] Plenty of clean water intake

## Nutritional Supplementation

### Vitamins

- [A] Multivitamin (high potency)—daily with meals; B-1, B-3, B-6, B-12, E, and folic acid are particularly important.
- [A] Vitamin C (best in ascorbate form with 5-10% bioflavonoids)—3,000 mg or more per day

### Minerals

- Zinc—15-60 mg per day (picolinate or methionate forms may be best)

### Enzymes and Digestive Aids

- [B] Betaine HCL—300-1200 mg per protein meal in those individuals who are deficient in gastric HCL
- [C] Friendly Intestinal Bacterial Flora (primarily Lactobacillus acidophilus and Bifidobacterium strains)
- [C] Pancreatin—used with protein meals for decreased allergenicity

### Amino Acids

- [B] L-glutamine—1-2 grams per day to nourish damaged intestinal cells
- [C] Easily digestible form of protein (either free form amino acids or rice protein concentrate)

### Other Nutrients

- [B] Omega-3 Fatty Acids ("MaxEPA" or Eicosapentaenoic acid)—4-6 grams per day
- [B] Omega-6 Fatty Acids (gamma linoenic acid as found in evening primrose oil, borage seed oil, and flax seed oil)—1 gram four times per day
- [C] Fructo-oligosaccharides (FOS)—taken with beneficial intestinal flora supplements to enhance their survival

### Herbs

- [B] Deglycyrrhizinated Licorice—760-1520 mg between meals for 8-16 weeks for the treatment of peptic and duodenal ulcers
- [B] Rhubarb has been found to reduce bleeding in ulcers.
- [B] S-methylmethionine as found in raw cabbage juice—1 liter of raw cabbage juice per day helps heal duodenal and peptic ulcers
- [C] Bilberry (Vaccinium myrtillus)—80-160 mg three times per day if anthocyanidin content is 25%, to help heal gastric ulcers

## Other Therapeutic Aids

- [A] Avoidance of environmental contaminants, chemical pollutants, inhalant allergens, and toxic agents by using natural products at home and at work; if necessary, use HEPA air filters and replace mercury dental amalgams with less reactive alternatives. *No alcohol or tobacco products.*
- [A] Stress management including plenty of sound sleep and sufficient rest

- [A] Avoid steroids, antibiotics, antacids, non-steroidal anti-inflammatory drugs such as ibuprofen, acetaminophen, aspirin, and naprosyn unless specifically prescribed by a physician who is familiar with the protocols set forth here.
- [B] Chiropractic manipulation
- [B] Graduated, moderate, fun, conditioning exercise
- [B] Acupuncture

## PSORIASIS

[A] = high priority, [B] = second order priority, [C] = third order priority

### Helpful Functional Tests that Assist Treatment

- [A] Detailed history of the character, onset, and course of the symptoms
- [A] Diet/symptom diary to help determine food sensitivities, intolerances, and allergic reactions
- [A] ELISA/ACT™ blood tests for immunological reactivity to foods, inhalants, environmental agents, chemical pollutants, etc.
- [A] Comprehensive stool analysis can show disturbances in intestinal flora, parasitic infection, toxic bowel contaminants, and digestive dysfunction.
- [A] Therapeutic trial of Betaine HCL to produce digestive ease or [C] Hiedelberg capsule gastric analysis can be done to verify degree of HCL deficiency, if suspected.
- [A] Lifestyle Stress Inventory to assess the sources and effects of stress in order to make lifestyle changes to correct this element of the problem; physiological assessment to see if biofeedback may be of benefit can be a part of the stress inventory, as can a psychotherapeutic interview.

- [B] Traditional Oriental Diagnosis to determine if acupuncture might be of significant assistance
- [B] Hair analysis can help to evaluate a proper zinc/copper ratio.
- [C] Fatty acid analysis of blood can help identify disturbances in fatty acid metabolism.
- [C] Amino acid analysis of blood can help identify disturbances in amino acid metabolism.
- [C] Chiropractic examination to determine if joint fixations or trigger points are contributing factors that can be addressed with manipulation and therapeutic massage

### Diet

- [A] Vegetarian, organic, high fiber, low fat diet void of allergenic foods, simple sugars, alcohol, and chemical contaminants
- [A] Plenty of clean water intake

### Nutritional Supplementation

#### Vitamins

- [A] Multivitamin (high potency)—daily with meals. B-6, B-12, E, and folic acid are particularly important.
- [A] Beta-carotene—50,000 I.U. per day
- [A] Vitamin C (best in ascorbate form with 5-10% bioflavonoids)—3,000 mg or more per day

#### Minerals

- [B] Zinc—15-40 mg per day (picolinate or methionate forms may be best), if deficient
- [C] Chromium—200 mcg per day, if deficient
- [C] Selenium—200 mcg per day, if deficient

## Enzymes and Digestive Aids

- [A] Pancreatin—used with protein meals
- [A] Betaine HCL—300-1200 mg per protein meal in those individuals who are deficient in gastric HCL
- [B] Friendly Intestinal Bacterial Flora (primarily Lactobacillus acidophilus and Bifidobacterium strains)

## Other Nutrients

- [A] Omega-3 Fatty Acids ("MaxEPA" or Eicosapentaenoic acid)—10-12 grams per day
- [A] Omega-6 Fatty Acids (gamma linoenic acid as found in evening primrose oil, borage seed oil, and flax seed oil)—1 gram three times per day

## Herbs

- [B] Milk Thistle (Silybum marianum)—70-210 mg per day of the active ingredient, Silymarin
- [B] Bitter melon ( Momardica charantia)—2-4 ounces of fresh juice per day
- [B] Cayenne pepper (Capsicum frutescens)—Topical application of active ingredient, Capsaicin, usually in a 0.025-0.075% ointment
- [B] Prosicur® (Oleum Horwathiensis)—This is a topical application of the herbs: garlic, yarrow, calendula, dandelion, nettle, and veronica.
- [B] Psoralea coryliforia—Psoralens, the active ingredient, when combined with ultraviolet light A is helpful.
- [B] Sarsaparilla (Smilax Sarsaparilla)—250 mg three times per day of the powdered extract or 1-4 grams three times per day of the dried root

## Other Therapeutic Aids

- [A] Avoidance of environmental contaminants, chemical pollutants, inhalant allergens, and toxic agents by using natural products at home and at work. If necessary, use HEPA air filters and replace mercury dental amalgams with less reactive alternatives. *No alcohol or tobacco products.*
- [A] Stress management including plenty of sound sleep and sufficient rest with possible combinations of psychotherapy, biofeedback and hypnosis for optimal results
- [B] Graduated, moderate, conditioning exercise
- [B] Exposure to sunshine and warmth
- [B] Acupuncture
- [C] Chiropractic manipulation

## RHEUMATOID ARTHRITIS

[A] = high priority, [B] = second order priority, [C] = third order priority

### Diagnosis

Differential Diagnosis: Consider and rule out Sjogren's Syndrome, Systemic Lupus Erythematosus, Anemia of Chronic Disease, and Gout.

Prime criteria in descending order of importance: subcutaneous nodules, positive x-ray findings, symptoms begin under age of 35, positive synovial fluid inflammation tests, symmetrical joint swelling, inflammation of metacarpal-phalangeal joints or wrists or ankles or elbows or proximal interphalangeal joints or multiple joints, positive sedimentation rate, and positive agglutination test for rheumatoid factor titer.

## Helpful Functional Tests that Assist Treatment

- [A] Diet/symptom diary to help avoid food sensitivities, intolerances, and allergic reactions

- [A] ELISA/ACT™ blood tests for immunological reactivity to foods, inhalants, environmental agents, chemical pollutants, etc.

- [A] Therapeutic trial of Betaine HCL to produce digestive ease or [C] Hiedelberg capsule gastric analysis can be done to verify degree of HCL deficiency.

- [B] Thyroid function tests may be helpful in identifying the 30% of rheumatoid sufferers that have thyroid dysfunction. The Barnes morning basal temperature test may be more helpful than standard blood tests for identifying borderline cases.

- [B] Blood and hair analysis can help identify disturbances in mineral metabolism and deficiency or excess. This is particularly important with respect to copper, zinc, selenium, iron, and the toxic heavy metals.

- [B] Chiropractic examination to determine if joint fixations or trigger points are contributing factors that can be addressed with manipulation and therapeutic massage

- [B] Lifestyle Stress Inventory to assess the sources and effects of stress in order to make lifestyle changes to correct this element of the problem; physiological assessment to see if biofeedback may be of benefit can be a part of the stress inventory, as can a psychotherapeutic interview.

- [B] Traditional Oriental Diagnosis to determine if acupuncture may be of benefit

- [B] Comprehensive stool analysis can show disturbances in intestinal flora, toxic bowel contaminants, and digestive dysfunction.

- [C] Fatty acid analysis of blood can help identify disturbances in fatty acid metabolism.

- [C] Amino acid analysis of blood can help identify disturbances in amino acid metabolism.

- [C] Microbiological examination of aspirated synovial fluid in affected joints to identify mycotic infection

## Diet

- [A] Vegetarian, low fat, low saturated fat, low in simple sugars (sweets), high fiber void of allergenic foods

- [C] Increase foods containing sulfur— Choose from eggs, beans, fish, Brussels sprouts, onions, garlic, cabbage, brewer's yeast, and nuts.

## Nutritional Supplementation

### Vitamins

- [A] Multivitamin (high potency)—daily with meals; B-12 and folic acid are particularly important.

- [A] Vitamin C (best in ascorbate form with 5-10% bioflavonoids)—3,000 mg or more per day

- [A] Pantothenic Acid—500-2000 mg calcium pantothenate per day (start at lower dose and gradually increase)

- [C] Vitamin K (menadione)—5-10 mg per day

### Minerals

- [A] Boron—5-10 mg per day

- [B] Zinc—10-50 mg three times per day (since zinc and copper are antagonists biochemically, it is sometimes difficult to maintain a good balance of these two minerals; a periodic hair and/or blood analysis may be helpful)

- [C] Copper salicylate—64-128 mg per day for maximum 10 days

- [C] Selenium—200 mcg per day (if excessive levels exist in whole blood or hair analysis, supplementation should cease)

## Enzymes and Digestive Aids

- [B] Friendly Intestinal Bacterial Flora (primarily Acidophilus and Bifidobacterium strains)
- [B] Bromelain—250-1000 mg (or 150-600 G.D.U.) three times per day away from meals
- [B] Pancreatin—1400 mg three times per day away from meals
- [B] Betaine HCL—300-1200 mg per protein meal in those individuals who are deficient in gastric HCL

## Amino Acids

- [C] L-Histidine—1 gram 2-3 times per day between meals
- [C] Tryptophan—1-2 grams per day between meals
- [C] D,L Phenylalanine—400-1500 mg three times per day taken 1/2 hour before meals

## Other Nutrients

- [B] Bioflavonoids (primarily Quercitin and Catechin)—1000 mg or more taken with vitamin C
- [B] Glycosaminoglycans—1-3 grams three times per day
- [B] Omega-3 Fatty Acids ("MaxEPA" or Eicosapentaenoic acid)—4-20 grams per day
- [B] Omega-6 Fatty Acids (gamma linoenic acid as found in evening primrose oil, borage seed oil, and flax seed oil)—1 gram four times per day

## Herbs

It is often wise to find an experienced physician who can intelligently prescribe botanical preparations to aid rheumatoid arthritis sufferers.

- [C] Chinese skullcap (Scutellaria baicalensis)
- [C] Chinese Thoroughwax (Bupleuri falcatum)
- [C] Devils claw (Harpoagophytum procumbens)
- [C] Feverfew (Tanacetum parthenium)
- [C] Ginseng ( Panax ginseng and Eleutherococcus Senticosus)
- [C] Licorice (Glycyrrhiza glabra)
- [C] Tryptergium wilfordii Hook F
- [C] Turmeric (Curcuma Longa) with the active ingredient curcumin
- [C] Yucca Saponin extract

## Other Therapeutic Aids

- [A] Avoidance of environmental contaminants, chemical pollutants, inhalant allergens, and toxic agents by using natural products at home and at work; if necessary, use HEPA air filters and replace mercury dental amalgams with less reactive alternatives.
- [B] Acupuncture
- [B] Chiropractic manipulation (not of acutely inflamed or unstable joints, though)
- [B] Stress management and transpersonal psychotherapy
- [C] Monochromatic blue light reduces pain levels. Skin exposure is effective, but exposure of eyes may be more so. Filtering out other wavelengths during exposure seems to increase effectiveness.
- [C] Antimycotic pharmaceuticals for the treatment of infected joints

# APPENDIX

## PARENTING / CHILDREN'S HEALTH

*There are only two lasting bequests we can give our children.*
*One is roots, the other wings.*

**Hodding Carter**

This book has focused primarily on adult holistic health. Most of the same principles and paths to wholeness can be applied directly to children. But obviously each aspect of health is substantially different from the others. It would take another volume of similar size to do justice to the subject of developing wholeness in our children. Until that volume is written, we will use this chapter to touch upon some of these important areas so that the reader can adapt the recommendations for adults to children.

Holistic health with respect to children begins before conception. Parental nutrition, drug use, physical health, health care practices, education, psychological make-up, stress levels, economic status, contamination with environmental toxins, and spiritual practices and values, are all fields of influence that affect the sperm, the egg, and the site in which the fertilized egg develops. These influences continue as the child is born and grows. We must give adequate attention to these issues if health care is to advance. In the past we have not done this, and tragic results have been imposed on our children.

Proper care of our children is a perfect example of preventive health care. So many of the dysfunctions and ills of adult life have their roots in childhood.

## PHYSICAL HEALTH

*The best thing about being young is*
*if you had to do it over again,*
*you'd still have time.*

**Unknown**

Maternal and childhood nutrition are more important than the standards of care in modern medicine admit. Children will become much healthier if we use the nutritional guidelines in this book and those detailed in the recommended resources. The official guidelines we have now are far too conservative and out-of-date.

*At least 60 % of American children have milk allergies or sensitivities.*

344

Exercise guidelines for children and pregnant women will continue to be refined over the years. As we understand more the importance of assessing *function* rather than just treating symptoms, we will look anew at what sports and exercise do for young people. The future consequences of athletic stress and injury will alter our views on what games and activities are appropriate for young people. When more research is done, a reemphasis will have to be made. More attention will be given to teaching *many* students a variety of healthy sports for life. Less emphasis will be given to collision, contact, and competitive sports for a few when they are found to be more damaging than we generally realize today.

Natural therapeutic alternatives will be used more often, rather than medicine and surgery, because adverse drug reactions and complications can be greater with children than with adults. As more research comes to light, manipulative therapy for pregnant women and children of all ages will take on increasing importance. Acupuncture will be more accepted and utilized. Full spectrum lighting will become mandatory in classrooms because of its powerful overall affect on many psychological, intellectual and physiological functions in children. Neurosensory Development Training will evolve into a much more widely used protocol for improving neurohormonal function.

## ECONOMICS

*There is no such thing a nonworking mother.*
**Hester Mundis**

Economics powerfully affects the health of children, particularly the poor.

*5,500,000 American children under 12
go hungry every day.
An additional six million children are
underfed due to poverty.
20% of American children live below
the poverty level.*

More needs to be done to insure that economic disadvantage does not adversely affect children of the future.

## EDUCATION

*Do not limit a child to your own learning,
for he was born in another time.*
**Unknown**

Dramatic improvements are being made in holistic education. Unfortunately, successful innovations are available only to a select few. Many changes need to take place before high quality education will become available on a broad basis. Teachers must be respected more and paid more. They also must be educated better and held accountable for the quality of their efforts. Student assessments could be improved, but we needn't wait for new evaluation tools before we institute what we already know are superior learning environments and techniques. Nutrition and allergy will be seen more as important facets of the educational process. Multi-sensory learning will be more widely used to accommodate those children who process information better through auditory and kinesthetic modes than visual ones.

Parental education with regards to pre- and peri-natal care, child development, effective parenting practices, child health care, and child abuse is the most important route to improved health for children in the future. So much needs to be done with just the knowledge that is available now. And exciting new information is emerging in this field daily.

*Kids Learn by Example.*
*Children Learn What They Live.*

*If children live with criticism*
*they learn to condemn.*
*If children live with hostility*
*they learn to fight.*
*If children live with ridicule*
*they learn to be shy.*
*If children live with shame*
*they learn to feel guilty.*
*If children live with tolerance*
*they learn to be patient.*
*If children live with encouragement*
*they learn confidence.*
*If children live with praise*
*they learn to appreciate.*
*If children live with fairness*
*they learn justice.*
*If children live with acceptance and friendship*
*they learn to find love in this world.*

**Dorothy Law Noble**

## PSYCHOLOGICAL AND RELATIONSHIP HEALTH

*Allow children to be happy in their own way,*
*for what better way will they ever find?*

**Dr. Johnson**

The psychological needs of children will receive much more attention in the future. With each day we are learning more about the strong importance of early psychological influences on future health. Early relationships, particularly those with family members, are crucial elements in the development of a healthy psyche. Mechanisms for enhancing these early influences will become more widely known and utilized. Ironically, this new knowledge about the importance of family dynamics in early development comes at a time when there are more and more broken homes.

## GOVERNMENTAL HEALTH

*Native American Iroquois, when making important decisions, would traditionally consider how their actions would affect the 7th generation of children.*

As a society we have an obligation to see to it that governmental organizations protect our children. Children do not have enough good representation in the legislature to enact programs for their benefit. We are now leaving our children with a legacy of poverty, psychological trauma, pollution, ignorance, and distorted values. We have not maintained our country's infrastructure but have sucked the life out of it for our own benefit. It will cost our children untold billions of dollars to rebuild what we have destroyed. We have amassed billions more in national debt which they will have to pay. The millions of children we have malnourished over the years, and their children, will suffer lifetimes of lost potential. Our psychodynamic faults will be passed to our children if we do not correct our own psychological and relationship problems. By not investing in better education, we are sentencing our children to unimaginable lost potential for generations to come. America has the worst child care provisions of any industrialized nation except South Africa. We are leaving to our children radioactive and toxic waste which will remain deadly and nearly impossible to manage for tens of thousands of years. We are bequeathing a set of values that encourages competition over cooperation, egotism over common welfare. We are also giving our children a government in gridlock, unable to grapple with these issues.

## ECOLOGICAL HEALTH

*Teaching a child not to step on a caterpillar is as valuable to the child as it is to the caterpillar.*

**Bradley Miller**

We are beginning to recognize the enormous impact our environment has on our health. Children and fetuses are particularly vulnerable to their physical environment just because of their high cellular growth. Environmental contaminants can have profound adverse effects upon these growing tissues, particularly since DNA is so susceptible to errors in replication under these conditions. Lead, mercury, aluminum, pesticides, alcohol, tobacco smoke, drugs, and radiation are all found to be much more dangerous than previously thought.

Allergies, too, pay a more important role in the etiology of diseases which start in childhood. Hidden allergies, either to food or inhalant or contact substances, have a dominant causal influence on infections, especially upper respiratory tract and chronic otitis media (ear infections), behavioral difficulties such as hyperactivity, and learning problems.

Allergies may also be implicated in Sudden Infant Death Syndrome.

It is exciting to see all the great new activities for children centering around ecological awareness. They need to learn what their preceding generations did not—we must protect the Earth, our home.

*We don't inherit the land from our ancestors,*
*we borrow it from our children.*
**Old Proverb of Unknown Origin**

Those with children should pay particularly close attention to the recommendations and resources in the chapter on Ecological Health.

## SPIRITUAL HEALTH

*Children can be conceptualized as mirrors.*
*If love is given to them, they return it.*
*If none is given, they have none to return.*
*Unconditional love is reflected unconditionally,*
*and conditional love is returned conditionally.*
**Ross Campbell**

The spiritual development of children has been a concern for parents since ancient times. Parents, educators, and religious leaders are realizing that children learn best not by memorizing passages in a book, but by different kinds of activities in relationship with the world and the environment.

Seeing their parents behave in spiritually virtuous ways teaches them much more than repeating biblical phrases. Actively enjoying and protecting nature, cooperating in an assortment of activities with a variety of different people, expressing feelings freely, and just being present to life's wonders have long-lasting benefits for our children's spiritual development, as well as our own.

## HIGHEST PRIORITY HEALTH ENHANCEMENT ENDEAVORS FOR CHILDREN

1. Parent effectiveness training.
2. Ideal nutrition for pregnant mothers and children of all ages.
3. Chiropractic care for children will prevent untold suffering and illness, and the effects will have important ramifications into adulthood.
4. Parents should do a child safety check including the following rules:
   a. Always have children properly secured with safety restraints in automobiles.
   b. Eliminate toxic substances from the home and school. This includes secondhand tobacco smoke, alcohol, chemical cleansers, pesticides, lead, radon, formaldehyde, allergenic foods, etc.
   c. Ensure that firearms are not accessible.
5. Family counseling can be sought at times when conflicts seem too confusing to resolve unassisted.
6. Love!

## PARENTING / CHILDREN RESOURCES

★ Denotes Best of the Best Resources

## Birthing and Newborn

*Throw a ring of wood into the ocean.*
*There is a blind turtle in the sea that rises*
*to the surface for air every 100 years.*
*His chances of coming up with his head*
*inside the ring are greater than the chances*
*of a particular life form being human.*
*This is how precious a human life is.*

**The First Great Difficulty of Life,**
**according to Buddhism**

### *Books*

Buttram, Harold. *For Tomorrow's Children: A Manual for Future Parents.* 1990. Available from Preconception Care, Inc., P.O. Box 357, Blooming Glen, PA 18911.

Chamberlain, D. B. *Babies Remember Birth: And Other Extraordinary Scientific Discoveries About the Mind and Personality of Your Newborn.* Ballantine Books, 1990.

Eisenberg, Arlene; Murkoff, Heidi; Hathaway, Sandee. *What to Expect the First Year.* Workman Publishing, 1989.

Eisenberg, Arlene; Murkoff, Heidi; Hathaway, Sandee. *What to Expect When You're Expecting.* Workman Publishing, 1991.

Goldsmith, Judith. *Childbirth Wisdom from the World's Oldest Societies.* Congdon & Weed, 1984. Available from East-West Natural Health Books, 17 Station St., Brookline, MA 02147; (617) 232-1000.

Grof, Stan. *Beyond the Brain: Birth, Death, and Transcendence in Psychotherapy.* State University of New York Press, 1985.

Janov, Arthur. *Imprints: The Lifelong Effects of the Birth Experience.* Coward-McCann, 1983.

Jones, Carl. *Alternative Birth.* Tarcher, 1991.

Korte, Diana and Scaer, Roberta. *A Good Birth, A Safe Birth: Choosing and Having the Childbirth Experience You Want.* Harvard Common Press, 1992.

Leboyer, Frederick. *Birth Without Violence.* Random House, 1975.

Leach, Penelope. *Your Baby and Child.* Alfred A. Knopf, 1989.

*Moonflower Birthing Supply Catalog,* P.O. Box 128, Louisville, CO 80027.

Odent, Michael. *Birth Reborn.* Pantheon, 1984.

Peterson, Gayle. *An Easier Childbirth: A Mother's Workbook for Health and Emotional Well-Being During Pregnancy and Delivery.* Tarcher, 1991.

Spock, Benjamin. *Dr. Spock's Baby and Child Care.* Simon & Schuster, 1992.

Verny, Thomas. *The Secret Life of the Unborn Child.* Sphere Books, 1982.

Walker, Peter. *The Book of Baby Massage.* Fireside, 1988.

*Born Dancing: How Intuitive Parents Understand Their Baby's Unspoken Language.* Harper & Row, 1987.

### *Periodicals*

*Children are God's apostles, day by day*
*sent forth to preach of love, and hope,*
*and peace.*

**James Russell Lowell**

*For Tomorrow's Children,* Newsletter available from Preconception Care, Inc., P.O. Box 357, Blooming Glen, PA 18911.

*Lamaze Magazine,* Lamaze Publishing, 4 Byngton Place, Norwalk, CT 06850; (800) 832-0277.

★*Mothering,* P.O. Box 1690, Santa Fe, NM 87504; (505) 984-8116; (800) 827-1061; (800) 545-9364.

### *Videos*

*There never was a child so lovely but*
*his mother was glad to get him asleep.*

**Ralph Waldo Emerson**

*Baby Basics.* VidaHealth Communications, 1987; (800) 524-1013.

*Baby Massage and Exercise.* Morel Media, 1989; (800) 333-0901.

Brazelton, T. Berry. *Infant Development.* Johnson & Johnson, 1987.

Brazelton, T. Berry. *Infant Health Care.* Johnson & Johnson, 1987.

Daniels, Karil. *Water Baby: Experiences of Water Birth.* Point of View Productions, 2477 Folsom St., San Francisco, CA 94110.

*Water Birth Video,* Star Publishing, P.O. Box 161113, Austin, TX 78716.

## *Organizations*

*Nature makes boys and girls lovely to look upon*
*so they can be tolerated*
*until they acquire some sense.*

**William Lyon Phelps**

American Academy of Husband-Coached Childbirth—
(800) 423-2397; (800) 4-A-BIRTH (in California).

American College of Nurse Midwives, 818 Connecticut
Ave. NW, Suite 900, Washington, DC 20006; (202)
728-9860.

American Society for Psychoprophylaxis in Obstetrics
(ASPO/Lamaze), 1200 19th St. NW, Suite 300, Washington, DC 20036; (800) 368-4404; (202) 857-1128
(in DC); (202) 857-1130. Non-profit organization
promoting prenatal care, Lamaze type childbirth,
and parenting education.

Association of Birth Psychology, 444 E. 82nd St., New
York, NY 10028; (212) 988- 6617. Publishes *Birth
Psychology Bulletin*.

Informed Birth and Parenting, P.O. Box 3675, Ann
Arbor, MI 48106; (313) 662-6857. Provides books,
videos, and a midwife referral service.

International Association for Childbirth at Home, Family
Birth and Wellness Center, 1989 Riverside Dr., Los
Angeles, CA 90039; (213) 663-4996. Publishes *Birth
Notes*.

International Association of Parents and Professionals
for Safe Alternatives in Childbirth, Rt. 1, Box 646,
Marble Hill, MO 63764-9725; (314) 238-2010.

International Childbirth Education Association, P.O.
Box 20048, Minneapolis, MN 55420-0048; (612) 854-
8660 (General Information); (800) 624-4934 (Book
Orders).

Lamaze, 372 Danbury Rd., Wilton, CT 06897; (203) 834-
2711.

Midwives Alliance of North America, P.O. Box 175,
Newton, KS 67114; (316) 283-4543.

Planned Parenthood Federation of America, 810 Seventh Ave., New York, NY 10019; (800) 829-7732;
(212) 541-7800.

Preconception Care, Inc., P.O. Box 357, Blooming Glen,
PA 18911. Supports responsible, progressive, preventive preconception health care efforts for the
benefit of our children.

## **Parent / Child Health Resources**

*Your children are not your children.*
*They are the sons and daughters*
*of Life's longing for itself.*

**Kahlil Gibran**

### *Books*

Armstrong, Thomas. *Awakening Your Child's Natural
Genius: Enhancing Curiosity, Creativity, and Learning Ability*. Tarcher, 1991.

Auerbach, Stevanne. *The Whole Child: A Sourcebook*. G.
P. Putnam's Sons, 1981.

Biracree, Tom and Nancy. *The Parent's Book of Facts*.
Facts On File, 1989.

Bishop, Bob and Thomas, Matt. *Protecting Children
from Danger: Building Self-Reliance and Emergency Skills without Fear*. North Atlantic, 1993.

Capacchione, Lucia. *The Creative Journal for Children*.
Shambhala, 1989.

Catchpole, Terry and Catherine. *The Family Video
Guide*. Williamson Publishing, 1992.

Cella, Catherine. *Great Videos for Kids*. Carol Publishing,
1992.

Christopher Gail. *Anchors for the Innocent: A Single
Parent's Guide to Raising Children*. Noble Press,
1992.

Conners, C. Keith. *Feeding the Brain: How Foods Affect
Children*. Plenum, 1989.

Cooper, Kenneth. *Kid Fitness: The Complete Shape-Up
Program from Birth Through High School*. Bantam,
1992.

Crook, William. *Help for the Hyperactive Child*. Professional Books, 1991.

Crook, William and Stevens, Laura. *Solving the Puzzle of
Your Hard-to-Raise Child*. Random House, 1987.

Dreikurs, Rudol. *Children: The Challenge*. Penguin,
1991.

Edwards, Sharon and Maloy, Robert. *Kids Have All the
Right Stuff*. Penguin, 1992.

Firkalay, Susan. *Into the Mouths of Babes: A Natural
Foods Cookbook for Infants and Toddlers*. Better-
way Books, 1984.

Doan, Marilyn. *Starting Small in the Wilderness: The
Sierra Club Outdoors Guide for Families*. Sierra Club
Books. How to introduce kids to nature through
camping.

Fiske, Edward. *Smart Schools, Smart Kids: Why Do Some
Schools Work?* Simon and Schuster, 1991.

Fitzpatrick, Jean. *Something More: Nurturing Your
Child's Spiritual Growth*. Viking Penguin, 1992.

RESOURCES

Fontana, Vincent. *Save the Family, Save the Child*. NAL-Dutton, 1992.

★ Galland, Leo. *Superimmunity for Kids*. Copestone Press, 1988.

Hamburg, David. *Today's Children: Creating a Future for a Generation in Crisis*. Times Books, 1992.

Humphrey, J.H. and Humphrey, J.N., ed. *Controlling Stress in Children*. Charles C. Thomas, 1988.

James, Walene. *Immunization: The Reality Behind The Myth*. Greenwood, 1988.

Jeffrey, Nan and Kevin. *Adventuring with Children*. Foghorn Press, 1992. Outdoor activities with kids.

Kozol, Jonathan. *Savage Inequalities: Children in America's Schools*. Crown, 1991.

McClure, Vimala. *The Tao of Motherhood*. Nucleus Pub., 1991.

McClure, Vimala. *Infant Massage: A Handbook for Loving Parents*.

Metzger, Mary. *Whole Child Catalogue: A World of Products for Kids from Birth to Age Five*. Doubleday, 1990.

Metzger, Mary and Whittaker, Cinthya. *The Childproofing Checklist: A Parent's Guide to Accident Prevention*. Doubleday, 1988.

Miller, Ron. *Guide to Resources in Holistic Education*. Holistic Education Press.

Miller, Ron, ed. *New Directions in Education: Selections from Holistic Education Review*. Holistic Education Press, 1991.

Miller, Ron. *Renewal of Meaning in Education: Responses to the Cultural & Ecological Crisis of Our Time*. Holistic Education Press, 1993.

Miller, Ron. *What Are Schools For?* Holistic Education Press, 1992.

Mintz, Jerry. *Handbook of Alternative Education*. MacMillan, 1994.

Neustaedter, Randall. *The Immunization Decision: A Guide for Parents*. 1990. North Atlantic Books, 2800 Woolsey St., Berkeley, CA 94705.

*The Non-toxic Baby*, from Natural Choices, 204 N. El Camino Real, Suite E214, Encinitas, CA 92024; (619) 632-1335.

★ Oppenheim, Joanne and Stephanie. *The Best Toys, Books and Videos for Kids*. HarperCollins, 1994.

Pearce, Joseph Chilton. *Evolution's End: Claiming the Potential of Our Intelligence*. HarperCollins, 1992.

Pedersen, Anne and O'Mara, Peggy, ed. *Schooling at Home: Parents, Kids, and Learning*. John Muir Publications, 1990.

Perry, Susan. *Playing Smart: A Parent's Guide to Enriching, Offbeat Learning Activities for Ages 4-14*. Free Spirit Publishing, 1990.

Rapp, Doris. *Is This Your Child? Discovering and Treating Unrecognized Allergies*. William Morrow and Co., 1991.

Rapp, Doris and Bamberg, Dorothy. *The Impossible Child in School, at Home: A Guide for Caring Teachers and Parents*. Practical Allergy, 1988.

Reynolds, Cecil and Kamphaus, Randy. eds. *Handbook of Psychological and Educational Assessment of Children: Personality, Behavior, and Context*. Guilford Press, 1990.

Rowland, Thomas. *Exercise and Children's Health*. Human Kinetics, 1990.

Schmidt, Michael. *Childhood Ear Infections: What Every Parent and Physician Should Know*. North Atlantic, Berkeley 1990.

Schmidt, Michael. *Beyond Antibiotics: Healthier Options for Families*. North Atlantic, 1992.

Schoemaker, Joyce and Vitale, Charity. *Healthy Homes, Healthy Kids: Protecting Your Children from Everyday Environmental Hazards*. Island Press, 1991.

Sisson, Edith. *Nature With Children of All Ages: Activities and Adventures for Exploring, Learning, and Enjoying the World Around Us*. Prentice Hall, 1990.

Tsang, Reginald and Nichols, Buford, ed. *Nutrition During Infancy*. Hanley & Belfus, 1988. More oriented for health professionals.

Turecki, Stanley and Tonner, Leslie. *The Difficult Child*. Bantam, 1989.

Vissel, Barry and Joyce. *Models of Love: The Parent — Child Journey*. Ramira, 1986, Ramira Publishing, P.O. Box 1707, Aptos, CA 95001. Great for those who are seeking to unfold spiritually with their children.

Weiner, M.A. *Healing Children Naturally*. Quantum Books, 1993. Quantum Books, Box 2056, San Rafael, CA 94912-2056.

Yntema, Sharon. *Vegetarian Baby*. McBooks, 1984.

## *Periodicals, Reviews, and Catalogs*

*Blessed be childhood, which brings down something of heaven into the midst of our rough earthliness.*

**Henri Frederic Amiel**

★ Buckleitner, Warren. *High/Scope Buyer's Guide to Children's Software*. High/Scope Press, annual.

Buttram, Harold. "Protecting Children from Toxic Environmental Chemicals." *Townsend Letter for Doctors* (April, 1993): pp. 312-15.

*Children's Software Revue,* Active Learning Associates, 520 N. Adams St., Ypsilanti, MI 48197; (313) 480-0040; Fax (313) 480-2260.

"Contaminated Classrooms: When Learning Becomes Lethal." *Townsend Letter for Doctors* (Jan, 1993): pp. 114-18.

Educational Resources, 1550 Executive Dr., Elgin, IL 60123; (800) 624-2926; Fax (708) 888-8499. Educational software.

EDUCORP, 7434 Trade St., San Diego, CA 92121-2410; (619) 536-9999; Fax (619) 536-2345. Educational computer resources.

*Global Child Health News & Review,* #113-990 Beach Ave., Vancouver, BC Canada V6E 4M2.

*Growing Without Schooling.* A bimonthly publication from Holt Associates on home schooling and educational reform.

★ *Holistic Education Review,* Holistic Education Press, P.O. Box 328, Brandon, VT 05733-1007; (802) 247-8312; orders (800) 639-4122.

*The Learning Company Catalog,* 6493 Kaiser Dr., Fremont, CA 94555; (800) 852-2255. Educational software.

*Montessori Observer.* A bimonthly publication from the International Montessori Society.

*Montessori News.* A tri-annual publication from the International Montessori Society.

*Options in Learning,* Alliance for Parental Involvement in Education, P.O. Box 59, E. Chatham, NY 12060-0059; (518) 392-6900.

*Preventing Sexual Abuse.* A quarterly publication from S.A.F.E. Institute, 1225 N.W. Murray Road, Suite 214, Portland, OR 97229.

*Rethinking Schools,* 1001 E. Keefe Ave., Milwaukee, WI 53212; (414) 964-9646. A quarterly journal of progressive education transformation.

Rodriguez, Juan and Brown, Stuart. "Childhood Injuries in the United States." *American Journal of Diseases of Children* 144 (June 1990).

★ *Self Help for Kids Catalog,* Free Spirit Publishing, 400 1st Ave., Suite 616-52, Minneapolis, MN 55401-1730; (800) 735-7323; Fax (612) 337-5050. A great resource for healthy children.

Sunburst Communications Catalog, 101 Castleto St., Pleasantville, NY 10570; (800) 321-7511; Fax (914) 747-4109. High quality educational software.

## Organizations

*Children need models
more than they need critics.*

**Joseph Joubert**

Academy for Education Development; (212) 243-1110. Provides financial as well as other assistance to a variety of agencies working on educational issues of children.

Alliance for Parental Involvement in Education, P.O. Box 59, E. Chatham, NY 12060-0059; (518) 392-6900. Publishes *Options in Learning,* a diverse discussion of educational issues.

Child Find of America, Inc.; (800) 426-5678, looks for missing and abducted children; (800) 292-9688, provides crisis mediation and prevention information in parental abduction.

ChildHelp/IOF Foresters National Child Abuse Hotline; (800) 4-A-CHILD; (800) 2-A-CHILD (TDD).

Children's Defense Fund, 25 E St. NW, Washington, DC 20001; (800) CDF-1200; (202) 628-8787. Informs public of the needs of children.

Covenant House Nineline; (800) 999-9999. Crisis line for youth, teens, and families with various problems. Includes a local referral service.

Dissatisfied Parents Together (DPT), c/o Barbara Fisher, Box 563, 1377 K St., N.W., Washington, DC 20005. Activist parents who have seen some of the damage that vaccinations can cause and are trying to remedy the situation.

Family Resource Coalition; (312) 341-0900. A national network of family service organizations based in local communities providing information and other services to help children's total health.

Friends Council on Education, 1507 Cherry St., Philadelphia, PA 19102; (215) 241-7245.

Holt Associates, 2269 Massachusetts Ave., Cambridge, MA 02140; (617) 864-3100. A clearinghouse for home schooling information and resources.

★ Institute for Childhood Resources, c/o Stevanne Auerbach, 220 Montgomery St., No. 2811, San Francisco, CA 94104; (415) 864-1169.

International Montessori Society, 912 Thayer Ave., Silver Spring, MD 20910; (301) 589-1127.

National Center for Education in Maternal and Child Health, 2000 15th St. North, Suite 701, Arlington, VA 22201-2617; (703) 524-7802. Produces a wide variety of free or inexpensive publications on this topic.

National Child Abuse Hotline (24 hour); (800) 422-4453.

National Child Safety Council Childwatch; (800) 222-1464.

RESOURCES

National Clearinghouse on Child Abuse and Neglect, P.O. Box 1182, Washington, DC 20013; (800) 394-3366; (703) 385-7565 (in Virginia).

National Collaboration for Youth, 1319 "F" St., Washington, DC 20004; (202) 347-2080. Public education organization addressing multiple levels of health issues.

National Committee for the Prevention of Child Abuse, 332 S. Michigan, Suite 1600, Chicago, IL 60604; (312) 663-3520. An information network providing data on child abuse to direct service organizations in the U.S.

National Maternal and Child Health Clearinghouse, 8201 Greensboro Dr., Suite 600, McLean, VA 22102; (703) 821-8955. Distributes a wide variety of free or inexpensive publications on this topic.

National Organization of Single Mothers, P.O. Box 68, Midland, NC 28107-0068; business office (704) 888-2337; Hotline for single mothers (704) 888-KIDS. Publishes the newsletter *Single Mother*. Ask for a free sample copy. Regional networking groups are open for membership throughout the U.S.

National Runaway Hotline, 308 N. Lincoln, Chicago, IL 60657; (800) 231-6946.

United Nations Children's Fund; (212) 326-7000. Information network, lobbying agency, and fund-raising organization for the benefit of the children of the world. Publishes *The State of the World's Children*.

Waldorf Institute, 260 Hungry Hollow Rd., Spring Valley, NY 10977; (914) 425-0055. The Institute supports Rudolf Steiner's approach to the natural intellectual and spiritual development of children.

Youth Crisis Hotline (teen issues); (800) 448-4663.

## Suppliers of Educational Materials and Toys

*Having children is like having
a bowling alley installed in your brain.*

**Martin Mull**

Back to Basics Toys, 2707 Pittman, Silver Spring, MD 20910; (800) 356-5360.

Childcraft, P.O. Box 29156, Mission, KS 66201; (800) 631-5657.

The Children's Software Co., 5505 Connecticut Ave. N.W. #333, Washington, DC 20015-2601; (800) 556-5590.

Coalition for Quality Children's Video, 535 Cordova Rd., Suite 456, Santa Fe, NM 87501; (505) 989-8076.

Facets Kids Video Catalog, 1517 W. Fullerton Ave., Chicago, IL 60614; (800) 331-6197.

Hearth Song, 6519 N. Galena Rd., Peoria, IL 61614; (800) 325-2502.

Holcombs Educational Materials, 3205 Harvard Ave., Cleveland, OH 44105; (800) 362-9907.

Humungous Entertainment, 13110 NE 177th Pl. #180, Woodinville, WA 98072-9965. Educational software company.

Natural Baby Company, 816 Silvia St., Trenton, NJ 08628; (800) 388-BABY.

New World Education Book Collection, Welsh Products, P.O. Box 845, Benicia, CA 94510.

Toys To Grow On, P.O. Box 17, Long Beach, CA 90801; (800) 542-8338.

*In automobile terms, the child supplies the power,
but the parents have to do the steering.*

**Benjamin Spock**

# TECHNOLOGICAL HEALTH

*The cloning of humans is on most of the lists of things to worry about from Science,
along with behavior control, genetic engineering, transplanted heads, computer poetry
and the unrestrained growth of plastic flowers.*

**Lewis Thomas**

The Web of Wholeness which we have been discussing has many elements and relationships. For the sake of clarity we have chosen to explore only a certain number of these parts and interconnections. One aspect which was not incorporated into the total discussion was the one concerning our technological health. We touched on the subject indirectly with references in the sections on economics, intellect, and ecology. The topic is important enough to amplify in further discussion.

At every level of our being, from the individual to the family and the community, our national identity, even our global totality, uses technology of different types to varying degrees, and with diverse levels of sophistication. We use so much technology that we may be unaware of its total impact on our lives. Sometimes the type of technological support we use is needed. At other times the level of technology is not enough to promote adequate health. On some occasions technological sophistication is excessive and/or counterproductive.

*Progress might have been all right once
but it has gone on too long.*

**Ogden Nash**

As individuals, we must become aware of technology in our daily lives and decide if it is appropriate and health enhancing, insufficient or excessive, helpful or counterproductive. Does it release energy and time for other more worthwhile activities, or is it more stressful and consuming than it is worth? And what relationship does it establish between each individual and his or her environment? What relationship does a particular piece of technological wizardry create between people?

Electric toothbrushes, electric can openers, hair dryers, curling irons, electric screwdrivers, food processors, coffee makers—are they worth the expense, the hassles, the cumulative exposure to electromagnetic radiation? There is something to be said for simplicity.

There are some aspects to drying clothes on a line in the sun and fresh air that, when compared with the expense and ecological travesty of a gas or electric clothes dryer, makes the convenience of modern technology less substantial.

*Teach us Delight in simple things,
And Mirth that has no bitter springs.*

**Rudyard Kipling**

Microwave ovens are very convenient for fast paced lifestyles. But maybe we lose more in the hectic pace than what is healthy. Microwave ovens are expensive. They are energy hogs. More time is needed to work enough to pay for this. Many of the quick, ready-to-eat dinners that are specially made for microwave cooking are unhealthy nutritionally. When deliberate, mindful, loving food preparation is replaced with a grab-it-and-run mentality, more health is lost than just what can be quantified by nutritional standards.

Observe some of the benefits and disadvantages of different levels of transportation technology. The automobile, airplane, and travel in space are technological events that have radically changed all of humanity and the planet. Some of their consequences for our health have been negative, some positive.

*Horsepower was a wonderful thing
when only horses had it.*

**Unknown**

The automobile has expanded our world and integrated people from different locales and cultures. This may be viewed as a positive influence because it created unity. But the automobile has also been responsible for making communities *too* mobile and impermanent, breaking the bonds of family and community. The environmental havoc which the internal combustion engine has produced is enormous. Air pollution, oil spills, paved-over land, and urban sprawl, destroying agricultural land and natural resources, have tremendous adverse health effects. The direct damage to human life and limb is also astronomical. The United States has more casualties each year due to auto collisions than ten years worth of military casualties in Vietnam.

*Our national flower is*
*the concrete cloverleaf.*

**Lewis Mumford**

On the one hand the American trucking industry is so extensive that it can with relative ease transport any product from one part of the country to another in a short period of time; that has significant health advantages. Distribution of food and health care products helps our physical health. Efficient postal service makes our government and businesses run more healthfully, not to mention the help it gives us to keep in touch with friends and family. But on the other hand local economies, most notably agriculture, can be undermined by shipping cheaper, foreign-made products into a region. Trucking in itself is not the most health promoting occupation. A trucker's health is often in jeopardy because of the stresses of long distance driving. Everyone who ventures out onto our highways is at greater risk when such large vehicles are barrelling down the road. Overworked truck drivers who doze off at the wheel, and poor truck maintenance compound the problem.

Similar correlations can be drawn when considering air transportation. There are advantages and disadvantages to that mobility. At the same time that it brings people closer together it pulls people further apart. Rapid helicopter life-flights save lives on a daily basis. During wartime, military air power is the most life threatening technology. Jet fuel poisons our air and destroys our atmospheric ozone every minute of every day.

*Technological progress is like an axe*
*in the hands of a pathological criminal.*

**Albert Einstein**

Space travel expands our knowledge about ourselves and our place in the universe. But some say the money spent looking outward to other planets and galaxies might have been better spent on efforts to look within and solve the problems on our home planet. In fact, the first picture taken of our colorful Earth island against the black backdrop of deep space may have been the most important look that all our space investigations took. It gave everybody on this life-filled orb a new perspective on the term "Spaceship Earth," and a new recognition of how valuable it is to care for our home. And as satellites monitor ozone depletion in an effort to protect the planet, military intelligence uses other satellites to more efficiently kill people. Other satellites keep viewers glued to the Home Shopping Network so they can buy every imaginable piece of unnecessary junk ever devised by obsessive marketing minds.

*The scientific theory I like best is that the rings*
*of Saturn are composed of*
*lost airline luggage.*

**Mark Russell**

Other telecommunication advances have revolutionized the world. Few would argue against the benefits that the radio and telephone have given humanity. But television brings with its advantages a possibly longer list of detriments which are enumerated in Jerry Mander's book, *The Four Arguments for the Elimination of TV.*

We must meet these issues where they are relevant and can be changed. For each individual it is not too useful to debate *whether* automobiles, airplanes, television, or any other technological advancement is ultimately healthy *or* unhealthy when all the debating points are summed up, because that evaluation is not likely to make an appreciable impact on the existence of that technology. Cars, TV's, and gadgetry are going to be here for a long time no matter how much we debate the pros and cons. It is important to evaluate *how* we each use these technologies in daily life.

It might be less important to debate *if* we should use light bulbs and more meaningful to evaluate *which* light bulbs are the most energy efficient and imitative of natural full spectrum sunlight. The more relevant and practical question is not, "Should there be cars?" but, "How do I manage my transportation alternatives? When should I use mass transit? If I decide on automobile transportation, what kind of healthy technological support will I include—fuel economy? Airbags? Anti-lock brakes? Headrests? Electricar?"

Maybe I will choose to let the technology of modern day fabric manufacturing weave me a store bought shirt rather than spin the fiber and weave the fabric on a handmade loom and then stitch it by hand. Or, I might choose not to use the technology of synthetic fabrics and simply buy a shirt of 100% cotton.

A doctor may choose to use computerized diagnostic and treatment expert systems to enhance her health care services. She may see the value in having her children educated with the use of computers, but feel that computer games or computer shopping are too detrimental to have that technology enter her family's life.

Each of us has to draw lines as to which technology is healthy and which is not, which we will choose to use and which we will choose to avoid. But we can make those choices only if we are educated about the ramifications of technology and are aware of the many ways it affects our life and health.

*For people who like peace and quiet a phoneless cord.*

**Unknown**

We must also make these choices for our collective health. Is it worth it for our society to deal with the unimaginable complexity, cost, and danger of nuclear power so that we can produce heat a million degrees Fahrenheit to boil water to spin turbines, so that electricity can be shipped hundreds of miles (40% of which is lost through the transmission lines) to someone's hair curler? Some have likened this technological overkill to cutting butter with a chainsaw, not very cost-effective—particularly if all the money the government used to subsidize the nuclear industry had been put to alternative, safe, renewable energy sources so that each individual dwelling had its own, decentralized power source.

*I do not think that the measure of a civilization is how tall its buildings of concrete are, but rather how well its people have learned to relate to their environment and fellow man.*

**Sun Bear of the Chippewa Tribe**

The technology of mega agri-businesses is another issue we must face on both an individual basis and collectively. Personally, the decision might center around whether to buy locally grown organic produce at higher gross cost but cheaper net cost per unit of nutritional quality, or buy inexpensive supermarket chain food requiring pesticide use, long distance shipping, excessive fossil fuel expenditure, and poor land use management.

At the same time that we rave with amazement over high-tech medical procedures to save lives in extreme situations, we seriously debate the economic, moral, practical, and spiritual wisdom of when that technology should be used. These are questions that we have to answer on an individual basis by making living wills and by raising questions which we have to grapple with as a society.

Health care professionals and the lay public have at their disposal ever-increasing technological advantages with the rapid expansion of the information superhighway:

- specialized, health-related computer bulletin boards
- on-line health forums
- interactive faxing
- diagnostic and treatment software
- drug-interact software to reduce complications in medication prescription
- outcomes databases for more cost-effective decision making
- interactive lifestyle and risk assessments
- computer-aided medical literature searches
- real time video consultation with specialists

Individuals now have at their fingertips vast amounts of helpful information to better take care of their own health. Doctors, therapists, and health educators have powerful tools for keeping up with the most current clinical knowledge, consulting with specialists, and communicating with each other and their clients.

Everybody needs to make continual reassessments of how technology will be used to make us whole. To make informed choices use the resources that follow.

*It is not enough to be busy; so are ants.*
*The question is: What are we busy about?*

**Henry David Thoreau**

---

## TECHNOLOGICAL HEALTH RESOURCES

*If there is technological advance without social advance,*
*there is, almost automatically, an increase in human misery.*

**Michael Harrington**

★ Denotes Best of the Best Resources

### Books

★ Carnes, Alice and Zerzan, John. *Questioning Technology: Tool, Toy, or Tyrant.* New Society Publishers, 1991.

★ Darrow, Ken and Saxenian, Mike. *Appropriate Technology Sourcebook.* Volunteers in Asia, 1993. Available from Volunteers in Asia/Appropriate Technology Project, P.O. Box 4543, Stanford, CA 94305; (800) 648-8043.

★ Glendinning, Chellis. *When Technology Wounds: The Human Consequences of Progress.* William Morrow and Co., 1990.

★ LaFollette, Marcel and Stine, Jeffrey. *Technology and Choice.* University of Chicago Press, 1991.

Lovins, Amory and Lovins, Hunter. *Brittle Power: Energy Strategy for National Security.* Brick House Publishing Company, 1982.

Mander, Jerry. *Absence of the Sacred: The Failure of Technology and the Survival of the Indian Nations.* Sierra Club Books, 1991.

Mander, Jerry. *The Four Arguments for the Elimination of TV.* Morrow, 1978.

★ Schumacher, E. F. *Small Is Beautiful: Economics as if People Mattered.* Harper Collins, 1989.

Shrag, Robert. *Taming the Wild Tube: A Family's Guide to Television and Video.* U of NC Press, 1990.

Street, John. *Politics and Technology.* Guilford, 1992.

### Periodicals

*One has to look out for engineers—*
*they begin with sewing machines and*
*end up with the atomic bomb.*

**Marcel Pagnol**

*Adbusters,* Adbusters Media Foundation, 1243 W. 7th Ave., Vancouver, BC V6H 1B7, Canada; (604) 736-9401; Fax (604) 737-6021. In depth analysis of the detrimental impact of advertising.

★ *Appropriate Technology Journal,* 103-5 Southampton Row, London, WCI 4HH, UK.

*The Futurist,* World Future Society, 7910 Woodmont, Av., Suite 450, Bethesda, MD 20814; (301) 656-8274.

*Technology and Culture,* U. of Chicago Press, Journals Div., P.O. Box 37005, Chicago, IL 60637; (312) 702-7600.

*Technology Review;* (800) 877-5230.

*Tough Questions,* from Student Pugwash USA, 1638 R St. NW, Suite 32, Washington, DC 20009-6446; (202) 328-6555. Discusses the social and ethical aspects of technology.

*VITA News,* 1600 Wilson Blvd., Suite 500, Arlington, VA 22209; (703) 276-1800. Information about Volunteers in Technical Assistance.

## Organizations

*The machine does not isolate man from*
*the great problems of nature*
*but plunges him more deeply into them.*

**Antoine de Saint-Exupery**

★ Center for the Study of Commercialism, 1875 Connecticut Ave., NW Room 300, Washington, DC 20009-5728; (202) 797-7080.

Computer Professionals for Social Responsibility, P.O. Box 717, Palo Alto, CA 94301; (415) 322-3778; Fax (415) 322-3798; Internet: cpsr@csli.stanford.edu.

★ Energy Efficiency and Renewable Energy Clearinghouse, P.O. Box 3048, Merrifield, VA 22116; (800) DOE-EREC. Provides fact sheets on various energy conservation subjects and handles telephone inquiries, whether technical or general.

★ Intermediate Technology Development Group, 777 United Nations Plaza, Suite 3C, New York, NY 10017; (212) 953-6920. Their publications catalog has many great resources.

Office of Technology Assessment, Publications Order, U.S. Congress, Washington, DC 20510-8025; (202) 224-8996. Their current publications catalog contains many sources of excellent information on new technologies and their impact on our health.

★ Trans-National Network of Appropriate/Alternative Technology (TRANET), P.O. Box 567, Rangeley, ME 04970; (207) 864-2252. Appropriate technology clearinghouse.

## Computer Networks

*We have the power to make this*
*the best generation of mankind*
*in the history of the world—*
*or to make it the last.*

**John F. Kennedy**

*Awakening Technology,* Awakening Technology, 695 Fifth St., Lake Oswego, OR 97034; (503) 635-2615; Fax (503) 636-0106; Internet: p+t@awaken.com. Computer conference seminars to unlock human potential. Some related to ecology, like "Earth and Spirit."

*ECHO,* 97 Perry St., Suite 13, New York, NY 10014; (212) 255-3839. East coast version of the WELL.

HealthDesk Corp., 1801 Fifth St., Berkeley, CA 94710; (510) 843-8110; Fax (510) 845-8305. Interactive health information systems for health care providers and the lay public.

*The Meta Network,* 2000 N. 15th St., Suite 103, Arlington, VA 22201; (703) 243-6622. Eclectic, computer conferencing service.

*PeaceNet / EcoNet,* Institute for Global Communications, 18 De Boom St., San Francisco, CA 94107; (415) 442-0220. Computer conferencing systems with sub groups like ConflictNet, and Global Action Net.

*The WELL,* 1750 Bridgeway, Sausalito, CA 94965; (415) 332-4335; modem (415) 332-6106. Broad range of progressive topics with participation from a wide variety of individuals. Environmentalism, health, art, music, spirituality.

Ed Krol's *The Whole Internet: User's Guide and Catalog* from O'Reilly and Associates of Sebastopol, California is a good guide to accessing these computer networks.

See also the computer related resource sections in the chapters on Holistic Health, Ecological Health, Psychological Health, and Relationship Health.

# AGING, DYING, DEATH

*The Five Remembrances*
*1. I am of the nature to grow old. There is no way to escape growing old.*
*2. I am of the nature to have ill health. There is no way to escape having some illness.*
*3. I am of the nature to die. There is no way to escape death.*
*4. All that is dear to me and everyone I love are of the nature to change.*
*There is no way to escape being separated from them.*
*5. My actions are my only true belongings. I cannot escape the consequences of my actions.*
*My actions are the ground on which I stand.*

**Buddhist prayer**

## AGING

*A child's world is fresh and new and beautiful,*
*full of wonder and excitement.*
*It is our misfortune that for most of us*
*that clear-eyed vision, that true instinct for*
*what is beautiful and awe-inspiring, is dimmed*
*and even lost before we reach adulthood.*
*If I had influence with the good fairy*
*who is supposed to preside over*
*the christening of all children,*
*I should ask that her gift to each child*
*in the world be a sense of wonder*
*so indestructible that it would last*
*throughout life, as an unfailing*
*antidote against boredom*
*and disenchantments of later years,*
*the sterile preoccupation with things*
*that are artificial, the alienation from*
*the sources of our strength.*

**Rachel Carson**

There is no escape from growing old. But it is possible to grow old in a way that is not plagued by decades of disease, pain, suffering, unhappiness, and unfulfilled dreams.

*It should be the function of medicine to have*
*people die young as late as possible.*

**Ernst L. Wynder, M.D.**

The purpose of holistic health practices should be, in part, to diminish the aging process in such a way as to reduce the incidence and severity of illness and dysfunction until the very later stages of life. Health enhancement activities are life enhancement activities—encouraging full participation in all aspects of life right up to the end.

*How do I want to die?*
*At any age above the century mark I want*
*to be shot by a jealous husband.*

**Unknown**

Carlos Castenada's mentor gave good counsel to keep death at one's shoulder. It is a short time we have on this earth in these bodies. It is wise to live in a way that will help us fully develop every aspect of life.

The best way to age gracefully is to age as healthfully as possible. Transitions in life are frequently difficult. Often the transitions in later years are some of the most trying. Some aids to this process can be found in the resources at the end of this section. Of particular interest might be Health Hazard Appraisals for the determination of health risks and how they can be minimized. Also clinical measurements of biological age in comparison to chronological age can tell us if we are younger or older than our actual years and identify methods for reducing our biological age.

## Factors for Increased Health and Fulfilling Longevity

The following are proven to extend health into the senior years and increase longevity.

- Proper diet (see Nutrition section of this book). Pay particular attention to reducing calories and increasing nutrient rich foods. Nutrient supplementation is also of strong value. Refer to the anti-aging section in Elson Haas' book.

- Regular physical activity.

- Non-perpetuation of difficult emotions— Understanding and effectively dealing with anger, fear, hatred, resentment, greed, confusion, and doubt without denying their presence when these emotions arise. This is a real key to aliveness.

- Cultivation of positive psychological traits— joy, humor, confidence, courage, patience, empathy, friendliness, decisiveness, autonomy, tolerance, spontaneity . . .

- Fulfilling relationships with friends and family.

- Meaningful contribution to community and society—A purpose for living beyond personal gain.

- Stimulating environment with a minimum of harmful stresses.

- Strong ability to cope with change and loss.

- Minimal exposure to environmental toxins (tobacco and alcohol are the worst culprits).

- Optimistic anticipation of a long, meaningful life.

*Gene Fowler, the writer, visited W. C. Fields*
*shortly before his death.*
*Fowler found his ailing old crony*
*sitting in the garden reading the Bible.*
*"I'm looking for loopholes,"*
*Fields explained shyly.*

**Unknown source**

## DYING AND DEATH

*What the caterpillar calls the end of the world,*
*the rest of the world calls butterfly.*

**Richard Bach**

There is no way to escape the death of the physical body. If the physical body is what we think we are, then the end of that can be frightening. What we have been learning in this book is that there is a different Self we can identify with that will help us to better health and fuller life. It is also a recognition which will help us confront death.

Usually, we first make intimate contact with death as a friend or loved one lies dying or dies suddenly. Watching someone close to you being transformed by the dying process arouses many emotions, thoughts, and bodily reactions. We not only feel for his or her loss but our own. Fear, anger, resentment, vulnerability, and disappointment can flood us in wave after wave of intense feeling. Recognizing these emotions, communicating them to others, and integrating them into our rapidly changing relationship with the dying individual are necessary and rewarding for all concerned.

It is a dramatic transition and often a difficult time. We have dual responsibilities at these times. One is to be as supportive and helpful to the dying individual as possible in his or her final days and hours. The other responsibility is for our own psychological well-being. Getting guidance in effectively and healthfully dealing with these transformations can be very helpful. Use the excellent practical resources at the end of this section whenever death is an issue in one's life, and use them well before a death crisis arises. For the sudden death of a loved one is sometimes the most difficult experience to recover from if one does not have the wisdom to adequately deal with it.

*Whatever prepares you for death*
*enhances life.*

**Stephen Levine**

Our modern technological disease care system has brought us miraculous lifesaving techniques. Unfortunately, the technology did not give us the wisdom to use it in a rational, compassionate manner. Thousands of people are kept alive with expensive treatments even when there is no hope of recovery. Billions of dollars are spent in futile attempts to keep people alive who will unquestionably die within a few days or weeks. Often expensive, heroic efforts are expended in the last days of one's life where the treatment is worse than the disease or the natural dying process.

Advances in computerized "outcomes" research will continually give better information to doctors and family members regarding the likelihood that a given treatment will be worth the expense and trauma involved. A doctor approaches the family of a dying person in the hospital and says, "When we put the facts of his condition into our computer it showed a 5% possibility of surviving more than two weeks if we perform $600,000 worth of procedures, which—if successful—will leave him bedridden and hooked up to a machine for the rest of his life." This makes it easier to make a decision. But what makes for even easier decision-making at these times is when every family member has a "living will" drawn up that gives specific instructions to doctors and loved ones regarding what efforts should or should not be engaged to prolong life in the event of grave illness. These living will forms can be obtained from the Society for the Right to Die or Nolo Press.

If we truly have a deep understanding of life, death is not a macabre tragedy to fear. It is a transition in the form of the body, while the essence of Life permeates all in a unifying Oneness which does not die but continually transforms itself. This is part of the Web of Wholeness.

*People who fear Death*
*Mistake their life for a fragile glass bulb*
*That dies when the tungsten burns out.*
*If they only knew*
*Their Life is the Light of the Universe*
*that never dies.*

**Thomas M. Collins**

## AGING, DYING, DEATH RESOURCES

*To everything there is a season, and a time to every purpose under the heaven.*

**from Ecclesiastes**

## Aging

*None are so old as those who have outlived enthusiasm.*

**Unknown**

### Books

Birkedahl, Nonie. *Older and Wiser: A Workbook for Coping with Aging.* New Harbinger, 1991.

Carlsen, Mary. *Creative Aging: A Meaning Making Perspective.* Norton, 1991.

Cheney, Walter; Diehm, William; Seeley, Frank. *The Second 50 Years.* Paragon House, 1992.

Cole, Thomas. *The Journey of Life: A Cultural History of Aging in America.* Cambridge University Press, 1992.

Dean, Ward. *Biological Aging Measurement—Clinical Applications.* Available from Center for Bio-Gerontology. Contains descriptions of the tests in detail with sources for obtaining the equipment needed to run them.

Evans, William and Rosenberg, Irwin. *Biomarkers—The 10 Determinants of Aging You Can Control.* Simon & Schuster, 1991.

Gerzon, Mark. *Coming Into Our Own: Understanding the Adult Metamorphosis.* Delacorte Press, 1992.

Goldman, Connie. *The Ageless Spirit.* Ballantine, 1992.

Haas, Elson. *Staying Healthy with Nutrition.* Celestial Arts, 1991. Has a good chapter on anti-aging strategies.

Heynen, Jim and Boyer, Paul. *One Hundred Over One Hundred.* Fulcrum Pub., 1990.

Hoffer, Abram and Walker, Morton. *Smart Nutrients: A Guide to Nutrients That Can Prevent and Reverse Senility.* Avery, 1994.

Lewis, Carole and Campanelli, Linda. *Health Promotion and Exercise for Older Adults.* Aspen, 1990.

Pretat, Jane. *Coming to Age: The Croning Years and Late-Life Transformation.* Inner City Books, 1994.

Walford, Roy. *The One Hundred and Twenty Year Diet.* 1991.

Weindruch, Richard and Walford, Roy. *The Retardation of Aging and Disease by Dietary Restriction.* Charles C. Thomas, 1988.

Wolfe, Sidney; Hope, Rose-Ellen; and Public Citizen Health Research Group. *Worst Pills, Best Pills: The Older Adults Guide to Avoiding Drug Induced Death or Illness.* Public Citizen, 1993.

## Periodicals

**To keep the heart unwrinkled, to be hopeful, kindly, cheerful, reverent—that is to triumph over old age.**

**Thomas Bailey Aldrich**

*Aging and the Human Spirit Newsletter,* c/o Diane Pfeil, Institute for Medical Humanities, University of Texas, Suite 2.210 Ashbel Smith, Galveston, TX 77555-1311; (409) 772-2376.

## Computer Databases

**As we grow old . . . the beauty steals inward.**

**Ralph Waldo Emerson**

AgeLine. From AARP; thousands of documents on age-related health subjects updated monthly and dating back to 1978.

## Organizations and Workshops on Aging

**Within, I do not find wrinkles and used heart, but unspent youth.**

**Ralph Waldo Emerson**

Alliance for Aging Research, 2021 K St., N.W., Suite 305, Washington, DC 20006; (202) 293-2856; Fax (202) 785-8574. Promotes health and independence of the elderly through medical research on aging.

American Academy of Anti-Aging Medicine, P.O. Box 146571, Chicago, IL 60614-2013; (312) 975-4034; Fax (312) 929-5733. Health professionals interested in extending and enhancing human life.

American Aging Association, 2129 Providence Ave., Chester, PA 19013; (215) 874-7550.

Center for Bio-Gerontology, P.O. Box 11097, Pensacola, FL 32524; (904) 484-0595. Does research on the analysis of biological age and develops programs to retard the aging process. They can be contacted for information about which functional capacity tests are most accurate at determining the aging process and which protocols are best for extending life.

Center for Intergenerational Learning, Temple University, 1601 N. Broad St., Philadelphia, PA 19122; (215) 204-6970. Explores the value of multigenerational interactions.

Elder Hostel, 75 Federal St., 3rd Fl., Boston, MA 02110; (617) 426-7788.

Gray Panthers, 6342 Greene St., Philadelphia, PA 19144; (215) 438-0276. Elder activists.

National Institute on Aging Information Center; (800) 222-2225; in Maryland, (301) 587-2528; Fax (301) 589-3014.

Spiritual Eldering Project, P'nai Or Religious Fellowship, 7318 Germantown Ave., Philadelphia, PA 19119; (215) 242-4074. Emphasizes engagement in the present from a proper perspective of the past for future growth and wholeness—of self and the world.

Look in the phone book for a local area Agency on Aging or obtain that number from the Office for the Aging in each state capitol. This organization has numerous services assisting the elderly with important aspects of health care.

**Birth is not a beginning; death is not an end.**

**Chuang-tzu**

## Dying and Death

### Books

**Bury me when I die
beneath a wine barrel in a tavern.
With luck the cask will leak.**

**Moriya Sen'an**

Ahronheim, Judith. *Final Passages: Positive Choices for the Dying & Their Loved Ones.* S & S Trade, 1992.

Carlson, Lisa. *Caring for Your Own Dead: A Final Act of Love.* Upper Access Publishers, 1987. Upper Access Publishers, P.O. Box 457, Hinesburg, VT 05461; (800) 356-9315.

Doore, Gary, ed. *What Survives?: Contemporary Explorations of Life after Death.* Tarcher, 1990.

RESOURCES

Duda, Deborah. *Coming Home: A Guide to Dying at Home With Dignity.* Aurora Press, 1987. Best practical guide for supporting a dying loved one.

Gonda, Thomas and Ruark, John. *Dying Dignified: The Health Professional's Guide to Care.* Addison-Wesley, 1984.

Humphrey, Derek. *Dying With Dignity: Understanding Euthanasia.* Carol Pub., 1992.

Kapleau, Philip. *The Wheel of Life and Death: A Practical and Spiritual Guide to Death, Dying, and Beyond.* Doubleday, 1989.

Kubler-Ross, Elizabeth. *On Death and Dying.* MacMillan, 1970.

Levine, Stephen. *Who Dies?* Doubleday/Anchor, 1982.

Levine, Stephen. *Meetings at the Edge.* Doubleday, 1988.

Levine, Stephen. *Healing Into Life and Death.* Doubleday, 1988.

Morgan, Ernest and Jenifer. *Dealing Creatively with Death: A Manual of Death Education & Simple Burial.* Barclay House, 1990.

Nearing, Helen. *Loving and Leaving the Good Life.* Chelsea Green, 1992.

Nolo Press, 950 Parker St., Berkeley, CA 94710; (800) 992-6656; (510) 549-1976. This publisher of legal self help books has a number of books and a computer software program for making your own will.

Schneider, Miriam and Sellicken, Jan. *Midwives to the Dying.* Angel's Word, 1992.

Nuland, Sherman. *How We Die: Reflections on Life's Final Chapters.* Knopf, 1994.

Sogyal Rinpoche. *The Tibetan Book of Living and Dying.* Harper/Collins, 1992.

Weber, Doron. *The Complete Guide to Living Wills.* Bantam, 1991.

## *Videos*

*Deathing: An Introduction to Conscious Dying.* Available from Hartley Film Foundation, 59 Cat Rock Road, Cos Cob, CT 06807; (203) 869-1818; (800) 937-1819; Fax (203) 869-1905.

## *Organizations and Workshops*

*The Native American term for "death" is the "Great Return" or more accurately "making the Earth split, Spirit returning, Earth remaining."*

**Unknown**

Choice in Dying, 200 Varick St., 10th Floor, New York, NY 10014; (800) 989-9455; (212) 366-5540. Provides "advanced directive" forms, for each state, to help your family and physicians carry out your wishes of dying with dignity.

Concern for Dying, 250 West 57th St., New York, NY 10107; (212) 366-5540.

*Conscious Living / Conscious Dying Workshops* with the Levines. Contact Grace Productions, 1615 24th Ave., San Francisco, CA 94122; (415) 753-5755.

Hemlock Society, P.O. Box 11830, Eugene, OR 97440-4030; (503) 342-5748. Information on active euthanasia for the terminally ill and seriously incurably ill. Publishes *Timelines.*

*Life, Death, and Transitions Workshops* sponsored by The Elizabeth Kubler-Ross Center/Shanti Nilaya, S. Rte. 616, Head Waters, VA 24442; (703) 396-3441.

Living / Dying Project, 75 Digital Dr., Novato, CA 94949; (415) 884-2343; Fax (415) 884-2342. Teaches volunteers to work with the dying.

National Hospice Organization, 1901 N. Moore St., Suite 901, Arlington, VA 22209; (703) 243-5900. For information and referral to nearly 2000 hospices nationwide—(800) 658-8898.

Society for the Right to Die, 250 W. 57th St., New York, NY 10107; (212) 366-5540. Living will forms are available through the Society.

**Benjamin Franklin's Epitaph**

*The Body of B. Franklin, Printer,
Like the Cover of an Old Book,
Its Contents Torn Out And Stripped of its
Lettering and Guilding,
Lies Here
Food for Worms,
But the Work shall not be Lost,
For it Will as He Believed
Appear Once More
In a New and More Elegant Edition
Revised and Corrected
By the Author.*

# ULTRA-LOW COST HEALTH ENHANCEMENT STRATEGIES

*Frugality is the sure guardian of our virtues.*
**Proverb of Unknown Origin**

There is a great need for everyone to adopt holistic health care alternatives. Those who can benefit the most often do not have the economic resources to invest heavily in *any* health care endeavor. Fortunately, some of the most powerful health enhancement strategies are often the least expensive to participate in. Even more often people will save money by altering their present lifestyle and substituting the recommended low-cost guidelines for healthy life change. The reduced illness and fewer doctor bills, the greater work productivity that results from these health promoting undertakings, will more than compensate for some of the nominal expenses incurred.

Below are listed some very significant suggestions for inexpensively instituting dramatic improvements in all aspects of one's health.

## PHYSICAL

### Safety

Cost: $0

Abide by all the auto and highway safety rules. Seat belts, shoulder harnesses, and headrests are a must.

Be safety conscious around the home, at work, and while at play. Read: Hax, Elizabeth (ed.). *The Home Book: A Guide to Safety, Security, and Savings in the Home.* Public Citizen and Jacobson, Michael and Lefferts, Lisa. *Safe Food: Eating Wisely in a Risky World.* Living Planet Press, 1991.

Practice good food preparation hygiene in the kitchen and avoid being one of the millions of cases of food poisonings each year.

Avoid violent people, stay away from guns, shun taverns, don't drink alcohol or take drugs.

### Nutrition

Cost: Save $

Follow the Nutrition Guidelines in the chapter on Nutrition. If the recommendation to buy organic is omitted, this type of diet will be the least expensive and most nutritious diet available. The most expensive foods are also the ones that have negative health effects—junk foods, fast foods, convenience foods, fats, sugars, red meats, alcohol, caffeine, carbonated beverages.

Obtain cookbooks and nutrition books, magazines, and newsletters from your library. Encourage your librarian to carry all of this book's recommended resources.

### Exercise

Cost: A good pair of walking shoes, Lifeline Gym exercise tubing, and *Auto Stretching: The Complete Manual of Specific Stretching* by Olaf Evjenth and Jern Hamberg (Alfta Rehab Forlag, 1989). $130 up front, but it will be repaid in the first few months of increased health and vitality.

Walking briskly for at least 30 minutes every day is the most cost effective exercise available. Wearing comfortable shoes that provide good support is helpful. Read *Walking Medicine: The Lifetime Guide to Preventive & Therapeutic Exercisewalking Programs* by Gary Yanker and Kathy Burton (McGraw-Hill, 1990). Walking or riding a bicycle to work is an excellent way to obtain good, regular exercise and save money on transportation. This accommodates the aerobic portion of fitness.

For flexibility, use the book *Autostretching* five days per week to provide balanced flexibility to all parts of your body. Do not neglect this important aspect of physical health.

For strength training, obtain a Lifeline Gym, preferably with a foot attachment (or similar rubber tubing device listed in the Exercise resource section). Using this for 30 minutes, 2-3 times per week, will keep muscles toned, strong, fit, and balanced, if done in an intelligent manner utilizing the strength training principles detailed in the exercise resource section of the book. These resources can be obtained from your local library. For everyone except the elite athlete, this form of strength training is as good as can be acquired in any gym or fitness spa.

### Biological Rhythms and Sleep

Cost: $0

Get plenty of sleep. Sleep deprivation causes illness, accidents, and lost productivity.

Get plenty of sunshine. Be careful not to burn, but daily exposure to unimpeded sunlight, particularly through the eyes, is instrumental in maintaining normal biological rhythm and biochemical balance. This will also enhance emotional balance and mental acuity.

## ECONOMIC

Cost: Save $

Be clear as to the difference between necessities and nonessentials. Don't buy impulsively. Don't even listen to radio or television commercials or allow your children to be programmed in such a destructive way.

Plan ahead. Buy items when on sale as much as possible. Avoid the more expensive brand name items when alternatives will be less expensive and of equal quality. Thrift stores run by charitable organizations like Salvation Army and Goodwill are often wise places to shop, in addition to being places whose proceeds help those less fortunate.

Keep a budget. Use the suggestions given by Fernandez. (See resources in the chapter on Economic Health.) Your librarian may be able to acquire it.

Remember that life has little to do with acquiring and more to do with loving.

## HEALTH CARE

Cost: Save $

The more one participates in self-care wisely, the less health care intervention by expensive professionals will be needed.

That first means becoming informed. Obtain the resources you feel are of the highest priority from your local library. Then use the recommendations from "The Best of the Best Resources" and do the same. Then continue reading and keeping informed with all the other resources recommended.

Then the real key comes—actively using that information for your health benefit—eating right, exercising, doing self psychotherapy, meditating, being mindful. . . .

## TRANSPORTATION

Cost: Save $

Walk, bicycle, use mass transit, car pool, and if auto travel is necessary, buy good used cars with shoulder harnesses, seat belts, and head rests which get good gas mileage. Keep tires inflated at the upper end of the recommended range.

## EDUCATION

THE SINGLE MOST IMPORTANT, COST-EFFECTIVE HEALTH ENHANCEMENT STRATEGY IS TO BE CONSTANTLY INFORMED ABOUT YOUR HEALTH.

We are fortunate to live in a society with such ready access to information. Although libraries have been cutting back hours and do not always have the best stock of the most recent, relevant health care resources, they do provide one of the best resources in the world for excellent *free* health care advice.

Obtain the resources mentioned in this book from the Library. Recommend to your librarian that they carry all these important works. The periodicals are particularly important to keep up-to-date with the rapidly changing information in various health related fields.

Also take advantage of free or inexpensive community classes given through the local community center or community colleges. Many nutrition or health food stores sponsor free cooking classes.

Job training for a career that will be healthier, as well as more economically supportive, is often some of the wisest education that can be gained from a health enhancement perspective.

## PSYCHOLOGICAL

Cost: $0

Obtain the resources from the library and work in this aspect of health regularly with self exercises.

Use the nutritional guidelines in order to establish proper brain biochemistry for good psychological function.

Get plenty of sunshine for the same reason.

Work at avoiding stresses in life. Don't complicate life.

Practice relaxation exercises daily.

Surround yourself with emotionally supportive friends and family. Avoid troublesome people.

## RELATIONSHIPS

Cost: $0

Avoid harmful, abusive relationships.

Obtain and utilize the resources found in the chapter on Relationship Health from your library.

Look for and attend the many free or inexpensive relationship classes put on in your community.

## ENVIRONMENT

Save $

Use the energy saving recommendations found in the resource section of the Ecological Health chapter.

Avoid pollutants. Use Dadd-Redalia's book, obtained from the library. Cigarette smoke is the worst culprit, alcohol is next.

Avoid allergy provoking substances, particularly synthetic chemicals and foods.

Spend plenty of time in Nature. Go on outings with the Sierra Club.

Don't live in big cities. Their pollution, crime, expense, and stress are too damaging to health. The "apparent" economic advantages are seldom worth it.

## SPIRITUAL

Cost: $0

Sit in silent observation twice daily. Use the guidelines obtained from the resources in the chapter on Spiritual Health.

Read spiritually or philosophically inspiring writings everyday, even if it's only a sentence or a simple quote.

Spend time with others who will support you in your spiritual practices and activities.

Be kind. Help others. Make sure the words you speak are always constructive.

Spend a little time each day to appreciate and be thankful for all the joys and good things in life.

Be truthful.

*Men do not realize how great an income thrift is.*

**Cicero**

# RETREATS

## FINDING RETREATS

*Nowhere can man find a quieter or more untroubled retreat than in his own soul.*

**Marcus Aurelius**

Benson, Jack. *Transformative Adventures, Vacations & Retreats: An International Directory of 300+ Host Organizations.* New Millennium Publishing, 1994.

Kelly, Jack and Marcia. *Sanctuaries: A Guide to Lodgings in Monasteries, Abbeys, and Retreats of the United States.* Bell Tower / Harmony Books, 1991, 1993.

Morreale, Don. *Buddhist America: Centers, Retreats, Practices.* John Muir Publications, 1988; (800) 888-7504.

North American Retreat Directors Association, Stony Point Center, 17 Crickettown Road, Stony Point, NY 10980; (914) 786-3825.

Ram Dass. *Journey of Awakening: Meditator's Guidebook.* Bantam, 1990. Sound advice for spiritual seekers with extensive list of multi-denominational meditation groups and retreat centers.

Spa Finders, (800) ALL-SPAS, provides booking services to many spas and sells a helpful book, *The Spa Finder Catalog.*

Rudee, Martine and Blease, Jonathon. *Traveler's Guide to Healing Centers and Retreats in North America.* John Muir, 1989.

## RETREAT FACILITIES

*Let my mind become silent,*
*And my thoughts come to rest.*
*I want to see*
*All that is before me.*
*In self-forgetfulness*
*I become everything.*

**Joseph Cornell**

Breitenbush Hot Springs Retreat and Conference Center, P.O. Box 578, Detroit, OR 97342; (503) 854-3314.

Chinook Learning Center, P.O. Box 57 Clinton, WA 98236; (206) 321-1884; (206) 467-0384.

Elat Chayyim: The Woodstock Center for Healing and Renewal, P.O. Box 127, Woodstock, NY 12498; (800) 398-2630.

Esalen Institute, Big Sur, CA 93920-9616; (408) 667-3000.

Feathered Pipe Ranch, Box 1682, Helena, MT 59624; (406) 442-8196.

Findhorn Foundation, Cluny Hill College, Forres IV36 ORD, Scotland; (0309) 72288; phone : 0309 673655.

Gatehouse Retreat Center, 1236 Vista Dr., Mt. Shasta, CA 96067; (916) 926-5752.

Glyn Foundation, Gaunts House, Wimborne, Dorset, BH21 4JQ, UK; phone: 0202 841522.

Heartwood Institute, 220 Harmony Lane, Garberville, CA 95542; (707) 923-2021; (707) 923-5000.

Hollyhock Farm, Box 127, Manson's Landing, Cortes Island, BC VOP 1KO Canada; (604) 935-6465; (604) 935-6533.

Interface, 55 Wheeler St., Cambridge, MA 02138; (617) 876-4600.

Jughandle Creek Farm and Nature Center, P.O. Box 17, Caspar, CA 95420; (707) 964-4630.

Kalani Honua, RR2, Box 4500, Pahoa, HI 96778; (800) 800-6886.

Lama Foundation, Box 240, San Cristobal, NM 87564; (505) 586-1269.

Mendocino Woodlands, P.O. Box 267, Mendocino, CA 95460; (707) 937-5755.

Mount Madonna Center, 445 Summit Rd. Watsonville, CA 95076; (408) 847-0406.

Naropa Institute, 2130 Arapahoe Ave., Boulder, CO 80302; (303) 444-0202.

Oasis Center, 7463 N. Sheridan Rd., Chicago, IL 60626; (312) 274-6777.

Ocean Song, P.O. Box 659, Occidental, CA 95465; (707) 874-2442.

Ojai Foundation, 9739 Ojai-Santa Pould Rd., Ojai, CA 93024; (805) 646-8343.

Omega Institute for Holistic Studies, 260 Lake Drive, RD 2, Box 377, Rhinebeck, NY 12572; (800) 944-1001 or (914) 266-4444 and in summer (914) 266-4301.

Open Center, 83 Spring Street, New York, NY 10012; (212) 219-2527.

Orr Hot Springs, 13201 Orr Springs Road, Ukiah, CA 95482; (707) 462-6277.

Pocket Ranch Institute, P.O. Box 516, Geyserville, CA 95441; (707) 857-3359.

Rainbow Ranch, 3975 Mt. Home Rd., Calistoga, CA 94515; (707) 942-5127.

Rowe Camp and Conference Center, Kings Highway Road, P.O. Box 273, Rowe, MA 01367; (413) 339-4954.

Saint Benedict's Monastery, 1012 Monastery Rd., Snowmass, CO 81654; (303) 927-3311.

Saratoga Springs Retreat, 10243 Saratoga Springs Rd., Upper Lake, CA 95485; (800) 655-7153.

Schumacher College, The Old Postern, Darington, Totnes, Devon, TQ9 6EA, England; (0803) 865934.

Shenoa Retreat and Learning Center, Box 43, Philo, CA 95466; (707) 895-3156.

Sierra Hot Springs, Cambell Hot Springs Rd., Sierraville, CA; (800) 994-3770; (916) 994-3773.

Tanager Foundation, P.O. Box 18283, Reno, NV 89511; (702) 827-1203.

Tassajara Zen Mountain Center. Contact San Francisco Zen Center, 300 Page St., San Francisco, CA 94102; (415) 431-3771.

Wainwright House, 260 Stuyvesant Ave., Rye, NY 10580; (914) 967-6080.

Wellspring Renewal Center, P.O. Box 332, Philo, CA 95466; (707) 895-3893.

Westerbeke Ranch Conference Center, 2300 Grove, Sonoma, CA 95476; (707) 996-7546.

White Sulphur Springs Resort and Spa, 3100 White Sulphur Springs Rd., St. Helena, CA 94574; (707) 963-8588; Fax (707) 963-2890.

Wilbur Hot Springs, 3375 Wilbur Springs Rd., Williams, CA 95987; (916) 473-2306.

Wildwood Retreat, P.O. Box 78, Guerneville, CA 95446; (707) 632-5321; Fax (707) 632-5975.

Windstar Foundation, 2317 Snowmass Creek Rd., Snowmass, CO 81654; (303) 927-4777.

*There is one spectacle grander than the sea,*
*that is the sky;*
*There is one spectacle grander than the sky,*
*that is the interior of the soul.*

**Victor Hugo**

RESOURCES

# SPECIAL SUBJECT RESOURCES

## AIDS

### Books

Kidd, Parris and Huber, Wolfgang. *Living With the AIDS Virus: A Strategy for Long-Term Survival.* HK Biomedical Inc., P.O. box 8207, Berkeley, CA 94707.

Konlee, Mark. *AIDS Control Diet.* Available from Keep Hope Alive, P.O. Box 27041, West Allis, WI 53227.

Siano, Nick and Lipsett, Suzanne. *No Time to Wait: A Complete Guide to Treating, Managing, and Living with HIV Infection.* Bantam, Doubleday, 1993.

### Periodicals

*AIDS/HIV Treatment Directory,* AmFAR—TIS, 733 third Av., New York, NY 10017-3204; (800) 39-AmFAR. Quarterly reports about new treatment alternatives.

### Organizations

AIDS Alternative Health Project, 4753 N. Broadway, Suite 1110, Chicago, IL 60640; (312) 561-2800. Clinic offering multidisciplinary, natural therapies for health improvement for those with HIV.

Gay Men's Health Crisis, 129 W. 20th St. New York, NY 10011; (212) 807-6664.

National AIDS Information Clearinghouse, P.O. Box 6003, Rockville, MD 20850; (800) 458-5231; (800) 243-7012 (TTY/TDD); International line (301) 738-6616; Fax (301) 217-0023 .

Project Inform, 347 Dolores St., Suite 301, San Francisco, CA 94110; (800) 822-7422; or in California (800) 334-7422, (415) 558-9051.

## Alzheimer's Disease

Alzheimer's Association; (800) 272-3900.

Alzheimer's Disease Education and Referral Center; (800) 438-4380.

Warren, Tom. *Beating Alzheimer's: Steps Towards Unlocking the Mysteries of Brain Diseases.* Avery Publications, 1991.

Brennan, Patricia. "Computer Networks Promote Caregiving Collaboration: The ComputerLink Project." *Consumer Health Informatics.* Self-care Productions, 1993. ComputerLink Project is a computer network for caregivers of Alzheimer's patients. For more information contact Patricia Flatley Brennan,

Case Western Reserve University, 2121 Abington Road, Room 304F, Cleveland, OH 44106-4904; (216) 368-5130; Fax (216) 368-3813; E-Mail: pfb@po. CWRU.

## Arthritis

di Fabio, Anthony. "Arthritis." *Townsend Letter For Doctors* (Dec. 1993): 1194-1209.

di Fabio, Anthony, et al. "Candidiasis: Scourge of Arthritics." *Townsend Letter for Doctors* (Jan 1994): 64-75.

Scammell, Henry and Brown, Thomas. *The Arthritis Breakthrough: The Road Back.* M. Evans & Co., 1993.

## Autism

### Books

Williams, Donna. *Nobody Nowhere.* Random House, 1992. A description of the disease from a high-functioning autistic.

### Organizations

Autism Research Institute, 4182 Adams Ave., San Diego, CA 92116; (619) 281-7165. A good resource center.

Autism Services Center, Prihard Bldg., 605 9th St., P.O. Box 507, Huntington, WV 25710-0507; (304) 525-8014. Another excellent resource center.

Autism Society of America, 7910 Woodmont Ave., Suite 650, Bethesda, MD 20814-3015; (301) 657-0881; (800) 3-AUTISM; Fax (301) 657-0869. This is an information resource center which publishes a quarterly newsletter, *Advocate.*

## Brain Enhancement

Tools For Exploration, 4460 Redwood Highway, Suite 2, San Rafael, CA 94903; (800) 456-9887. Innovative but unproven brain enhancement technology.

Quantum Link, 8665 East Miami River Rd. Cincinnati, OH 45247; (800) 531-9283. Brainwave stimulating audiotapes with specific enhancement orientations.

# Cancer

## *Books*

Austin, Steve and Hitchcock, Cathy. *Breast Cancer: What You Should Know (But May Not Be Told) About Prevention, Diagnosis, and Treatment*. Prima, 1995.

Cantwell, Alan. *The Cancer Microbe*. Aries Rising Press, 1990.

Fink, John. *Third Opinion: An International Directory to Alternative Therapy Centers for the Treatment and Prevention of Cancer*. Avery Publishing, 1988.

Fiore, Neil. *The Road Back to Health: Coping with the Emotional Aspects of Cancer*. Celestial Arts, 1990.

Holland, Jimmie and Rowland, Julia (eds.) *Handbook of Psychooncology: Psychological Care of the Patient with Cancer*. Oxford U. Press, 1989. For health care professionals.

Lerner, Michael. *Choices in Healing: Integrating the Best of Conventional and Complementary Approaches to Cancer*. MIT Press, 1994.

Moss, Ralph, *Cancer Therapy: The Independent Consumer's Guide to Non-Toxic Treatment and Prevention*. Equinox Press, 1992. From People Against Cancer, P.O. Box 10, Otho, IA 50569; (800) NO-CANCER.

Prasad, Kedar. *Vitamins Against Cancer*. Healing Arts Press, One Park St., Rochester, VT 05767.

Prasad, Kedar and Meyskens, F. *Nutrients and Cancer Prevention*. Humana Press, 1990.

Quillan, Patrick. *Beating Cancer with Nutrition*. ImpaKt Communications, P.O. Box 12496, Green Bay, WI 54307-2496; (800) 477-2995.

Rogers, Sherry. *Wellness Against All Odds*. Prestige Publishing, 1994.

Walters, Richard. *Options: The Alternative Cancer Therapy Book*. Avery, 1993.

## *Organizations*

Cancer Control Society, 2043 Berendo St., Los Angeles, CA 90027; (213) 663-7801. Non-profit informational service that includes alternative cancer treatments.

Foundation for Advancement in Cancer Therapy, P.O. Box 1242, Old Chelsea Station, New York, NY 10113; (212) 741-2790. Alternative cancer therapy clearinghouse.

International Association of Cancer Victors and Friends, temporary address: 515 W. Sycamore, El Segundo, CA 90245; (310) 822-5032.

# Candidiasis

## *Books*

Crook, William. *The Yeast Connection: A Medical Breakthrough*. Professional Books, 1983.

Truss, Orian. *The Missing Diagnosis*. Orian Truss, 1983. Available from C. Orian Truss, M.D., 2614 Highland Ave., Birmingham, AL 35205.

## *Journal Articles*

di Fabio, Anthony, et al. Candidiasis: Scourge of Arthritics" *Townsend Letter for Doctors*. Jan 1994; pp. 64-75.

## *Organizations*

Candida Research and Information Foundation, P.O. Box 2719, Castro Valley, CA 94546.

# Cardiovascular Diseases

## *Books*

Brecher, Harold and Brecher, Arlene. *Forty Something Forever: A Consumer Guide to Chelation Therapy & Other Heart Savers*. Healthsavers Press, 1992. Healthsavers Press, P.O. Box 683, Herndon, VA 22070; (703) 471-4734.

Locke, Steven and Hornig-Rohan, Mady. *Psychological and Behavioral Treatments for Disorders of the Heart and Blood Vessels: An Annotated Bibliography*. Available from The Fetzer Institute.

Ornish, Dean. *Dr. Dean Ornish's Program for Reversing Heart Disease*. Random House, 1990.

Rath, Mathias. *Eradicating Heart Disease*. Available from Health Now, 387 Ivy St., San Francisco, CA 94102; (800) 624-2442.

## *Journal Articles*

"Bibliography on Mechanism of Action of EDTA" *Townsend Letter for Doctors*, May, 1994; pp. 476-79.

Cranton, Elmer. "A Texbook on EDTA Chelation Therapy" *Journal of Advancement in Medicine*. 1989; Vol. 2: # 1&2.

## *Organizations*

American Board of Chelation Therapy, 70 W. Huron St., Chicago, IL 60610; (312) 787-2228. Certifies chelation therapists.

American College of Advancement in Medicine, 23121 Verdugo Drive, Suite 204, Laguna Hills, CA 92653; (800) 532-3688; (714) 583-7666. Professional organization which trains physicians in chelation therapy.

American Institute of Medical Preventics, 405 Kains Ave., Albany CA 94706; (510) 526-3232. Professional organization involved with chelation therapy research.

Linus Pauling Heart Foundation, 440 Page Mill Road, Palo Alto, CA 94306.

## Chronic Fatigue Immune Deficiency Syndrome

### *Books*

Culbert, Michael. *Conquering the Crippler*. Available from American Biologics, 1180 Walnut Ave., Chula Vista, CA 91911; (800) 227-4473.

★ Rosenbaum, Michael and Susser, Murray. *Solving the Puzzle of Chronic Fatigue Syndrome*. Life Sciences Press, 1992. The best single book on the subject.

Goldstein, Jay. *Chronic Fatigue Syndromes: The Limbic Hypothesis*. Haworth Press, 1993.

Vayda, William, et al. *Chronic Fatigue: The Silent Epidemic*. Simon & Schuster Australia, 1991.

### *Periodicals*

Bradley, Alexander and Lord, Richard. "Treatment of Chronic Fatigue Syndrome with Specific Amino Acid Supplementation." *Journal of Applied Nutrition* 46:3 (1994): 74-78.

*Journal of the Chronic Fatigue Syndrome*. Haworth Medical Press, 10 Alice Street, Binghamton, NY 13904-1580; (800) 342-9678.

### *Organizations*

CFIDS Association, P.O. Box 220398, Charlotte, NC 28222-0398; (704) 362-CFID; (800) 442-3437. Publishes the *CFIDS Chronicle* on a quarterly basis.

Environmental Health Network, P.O. Box 1155, Larkspur, CA 94577; (415) 541-5075. Publishes *The Reactor*.

## Detoxification

Gard, Zane and Brown, Erma. "Literature Review and Comparison Studies of Sauna / Hyperthermia in Detoxification," *Townsend Letter for Doctors*. #107: June 1992, 470-8.

Gard, Zane and Brown, Erma. "Literature Review and Comparison Studies of the Sauna and Illness," *Townsend Letter for Doctors* 108 (July 1992): 650-60.

Gard, Zane and Brown, Erma. "Literature Review and Comparison Studies of Sauna Hyperthermia in Detoxification. *Townsend Letter for Doctors* 111 (October 1992): 844-53.

Zane R. Gard, M.D., P.O. Box 1791 Beaverton, OR 97075-1791. For more information on Dr. Gard's BioToxic Reduction Program for the medically supervised elimination of toxic substances (recreational drugs, medicines, industrial pollutants, pesticides) from the body.

## DMSO

Walker, Morton. *DMSO—Nature's Healer*. Avery, 1993.

## Epilepsy

Reiter, Joel; Andrews, Donna; Janis, Charlotte. *Taking Control of Your Epilepsy: A Workbook for Patients and Professionals*. The Basics Publishing Co., 1987. Available from Andrews/Reiter Epilepsy Program, Inc., 550 Doyle Park Dr., Santa Rosa, CA 95405.

## Hypothyroidism

Langer, Stephen with Scheer, James. *Solved: The Riddle of Illness*. Keats, 1984.

## Life Threatening Illness

Fink, John. *Third Opinion: An International Directory to Alternative Therapy Centers for the Treatment and Prevention of Cancer*. Avery Publishing, 1988. Many of these centers treat other serious and degenerative diseases.

Siegel, Bernie. *Peace, Love, and Healing: Bodymind Communication and the Path to Self-Healing: An Exploration.* Harper & Row, 1990.

## Multiple Sclerosis

DeVries, Jan. *Multiple Sclerosis.* Mainstream Publishing, Edinburgh, 1985.

## Music and Healing

### *Books*

Campbell, Don. *Music and Miracles.* Quest, 1992.

Campbell, Don. *Music: Physician for Times to Come.* Quest, 1992.

Campbell, Don. *The Roar of Silence: Healing Powers of Breath, Tone, and Music.* Quest, 1992.

Lingerman, Hal. *The Healing Energies of Music.* Quest, 1992.

Lingerman, Hal. *Lifestreams.* Quest, 1992. How to blend meditations with music.

Spintge, Ralph. *Music Medicine.* MMB Music, 1992.

### *Audio and Video Tapes*

Campbell, Don and Wilson, Tim. *Healing Powers of Tone and Chant.* Audio.

Campbell, Don. *The Roar of Silence.* Video.

### *Audio and Video Tape Catalogs*

Alcazar, P.O. Box 429, Waterbury, VT 05676; (800) 541-9904. Expansive catalogue with tunes from nearly every genre to put a song in one's heart.

Backroads Distributors, 417 Tamal Plaza, Corte Madera, CA 94925; (800) 825-4848. Their *Heartbeats* catalogue has approximately 2,500 titles of great music that can help one to wholeness.

Sounds True, 735 Walnut St., Boulder, CO 80302; (800) 333-9185.

### *Organizations*

American Association for Music Therapy, P.O. Box 50012, Valley Forge, PA 19484; (215) 265-4006; Fax (610) 265-1011. Publishes *International Newsletter of Music Therapy* and *Music Therapy Journal.*

National Association of Music Therapy, 8455 Colesville Road, Suite 930, Silver Springs, MD 20910; (301) 589-3300.

## Osteoporosis

Appleton, Nancy. *Healthy Bones: What You Should Know About Osteoporosis.* Avery Publishing, 1991.

★ Gaby, Alan. *Preventing and Reversing Osteoporosis.* Prima, 1994.

## Parasites

Gittleman, Ann. *Guess What Came To Dinner—Parasites and Your Health.* Avery, 1993.

## Schizophrenia

Hoffer, Abram. *Common Questions On Schizophrenia and Their Answers.* Keats, 1987.

Canadian Schizophrenia Foundation, 16 Florence Ave., Toronto, Canada M2N 1E9: (416) 733-2117.

★ Pfieffer, Carl; Mailloux, Richard; and Forsythe, Linda. *The Schizophrenias: Ours to Conquer.* Bio-Communications Press, 1988.

Torrey, E.F. *Surviving Schizophrenia: A Family Manual.* Revised Edition; Harper & Row, 1988.

## Sports Health and Exercise Physiology

American College of Sports Medicine, 401 West Michigan St., Indianapolis, IN 46202; (317) 637-9200. Publishes *Medicine and Science in Sports and Exercise,* a professional journal.

*Sports Medicine and Exercise Physiology Catalog* from Brown and Benchmark Publishers, 2460 Kerper Boulevard, Dubuque, IA 52001; (800) 346-2377. Books, videos, and software.

Human Kinetic Publishers, P.O. Box 5076, Champaign, IL 61825-5076; (800) 747-4457; (217) 351-5076; In Canada: Human Kinetics, Box 224040, 1275 Walker Rd., Windsor, Ontario N8Y 4Y9; (519) 944-7774. Provides a wide array of books, journals, and software on every aspect of exercise.

RESOURCES

## Sudden Infant Death Syndrome

National Sudden Infant Death Syndrome Resource Center, 8201 Greensboro Dr., Suite 600, McLean, VA 22102; (703) 821-8955; Fax (703) 821-2098.

## Vision

College of Optometrists in Vision Development, P.O. Box 285, Chula Vista, CA 91912; (619) 425-6191. Professional organization of progressive optometrists knowledgeable about vision therapy.

Optometric Extension Program Foundation, Inc., 2912 Daimler St., Santa Ana, CA 92705; (714) 250-8070. Professional organization of progressive optometrists knowledgeable about behavioral optometry.

Parents Active for Vision Education, 7898 Broadway, Lemon Grove, CA 91945-1801; (619) 464-0687.

## Women's Health

### *Books*

Anderson, Ruth and Hopkins, Patricia. *The Feminine Face of God: The Unfolding of the Sacred in Women.* Bantam, 1991.

Aspen Reference Group. *Women's Health Patient Education Resource Manual.* Aspen Publishers, 1994.

Boston Women's Health Book Collective Staff. *The New Our Bodies, Ourselves.* Simon & Schuster, 1992.

Cerra, Francis. *Why Women Pay More.* $10 from P.O. Box 19366, Washington, DC 20036.

Hudson, Tori. *Gynecology and Naturopathic Medicine: A Treatment Manual.* TK Publications. Available for $31.50 from TK Publications, 19135 SW Butternut St., Aloha, OR 97009; (503) 591-5428.

King, Theresa, ed. *The Spiral Path: Explorations in Women's Spirituality.* Yes Int'l, 1992.

Media Network. *Choice: Women's Reproductive Freedom and Health.* A media guide to 80 films and videos. Available from Media Network, 39 W. 14th St., Suite 403, New York, NY 10011; (212) 929-2663; (212) 929-2732.

Media Network. *In Her Own Image.* A media guide to 82 films and videos on women and community development. Available from Media Network, 39 W. 14th St., Suite 403, New York, NY 10011; (212) 929-2663; (212) 929-2732.

Mendlesohn, Robert S. *Malepractice: How Doctors Manipulate Women.* Contemporary, 1982.

Silver, Lynn and Wolfe, Sidney. *Unnecessary Cesarean Sections: How to Cure a National Epidemic.* Public Citizen, 1989.

West, Stanley. *The Hysterectomy Hoax.* Doubleday, 1994.

Wolfe, Sidney and Jones Rhoda. *Women's Health Alert: What Most Doctors Won't Tell You About.* Addison-Wesley, 1991.

### *Periodicals*

*Healthy Woman,* Rodale Press, 33 E. Minor St., Emmaus, PA 18098; (610) 967-5171. Quite diverse health information. Could be better with some chiropractors and naturopathic physicians on the health advisory board and a bit less emphasis on medicinal recommendations and advertisements.

*Journal of Women's Health,* Mary Ann Liebert, Inc., 1651 Third Ave., New York, NY 10130-0060; (212) 289-2300.

*Journal of Women & Aging,* Haworth Press, 10 Alice Street, Binghamton, NY 13904-1580; (800) 342-9678.

*Women & Health,* Haworth Press, 10 Alice Street, Binghamton, NY 13904-1580; (800) 342-9678.

"Women's Health Update" (a regular section in *Townsend Letter for Doctors* by Tori Hudson, ND).

### *Organizations*

Fertility Awareness Service, Box 986, Corvallis, OR 97339; (503) 753-8530.

National Women's Health Network, 514 10th St. NW, Suite 400, Washington, DC 20004; (202) 628-7814. Women's Health clearinghouse that provides health educational material and publishes a newsletter.

Office of Research on Women's Health, National Institutes of Health, Building 1, Rm 201, Bethesda, MD 20892; (301) 402-1770.

Women's Sport Foundation: (800) 227-3988. Provides information on women's sport, fitness and sports health.

# EPILOGUE

Symptoms are primarily late warning signals indicating that dysfunction is occurring. Attention needs to be focused on the underlying causes of dysfunction rather than the symptoms.

An illness has many causes and maintains itself from many sources.

Health improvement depends primarily on pursuing a responsible lifestyle and making changes in behavior; it also depends on a community and a society which provide freedom and education while protecting health; it depends lastly on health care practitioners.

Multifaceted, interdisciplinary approaches are the future form of health care. Instructional assistance for self-care will be the most significant element.

All aspects of our being are intimately intertwined. Finding a balance among all these elements marks a Life of Wholeness. This entails the wise selection of efforts to support those aspects of health that will have the most powerful impact on overall wholeness.

So as we travel this Path of Wholeness, our consciousness expands to embrace an all-encompassing "I"—more than an individual self, more than a bag of bones and juice, personal thoughts, and agendas. When our consciousness does this, we also abandon our overemphasis on "disease care." As we realize our True Self and understand the complex interconnections of cause and effect that govern the processes of Life, our actions are transformed in positive directions. We evolve more holistic ways to care not only for the personal self, but also for parts of our larger Self—family, community, Gaia, the universe.

The more individuals who walk this high road, the more it becomes a preferred route for others. It is important to point the way to those who are usually followers in progressive movements—doctors, government officials, business executives, men in power—even though they may be erecting major autobahns in the opposite direction.

Then the holistic path can become a highway to be travelled by institutions—hospitals, churches, the U.S. justice system, insurance companies, big businesses, the U.S. Forest Service, and so on.

Be a leader. Clear a path for others with your responsible health consciousness.

# INDEX

# ABOUT THE AUTHOR

Thomas M. Collins, D.C., is a chiropractic physician in Sonoma County, California. In his sixteen years of private practice, he has incorporated many natural health approaches into his care of clients, including:

- health education
- nutritional prescription
- exercise rehabilitation
- musculoskeletal manipulation
- psychological and lifestyle counseling
- meditation
- stress management
- botanical medicine
- acupuncture
- biofeedback
- light therapy
- cranial electrical stimulation

# HEALTH TRANSFORMATIONS

Health Transformations is a consulting service established by Dr. Collins for the purpose of advising individuals and groups who want to travel on this journey of Transformation and Wholeness.

Dr. Collins' background includes nineteen years of experience providing holistic health care services. Combined with his skill and knowledge are complex computer expert systems, vast databases, and a network of multi-discipinary health professionals. This unique combination makes it possible to help people with problems ranging from the simple to the complex.

For those who are seeking more personalized guidance than is contained in this book, a consultation can be very valuable. This can even be done by phone and fax.

Dr. Collins is also available for groups with special needs. Workshops or retreats using the principles and practices presented in his book can

be arranged to suit an organization's needs. This can be an ideal way for individuals or support groups, professional associations and companies, to make great strides in their health, service to others, and productivity.

For more information contact:
Thomas M. Collins, D.C.
P.O. Box 602
Cotati, CA 94931
(707) 795-0692
M-F 9-5 Pacific Time

Use this address also for assistance in up-dating any resource information such as a change in address or phone number for future editions of this Resource Guide. If there are resources which you think should be included, please send a copy of the book, a sample of the periodical, or a detailed description of an organization and its services.